The United States
1¢ Franklin
1861-1867

and an Introduction to the
Postal History of the Period

———■———

Don L. Evans
with contributions from C.W. Bert Christian

Published by *Linn's Stamp News*, the largest and most informative stamp newspaper in the world. *Linn's* is owned by Amos Press Inc., 911 Vandemark Road, Sidney, Ohio 45365. Amos Press also publishes *Scott Stamp Monthly* and the Scott line of catalogs. Illustrated on the cover of this book is the 1861 1¢ Franklin (Scott 63). This book's cover was designed by Veronica Schreiber.

Copyright Linn's Stamp News, 1997

Evans, Don L.
    The United States 1¢ Franklin, 1861-1867 : and an introduction to the postal history of the period / Don L. Evans with contributions from C.W. Bert Christian.
       p. cm.
    On t.p. "cent" appears as the cent symbol.
    Includes bibliographical references and index.
    ISBN 0-940403-70-6. -- ISBN 0-940403-71-4
    1. Postage stamps--United States--History--19th century.
    2. Postal service--United States--History--19th century.
I. Christian, C.W. Bert (Calvin W. Bert) II. Title.
HE6185.U5E93 1997
769.56`973--dc21   97-959
                                                                                              CIP

Dedication

In memory of my good friend and philatelic mentor, C.W. "Bert" Christian, who introduced me to the joys of collecting postal history, and who shared with me a special fascination for the 1¢ Franklin of 1861.

and

To my wife, Alyce. Her great curiosity about all things philatelic, and her knowledge, advice and support, have made the writing of this book a pleasure.

Acknowledgments

In gathering facts and material in preparation for writing this book, I have been extremely fortunate. Many of the present-day outstanding researchers and collectors of 19th-century philately have generously given of their expertise and provided material for this volume.

Richard B. Graham, the dean of writers about postal history of the Civil War period and longtime editor of the 1861-69 Period section of the *Chronicle* of the U.S. Philatelic Classics Society has been closely associated with the manuscript since its inception. His guidance, suggestions and critical reviews have contributed greatly to the accuracy and breadth of the information contained, and his provision of photos and material from his personal files and extensive collection has been invaluable.

Richard F. Winter, immediate past president of the U.S. Philatelic Classics Society and an author and acknowledged authority on transatlantic foreign mails, provided me with sources of information, and a helping hand in understanding the fascinating intricacies of the foreign mail system. His knowledgeable critiques helped immeasurably in improving my explanations and eliminating errors.

James E. Lee opened his entire award-winning collection of 1861-67 1¢ covers to me, and provided photos and information for inclusion in the book.

Robert B. Meyersburg, an outstanding expert on the private and government carrier systems of the United States, critically reviewed the chapter on his specialty, and provided much useful material, as did Hubert C. Skinner for the section on cancellations, and Richard F. Frajola for the section on Western mails.

Dale Pulver helped clear up ambiguities in the Mexican mail system, and Barbara Mueller assisted with facts regarding the early days of the registered mail service.

Scott Trepel and Ken Lawrence both provided insight into the controversial Z-grill debate that is now under way, and William Weiss helped with a critical review of the section on patriotic covers.

Stanley Bierman graciously opened his superb philatelic library to me for research and provided many needed illustrations, as well as information from his writings on the lives of famous philatelists.

Others who generously provided their expertise or material, or both, include James Bruns, Ronald Burns, John Chapin, Walter Cole, Guy Dillaway, Joseph Geraci, Bruce Hazelton, John Hotchner, Clyde Jennings, Alvin and Marjorie Kantor, the late Susan McDonald, John Mahoney, William Maisel, James Milgram, Cornelis Muys, Michael McClung, Randy Neil, Henry Nowak, Stanley Piller, Joseph Rorke, Perry Sapperstein, Norman Sachat, Richard Searing, Edward J. Siskin, Thomas Stanton, Robert Stets and Nathan Zankel.

I wish to thank the many auction firms that provided both information and illustrations from their sales. These include Christie's New York, Richard C. Frajola Inc., Steve Ivy Philatelic Auctions, John W. Kaufmann Inc., Robert G. Kaufmann Auction Galleries, Daniel F. Kelleher, Herb La Touchie Auctions, Lionel S. Newman Auctions, Robert A. Siegel Auction Galleries, William Weiss Philatelics and Richard Wolffers Auctions.

The debt owed to philatelic associations and their publications is tremendous and can never be satisfactorily acknowledged. There are hundreds of references in this volume to information from issues of the *Chronicle* of the U.S. Philatelic Classics Society. Material from the *Essay-Proof Journal* of the Essay-Proof Society, the New York Collectors Club's *Collectors Club Philatelist*, American Philatelic Congress' *Congress Book*, the American Philatelic Society's *American Philatelist* and the *United States Specialist* of the Bureau Issues Association also contributed substantially to this work.

Various publishers have been generous in their support and permission to use material from their publications. These include Quarterman Publications Inc., which has reprinted many of the major out-of-print philatelic works of authors such as Clarence Brazer, Delf Norona, Carroll Chase and Maurice Blake, and whose editions have been a primary source of information for this effort. David G. Phillips provided permission for material from Lester C. Brookman's *United States Postage Stamps of the 19th Century* and his *American Illustrated Cover Catalog*. The publisher of *Mekeel's Weekly Stamp News*, and the publishers of *Linn's Stamp News* and *Linn's Handbook Series* have authorized the reproduction of material from their publications. Many other books and publications, too many to conveniently list here, have also provided information and illustrations for the text.

I have tried to identify the source of all material in the text and illustrations, and to ensure that proper credit is given, and apologize for any instance where this might have been inadvertently omitted. Those illustrations of material where the caption does not indicate a source are from my personal collection.

Special thanks are due to the late C.W. "Bert" Christian and to his wife, Louise Christian. Bert's international award-winning collection of the 1861 1¢ Franklin was loaned to me in its entirety for research and reproduction. His extensive meticulous notes and philatelic library were also made available to me, and provided a major source of information not obtainable elsewhere. Louise provided all of the logistic support to make this possible as well as offering me the warm hospitality of their home. Bert passed away shortly before the date of publication for this volume and did not have the opportunity to see it in its final form. He did, however, have draft copies of the manuscript and fortunately was aware of the importance of his contributions of material and expertise to the content of the book.

The unenviable task of being the first person to read each chapter as it was completed fell to my wife, Alyce. She has been instrumental in removing many of the errors and inconsistencies that appeared in the drafts, in correcting poor syntax and pointing out many instances where my explanations were confusing or just plain boring. The reader will reap the benefits of the many hours that she spent in reviewing this long manuscript, and she has my personal affection and appreciation for her knowledgeable support and discerning eye.

Finally, I want to express my appreciation to my publisher, Michael Laurence, and to my editor, Donna O'Keefe Houseman. Their exceptionally competent support and long hours of effort have made my part of the final production of this volume a pleasurable experience.

Don L. Evans

Introduction

By Michael Laurence

Don Evans' comprehensive coverage of the United States 1¢ Franklin stamp of the 1861-67 series fills a long-standing void in philatelic literature.

The previous stamp series of 1851 and 1857 are superbly covered in works originally created in the early decades of the 20th century by Carroll Chase (on the 3¢ stamps) and Stanley Ashbrook (on the 1¢ stamps). Quite surprisingly, there's been nothing comparable for the subsequent stamp issues of 1861-67.

Evans' book is thus an important landmark in the literature of classic U.S. stamps. Although the book concentrates on the lowest denomination of the 1861 series, the 1¢ stamp is found in combination with all the other values and was used in every conceivable postal application. This opens the text to a discussion of the complete range of philatelic lore for the mid-century period, and results in an encyclopedic introduction to virtually all aspects of the postal history of the era. Examples of all types of postal use are described and illustrated, together with citations from the applicable Postal Laws and Regulations and other directives that governed usage.

Despite being neglected in the literature, the 1861-67 stamps are an especially interesting series of stamps. The Civil War made new designs necessary and required the demonetization of previous issues, all to prevent use of old stamps in the hands of the Confederates. Covers bearing the 1861 stamps reflect not only the exigencies of war, but also the striking and rapid advancements in western settlement, in transcontinental mail service, and in rail transportation generally.

The very first printings of the new stamp designs, as samples for the contract competition, resulted in impressions that for many decades were considered to be a rare regular issue, the "premieres gravures." Examples to this day command exotic prices.

The 1¢ stamp design was also used to print many colorful and attractive samples for experimental patent stamps, designed to prevent cancel-washing and reuse. As part of this quest, 1867 saw the first printings of U.S. stamps with impressed grills, in which the 1¢ value figured prominently. Proof and essays, with many different collectible aspects, also abound for the 1¢ Franklin, and Evans treats them all extensively.

The 1860s saw major changes in postal laws and postal service. Instituted for the first time were free carrier service, money orders and a standard domestic postal rate regardless of distance. The volume of foreign mails increased dramatically, as many new international postal treaties were concluded. These changes created some fascinating transoceanic covers, well-represented by the 1¢ Franklin, which Evans discusses in detail.

It's my belief that this book will do for the 1861 stamps what Chase and Ashbrook did for the previous issue. If there's something you want to know about the 1¢ stamp of 1861-67 or the postal practices of its era, you'll most likely find the answer within this volume. Additionally, Evans has an open and friendly prose style; he has written an engaging book that's easy and even fun to read.

Preface

The primary goal of this work is to present in a single volume the majority of available and pertinent information on the 1¢ Franklin of the 1861 issue and the associated postal history of the era.

From an information base consisting of most of the published information on these subjects, the author has distilled the relevant data, and where possible, resolved conflicts or provided new conclusions where the facts so indicate.

An attempt has been made to include in the scope of this book, a picture of the lifestyles and technology of the 1860s, and the effect of the early philatelic pioneers on the acquisition of material and the present-day state of knowledge, as well as acknowledging the contributions of the many 20th-century scholars and collectors who have provided so much information for this volume.

While the book concentrates on the 1861-67 Franklin, the information presented is also applicable, in most cases, to all other denominations of the series, and to general mid-19th-century postal history.

In putting together a book with a comprehensive coverage of many philatelic areas, and the necessary reliance on numerous secondary sources, it is to be expected that some errors and incorrect information will find its way into print. Also, facts that are relevant and important can be inadvertently overlooked.

The author has made every attempt to eliminate these errors by checking and cross-checking, and by having experts in specialized areas critically review sections of this work, but it would be naive to believe that they have all been identified and corrected. Much information has been written and rewritten throughout the years so there is also the probability that some errors have been repeated by various authors in different publications, and the unanimity of agreement in those writings does not necessarily guarantee validity. New philatelic discoveries are being made every day, and some may invalidate conclusions presented here. There is no last word in scholarship, so the search for completeness and accuracy is never finished.

With the above caveats in place, the author would like to invite the readers of this document to join with him to make corrections and additions where needed. Please advise, in care of the publisher at the address below, of any errors of commission or omission that you may note. Also new information and illustrations are solicited.

Responses to this request will be considered for inclusion in any revised edition or supplement to this work that may be produced. The sources of all new material will, of course, be properly credited.

In this volume, the beginning chapters concentrate on the 1¢ Franklin stamp and the circumstances surrounding its conception, manufacture and distribution. The latter chapters discuss examples of the many uses of the stamp, and in so doing provide a comprehensive introduction to the postal history of the mid-19th century. All illustrated examples of covers include the use of the 1861-67 1¢ Franklin, exclusively or in combination with other stamps. Chapter 6 is a special chapter that summarizes rates and postal procedures, and is formulated for quick reference.

To avoid the necessity for excessive cross-searching through the volume to extract desired information, each chapter is written to stand on its own, and for that reason the reader will notice that there is some duplication in the text and illustrations. For example, a cover shown to illustrate a certain type of marking may be shown again in another chapter to provide an example of a scarce type of use.

Unless otherwise identified, all 1¢ stamps shown on covers or in illustrations are Scott 63, all 3¢ stamps are Scott 65 and all 10¢ stamps are Scott 68. To avoid unnecessary repetition, these identifications may not always be noted in the captions. All other issues or denominations are specifically described.

References to sources of information are described in the text, or noted at the end of a discussion. For example, a source may be identified by a "[7:254]." This means that the source is from a book or article listed as item 7 in the compilation of sources that is included at the end of each chapter, and that the material is from page 254 of that source.

Don L. Evans
c/o Linn's Stamp News
P.O. Box 29
Sidney, OH 45365-0029

Contents

Chapter 1: The 1861 Contract and the First Printings 1
   The Union Breaks Up 1
   The New Contract 2
   The Mystery of the Premieres Gravures 6
   Essays of the 1¢ Design for the 1861 Contract 10
   Toppan, Carpenter & Company Essays 11
   National Bank Note Company Premiere Gravure Essays 12
   References 15

Chapter 2: The Issued 1¢ Stamp of 1861 17
   Design 17
   Stamp Production 18
   Proofs 22
      Progress and Engravers' Die Proofs 24
      Large Die Proofs 24
      Plate Proofs 26
   Plates and Multiples 29
   Colors 30
   Varieties and Production Errors 34
   References 38

Chapter 3: The Grilled Issues of 1867-69 41
   History of the Grilled Stamp 41
   Production of Grilled Stamps 43
      A Grill 45
      B Grill 45
      C Grill 46
      D Grill 46
      Z Grill 46
      E Grill 48
      F Grill 50
   Grilled Essays 52
   Counterfeit Grills 54
   The End of the 1867 Grills and the Beginning of the 1869 Pictorial Issue 55
   References 56

Chapter 4: Experimental and Patent Printings 59
   Introduction 59
   Bowlsby Patent and the Coupon Essays 59
   The Lowenberg Patent 62
   Wyckoff Patent 64
   Macdonough Patent 65
   Gibson Patent 66
   Summary 66
   References 67

Chapter 5: Special Printings 69
   Specimen Overprints 69
      Small Specimen Overprint 69
      The 15mm Specimen Overprint 70
      Manuscript Overprint 71
      Large Block-Letter Overprint 71

Control-Number Overprints	72
The Reissue of 1875	72
Plate Proofs on Cardboard, 1879-93	76
The Atlanta Color Proofs	77
The 1895 Atlanta Proofs	78
The Envelope Essay	82
1900 Paris International Exhibition	82
The Roosevelt Small Die Proofs of 1903	83
Panama-Pacific Die Proofs	85
References	88
Chapter 6: Summary of Postal Rates and Procedures	**89**
Introduction	89
Advertised Mail	90
Books	90
Branch Post Offices	91
Canceling	91
Carriers	91
Circulars	92
Classes of Mail	92
Collect/Underpaid	92
Dead Letters	93
Drop and Local Letters	93
Forwarding	94
Franked and Other Free Mail	94
Letters	95
Money Orders	95
Newspapers	95
Pamphlets	95
Registered Mail	95
Ship, Steamship and Steamboat Letters	96
Soldiers' and Sailors' Mail	96
Stamped Envelopes (Postal Stationery)	96
Supplementary Mail	97
Transient Mail	97
Way Letters	97
Note	97
Domestic Postal Rates & Fees 1860 to 1870	98
References	100
Chapter 7: Postal Markings	**101**
Introduction	101
Town and Date Markings	102
Received Markings	106
Railroad Postmarks	106
Auxiliary Postal Markings	110
Delayed-delivery Markings	110
Undelivered Mail	112
Forwarded Mail	114
Missent Mail	115
Dead Letter Office	117
Due Markings	118
Leominster Labels	121
Free	122

    References 125
Chapter 8: Cancellations 127
    Introduction 127
    Fancy Cancellations 128
    Manuscript Cancellations 133
    Postmarks Used as Cancels 135
    Precancels 137
    Patent Cancels 139
    Colored Cancels 147
    References 148
Chapter 9: The Demonetization Period and First Uses 149
    Demonetization 149
    First Uses of the 1¢ Franklin of 1861 152
    Demonetization Across the United States 156
    'Old Stamps Not Recognized' 159
    Old Stamps Accepted 162
    References 162
Chapter 10: City Carrier Collection and Delivery 163
    Introduction 163
    The Post Office Carrier System 164
    New York City 166
        Carrier Markings and Local Service 167
        Collection for Delivery to the Mails 171
    Brooklyn, New York 175
    Philadelphia 175
    Boston 186
    Baltimore and Washington, D.C. 189
    Carrier Service in Other Cities 191
    Branch Post Offices 193
    Prepayment of Carrier Delivery Fee 197
    Epilogue 199
    References 200
Chapter 11: Drop Letters 203
    References 212
    Introduction 213
Chapter 12: Circular and Transient Mail 213
    Domestic Circular Mail 214
    Circulars to Foreign Destinations 218
    Newspapers 223
    Newspapers and Periodicals to Foreign Destinations 227
    References 229
Chapter 13: Special Services 231
    Registry Service 231
    Ship, Steamship, and Steamboat Mails 236
        Ship Letters 236
        Steamship Mail 239
        Steamboat Letters 242
    Way Letters 244
    Supplementary Mail 247
    References 251
Chapter 14: Armed Forces and War-related Mails 253
    Armed Forces Mail 255

    Occupation Covers 266
    Patriotic Envelopes 273
    Sanitary Commission Covers 288
    References 292

Chapter 15: Illustrated Covers 295
    Introduction 295
    Advertising Covers 295
    City and State Illustrated Covers 301
    Valentines and Love Letters 304
    References 308

Chapter 16: Transcontinental and Western Mails 309
    The Early Years 309
    Transcontinental Mail by Steamship 312
    The Overland Mail and Western Express Companies 313
    Territorial Mails 325
    References 330

Chapter 17: Foreign Mails 331
    Transatlantic Mails 333
    British Treaty Mails 334
    The Postal Conventions of 1868 340
    The British Conventions of 1868 and 1870 341
    The French Mails 341
    Mail under Conventions with the Germanic States 347
        Bremen Convention 349
        Hamburg Convention 349
        Prussian Convention 350
    Belgian Conventions of 1859 and 1868 355
    The Netherlands (Holland) Convention of 1868 355
    Switzerland Convention of 1868 355
    Italian Convention of 1868 355
    Mail to Canada and the British North American Provinces 356
        Canada 357
        New Brunswick 361
        Nova Scotia 363
        Newfoundland and Prince Edward Island 367
        Vancouver's Island and British Columbia 367
    St. Pierre & Miquelon 370
    Mexico 371
    Central and South America 373
    New Granada (Colombia) 373
    Chile 374
    In Conclusion 374
    References 374

Chapter 18: Monetary and Revenue Use 377
    Monetary Use 377
    Revenue Use 381
    Revenue Stamps Used for Postage 385
    References 388

Chapter 19: Miscellaneous, Odd and Unusual 389
    Odd-Shaped Envelopes 389
    Leeds & Franklin Patent Envelopes 389
    Turned Covers 397

  1¢ Franklin Bisect Use 398
  References 398
Index **401**
About the Author **419**

CHAPTER 1

The 1861 Contract and the First Printings

The Union Breaks Up

In the early months of 1861, the storm clouds of the Rebellion were fast gathering over the eastern seaboard of the United States. Abraham Lincoln had been sworn in as president on March 4, and five days later he appointed Montgomery Blair as postmaster general. While the political prominence of the Blair family was a factor in the selection, it was an excellent choice. Blair governed the Post Office Department with skill and success during his tenure. Many problems faced the Post Office Department at that time. It had been operating at a huge loss, it was hampered by a politically appointed bureaucracy, and most importantly, something had to be done about mail to the seceding states and their post offices.

Postmaster General Blair was a leading member of an influential family that served in many important political and government positions. His father, Francis P. Blair, had been a member of President Jackson's kitchen cabinet, and had participated in the founding of the Republican Party. His brother, Francis P. Blair Jr., helped organize the Free Soil Party, and worked to retain Missouri within the Union. He also raised troops in Missouri and subsequently served in the Civil War as a major general.

Montgomery Blair graduated from the U.S. Military Academy in 1835 and took part in the Seminole War before resigning from the service. He conducted a successful law practice with his brother in St. Louis and was the counsel for Scott in the famous Dred Scott case.

His management of the Post Office Department from 1861 to 1864 was efficient and innovative. He instituted many changes that improved the postal service, and it was his recommendations that resulted in free carrier delivery, a single domestic postage rate regardless of distance, improved registration procedures and better foreign postal agreements. He also selected outstanding individuals for his assistant postmasters general. Lincoln could hardly have made a better choice. **Figure 1-1** reproduces a Civil War-era photograph of Montgomery Blair.

With the likelihood of war increasing with each day, concern for the possible loss of revenue to the United States from the illegal sale of the the large number of postage stamps and envelopes that were in the hands of Southern postmasters became an important issue. In addition, mail between the South and the North was a likely conduit for information, funds and other support to the rebellious states.

The decision was made to issue a new series of stamps that would be significantly different in appearance than those currently in use. After distribution of the new issue to post offices, and allowing a short period for the exchange by the public of old stamps for the new issue, the 1851-57 stamps were to be demonetized and disallowed for postage use. The timing for a new issue was fortuitous. The current contract with Toppan, Carpenter and Company was to expire on June 10, 1861, and it was also possible that a competitive procurement might result in a lower-cost contract for the production of stamps.

This decision to print new stamps sparked a series of events that would be revisited many times by philatelic researchers a century later in an attempt to resolve the actual facts surrounding the printing and issuing of the new series. The solving of the mystery of the premieres gravures, which are also known as the First Designs or August issues of 1861, was a major goal of these investigations.

In February, delegates from six seceding Southern states met in Montgomery, Alabama, and by the evening of February 8, 1861, they had formed the Confederate States of America. On April 12, 1861, Fort Sumter was fired upon, and the Civil War became a reality.

Despite these hostile actions, mail service was still being provided to the South. The splitting of the Union demanded a swift response on the part of the Post Office Department to safeguard the postal resources in the hands of the South and to prevent the mails from being used to further the cause of the Confederacy. Of course it was also true that much useful information accrued to the North from sources in the South, so there were some mutual advantages in maintaining the postal service.

Somewhat surprisingly, in spite of the dissension and bitterness surrounding the breakup of the Union, there was a strong sense of responsibility evidenced by the Southern postal authorities. The Confederate postmaster general, John H. Reagan, issued a proclamation, dated

Figure 1-1. Montgomery Blair: Lincoln's postmaster general, 1861-64.
(U.S. Government Printing Office)

1

May 13, 1861, that stated, in part:

> "All postmasters are hereby required to render to the Post Office Department at Washington, D.C., their final accounts and their vouchers for postal receipts and expenditures, up to the 31st day of this month, taking care to forward with said accounts all postage stamps and stamped envelopes remaining on hand, belonging to the Post Office Department of the United States, in order that they may receive the proper credits therefore, in the adjustment of their accounts."

While this proclamation resulted in some stamps being returned to Washington, not all postmasters complied, and there remained large stocks of the 1851-57 issues that were found in Southern post offices after the war. A substantial number of these recovered stamps eventually found their way into philatelic hands [1:66].

At this time, even though mail services were still being conducted between the North and the South, with many disruptions and some loss of mail, the Confederacy was rapidly establishing its own postal system, and as early as March 4 had requested from the American Bank Note Company samples and prices for postage stamps. The company was later criticized in the press and in Congress for replying to the CSA request, but defended its action by noting that such negotiations had taken place prior to the declaration of hostilities and also before either government advertised for a stamp contract [2:155].

With the continuing deterioration of relationships with the seceding states, Postmaster General Blair finally ordered the cessation of mail services on May 27, 1861, to become effective on May 31. Quoting from a transcript of the original manuscript directive, furnished to the author by Richard B. Graham:

> "All Postal Service in the States of Virginia, North Carolina, South Carolina, Georgia, Florida, Alabama, Mississippi, Louisiana, Arkansas, and Texas will be suspended from and after the 31st instant.
> Letters for Offices temporarily closed by this order will be forwarded to the Dead Letter Office, except those for Western Virginia, which will be sent to Wheeling."

At this time, General Blair notified all post offices in the South to return to Washington their stamps, stamped envelopes, and money they had collected for stamps. This was two weeks after the CSA postmaster general had issued his similar directive. It is interesting to note that although Western Virginia remained in the Union, it was another two years before it became the state of West Virginia, and legally separated from Virginia.

Examples of correspondence directed to the South subsequent to Postmaster General Blair's directive are scarce and sought-after Civil War postal history items. **Figure 1-2** shows a striking cover that was offered in the Wolffers sale of January 26, 1983. It is from New York, addressed to Aberdeen, Mississippi, and demonstrates an unusually late attempt to send mail to the South. The oval "MAILS SUSPENDED" marking was applied at the Dead Letter Office to mail that could be returned to the sender. General Blair noted in his 1861 Report to Congress that 46,697 letters were thus stamped and returned. The 1862 Report listed an additional 21,000 returned letters [3:390].

The New Contract

Concurrent with the momentous events of the beginning of the Civil War, activities to procure a new contract for the production of a new issue of postage stamps continued.

It should probably be mentioned at this point that a significant amount of space in this chapter will be devoted to the details of the contract and the initial production of the 1861 issue. The principal reason for the unusual emphasis on this aspect of the issue is the question of the rightful position of the premieres gravures in the pantheon of 1861 stamps. The very high value of premieres gravures, and the questions and controversy that for many years have surrounded their origin, makes the determination of their proper description both important and philatelically interesting.

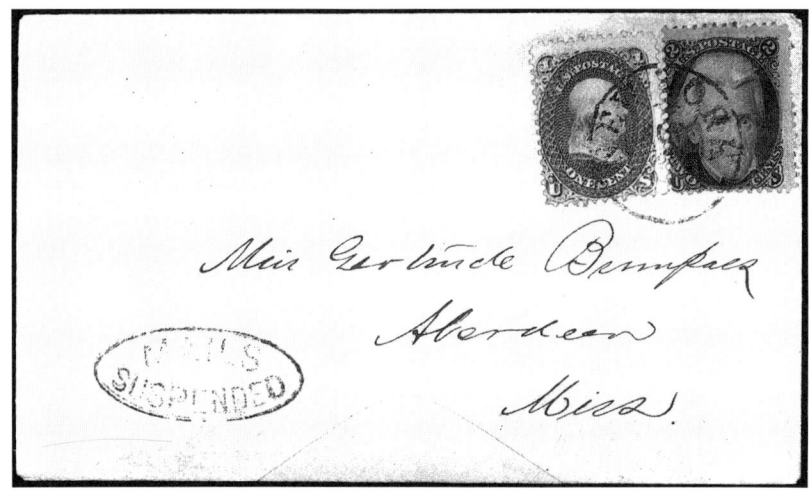

Figure 1-2. A scarce MAILS/SUSPENDED marking on Northern cover to Confederate addressee showing the 3¢ domestic rate with a 1¢ 1861 and a 2¢ 1861 Jackson. Reported to be a unique usage with the 1863 Black Jack.
(Photo from a Richard Wolffers Inc. auction)

The contract for the production of postage stamps at that time was held by Toppan, Carpenter & Company, whose original 1851-57 contract had been extended to June 10, 1861. While there was no apparent dissatisfaction with its performance, an advertisement by the Post Office Department for bids relating to the production of a new issue of postage stamps was approved on March 27, 1861, and placed in leading newspapers.

The content of the advertisement for proposals is quite long and detailed. Of primary philatelic importance are the following excerpts:

Figure 1-3. **Designs prepared by the American Bank Note Company for the 1861 contract bid.**
(C.W. Brazer photos, courtesy of Quarterman Publications Inc.)

"POST-OFFICE DEPARTMENT, March 27, 1861.

PROPOSALS for POSTAGE STAMPS,—Proposals will be received until 12m of 30th April next for furnishing Postage Stamps of the general style and description of those now in use, on suitable paper of the best quality, for a term of six years, commencing 1st. July next . . .

The heads of Washington and Franklin are to be preserved as the leading designs; the former on all stamps except those of one cent and thirty cents on which are to be the head of Franklin. On all of the stamps the denomination must be given distinctly in figures as well as letters, and the whole work must be executed in the best style of line engraving on steel . . .

Each bid is to be accompanied with a specimen of the style of engraving, and the quality of paper to be furnished, which will be submitted to a board of disinterested experts or artists for examinations; and the accepted bidder, before the final consummation of the contract, will be required to prepare designs and furnish proof impressions of the engravings of the several denominations of the stamps . . .

. . . dies and plates are to be the property of the United States for the service of the Post Office Department . . .

No bids will be considered except from parties who have actually been engaged in the business of copper plate and steel engraving and printing and are thus engaged at the time of bidding, . . .

M. Blair
Postmaster General" [2:165-6]

It should be noted that having the head of Jefferson on the 5¢ denomination was not mentioned in the advertisement. This oversight was corrected in later negotiations with the accepted bidder, and the submitted designs did include the Jefferson head.

Competition was strong between the leading bank note companies to obtain the contract. The call for proposals favored Toppan, Carpenter & Company, the incumbent, since there were no changes required for the engraved heads or style of the stamps, and only the addition of the denominations in figures needed to be done to the 1857 dies for them to conform to the new requirements.

The National Bank Note Company, on the other hand, was a relatively new company with only a limited supply of engraved dies and equipment in place. It was, however, a dynamic organization, and went to a significant amount of expense and labor to produce high-quality entries for the competition.

The American Bank Note Company had all the dies and resources of the several companies from which it had been formed a few years previously, including the old Bald, Cousland & Company vignettes and frames that it submitted as part of its bid. Its proposed designs were relatively incomplete and, in some cases, did not meet the proposal requirements. All of its submissions were in the 3¢ or 5¢ denominations, and therefore do not really fall within the primary scope of this text. However, for information, an illustration of two of its submissions is shown in **Figure 1-3.** A complete description of these proposed designs may be found in Brazer's catalog [4:31-33].

The middle of the 19th century produced some of the best and most prolific engravers in the United States, and most were engaged in the production of bank notes and postage stamps. Conditions and equipment for the engraving of steel dies had progressed rapidly over the previous 10 years, and at the time of the preparation of the 1861 dies, the engraver could be assured of well-lit and comfortable quarters in which to pursue his craft. **Figure 1-4** shows a woodcut that depicts the engraving room in a contemporary bank note firm.

Figure 1-4. **The engraving room in an 1860s-era bank note firm, where stamp vignettes and other pictorial engravings were made.**
(*Harper's New Monthly Magazine*, February, 1862)

Other than the three largest firms that entered bids, the remaining bank note and engraving companies that still existed as independent companies after the previous decade's amalgamations were all too small or lacked the necessary facilities and experience to actively bid for the contract.

The essays produced by the two major competitors, Toppan, Carpenter & Company and The National Bank Note Company, will be considered in depth in a following section.

At the close of 1861, the postmaster general, in his annual report dated December 2, 1861, mentioned the causes for and the advantages of the new issue of stamps. The report stated:

> "The contract for the manufacture of postage stamps having expired on the 10th of June, 1861, a new one was entered into with the National Bank Note Company, of New York, upon terms very advantageous to the department, from which there will result an annual saving of more than thirty per cent, in the cost of the stamps.
>
> In order to prevent the fraudulent use of the large quantity of stamps remaining unaccounted for in the hands of postmasters in the disloyal States, it was deemed advisable to change the designs and the colors of those manufactured under the new contract, and also to modify the stamp on the stamped envelopes, and to substitute, as soon as possible, the new for the old issue. It was the design of the department that the distribution of the new stamps and envelopes should commence on the first of August, but, from unavoidable delays, that the latter did not take place until the 15th of that month." [5:571-2]

The cost of purchasing stamps did decrease substantially. The previous contract with Toppan, Carpenter & Company called for a payment of 18¢ per thousand stamps; whereas in the new contract with the National Bank Note Company, the price was reduced to 12¢ per thousand.

Only 18 weeks transpired between the call for proposals and the delivery of the first stamps. This is a relatively short time, and much work relating to the new issue was accomplished during this period. Undoubtedly the National Bank Note Company was aware that the stamp contract would expire in June, and it is possible that it may have started work in preparing for the engraving of the essay dies earlier than March 27, 1861, but in any event, the preparation of a complete new series of stamps in such a short time is a remarkable achievement.

Very few records exist concerning the events that took place during those 18 weeks. This lack of documentation contributed substantially to the differences in philatelic opinions concerning the status of the first essays as possible postage stamps, and cloaks the period with somewhat of an air of mystery. The few records that do remain are primarily from the letter files of the U.S. Post Office Department and articles from newspapers published at that time. The bank note company records are reported to have been destroyed in a fire sometime in the latter part of the 19th century. Part of the story can be pieced together, but the lost directives and letters from the Post Office Department to the National Bank Note Company hold the key to many of the unanswered questions.

It is not known exactly what sample or samples the National Bank Note Company submitted with its bid. It is the author's opinion that it is unlikely that die essays of any of the required designs were submitted. This conflicts with Brazer's statement in his 1941 article where he assumes that die essays for all eight values were submitted with the bid. The request for proposals did not require the designs, and a letter to the Post Office Department from the National Bank Note Company on May 18, 1861, stated that the engravers had all of the heads in hand, except for the 24¢ and 30¢ values [5:53]. This is more than two weeks after the opening of the bids on April 30, 1861, and it seems unlikely that engravers would just be starting on designs that supposedly had been submitted with the bid. Of course it is entirely possible that dies with the required heads that previously had been used for stock certificates or bank notes could have been available from National's vaults.

When the bids were opened, it may be assumed that they were evaluated with respect to the conditions of the request for proposals and that the submitted samples were examined by the "board of artists" mentioned in the original specification. Some days later, an official notice appeared in a New York newspaper, as follows:

> "POST OFFICE DEPARTMENT
> MAY 10, 1861
>
> Accepts proposal of the National Bank Note Company for Postage Stamps at twelve cents (12¢) per thousand stamps, . . .
>
> It is further provided, agreeably to the terms of the advertisement . . . that before closing a contract the National Bank Note Company shall prepare designs and furnish impressions of the several denominations of stamps, in sheets, perfectly gummed and perforated . . .
>
> M. Blair
> P. M. General" [6:52]

The wording of the above notice is an indication that the Post Office Department had not seen at this date the proposed designs, and that the competition winner was now expected to proceed with the engraving and printing of designs for approval before a contract would be signed.

There is no doubt from this time on there was frequent and continuing communication between the Post Office Department and the National Bank Note Company, and probably a dialog concerning the nature of the designs had been established between the two organizations. Daniel M. Boyd, who had been the government's stamp agent with Toppan, Carpenter & Company, was

Figure 1-5. A typical printing room of a large bank note firm. Many hand presses were required, and all inking was done by hand. Steam printing presses were just beginning to be used at this time.
(*Harper's New Monthly Magazine*, February 1862)

assigned to the National Bank Note Company, probably upon the completion of the previous contract on June 10, 1861. He occupied an office in the new contractor's facilities and functioned as the Post Office Department's on-site representative. The primary contact in Washington was A.N. Zevely, the third assistant postmaster general. Zevely was a dedicated public servant and was instrumental in the conduct and actions of the Post Office Department in the area of postage stamps for many years.

Three days later, on May 13, National sent a letter to Zevely stating that it had not yet received the memoranda of understanding that was to have been sent, but was progressing in the meantime.

On May 18, the bank note company informed Zevely that it was considering moving to new premises and also suggested that it might be desirable to use portraits other than Washington for the 24¢ and 30¢ values. John Adams, John Q. Adams, Madison and Jackson were suggested as possible alternatives [6:53].

The new facilities mentioned were located at 1 Wall Street, New York, and had been equipped and furnished for the production of stamps by Charles F. Steel, who had joined the National Bank Note Company. **Figure 1-5** shows a woodcut depicting a typical printing room in an 1861-era bank note firm.

The next letter of import was dated June 15, to the third assistant postmaster general, and signed by J. Macdonough, the new secretary of the National Bank Note Company.

"Dear Sir:

Your favor of 14th inst. received.

We have preserved the portraits and busts of Washington, Franklin and Jefferson, on the respective stamps as now used, but have entirely changed the form and design of the stamps; while the portraits, engraved carefully by our best artists from direct daguerreotypes of Stuarts paintings & etc., will make the whole stamp strikingly different from those now in use.

We have engraved in addition to the usual lettering on each stamp, the denomination in figures, plainly and clearly, on each of the upper corners, and "U S" on the lower corners.

All of the engraving will be finished by next Wednesday (sic. June 19th) and we will forward for your inspection immediately after proofs from the dies in black and in various colors — we have already transferred and completed the plates of the 10 and 90 cents.

We have in our employ now the best workmen and girls from the establishment of Messrs. T.C. & Co: and soon as our machinery is completed we shall be enabled to go forward without any interruption.

Very respectfully
Your Obt. Servt.
J. Macdonough
Secretary" [6:54]

The final letter in this series was dated July 27, 1861. It mentioned that difficulty had been encountered in obtaining the desired color of the 3¢ value, but that the problem had finally been resolved, having on that afternoon achieved the "precise tint" desired by the Post Office Department, and that the printers thought that it could be printed. The letter also requested that the date for delivery of the first stamps be postponed from August 1 to August 15 so an adequate supply of the 3¢ stamps in the new color could be made available. It did, however, stipulate that printing would continue, and that specimens of all of the stamps complete would be sent on the following Monday (July 29). This would be prior to the August 1 date that was the required date for the first delivery. The letter also implied that sufficient stamps would be available for distribution at that time in case the request for delay was not approved, but that the previously printed red 3¢ stamps would have to be used instead of the new color that had been just achieved. The request for a delay was evidently approved. Norton York, in an excellent article [6:55], stated that the stamp agent of the Post Office Department, Daniel Boyd, accepted, on August 16, the first delivery as order number 1, consisting of more than 5,000,000 stamps including all of the eight denominations. These were from plate 6 for the 24¢, plate 7 for the 30¢ in the premieres gravures design, and plates 9 to 18 with the new designs. (The differences in the design of the 1¢ denomination will be detailed in the next section.)

Distribution of the stamps followed shortly thereafter, and it is accepted that the first day of use was Saturday, August 17, 1861. The illustrated off-cover 1¢ Franklin (see **Figure 1-6**), which has a legible "Aug/17/1861" Baltimore datestamp, was for many years the earliest known use of the 1861 issue. A 3¢ stamp on-cover, also dated August 17, from Baltimore, was later discovered. This reinforces the assumption that this is probably the earliest possible date of use and that Baltimore was one of the first cities to receive any of the new stamps.

Further verification of this fact, and probably the

Figure 1-6. Off-cover example of earliest-known use. Stamp is canceled with a Baltimore, Maryland, circular datestamp showing a date of August 17, 1861.
(Christie's New York auction photo)

best contemporary evidence that the new stamps were available on this date, can be found in advertisements in a Baltimore newspaper. On Saturday, August 17, 1861, the following advertisement appeared in the *Baltimore American and Commercial Advertiser* [7:123]:

"Post Office Notice

The public are hereby notified that the Postmaster at Baltimore will be prepared from this date to Exchange ENVELOPES and STAMPS of the new style for an equivalent amount of the old issue, up to THURSDAY, the 22nd instant, after which the old issue will not be received in payment of letters mailed at this office.

WM. PURNELL, Postmaster
Baltimore, Md."

A following news item appeared on Monday, August 19:

"EXCHANGE OF POST OFFICE STAMPS.— On Saturday the stamp department of the Baltimore Post Office was literally besieged with crowds of persons anxious to exchange the old style stamps for the new ones now issuing by the Department. Several extra clerks were required to attend to the demands, as some of the claimants had large quantities of stamps with them. All persons holding them should have them promptly exchanged, otherwise they may lose their value. Mr. Purnell, by way of accommodation, has extended the time of exchange for the smaller post offices to the 17th of September."

All of the actions related above, after the acceptance of the National bid on May 10, 1861, took place under a memorandum of understanding between the Post Office Department and the National Bank Note Company. The actual six-year contract was not signed until November 5, 1861, but it established August 15 as the beginning date for the contract. As far as is known, no funds were supplied by the government prior to the signing of the contract in spite of the fact that the National Bank Note Company had previously delivered many millions of stamps.

The Mystery of the Premieres Gravures

Were they issued stamps, essays, samples, labels or specimens? All of these names at one time or another have been given to the premieres gravures by recognized philatelic scholars.

The fact that the stamps of the 1861 issue existed in more than one design was first established a few years after the initial printing of the issue. The 3¢ and the 12¢ values were the first to be discovered, probably because the variation between the issued designs and the premieres gravures was most evident in these values. Extra corner ornaments had been added to each of the designs, and the frame now took on a more rectangular appearance. Examples of these values without these corner ornaments had also been found with full gum, perforated and printed on a thin semitransparent paper. Initially these items were regarded as printed essays, an excellent choice, as later research has shown.

On May 26, 1896, John N. Luff, the most eminent philatelic scholar of his day, presented a paper before the National Philatelic Society. In this paper he made the claim that there were two distinct printings of the 1861 issue, each with slightly different designs (with the exception of the 24¢ and 30¢ values), and that all of the values had done postal duty [2:153]. He evidently based his conclusions on the fact that the 10¢ value had been found postally used with a slightly different design and that subsequent research had discovered unused perforated and gummed examples with small but definite variations in all of the remaining designs except the 24¢ and 30¢ values. It should be noted that the known used examples of the 10¢ value with the premiere gravure design were printed on a thinner and more transparent paper than the regularly issued 10¢ stamps, and that all of the other values that were discovered with the premiere gravure designs were found on a similar hard and thin, semi-transparent paper. The variations in the designs are now well-known and documented.

Six years later, in 1902, John Luff (see **Figure 1-7**) published his magnificent study, *The Postage Stamps of the United States*. This was the first successful attempt to assemble and publish the available information on U.S. postal issues to that date. Luff's book served as the philatelic bible for many years. It is still a basic source for much information. Unfortunately, Luff continued to hold to his belief that there had been two issues of stamps. He postulated that the premiere gravure designs had been issued prior to August 15 and that the regular or second designs followed later because the original designs had not met with approval by the postal authorities. This idea was further promulgated by the inclusion of the premieres gravures in the Scott *Standard Postage Stamp Catalogue* as a separate issue. These listings appeared as early as 1911 and remained basically unchanged until recently. Luff was employed by the publishers of the Scott catalog until his death in 1938. His philatelic stature and his relationship with the publishing of the catalog undoubtedly were instrumental in continuing the listing of the premieres as stamps. It is difficult, however, to understand why the listing continued for more than 50 additional years after his death in spite of research results that conclusively proved that the premieres were finished essays. Of course there is the possibility that the extremely high value of tens of thousands of dollars that had accrued to some of the premieres, and the philatelic and financial stature of many of the individuals who owned these rare items, may have been an influencing reason to retain the stamp status of the premieres instead of their being designated as essays.

In his 1902 book, Luff remarked: "When it was first discovered that this issue was composed of two series, it was believed that the stamps of the second types were not ready for use until September 1861. Thus the two series were designated as the August and September issues, respectively, but from the information supplied by the cancellations we perceive that these titles are incorrect and must be abandoned." The cancellations that Luff refers to are the many examples of the various values that were found canceled on covers and dated in the second half of August. In spite of his suggestions to abandon the August and September nomenclature, these descriptive titles were frequently used for another half-century and are still occasionally encountered.

Figure 1-7. John N. Luff (1860-1938), the father of United States philatelic research. From *Postmaster's Provisional Stamps*, Scott Stamp and Coin Company, 1937. (Courtesy of Dr. Stanley M. Bierman)

The situation of 1906, with the premieres being generally accepted as an officially issued stamp, continued until about 1935, when Stanley B. Ashbrook and Clarence W. Brazer began to publish results of their investigations that cast serious doubt on the authenticity of the premieres as stamps. Many of the leading philatelic scholars of the U.S. classic stamps became involved in the controversy. On one side, supporting the Luff theory, were Luff, of course, and Philip H. Ward Jr. who was a well-known dealer and stamp expert (coincidentally also the owner of many of the more important premieres gravures), and the editors of the Scott *Specialized Catalogue of United States Stamps*. On the dissenting side were Ashbrook and Brazer, as previously stated, and also Elliott Perry and Cyril dos Passos. Many articles were written by these individuals, arguing the pros and cons of the situation. Later, the dissenting side was joined by additional scholars such as Norton D. York, whose article, "The Oneness of the 1861-1862 Regular Postage Stamp Issue," appeared in the 33rd *American Philatelic Congress Book* for 1967. Later, Dr. Howard S. Friedman joined the fray with a masterfully written summary article titled "The 1861 Holocaust," which appeared in the *Essay-Proof Journal* for the spring of 1975. Only dos Passos and Perry were still alive of the original group, and no major proponents for the Luff theory remained, with the exception of the Scott catalog, which continued the listing of the premieres as stamps without wavering.

Elliott Perry finally decided that the questions should be put to rest and authored a comprehensive article titled "The Whole Truth About the So-Called First Designs or Premieres gravures or August Issue of the United States, 1861." This was published as a series of three articles beginning in the fall of 1970 in the *Essay-Proof Journal*. At Perry's request, dos Passos published a summary article on Perry's series in the winter 1972, number 113, *Essay-Proof Journal*.

The banner continued to be carried by other contemporary philatelic scholars, and the current dean of Civil War-era postal historians, Richard B. Graham, wrote several articles urging reclassification of the premieres from stamps to essays and the concurrence of the Scott catalog in this change. Until recently, Graham was the 1861 section editor of *The Chronicle* of the United States Philatelic Classics Society, a position he held for more than 29 years. In this capacity, he was instrumental in bringing this extended dispute to a reasonable conclusion. His summary article, "The Premiere Gravures Controversy of Past Decades," appeared in the August 1992 issue of *The Chronicle* [8:187]. The 1992 Scott U.S. specialized, under new ownership by the Amos Press (parent company of *Linn's Stamp News*) and a new editorial staff, finally recognized the true nature of the premieres gravures, and they are now comfortably listed with their related essays. However, there is no doubt they are still a special class of essay printing and should not be confused with the more common sample impressions by an engraver desiring to check his work.

The above discussion has covered much of the historical aspects of the premieres gravures controversy but has said little about the essays and stamps themselves and the actual chain of events that produced them. Some of these events were chronicled in the section on the 1861 contract, but it is advisable to look at the sequence of production activities leading up to the initial distribution of the stamps. Over the years since Luff's original paper, much correspondence and many pertinent newspaper articles have come to light, so a reasonably factual story can be told. The chronology of events is essentially as follows:

March 27, 1861: Request for bids for a stamp contract. Bidders required to furnish a specimen of the style of engraving, and the quality of paper to be used. Note that there was no requirement for essays of the designs to be submitted. This requirement came later in the announcement where it required the accepted bidder to prepare designs and furnish proof impressions of the several denominations.

May 10, 1861: The Post Office Department accepted the bid of the National Bank Note Company and assured them (verbally?) of a contract to begin on June 11, 1861. A newspaper report of this acceptance noted that before the contract was closed, it would be necessary for the bank note company to furnish impressions of the designs for the several denominations in sheets, perfectly gummed and perforated. It is most probable that it was this requirement that led to the preparation of the sheets that eventually became the notorious premieres gravures.

June 15, 1861: National informs the Post Office Department that all of the engravings will be completed by June 19, and immediately after, die proofs in black and various colors will be forwarded to the Post Office for inspection, and that the plates for the 10¢ and 90¢ values were already complete. This implies that National already had nominal approval for the designs, at least for the 10¢ and 90¢, or were confident that its submission would be approved. Note that finished sheets have still not been submitted, nor is there any evidence of a legal contract.

The date of submission of these finished sheets of the premieres is not known, but if the die proofs were submitted as promised shortly after June 19, and the examining board approved the designs and colors without undue delay, approval could have been forthcoming by the end of the month. At this time, National could have commenced production of the premiere gravure sheets.

A very important fact surfaces at this point. In preparing the plates from the dies, the same spacing was used for all of the designs. The plates were laid down with 21.5mm horizontal and about 26mm vertical spacing on centers for all values. This resulted in all of the denominations (except the 24¢ and the 30¢, which were smaller designs) in having very narrow spacing between the stamps with not enough room for perforations. Brazer thought this technical oversight resulted from the inexperience of the National Bank Note Company in the production of postage stamps. The importance of this fact is that new plates with altered designs and larger spaces between the designs for all denominations except the 24¢ and the 30¢ were later produced to print the regular issue.

The finished plate proofs of all the premiere gravure designs were printed on a thin semitransparent paper, perforated and gummed. The gum was a dark brown and, according to Brazer, was inexpertly applied. These finished sheets of plate proofs were submitted for approval to the Post Office Department in colors similar to the final-issue colors, except that the inks used for the proofs were the more expensive inks reserved for die and proof impressions. These resulted in colors that were richer and better impressions than would be found later on the regular issues. Examples from some of these finished premiere gravure sheets have been found in more than one hue. Brazer reported in 1941 that he had four shades of red of the 3¢ value in his reference collection. Whether more than one color shade for each value was submitted to the Post Office for consideration is not known. The submitted color for the 1¢ denomination was a deep indigo and is an exceptionally attractive color.

It was on this phase of the stamp production where much of the controversy centered. Many philatelic students believed that the Post Office requested changes to the designs (except the 24¢ and 30¢) because they had an "unfinished look," and that National then engraved new dies and prepared new plates, which became the "second" or issued designs. While it is certainly possible, even likely, that some changes were proposed, most of the changes that resulted were so minor in nature that they escaped the observant eyes of collectors for more than 35 years after they were issued.

It is the opinion of this author that the changes that were made to the original dies and plates were, in the main, not the result of dissatisfaction with the original designs, but resulted from two other considerations.

First, regulations of the period required that dies used for issued postage stamps become the property of the Post Office Department. The premiere gravure dies were the property at that time of the National Bank Note Company, and the Post Office Department, not having a contract, had no legal control over the distribution of emissions from these dies or the finished plate proofs. The Post Office Department, therefore, requested/ordered National to change the designs for the "to be issued stamp" in some way to make them distinctive from the original submissions. The engravers of the National Bank Note Company took this opportunity, as most artists would, to make changes not only to provide a slightly different design, but also to improve the overall appearance. This resulted in the large changes in the 3¢ and 12¢ to fill out a rectangular frame, and the minor changes to satisfy the Post Office's directive in the other denominations.

Second, the excessively narrow spacing between the stamps for most of the values also provided a reason to produce new plates instead of re-entering the original plates with a touched-up die. The exceptions to this, of course, are the 24¢ and 30¢ designs. Only one plate (the original premiere gravure plate) was produced for each of these values. The only changes in the design, according to Brazer, were a result of small engraving improvements that were made to the 24¢ premiere gravure die and re-entered into the original plate. Brazer makes no mention of any changes to the 30¢. However, in his comprehensive 1941 book, *Essays For U.S. Adhesive Postage Stamps*, he does note that finished, i.e., gummed and perforated, copies of the 24¢ and the 30¢ values on transparent paper had not been recorded as of that date. No subsequent findings have been reported, and it may be assumed that these two denominations do not exist as finished premieres gravures.

It has been suggested that the dies for the 24¢ and 30¢ were not completed in time for the sample sheets to be sent to the Post Office Department with the other finished premieres, and that by the time they were ready and sample sheets prepared, the contract was in effect, thereby negating the requirement to alter the designs to differentiate from precontract dies. This is certainly a reasonable hypothesis and would explain why these two values were the only ones where all of the regular issues were printed from the original premiere gravure plates.

It took almost a century to reach the present agreement on the status of the premieres gravures. They are all essays except for the 10¢ value. The 10¢ premiere gravure, plate 4, was used, probably in September of 1861, to print a large number of stamps. This printing was issued and postally used. The reason for this unexpected use is not known, but it is generally assumed that the premiere gravure plate was mistakenly put into the presses, and no one at the time noticed the error. The 10¢ printed on the premiere gravure paper and in the original color is still considered an essay, while the later printing has the status of a regular stamp issue.

It is interesting to compare some of the Scott catalog entries for the 1861 issue over the years. The U.S. specialized for 1932 lists the premieres gravures as the "First Issue," with a date of issue for all denominations of August 17, 1861, and assigns numbers 55 through 62 to the different values. Prices for used copies of the 10¢ and 24¢ are listed. The actually issued stamp is listed as the "Second Issue" and has dates of issue ranging from August 18, 1861, for the 3¢, to October 8, 1861, for the 24¢. The date of issue for the 1¢ value is listed as "Sept. 24, 1861." This is difficult to understand since by this time thousands of covers with dates that preceded these published dates were available for reference.

By 1973 some minor changes had been made to the listings. A new number, 62B, with an issue date of "Sept. 17, 1861," had been added to identify the issued printing of the 10¢ premiere gravure, and it was noted that the design on thin semitransparent paper did not exist in used condition. A note preceding the premieres gravures now stated that "It is doubtful that Nos. 55-62 were regularly issued." The titles "First" and "Second" issue were eliminated, and the issued dates for the regular issue were changed for some denominations.

No further significant changes were made in the listings until the ownership of the Scott catalog changed. The 1991 U.S. specialized under the new ownership of Amos Press Inc. discarded the long discredited idea of two issues, and the premieres gravures were moved to a new section entitled "Special Printings." This was a reasonable choice since there is no doubt the premieres were a special printing, solely for the purpose of satisfying the precontract requirements. No changes in the numbers assigned to the premieres were made. It did, however, leave in abeyance the question of whether the premieres were essays or stamps. For the record and for the purposes of this volume, the following definition of an essay, as stated by Brazer, will be used: "An essay is a design submitted in stamp form but not accepted for issuance in that form."

The Scott U.S. specialized catalog for 1992 made the final change. The premieres gravures were listed in the essays section, along with their die and plate proofs. The Scott numbers were changed to reflect this new categorization, and the 1¢ Franklin in indigo on semitransparent paper, perforated 12 and gummed, now became 63-E11e. The premieres gravures thereby suffered a severe, but correct, change in stature and description, but continue to shine as one of the most sought-after printings of the classic era.

Collectors are urged to visit in greater detail this controversy and the philatelic detective work involved in reaching the present level of knowledge by reading some or all of the many articles on the subject. A reasonably complete listing of these very interesting writings is presented at the end of this chapter. These articles provided the source for the bulk of the information that has been presented here, and their contributions are gratefully acknowledged.

To complete this section, it seems only fitting to present a close look at the famous and elusive 1¢ indigo premiere gravure, which caused so much debate and controversy over the past century. An enlarged photo of this essay (or sample or special printing) is shown in **Figure 1-8**. Just how and when these items entered the philatelic market is not known, but it seems unlikely, as has been suggested, that the Post Office Department sent them to foreign countries as samples of the new issue since it had no other copies of the stamp available for that purpose in early August 1861. It is difficult to understand why there would be such a hurry to get the new designs into the hands of foreign postal authorities. After all, the old 1857 stamps would still be valid for postage for some time, pending the completion of the demonetization actions, and the new designs would have become available for samples in quantity in about two more weeks.

Estimates of the number of examples of the 1¢ premiere gravure presently in philatelic hands range from 15 to 20 copies. Although this essay has been listed by Brazer as very rare, and the auction realizations are in the five figure range, the frequency with which it appears on the market suggests that a designation of "scarce" would be more appropriate. All copies that the author has seen of the finished premiere gravure have been poorly centered, and it is not believed that any copies with really good centering exist.

The Robert A. Siegel auction of October 3, 1992, offered an indigo premiere gravure with a portion of a target cancel on the upper-left corner of the design. The item has full original gum, and the cancel is possibly of an experimental nature, or was applied to insure that the sample design would not be used for postage.

There are two questions that are still not answered to the author's satisfaction. How and when did the premieres gravures enter the philatelic market? None was identified until some years subsequent to their printing, and many of the early finds surfaced in Europe. The other question is: If the "sample" sheets were to be of the "best quality," why are so many examples of the premieres gravures found to be poorly centered copies? Certainly, the National Bank Note Company, which worked so hard in other aspects to prepare a superior product, must have realized that the perforations were not well-executed. These questions pose interesting avenues for further exploration.

Essays of the 1¢ Design for the 1861 Contract

In addition to the finished sheets of the premieres gravures that were extensively discussed in the previous section, the competing bank note companies produced other proofs of their submitted designs. Although a newspaper article of the period reported that six companies (probably a journalistic error) had competed for the contract, essays from only three companies have been recorded. Two of these companies were Toppan, Carpenter & Company and the National Bank Note Company. The other bidder, the American Bank Note Company, did not produce an essay for the 1¢ value.

All of these essay examples range in availability from scarce to very rare, and most of the following descriptions are from listings compiled by Clarence W. Brazer (**Figure 1-9**) from his reference collection. Brazer possessed the most comprehensive modern holding of U.S. essays and proofs, and this collection provided the source for his definitive catalog, *Essays for U.S. Adhesive Postage Stamps*, originally published by the American Philatelic Society in 1941. It is now available in a 1977 reprint by Quarterman Publications Inc.

Figure 1-8. An example of the famous and scarce 1¢ indigo premiere gravure. It is better centered than most. (Photo from Steve Ivy Auctions, March 1988)

In early January 1951, most of Brazer's stock was stolen from his office. Although many items from this theft have recently surfaced on the philatelic market, it is too early to determine if all of his reference collection of scarce and frequently unique essays and proofs will again be available to the philatelic world. It is fortunate, however, that Brazer wrote extensively and published the results of his studies in numerous articles for various publications, thereby preserving much of this invaluable information for scholars and collectors. Many proof and essay items in Brazer's personal collection, which escaped being pilfered in the office burglary, were later sold by Brazer's widow to Morton Dean Joyce, who kept the collection intact during his lifetime. Subsequent to Joyce's death, the Clarence Brazer collection of U.S. essays and proofs was offered for sale in a 1990 Siegel auction, and many unique and rare items became available for the first time in many years.

Figure 1-9. Dr. Clarence W. Brazer.
(Courtesy of James Bruns)

Falk Finkelburg, who had been a colleague of Brazer, became the leading expert in U.S. essays and proofs subsequent to Brazer's death in 1956. Finkelburg coordinated a revision and update to the Brazer catalog that was published over a period of time during the 1970s in the *Essay-Proof Journal*. The Brazer catalog and the Finkelburg revisions, along with their published articles, provide the original sources for most of the information currently available for the 1¢ essays and proofs.

Scott Publishing Company, in the 1992 edition of the U.S. specialized catalog, for the first time published a compendium of essays to compliment its previously issued listing of U.S. proofs, and assigned Scott numbers to the items.

The following descriptions of the 1¢ essays for the 1861 contract bid will be identified with both their Brazer and Scott numbers.

Toppan, Carpenter & Company Essays

For the 1851 and 1857 contracts, Toppan, Carpenter & Company had produced a series of master dies for all of the denominations. As previously mentioned, numerical values were added to these designs (except the 10¢ and 30¢, which already had numbers) to satisfy the bid requirements for the 1861 issue. These essay die proofs were printed in colors similar to those of the 1857 issue and also in black. Examples of the completed dies printed on India, old proof paper and old ivory paper exist, as well as some impressions from the progress and trial dies. They are very rare from the original 1861 printings, but examples from the 1903 Schernikow reprints can be more easily obtained. An example of an original 1861 essay in blue on India paper is shown in **Figure 1-10**.

About 1899 Ernest Schernikow, who at that time was secretary of the Hamilton Bank Note Company of New York, purchased from the dissolution assets of the Philadelphia Bank Note Company many of the dies and plates of that company. The Philadelphia Bank Note Company earlier had absorbed the Butler and Carpenter Company, and its inventory included the original Toppan, Carpenter & Company dies for the 1861 essays. Schernikow offered these for sale to his firm, but the offer was not accepted. In 1903, to recoup his costs for the dies and other items, he caused to have printed a limited number of copies from various

Figure 1-10. Toppan, Carpenter & Company original essay for the 1861 contract. This example, in dark blue on India paper, is cut to size, as usual.

dies on different papers and in many colors. These reprints were then offered to stamp dealers and others as a limited edition, and the dies were reportedly then destroyed by dropping them into a river.

Although the 1903 Schernikow reprints have no status as an official issue, they are presently welcomed as a legitimate philatelic item, most likely because the 1861 originals are practically unobtainable, and in some cases no longer exist. The reprints are attractive printings, and the many colors and the various papers used for the printings form a colorful and interesting display of early engravings and stamp design. According to the Brazer catalog and the Scott U.S. specialized , 10 sets of reprints were made from various stages of the dies in about 16 colors, with a smaller number and fewer colors being reprinted on colored card, bond and pelure papers. With a total of 200 to 300 examples of the reprinted 1¢ essays originally available, they are not rare and are frequently seen in auction catalog offerings. A complete listing of all of the die, color and paper combinations, based on the original Brazer descriptions, is available in the 1992 through 1996 Scott U.S. specialized catalogs, and will probably be continued as a standard listing. Illustrations of the four stages of the 1¢ essay die available in the Schernikow reprints are shown in **Figure 1-11**.

Although these reprints were made from a completed essay die, Schernikow was able to simulate the effect of progressive die prints by using a technique known as "breakdown dies." Printings were first made from the original die, and these constituted the completed die series. A transfer roller was then made from the die, and parts of the design were machined off the raised surface so that the third stage of the design remained. A lay-down die was then made, and another series of prints was made. The process was repeated for the second and first stage of the die by selectively machining off more of the design from the roller until only the vignette remained. In this manner, by working the process in the reverse of the original engraving sequence, a series of progressive die impressions was achieved.

National Bank Note Company Premiere Gravure Essays

The premiere gravure proofs produced by the National Bank Note Company include not only the gummed and perforated plate proofs that were produced as a sample for the Post Office Department, but also die and plate proofs in the issued color and in trial colors. These are all scarce and seldom come on the market. They are important to collectors of the 1¢ Franklin for they show in

Figure 1-11. Schernikow reprints of progressive die impressions for the 1861 contract essay listed by Scott and Brazer catalog numbers.

Sc. 63-E1, Br. 55E-Aa

Sc. 63-E2, Br. 55E-Ad

Sc. 63-E3, Br. 55-Af

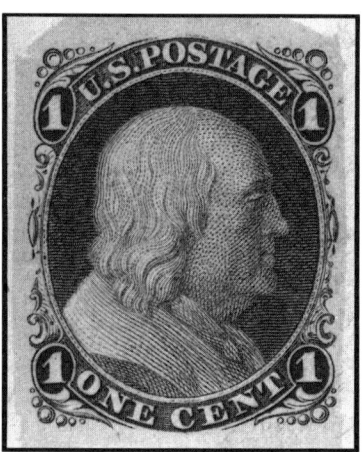

Sc. 63-E9, Br. 55-Al

detail the state of the die before the small changes were made that resulted in the issued design.

The enlarged photographs in **Figures 1-12** and **1-13** show the principal differences in the states of the premiere gravure and the completed die.

The primary changes that were made to the die were the recutting and strengthening of some lines, and some small additional engraving. The easiest identifying changes to see, in addition to the small dash of added color (C), which has been the description of the change appearing in the Scott catalogs for many years, are the stronger lip lines (F), which give a more incisive look to Franklin's mouth, and the extension and addition of vertical lines in the corner ovals (A and B).

More minor, but still observable changes include the strengthening of the outermost line of the oval surrounding the vignette (D). Although the recutting of the line is not disputed, some care must be taken with this identifying feature. Strong and well-inked proof printings of the premiere gravure will sometimes show oval lines that appear stronger than those shown in less carefully produced proofs of the completed die. Other changes are shown and described in the photographs.

A very interesting, and probably unintentional, variation from the original die was first recorded by C.W. Christian. It is a short small scratch (E) that emanates from the outer line of the upper-right oval. It was possibly made by a slip of the engraver's tool and can be identified under magnification in any clear printing of the completed issue die.

Christian's comparative studies of the dies have been published in several philatelic publications, including the winter 1972 issue of the *Essay-Proof Journal*, and much of the information included here is based on these studies.

Die proofs showing an intermediate stage between the premiere gravure die and the completed die are, according to Brazer [2:157], in existence. They must be very rare since this author has never seen an actual copy and has seen only one auction listing. The intermediate die, as described by Brazer, has the reworked corners, but the strengthening of the outer oval framelines had not yet been done. His description lists these essays as being on India paper and being in the following colors: dull red, orange, yellow, brown, green and blue.

Another interesting mark on the premiere gravure die is a very small horizontal line about 2mm in length located 2mm above the top of the design and about 5.5mm to the left of the top center. This mark is readily apparent on all proofs. The mark carries through to the accepted-design die and also to the reprint die for plate 56. It can be seen on most well-inked and clear copies of the proofs

Figure 1-12. Premiere gravure design from a large die proof in black.
(C.W. Christian collection)

Figure 1-13. Issued design.
A-Vertical shading lines in numeral area lengthened and new lines added.
B-Lengthened vertical shading in back of U and S, and lines added.
C-Added dash.
D-Outer line of oval strengthened.
E-Scratch on the die, slightly intensified for viewing.
F-Lip lines strengthened.

and issued stamps. To the author's knowledge, this particular mark has not been previously reported.

The following descriptions include all Brazer (including the Finkelburg update) and Scott-listed premiere gravure essay proofs, plus unlisted proofs known to the author. With the inclusion of these essays in the Scott catalog, the Scott numbers have become the preferred identification criteria, and the Brazer numbers are need primarily for research and cross-referencing.

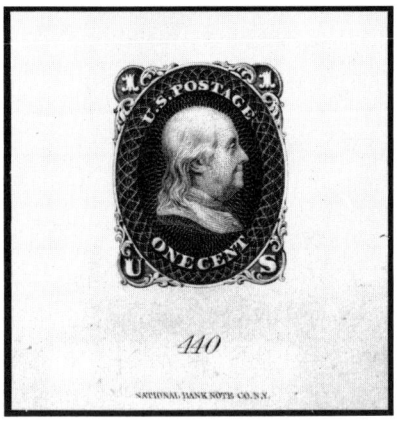

Figure 1-14. Scott 63-E11a, Brazer 55E-Ba

National Bank Note Company
Premiere gravure die 440
Size 58x56mm
Vignette engraved by Joseph Ives Pease
Frame by Cyrus Durand

Scott 63-E11 (Brazer 55E-B)
a. die essay on India paper
   indigo (unlisted in Brazer)
   black (rare) (see **Figure 1-14**)
   ultramarine (very rare)
b. small die essay on white wove paper (28x31mm)
   indigo (unlisted in Brazer)
c. plate essay on India (Brazer 55E-Bb)
   indigo
   blue
   ultramarine
   violet-ultramarine
d. plate essay on semitransparent stamp paper
   (Brazer 55E-Bba)
   ultramarine
e. plate essay on semitransparent stamp paper,
   perforated 12 and with gum
   (Brazer 55E-Bc) (rare)
   indigo (the finished essay, formerly Scott 55,
      see **Figure 1-8**)

In addition to this listing, the author has a Scott 63-E11c in ultramarine on stamp paper and another ultramarine essay that is perforated and gummed. The identification of the paper on this last item is not conclusive, but it may be a proof paper.

Scott also lists a 63-E-10, a black die frame essay with blank areas for the remainder of the design (no illustration available).

The Finkelburg revision to the Brazer catalog lists as 63E-Ba an impression in black of a sample drawing, die size unknown. It is listed as being very rare (see **Figure 1-16**).

Figure 1-17 shows a completed essay die, except that there are 1mm blank squares where the numerals would normally be.

Examples of the premiere gravure design from various types of impressions are shown in the following illustrations.

The plate 1 strip of four in ultramarine on India paper, shown in **Figure 1-15a**, was previously part of the Burroughs essay-proof collection. It was then auctioned February 1956 in the Robert P. Hackett sale by H.R. Harmer of New York. Subsequently, it appeared in a September 1988 Christie's sale. For many years this was the only plate number multiple of the premiere gravure proofs that the author had seen or recorded. However, in the spring of 1994, a plate block of eight, also in ultramarine, but mounted on the original cardboard backing (**Figure 1-15b**), was offered in a Weiss Philatelics auction. These two companion pieces may make up the only surviving plate number multiples of the 1¢ premiere gravure proofs.

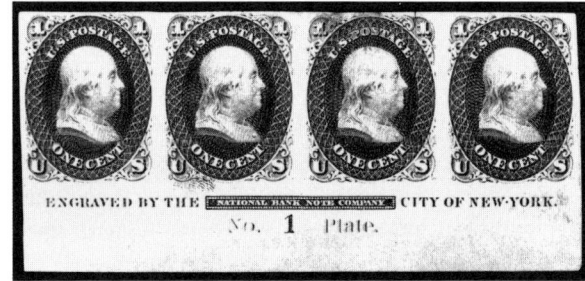

Figure 1-15a. Plate number 1 plate proof on India, strip of four. Ultramarine (rare).

Figure 1-15b. Plate number 1, plate proof on India, block of eight. Ultramarine (rare).

Figure 1-16. Brazer 63E-Ba.

Figure 1-17. On India paper, die sunk on card. Die size 47mm by 55mm. Black (rare).

Both the strip and the block show the very narrow spacing between the stamps that was a feature of the first plate. Elliott Perry reported on an intensive study of the gutter spacing for the premieres in an article in *The Essay-Proof Journal*, 109, titled "The Whole Truth." He noted the following figures for the 1¢ value:

Premiere gravure die 440, plate 1
  Height: Design 25.0mm plus gutter 1.5mm,
         total 26.5mm
  Width: Design 19.0mm plus gutter 2.5mm,
         total 21.5mm
Second design die 440, plates 9 and 10
  Height: Design 25.0mm plus gutter 3.0mm,
         total 28.0mm
  Width: Design 21.0mm plus gutter 2.0mm,
         total 23.0mm

These values compare closely with an independent study that the author conducted some 20 years later. Although the gutter spacing for plates 9 and 10 was increased substantially for the vertical measurements, the spacing was still too limited, and this resulted in the majority of the copies of the issued stamp having perforations that cut into the design. It is believed that a further increase in spacing was not possible because the printing presses being used could not accept a larger size plate, so the 200 designs per plate had to be accommodated in the available space. It was not until the reissue of 1875, when the plates were made with only 100 designs to each plate, that the gutter spacing was increased to 2.6mm in both directions, and printings resulted with beautifully margined stamps.

In the same Christie's auction of September 28, 1988, a copy of an indigo plate proof on India paper with an experimental blue cancel was offered. From the catalog photo, the cancel seems to be a blurred cork smudge, but actual inspection may show some design to the cancel.

One of the most outstanding auction sales of recent times with respect to essays and proofs was the previously mentioned Robert A. Siegel auction of June 27-29, 1990. This sale featured many surviving items from the Brazer collection. It included one-of-a-kind items and provided an unparalleled opportunity for many collectors to add some of these elusive items to their collections. One of the offerings was a black die proof on India, sunk on card, featuring the rare intermediate state of the die, previously described here from Brazer's notes. Brazer did not mention one in black, but his description of the die matches the auction description of the above item. Since this item supposedly came from the original Brazer collection, it may be a previously unreported example of this intermediate state of the die.

Another example of an unusual premiere gravure item is the hybrid proof. A plate proof of the premiere gravure on India paper and cut to size is mounted on a die-sized piece of India paper. The combination is then die sunk on card. While this is standard procedure for a low-cost method of producing simulated large die proofs in quantities, why it was done for the premiere gravure die is an interesting question.

During the short period of approximately six weeks or less that the premiere gravure die 440 was in existence before it was modified to the issued die state, all essay impressions of the 1¢ National design shown or described in this chapter must have been made, and no additional printings could have later been made from the original die. The disposition of the transfer roller and printing plate 1 is not known, but it has been assumed that they were softened and reused for other purposes. No reference has been made by any philatelic researcher to later printings of the 1¢ premiere gravure, so it may be accepted as an almost certainty that the design on the original essay die, and any transfers or plates made from it, have long since passed into history and no longer exist.

References

1. Luff, John N. *Postage Stamps of the United States*. Quarterman Publications, 1981. (Reprinted from the original 1902 publication by Scott Stamp and Coin Company).

2. Brazer, Clarence W. "History of the Preparation of the United States 1861 Stamps." *Essay-Proof Journal* No. 84.

3. Alexander, Thomas J. Ed. *Simpson's Postal Markings 1851-61* (The Civil War by Richard B. Graham). U.S. Philatelic Classics Society, 1979.

4. Brazer, Clarence W. *Essays For U.S. Adhesive Postage Stamps*. Quarterman Publications, 1977.

5. Wierenga, Theron. Reprint of the *Report of the Postmaster General for 1861*. 1977.

6. York, Norton D. *The Oneness of the 1861-1862 Regular Postage Stamp Issues*. 33rd American Philatelic Congress, 1967.

7. Perry, Elliott. *Pat Paragraphs*. Bureau Issues Association, 1981.

8. Graham, Richard B. "The Premiere Gravures Controversy of Past Decades." *Chronicle*. August 1992.

CHAPTER 2

The Issued 1¢ Stamp of 1861

Design

In his 1904 *Postage Stamps of the United States*, Luff quoted from an official description of the stamp design:

"... The portrait is probably intended as a copy from Rubricht." This quotation was accepted as fact and was repeated through the years by catalogs and by philatelic researchers as the source of the Franklin design on the 1¢ denomination.

During the late 1920s, E. Tudor Gross, the first and one of the foremost specialists in the 1861 1¢ Franklin, embarked on an extended search for the origin of the Franklin portrait featured on the stamp. Gross was exhaustive and meticulous in acquiring his information. After hundreds of letters to museums and other sources of information, and field trips to view statues and busts of Franklin, he finally resolved the matter to his satisfaction and published his findings in an article titled "Hunting for Franklin" in the October 1928 issue of *The American Philatelist*.

Gross searched without success for any information concerning an artist, sculptor or engraver by the name of Rubricht. During his quest, Gross learned that a marble bust of Franklin, which resembled the features on the stamp design, was on display at the Metropolitan Museum of Art in New York (**Figure 2-1**). After carefully comparing photos of the bust taken from different angles with the Franklin portrait on the 1¢ stamp, he was completely satisfied that this bust was the origin of the design. The sculpture was done in marble by the famous artist, Antoine Houdon, in 1778. An illustration of the bust in profile that duplicates the view shown on the stamp is shown in **Figure 2-2**.

Figure 2-3. James Macdonough, designer of the 1861 series of stamps.
(From a late engraving by the American Bank Note Company)

Who or what was Rubricht remains a mystery. It has been considered to be just an error by a clerk or by the individual who prepared the official description, but there is another possible explanation. In following up on some of the Tudor Gross research, this author found that a red chalk or crayon drawing can be referred to as a rubric. Maybe the rendering used by the engraver for the design portrait was a crayon drawing of the Houdon bust, and the word "rubric" was incorrectly copied as "rubricht."

The 1861 1¢ Franklin was designed, as were all of the 1861 issue stamps, by James Macdonough (**Figure 2-3**). At that time he was secretary of the National Bank Note Company, and later was president of the American Bank Note Company from 1887 to 1901. In the early days of the bank note companies, the officers of the firms frequently were artisans and craftsmen in the printing trade foremost, and businessmen to a lesser extent. Macdonough was a prime example of the combination of craftsman and entrepreneur. In addition to his design work, he also investigated novel ways of printing stamps with fugitive inks, and some of his patented methods were applied to experimental printings of the 1¢ Franklin.

The vignette was engraved by Joseph Ives Pease (**Figure 2-4**), a famous bank note and stamp engraver who also engraved all of the portraits for the 1851-57

Figure 2-1. The Houdon bust of Benjamin Franklin.
(Metropolitan Museum of Art, New York City)

Figure 2-2. Left profile of Houdon bust (reversed image).
(Courtesy of *The American Philatelist*)

Figure 2-4. Joseph Ives Pease, vignette engraver.
(From the *Essay-Proof Journal*)

17

issues, as well as the 1¢, 30¢ and 90¢ denominations of the 1861 issue.

The frame was engraved by Cyrus Durand, and the lettering was by David M. Cooper. It is not at all unusual to have different engravers involved with the preparation of a single die. In general, engravers specialized in specific types of engraving, such as portrait, lettering, and even lathework. In large firms such as the National or American Bank Note companies, there might have been several engravers, each of whom specialized in a different kind of lettering. One may have been a specialist in Spencerian or script, while others were expert in block lettering, numerals and other areas.

Lathework, the complex mathematical design constructed from arcs, circles and lines that surrounds the vignette, was first introduced in the United States with the 1851 issue, and played a large part in the achievement of intricacy in many stamp designs. Complexity of design was a goal for both stamps and bank notes. By incorporating extremely fine detail into the engraving, it became much more difficult to counterfeit.

Jacob Perkins' development in the early 1800s of the geometric lathe-engraving device provided the designers with a tool that could quickly produce engraved patterns of great regularity, complexity and beauty — all features that were important in stamp design. This ingenious machine was further perfected by Durand, who did the work for the 1861 1¢ [1:78]. In the year 1861, the geometric lathe was a marvel of advanced machine design (**Figure 2-5**). With a cost in excess of $10,000 and a construction time of three years, it was not likely that counterfeiters would be able to obtain a similar device that would

Figure 2-5. Lathe room where geometric designs were engraved.
(*Harper's New Monthly Magazine*, February 1862)

duplicate the stamp engraver's precision work.

Stamp Production

The 1861 Franklin was printed in intaglio from steel plates that contained 200 exact copies of the master die. The printed sheet measured approximately 12 inches by 18 inches, including margins of approximately one-half inch surrounding the printed design. Each sheet was divided vertically, probably after gumming, into two panes to facilitate handling and shipping. There is some question as to whether the sheet was divided before or after perforating. Contemporary accounts vary in describing the sheets that were being perforated as containing either 100 or 200 stamps.

For a detailed and very comprehensive guide to the technical aspects of the design and production of stamps, the reader is recommended to the excellent work by L.N. and M. Williams, titled *Fundamentals of Philately*. This book is one of the APS handbook series, and can answer most of the questions regarding philatelic technology [2].

At the beginning of production in 1861, the National Bank Note Company used a total of nine presses, six of them driven by steam, and they operated both day and night to satisfy the demand for the new issue. Approximately 33 employees were engaged in the production of stamps, and this number probably did not include designers, engravers, watchmen and other employees peripheral to the actual stamp-production process. About a third of the employees were women.

After removal from the printing presses, the sheets of stamps were taken to the drying room where they were dried at a temperature of about 120 degrees. After drying, they were gummed. This is a particularly difficult process, and owed its satisfactory accomplishment to the skill of the women appliers as much as it did to the composition of the adhesive. Each sheet to be gummed was laid on a wooden or steel frame somewhat smaller than the paper so that the edges would not receive gum and present a later handling problem. The operator gummed the sheet by hand with a large, but finely bristled brush, and the sheets were then placed in frames on a drying rack. During that period of production, enough frames and racks were available for as many as 5,000 sheets of gummed stamps to be dried simultaneously. Following the drying process, the sheets were smoothed in a hydraulic press and readied for the perforation process.

The stamp is perforated 12, a departure from the standard 15 gauge perforations of the 1851-57 series. Although no documentation seems to exist that explains

Figure 2-6. Treadle-operated perforator with the hand-gumming operation being performed in the background. (Contemporary woodcut from 1862 *Harper's New Monthly Magazine*)

why the change was made, it has been generally accepted that the wider-spaced perforations were used to avoid the unwanted separation that occurred with the earlier issue while the stamps were still in sheet form. Perforations were done on a hand-operated perforating machine similar to that developed by Bemrose and Sons in England some years previously. One of the Bemrose machines had been purchased in 1856 by Toppan, Carpenter & Company for the amount of $150 for use in its production of the 1857 issue. It originally was set up for rouletting and had to be revised by Toppan, Carpenter to punch perforations. An interesting account of the early correspondence concerning this purchase is available in Chase's book on the 3¢ 1851-57 stamp [3:164].

Either an additional machine was later purchased by the National Bank Note Company from Bemrose, or a pirated version was constructed. It has been reported that at that time the Bemrose machine was not yet patented in the United States. Norton York suggested that if it were a pirated design, the change from 15 to 12 gauge perforations would have reduced the number of pins and precision matching holes that had to be machined into the device by about 20 percent, and consequently substantially decreased the cost of manufacture [4:5].

A woodcut of a contemporary device in use is shown in **Figure 2-6**. From the drawing of the perforating machine, it appears that the size of the paper being perforated is more the size of a nominal pane of stamps rather than the larger sheet. This conclusion is further reinforced by Stanley Brookman when he describes the Toppan, Carpenter & Company machine as being limited in width for acceptance of sheets and a contributing factor to the use of small-size plates and the consequent narrow gutter margins that resulted [5:182]. However, Winthrop Boggs, in a comprehensive article on early perforating machines [6:30], firmly states that the National Bank Note Company perforated the 200-subject sheet before it was cut into panes. Considering that straight-edge copies of the 1¢ are common, and that straight edges are normally the result of cutting the sheet in two after perforating, the conclusion can be reached that this is a true statement.

The American Bank Note Company was at the same time engaged in the production of stamps for other countries such as Mexico and Newfoundland, and in its operation, the sheets were divided before perforating. This may account for some of the confusion resulting from a reading of the contemporary literature.

The perforating machine was powered by a foot-operated pedal that turned two meshing cylinders. One cylinder contained pins that punched the paper, and the other lower cylinder had carefully drilled holes that precisely fitted with the pins. The punched paper debris fell into the bottom hollow cylinder and was safely removed from the operation. Each pair of matching cylinders could be spaced as desired on the supporting shaft and adjusted to the required spacing between stamps. Obviously, since the spacing was different for the vertical and horizontal perforating operations, all of the cylinders had to be repositioned whenever the direction was changed. This was a time-consuming process, and generally all of the gummed sheets available would be perforated in one direction. Then the spacing would be changed, and the sheets would be perforated in the other direction.

Evidently only one machine was used, and this device, according to Luff and others, was the production bottleneck that restricted the output of stamps. During times when large numbers of stamps had to be produced, the machine must have been in constant use. It is surprising that another machine was not acquired or built to facilitate production by setting each to perforate in one direction only, although this was certainly done in later years.

The contents of a memo [7:67] from James Macdonough to Charles F. Steel, who was in charge of stamp production for the company, is quoted as follows:

"Sept. 12th, 1861
U. S. Postage Stamp Department.
Charles F. Steel, Manager.

Sir.
You are directed to put in force the following arrangement.

Daily task for expert perforators 7,500 sheets per day — for which will be paid $5.00 per week.

Overwork will be paid at the rate of 12½ cents per 1,000 sheets, unless the amount perforated beyond the daily task shall read 2,500 sheets, in which case 20 cts per 1,000 sheets will be paid.

Daily task for expert gummers 1,000 sheets per day — for which will be paid $4.00 per week.

Overwork will be paid at the rate of 12½ cts per 100 sheets.

All capable of performing the daily task shall be considered 'Expert' and paid accordingly.

J. Macdonough, Secretary"

The quoted arrangement for perforating requires that the operator perforate a sheet in one direction approximately every 2½ seconds (assuming a 10-hour work day). This is obviously a difficult-to-achieve goal. Records of the company during this period show that the stamp production rate was about 2,250 sheets per day. This is about one-third of the number dictated by the Macdonough memo, and a more reasonable target.

Another contemporary account concerning the perforation operation appears in the descriptive text accompanying a woodcut of the perforator previously illustrated in Figure 2-6. This text from the February 1862 *New Harper's Magazine* is quite illuminating, and is quoted here:

> ". . . In a small room we find a machine, for the invention of which almost every one has daily cause to be thankful. It is used to perforate those little holes in a sheet of postage stamps which enable us to separate them so readily. It consists of a couple of cylinders revolving together. The upper one is studded over with little punches which fit into holes in the lower one. A sheet of stamps — already gummed, dried, and pressed — is passed between these cylinders, and each punch cuts out a piece; the lower cylinder being hollow these pieces fall into it and do not clog the punches. A hundred stamps are usually printed on a sheet, and 250 of these sheets can be perforated in an hour. As simple as this machine is, no one hit upon it for years after the introduction of stamps."

The rate of perforating mentioned in this article agrees much better with the recorded stamp production volume, particularly if the perforating operation was the limiting factor in the production of stamps as Luff claimed.

Another description of the perforating operation was reported in a contemporary newspaper article in the *New York Evening Post* of August 24, 1861, and was reprinted in Elliott Perry's *Pat Paragraphs* [8:98-99]. A portion of this article follows:

> ". . . PERFORATION
> The perforation of the spaces between the stamps, so as to facilitate dividing them, as well as to promote by the roughness of the edges, their adhesion, is a rapid and peculiar operation. It is done by means of revolving cylinders, armed on the surfaces with rows of circular cutting instruments, and which, as the sheets pass, produce rows of holes. Each sheet is drawn twice though the machine in different directions, cutting completely around every stamp.
> The sheets are afterward divided, leaving one hundred on each half . . ."

Reporters of that day were probably no better in reporting facts than they are now, and there is at least one error in this account. All stamps were definitely not perforated on all sides. There was one vertical row in the center of the 200-impression sheet that received no perforations, leaving two columns of stamps with perforations on only three sides. This was the position where the sheet was divided into two panes. Most likely the sheet had been previously cut in two, and there was no necessity to perforate the outside edge. Of course, it is possible that a set of perforating cylinders could have been removed from the centerline and the sheets cut later, but this is unlikely, for the reasons earlier stated.

The final stage in the production of the stamps was the counting and packaging of the printed sheets. This was done under the careful supervision of Daniel M. Boyd, the Post Office Department's official stamp agent, who maintained an office at the bank note company. At the completion of this task, the boxes of completed stamps were transferred to the possession of the stamp agent for required distribution. At this point, most of the stamps were sent directly to requesting post offices. Any excess to current distribution requirements were stored securely on the premises or sent to the Post Office at Washington for further action.

Security and care were important elements throughout the entire operation. Printing plates were stored in guarded and locked rooms and could be removed only with the cognizance and permission of the stamp agent. All sheets of paper were counted before use by the printers, and each sheet had to be later accounted for as a completed product or scrap. The dies and the printed stamps were the property of the government, and every precaution was taken to insure that there was no possibility for fraud or theft.

During the first third of the 20th century, the only figures that were available to collectors for the number of stamps that were printed for the 1861 issue were the tables published in Luff's 1904 *Postage Stamps of the United States*. Luff stated that his figures were from the records of the stamp agent, and a listing of the published quantities for the 1¢ denomination follows:

1861	
Aug. 16	1,623,000
Aug. 17-31	3,096,900
Sept. 1 to Nov. 29	12,577,900
Nov. 29 to Dec. 31	3,838,500
Total 1861	21,136,300
1862	47,548,800
1863	36,930,400
1864	1,453,570
1865	4,525,700
1866	7,843,800
1867	10,330,000
	(includes some grilled stamps)
1868	3,774,400
	(January through March)
Grand total	133,542,970

In the same volume, Luff also reported the number of stamps that had been issued to the post offices during the same period. These figures were extracted from the annual reports of the postmaster general, and reflect amounts for a fiscal year (July 1 of the previous year through June 30 of the current year) in contrast to the above table, which is for calendar years. A summary of Luff's report follows:

    FY 1862   60,021,250
       (This includes some 1857 stamps for July and August of 1861.)
    FY 1863   69,854,000
    FY 1864   2,096,300
    FY 1865   2,120,800
    FY 1866   7,450,600
    FY 1867   8,970,500
    Total   49,513,450

Even considering the numbers of the 1857 issue that were delivered to the post offices during the last two months of the previous contract, the discrepancy in the totals printed and delivered is probably in the order of 16,000,000. This is a lot of stamps, and for some reason, the difference was not questioned in the philatelic literature until some corollary research by Elliott Perry was conducted in the 1930s.

Beginning in 1931, Perry started a campaign to learn all that he could about the facts surrounding the initial issue of the 1861 series. He had strong doubts regarding the Luff claim that the premieres gravures were issued stamps, and he wanted the factual information to substantiate his theory.

One of the important pieces of information was the actual number of stamps printed during the early days and months of the contract so that he could ascertain if there was a likelihood of the premieres gravures being printed in any quantity. The National Bank Note Company had eventually been absorbed by the American Bank Note Company, and all of its existing records became a part of the American Bank Note Company files.

Perry contacted D.E. Woodhull, president of the American Bank Note Company and received from him copies of National Bank Note Company "orders," which showed the numbers of stamps that were delivered to the stamp agent on specific days. By carefully comparing these figures with those published by Luff, Perry was able to show that for some reason Luff had neglected to include the correct number of stamps delivered during September 1861. In fact, he had missed most of the "orders" for that month [8:104-108]. The shortfall amounted to 9,531,600 1¢ stamps. This number, together with the quantities of stamps on hand at the end of the fiscal year that had not yet been delivered to the post offices, could resolve most of the the discrepancy in Luff's report.

About five decades later, the subject was again visited by William K. Herzog, a dedicated philatelist with a deep knowledge of the 1861 issue. Herzog carefully compared the various sources of information, and cross-checked the figures from Perry, Luff and the postmaster general's reports. His conclusion was that 152,205,250 1¢ stamps of the 1861 issue had been delivered to the post offices during the period from August 16, 1861, to March 31, 1868 [9:85-86]. This included a small number of grilled stamps that supposedly were not separately listed in the fourth quarter of 1867. These same grills were included in the Luff figures and possibly in the Perry results.

A fourth, and different figure has been published by Lester Brookman in his *United States Postage Stamps of the 19th Century* [5:7]. Brookman estimates that 138,000,000 were issued. No specific source for this number is mentioned. An early 1941 article by E. Tudor Gross states, without citation of source, that about 130,000,000 of the ungrilled stamps were issued.

We now have, in round numbers: Luff (stamp agent report) 134,000,000; Luff (postmaster general report) 150,000,000; Perry (National Bank Note Company orders) 144,000,000; Herzog 152,000,000; Brookman with 138,000,000; and Gross with 130,000,000. While some of these figures refer to stamps printed and delivered to the Post Office Department and the remainder refer to the number disbursed by the Post Office to individual post offices, the two amounts should agree closely since there are no records of any large number of the 1¢ stamps being destroyed by the Post Office Department. Reviewing Herzog's methodology in determining his results, it appears that his figures should be considered to be reasonably accurate and given substantial weight in comparison with the other estimates.

Knowing the exact number of stamps issued has limited philatelic value, and a few percent difference one way or the other is not significant for most purposes. It is always nice to be able to pinpoint with great accuracy the exact numbers, but in this author's opinion, a general estimate of 150,000,000 for the issued quantity will suffice.

It is interesting to note that the great majority (80 percent) of the 1¢ stamps were issued prior to June 30, 1863. There are two reasons to account for this. First, it was necessary to initially provide a stock of 1¢ stamps at all post offices since the 1¢ was the required postage for drop, transient and carrier mail. Secondly, the rate for each of these services was raised to 2¢ in July of 1863, and the 2¢ Jackson was issued. This obviated the need for so many 1¢ stamps, and the issued numbers dropped dramatically. A subsequent decrease in 1865 of the drop-letter rate to 1¢, at post offices without carrier service, reinstituted a limited need for penny postage, and this is reflected in some increase in deliveries from 1865 through 1867.

There were about 12 times as many 3¢ stamps issued as 1¢ stamps; however, the number of 1¢ stamps that are now available to collectors, particularly in used condition, is a much smaller percentage of the 3¢ value than the originally issued amounts would predict. A figure of merit would be that the 1¢ is about 100 times scarcer than the 3¢ 1861. The probable reason for this difference is that many more of the 1¢ stamps were destroyed after use. The penny stamp was used mainly on circulars, transient mail and local letters. These were all categories of mail that were less likely to be saved than out of town correspondence. The dustbins of yesteryear probably received a larger share of 1¢ Franklins than they did of the other denominations of the 1861 series.

Proofs

At this point, to avoid any possible misinterpretation, the terms proof, essay and stamp will be defined for the purposes of this text. Over the years, many varying definitions have been given for these terms, many of them overlapping or conflicting. Brazer, in his articles and books, proposed a simple, but all-inclusive, set of definitions that will be used as the basis for the terms as used here. The following definitions will be adhered to during this work:

Essay: Any drawing or impression of a stamp design that differs from the design appearing on the approved stamp that is sold to the public for postal use.

Proof: Any impression of a stamp design, other than the issued stamp itself, where the design is exactly like the design of the officially approved and issued stamp. Proofs are not produced for sale to the public, or for postal use.

Stamp: An impression that results from a printing of the approved plate and that is printed in the approved color on stamp paper, gummed and perforated, and produced for sale to the public for postal use.

Note that there are no restrictions concerning the material on which the impression is printed or the time when the printing was done.

There are several types of proofs that are known to have been made from the 1¢ die or plates. In this section, all of the proofs known to the author will be discussed with the exception of those die or plate proofs that were specially ordered by the Post Office Department for particular uses, such as the die proofs for the display at the Atlanta Cotton Fair in 1881, or the cardboard proofs that were made for free distribution to congressmen and others during the period of 1879-95. These special-order proofs will be included in the chapter on special printings.

During the course of producing a stamp, the engravers, the platemakers and the printers each had a need for impressions from their work at all stages of production. In addition, examples of the finished engraved print were used for the purpose of official approval, for special gifts and official presentations or displays, and as samples of the company's product.

A proof is the most beautiful example of the stamp engraving. It is printed with particular care on special paper, and with high-quality ink. The die or plate is normally in new condition, and the proof impression becomes an outstanding piece of intaglio art.

Through the years, collectors have recognized the outstanding quality of the proof impressions, and they have become a part of some of the most impressive philatelic collections. The question of how the proofs and essays came into philatelic hands has been the subject of many investigations and articles. It must be remembered that in the early period of stamp production, proofs were not considered to have any particular value, and no accounting was kept of their production. This was just the opposite from the situation with the actual postage stamp, where careful records and controls were maintained. Early proofs and essays were saved as souvenirs by individuals connected with the production process, and some copies were retained for the bank note company's records.

Because of their artistic merit and beauty, proofs and essays aroused the acquisitive instincts of the people who had access to these items. Model drawings and progressive die proofs were considered to be the property of the artists and engravers, and were retained in their possession, frequently to pass into philatelic hands many years later when heirs disposed of the property. A signed copy of the approved die proof was usually given to the principal engraver. Large die proofs were bound into books and given to bank note company and Post Office Department officials. Sheets of plate proofs were placed in company files for record, and scrap with unfinished or poorly executed designs was carried home by workmen as souvenirs. All of these sources contributed to the substantial, but limited, number of essays and proofs that exist today. At the end of the Civil War, the National Bank Note Company engaged in the production of many experimental and patented ideas, primarily for the purpose of insuring that canceled stamps could not be reused. Most of these printings eventually became philatelic property. In addition, many of the special printings of proofs that were requested by the government found their way into private hands, and these have provided collectors with some of the most sought-after proofs.

The approved dies and plates of the 1861 issue were the property of the government, but they remained in the custody of the bank note company after the completion of the contract. Over the years, bank note officials had many special proofs pulled from the master dies. Henry G. Mandel (**Figure 2-7**) was the official counterfeit and color expert for the American Bank Note Company during the last two decades of the 19th century and, in this position, had easy access to the dies in the company vaults. He also had a close working and personal relationship with many officials in the Post Office Department and the Bureau of Engraving and Printing, as well as with many of the engravers and artisans in the bank note company. Mandel was an avid collector of essays and proofs, and used all of his sources to accumulate the most complete and outstanding collections of original drawings, essays and proofs that had ever been assembled up until that time.

Figure 2-7. Henry G. Mandel (Courtesy of the Essay-Proof Society)

By this time, the National Bank Note Company had merged with the Continental Bank Note Company, which was subsequently acquired by the American Bank Note Company in 1879, so now all of the dies, plates, die proofs and thousands of sheets of plate proofs from the National Bank Note Company's archives, including those of the 1861 1¢ issue, were now in the possession of the American Bank Note Company.

Mandel took full advantage of this situation and, with the apparent approval of James Macdonough, the company's president, had many special proofs made from the official dies for his personal use. It is reported that he had a private proof press installed in his office. When he wanted a special item, he would instruct one of his associates to bring up a particular die from the vaults, and he would have an impression made from it [10:190]. He acted as an adviser to the Post Office Department, and was instrumental in arranging and coordinating the U.S. postal exhibit at the Paris Exposition in 1900. He also prepared large books of essays and proofs for officers and directors of his company, and in 1903, he was an adviser to the Bureau of Engraving and Printing during its preparation of the famous small die proofs for the Roosevelt presentation albums.

When the Bureau of Engraving and Printing acquired the contract for stamp printing in 1894, all of the plates that were then in the possession of the private bank note companies were returned to the Post Office Department, and some time shortly before July of the same year, BEP destroyed all of these plates. Consequently, no plate proofs of prior issues could subsequently be printed from the original plates [11:136].

Mandel's most significant transfer of proof material into private ownership was accomplished via the research activities of John N. Luff. In about 1895, Luff was associated with the Scott Stamp & Coin Company in New York, and had begun an ambitious project to collect all of the information available on U.S. stamps into an authoritative and comprehensive work. The culmination of his efforts was, of course, his magnificent *Postage Stamps of the United States*, which is a fundamental source for almost all research on early U.S. stamps that has occurred since its publication in 1902. It also provided the information for the U.S. section of the Scott *Standard Postage Stamp Catalogue*, which was edited by Luff for many years.

To help him classify and describe the various issues, Mandel provided Luff with reference sheets of India plate proofs from the files of the American Bank Note Company. Although, information on the specifics of this action is scarce, it appears that the transfer met with the approval of the Post Office Department, which was very supportive of philatelic research projects, and with the American Bank Note Company officials. Whether the sheets were just loaned to Luff or given to him is not clear, but they were evidently never returned to bank note company files. It has been reported that the floor of Luff's office had on it a stack of India proof sheets that was more than 3 feet high. Since India paper is normally just a couple of thousandths of an inch thick, this would suggest that there may have been several thousand sheets of proofs.

Brazer noted in the *Essay-Proof Journal* for January 1956 that he had been told that these proofs were turned over to J.C. Morganthau and John W. Scott for sale. By about 1905, most of these proofs became a part of the collection of Senator Ernest Ackerman and the source for the majority of India proofs that are now available.

There were other famous collectors of the period who amassed many of the existing proofs and essays into extensive collections. E.H. Mason was one of the first to develop a catalog of essays that described his holdings. These provided the initial base for Brazer's comprehensive catalogs that were written 40 years later. Other collectors, such as William A. Smith Jr.; Joseph E. Ralph, who was a director of the Bureau of Engraving and Printing; and, of course, the Earl of Crawford, whose proof collection eventually surpassed any other that has ever been assembled, all contributed to the organization and conservation of essay and proof material. Almost all of this material, with the exception of the Ackerman India proof sheets, eventually funneled into the vaults of the Nassau Stamp Company of New York. John Klemann was the proprietor of the company, and under his guidance it became the principal source of essay and proof material for collectors worldwide. The great holdings that previously existed in individual collections, for the most part, have been widely disseminated into the albums of thousands of collectors.

As the appreciation for the value and artistry embodied in proof material spread, the number of requests to the Post Office Department and the Bureau of Engraving and Printing for samples increased. The generous distribution that marked the earlier years slowed, and by 1909, the government prohibited the distribution of essay and proof material. This prohibition remained in force with some exceptions, such as the Farley days of the Franklin D. Roosevelt administration. Most material of an essay or proof nature dates from the time of the bank note companies, and very little has come into private ownership since the Bureau of Engraving and Printing assumed responsibility for stamp production.

An interesting account from a 1949 article in the *Essay-Proof Journal* titled "How Early U.S. Essays & Proofs Became Available" gives a quotation from a paper delivered to the Boston Philatelic Society on April 21, 1896, by F. Trifit, a leading Boston stamp dealer who began collecting and selling stamps in 1862. An abbreviated excerpt from this paper, which describes how some material from the Post Office Department was transferred into private hands, is quoted below. Wording within brackets are this author's additions.

"At an early period I established friendly relations with the Post Office Department through the Third Assistant Postmaster General. The first I remember was Mr. Zevely [to 1868]; then came [1868-72] Mr. Terrell; for a brief period [?], Mr. Hazen [1878-93] and, under Pres. Hayes, Mr. Barber [1875]. Nothing in the way of information, proofs or essays but what I could get through them. In all those years their chief clerk was Mr. Wm. M. Ireland, a liberal minded man, much interested in stamps and Post Office matters with which he had been connected since the forties. It was through him in 1876 I was intrusted with the entire government collection gathered by his efforts from all parts of the world. This I arranged in two magnificent volumes, adding to its treasures stamps valued at that time at fully three thousand dollars. When completed I took it to Washington and presented it to Mr. Barber for the Department. He was very much pleased with the magnificent gift and was sorry he could give me in return only some old stamps held as waste paper, and some proofs and essays, all of which he considered but ill repaid me for my labors. If I had locked them up in a safe and lost the combination until now, what would I have found?

18 sheets of each of the eight values of 1851-60

120 complete sets of the officials, including all of the high-value State in sheets.
150 each of the compound envelopes with and without patent lines.
Thousands of all the old envelopes. [These were probably the demonetized envelopes left in stock in 1861.]
1847 to 1869 reprints in sets by the hundred, Essays, Proofs, Specimens, etc., etc."

While the remuneration was largess in the extreme by today's standards, it was very little at a time when proofs and similar items had little or no value. It was the only way that the Post Office Department could pay for services connected with the National Stamp Collection since no funds were budgeted or allocated to that enterprise, and all accessions were by gift or barter.

Descriptions of several types of proofs that are known to have been made from the 1¢ die or plates are etailed in the following sections.

Progress and Engravers' Die Proofs

Normally, upon the approval of the stamp design, the vignette engraver begins the engraving of the die on a steel block with dimensions of about 2 by 2½ inches. During the progress of engraving, proofs may be taken to check the results of the engraver's work, and similar progress proofs may be taken at later stages, showing the work of the frame and lettering engravers. At the completion of the die engraving, and before hardening of the steel, one or more large die proofs are made. Each engraver was entitled by policy to a copy of his work, and these die proofs were frequently signed by the artisans and retained in their possession. These were called "engravers' proofs."

In the case of the 1861 1¢ Franklin, all of the progress proofs would have been made from the premiere gravure die during its engraving. There is no record of any of these surviving to the present nor, to the best of the author's knowledge, do any copies presently exist of signed engravers impressions, either from the premiere gravure or the issue die.

Large Die Proofs

A large die proof is the most beautiful of all the printings of the stamp design. For large die proofs of the late 19th century or early 20th century, specially prepared inks, usually of better quality than the production inks, a new die with no signs of wear, fine India paper that takes a precise impression, a special proof-press and a skilled operator all combined to produce these outstanding prints.

In making these proofs, the die was carefully inked; then the surface was wiped clean, first with a soft rag, and then with the hand. This removed all traces of ink except that remaining in the engraved recesses. The die was placed on the bed of the press and covered with a dampened piece of India paper, usually trimmed to about the size of the die. India paper is very thin and extremely fragile when wet, so it was necessary to cover it with a backing, which was usually a soft thin piece of white cardboard about 6 inches by 8 inches in size. The heavy roller of the proof press was now passed over the assemblage, and the result was a large die proof on India paper, adhering to the card backing, and with a die sinkage of the size of the die block.

After the engravers were satisfied with the die in all respects, large die proofs were made for approval, usually in the desired color for the issue, but possibly in different shades or colors for consideration by the Post Office Department. These normally were submitted to the third assistant postmaster general, whose office oversaw the design and production of stamps. After approval of the engraving and selected color, the large die proof was usually signed and dated by the approving official. The die was then hardened and new proofs were pulled in the approved color for final checking. This was necessary since, during the hardening process, damage to the die could occur. Unfortunately, no copies with the "officially approved" notation and signature for the 1861 1¢ Franklin are known to presently exist. Possibly some of these missing items may still be around, but residing in someone's very private collection or in the attics of descendants of some of the early engravers or bank note company officials.

An example of a large die proof in the issued color is illustrated in **Figure 2-8**. All dies were numbered, and the number 440 for the 1861 1¢ die (both the premiere gravure and the issued design) was assigned. The number is placed below the design on the die and is accompanied by the logo of the National Bank Note Company.

A large die proof, printed in black on glazed ivory card, and die sunk, was offered for sale in a 1995 Kelleher auction. This item has not previously been recorded and may be unique. It is slightly reduced from the full-die size and measures 49mm by 69mm. The die sinkage is visible at both the top and bottom of the proof. The surface of the ivory card is unusually glossy. Below the design appears an albino impression of the "440" die number and the National Bank Note Company logo. When this proof was struck, and why it was printed on such an uncommon material, is unknown. The impression is extremely sharp and clear.

Another type of die proof is known as an "autographed proof." As the name implies, these were large die proofs with the autographs on their face. Mandel assembled an extensive selection of these items by having large die proofs in his collection autographed by the engravers. The engraver of the frame and letters usually signed in pencil in the lower-left corner, the vignette engraver in the right-hand corner, and the designer at the top. It seems likely that such an item would exist for the 1861 1¢ since Macdonough was the designer, and the die proof most probably was available to Mandel. But again it is a missing proof.

Hybrid die proofs are somewhat more common than the standard large die proof. A hybrid proof was made by trimming a plate proof close to the design, mounting this trimmed proof on a sheet of approximately die-sized India paper with possibly a light sprinkling of flour as an adhesive. It was then placed, with a card backing, over a blank die block, and the combination was subjected to the pressure of the proof press. The result closely resembles a normal large die proof, but careful examination will disclose a visible impression the size of the cut-out proof on the back of the card. This results, of course, from the extra thickness caused by the proof.

Hybrid dies were made as a cost-effective substitute. The bank note companies were not paid additionally for their manufacture of the many proofs that the Post Office Department requested from them, so when a large number of large die proofs were requested, it was much easier to make them in the hybrid form. This bypassed the inking and wiping stage entirely with a substantial savings in time and material.

Figure 2-8. Die 440. Large proof in the issued color, on India paper, die-sunk on cardboard.

  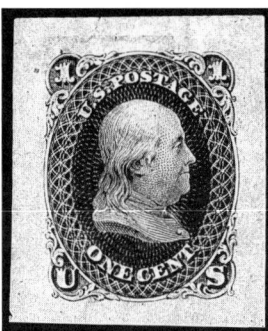

Figure 2-9. Small die trial color proofs of the issued design. Also shown in color section.

Trial color proofs on India were probably also made in large die form. All recorded copies have been trimmed so that the margins are relatively small (about 3mm) and consequently are classified as "small die proofs." They are extremely rare. The Scott 1996 catalog lists five colors: black, red, brown, green and orange, and designates them as 63TC(2). The author's collection has a dull red, green and an orange example of these small die proofs. These were obtained from the sale of the Brazer collection and may be unique. Photos of these particular items are shown for reference as **Figure 2-9** and again in the color section to illustrate the actual colors. Referring to the previous discussion on page 13, it is possible that these proofs are the progressive die proofs that Brazer described. However, after careful examination, the author has been unable to ascertain any variation in the outer framelines from the final die configuration.

Although there are many other trial-color impressions of the 1861 1¢ Franklin listed in the Scott catalog, they are all plate printings that were printed in various colors to demonstrate several patent ideas. These will be discussed in Chapter 4. The multicolored Atlanta small dies on thin card are better described as special printings and are reviewed in Chapter 5.

With respect to their rarity, trial color die proofs of this issue are very underpriced. Although proofs and essays have come a long way from their early beginnings of no value toward reaching their proper place in the price structure of philatelic items, they are still priced at levels much less than their beauty and rarity should dictate.

Plate Proofs

After the original die was approved and hardened, it was placed on the bed of a transfer press so that a roller of soft steel could be mounted above it and rolled or rocked into the die block under tremendous pressure. The soft steel of the roller was forced into every engraved line in the die, and a resulting mirror image of the engraved die was formed in relief on the roller.

Transferring designs by means of the transfer press was a long and exacting process. Each time the hardened image was rocked into the recipient metal, a little more of the design was transferred. The entry procedure was repeated many times for each image before the design was properly duplicated, and making of a transfer roller could take several days of a craftsman's time.

Several reliefs were normally made on the surface of a single roller. The reliefs were spaced so that the distance between them was the same as the planned distance between images on the printing plate. The transfer roll was then checked for flaws, such as scratches and extraneous bits of metal or incomplete entries. If it was found to be satisfactory, it was hardened. From the hardened transfer roll, several duplicate dies were made by reversing the procedure in the transfer press. These dies were known as "lay-down" or "working" dies. The original die was then designated as the "master die" and placed in secure storage in the event that the working dies and the transfer roller were damaged or lost.

The designs on the transfer roller were then entered on a steel plate. A skilled worker called a siderographer carefully measured and marked the plate so that he could correctly position the transfer roller to enter all the necessary designs onto the plate with the transfer press (**Figure 2-10**). These markings are the source of position dots and lines present on most proofs and occasionally seen on the issued stamps.

The plate for the 1861 1¢ contained 200 subjects arranged in 10 rows of 20 subjects each. After entering the subjects on the plate, the marginal markings were added, probably from a specially prepared transfer roller that contained the necessary inscriptions. In this case they consisted of a 42mm boxed logo with the words "National Bank Note Co. New York" placed at the top center of each pane, and on the right margin of the right pane and the left margin of the left pane. Centered at the

Figure 2-10. Transfer room. Note the Fresnel light-concentrating lenses at the lower part of the windows to provide improved illumination for the exacting work of transferring engravings.
(*Harper's New Monthly Magazine*, February 1862)

Figure 2-11. Plate margin markings. The top photo shows the marking found at the top and sides of the plate, and the lower photo is an enlarged reproduction of the bottom margin logo and plate number marking.

bottom of each pane is a 28.5mm "National Bank Note Company" boxed logo preceded by the words "Engraved by the" and followed by "City of New York." Below the logo is the plate number inscription. It is probable that the plate number was engraved directly on the plate. See **Figure 2-11** for an illustration of these markings.

Upon completion of the plate entries, a proof impression on India paper was made, usually in the color selected for the issued stamp but in trial colors if required. This plate proof was carefully inspected for any defects, which, if found, were corrected before proceeding. If sat-

isfactory, the proof sheet was signed and placed in the Post Office Department files for record. Additional proofs were pulled for the files of the National Bank Note Company. According to Friedman, it is probable that most of the 19th-century U.S. plates were not hardened, although this author has not found any separate confirmation of this.

Brazer contends that all India proofs were printed "contemporaneously with or before the stamps." This is in strong contrast to die and cardboard plate proofs, which are known to have been printed at various times

Figure 2-12. Matched pair of marginal blocks of 12 plate proofs on India paper from plate number 56. (C.W. Christian collection)

subsequent to the printing of the original stamp. As previously mentioned, the majority of the India plate proofs now available to collectors originated from the files of the National Bank Note Company and came down through the years via Luff, Crawford, Ackerman, Lilly and, more recently, from the vaults of the Weill brothers of New Orleans.

The India plate proofs are listed by Scott as 63P3, and a notation at the end of the listing states that these proofs are priced for examples from the 100-subject plate that was made for the 1875 reissue. Some of the 1¢ India proofs are also from the earlier regular-issue plates and can be distinguished by their characteristic narrow gutters. Of course to make this distinction it is necessary to have a multiple-impression example. The author has a horizontal pair that shows the narrow separation, and in the chapter on special printings, a plate 27 imprint block on India paper is illustrated in Figure 5-13. Large multiples of the India proofs are scarce, but it is quite possible that some complete sheets still exist from the 1967-68 Josiah K. Lilly sale.

In the C.W. Christian collection there is a striking set of matched India blocks of 12 from the reissue plate 56. The photo shown as **Figure 2-12** illustrates the right and left pane inscriptions as well as the expanded spacing between the stamps and the larger plate margins that were possible with the 100-subject plate.

Scott lists 63P3 in blue only, while Brazer records blue, ultramarine, pale blue and dark blue. In the author's experience, the range of colors is not great, and a true ultramarine has not been seen. But since Brazer advertised a block of four of the ultramarine for sale in 1956, it is certainly probable that plate proofs in the ultramarine shade do exist.

A Kelleher auction of November 8, 1978, described a horizontal proof pair on bond paper, but in general, varieties in plate proof examples are minimal.

A word of caution should be injected at this point. The most dangerous fakes of U.S. stamps are those that are manufactured from India and card proofs. In the early years, proofs were very inexpensive, and of course, the designs duplicated those of the actual stamp in every detail since they were printed from the same plates. In the case of card proofs, the faker shaved the card until it was approximately the thickness of the issued stamp. For India proofs, additional paper backing was added. After achieving the desired thickness, the proof was perforated and offered as a genuine stamp. Most of this type of work is reported to have been done in Europe, which around the turn of the century possessed a considerable number of artisans who were busy altering and counterfeiting stamps for sale to unwary collectors.

Fortunately, it is not particularly difficult to distinguish these proof fakes. Card proofs, even when shaved, still retain the uneven density of the cardboard. When the "stamp" is held up to the light, the paper transmits the light unevenly, and a mottled appearance is noticeable. C.W. Christian also recommends floating the item gently on watermark fluid. A genuine stamp will sink in seconds, whereas a cardboard fake may take minutes. In the case of India paper fakes, the additional thickness is achieved by gluing a thin backing to the India paper. The glue alters the characteristics of the paper. When the fake is floated on watermark fluid, the saturation by the fluid is very uneven. In addition, under strong magnification, it is sometimes easy to see the two layers of paper when the edges are carefully examined.

The fake perforations also provide clues to distinguish fakes, as does the gumming process (although all altered proofs are not necessarily gummed).

The alerting signal in spotting an altered proof is that the design impression is exceptionally sharp and

Figure 2-13. Fake "finished premiere gravure" manufactured from an India proof. (C.W. Christian collection)

clear. Also, the margins are generally even and relatively large. Very few genuine stamps achieve the clarity of color and the detail in the printing that are characteristic of proofs, particularly proofs that were printed on India paper.

In the case of the 1¢ 1861, the most likely subject for fraud would be an attempt to manufacture a copy of the finished gummed essay of the premiere gravure from an India proof with the same design. This would increase its potential sales price by several thousand percent. **Figure 2-13** illustrates an example of one of these fakes. Examination against a bright light shows the unevenness of the India paper, but the most telling error by the faker is that he selected a premiere gravure essay proof in the ultramarine shade for his alterations. The finished essay is only found in indigo. As always, knowledge of stamps is one of the best protections against being cheated. Another possible target might be the 1875 reprint. Here, the unique shade of the reprint and the very white paper upon which it is printed could differentiate a true copy from a fake. This is in addition, of course, to all the other indicators that have been mentioned.

A selection of 1¢ proofs adds distinction to any collection, and a comprehensive showing is a must for any specialist in the stamps of this period. No more will ever be made. These outstanding examples of the engravers' and printers' art are not only beautiful, but their rarity continues to increase as examples are lost to theft, carelessness and the elements.

Plates and Multiples

For many years, respected philatelic authorities have listed the plates used to print the 1861 1¢ Franklin (Scott 63) to be plates 9, 10, 22, 25 and 27. The earliest mention of these numbers appears in Luff's 1902 work on U.S. stamps, and these numbers are repeated in Brookman. Examples of stamps or multiples with attached plate numbers are very scarce. In 1992 this author made a compre-

hensive survey of all the records at his disposal that described or illustrated a 1¢ Franklin single or multiple showing a plate number. The results were very meager, and no examples with plate 22 or 25 could be found. This raised the interesting possibility that these two plates had never seen actual use, and that even if they had been prepared, they could have been damaged in some way, and there had been no necessity for replacing them. Working with this premise, an article was written for the *Chronicle* [12:183-87], which described the search for the missing plates, and which called for readers to offer any information concerning them. Unfortunately, there was no response to this request. This, of course, does not rule out the possibility that plates 22 and 25 were used, but it further supports the supposition that they may never have been used in the printing presses.

John C. Chapin's definitive listing of plate blocks [13] shows no listing for numbers 22 and 25, but the few blocks listed do underscore the scarcity of plate number multiples of the 1861 1¢ (Scott 63) and the 1867 grilled issues (Scott 86, the E grill, and 92, the F grill). After an extensive survey of the literature and queries of the philatelic public, Chapin was able to locate only a total of eight plate multiples of Scott 63: two for plate 9, two for plate 10 and four for plate 27. The E grill was represented by one plate 10 example, and the F grill by a single plate 27 block.

The largest multiple recorded by Chapin is a complete pane of 100 subjects. This is a left pane from plate 27, and was listed in the November 19, 1970, Siegel auction. Chapin indicates that this item previously formed part of the Green and Neinken collections. The next largest is a block of 98 (positions 9 and 10 missing from the pane) from plate 9, the first plate to be used. This is an ex-Lilly item, and was recorded in a September 14, 1967, Siegel auction.

Next are two blocks of 20 (10 by 2), one from plate 9, sold from the Y. Souren collection by H.R. Harmer in 1951 for $90 (a wonderful buy). The other block of 20 is from plate 27 and is illustrated in **Figure 2-14**. Two blocks of 12 are listed, both from plate 27, and the list finishes with two used strips of three, each from plate 10. One of these used strips is found on an 1863 cover from Bryant, Illinois, and is the only known example of a plate number multiple on cover. This is shown in **Figure 2-15**. In addition to the above listings, there is a block of 12 from plate 9 that is in the Christian collection. This item is shown in **Figure 2-16.**

The catalog from the November 12, 1993, Richard E. Drews auction pictured an unused four-by-five block, plate 10, multiple that has not before been listed. The selvage is trimmed at the bottom, and only the top half of the "10" is visible. However, there is no doubt as to the

Figure 2-14. Plate number 27 block of 20, lower-left pane.

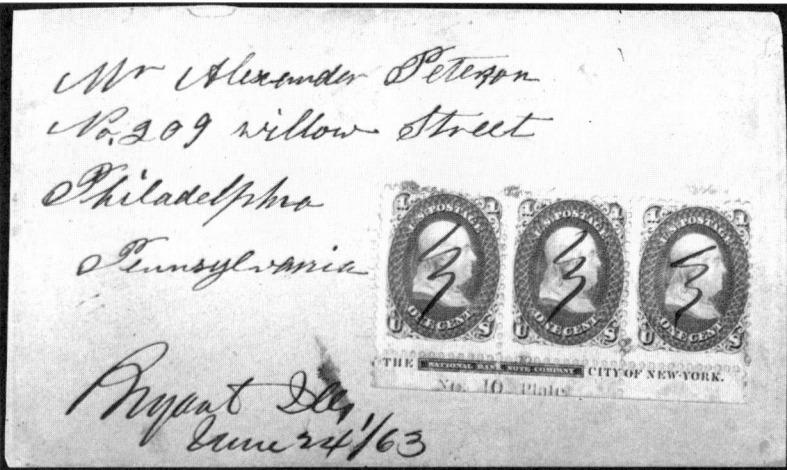

Figure 2-15. Very rare, possibly unique, plate number strip on cover. Mailed June 24, 1863, at the 3¢ letter rate, from Bryant, Illinois, to Philadelphia, Pennsylvania.

identification.

Other known examples of plate numbers exist on single stamps, both used and unused. All that this writer has recorded carry one of the known plate numbers, 9, 10 or 27.

For a stamp with an issue amount of 150,000,000 stamps, this is an astonishingly small number of plate number examples. Consequently, plate-inscription multiples carry large premiums, and their scarcity dictates that they will not be found in many collections.

Used blocks of four on cover are also very scarce. It is reported that fewer than five examples are known where the block is on the face of the envelope. An example of one of these rare covers is shown in Chapter 10, Figure 10-43.

Only two blocks of six, used on cover, have been recorded by the author. One is addressed to Montreal, Canada, via New York, and was transported outside the mails. An illustration of this unusual cover is shown in Chapter 13, Figure 13-6. The other was listed in a Robert G. Kaufamnn sale in 1981. The partial illustration showed a block of six affixed sideways on the left side of a cover originating at Port Royal, South Carolina. The date and destination are not complete in the illustration.

One block of 15 stamps is recorded on a domestic cover from Warrensburgh, Missouri, to St. Louis, Missouri. The total franking on this large orange cover is 18¢ for a six-times rate with the block of 15 plus a vertical pair and single of the 1¢ Franklin. All stamps are on the reverse of the cover. It was offered by Christie's in New York in a June 25, 1996, auction.

The largest number of the 1¢ Franklin to be used on cover is reported to be 30 copies on a large registered cover from Philadelphia, dated March 28, 1865. This item is discussed in the registered letter section of Chapter 13 and is illustrated as Figure 13-3 of that chapter.

Unused multiples of 15 or more impressions are scarce, and those with more than 20 impressions are rare. To the author's knowledge, no census of these multiples has ever been compiled, other than the plate number multiples referred to in the preceding discussion. **Figure 2-16b** shows a top sheet margin block of 30 that was offered in the March 15, 1989, Christie's New York auction of the Walter C. Klein collection.

Colors

Color is a very important characteristic of a stamp. However, the color perceived also depends very much on the person looking at the stamp, the quality of the illumination, the surrounding colors, and the paper on

Figure 2-16. A plate number 9 block of 12. (C.W. Christian collection)

Figure 2-16b. Top sheet margin block of 30, dark blue shade. From the Walter C. Klein collection. Multiples of more than 20 impressions are rare. (Christie's New York auction photo)

which the stamp is printed. With so many variables, it is difficult to accurately define a specific color for a specific stamp. Scientific instrumentation exists that can break down any color into its component wavelengths and also determine the constituents of the ink, therefore precisely identifying a color and the material that produces the color. These are not available to most collectors, and the observational method of color determination remains the most widely used.

Several good books are available that can aid the collector. These include the *Methuen Handbook of Color* [14], which contains color plates for matching colors, and R.H. White's *Encyclopedia of the Colors of United States Postage Stamps* [15]. The latter is an excellent reference work that contains color photos with a high degree of fidelity of U.S. stamps along with analyses and descriptions of the major color varieties.

To properly describe colors, and to understand the meaning of these descriptions, it is advisable to be familiar with the color descriptors and their precise meanings. There are three basic qualities in a color by which it can be completely described. These are its hue, chroma and value. Hue is how we distinguish one color from another, e.g., red, yellow, blue-green, and so on. (Hue is also frequently referred to as "color" or "shade.") Chroma is the strength or weakness of a color and is a measure of how far the color varies from a neutral gray. The terms brightness and dullness are frequently used interchangeably for chroma. The third measurement is value, which is an indication of how dark or light the color is. A low value is dark and a high value refers to light. Intensity is an equivalent term in common use for value.

In this book, an attempt will be made to use the same set of descriptors throughout. These alternatives will be color and shade for hue, brightness for chroma, and intensity for value. Terms like the adjectives pale and dark are self-explanatory and denote an evaluation of the chroma and value.

The recommended way to view and compare colors is to view them under a white light corresponding to a color temperature of approximately 5,500°K. Sylvania markets an acceptable fluorescent light (model F 14 T12-D) that may be used in a desk lamp for this purpose. The stamp should be viewed on a background of neutral gray, and if it is on cover, the surrounding area should be masked with gray card. The reference stamp to which the sample is being compared should be placed as close as possible to the subject stamp. Since the paper that the 1861 stamps are printed on varies in both hue and texture, every attempt should be made to concentrate on the color of the ink itself without being influenced by the background paper. In spite of all of the care and precautions that may be taken, assessing colors and their variations remains a very subjective procedure.

Pigments for the inks used in the 1861 series of stamps were made from natural materials, both organic and mineral. They were prepared by hand, and in relatively small batches (**Figure 2-17**), which resulted in many variations in the shades of blue used for the issued stamp. Besides the differences in color caused by the inconsistency of the raw materials, and variations in the manual procedures used in making the ink, formulas for the ingredients were, at times, purposely changed to attain a more satisfactory color.

In addition to the color, the thickness of the ink was very important. It had to be soft enough so that it could be forced into all of the minute recesses of the engraved plate, but at the same time not so fluid as to run. At the completion of its preparation, the batch of ink was extremely viscous to the point where it was barely malleable. Before it was used, it had to be heated so it could be applied to the plate, which was also heated. The application was done by hand with the printer warming and working a small amount of ink, and then applying it to the plate so that every line of the intaglio design was filled with ink. Excess ink was then wiped from the surface of the plate, first with a cloth and then expertly with the hand. This was a critical operation, and incomplete wiping resulted in those examples of stamps that show a light shading of the stamp color over their entire surface.

The amount of ink used was also important. Since several impressions were made before re-inking, it was necessary to insure that sufficient ink was used to avoid lightly printed or "dry" printings, and to avoid the necessity for frequent re-inking. In addition to the dry prints,

Figure 2-17. Contemporary woodcut of a mill used to grind pigments for ink. Note the belts that provide power to the grinder, a very early use of steam to power machines in the printing trade.
(*Harper's New Monthly Magazine*, 1862)

other printing variations were caused by improper inking and handling. Blank or light areas resulted from incomplete inking, and offset impressions on the reverse side were made when sheets of printed stamps were piled on each other before the ink was sufficiently dry.

The 1861 1¢ Franklin is basically printed in one primary color, and that is blue. It exists in many shades of blue, and in varying intensities and degrees of brightness.

The 1996 Scott catalog lists the stamp (Scott 63) in five shades: blue, pale blue, bright blue, ultramarine and dark blue. Previous editions had included the indigo shade. All six shades are also listed in Brookman. The elimination of the indigo from the current listing is a matter for debate. Indigo, for the purposes of this book, and in the author's opinion, is a blackish blue, and there are certainly examples that fit this designation. It is interesting to note as an aside that 300 years ago Sir Isaac Newton defined indigo as one of the primary colors and placed its hue midway between blue and violet.

Scott lists the ultramarine (63a) and the dark blue (63b) as separate varieties with a substantial premium attached to each.

The Philatelic Foundation, according to William K. Herzog [16:116-18], has never certified an indigo 1¢ 1861, and has a policy that it will not certify one until its expertizers are shown an unused, original-gum copy that matches the indigo shade of the finished premiere gravure. This in the author's opinion seems to be an unduly restrictive policy, but if the expertizers want to call the indigo shades of the 1¢ Franklin a dark blue, it really doesn't matter much. It remains an attractive shade that is elusive. Herzog also commented that indigos are "almost unattainable," which seems to be a true observation. White, in his color encyclopedia, illustrates a used copy of the 1¢ that he labels as indigo, and the author agrees with this designation. Three or four stamps in the author's collection would, in his opinion, fall within the indigo classification, and there is no doubt they are very difficult to find.

The ultramarine color is also extremely scarce. White illustrates several ultramarines and comments that they all seem to have a reddish hue. In the author's experience, the ultramarine shade appears to have a pastel look and is an extremely attractive color.

A reference ultramarine that the author uses for comparison studies is the color of the ultramarine printing of the premiere gravure large die proof. This item is very rare, possibly unique, and it is shown in **Figure 2-18**. It is also shown in the color section to provide the reader with an example of this scarce shade. The shade of this reference appears to closely match color 20 C 6, as

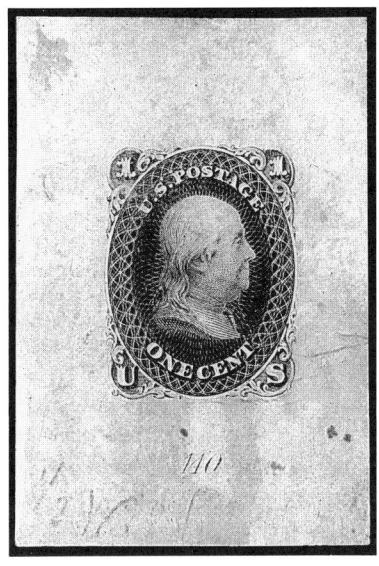

Figure 2-18. Large die premiere gravure India proof in ultramarine (rare). Also shown in color section.

shown in the *Methuen Handbook of Color* [14]. Another good reference is the ultramarine printings of the India paper plate proofs of the premiere gravure design. The intensity of the ultramarine on these India proofs is slightly brighter than that on the previously discussed die proof.

Comparing both reference examples to the ultramarines shown in White's study [15: plate I-13], the author finds that the proof examples appear to be a bit more purple than the White ultramarine examples.

When using proof examples of colors for comparison, it should be remembered that the paper and quality of ink used for the general issues, as well as the care with which they were printed, was different and less exacting. Therefore, a one-to-one correlation should not be expected. However, the proof examples are a good place to begin to identify the ultramarine and indigo shades.

The actual stamps this author considers definitely to be ultramarine have the shades that are pictured in the White book as the middle two 63a examples in row two of plate I-13. These correspond with Methuen color samples 21 D 5 and 21 D 6. According to Herzog [16:117], this is also the sample designation that describes the Philatelic Foundation reference stamp for the 1¢ 1861 ultramarine.

The remaining shades are all comparatively plentiful, and a color expert can identify dozens of slight variations in color, intensity and brightness. This is to be expected with the frequent mixing of ink pigments that occurred. The author has some examples in his personal collection that seem to have a greenish-blue hue. No mention of a tendency toward green is made in any published list of colors, so these may be color changelings or post-printing color change. Some envelopes of the 19th

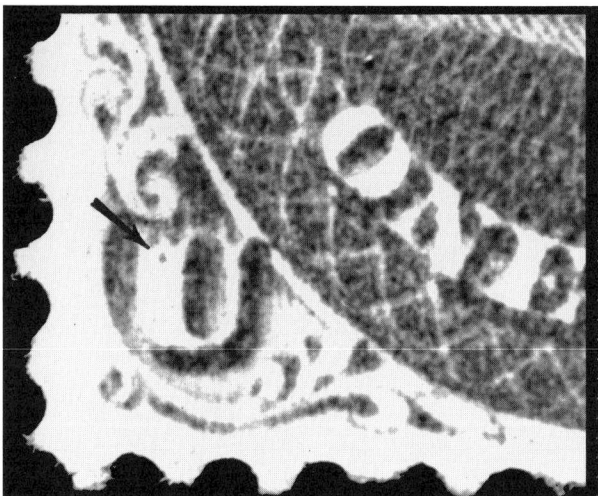

Figure 2-19. Enlarged photo of the "U" in the lower-left corner of the stamp, showing the dot error in plate 9.

Figure 2-20. Reverse side of the rare "printed on two sides" variety. (Harmer's, San Francisco, auction photo, January 11, 1986)

century are known to contain small amounts of cyanide, and this can react with the blue colorant to produce a greenish tint [15:28]. In general the blues are relatively stable and do not experience the environmental changes that affect so many of the violet colors and iron-oxide pigments.

No attempt to illustrate the many minor color variations will be made here. Accurate color reproductions are exceptionally difficult to achieve, and if they are not completely accurate, they serve little purpose.

Varieties and Production Errors

There are very few different printing varieties of the 1861 1¢. A major variety is the "dot in U," which receives its name from a small dot that is found in the "U" in the lower-left corner of the stamp as shown in **Figure 2-19.** This variety is found only on stamps from plate 9, the first plate. Since the dot is found in all the positions on this plate, the flaw must have occurred in the die from which the transfer roller was made. This would have resulted in a raised dot on the roller, and consequently a depression that would receive ink in each image on the plate. Somewhere early in the printing history, the dot must have been noticed, and the flaws removed from the roller, or a new roller made, and a new plate made without the distinctive dot. It is unfortunate that there are not enough available stamps that can be positively identified to be from plate 9 to better determine exactly when the dot ceased to exist. It can definitely be said, however, that it is in plate 9 and is not in the subsequent plates.

Scott lists a double transfer, which the author has not seen. The only other recorded plate error is a cracked-plate error on a dark blue stamp. The stamp is on an 1862 cover addressed to Carrollton, Illinois. The crack runs diagonally from the top left to the bottom right. This may be a unique example of this plate fault [17].

The stamp is known printed on both sides, and it is listed in the Scott U.S. specialized as 63e. Only two examples of this error are known to the author, and they both appear to have come from the same sheet. One was sold at a 1966 Higgins and Gage auction in Los Angeles for $177. At that time it was described as having come from the Hugh Clark collection. A photocopy of the catalog offering exists, but unfortunately, it is not good enough to reproduce as an illustration. The other recorded copy was sold in a 1986 Harmer's auction and purchased by the well-known San Francisco dealer, Stanley Piller. A photo of this example is shown in **Figure 2-20.**

Only one example of the 1¢ is reported to exist in imperforate condition. It is part of a unique complete imperforate set of all 10 values for the 1861-67 issue. Many of the denominations have small inked crosses on them, although the 1¢ value is without this marking. Two other sets of imperforates are reported, but both are missing the 1¢ value. The three sets evidently were part of sample or specimen sheets of the 1861 series, as suggested by the inked markings that are similar to those frequently added to specimens or samples. The date or purpose for

Figure 2-21. Unique imperforate copy of the 1¢ 1861. The stamp is unused, but it appears that the ink was smeared before drying. (Steve Ivy Philatelic Auctions)

Figure 2-22. A horizontally imperforate plate number 10 single on a Chicago cover, paying the 1¢ drop rate. (Christie's of New York, photo)

Figure 2-23. Examples of vertical and horizontal double perforations.

which these were printed is not known.

The complete set was offered in a 1988 Daniel F. Kelleher auction (price realized was $18,000) and again later in the same year at a Steve Ivy auction with an estimated value of $20,000-$40,000. The auction description states that the set was sold in 1922 by J.C. Morganthau & Company, and that it more recently had been a part of the Rudy Wunderlich collection. Although single copies of imperforate stamps are difficult to authenticate, all stamps in this set have been certified by the Philatelic Foundation as genuine. **Figure 2-21** shows the 1¢ from this set.

The Scott U.S. specialized also lists a vertical pair, imperforate between, as Scott 63d. The origin and present location of this item is not known to the author. Another example of a rare horizontally imperforate 1¢ blue, on cover, sold for $7,475, including the 15-percent buyer's premium, in the September 1993 Christie's auction of the Ishikawa U.S. classics collection. This stamp, although not a multiple, also shows the bottom plate margin with no perforations between it and the stamp. This verifies that it is horizontally imperforate on the bottom, and the large imperforate top margin is highly suggestive that it is also imperforate at the top. The stamp is tied to a cover with a blue Chicago circular datestamp and has a matching oval backstamp with the notation, "HALF HOUR DROP LETTER DELIVERY." A reproduction of the catalog photo of this gem is shown in **Figure 2-22**.

Most of the production errors associated with the stamp are a result of the perforating operation. As stated earlier, perforating was done manually with a relatively primitive device. It was powered by a foot treadle similar to that of a sewing machine. A single machine perforated all of the stamps for the National Bank Note Company, at least in its early years of printing stamps. Since sheets of stamps had to be fed through the machine twice, once horizontally and once vertically, and the perforator had to be reset between these operations, there were significant opportunities for error. The most common error is the double perforation. A sheet is fed through the machine twice, either by mistake or to correct a misperforation. Examples of double perforation errors are illustrated in **Figure 2-23**. Two sets of parallel holes result, which are usually just a couple of millimeters apart. No examples of double perforations in both vertical and horizontal directions on the same stamp are recorded.

Although almost all of the stamps of this issue are poorly centered, there do not seem to be any extreme examples of perforation errors where the perforations are in the middle of the stamp.

In the early 1920s, E. Tudor Gross began his initial acquisitions of the 1¢ Franklin and concentrated on finding exceptionally well-centered copies of the stamp. He was very surprised that the number of stamps that we would now describe as superb were so few in number. He had not at that time made a decision to specialize in the

Figure 2-24. A preprinting fold resulted in this extraordinary production error. (From a photo by Clyde Jennings)

stamp, as he later did, but was simply looking for fine copies of a stamp he particularly liked. Some years later he made a calculation based on the number of superb stamps he had been able to find relative to the total number of stamps that seemed to be in philatelic hands. He came up with an estimated conclusion that there were fewer than 3,000 superb copies in existence [18:263].

This number does not seem to be unreasonable, and it is certainly true that the stamp is very scarce with very fine to superb centering. Auction realizations for these gems reflect their scarcity and bring many times the price of an average fine copy.

Perforation errors that come from sheets of stamps being accidentally folded prior to perforating result in some unusual errors. The most spectacular error of this kind that this author has ever seen is shown in **Figure 2-24**. This marvelous find was at one time in the Clyde Jennings collection. It is an unused copy, and it is the only unused perforation error of this type that this author has seen.

Another interesting example of this type of error is from the C.W. Christian collection and is shown in **Figure 2-25**.

Because the space between the perforating rollers had to be readjusted between the horizontal and the vertical perforating operations, there were occasions when these adjustments were not done properly, and the distance between perforations was not uniform. This could lead to stamps with very small or very large margins. Also, since the sheet was positioned for entry into the perforating rollers by a guide, misplacement of this guide could cause the perforations to all be made to one side or the other of the desired location.

Two examples of unusual stamps that resulted from these types of mistakes are shown. **Figure 2-26** illustrates a stamp with extremely wide vertical margins. Traces of the adjoining stamps are visible on both sides. The stamp is probably the result of the sheet being fed through the perforator with an incorrectly positioned guide. This misplaced the vertical perforations to the right. The large left margin is most likely the edge of the pane in a case where the sheet was not divided into two equally sized panes.

Figure 2-27 shows an example on cover of a somewhat scarce "midget." The width of this stamp is less than 75 percent of that of a normal average stamp. While it could be the result of poorly spaced perforating rollers, C.W. Christian is of the opinion that the stamp initially had at least one double vertical perforation, and that the user separated the stamp using the inside perforations. This is a reasonable explanation for the cause of this very emaciated stamp.

Another type of perforation error is "slanted perforations." These result from the pane being fed into the perforator at a slight angle. The author has in his collection a strip of three stamps where the horizontal perforations slope down to the left. This error is normally quite slight. Any large misalignment during the insertion process would not allow the pane to feed properly between the rollers.

Examples of a class of errors called simple preprinting folds are not particularly scarce. When the dampened

Figure 2-25. A "wild perforation" error on cover. Although partially obscured by the cancel, there is a diagonal line of perforations also in the lower-left corner of the stamp. Mailed at the drop rate of 1¢ for local delivery at Brandon, Vermont.
(C.W. Christian collection)

sheet of paper was placed on the plate it contained a small, probably unnoticed, fold. Subsequently, when the sheet was dried and pressed after printing, the unprinted portion under the fold was exposed. Most of these printing errors show the results of very small folds of 1mm or 2mm in width, but examples that the author has seen have blank areas as large as 5mm. **Figure 2-28** shows a photo of a vertical preprinting fold. This type of error can be distinguished from a similar-looking unprinted area, caused by some type of debris on the paper before printing, by the distortion that it causes in the design. In the example shown, the width of the design has been in-

Figure 2-26. An oversize copy of the 1¢ 1861 stamp. (C.W. Christian collection)

Figure 2-27. An exceptionally narrow copy of the 1¢ Franklin, resulting from a perforation error. The cover, from St. Louis, Missouri, to Quincy, Massachusetts, is dated March 5. It is also franked with the 1863 2¢ Jackson to make up the 3¢ domestic letter rate. (James Lee collection)

creased by the thickness of the fold. This would not be the case if a small fragment of paper or other material had caused the blank area.

The last category of varieties is the paper varieties. The 1861 1¢ stamp is found on slightly varying thicknesses and colors of wove paper with an average thickness of about 0.004 inches, and a relatively hard and crisp surface. Because of the lack of strict production standards for paper during that period, the characteristics of the paper changed slightly from time to time. There is no strong correlation between the properties of the paper and the time of printing, with the exception of a very thin paper that was at times used for the E and F grills. The same type of statement may be made for the gum that was used. It varied in color from a pale yellowish white to a brownish color, and the variations appear to be random.

One paper that was used is distinctive. This is laid paper, and the stamp is known to have been printed on both horizontally and vertically laid paper. Examples are

scarce and are somewhat difficult to identify by casual observation. For this reason, there may be more examples around than would be indicated from a census of auctions and other listings. The horizontal paper variety seems to be significantly scarcer than the vertical paper, and this writer has seen only two examples of horizontally laid paper with the 1¢ Franklin. Both are used, and one is on cover with a New York City "11 OCT" red carrier marking as a cancellation.

Figure 2-28. A typical preprinting fold.

Figure 2-29. Front and reverse of a block of six on vertical laid paper. (From a C.W. Christian photo)

The largest multiple on laid paper known to the author is a block of six illustrated in an article titled "One Cent 1861 Stamps on Vertically Laid Paper" in the May 1975 issue of the *Chronicle*. Curiously, a different block of six, and a block of four on vertical laid paper have appeared in different sales.

All of these blocks, including the one pictured in the *Chronicle*, are canceled with the same design (**see Figure 2-29**). This suggests that they originally were all part of a single larger multiple. The *Chronicle* article reported that the cancel was from a Kansas town.

References

1. Brazer, C.W. *Essay-Proof Journal*. Number 122. 1974.

2. Williams, L. N. and M. *Fundamentals of Philately*. The American Philatelic Society Inc. 1971.

3. Chase, Carroll. *The 3¢ Stamp of the United States, 1851-1857 Issue*. Reproduction of the revised original 1929 edition. Quarterman Publications Inc. 1975.

4. Brookman, Lester G. *The United States Postage Stamps of the 19th Century*. Volume I. H.L. Lindquist Publications Inc. 1966.

5. Brookman, Lester G. *The United States Postage Stamps of the 19th Century*. Volume II. H.L. Lindquist Publications Inc. 1966.

6. Boggs, Winthrop S. "Early American Perforating Machines and Perforations 1857-1867." A reprint from *Collectors Club Philatelist*, Volume 33. Unitrade Press, Ontario, Canada. June 1982.

7. Haverbeck, H.D.S. "The Grill and Other Patents of Charles F. Steel Relating to Postage Stamp Production, 1867-1875." *Collectors Club Philatelist*. Volume XXXV, Number 11.

8. Perry, Eliott. *Pat Paragraphs*. Bureau Issues Association Inc. 1981.

9. Herzog, William K. *The Congress Book*. American Philatelic Congress Inc. 1978.

10. Bierman, Stanley M. *The World's Greatest Stamp Collectors*. Linn's Stamp News, Sidney, Ohio. 1990.

11. Brazer, C.W. *Essay-Proof Journal*. Number 47. 1955.

12. Evans, Don L. *The Chronicle*. 155. August 1992.

13. Chapin, John C. *A Census of United States Classic Plate Blocks*. The Collectors Club of New York, New York. 1982.

14. *Methuen Handbook of Colour*. Third Edition, Eyre Methuen Ltd. 1978.

15. White, R.H. *Encyclopedia of the Colors of United States Postage Stamps*. Volume I. Philatelic Research Ltd. 1981.

16. Herzog, William K. "1¢ 1861 Ultramarine and Indigo Shades." *Chronicle*. Number 106. May 1980.

17. Hines, Stephen. Private communication. 1982.

18. Gross, Tudor E. "The U. S. 1¢ 1861." *Mekeel's Weekly Stamp News*. April 21, 1941.

CHAPTER 3

The Grilled Issues of 1867-69

History of the Grilled Stamp

This particularly interesting group of printings was the result of the continuing concern of the Post Office Department that postally used stamps were being cleaned and reused. This had been an item of worry for the Post Office Department from the beginning of the use of the adhesive postage stamp. Policies were enacted and regulations were passed to ensure that every stamp that passed through the mail received a cancellation, preferably with a heavy black ink that would be difficult to remove, but these regulations and policies were not always carefully followed. Small post offices were not furnished canceling devices by the Post Office, and many of them canceled stamps with a pen. Some offices used a datestamp for a canceling device, and some used ink that was easily removed.

While it is unlikely that the amount of loss from illegal reuse of stamps was high, the well-publicized concern of the Post Office Department did spark the inventive spirit of the mid-century Yankees. Many ideas were proposed, and some patented, for schemes to make canceled stamps difficult to use again. Only one of the many ideas submitted to the Post Office was actually approved for use in the production of stamps for public use. That was the patent for the grilled or embossed stamp. Other ideas that only reached the experimental stage and involved the 1¢ Franklin design will be discussed in later chapters.

The inventor and driving force behind the grilled stamps produced for the Post Office Department between 1867 and the early 1870s was Charles F. Steel. Steel had a lot of experience in the production of stamps and was highly entrepreneurial. Much of what is known about the development and manufacture of the grilled stamps has been obtained from a study of his correspondence with the Post Office Department.

Steel originally was employed by Toppan, Carpenter & Company at Philadelphia in 1855. When the stamp contract was transferred to the National Bank Note Company in 1861, Steel went to New York where he, in his words, ". . . fitted up the establishment for the work, and was their Superintendent for twelve years . . ." His relationship with the bank note companies was somewhat that of an independent subcontractor for the production of stamps. At the same time, he was a salaried worker and seemed to have been considered to be an employee. This working relationship is unusual by today's practices, and

it did allow Steel extra freedom in his activities. In 1873 the National Bank Note Company lost the contract to the Continental Bank Note Company, and Steel repeated his performance of the previous decade. He "fitted up" the Continental establishment for the printing of stamps and became its supervisor, licensing his grill patent to Continental for an additional annual stipend. Four years later the interest in grilling stamps had all but vanished, and Steel left Continental and formed his own organization, The Franklin Engraving and Printing Company, of which he became president. Steel later bid for the 1889 production contract for the printing of U.S. stamps. Although his bid was the lowest submitted, it was thrown out on a technicality. Steel sued, and the problems resulting from the controversy were a factor in the government's decision to transfer its stamp business to the Bureau of Engraving and Printing, where there would be no more squabbling over contracts [1:85].

Many serious and competent philatelic scholars have written extensively concerning the grilled issues, and there will be no attempt here to reproduce the many findings, facts and assumptions that are detailed in their writings. Instead, it will be the goal of this section to highlight the most important and interesting aspects of the published research, and to illustrate some of the main features of the 1867 1¢ grilled issue and the associated experiments and essays.

The reader who desires additional information is advised to consult the work of Lester G. Brookman, who in his *United States Stamps of the 19th Century*, comprehensively reported just about all the information that was known about grills at that time (1966). Very few additional facts have come to light since then. In addition to his personal investigations, Brookman was assisted in his effort by Elliott Perry, H.L. Wiley, John Klemann and Clarence Brazer. Also the works of William Stevenson (who was one of the most ardent and accomplished philatelists in the field of grills), John Tiffany, J.B. Leavy and John Luff provided data for his presentation [2:67]. It is obvious from the listing of names that many of the most famous collectors of earlier years were interested in and wrote on this subject.

Another excellent and more contemporary source of information is "The Story of the United States Grilled Postage Stamp" by William K. Herzog, in the *American Philatelic Congress Book* for 1978 [3:67-103]. Herzog is a talented collector whose article is marked by extensive and detailed research into the facts and suppositions surrounding the issuance of the grilled stamps. An even later entry into the roster of philatelic scholars who have investigated the grilled issues is Scott R. Trepel, who wrote an outstanding article on the early grills. The article appeared in the *Chronicle* in 1987 [4:118-125].

Returning to the discussion of grills, the first evidence of an interest by the government in producing a grilled stamp is reflected in a letter dated December 13, 1865, from A.N. Zevely to Steel at the main office of the National Bank Note Company at 1 Wall Street in New York [1:68]. The letter reads as follows:

"Dear Sir.

Yours of the 11 inst. is received, This Department wants a postage stamp from which it will be impossible to remove canceling marks without destroying it. If you establish your claim to such an invention, it might be introduced thro' the National Bank Note Co. As to compensation the Postmaster General would consult Congress. Or he might negotiate subject to the approval of Congress. It will be necessary to continue the manufacture in present hands, and your better plan might be to arrange with the contractors. If then your stamps and the price suited the Postmaster General, he might ask the necessary legislation.

Very Respectfully
A. N. Zevely
3rd Ast PMG"

A week later, another letter was sent to Steel from Zevely, evidently in response to grilled samples that Steel had furnished.

"Sir:

Acknowledging the receipt of the samples furnished by you with which I am favorably impressed, I have to state that no definite judgement can be formed of their actual merits until they shall have been passed through certain practical tests. The best of tests would be this: that you make arrangements with the National Bank Note Co. to manufacture a certain number of these stamps to be sent out, sold and used, as the present stamps. If they prove to be what is wanted this fact would soon become apparent and the Department would be prepared, after such a successful trial, to enter into arrangements for their adoption."

Following this letter is an extended period of more than a year during which no action seems to have been taken with regards to Zevely's suggestion concerning the production of some grilled stamps for field trials.

It is known, however, that Steel continued some of his experiments, and by the summer of 1867, some examples of grilled postage stamps of the 1861 issue had been produced for actual postal use.

A year and a half after the initial letters, official documentation with reference to grilling stamps again made its appearance. The Post Office Department was apparently satisfied with the experimental samples that had been produced, and the actual trials in the mail that resulted in the presently known August 1867 uses of the 3¢ denomination with the overall grill. The original six-year contract with National Bank Note Company for the production of stamps was due to expire on August 15, 1867, and the government extended the contract for a period of one year, with a provision for the production of a new style of postage stamp at an increased cost. The contract extension was not the result of a competitive bid, but rather by an order by the postmaster general as detailed in the following August 16, 1867, letter from Zevely to the Post Office auditor, McGrew [3:73].

"I have the honor to transmit herewith a copy of the order of the Postmaster General, issued yesterday, under the seventh section of an Act of Congress approved June 12, 1866 — accepting the proposal of the National Bank Note Company of New York to furnish a new style of postage stamps, for one year from this date, at the rate of twenty cents per thousand; and also providing for the continuance of the contract, which expired yesterday, with said Company, for furnishing the present style of postage stamps at Twelve cents a thousand . . ."

The "new style" of postage stamps referred to was undoubtedly the grilled stamps, and the increase in fee was to compensate the National Bank Note Company for the additional production costs that would be incurred. The above referenced Act of Congress contained a provision that allowed the postmaster general, at his discretion, to approve new kinds of postage stamps, to modify contracts for producing these stamps, and to allow the contractors additional sums to cover increased expenses. This act provided the postmaster general with a great deal of authority to make personal decisions, and may have been the result of convincing Congress of the advisability of changing the style of the current stamps to a grilled variety.

On October 8, 1867, Zevely resumed correspondence with Steel, and wrote that he had requested National Bank Note Company to send him samples, and that his purpose was to send out a million or more as soon as possible. He also reiterated his support for the invention and mentioned that the postmaster general was pleased with it (at this time the postmaster general was Alex W. Randall), and that Steel's patent had been ordered and would be issued in a week or so.

In accordance with Zevely's promise, on October 22, 1867, a patent was granted to Charles F. Steel for the "embossing" of stamp paper to improve its adhesion and to prevent the removal of canceling inks. In the patent application, Steel proposed that the stamp paper first be gummed and dried, then embossed between plates or rollers, pressed to flatten the paper and finally printed with the stamp design.

The above sequence evidently had some drawbacks. It is possible that the designs did not print well on grilled paper, even though the grill impressions were supposed to be flattened out. The actual procedure used for production printed the stamp first, then the sheet was gummed and dried, pressed, grilled, perforated and finally pressed again under very high pressure.

From this date on, actions to put the grilling idea into practice seemed to accelerate. On October 23, 1867, Zevely wrote to Steel that he had been advised by Boyd (the government stamp agent at New York) that the printing of a trial run of stamps with grills was under way and that they would be fairly tested along with any other samples Steel might offer. He also suggested that the grilling should be tried in combination with Macdonough's idea. It is possible he is here referring to the patent by James Macdonough for the use of fugitive glycerine inks for printing. (Macdonough's patent will be reviewed in the following chapter on experimental printings.) Zevely went on to state that surface printing was wanted. Fortunately, this idea was never adopted, and the beautifully engraved designs continued to be used.

In the latter part of 1867, other letters show that National Bank Note Company received the exclusive right to use the Steel patent for a royalty of 3¢ per 1,000 stamps, pursuant to a requirement by the Post Office Department to grill the postage stamps. Until this time, Steel's contract afforded him a salary of $2,500 per year. Records show that approximately 350 million grilled stamps were produced in 1868, and the royalty on this number of stamps would increase Steel's income by more than $10,000, which was a substantial sum for that period.

Additional letters indicate that National Bank Note Company was contemplating a change in the design for the issue, and was considering a lithographed stamp with an ornate frame and a large numeral for the denomination in the grilled center, similar to the essay shown in **Figure 3-1**. No essays exist with the 1¢ value in the center, but a 1¢ frame essay with blank center was produced and will be illustrated later in this chapter.

Support by the postmaster general for the change

Figure 3-1. Lithographed frame with grilled center and embossed denomination. This was proposed to the National Bank Note Company by Steel as a trial design for a grilled stamp.
(Brazer)

to grilled stamps was documented in his Annual Report to Congress, dated November 26, 1867, which stated:

"Experiments are in progress with a postage stamp printed on embossed paper, which seems to afford good security against fraud. The fibres of the paper being broken, canceling marks almost necessarily penetrate, so that they cannot easily be removed without destroying the stamp. The adhesive properties are also promoted and other advantages secured which commend the invention to favorable notice."

While there is evidence that a number of grilled stamps were sold and used during the latter part of 1867 (not necessarily including E and F grills), these were not separately accounted for by the stamp agent at New York, and evidently were produced without additional compensation. They were probably part of the "experimental phase" to demonstrate the effectiveness of the grilling process. Beginning in January 1868, large numbers of grilled stamps were delivered to the Post Office Department, and records of their production were established. Although these records do not differentiate between types of grills, they do provide information concerning the total number of grilled stamps that were printed. It should be noted that while most catalogs and other references refer to these grilled issues as the issues of 1867, they should more properly be identified as the issues of 1868. The years of 1868 and 1869 encompassed the years during which National Bank Note Company officially delivered grilled stamps to the Post Office Department under its contract. To avoid any misunderstanding or conflicts, this text will continue to refer to the grilled issues as the issues of 1867.

Production of Grilled Stamps

In his application for a patent, Charles F. Steel made little or no reference to the devices that would be needed to produce a grilled postage stamp. The sum total of the information that he provided in this regard are his patent statements [2:69]:

"I then press the entire sheet between embossed plates, or pass it through between embossing-rollers."

and

"I do not deem it necessary to describe the devices for embossing, flattening, printing, etc., as they may be of any convenient character known to mechanics . . ."

It is unfortunate from the viewpoint of present-day collectors that Steel did not better describe the procedures for manufacture, since there are no known drawings or detailed descriptions of exactly how the grilling process was accomplished. The current level of knowledge concerning these operations is the result of careful examination of the final stamp product and hypothesizing what must have been done to achieve it.

The only recorded contemporary account of the grilling process is very general in nature but does provide a bit of information. In the *American Journal of Philately* for October 20, 1868, an article by Cosmopolitan, titled "How Our New Postage Stamps are Made," describes the operation in the following manner:

> "After receiving the gum they are placed on wire frames and deposited in the drying room, where they remain until entirely dry. This operation being finished, they are consigned to the 'embosser,' who, with a remarkably complicated and delicate machine leaves the little square chequer board marks we see upon our stamps. After passing through the embossing press they are perforated . . ."[3:68]

While the article doesn't shed much light on the process, it does establish that the embosser or grilling device was complicated and delicate, at least in the eyes of the writer.

It is the accepted conclusion of the majority of collectors who have made a study of grills that the embossing or grilling was done by passing the sheet of stamps between a flat bed of soft material such as cloth, leather or even lead, and a steel roller on whose surface the grilling design had been formed. There are two basic types of rollers, and the appearance of grill design on these rollers is shown in **Figure 3-2**, which is taken from Brookman's work [2:92]. The female grill roller was made, probably in some type of transfer press or lathe, by impressing into a soft steel roller the design of the grill from a master die or knurl. A knurl is a hardened steel wheel with pyramidal bosses whose design could be transferred, making depressions on the roller. The male roller was probably made by machining the bosses directly on the roller, and resulted in pyramidal protrusions that produced indentations when applied to the sheets of stamps.

Sheets to be grilled were normally passed through the grilling apparatus face up. As a consequence, when the roller with the female depressions was used, the grilled stamp emerged with the points of the pyramidal concavity facing in the up position, and conversely, the male

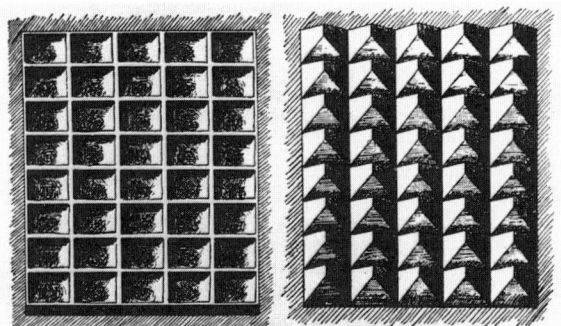

Figure 3-2. Female grill   Male grill

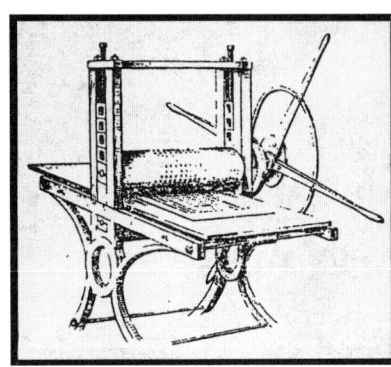

Figure 3-3. Conceptual drawing by Brookman of a possible embossing device.

roller bosses produced points-down designs.

Although the construction of the grilling machine is not known exactly, Brookman pictured a hypothetical device (shown in **Figure 3-3**) adapted from a proof press, which would produce grilled stamps with the characteristics observed in the various grills. The roller was mounted on the press above the bed. The bed consisted of a relatively soft material and the sheet of stamps to be grilled was drawn between the embossing roller and the bed, under pressure, by turning the roller. The soft material of the bed forced the paper up into the depressions of the female roller or between the bosses of the male roller and produced a resulting grill.

The characteristics of the grills formed by the male and female rollers differ. As previously stated, those with the points of the individual impressions pointing up are made with the female grill (with some rare exceptions that will be discussed later), and those made with the male grill result in points-down grills. The grill impression of the male roller is generally much sharper than the female and results in an X-shaped design in the middle of each of the squares as a consequence of the pressing out of the pyramidal indentation subsequent to the grilling process. The sharper impression results from the fact that for the male impression, the bosses on the roller force the paper into the soft bed, and the shape of the boss is exactly duplicated in the paper.

For the female-roller case, the soft material of the bed forces the paper up into the depressions on the roller, but the bed does not seem to deform sufficiently to ensure that the paper is pushed into the far recesses of the die. The more rounded impressions from the female roller are sometimes referred to as biscuit grills. Another general characteristic of the female grill shows evidence of fractures in the paper at the tip of the depression. This is probably caused by the paper stretching as it is forced into the depression with some slight tearing at the point of maximum stress.

For both male and female rollers, it is now believed that the shape of the die boss or depression is approximately the same, but mirror images of each other, and the differences in the appearance of the resulting grills are due to the considerations described above.

It should be mentioned at this point that the pyramidal shape of the grill design is not a perfect pyramid. For the male (D, E and F) rollers, the rectangle forming the base of the pyramid is a bit longer in the vertical direction, and the top of the pyramid is slightly truncated, resulting in an observable vertical ridge at the tip of the grill design whose length is about one-third the height of the grill unit. Because the tip of the female design used for the A and C grills is not as clearly defined, the existence of ridges is not as readily apparent.

The letters that characterize the various grills were assigned by William Stevenson during his extensive research on grilled stamps during the early part of the 20th century. The alphabetical identification of the grills was assigned in chronological order with respect to when he thought they were produced. The exception is the Z grill. Stevenson was not sure where it belonged in the chronology so he arbitrarily gave it a designation that probably would never be needed by any other grill. While all grills of the 1867 issue are not found on the 1¢ Franklin, a compilation of the 1867 grill types and their characteristics will be listed and illustrated for completeness:

Figure 3-4. Unlisted A grill essay on the 1¢ design, accompanied by a blank, gummed-paper essay with the same grill.
(C.W. Christian collection)

A Grill

Points up, overall grill. This is the first grill and was produced for trial postal use. It was embossed only on the 3¢, 5¢ and 30¢ 1861 denominations (Scott 79, 80, 81), and a significant number of the 3¢ sheets and a few of the others were sold and used. Several covers dated in August of 1867 are known from various parts of the country. The earliest use is recorded as August 13, 1867, on a 3¢ cover from Buffalo, New York [1:97]. While used copies of the 5¢ and 30¢ values exist, they are not known on cover. All of these examples are rare, and several resided in the Ishikawa collection.

The experimental trial of this grill found it to be unsatisfactory. When the entire sheet was grilled, the embossing weakened the perforations to an extent that caused uneven and jagged borders on the individual stamps when they were separated. Changes were then made to the grill size on the roller, which resulted in the smaller C grills.

The A grill is known on the 1¢ Franklin only as an essay, and is an unlisted variety. This is a points-up grill and was produced by a male roller. The grill is strongly embossed and shows no evidence of being pressed after grilling. According to James E. Lee, a well-known collector and dealer in philatelic literature and postal history, four copies are known, all of which originated from a single block in the Worthington collection. One of these is presently in the C.W. Christian collection, and a photograph of this item is illustrated in **Figure 3-4**. Shown also is a blank, gummed-paper essay with the same grill. This essay grill is reported by Brookman and Christian to differ slightly from the issued A grill, with the individual grill units being square in shape in contrast to the rectangular boxes of the issued grill, and the rows of grills being farther apart. This is not surprising since they are now considered to have been made from different rollers.

B Grill

Points up, grilled area about 18mm by 15mm (horizontal measurements are given first), 22 by 18 points up. The grill impression probably was made from a male embosser. The B grill is the mystery grill of the series. Its existence as a genuinely issued stamp has been debated. The 1996 Scott U.S. specialized lists it as Scott 82, on the 3¢ only, in used condition, with a value of $100,000. The catalog states, "The four known copies of No. 82 are valued in the grade of fine." An example known as the Luff/Worthington copy is an essay, in the opinion of Brookman [2:128] and others. Brookman discusses the pros and cons of the validity of this item at length, and also shows an 1869 cover from Mason, Texas, to Darmstadt, Germany, with four 3¢ 18mm-by-15mm B grills, which he claimed to be genuine, and to be the only known examples of this grill. These stamps, unfortunately, were

Figure 3-5. Unique 1¢ blue essay, C grill with points down. Ex-Worthington. (Courtesy of Christie's, New York)

later removed from the cover and sold to separate owners so that multiple ownership of this grill rarity could be possible. But in the process a wonderful postal history item was destroyed. One of the stamps became a part of the Ishikawa collection, as reported by Calvet M. Hahn [5:252]. The stamps are considered by current experts to be genuine and possibly the only B-grill stamps in existence.

The dilemma of a supposedly early type of experimental grill being used as late as 1869 is considered by Trepel in his *Chronicle* article with the conclusion that it was entirely possible [4:120]. This will be discussed further in the latter part of this chapter.

There are no examples of a B grill on the 1¢ Franklin.

C Grill

Points up, about 13mm by 16mm, 16 to 17 by 18 to 21 points. This grill has all of the characteristics of the A grill except size. The size was reduced from the A grill to eliminate the problem of weakened perforations. The original female-grill roller was altered by having strips of the grill design removed by grinding or planing in both directions. This resulted in a roller with small islands of grill design remaining, and separated so that each stamp would receive the impression from a single area during the grilling process. In some places the original roller was not completely erased in the planed regions, and the partial design that remained resulted in some examples that resemble B grills in size. On occasion, these have been sold as such.

The 1¢ value is not known as an issued stamp with the C grill. It is known, however, as an essay, grilled with points down and points up. The 1996 Scott U.S. specialized lists the essay and prices it at $4,000 for both points-up and points-down grills. This essay is very rare, and a copy, originally from the Worthington estate, sold in a November 1972 Robert A. Siegel auction for $27,000. At that time it was listed as a regular stamp variety, Scott 82A. Eighteen years later, the same item reappeared in the Christie's auction of October 25, 1990. It was described as an unlisted C-grill essay with Philatelic Foundation certificate, and the only copy known. The price realized was $3,500. An illustration of this item is shown in **Figure 3-5**. Trepel [4:121] also shows a 1¢ C grill with points up and states that both of these variations appear to have been made with a male roller.

D Grill

The D grill and following varieties of grills were all made with male rollers and, in general, exhibit more sharply defined tops to the pyramidal impressions and more definite "x" marks where the grill impressions were pressed out in the final stage of the printing process.

The D grill has points down and a grilled area of about 12mm by 14mm, with 15 by 17 to 18 points.

According to Brookman, there were an estimated 700,000 copies of the D grill produced on the 2¢ and 3¢ values. For such a small total printing, there must have been something about the grill that did not meet the desired criteria, for the grill roller may have again been altered after this limited printing.

There are no examples of the 1861 1¢ Franklin with the D grill on issued stamps or essays.

Z Grill

Points down, grill area about 11mm by 14mm, 13 to 14 by 18 points.

The philatelic history surrounding the 1¢ Franklin with a Z grill (Scott 85A) is fascinating, and this interest is compounded by the fact that it is considered to be the rarest and most valuable of all U.S. stamps. Two copies are known, and only one is in private hands. That copy currently has a market value in the six-figure range, and both the philatelic and popular press follow its provenance from owner to owner. It is the United States' equivalent of the British Guiana 1¢ magenta.

Over the past several years, the validity of the single copy in private hands has been questioned. This controversy will be discussed in some detail later in this section.

The Z grill was made from a new roller, and as far as can be determined, this same roller was used for all of the Z-grilled stamps that were issued for the 1867 series. The roller was a male roller with the characteristics of the D, E and F rollers, except for the orientation of the short ridge that marked the tip of the truncated inverted pyramid in each grill element. In the Z grill, this ridge is horizontally oriented, while the ridges in all other grill types are in the vertical direction and parallel to the sides of the stamp. For comparison and identification, a photo of the reverse side of a 12¢ denomination of the 1867 issue with a clear Z grill is shown in **Figure 3-6**.

The Z grill was first reported in 1914 by Stevenson during the course of his intensive research into the grilled issues. At the time of discovery, he did not know its position in the chronological sequence of grills, as previously mentioned. As a result of continuing investigations, he came to the conclusion that the proper place for the Z grill was probably between the D and E grills, or at least in that general time frame. In one of his listings, Stevenson stated that he had two copies of the 1¢ Z grill, both of them in used condition.

In 1917 Elliott Perry acquired Stevenson's collection of grilled stamps and immediately sold the 1¢ Z grill to Benjamin K. Miller. Perry noted that there was only one example of the 1¢ Z grill in the material he had purchased from Stevenson, so the fate of the other copy that Stevenson had listed is unknown.

About 1925, Miller donated his collection to the New York Public Library. Perry was hired to mount it and prepare it for exhibition, and sections of it were displayed over the years by the library. Unfortunately, a series of thefts caused the collection to be removed from exhibition and stored in a secure location. The items in the collection are not presently available to anyone for viewing or study. At the time the collection was mounted, there was no special significance attached to the 1¢ Z grill. It was grouped with the other grills of the issue. No photograph of this particular grill is available, and most philatelic experts who have had the opportunity to examine it are no longer alive. One exception to this is Scott Trepel, who has seen the stamp and described it to the author as follows:

> "The Miller copy has a distinct grill and is printed on heavy paper. It is canceled with a seven-bar circular grid."

It is extremely unfortunate that this very important stamp cannot be made available for expert testing that would establish the precise characteristics of the stamp. Since this is the stamp that defined the 1¢ Z grill, it must be considered to be genuine and could be the fundamental reference against which any other 1¢ Z grill would be measured.

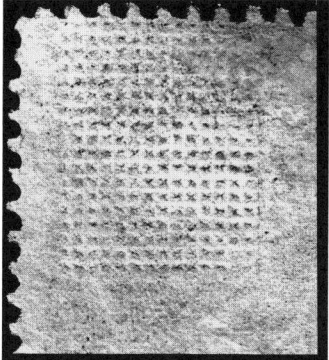

Figure 3-6. Reverse side of a 12¢ 1867 stamp with a Z grill.

For many years it was considered to be unique, but about 40 years (1957) after the initial discovery, Brookman discovered another copy while examining a selection of stamps from Henry Kuhlman of Chicago.

After finding the second copy, Brookman met with Perry, who had previously examined the Miller Z grill, to confirm the identification of the new find. Perry agreed that it was definitely a genuine Z grill. Later, Brookman sold his copy to Wilbur Schilling who became the first and probably only person to ever own a copy of each of the grilled stamps of the 1867 series.

The Brookman/Schilling copy has a double grill, which makes it unique in that regard. Unfortunately, this writer has not had the opportunity to examine or photograph this 1¢ Z grill. An illustration from a Philatelic Foundation certificate photo is shown in **Figure 3-7**. This copy has been certified genuine by the Foundation in 1957, 1975 and again in 1986.

In spite of these findings, there has been some discussion regarding the possibility that the Brookman/Schilling copy is not a true Z grill. This controversy is primarily based on the fact that the Philadelphia town marking that cancels the stamp is a type that is not known to have been used as late as 1868 when the earliest possible use of the Z grill occurred.

Very late accidental or casual use of markings that have been out of use for years are known in many cases, and this does not automatically suggest that the grill is not genuine. However, the use of this outdated canceling

Figure 3-7. A 1¢ Z grill. Front and back photos from the original Philatelic Foundation certificate. (Brookman)

device does require consideration and should be factored into any evaluation of the authenticity of this item.

Ken Lawrence takes a cogent historical look at the history of the 1¢ Z grills in an article titled, "The 1 Cent Z Grill Mystery" in the 1995 *Congress Book* of the American Philatelic Congress. He presented the possibility that the Brookman/Schilling copy is actually the "other" 1¢ Z grill Stevenson had noted in his 1916 listing. He hypothesized that Stevenson decided that this copy was not a true Z grill and relegated it to his reference collection, where it remained until after his death on December 25, 1956. The copy then was acquired by the Chicago dealer Kuhlman, who sold it to Brookman, who, in turn, sold it to Schilling, where it embarked on its journey to its present notoriety.

This plausible scenario has one serious drawback. Why would anyone prior to 1916 want to fake a Z grill? It was not even known as a grill variety at that time, and consequently would not have had any price advantage over the more common grill types. The Z grill on the stamp is the same as the genuine Z grills on other denominations of the series, as attested to by the repeated PF certificates, so if it were faked, it certainly was an exceptionally expert job. All Z grills are scarce enough that finding one to copy would have been difficult.

The last word on this controversy is yet to be written, but with the evidence presently available, it seems prudent to accept the PF certificates of authenticity as fact.

The Z grill is known on the 1¢, 2¢, 3¢, 10¢, 12¢ and 15¢ denominations, and on many essays. A large number of grilled essays, on different colored paper, were produced in the 12¢ value. The Z grill is scarce to rare in all denominations.

E Grill

Points down, with a grilled area of about 11mm by 13mm, with 14 by 15 to 17 points.

This is the first grill to be regularly issued with the 1¢ stamp design

Figure 3-8. Outstanding example of a 1¢ E grill.
(Steve Ivy Auction, December 15, 1990)

(Scott 86). It is probable that a new roller with the smaller-size grill was prepared for this variety. By decreasing the area of a grill, the pressure from the grill roller was concentrated on a smaller area, making it easier to break the fibers of the paper.

The number of 1¢ stamps printed with the E grill was relatively small. Brookman estimates the total production to be 3,000,000 copies. Because of this small printing, and the decline in workmanship in the late 1860s, which resulted in many poorly centered copies, it is a difficult stamp to find in very fine condition. Choice copies demand a great premium. A photo of a beautiful example of this stamp is shown in **Figure 3-8**. This is the most outstanding copy this writer has seen.

The E grill was printed in two shades of blue: a normal blue and a dull blue. Neither shade is scarce. The earliest-known use of the 1¢ E grill is on an 1868 cover from Lawrence, Kansas, dated March 9. The year is established from the March 11, 1868, receiving stamp (**Figure 3-9**).

Multiples exist but are scarce. Brookman writes that an unused top imprint block of 50 was in the Worthington sale and that a used block of 18 was sold in a Robert A. Siegel sale in 1964. Whether these have been subsequently broken up is not known to the author, who has an unused top margin imprint block of six in his collection

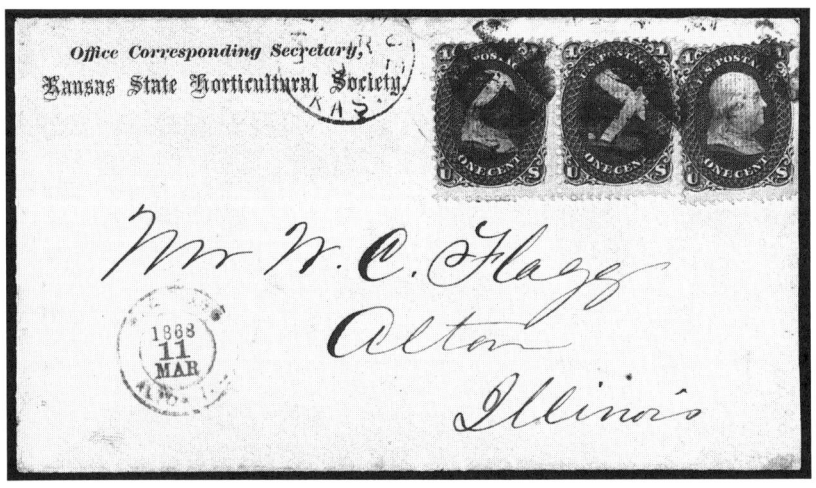

Figure 3-9. Earliest-known use of the 1¢ E grill. Lawrence, Kansas, to Alton, Illinois, on March 9, with a receiving mark of March 11, 1868, validating the year of use. Three (Scott 86) making up the 3¢ domestic letter rate.
(James E. Lee collection)

Figure 3-10. E grill top inscription block of six.

Figure 3-11 illustrates the E grill as seen on the reverse of an unused copy of Scott 86.

In the latter period of production of this stamp, very thin paper was used on occasion. It is thought that the thin paper was used to increase the fiber destruction caused by the grill and consequently to increase its absorption of ink

Grill varieties or errors are found on the 1¢. They are scarce, but obtainable. The stamp is known with a double grill, a split grill and an inverted grill. Examples of these varieties are illustrated for comparison with the normal E grill that is shown in **Figure 3-11**.

Double grills are produced when the sheet of stamps is fed through the grilling apparatus twice, and the additional pass results in another grill impression, which is usually offset from the one that was received in the first pass. **Figure 3-12** illustrates this variety.

Split grills result from the sheet not being positioned properly when fed into the embosser. This results in two separate partial grills on one stamp as shown in **Figure 3-13**.

(see **Figure 3-10**).

Plate number blocks are very rare. Only one was recorded by Chapin in his *Census of U. S. Classic Plate Blocks*. This is a horizontal block of eight from plate 10. It was sold in 1950 in a Harmer's auction, and was described as previously being in the Hind, Brigham and Moody collections. Its present location is unknown to the author. Luff was unable to record any plate numbers for the E-grill printings, nor have any other philatelic investigators identified any, so it is not known if any plates other than plate 10 were used.

Inverted grills are very scarce and result from the stamp sheet being folded before it goes through the machine. The effect is that where the paper is folded, the grill will be impressed on two layers of paper with one layer being upside down. The end result is a points-up grill instead of the normal points-down grill on the inverted layer. If the fold is not at right angles to the edges of the sheet, as is normally the case, the inverted grill will be oblique to the sides of the stamp. Grills impressed in the areas along the crease would result in a stamp having two grills — one inverted, and the other normal. Both of these impressions will be incomplete, one probably ob-

Figure 3-11. Reverse of a 1¢ Franklin with a normal E-grill impression.

Figure 3-12. Reverse of a 1¢ Franklin showing a double E grill.

Figure 3-13. Reverse of a 1¢ Franklin with a split E grill. The second partial grill shows two rows at the top of the stamp.

Figure 3-14. An inverted E grill with points up. This was caused by a folded sheet being grilled. The grill is tilted approximately 5 degrees from the vertical. (W.K. Herzog)

Figure 3-15. A magnificent copy of the 1¢ F grill. (Steve Ivy auction photo)

lique to the other.

Of course, it would be entirely possible for a sheet of stamps to be fed upside down into the grilling press. This has been discounted by most investigators because of the scarcity of the inverted error. Two hundred of them would have been produced each time a sheet of stamps was fed into the embosser face down. If it ever did happen, it must have been a very rare occurrence.

A 1¢ stamp with an inverted E grill is shown in **Figure 3-14**. This indistinct photo is taken from an interesting article on this subject by William K. Herzog [6:185]. Unfortunately there is no photo available of the reverse side. This same stamp was offered for sale in the November 27, 1979, John W. Kaufmann auction as an inverted F grill. With Herzog's record of careful scholarship, the author is inclined to consider that the Kaufmann auction description was a typographical error.

A variation on this type of error is caused by a wrinkle type of fold similar to those that cause preprinting fold errors on stamps. In this case there are actually three layers of paper being grilled at the same time. This fold is normally quite small, a few millimeters or so, and when the paper is unfolded, an oversize grill results. Of course, one strip of the grill is inverted and bordered on both sides by normally impressed portions of the grill. Due to pressing in the final stage of production, the inverted portion is frequently not noticed as being different from the rest of the grill, and a grill with previously unreported dimensions is thought to have been discovered. This type of error has produced some spectacular freaks, but the author has not seen an example on the 1¢.

F Grill

Points down, grill area about 9mm by 13mm, with 11 to 12 by 15 to 17 points (Scott 92).

Like the E grill, this stamp is extremely difficult to find well-centered and in choice condition. The deteriorating quality control that occurred during its production resulted in ragged and off-center perforations. One of the finest examples of the stamp this writer has seen is pictured in **Figure 3-15**. This was offered in the same Steve Ivy auction of December 1990 that offered the E-grill gem pictured in the previous section.

The F grill is the smallest of all the grill sizes used on the 1867 series of stamps. The small size probably resulted in the most satisfactory of the grills, and the number of F grills that were produced exceeded the figures for any other grill type. Brookman estimates that 7,000,000 1¢ F grills were made. It is found in three major shades: blue, dark blue and light blue. Some examples of the dark blue approach an indigo in appearance. The stamp was also printed on both a regular weight and a very thin paper, as was the E grill. The percentage of thin-paper copies with the F grill seems to be much greater than those with the E grill.

The variations in sizes of the grill impressions for any individual grill type were a result of inaccuracies in machining the rollers from a previous configuration. When the size of a grill was reduced, parts of the grill design were machined off in both directions. A variation of a point or two in either direction was not of great consequence, and evidently no attempt was made to attain exact uniformity. At times a line of grill points was terminated within a grill area, resulting in a partial line of points. Since the stamps were flattened after grilling, and also because the later emissions of the grills were not as carefully manufactured, many grill impressions are very weak and some incomplete. Great care must be taken to establish the identity of some of these weaker impressions.

The Grilled Issues of 1867-69

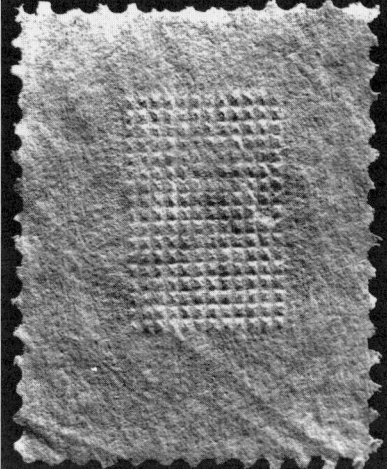  

Figure 3-16. Reverse of a 1¢ Franklin (Scott 92), showing a normal F grill.

Figure 3-17. Reverse of a 1¢ Franklin with a double F grill. The second grill is at an angle of 20° with the first.

Figure 3-18. Reverse of a 1¢ Franklin showing the unusual combination of a double and split F grill.

Scott lists the F grill with a double transfer. The nature of this transfer is not known to the author. Examples of grilling errors are also known, including double and split grills and a rare combination of the two.

A normal F grill is shown in **Figure 3-16**. An unusual double grill is shown in **Figure 3-17**. The first impression is aligned at an angle of about 12° from the vertical. This stamp was produced by feeding the sheet into the embosser at an angle during the first pass. The operator evidently noticed the error and removed the sheet to reposition it for the second pass. However, the alignment was still not completely corrected, and the next pass produced another oblique grill. Because the two impressions are not displaced horizontally, it can be assumed that this error occurred in the first row of stamps being grilled, and it may be that only a single row was grilled before the operator noticed the initial misalignment.

A rare combination of two errors also exists. It occurs when a sheet is misfed on one pass, a split grill is impressed and the sheet is passed through the embosser again to produce a double grill. An example of this error is pictured in **Figure 3-18**.

Large multiples are rare. A *Chronicle* description of the Ishikawa International Grand Prix collection, reported an unused block of six that was thought to be originally from the Hind collection and the largest unused multiple known [7:253]. The latter statement is incorrect, for a block of nine does exist and is shown in **Figure 3-19**.

However, only one plate block has been reported, and this may be the block that was being described. It is a block of six, plate number 27, and is shown in **Figure 3-20**. It was sold in an April 5, 1980, Robert A. Siegel auction, where it realized a hammer price of $18,700. It later appeared in the Ishikawa collection and was then sold in the 1993 Christie's Ishikawa sale for $12,650.

As with all of the grills, used large multiples on cover are scarce. In a 1986 Wolffer's auction, a block of 12 plus three singles, used to pay the 15¢ rate on an 1869 cover to Switzerland, was offered. This is the largest used multiple of the F grill for which the writer has any record.

Figure 3-19. F-grill block of nine.

This cover, which was recently shown to the author by Stanley Piller, originated at San Jose, California, on August 21 (1869). It is addressed to Locarno, Switzerland, and was marked at San Jose with a manuscript "Paid 15." It received a BR TRANSIT PAID ALL marking, dated August 31, at the New York exchange office. All the stamps are on the reverse of the cover. The reverse also shows a transit marking from Basel, Switzerland, dated September 12, 1869, and a receiving mark at Locarno, dated two days later.

The earliest-reported use of an F grill on cover is illustrated in **Figure 3-21**. This drop-letter use of a small lady's cover was postmarked at Dansville, New York, on August 11 (1868). The year of use is established from a dated letter enclosure. The grill impression is exceptionally sharp and well-defined, with 12 by 16 points. This cover was first reported in 1990 by Henry Nowak and precedes the previous earliest-known cover of November 24 (1868) from Princeton, Illinois, listed by Herzog [3:97].

It would not be surprising if even earlier 1¢ grilled Franklin earliest-known-use covers were found. While there are a significant number of examples of the grilled stamps on cover, most postmarks of this period did not contain a year date, and the only way to determine the year is from docketing or dated enclosures. Covers with either of these features are scarce. No E or F grill on cover for any of the denominations of the 1861-67 issue is known with a year date of 1867, and it is accepted that these grills were not delivered to the Post Office Department until 1868.

Figure 3-20. Unique F-grill plate number 27 block of six.
(Robert A. Siegel auction photo)

Grilled Essays

There were a large number of essays produced for the grilled issues, both for testing and for samples. A limited number of these essays were produced with variations on the 1¢ Franklin design, and they are all scarce to rare. They are listed here, separate from the grills in the preceding sections because they are impressed on essays of the 1¢ stamp rather than the issued design. In addition, some of these essays were produced without being grilled. They are included in this enumeration because they were produced at the same time as the grilled essays, and also for consistency since both Brazer and Scott also include them with their descriptions of the grilled essays.

Although it is impossible to date exactly when these essays were made, the variations in the grills give some information on the probable chronology of their production.

Bowlsby essay: The earliest impression is the "C" type 13mm by 16mm, points-up grill, embossed on a red Bowlsby essay (Scott 63-E13e).

Figure 3-21. Earliest-known use of a 1¢ F grill (Scott 92) on cover. This is an example of a drop use at Dansville, New York, at the 1¢ rate for post offices without carrier service. The cover is postmarked August 11 (1868). The year of use was established by a dated enclosure.
(Henry Nowak collection)

Figure 3-24. Frame-only die essay, printed in red-brown on deep yellow paper. Grilled 14 by 17 points down. (Barry Rieger auction photo)

Figure 3-22. Bowlsby essay, embossed with a C grill on upper and lower sections of the essay.

Figure 3-23. Frame-only die essay of the 1¢ Franklin with safety underprint.

Figure 3-25. Frame essay with monogram in center. Grilled 11 by 13, points down. Printed in red brown. (Brazer)

This essay is on gummed, white paper, and was considered by Brazer to be scarce. An illustration of this item is shown in **Figure 3-22**. The use of a grill on a Bowlsby essay seems to be completely inappropriate since the Bowlsby essay was designed to eliminate the need for canceling; therefore, there certainly would be no requirement for a grill. The Bowlsby essay is described in greater detail in Chapter 4.

Frame-only essays: Rare die essays with the center of the 1¢ Franklin design left blank. The grills are points down with some variation in the grill sizes.

Scott lists these die essays as follows:
"79-E29 One Cent frame only.
a. Die on thin crisp paper underprinted with a safety design. Printed in black on dull olive-green. (See **Figure 3-23**).
b. Die on pink paper, 18x13mm points down grill, imperforate, gummed. Printed in red-brown.
c. Die on pink laid paper, no grill. Printed in red.
d. Die on pale pink paper, no grill. Printed in red-brown.
e. Die on transparent paper, no grill. Printed in red-brown.
f. Die on thick yellow paper, no grill. printed in red brown.
g. Die on thin transparent white paper, 11x13mm points down no grill, perforated 12, gummed. Printed in red-brown. (Brazer 86E-Ac).
h. As above, but imperforate."

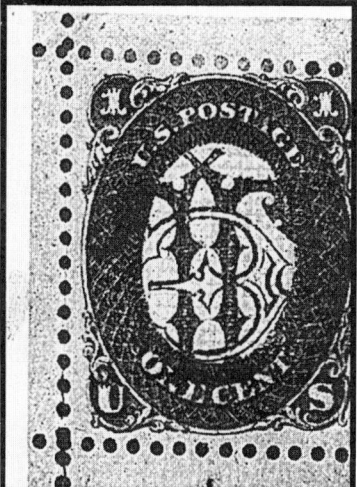

A similar, but unlisted variety was offered in a Barry Rieger auction in October 1983. This item was gummed and printed on a deep yellow paper with a 14-by-17 points-down, heavily embossed grill. A reproduction of the auction catalog photo is shown as **Figure 3-24.**

Monogram essay: (Scott 79-E79i) Similar to the above frame-only essays, but the center contains a monogramlike design, otherwise identical to 79-E79g (Brazer 86E-Ad). This essay is illustrated in **Figure 3-25.**

Bicolor Essay: Typographed and supposedly printed in 1868 (Scott 79-E33). The frame of the 1¢ 1861 is printed as a negative of the normal frame design. The frame is printed in pink, and the vignette is printed in dark blue over pink. (The vignette appears to be a portrait of Washington, similar to that on the 1861 10¢ denomination.) Brazer lists this item as 92E and attributes it to George T. Jones as part of his contract proposal dated July 20, 1868. The essay is shown in **Figure 3-26**.

It seems inappropriate and somewhat confusing for the Scott U.S. specialized to list the above items under the designator 79-E. They were produced in the time period of the E grill (Scott 86) and F grill (Scott 92), and it would make more sense to assign one or both of these numbers to the essays, as was done by Brazer. Using 79, which is also the Scott designation for the 1861 3¢ A grill, is misleading.

All of the above essays evidently were produced in very small numbers (except for the Bowlsby grilled essay), and it is doubtful that more than two or three of any of them are presently in philatelic hands.

Figure 3-26. Bicolor essay, typographed.
(Brazer)

Counterfeit Grills

The grilled stamps of the United States is one of the few areas, along with fancy cancellations and postal history items, where fakers have somewhat successfully plied their trade with respect to the postal issues of this country. The relative scarcity of grilled stamps has not allowed a great deal of familiarity with their characteristics to be achieved by the general collector. The very high value of some grills and the advanced price over ungrilled copies common to all grills have provided an incentive for the application of counterfeit grills to otherwise genuine stamps. As with all counterfeits, personal knowledge or the advice of a knowledgeable expert in the field is the best protection. For some reason, fakers frequently seem to make major errors, such as impressing an 1868 type of grill on an 1861 stamp and affixing it to a pre-1868 cover. These errors provide the careful buyer with a degree of protection.

One of the more comprehensive articles to appear on the subject of the 1861 counterfeit grills was written by C.W. Christian and appeared in three parts in the *American Philatelist* for May, July and September of 1983, as part of the "APS Project Fakes" series. Most of the fakes described are on denominations other than the 1¢, but many types of fake grills are described and illustrated, and the information is applicable to all grilled stamps.

One well-executed counterfeit of the 1¢ Z grill is described in the series. It is heavily embossed and accurately reproduces the characteristic Z grill. However, there is a faint extra row of points in addition to the maximum of 18 rows for the genuine grill. The faker also tried to simulate the penetration of canceling ink and applied too much ink to the back, which resulted in the ink smearing on the reverse side beyond the grill boundaries. Trying to counterfeit the 1¢ Z grill would take a lot of confidence or a lot of ignorance. When only one or two copies of an item are known, it is a certainty that any new copy reported would immediately receive a detailed and expert examination.

An attempt to fake an unused 1¢ C grill is shown in **Figure 3-27**. This is a 16-by-22 points-down grill and, from a casual observation, is reasonably well-executed. There is one more line of grills in the vertical direction than there should be, but it is known that when the C grill was made from the overall grill roller that some of the original grill design remained at the periphery of some of the C grill areas, so it would be possible to have a larger grill that had not been previously recorded. There is no evidence that the grill underwent any pressing after it was embossed, but that could be true for an essay or experimental grill. The fundamental error is in the shape of the grill elements. They show neither the correct biscuit shape from a female roller, nor the sharp truncated pyramid of the male roller. Instead, the impressions are somewhat box-shaped and, from the front, give a colum-

Figure 3-27. Front and back of a 1¢ 1861 showing a counterfeit C grill.
(C.W. Christian collection)

nar appearance.

A simple check will immediately identify most bogus grills:

1. Measure the size of the grilled area, and count the points in each direction. Do they match with cataloged or recorded grills?

2. Are the points in the correct direction?

3. Are the sides of the grill parallel with the stamp border? A large number of fakes have the grill design oriented at a slight angle to the borders of the stamp.

4. Is the grill made up of several small grills applied separately? Many counterfeiters made only a very small grilling tool, which they impressed repeatedly on the stamp to obtain the desired size of grill. This operation was probably done by hand, and the resulting grills show variations in continuity and orientation. No genuine grill was ever produced in this manner. **Figure 3-28** shows a fake A grill.

5. Does the shape of the individual grill elements match the known grill shapes?

A stamp can fail all of the above tests (except number 4) and still be genuine. It is always possible to dis-

Figure 3-28. A fake A grill produced by repeated applications of a small grilling device.
(C.W. Christian photo)

cover a new variety, but also it is very unlikely. However, if the stamp fails any of the tests, caution should be exercised.

Fake grills exist, but the great majority of grills on the market are genuine. The writer has only purchased one fake grill during many years of collecting, and that was contained in a large collection from Europe. A little care and a reasonable amount of knowledge will provide all of the protection that is normally needed.

The large numbers of combinations and permutations of the grill designs, and the almost total lack of contemporary records concerning their production, make the study of grills very challenging and subjective. Grills have interested most of the major philatelic students over the years, and a great amount has been written about them. Much of this writing contains data and theories that are contradicting, and many suppositions have been put forward. This writer has not tried to argue the case for one theory or another, but rather has attempted to present in a limited amount of space those conclusions that appear to be the most logical (in his opinion), and which support a reasonable scenario of events. Omissions and errors undoubtedly exist in this discussion. Further research and discoveries may reverse some presently held theories, but that is the nature of historical investigations of all types.

The End of the 1867 Grills and the Beginning of the 1869 Pictorial Issue

Letters exist that show that the officers of the National Bank Note Company were probably never too enthusiastic about the advisability of grilling stamps. This may be one reason why so little was done between 1865 and 1867 to implement the idea, in spite of the documented interest of the Post Office Department. By 1868, the Post Office also began to have some doubts about the effectiveness of grilling as a means of preventing the reuse of stamps. On November 2, 1868, Zevely, the third assistant postmaster general, wrote to Steel about his new patent for the use of a double-paper printing to prevent the cleaning of stamps, suggesting that he investigate its effectiveness as a replacement and improvement to grilling. Zevely also suggested that National Bank Note Company conduct some experiments. The requirement for grilling stamps in 1868 seems to have become more of a political and contractual consideration than a production advantage.

As previously discussed, the 1861 contract with National Bank Note Company expired on August 15, 1867. It was renewed at that time for a period of one year by order of the postmaster general with an included provision for grilled stamps. At the end of the year's extension, it was evidently extended again for a short period until an entirely new contract was signed, although no documentation reflecting this has come to the author's attention. It is known that on June 22, 1868, an official advertisement was published requesting bids for the production of a new postage stamp. The contract was scheduled to commence on September 22, 1868 [2:150]. Bids were to be submitted by July 22, 1868. The portions of the advertisement that are of particular interest to this discussion are:

"... The stamps must be prepared in such a manner that any attempt to remove them from a letter or packet

will so mutilate them as to render them useless.
   Special proposals for stamps on embossed paper as now in use are invited . . .
   There should be a variety in size as well as the designs of the stamps . . ."

On the day after the advertisement, Postmaster General Alex W. Randall ordered the formation of a committee to review and report on the relative merits of samples submitted with the proposals. The members of the committee were Dr. George C. Schaeffer, librarian of the Patent Office; John B. Guthrie, special agent of the Treasury Department; Dr. Benjamin F. Craig, Army Medical Museum; and A.N. Zevely, third assistant postmaster general.

There were four respondents to the call for bids, and the resulting bids in order of cost were National Bank Note Company, with the highest bid, followed by the American Bank Note Company, then the bid of George T. Jones (for typographed bicolored stamps) and the lowest bid by Butler & Carpenter.

The committee found that the two lower bidders had presented samples that were inferior in quality to those of the two top bidders, and that the bid of National Bank Note Company demonstrated superior workmanship. They also stated reservations concerning the merits and costs of embossing [3:79].

The president of the National Bank Note Company informed the Post Office Department that it had the exclusive right to use the Steel patent for grills, and it seems that this fact gave Postmaster General Randall the rationale to use his discretionary power to award the contract to National Bank Note Company, even though it was the highest bidder. It seems very likely that he personally wanted National Bank Note Company as the contractor for stamp production, and the grilling issue was only a means by which he could justify the selection. His award stipulated that the embossing would be provided free of additional charge.

Because of the somewhat unusual circumstances surrounding the award of the contract, the lowest bidder, Butler & Carpenter, filed a protest. A Congressional committee investigated the matter, but found in favor of National Bank Note Company.

The awarding of the four-year contract for new stamps to the National Bank Note Company was announced on October 3, 1868, and it became effective on December 12, 1868. Curiously, the original National Bank Note Company proposal had called for a price of 27½¢ per 1,000 grilled stamps. Postmaster General Randall had stated that there would be no surcharge for grilling, i.e., 25¢ per thousand, when he announced the award, but the final contract awarded a price of 25½¢ per thousand, and all stamps were to be grilled.

The above discussion of the contract for the new stamps of the 1869 series is relevant to the 1861-67 series because the old stamps continued to be furnished to the Post Office Department long after the new contract was in force. Letters and advisories as late as March 2, 1869, were sent to postmasters stating that all of the old stamps were to be used before the new stamps would be supplied. Large stocks of grilled stamps produced during the 1867-69 period, and maybe even some of the ungrilled 1861 stamps, were still in the inventory of the National Bank Note Company. Obviously, it would be to its financial advantage to deliver these to the stamp agent and to receive payment for them.

Richard B. Graham brought the above situation to the author's attention and also discussed its importance in some supplementary comments to the Scott Trepel *Chronicle* article previously referenced. Graham felt that since it would be advantageous to the company to sell all of its old stamps, National Bank Note Company probably emptied its vaults and drawers of the remaining 1861-67 stamps in its possession. This could have possibly included sheets of the early experimental grills and could account for the appearance in 1869 of items like the Mason, Texas, B-grill cover [8:125-7].

On March 19, 1869, the first of the 1869 Pictorials were supplied to the stamp agent, and the sale of the 1867 grilled issues became mixed with those of the new issue. Herzog [3:80] reports that more than 3,000,000 of the old 1¢ grilled stamps were issued to post offices in the first quarter of 1869 and almost 500,000 in the second quarter.

Although the new 1869 issues continued to be embossed, the desire of the Post Office Department for grilling definitely had diminished. A new postmaster general, John A.J. Creswell, and a new staff of assistant postmasters general had been appointed, and grilling no longer seemed to be an important issue.

The quality control in the production of grills continued to decline until the embossing on many stamps was extremely faint or missing, and in the spring of 1870, the National Bank Note Company began phasing out the production of embossed stamps. Thus ended a very interesting period in stamp history.

References

1. Haverbeck, H.D.S. "The Grill and Other Patents of Charles F. Steel Relating to Postage Stamp Production, 1867-1875." *Collectors Club Philatelist*. Volume XXXV, Number 11. 1965.

2. Brookman, Lester G. *The United States Postage Stamps of the 19th Century*. Volume II. H.L. Lindquist

Publications Inc. 1966.

3. Herzog, William K. "The Story of the United States Grilled Stamps." *Congress Book*. 1978.

4. Trepel, Scott R. "The Three-Cent All-Over Grill Essays; Origin of the Trial Cancellation." *Chronicle* 134. May 1987.

5. Hahn, Calvet M. "Ishikawa's Display of the U. S. Grill." *Chronicle* 112. November 1981.

6. Herzog, William K. "Inverted 1¢ 'E' & 3¢ 'F' Grills." *Chronicle* 103. August 1979.

7. Hahn, Calvet M. "Ishikawa's Display of the U.S. Grills." *Chronicle*. November 1981.

8. Graham, Richard B. "Some Comments About the Used Experimental Grilled Stamps of 1867-9." *Chronicle* 134. May 1987.

The United States 1¢ Franklin 1861-67

CHAPTER 4

Experimental and Patent Printings

Introduction

One of the most colorful and interesting groups of printings of the 1¢ 1861 stamp resulted from the continuing concern of the Post Office Department with the possibility of losing large amounts of postal revenue when canceled stamps were cleaned and reused. The actual amount of loss was probably much less than the Post Office Department estimated, but its interest in the problem led to many ideas and patents to prevent the illegal reuse of stamps. Although the experimental printings and trials based on these patents were encouraged by the Post Office Department, none of the ideas was actually approved and put into general use except for the grills from the patent of Charles F. Steel, discussed in the previous chapter.

Little has been written concerning the experimental printings, although examples frequently appear on the market. There are few records, other than the patent applications that still exist, concerning the experimental printings. As a result, identification of specific copies with the patents is based only on observable correlation between the patent descriptions and the appearance of the stamp. C.W. Christian is one of the foremost investigators in this area. His survey of the subject was published in an article titled "Patent Improvements and Experiments of the Sixties" in the 1972 *American Philatelic Congress Book*. Sol Altman, another researcher in the field, wrote "Patent Papers Relating to the Improvement and Protection of United States Bank-Notes, Postage and Revenue Stamps," which appeared in the *Essay-Proof Journal*, Number 67 (1960). These two articles probably contain most of the meager information that is available on the 1¢ Franklin patent printings. Much of this chapter is based on information contained in Christian's earlier works.

In this section, information on the patents of George Bowlsby (whose ideas resulted in the most unusual and beautiful of the experimental printings), Henry Lowenberg, William Wyckoff, James Macdonough and Abraham Gibson will be presented. Patented ideas for preventing the reuse of stamps by using special canceling devices will be covered in the chapter on cancellations.

Bowlsby Patent and the Coupon Essays

On December 26, 1866, George W. Bowlsby of Monroe, Michigan, was granted patent 51782 for a novel, but not very practical, method to eliminate the reuse of postage stamps. His idea, essentially, was to tear off part of the stamp in order to cancel it. **Figure 4-1** is a reproduction of a page from the original patent document, and the following is quoted from the relevant portions of the patent application:

> "The nature of my invention consists of applying the adhesive substance to only a portion of the under surface of the stamp so that when the stamp is attached to the letter or other mailable matter it will leave the remaining part, which is not made adhesive projecting . . . that is, not adhering to the letter.
> It also consists in the tearing off of the projecting part of the stamp by the postmaster before the letter is put into the mail, and so totally destroying the stamp past all fur-

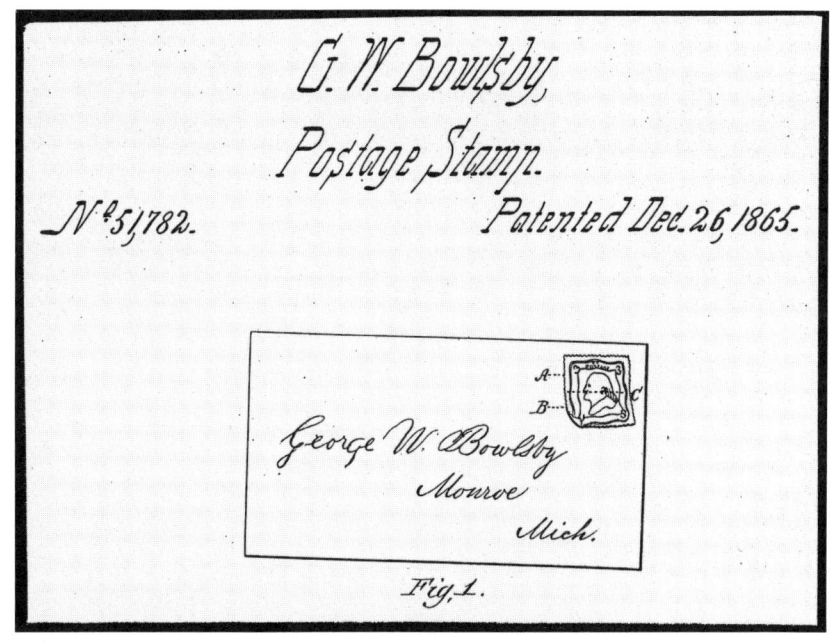

Figure 4-1. Part of the specification from the original Bowlsby patent application. (Courtesy of C.W. Christian)

ther recovery and use.

A B, Fig. 1, is the stamp. A is the upper half adhering to the letter. B is the lower half, to be torn off by the postmaster. C is the line of perforations across the middle of the stamp in the line of separation, to complete the tearing in a neat manner . . .

The object of this invention is to totally destroy the stamp, so that it cannot be washed or otherwise be cleaned and reused, as is now much done."

Though the Bowlsby patent is credited for the coupon essays, an example of which is pictured in **Figure 4-2**, it is apparent that the original idea was improved upon beyond the specification sketches by adding the coupon. Only the 1¢ Franklin design and die were used to make these particular experimental printings, and they are the most extensively printed of all of the patents. The coupon is approximately the size of the stamp, and is placed above the stamp design with the wording, "STAMP of no value without Coupon. COUPON to be removed only by the POSTMASTER." The success of the patent depended upon properly affixing the stamp to the envelope with the coupon extending free and readily accessible to be torn off at the post office. When the coupon was removed the stamp was effectively canceled. The basic flaws in the concept are readily apparent. The handwork necessary to properly detach the coupon to cancel the stamp would be more time-consuming and exacting than using a normal killer. Great care would have to be taken so the coupon would not be accidentally torn from the stamp during handling before the canceling operation.

The National Bank Note Company produced a variety of examples of the coupon essay. Large die essays were prepared in 12 colors, according to the Brazer catalog, and 14 colors as listed in the Scott U.S. specialized. These are exceptionally beautiful die proofs and are found on India paper, die sunk on card, and also on a thick white ivory paper. A color photo of one of these large die proofs is shown in the color plates.

On most of the large dies on India paper that the author has seen, there is a small script letter in pencil at the lower-right corner of the die block impression. These letters probably correlate with the colors of the proofs, but because of the scarcity of the die impressions, it has been impossible, to date, to definitely assign specific letters to every color. Large die proofs in the yellow-green color from James Lee's stock, the C.W. Christian collection and from the author's collection all show the letter "m" (see **Figure 4-3**), and the carmine proofs in the author's and the Christian collection show the letter "l." This is a fairly good indication that there is a definite correlation. The letters are faint on some examples and can only be approximately identified, but a careful exami-

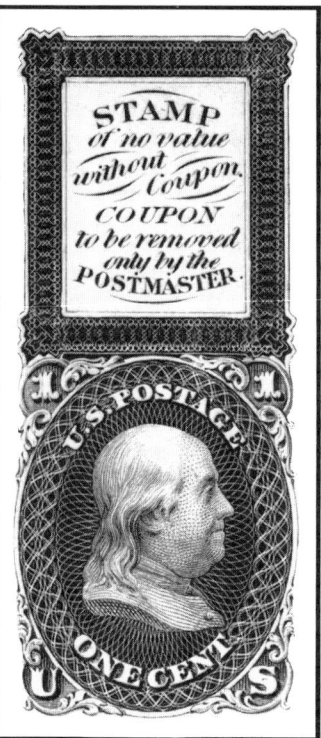

Figure 4-2. Bowlsby coupon essay, large die proof in black, die sunk on card. (C.W. Christian collection)

nation of those examples that were available for viewing shows the following correlations:

a. scarlet
c. green
e. brown
j. blue (identification is marginal)
l. carmine
m. apple-green

A plate was made from the die, and plate essays were also prepared. Some are completely perforated on all sides and between the stamp and coupon, others are perforated around and rouletted or imperforate between, and one variety is completely imperforate. These plate essays were printed in red and blue, and with and without gum. A variety is known on tissue or pelure paper, and one type is found with a C grill and gummed (see Figure 3-22). The grill is applied to both the upper and lower part of the essay as would be expected if an unaltered C-grill roller were used. The need for a grill to prevent reuse on a coupon patent that wouldn't be canceled anyway seems like overkill. Lee reports having a red plate essay with a split C grill, and further states that it is one of only two he has seen [1].

The Bowlsby coupon essays are listed in the Brazer essay catalog and in the Scott U.S. specialized beginning with the 1992 edition.

The following is a compilation of their listings with assigned catalog numbers:

Size of complete design 20mm by 47mm die size 57mm by 95mm.

Brazer 63E-B	Scott 63-E13	ONE CENT
a.	a.	Die on India, die sunk on card; (scarce)
		black
		red
		scarlet
		orange
		orange-brown
		brown
		yellow-green†
		green†
		blue
		violet
		red-violet
		gray
		gray-brown*
		dull orange-yellow*
		yellow-brown*
		blue-green*
		†Brazer only *Scott only
b.	b.	Die on white glazed (ivory) paper; (scarce)
		black
		dark-brown
		scarlet
		blue
c.		Plate on India paper; (scarce)
		black
d.		Plate on card; (scarce)
		black
e.	c.	Plate on pelure paper, gummed; (scarce)
		red
f.	d.	Plate on white paper
		red
g.	e.	Plate on white paper with grill 13mm x 16mm points up, gummed; (scarce)
		red
h.	f.	Plate on white paper, perforated all around and between stamp and coupon
		red
		blue
i.	g.	Same, but imperforate between stamp and coupon
		red
		blue
j.	h.	Same, rouletted between
		red
		blue

Large multiples are extremely difficult to obtain. A block of 30 of the plate essay in blue (Scott 63E-13f) was offered in a February 1977 Robert A. Siegel auction, and the largest multiple that this author has recorded is from a note written in 1914 by Edward H. Mason, an early essay collector. He stated that he had in his possession a sheet of the 1¢ coupon essays [2:58]. He did not give the number of impressions in the sheet, but it can be as-

Figure 4-3. Large India-paper Bowlsby die proof, die sunk on card. Printed in apple-green, with a manuscript "m" in the lower right, as an identifier. (Also illustrated in color.)

sumed that a pane of the coupon essays contained 50 impressions. The block of 30 (3 by 10) mentioned above shows the bottom and left margins as well as the pane separation at the right. Since the height of the coupon essay is twice that of the issued stamp, it would be likely that a plate of the essays would contain half as many impressions. This example shows no plate number or inscription, and none is known for copies of the coupon essay. **Figure 4-4** shows a beautiful, almost perfectly centered block of six in red.

One of the most curious examples that exists from this experimental printing is a canceled strip of three on part of a U.S. sanitary fair envelope. **Figure 4-5** shows a photo from the columns of Hugh J. and J. David Baker [3:244]. It is most likely that this item never went through the mails and was prepared as an example of how it would be used. The essays on the envelope are in blue and rouletted between the stamp and coupon. Both the stamps and their accompanying coupons are glued to the cover making it quite difficult for a postmaster to remove the coupon at the rouletting. In addition, sticking out as they do above the envelope would make it easy to damage the coupons before processing. This example is canceled with a circular grid marking. This, of course, should not be

Figure 4-4. Block of six of the Bowlsby patent essay (Scott 63-E13g), in red.
(C.W. Christian collection)

necessary with the Bowlsby patent.

The probability that the on-cover use is only a trial example is further enhanced by the existence of three other identical sanitary fair illustrated envelopes with copies of the Bowlsby essays attached. The essays are uncanceled, with examples in red and blue, and in both perforated and imperforate versions [4:114]. These three examples, in addition to the canceled version previously discussed, would comprise a complete set of color and perforation varieties, and may have been placed on leftover Civil War-era sanitary fair envelopes to add interest to a presentation of the Bowlsby patent.

The coupon patent was not a very useful idea, but it did result in many beautiful examples of the engraving and printing of the period, and provided some philatelic gems for collectors of the future.

The Lowenberg Patent

The Lowenberg patent, and the three additional patents whose descriptions follow, shared one principle in common. They all depended on a soluble substance that would dissolve if attempts were made to clean a canceled stamp.

Henry Lowenberg of New York City was granted patent 42207 on April 5, 1863. His idea was to coat the paper on which the stamp was to be printed with a soluble sizing or starch. The National Bank Note Company, using plate 27, printed experimental sheets for this patent, and examples in many colors are still readily available to the

Figure 4-5. Reduced cover showing use of the Bowlsby patent coupon stamp on cover. This is probably an experimental trial.
(From *Bakers' U.S. Classics*)

Experimental and Patent Printings

Figure 4-6. Enlarged view of the reverse side of a Lowenberg patent printing, showing characteristic ripples caused by the aged starch coating.

Figure 4-7. Front of a Lowenberg printing with the starch cracks and eroded design plainly visible.

collector. This experimental printing is listed in the Scott U.S. specialized as a trial color proof with catalog number 63TC5 if imperforate and 63TC6 if perforated. These stamps are printed on white wove paper and in many colors, although some colors are not known in both perforated and imperforate versions. Scott groups all of the printings from the patents by Lowenberg, Wyckoff and Macdonough under the 63TC5/6 category, with no attempt to distinguish between the patents, although there are distinctive differences. The printings are listed in 15 colors.

With the passage of years, the starch coating on many of the printings from the Lowenberg patent has become rough and crinkly, sometimes forming ridges and other times separating into small platelets similar to the cracking of mud in a puddle drying in the sun. The degree of roughness is probably a result of both the amount of starch used in the coating and the environmental conditions to which the stamp has been exposed during its lifetime. **Figure 4-6** is an enlarged photo of the reverse of one of these stamps showing the characteristic roughness of the starch coating. On the printed surface of many of the stamps, in addition to the roughness, the design frequently has partially eroded. The erosion is due to the stamp being exposed to moisture at some time, with the result that the design dissolved to some extent. This gives an appearance similar to that of a dry printing, and is very noticeable. **Figure 4-7** illustrates this condition.

It is difficult to obtain a perforated 63TC6 with good centering, and obtaining all of the colors with very fine or better centering is a real challenge.

Examples of the imperforate 63TC5 are much more common and easy to obtain. Both types are known in blocks of 12 with plate numbers and inscriptions. An attractive block is illustrated in **Figure 4-8**. These large multiples are scarce, and the largest group of them last came on the market in the 1990 sale by Robert A. Siegel of the Brazer collection. This sale offered 10 inscription plate number 27 blocks of 12, including both perforated and imperforate varieties. A couple of years earlier the Christie's sale of the Wunderlich essay/proof material included three plate blocks of 12 in the perforated variety. The author has seen a few other similar blocks, and a reasonable estimate of the total number of large plate number blocks is 15-20.

At the end of this section, all of the experimental printings from patents using soluble materials or inks are listed, along with the colors assignable to these patents.

In the fall of 1864, Lowenberg applied for, and was granted, a new patent for his well-known decalcomania stamps. His patent called for applying an adhesive substance to transparent paper, then printing the stamp de-

Figure 4-8. An imperforate inscription plate block of 12 of the Lowenberg patent essay.
(C.W. Christian collection)

The United States 1¢ Franklin 1861-67

Figure 4-9. An inscription plate number 27 strip of four, perforated 12, of the Wyckoff printing, in green. A similar item in brown is shown in the color section.

sign (in reverse) on the surface of the adhesive substance so that the design would be clearly visible through the transparent paper, and in the proper orientation, without coming in contact with it. When the stamp was applied to the surface of an envelope, the design would stick to the envelope, and any attempt to soak off the stamp so that it could be used again would result in the gum dissolving, and with it the image of the stamp. It was certainly a foolproof method for preventing reuse, but was never adopted by the Post Office Department. It was, however, briefly used in Prussia during 1866.

The 1861 1¢ in the decalcomania printing has been reported to exist by Falk Finkelburg [5:206], but this author has never seen one, nor is it listed in the Scott catalog. Many examples of the this patent do exist on the 1861 3¢ denomination. They are printed on "goldbeater's skin," which is a special paper treated with collodian to make it transparent. Since this process is similar to that used to make decalcomania designs, the name "decalcomania printing" has been given to this Lowenberg patent. The biggest drawback to the decalcomania experimentals with regards to their practical use was their extreme fragility and the transitory nature of the design. The paper tended to become brittle and crack, and the stamp image began to disappear when the slightest moisture came in contact with it during handling.

Wyckoff Patent

William C. Wyckoff of Brooklyn, New York, was granted patent 53723 on April 3, 1866. This patent resulted in some of the most attractive of the fugitive-ink patent printings. The term fugitive ink is often applied to all of the soluble-material patents since the inked design was definitely short-lived whenever it was dampened.

Wyckoff's patent proposed the idea of coating the paper with zinc oxide or pipe clay prior to printing, and as with the other patents, exposure to moisture or cleaning would dissolve the coating and the stamp impression.

The characteristics of this printing are a smooth surface and a very sharp impression. For examples printed in the issued color of the 1¢, it is impossible to tell them from the issued stamp by visual observation. Fortunately, as with all of these fugitive inks, a moistened toothpick can be gently applied to a small inconspicuous part of the design. If the ink disappears, it is an experimental printing. If the ink remains after light rubbing, it is a copy of the issued stamp. Since the experimental printing is less valuable than the unused issued stamp, particularly if well-centered, it is advisable to test any high-priced copies of the 1¢ Franklin for fugitive ink. A plate number 27 strip of four in dark green is shown in **Figure 4-9**. A companion piece, in brown, is illustrated in the color plates. These photographs illustrate the sharpness of image that was obtained with printings from the Wyckoff patent. No crinkling of the paper, such as that found in the Lowenberg starch-coated patent, is found on the Wyckoff copies. However, in cases where moisture has been present, some examples show evidence of faded or missing parts of the design. **Figure 4-10** shows a typical Wyckoff printing with some of the design eroded away.

The last two paragraphs, quoted below, of Wyckoff's patent application contain some interesting remarks regarding his comparison of his idea to that for the decalcomania patent by Lowenberg. It does not, however, mention the earlier starch-coating patent by Lowenberg, which was really more similar to the Wyckoff idea. The following is an excerpt from Wyckoff's "Letters Patent No. 53,723," dated April 3, 1866:

> "I am aware of the existence of a patent granted to Henry Lowenberg for self-canceling stamps; and I wish here to remark that my invention differs from his in very important particulars. It will be understood that I do not require or wish transparency of paper or material on which to print, but, on the contrary I leave the paper in its natural opaque condition and add to it some opaque soluble substance, for the reason that it is very difficult to obtain a good impression on a glazed surface or indeed on any gluti-

Experimental and Patent Printings

Figure 4-10. Two examples of the Wyckoff printing showing typical loss of design that can occur with moisture and rubbing.
(C.W. Christian collection)

Figure 4-11. Top inscription block of four of the Macdonough patent printing in light-brown glycerine ink.

nous surface. Stamps made thereby are impracticable for ordinary use, aside from the above disadvantage in printing for the reason that they are either sticky or too brittle, the latter being a great fault. Hence, to make such stamps on an extensive scale, as does the Government, is impracticable. The preparation of the material in a state ready for the impression is exceedingly expensive, the material receives the impression poorly, the sheets of stamps when printed are apt to stick together or break in pieces, and indeed much time would be consumed in the mere matter of handling and counting sheets of such stamps, and there would be some difficulty in counting them accurately; and these are no inconsiderable items, as is well known to those who do engraving and printing for the Government. I therefore wish it distinctly understood that I lay no claim to Mr. Lowenberg's invention. What I claim as my invention, and desire secure by Letters Patent, is—

Coating the side of the paper which is to receive the print of the postage or revenue stamp with a surface of water-color pigment or paint, or some sufficiently opaque or non-transparent surface as to receive a good impression from the types or plates, and at the same time be soluble in water, or other fluid, substantially as described.
WM. C. WYCKOFF"

Macdonough Patent

James Macdonough of New York City was issued patent 52869 on February 27, 1866, for "Improvement in the Manufacture of Ink for Printing Postage Stamps." Macdonough at this time was secretary of the National Bank Note Company, and in the future would become president of the American Bank Note Company. His invention was to make the printing ink from soluble materials so that attempts to clean a stamp would result in the destruction of the printed design.

In his patent specifications, Macdonough described his proposed "sensitive ink" in great detail. It was basically composed of glycerine as a carrier for the pigment, with the addition of other materials to reduce its solubility. While glycerine inks readily dissolve in water, acid and most other fluids, they are so fugitive in nature that they would not be practical without the addition of some sort of stabilizer. Macdonough proposed adding gelatine or dextrine or starch or other similar material to reduce the solubility. He considered the fact that the degree of solubility could be controlled and the ink tailored to a specific type of use to be a major advantage of his patent.

Experimental printings for this patent were printed only in brown, ranging from light brown to dark brown in appearance. The difference seems to be in the amount of dark-brown ink specks that are present on the stamp. It appears that for some reason the brown pigment was not ground to a fine powder before mixing with the glycerine carrier, and this resulted in a very pronounced speckling of color intensity on each stamp and a variation from stamp to stamp. The design characteristically has a blurred appearance, as shown in **Figure 4-11**, with none of the sharpness of detail found in the previous patents. The printings are found only imperforate. Large multiples are scarce, and this author has not seen a plate number example. Single copies are readily available, and blocks of four can be obtained.

Macdonough thought his patent had many advantages, primarily because no changes had to be made in the standard production process for the printing of postage stamps except for the mixing of a special ink. However, it shared many of the drawbacks of the other fugitive ink patents, and these plus the poor impressions obtained with the ink made it undesirable for use.

Gibson Patent

Among the simplest of the patents was the January 5, 1864, patent granted to Abraham J. Gibson of Worcester, Massachusetts. Gibson proposed to print a design in a fugitive ink, like the Macdonough patent. But his idea differed substantially in that he recommended printing the stamp as normally done with the intaglio process and regular ink, and then overprinting the stamp with a network of lines in a color different and preferably lighter than the issued-stamp color. This overprinting would be done with fugitive ink and could be accomplished easily by surface printing (letterpress or lithograph). Examples of the Gibson patent on the 1¢ Franklin are quite rare, and these have a pattern of red interlocking circles printed over the normal 1¢ blue stamp. This design is known as the "bedspring overprint," and an example is shown in **Figure 4-12**. Christian reported that he has personally seen three examples of this printing and is of the opinion that only one sheet was printed.

This idea had the simplicity of the Macdonough patent without the disadvantage of a degraded image. Its fatal fault was that if the overprint were washed off, the stamp would revert to the appearance of the 1861 stamp as issued. Therefore, to use the idea, all of the regular stamps would have to be demonetized and removed from circulation. Another problem that Gibson apparently did not consider is the ease with which a washed stamp could be overprinted again with the network design. Counterfeiting of washed stamps could have become a thriving business, and probably the Post Office Department would have lost a lot more money in that manner than it ever did from the washing-off of cancels.

Summary

A few general comments on the fugitive-ink patents and the experimental stamps that resulted from them are appropriate at this point.

The experimental printings are very attractive from a philatelic viewpoint, and the many colors in which they can be found add sparkle and variation to any exhibit or collection of the 1861 1¢ Franklin. There is probably no other U.S. stamp that offers such a wide diversity of colored experimental printings, and these rejected patent ideas provide a special benefit to the collector of this issue.

Although Scott lists 15 colors in total for both perforated and imperforate varieties, the exact number of distinctively different colors is somewhat hard to determine. For instance, the Scott listing in the orange category includes deep orange red, deep red orange, dark orange and yellow orange. Other describers have listed deep orange and orange red. All of these colors are similar, and exactly how many deserve individual listing is somewhat subjective.

Scott does not list the blue or light blue in perforated and gummed condition. This is definitely not correct since the author personally observed a beautifully centered block of four in the stock of Richard A. Champagne about a decade ago. This block was printed with fugitive ink, as Champagne illustrated by removing a small portion of the ink with a moistened applicator. Christian also has a similar block of four in his collection. It is the opinion of this author that there are as many perforated experimental copies in blue as there are in most of the other colors, but the majority of them reside in collections, masquerading as the issued stamp. This is not surprising. Not many collectors would touch their prized and valuable unused copies with a moistened swab for fear of damaging them, and where any negative outcome of the test would lead to disappointment. There are other indicators that will help distinguish the experimental printings from the issued stamp. The experimental printings are printed on a wove paper that is slightly thicker and softer than that of the issued stamp, and the paper is slightly whiter. Comparison of items with respect to these characteristic properties may give rise to, or allay, suspicions, but the water test is absolutely reliable and final.

The following is a list of experimental printings as listed under trial color proofs in the 1996 edition of the Scott U.S. specialized:

Color	63TC5 (imperf)	63TC6 (perf and gummed)
rose	x	x
deep orange red	x	x
deep red orange	x	
dark orange		x
yellow orange	x	
orange brown	x	x
dark brown	x	
yellow green		x
green	x	
blue green	x	x
gray lilac	x	x
gray black	x	x
slate black	x	
blue	x	
light blue	x	

As can be seen from this list, there are considerably more color varieties in the imperforate version than in the perforated and gummed versions. In addition to this list, the author would like to add the blue 63TC6

Figure 4-12. Gibson patent overprint of a red pattern in fugitive ink on the normal issued stamp. Also illustrated in the color section. (C.W. Christian collection)

discussed previously and a 63TC5, light-brown color, in which the Macdonough patent is printed. In the author's opinion, this is neither a dark brown nor an orange brown. The author also has a copy of a 63TC5 in a lake shade, much darker than the listed rose color. The red-orange shade seems to be the most common, while the gray lilac is the least common of the listed colors.

Some years ago, James Lee, a collector and dealer in U.S. postal history and philatelic literature, conducted a survey of the experimental printings and the colors in which they could be found. At that time he also queried the late Falk Finkelburg, whose reference collection of these items was unsurpassed, concerning colors. Lee's investigations verified all of the colors listed in the Scott catalog plus the addition of an olive green for the Wyckoff 63TC6, a dark blue for Wyckoff 63TC5 and 63TC6, and a brown for the Lowenberg 63TC5.

Based on the experience of the author and Christian in examinations of examples, and from correspondence with Lee and Finkelburg, the following characteristics may be assigned to each of the experimental fugitive-ink printings:

Henry Lowenberg starch-paper patent: sharp impression on a paper that is usually, but not always, rough and crinkly from the aged starch coating.

William Wyckoff patent: smooth surface with a very sharp impression.

James Macdonough patent: smooth surface with a blurred impression, imperforate, and printed only in a light-brown color with dark-brown specks of pigment.

Abraham Gibson patent: issued stamp overprinted in red with a fine network of intersecting 4mm circles.

References

1. Lee, James E. Personal communication. December 3, 1989.

2. Brazer, Clarence W. "E.H. Mason's Collection in 1914." *Essay-Proof Journal* No. 41 (1954).

3. Baker, Hugh J. and J. David Baker. *Baker's U.S. Classics*. U.S. Philatelic Classics Society, 1985.

4. Kantor, Alvin R. and Marjorie S. *Sanitary Fairs*. Scott Publishing Company, 1992.

5. Finkelburg, Falk. Revision to "Essays For U.S. Adhesive Postage Stamps" by Clarence W. Brazer. *Essay-Proof Journal* No. 132 (1976).

The United States 1¢ Franklin 1861-67

CHAPTER 5

Special Printings

Throughout the printing history of the 1861 1¢ stamp, the National Bank Note Company and its successors, including the Bureau of Engraving and Printing, made special printings of the plate or die for various purposes. Most of these were requested by the Post Office Department, but some appear to be in response to internal needs of the National Bank Note Company.

Included in this chapter are the specimen and control-number overprints, the 1875 reissue, 1879-93 cardboard proofs, 1881 Atlanta color proofs (plus the probable 1895 Atlanta printing), Roosevelt small die proofs and the Panama-Pacific small die proofs. While many of these items are called proofs within the broad definition of the word, they are really not proofs in the sense that implies an early hand-printing for the purpose of checking the die plate or color. These so-called "proofs" were printed at a later date to provide examples of the regular stamp issues, frequently in colors other than the issued stamp. Their principal use was for displays or special distribution by the government, or for demonstration by the bank note company of its product.

For that reason, the author has elected to discuss them in this section, separate from other proofs and essays. No matter what system of definitions is used to describe philatelic items or attributes, there will be some overlap between categories. In general, the simpler the definition and the broader its use, the more useful it is. Familiarity with the terms and their various meanings comes with experience. Excluded from this discussion are those printings of an experimental nature, specifically the Bowlsby essays and fugitive-ink experiments that were covered in the preceding chapter.

Specimen Overprints

The exact purpose for which most of the specimen overprints were made is unknown, and the distribution of these items is equally obscure. It may be possible that the overprinted stamps were planned for use as a sample of the issue to be distributed to foreign post offices. This was certainly the case for some specimen overprints of postal issues of the 1870s in connection with the Universal Postal Union. It is known that the bank note companies used specimens to demonstrate their capabilities to prospective customers.

John Luff states in his *Postage Stamps of the United States*, "On January 23rd, 1867, one hundred sets of the ten denominations of this issue were surcharged 'Specimen' in 'Old English' type. On February 28th, 1867, the same surcharge was applied to twenty thousand more sets. This was done by order of the Third Assistant Postmaster General. A few copies have been seen with the final letter of the surcharge inverted."[1:74] No copies of the inverted letter are presently known to this author. Although Luff refers to these as surcharges, they did not change the denomination of the stamp and are therefore overprints, not surcharges.

The source of Luff's information is unknown, and while the 100 copies for the small specimen overprints seems to be a reasonable number, the figure of 20,000 for a second printing with the larger overprint does not seem to correlate with the relative scarcity of the item. Recently the author accessed some information that seems to resolve this discrepancy.

Philip H. Ward Jr., writing in his column "U.S. Notes" in the November 7, 1952, edition of *Mekeel's Weekly Stamp News*, reproduced a communication dated January 27, 1893, and addressed to A.D. Hazen, the third assistant postmaster general, from his chief clerk. The letter provides the information that a large number of stamps, dating back as far as the 1851 issue and including more than 100,000 Confederate stamps that had been appropriated at the end of the war, had been in the Post Office Department files since the tenure of A.N. Zevely, and had now been destroyed in compliance with Hazen's orders. A certified list of the items destroyed followed and included an item for 18,800 specimen overprints of the 1¢ 1861. If Luff's original figure for a printing of 20,100 is correct, it leaves a balance of 1,300 copies unaccounted for. This number seems more in line with the present availability of the overprint.

There are four types of specimen overprints: the very rare small 12mm overprint and the more common 15mm overprint, both of which are found on the issued stamp; a very rare 43mm black manuscript overprint on a large die proof; and a rare 37mm double-line block-letter overprint found on some large die proofs.

Small Specimen Overprint

The 12mm overprint on a normal-color stamp is shown in **Figure 5-1**. This overprint is listed by Scott as 63S A, and is the rarest of the overprints. The single copy in the C.W. Christian collection is thought to be the only

69

Figure 5-1. Very rare, possibly unique, small 12mm "Specimen" overprint, with manuscript-inked cross. (C.W. Christian collection)

Figure 5-2. Counterfeit small "Specimen" overprint.

example of this rarity. This example was originally in the specimen collection of Clarence Brazer, and formed the basis for the initial Scott listing.

In the spring of 1937, Brazer sold his entire specimen collection to F.W. Pickard, and later reacquired the 1¢ small overprint when the Pickard collection was sold in 1944 by the Mercury Stamp Company. He subsequently sold it in 1951 to C.W. Christian, and in his sale invoice to Christian, he noted, in addition to the information stated above, that it was the Vinton E. Sisson copy and that it is unique. Careful examination of the photo will show a small manuscript "x" in black ink, just above the overprint.

The presence of this ink marking is interesting. Carroll Chase in his reference book on the 1851-57 3¢ stamp notes that the New York dealer, J.M. Bartels, purchased in the mid-1920s, a collection from the estate of a retired Washington postal employee [2:211]. In the collection was a copy of the 1¢ 1857 with a small specimen overprint showing a small inked cross above the overprint. It is possible that this stamp and the Christian copy came from the same source. Many copies of rare U.S. stamps and proofs have a small "x" in black ink, usually in the middle of the design. It may be that these items had their origin in Post Office Department files, where examples of special items had been marked with a small cross to prevent their use as postage. Another example of this type of defacement is seen in the rare set of imperforate stamps of the 1861 issue.

The reported uniqueness of the Christian copy maintained its position for many years; however, in January of 1993, a repaired stamp with the small overprint appeared in an auction sale. This stamp is better centered and has no manuscript "x" marking. At some time in its life, it was torn along the left edge. The tear has been expertly repaired and the stamp regummed. It now presents an excellent appearance, and the repair is unnoticeable to a casual inspection (see **Figure 5-2**). This author made the winning bid on the item and, after receipt, presented it to the Philatelic Foundation for expertizing. Unfortunately, it was determined to have a counterfeit overprint and was returned to the seller. This information is presented here as a cautionary note since it is entirely possible that this item may appear on the market again at some future date.

With possibly only one genuine example known of 63S A, the small overprint is one of the rarest of the 1861 1¢ issues, and is certainly a plum for the most discriminating collector. Considering its scarcity, it is considerably undervalued in the current Scott catalog.

About a decade ago, the author received a note from another 1¢ Franklin specialist, who mentioned that he possessed a copy of the small specimen overprint on a grilled stamp. The author has never seen this item and has some reservations about its authenticity. The small specimen overprint has not been previously reported on any of the 1867 grilled denominations.

The 15mm Specimen Overprint

While not plentiful, the larger overprint is not difficult to acquire as a single. Scott lists this item as 63S B, with the issued number of copies as 1,300 (in close agreement with the 20,100 copies printed as reported by Luff minus the 18,800 copies reported as destroyed in 1893). A subtype without the period is also listed and is probably very scarce. No examples of this variety have been seen by the author; however, Henry Nowak has reported a copy in his collection.

Multiples of the 15mm overprinted stamp are scarce. A spectacular inscription plate block of eight was sold in 1988 by Christie's, and an illustration of this item is shown in **Figure 5-3**. This is the largest multiple the author has seen. The fact that this block was printed from plate 27 adds credence to Luff's contention that the specimen overprints were printed in 1867, since most of the special and experimental printings of that period were from plate 27.

Figure 5-3. "Specimen" overprint (15mm) on a scarce multiple.
(Christie's, New York)

There are three single copies in the author's collection, and these copies all appear to be printed on different paper stocks. When viewed under ultraviolet light, the paper of two of the copies fluoresce, one with a greenish hue and one in a blue-white color. The third copy is on nonfluorescent paper. This suggests that there were three or more printings of the item, or that the printing was large enough that it would be probable that different paper stocks were used.

Manuscript Overprint

A manuscript overprint is known on a large die (65mm by 57mm) printing on India paper, die sunk on a 115mm by 133mm card backing. An albino embossed double circle with the inscription "National Bank Note Co. N.Y." is impressed below the proof design. This is an exceptionally beautiful item and possibly is unique. It may have been used as a display or presentation piece, or as a salesman's sample. Examples of this overprint on die proofs of other denominations of the 1861 issue were offered in the 1988 Christie's sale previously mentioned, and the manuscript overprint on each of them is slightly different in form. This particular Christie's sale contained an unusually large number of 1861 essays and proofs, and is a good reference source for the 1861-67 collector. It is reported that these items were from the Rudolph Wunderlich collection.

It is possible that the manuscript "Specimen" was applied to the die impression with a rubber stamp. This would explain the slight differences in the overprint on the various denominations. The 1¢ value in the Christian

Figure 5-4. Manuscript "Specimen" overprint on a large die proof.
(C.W. Christian collection)

collection is shown in **Figure 5-4**. The overprint on this example is 43mm in length.

Large Block-Letter Overprint

A 37mm large specimen overprint is recorded on a die impression, die sunk on a large card, and is most likely a page from a salesman's sample book. An example of this overprint is shown in **Figure 5-5**. The overprint varies in vertical placement on the die proof. Most usually it is found centered, but occasionally it is above or below center. The overprint is normally in black, but examples in red also exist.

At the bottom of the card, printed in a reddish-brown color, is the following inscription:
SPECIMEN
POSTAGE STAMP
FROM THE
NATIONAL BANK NOTE COMPANY
NO. 1 WALL STREET
NEW YORK

The exact number of examples of this item that exist is not known, but probably fewer than five of the red overprints and twice that number of black overprints can be found. **Figure 5-6** illustrates an example of an over-

The United States 1¢ Franklin 1861-67

Figure 5-5. Page from a salesman's sample book showing an India die proof with a large outlined block-letter specimen overprint. Also illustrated in the color section.

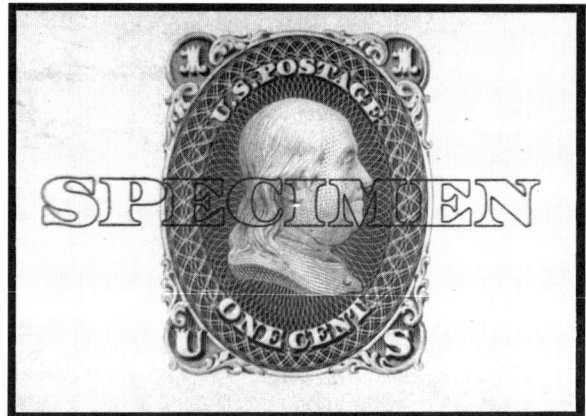

Figure 5-6. Block-letter specimen overprint on a large India die proof.

Figure 5-7. Control-number overprint in carmine. Also illustrated in the color section.

printed die proof that has been removed from its card backing.

Control-Number Overprints

Stamps in the issued colors and overprinted with a carmine number are known for all of the 1861-66 issue denominations. The purpose of the printing is not known, but it is surmised that it was an experiment to provide some means of keeping track of certain issues, thus the appellation "control."

The numbering scheme is of interest. The 90¢ value was overprinted with the sequence 1234, the 30¢ with 2345, the 24¢ with 3456, and so on, with the exception of the 15¢ value, until the 1¢ was reached and the numbers 9012 were used. The overprint on the 15¢ is 235 and does not fit with the normal numbering sequence. It may be that the control overprints were made subsequent to the 1863 Black Jack issue but before the 15¢ Lincoln was issued in 1866, and that a special printing of the 15¢ was made at a later date with an arbitrary number assigned to it.

It is accepted that probably only 100 impressions were made of these overprints. They are scarce as singles and rare in multiples. The author has seen blocks of four, but no larger multiples. A block of four of the 1¢ value (Scott 63S J) is pictured in **Figure 5-7**.

The Reissue of 1875

The Post Office Department continually received many requests from collectors for copies of stamps that were no longer available at the post offices. To fill these needs, the Post Office Department, in 1875, ordered a new printing of all current and previously issued stamps. Their issuance before the 1876 Centennial Exposition in

Philadelphia was coincidental.

The stamps from this printing fall into three categories: reprints, reissues and special printings. The reprints are new printings of those stamps that had previously been demonetized, such as the 1847 and 1851-57 issues. The reissues are new printings of those stamps that had earlier been removed from sale but were still valid for postage, and the special printings are for those issues still being sold in 1875. It has always been a mystery to collectors why the government specially printed copies of the then-current issues that were still available in local post offices.

As far as can be determined, these printings were not for sale at the Centennial Exposition, although a U.S. post office was maintained at the exposition. They were for sale only through the office of the third assistant postmaster general in Washington, D.C. Accounts of their sale were kept completely separate from all other stock, and the number sold of each denomination of every issue and the name of the purchaser were recorded. These records indicate that the first day of sale was February 23, 1875, and the last sale was made on July 16, 1884. Eight days later, the remainders were destroyed by order of the postmaster general. It was originally planned to make 10,000 copies of each denomination of each series (except for some high values of Official and newspaper stamps). Brookman refers to Luff as stating that these numbers were supplemented in some cases, particularly for low denominations, as dealers took advantage of an offer to buy $2 worth of any value [3:203].

The Post Office Department issued a circular, dated March 27, 1875, that described the 1875 printings, and how to obtain them. These special printings were to be ungummed and were to be available in sets of singles for each series. A reproduction of a portion of the sales circular is shown in **Figure 5-8**. This circular was evidently reprinted and distributed more than once. In his book [2], Carrol Chase illustrates a copy signed by Third Assistant Postmaster General E.W. Barber. Barber left office in August of 1875, therefore it is likely that this was the first of the circulars to be distributed. Chase also references another copy of the same circular, which was noted by Luff and signed by A.D. Hazen, a successor to Barber. Hazen held the post of third assistant postmaster general for only seven months, beginning in November 1892. Over the nine years that the special printings were offered to the public, it is probable that the circular was revised and redistributed several times to include additional new issues as they were added to the offering.

In addition to the information shown in Figure 5-8, the circular identified issues that could no longer be used for postage and listed the available Official and newspaper stamps. It also informed the prospective buyer that all specimens furnished would be ungummed (which of course was not the case), that the stamps would be sold by sets and that the minimum purchase was one complete set. It stipulated that stamps of one denomination of any issue would be sold in quantities of $2 worth or

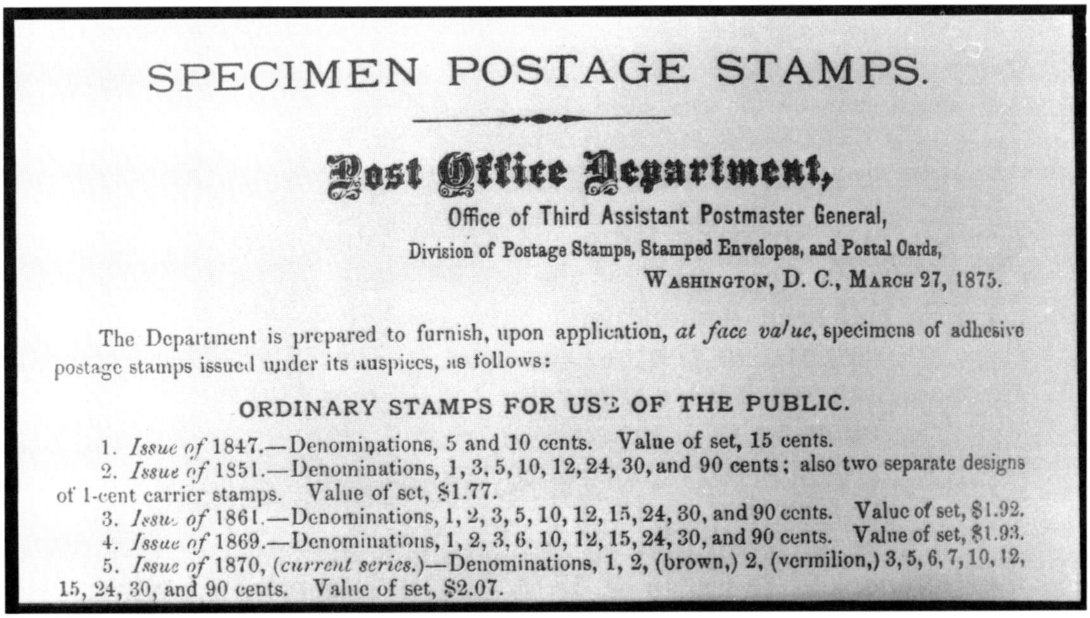

SPECIMEN POSTAGE STAMPS.

Post Office Department,
Office of Third Assistant Postmaster General,
Division of Postage Stamps, Stamped Envelopes, and Postal Cards,
WASHINGTON, D. C., MARCH 27, 1875.

The Department is prepared to furnish, upon application, *at face value*, specimens of adhesive postage stamps issued under its auspices, as follows:

ORDINARY STAMPS FOR USE OF THE PUBLIC.

1. *Issue of* 1847.—Denominations, 5 and 10 cents. Value of set, 15 cents.
2. *Issue of* 1851.—Denominations, 1, 3, 5, 10, 12, 24, 30, and 90 cents; also two separate designs of 1-cent carrier stamps. Value of set, $1.77.
3. *Issue of* 1861.—Denominations, 1, 2, 3, 5, 10, 12, 15, 24, 30, and 90 cents. Value of set, $1.92.
4. *Issue of* 1869.—Denominations, 1, 2, 3, 6, 10, 12, 15, 24, 30, and 90 cents. Value of set, $1.93.
5. *Issue of* 1870, (*current series*.)—Denominations, 1, 2, (brown,) 2, (vermilion,) 3, 5, 6, 7, 10, 12, 15, 24, 30, and 90 cents. Value of set, $2.07.

Figure 5-8. Reproduction of an excerpt from a Post Office Department circular, advertising sale of stamps from the 1875 special printing.
(Courtesy Quarterman Publications)

Figure 5-9. Unique example of the 1¢ 1875 reprint (Scott 102) used on cover. This registered cover was mailed at San Francisco on July 25, 1881, and addressed to Hanover, Germany. The cover is franked with a 1¢ reissue plus three 5¢ blue, a 6¢ pink and a 3¢ green of the Bank Note issues, for a total of 25¢. This paid the 10¢ registration fee plus 15¢ for a triple rate (3x5¢) letter postage to Germany under the UPU convention. (Wolffers Inc. auction photo)

Figure 5-10. Two postally used examples of Scott 102, showing the late-era cancellations.

more, and that no stamps would be sold for less than their face value.

The items purchased were sent in small white envelopes with a listing of the contents printed on the exterior. As it turned out, some were issued with gum and some without, and on various papers, which is quite understandable since the National, Continental and American bank note companies all were involved.

Surprisingly, the offer to provide these stamps met with limited response and much opposition. The public objected to paying face value for stamps that could not be used for postage (as was the case for the demonetized issues). Imagine the response if such an offer were made today.

When possible, the printing orders were given to the company that originally produced the stamp. In the case of the 1861 series, the National Bank Note Company was requested to reprint each of the denominations. Because of the unavailability of all the original 200-subject plates, new plates of 100 subjects each were made for some of the denominations, including the 1¢. The new plates had the advantage of allowing a larger gutter spacing between the stamps because of the smaller number of stamps on each plate. As a result well-centered copies with wide margins are much easier to obtain in the reissue. Although these new plates were supposedly made from the original dies or transfer rollers, the designs of the 2¢ and the 5¢ denominations have variations that distinguish them from the regular-issued stamp.

In the case of the 1¢ value, there does not seem to be any discernable difference in the designs. The author conducted an intensive investigation and comparison of the 1¢ regular issue and the reissue without finding any identifiable difference. Techniques used in reconnaissance-photo evaluation were used as well as standard methods of comparison. If any design difference does exist, it is extremely minute and not normally detectable.

Fortunately, there are some means to identify this reissue. The color is a quite distinctive and striking shade of ultramarine that once observed, can be used as a first-order selection criteria. The printing is sharp and clear from the new plate, and the paper is whiter than the normal issue. Many references mention a white crackly gum, although the author has not found this feature to be particularly distinctive. If the stamp is in multiples, the identification is absolute. The wider gutters are easily noted.

Post Office records indicate that 3,195 of the 1875 reissue of the 1861 1¢ denomination were sold. They were good for postage and can be found postally used. They are quite scarce in this condition and command a premium over the unused stamp. The author is aware of only one copy on cover. This was offered as a unique example in the Wolffers May 9, 1984, auction, and is on a cover addressed to Germany (see **Figure 5-9**). On off-cover stamps, the only way that the authenticity of used copies can be determined is from the use of a canceling device from the correct period or a cancellation by a postmark that shows the date. Examples of two postally used off-

Figure 5-11. Vertical imprint pair (Scott 102).

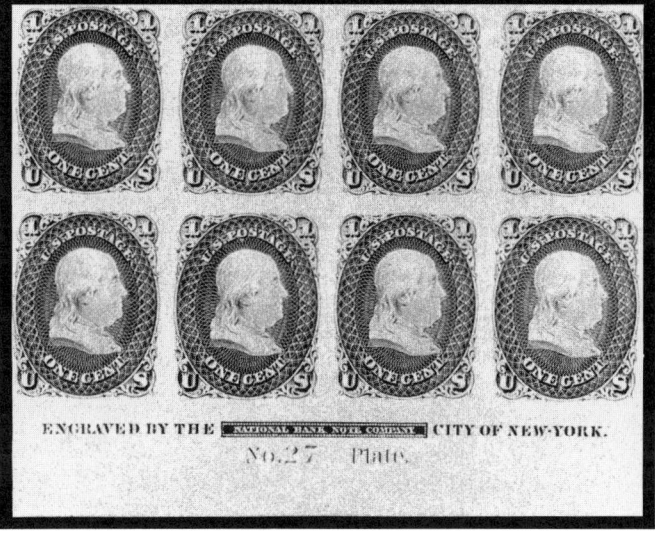

Figure 5-13. Plate proof on India (Scott 63P3), plate number 27.
(C.W. Christian collection)

miere gravure plate 1, the spacing for the general and grilled issues, and the improved spacing for the reissue plate.

Printing	Vertical	Horizontal
Premiere gravure (plate 1)	1.1mm-1.3mm	1.6mm-1.7mm
Regular issue (plates 9, 10, 27)	1.7mm-2.1mm	1.8mm-2.0mm
Reissue (plate 56)	2.6mm	2.6mm

These numbers differ slightly from values previously published by Perry and Luff; however, a significant number of multiples were measured by the author. The table reflects the results of these measurements. Stretching of paper, during and after printing, can result in some variations, but for most purposes the listed ranges of values can be used.

For many years, the Scott U.S. specialized listed the India plate proofs for the 1¢ 1861 issue as 63P3, and stated that all copies were from the reissue plate 56. This, of course, is not true. Plate proofs on India paper with the smaller gutter spacing of the regular issue do exist, and multiples showing this are in the author's collection. Those plate proofs where the gutter spacing can be determined to be that of the reissue plate should be listed as 102P3. In the Christian collection there is a plate 27 block of eight India proofs with the smaller gutter spacing (see **Figure 5-13**). This proves that all India proofs of the 1¢ are not from the reissue plate. It is likely that the reissue plate proofs are more numerous, but since there is currently no way to differentiate single copies, the question of relative abundance will probably remain unanswered.

The previous error in the Scott description has now

Figure 5-12. Rare multiple block of six of the 1875 reprint.
(Daniel Kelleher Co. auction photo)

cover copies are shown in **Figure 5-10**.

Since most copies were supposedly sold as singles, multiples are a true rarity. **Figure 5-11** shows a vertical imprint pair, and a block of six was offered in the June 5, 1980, Harmer sale (**see Figure 5-12**). This ex-Caspary block is the largest multiple that the author has recorded.

The new plate that was made for the 1¢ reissue was designated as plate 56. For comparison of the spacing, the following table shows the gutter spacing for the pre-

been corrected, and the existence of India plate proofs from both the original and the reprint plates is acknowledged in the current Scott catalog.

Plate blocks of the reissue stamp either do not exist or are extremely rare. John C. Chapin, in his exhaustive 1982 survey of classic plate blocks [4] was unable to find any examples or records of a plate block. This is not too surprising. Since the reissues were supposed to be sold in sets of singles for each issue, the selvage and plate numbers would probably normally be removed by the processing clerk before the stamps were assembled into sets. There were exceptions to this, as illustrated in Figure 5-11, but in the case of the 1¢ Franklin, all of the plate numbers seem to have been removed.

An India proof plate number block of eight has appeared on the market, first in the November 1967 Vahan Mozian sale and more recently in the September 1988 Christie's sale. This plate block has been privately perforated to resemble the reissued stamp and may be unique. A reproduction of the halftone photo in the Christie's auction catalog is shown in **Figure 5-14**.

The 1875 1¢ reissue is one of the most beautiful examples of the Franklin design. With its normally large and even margins, bright color and sharp impression, it is a wonderful classic stamp. In spite of the fact that only a relatively small number of these stamps were sold to the public, it is not particularly difficult to obtain, and the price is moderate. Probably 20 to 30 copies are offered at auction every year, and some individual sales may include several copies.

Plate Proofs on Cardboard, 1879-93

During the period between 1879 and 1893, there were five printings on cardboard of previously issued stamp designs to provide an inexpensive source of specimen stamps for distribution to the public and for special presentations. Also, there may have been another special printing in 1894 for the second Atlanta exposition (in addition to the multicolor issues on thin card for the first Atlanta exposition). These will be discussed in later sections.

These six printings are the source of all of the plate proofs on card in normal colors that are now in philatelic hands, excepting, of course, those examples from the multicolored 1881 Atlanta color proofs, which happen to also match the issued color.

It has been reported that the public was not very happy with the 1875 special printings, primarily because

Figure 5-14. Plate number 56, privately perforated India plate proof.
(Christie's New York auction photo)

they had to pay face value for the stamps, many of which were no longer valid for postage. Others had high denominations and were too expensive to buy for collections. This unhappiness provided the Post Office Department with a perceived need to find a cheaper way to provide stamp designs to collectors. In addition, it was desired to have an inexpensive source of stamp samples that could be made available for special presentations when the circumstances warranted.

These considerations resulted in the Post Office Department placing an order in September of 1879 with the American Bank Note Company for the production of 500 sets of each previously issued design to be printed in the issued colors on card. It is believed that by 1879 the American Bank Note Company had become the repository for all of the plates for U.S. stamp issues that were then in existence, including the plates used to print the 1875 special printings. These new printings were not perforated and were delivered in full or part sheets to the Post Office Department, where they were cut into singles and grouped into sets by year or type of issue and placed in small envelopes. The envelopes were printed with the words "PROOF SPECIMENS" and with a description of the contents.

There apparently were 17 different types of envelopes used to package the sets in this printing. These envelopes were then placed in presentation boxes and given to government officials, congressmen and others. Many of these, particularly those in the hands of congressmen, were then given to constituents and the general public. It seems likely that stamp collectors of the day would have besieged their congressmen for these proofs.

Special Printings

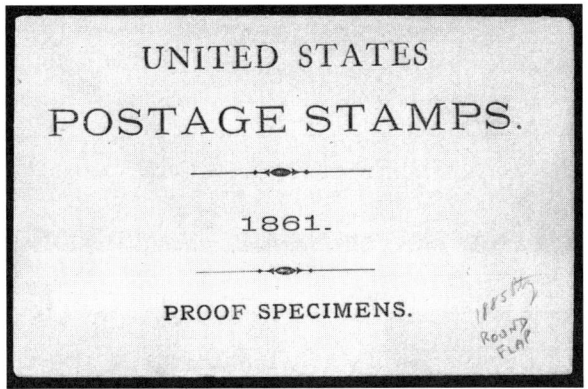

Figure 5-15. Example of an 1875 presentation envelope containing proofs of the 1861 issue.
(Courtesy of Weiss Philatelics)

In approximately October of 1885, a second printing of 500 more sets was ordered and delivered. This issue also included proofs of the new issues subsequent to 1879. According to Howard Friedman, a distinguished philatelic author and researcher who has written extensively on the subject of die and proof printings, the Post Office Department on January 14, 1885, ordered the American Bank Note Company to destroy all but one working plate of each series and denomination held by the company at that time [5:104]. This included the 1861 1¢; therefore, the single remaining plate must have been plate 56. The reader is urged to consult the various articles on proofs published by Friedman. They are very comprehensive and detailed, and he has collected many little-known facts that are of great interest to collectors and students of 19th-century stamps.

Five years later, in June of 1880, a third printing in the same number of sets was made, again adding the new issues. The process was repeated in January of 1893 and again in May of 1893. Most of the new orders seem to have been made to ensure that all new issues were included, and the last one evidently was made to include the 8¢ Columbian. (The Columbians were a popular set for which no-cost samples were in great demand.)

These five printings resulted in 2,500 plate proof copies of the 1861 1¢ Franklin being made available. The colors of the five printings, and the thickness of the cards on which they were printed vary to some degree. There have been many attempts to distinguish between the printings by using these characteristics. Brazer, from envelopes in his reference collection, assigned ranges of thickness and colors to the different issues [6:163]. Friedman did the same from measurements he had made [7:81]. There is a considerable overlap in the range of thicknesses attributed to each of the printings, and the color identifications are sometimes contradictory. Friedman makes the point, and this writer tends to agree with him, that the contents of the envelopes, even in Brazer's time, more than 50 years after their distribution, were not necessarily the same as they were originally.

The wording, design and size of the presentation envelopes differed in the various printings. The envelope size for the two earliest printings was 2¼ by 3⅝ inches, while those of the later printings were larger, 2⅞ by 5¼ inches. **Figure 5-15** shows an example of an envelope used for the 1885 presentations.

For philatelic reasons there is always the desire to assemble a set of items with outstanding characteristics. Wide and even margins and bright colors are in the greatest demand, and it is most probable that premium sets were constructed from sources originating in various printings. For these reasons, it does not seem to be of much philatelic use to try to assemble a complete set of the 1861 1¢ identified as originating in each of the issues. However, the color variations are substantial enough that it is worthwhile to attempt to collect a selection of colors, even if they cannot be assigned to a specific printing. According to Friedman, the colors range from a pale to a bright blue with the first printing as the most brilliant, the third the palest, the second the most intense and the fourth and fifth colors somewhere between the first and second printings. This is somewhat of a subjective approach and is, of course, dependent on the true printing origin of the examples.

As mentioned earlier, there was a likely, and generally not well-known, sixth printing of cardboard proofs that will be discussed in the next section.

The Atlanta Color Proofs

The Atlanta proofs are the most colorful of any of the special printings. The scope and beauty of this issue provides collectors a unique opportunity to see many of the early designs in colors differing from the original issue. It was a very limited printing, and consequently, examples are not particularly easy to obtain. In 1881 an International Cotton Exposition was held in Atlanta, Georgia. The Post Office Department planned to participate extensively in this event, and as a part of its exhibit ordered a special printing of all U.S. stamps from 1847 to 1880 for display. The order was placed with the American Bank Note Company, which at that time held the stamp printing contract, and also supposedly had possession of the remaining plates that had been used for the 1875 special printings.

Most of the designs, including the 1¢ 1861 (Scott 102TC) were reprinted in five colors (black, scarlet, green,

Figure 5-16. Rare set of blocks of the 1881 Atlanta card proofs in the five issued colors. Also illustrated in the color section.

brown and blue) on very thin white card of a thickness, as reported by Friedman, of 0.125mm-0.165mm. A complete set of the 1¢ 1861 Atlanta proofs in blocks of four is shown in **Figure 5-16**.

The colors are vivid, and the impressions are sharp and clear. The 1¢ was printed from the reissue plate, number 56, and it has been suggested that the sheet was then trimmed to remove the borders (and the plate number and inscription) for symmetry considerations [7:45-48]. It is also possible that the American Bank Note Company did not want to have a copy of its printing being displayed with the National Bank Note Company logo. In any case, plate numbers or inscriptions do not seem to exist on the Atlanta issues.

The story concerning the entry of the Atlanta printing into the philatelic market is interesting, but possibly not the whole truth. Friedman wrote, "Following the close of the exposition, a janitor was ordered to destroy the entire lot of sheets by burning them. At just that time a well-known stamp dealer of the period, Dr. J.A. Petrie of Phillipsburg, New Jersey, 'happened' by, and succeeded in acquiring the complete set of unburned sheets, of which only the five colors of the 1-Cent Post Office design had been destroyed. Thus was saved for the stamp-collecting world one of the great legacies of philately and one of the outstanding groups of special printings among U.S. proofs."

The coincidence of Petrie being on the spot at the right time, and the apparent disregard of the Post Office Department for not overseeing the destruction, makes this story a bit hard to believe. Petrie had a somewhat shady reputation, and it would be more likely to hypothesize that an arrangement with someone in the Post Office Department led to his procurement of these thousands of beautiful proofs. The Atlanta color proofs evidently stayed in Petrie's possession for some years before being dispersed. It is believed that the 1¢ Franklin sheets, in common with most issues, were cut into one block of eight, two blocks of four and the remainder into singles. The present existence of the blocks of eight of Scott 102TC is somewhat doubtful. The author has never seen one, and at one time in his collection had two blocks of four in black, while concurrently there was a block of four in black in the Christian collection. This seems to indicate that at least one of the blocks of eight was split, and a similar fate may have befallen the other colors. With only 100 copies available in each color, these Atlanta printings of the 1¢ Franklin exist in quantities comparable to the 24¢ Jenny airmail invert and, while not as famous or expensive, are a wonderful addition to a collection. Considering their beauty and scarcity, they are extremely undervalued at present.

The 1895 Atlanta Proofs

Friedman, in his article "The Atlanta Expositions and United States Philately" [5], writes at length concerning a little-known fact of philatelic proofdom. In 1895 another Cotton State and International Exposition was held in Atlanta. It was larger than the 1881 exposition and featured a special postal exhibition with displays by the United States and foreign countries. For the U.S. exhibit, the Post Office Department ordered a series of sheets or partial sheets of most previously issued stamp designs. These proof impressions were in normal or near-normal colors on white cardboard.

Exactly what happened to the displayed sheets after the close of the exposition is not known. Brazer and others assign their fate again to the infamous Dr. Petrie, who by this time had acquired an unenviable reputation for philatelic chicanery. The sheets are reported to have remained intact in Petrie's possession and were offered by him for sale in a 1903 circular from which is quoted the following information [8:26]:

"AN ABSOLUTELY UNIQUE COLLECTION
of all stamps ever issued by the United States Government in Cardboard — unique in the condition it is in being in entire sheets and includes all . . . from 1847 to 1893. The collection is complete with two exceptions, the One Cent 1890 and 15 Cent Department of the Interior. There are 208 varieties in sheets of 100 stamps each. More than 21,000 stamps in this collection.
THE PRICE IS $3,500."

The circular continues with a detailed description of the contents of the offering, including the 1861 issue, and a statement that if it was not sold as a unit, and enough interest was shown for individual parts, it would be broken up and sold in sets at prices listed. Dr. Petrie had been an assistant surgeon in the Navy during the Civil War [9], and a grainy, but interesting, photograph of him in uniform is shown in **Figure 5-17**.

Evidently there were no domestic takers for the offer, and Petrie set sail for England, where he sold his cardboard proofs plus some additional proof sheets to the Earl of Crawford [10:208].

In January 1913, in the first of a series of articles on the Crawford collection, in the *London Philatelist*, Edward Denny Bacon described these sheets in some detail and identifies them as being from an 1895 impression. Bacon was an English philatelic scholar of great merit, who for some years had been the curator of Lord Crawford's collection, and who later became curator of the Royal Philatelic Collection under King George V. He was well-known for his accuracy and attention to detail, so the 1895 date should be given substantial weight.

The sheets were part of a vast collection of proofs and essays owned by the Earl of Crawford. There is little doubt that this single collection housed the majority of the U.S. proofs and essays that were in private hands at that time, and that it was the most outstanding collection of these items that has ever been assembled.

In January of 1914, the earl died, and many of his philatelic holdings were subsequently dispersed. Along with many other proofs, the 1895 Atlanta sheets passed into the hands of John A. Klemann, the New York dealer, and eventually into the Ackerman and Lilly collections [5:105].

An unbroken sheet of 100 of the 1¢ 1861 cardboard proofs from the Lilly collection was sold in a 1967 Siegel auction. The sheet was from plate 56 and probably is the only source for 1¢ cardboard proofs in multiples.

The existence of this special printing is essentially a new piece of philatelic knowledge. Brazer contended in 1944 that the cardboard proofs in the Crawford collection were from the 1893 printings [8:136], and this opinion was shared by Friedman in his earlier writings.

However, in a contemporary article concerning the death of Klemann, the collection of cardboard proofs was referred to as the 1894 printing, but philatelic students assumed this later date to be a typographical error. In light of the presently known evidence, it seems likely the date was correct and that all of these sheets of cardboard proofs are from a printing for the 1895 Atlanta exposition.

Figure 5-17. Dr. James A. Petrie, in his U. S. Naval uniform as a Civil War assistant surgeon.
(*The Stamp Magazine*. 3:7. Norton House, London, 1937)

In 1941, Brazer had an opportunity to personally examine the Crawford proofs that were being sold from the Ackerman collection. He reported [11:136] that he was able to identify them as being from the "1894 final printing." This was a change from his earlier opinion that they were part of the 1893 issue.

The available evidence appears to substantiate the hypothesis that in 1894 the Post Office Department requested a set of cardboard proofs of all issues through 1894 from the American Bank Note Company. Until some written records concerning this order can be found, the details of this request will remain a philatelic mystery. It must have been one of the last printings from the 1875 reissue plates. All other plates had been previously destroyed by order of the Post Office. In 1894 the Bureau of Engraving and Printing assumed the responsibility for all future stamp printings and acquired the existing plates from the American Bank Note Company.

Shortly after acquiring the plates, BEP was ordered to destroy all of the plates that had been prepared by private bank note companies. This precluded any more plate impressions by plate 56, and to the best of the author's knowledge this was the last of the cardboard proof issues of the 1861 1¢ Franklin.

The Crawford plate proof sheets are probably the source of most, if not all, of the multiples of the cardboard proofs now in existence. For the 1¢ Franklin, multiples are very scarce. Until recently, the author had never seen an example of one, other than the auction illustration of the sheet of 100 that was sold in the 1967 Siegel sale.

In September of 1996, a large holding of partial sheets from the 1894 printing of cardboard proofs of the 1861 issues was offered for sale in an auction by Weiss Philatelics. The 1¢ Franklin was represented by a block of 30 impressions, showing the upper three rows of the sheet complete with top inscription. The 1¢ proofs show the characteristic wide spacing of plate number 56. This unique large multiple is illustrated in **Figure 5-18**.

The sale included examples of each of the denominations of the 1861-67 issue with the exception of the 2¢ value. The 1¢ (Scott 63P4), 3¢ (74P4, unlisted as a card proof), 5¢ (76P4), 10¢ (68P4), 12¢ (69P4) and 24¢ (78P4) values were each represented by top margin blocks of 30 proofs, including the margin inscription. The 30¢ (71P4) and 90¢ (72P4) were also top-margin blocks of 30 proofs, but without the top inscription, and the 15¢ (77P4) value was a magnificent lower half-sheet of 50 impressions, showing the bottom inscription and plate number.

Some additional information has recently been obtained that indicates that after the Lilly sheets were purchased in 1967 by the Raymond H. Weill Company of New Orleans, many, if not all, were sold to an Ohio proof dealer, Richard Taylor. A significant number of the cardboard proof sheets, including the 1861 issues, were subsequently cut into partial sheets. Those appearing in the Weiss sale were purchased from Taylor by an East Coast dealer and later consigned to the Weiss auction.

The provenance of these particular cardboard plate proof sheets is reported in such detail because of their uniqueness and colorful past. Unfortunately, now that they have been broken up, their journey through the philatelic world will be fragmented, and these proof gems, and their singularity will only be apparent in the surviving multiple copies. These can still be identified by being printed on cardboard or by the wider spacing between the impressions for some of the values compared to the original 1861 plate proof printings.

Obviously, the author's expressed hope that the 1967 Siegel sale sheets were still intact has been proven wrong (at least, as far as the 1861 issue is concerned); however, somewhere there are still large portions of these rare cardboard proof sheets that have yet to come on the market.

The proofs from the 1894 printing have not been listed by Scott as a separate issue. For one thing, there is probably no sure way to distinguish these printings from the well-known series of five printings of cardboard proofs between 1879 and 1893 (discussed in the previous section), and in addition, the source and exact date of this printing has not been definitely established.

The history of the 211 Crawford sheets of normal-color cardboard plate proofs, from their original printing to their present locations, is one of the more interesting tales of philately. Many prominent philatelic students, including Brazer, Friedman, Cabeen and others, have uncovered enough facts that now a summary of the likely sequence of events can be put together.

It can be assumed that the proofs originated in the press rooms of the American Bank Note Company, possibly in 1894. They were delivered to the Post Office Department, where they were prepared as an exhibit to be shown at the 1895 International and Cotton State Exhibition in Atlanta. Subsequent to the exhibition, the displayed sheets somehow found their way into the hands of Petrie. A few years later, probably about 1903, they were in the possession of the Earl of Crawford.

In this summary, it seems appropriate to say a few words about the various owners of these cardboard proofs through the years. They included some of the most outstanding collectors of this century, and their philatelic achievements are well worth recounting. For a much more complete telling of the philatelic lives of these individuals, it is recommended that the reader consult Stanley M. Bierman's books on the world's greatest stamp collectors, dealers, and scholars [10]. Bierman presents a wealth of information on both the people and the great philatelic items that passed through their hands in an interesting and readable manner.

James Ludovic Lindsay, the 26th Earl of Crawford and 9th Earl of Balcarres, the Premier Earl of Scotland, was an extremely gifted man. He was an outstanding scientist, an author, astronomer, medical researcher, a bibliophile who assembled one of the most outstanding private libraries in the world, and a sportsman. He was a "man of all seasons" and a true "renaissance man" in addition to being one of the greatest collectors of all time. A photo of the earl in the full regalia of a Scottish lord is shown in **Figure 5-19**.

The Earl of Crawford entered the philatelic scene in 1899, when he purchased the most impressive library of

Figure 5-18. Unique top-margin block of 30 plate proofs on cardboard, in blue. Part of the 1861 design 1¢ Franklin sheet of 100 impressions that was exhibited at the 1895 International and Cotton State Exhibition at Atlanta. (Weiss Philatelics photo)

philatelic references then in existence from the estate of John K. Tiffany. Tiffany was the founder of the American Philatelic Association (Society) and an outstanding collector, philatelic student and writer in his own right.

Five years later, at about the same time he purchased the Petrie sheets, the Earl of Crawford was able to acquire the magnificent collection of U.S. essays and proofs that had been formed by Henry G. Mandel. He then proceeded to apply his extraordinary talents and scientific approach to the task of properly describing and mounting all of this marvelous material. His approach was to arrange each issue with examples of the original designs, die proofs in various stages, plate proofs on India and card, the issued stamp in all its varieties, and finally reprints or reissues.

The items mounted in his albums were accompanied by very complete and detailed descriptions concerning their history and manufacture. Much of the earl's work was done while aboard his yacht, *Valhalla*, while en route to many of his scientific expedition destinations. In 1905 he sailed to New York, where he displayed his collection at the Collectors Club of New York. Many prominent collectors of the era had the opportunity to view the collection at that time and to see additional items onboard the *Valhalla*. John Luff reported on the collection and the display with many accolades, including a statement to the effect that it was the most professional display he had ever seen — a major compliment from the premier U.S. philatelic scholar of the day.

In January of 1914, when the Earl of Crawford died, the distribution of many of his philatelic holdings began. His magnificent library was bequeathed to the British Library, and parts of his collections were sold to various individuals. John Klemann, the proprietor of the Nassau Stamp Company and, at that time, the pre-eminent dealer in U.S. essays and proofs, set sail for England in the summer of 1914 to make an offer on the fabulous Crawford collection of U.S. stamps and proofs. A mutually acceptable price could not be agreed upon, and Klemann returned to the United States. Six weeks later word was received from the Crawford estate that Klemann's offer would be accepted. World War I was now in progress, and after some delay, Klemann was able to again sail to England in November of 1915, this time with the added problem of German U-boats. The transaction was final-

Figure 5-19. James Ludovic Lindsay, 26th Earl of Crawford and one of the philatelic giants of all time.
(From the *Philatelic Journal of America*. 23:283. C.H. Mekeel, 1913)

ized at the modest price of $60,000, and the philatelic gems were returned to the United States.

The collection, of course, also contained the cardboard proof sheets. These were kept intact in the Nassau Stamp Company vaults until 1918, when they were sold to Senator Ernest R. Ackerman, a wealthy New Jersey congressman. Senator Ackerman was another philatelic giant of the day. He assembled an outstanding collection that he bequeathed in part to the Library of Congress upon his death in 1931. The will stated: "I give and bequeath to the Library of Congress of the United States of America all Proofs of United States Stamps which shall be owned by me at the time of my death" [11:135].

The Ackerman heirs, realizing the tremendous value of this bequest, began actions to nullify the gift. For some reason, the U.S. Government did not seem to press its claim, and the situation remained in limbo for 19 years until the cardboard proofs were offered by the heirs, along with many other items, in a 1950 Harmer, Rooke and Company sale. In the interim, the Library of Congress in 1937 did receive three volumes of die and plate proofs (a small fraction of the total proof collection). This may have been the result of some compromise in the litigation, and in 1958 these three volumes were transferred to the Smithsonian Institution, where they still reside.

As a result of the Harmer, Rooke sale, the cardboard proofs were now in the possession of Josiah K. Lilly Jr., a pharmaceutical multimillionaire, who was following the footsteps of his philatelic predecessors in assembling a world-class collection based on earlier holdings and estates. Lilly died in 1966, and in the following year his monumental collection of stamps, essays and proofs was auctioned in a series of sales by the Robert A. Siegel organization. The fifth sale of this series in September 1967 listed 161 complete sheets of the cardboard proofs, including the 1861 1¢ value. This unique assemblage of plate proofs sold as a unit for the ridiculously low price of $34,000, and reflected the lack of interest in proofs at that time. The purchaser was the Raymond H. Weill Company of New Orleans, who was reported to have divided the sheets in 1972 and sold one-half to Richard Taylor, an Ohio dealer in proofs. The Weill brothers retained the other half. The proofs sold to Taylor are thought to have been further broken up and sold piecemeal in the philatelic market [10:198-250]. As discussed earlier, this is essentially correct.

So, ends the convoluted journey of a fabulous philatelic rarity.

The Envelope Essay

Another extremely rare printing that was a part of the Mandel and Crawford collections is a series of envelopes printed by the National Bank Note Company, probably during the latter part of the 19th century. These envelopes are generally referred to as "envelope essays," although they do not strictly fall within the definition of an essay since the printed design is identical to that of the issued stamp. In this author's opinion, including them in a category of "sample printings" would be preferable. They are printed in intaglio on envelopes measuring 148mm by 84mm.

Five of the envelopes were printed with the 1¢ 1861 Franklin design as the postage indicia, and four of them were printed with the 3¢ 1861 Washington design. One of the 3¢ values, in orange brown, on a white entire has the name and address of the National Bank Note Company printed at the upper left, and is gummed and sealed. All of the other examples are on plain envelopes and are without gum.

Figure 5-20 shows an example of the 1¢ envelope, with the Franklin design printed in blue on a cream-colored, laid-paper entire. There are two copies of this particular variety recorded, and it is the only variety where more than one example is known. The 1¢ is also found printed in brown on a cream entire, in brown on white and in deep carmine on white. The 3¢, in addition to the example already mentioned, is recorded as being printed in lake and deep brown red on white entires, and in dark green on cream.

The date and purpose of these printings is not known. It might be surmised that they were printed to demonstrate the kind of product that the National Bank Note Company could provide in the way of stamped envelopes, or possibly they were items specially printed by Mandel for his personal collection during the period when he was an official of the company. Many proofs and essays originated in this manner.

1900 Paris International Exhibition

The circumstances surrounding the postal exhibit at the International Exposition in Paris that opened on May 23, 1900, and details concerning the exhibited stamps and their subsequent fate remained a mystery until a few years ago when part of the remains from this exhibit were identified. The discovery is of particular interest to this study since a unique variety of the 1861 1¢ Franklin seems to have been included, and also because the plates from the 1875 special printings were used to produce the stamps for the early issues in the exhibit. The stamps may have come from proof remainders of the 1875 printings and/or from printings by the Bureau of Engraving and Printing, which by then had possession of the plates.

Very little has been recorded concerning the Paris exhibit, and the information included here has been primarily obtained from a 1982 *Chronicle* article [12:88-92], and from a discussion with Robert B. Meyersburg, the author of the article.

The U.S. Post Office Department was invited by the French postal administration to establish a postal station at the exhibition. The invitation was accepted, and in addition, the Post Office provided an exhibit of U.S. stamps for display. In his article, Meyersburg quotes a contemporary Washington newspaper article that described the exhibit as follows:

> "Assistant Postmaster General Madden has prepared and compiled under the direction and supervision of the Chief of the Stamping Division of the Post Office Department a full collection of postal stamps, beginning with the issue of 5-cent Franklin stamp and the 10-cent Washington stamp of the issue of 1847, and ending with the latest issue of the orange colored Cuban special Delivery stamp of 1900. The collection includes specimens of all of the stamps that were ever issued by the United States Post Office Department. They are artistically arranged on nine large pasteboard cartons and will be sent to the Paris Exposition to be added to the exhibit of the Post Office Department. The entire collection consists of about 600 specimens and the New York stamp expert who mounted the stamps says that the collection is worth at least $3,000."

After the exposition closed, the stamp exhibit disappeared, not to reappear until a half century later. In 1949 two boxes containing a number of pieces of cardboard upon which were glued samples of U.S. stamps turned up in Paris at one of the buildings in the Embassy complex. The boxes were turned over to the Post Office Department, which evidently had little interest and placed them in storage. Thirty-three years later, in 1982, the boxes of stamps were forwarded to the Smithsonian Institution for its possible use.

At that time, Frank Bruns was philatelic curator of the Smithsonian, and he requested that Meyersburg, who was an occasional volunteer philatelic consultant and assistant for the Smithsonian, try to salvage something from the remnants of 80 years of neglect. The boxes were full of scraps of grimy and insect-damaged pieces of cardboard covered with stamps. While the boxes did not con-

Figure 5-20. Rare example of the so-called "essay envelopes," printed by the National Bank Note Company, date of printing unknown. This stamp design is printed in blue on a cream-colored, laid-paper entire.

tain all of the stamps that were purported to have been in the Paris exhibit, there were plate proofs of the 1847 reproductions, 1857-60 and 1861-66 reprints, and the $5 Columbians, which were all glued in layers on the cardboard in decorative patterns of indeterminable design. The items were imperforate, as would be expected from proofs. The large multiples and strips were printed on India paper, while the single items, which evidently were used to separate the long strips in the overall design, were printed on a wove paper.

After several months of work, Meyersburg was able to separate the stamps from the cardboard, but most of them had been damaged by insects, mold or previous rough handling. Great care had to be taken with the project because many of the items were printed on India paper and consequently were very fragile. A limited number of respectable copies, however, were recovered, and among these were several copies of the 1861 1¢ Franklin. Some large blocks of the 1857-60 reprint proofs and strips of the same series were rescued, along with a number of 1861-66 and $5 Columbian reprint proofs. As a token of appreciation for his long and intensive efforts to recover these stamps, Meyersburg was given some of the duplicate items, and from this source, a small number have come onto the philatelic market.

The 1¢ 1861 from the Paris exhibit is a true blue in color and is printed on a very smooth, thin and hard paper. It has the normal margins for a single copy of the 1875 reprint plate proof but is distinguished by the fact that it is on wove paper instead of the usual India paper and is in a color different from the 1875 reprint. According to Meyersburg, there is only one copy of this exhibition proof in private hands.

During the first part of the 20th century, a number of exhibits of U.S. stamps and proofs were prepared for display at various expositions and special events around the world. In general, these exhibits were returned to the Post Office Department at the end of the event, where the stamps and proofs were demounted and filed to be used as a source of material for future exhibits. The items consequently soon lost their identity with any particular showing. It is fortunate that some of the material from the 1900 Paris exhibit, even though neglected and with major damage, has survived, along with its historical ties to a specific postal exhibit.

The Roosevelt Small Die Proofs of 1903

In December of 1902 through February 1903, the Post Office Department placed orders with the Bureau of Engraving and Printing for the preparation of 85 leatherbound albums containing small die proofs of most of the stamps produced by the United States from 1847 through 1902. The proofs were printed on a white wove paper and in the approximate colors of the issued stamp. Aniline inks were used, and each die proof was trimmed to produce margins of 3.5mm to 4.0mm. The proofs were then mounted in sets on thin gray card pages of approximately 7 inches by 11 inches. Each page was backed by a thick cardboard, and the page bordered with a half-inch strip of the backed gray cardboard. The pages were bound into a leather cover, and each page was burnished with gold on its three open sides. On the spine of the album, stamped in gold foil, was a four-line title: "UNITED STATES/POSTAGE STAMPS/1847-1902/PROOFS."

Each proof was mounted on the gray cardboard with a strong waterproof glue, and with pressure. They are almost impossible to remove from their backing, and many examples have been damaged in the attempt. The proofs of a particular issue were arranged in patterns on

Figure 5-21. A full page from the Roosevelt small die album showing proofs from the 1861 issue.
(Courtesy of Weiss Philatelics)

the pages of the album, but these patterns were not necessarily the same in all of the albums.

The entire ensemble made an impressive presentation piece, and on some of the album covers the name of the recipient was stamped in gold. As far as can be determined, the 1904 printings have received the name "Roosevelt" die proofs solely because they were printed during the term of Theodore Roosevelt. There is no indication that President Roosevelt requested or was specifically interested in their production, however, he is listed as one of the individuals who received an album. A photo of a complete page from the album is shown in **Figure 5-21**.

The 1861 blue Franklin is represented on two separate pages. One page supposedly showed the premiere-gravure designs of the 1861 issue, but the design of the 1¢ is not the same as the premiere. The 1¢ premiere gravure was simulated by printing it in a very dark blue, almost an indigo, but it was actually printed from the die used for the 1875 reissues. Three of the other values of the 1861 issue, the 3¢, 5¢ and 12¢, had part of their designs cut away to approximate the premiere-gravure designs. The second page showed the 1861 issue design in its approximately normal colors, with the 1¢ Franklin in a grayish-blue color.

An excellent research paper, written by Ronald A. Burns [13], has recently added new information on the printings of the Roosevelt and Panama-Pacific small die printings. He carefully reviewed the Bureau of Engraving and Printing records of these printings and published his findings in the referenced monograph.

He noted that the records showed at least 100, and sometimes more, proofs were pulled for each of the designs that were needed for the albums. Eighty-five of these were used in the Roosevelt albums, and some of the remainders may have been placed in additional albums for different purposes over the following years.

The proof-room records show that a total of 234 impressions for die 104 (the 1861 1¢ denomination) were pulled over a two-week period from January 20, 1903, to February 13, 1903. A number of these impressions were probably to check the dies and to obtain the correct color, and it could be assumed that about 200 of them were for the albums, 100 impressions of each of the two shades needed.

Figure 5-22 illustrates examples of these two varieties of the 1¢ proofs.

Most copies of the Roosevelt small die proofs have been cut from the original pages and have cardboard margins of approximately 2mm surrounding the trimmed proof. Considering the small number of these proofs that were printed, they are reasonably easy to acquire and are presently undervalued on the philatelic market. Complete albums are very scarce and command a high price.

Brazer wrote in the *Essay-Proof Journal*, Number 41, that he had copies of documents from the files of Arthur M. Travers, who was the chief clerk to Third Assistant Postmaster General Edwin C. Madden at the time the Roosevelt albums were produced. Among the documents was a paper that stated that on March 12, 1909, an

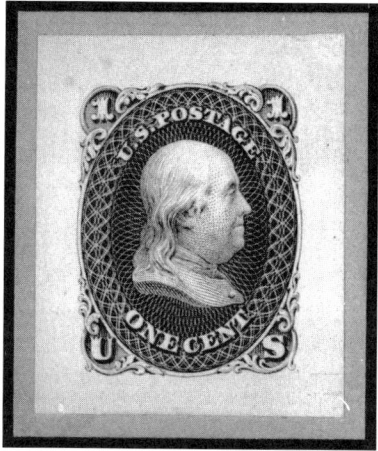 

Figure 5-22. Examples of the 1¢ 1861 issue. The dark blue printing on the left was to simulate the indigo premiere gravure, and the gray-blue printing on the right was for the issued stamp. Also illustrated in the color section.

album of small die proofs was "loaned and presented" by Postmaster General Meyer to the Massachusetts Historical Society, and other similar albums to Arthur M. Travers; Brooklyn Institute of Science and Art; the king of Italy; and the queen of Spain. The key word here is "loaned." Official policy established in 1904 prohibited the distribution of proofs, and a loan, even though it was understood that they would never be returned, was a way to circumvent the prohibition.

A listing of 74 recipients of the albums, with two copies to the previously mentioned Brooklyn Institute of Science and Art, includes the names of many important people of the period such as Elihu Root, secretary of war; Chauncey Depew, senator and president of the New York Central Railroad; Joseph G. Cannon, speaker of the House of Representatives; and Henry Cabot Lodge, one of the most influential senators at that time [14:36].

The 1¢ 1861 Roosevelt small die proof is listed by Scott as 63P2. It is listed in blue only, and possibly because of an oversight, the dark blue/indigo printing is not listed.

Panama-Pacific Die Proofs

The Panama-Pacific small die proofs of 1915 are the scarcest of all of the special printings of the 1861 Franklin design. James H. Bruns, director of the National Postal Museum and former curator of the National Philatelic Collection of the Smithsonian Institution, classifies them as among the most treasured rarities in the collection. They have been referred to as the "Gems of Proofdom," and there is little doubt that an example of this rare print-

ing is a jewel in any collection.

There is some doubt about the exact number of copies that are now in philatelic hands, and a search for information concerning the origin and distribution of these copies has interested some of the leading philatelic scholars for the past half-century.

Most of the information in this section has been garnered from a very complete and well-researched study by James H. Bruns, which was published in seven parts in the *Bureau Specialist* during 1988 and 1989 under the title "The Scarcity of Panama Pacific Proofs" [15]. Additional data is included from Francis J. McCall's article in the 1956 *Congress Book* [16], and from the previously cited series by Howard J. Friedman on U.S. die and plate proofs [17].

These special impressions were printed from die 104 in November of 1914 by the Bureau of Engraving and Printing at the request of the Post Office Department, and were to be used for a display at the 1915 San Francisco Panama-Pacific Exposition. The order, dated September 8, 1914, requested a die proof of each U.S. stamp issued from 1847 to date to be printed in the original colors on India paper, for a total of 413 proofs. The order was later revised to request two sets. One set was to be mounted and the other unmounted. The unmounted set was subsequently given to the National Postal Museum (Smithsonian) for its collection, and the total cost for preparing all of these proofs is recorded to have been $600.

BEP records, as reviewed and published by Ronald A. Burns [13:6], show the following for printing and disposition of the 1¢ 1861 design:

Printing date	Number printed	Disposition	Destroyed	Date
11-16-14	2	ink test	2	1-21-16
"	2	"	2	"
"	7	book	1	"
11-17-14	4	ink test	4	"
"	6	book	—	—

From a consideration of these numbers and dates, it seems reasonable to conclude that proofs in one of the two shades were printed on November 16, 1914, and that the other shade of blue was printed on the following day. Six copies of each shade remained after the test impressions were destroyed, and that is the maximum number of Panama-Pacific proofs that can exist.

The die proofs were actually printed on a soft wove paper with a coarse weave rather than on India paper, and each copy was trimmed to margins of 2.5mm to 3.0mm. Examples show the paper to have a distinct yellow tinge. Burns suspects that this may be the result of storage in sulfur-rich envelopes, and that the original printing may have been on white paper. The printing was done with synthetic aniline inks and in colors designed to reproduce those of the original 1861 issues. Photographs of examples of the two 1861 1¢ Panama-Pacific proofs are shown in **Figure 5-23**. Both proofs are printed in the issued design. The indigo or dark blue printing was used to simulate the premiere gravure (which in 1915 was still considered to be an issued stamp), and the actual issued stamp was represented by a lighter blue impression from the same die.

James Bruns carefully examined the Panama-Pacific proofs in the Smithsonian collection and reported that they generally share the characteristic of having small pin-prick indentations at the corners or along the sides of the design. These resulted from the use of a divider to establish the margins. Two more indentations are observed on each side to provide the guides for a straight-edge alignment for trimming with a razor. The distance between the points of the divider was a uniform $^3/_{32}$ of an inch.

The existence of the complete set in the Smithsonian collection is the result of a fortuitous chain of events. In 1912, the postmaster general ordered that the National Collection of United States Stamps, which was in the custody of the Post Office Department, be turned over to the National Postal Museum at the Smithsonian Institution. On December 12, 1914, Joseph B. Leavy, curator of the collection, visited the Post Office Department to ascertain if there were any copies available of stamps that were missing from the Smithsonian holdings. He had no success in his quest, but he did find out that there was a special printing of die proofs of all the issues to date under way at the Bureau of Engraving and Printing, and that the Post Office Department wanted his assistance in determining the correct chronology and colors for those yet to be printed. Upon returning to the museum, Leavy suggested to the secretary of the Smithsonian that he request from the third assistant postmaster general a set of these die proofs for the museum collection. The secretary, C.D. Walcott, made the request two days later, and the Post Office Department revised its original order to the BEP of one set to include an additional unmounted set for the Smithsonian.

Referring again to the data collected by Burns on the printing dates for the proofs, it is recorded that the 1861 designs had already been printed by the time Leavy visited the BEP, and his help would not have been available for color verification for that issue. The printing of proofs for the later issues continued until the early part of 1915, when the sets were delivered to the Post Office Department [13].

In summary, on November 16-17, 1914, ink-color-test impressions were pulled from the die for the 1861 design to determine the correct ink composition. These test impressions were recorded as being later destroyed. After the proper inks were mixed, 12 proofs were pulled, six each in two shades of blue. Presumably two sets of the best impressions were selected to fill the order, and the remainder of the proofs were trimmed and mounted in bound volumes for the Bureau files. It seems likely that some or all of these few file-copy proofs may be the source of the Panama-Pacific proofs now in the hands of philatelists.

The set of mounted proofs was delivered to the Post Office Department on February 2, 1915, and subsequently displayed at the Panama-Pacific Exhibition. The unmounted set was delivered the following month on March 20, 1915. The Smithsonian accession records show the receipt of its set on April 22, 1915. From that day, a complete set of the Panama-Pacific small die proofs has remained in the custody of the Smithsonian Institution.

The Post Office Department set was exhibited at the Panama-Pacific Exhibition and then returned to the Post Office's files. It is believed that it was used as the source for later exhibitions of U.S. issues. During the course of these exhibitions, worn and damaged copies were replaced, additional issues included, issues deleted, and the set assembled and reassembled to the point where it is difficult to know if any of the original copies from the exhibition display still exist. In any case the Post Office

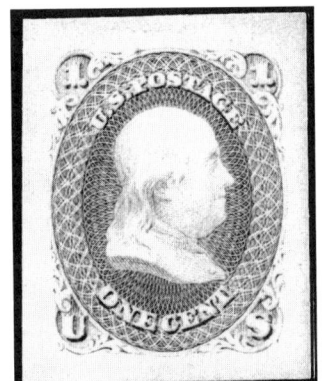 

Figure 5-23. Very rare Panama Pacific small die proofs. 1915 reprints of the 1¢ 1861 in pale blue (left) and dark blue (right). Very rare. Also illustrated in the color section.
(C.W. Christian collection)

Department holding has lost its identity as a set of the Panama-Pacific die proofs.

The 1915 die proofs have also been known as the "Southgate proofs," and there is good reason for this. Hugh M. Southgate was a prominent collector of the era and one of the founders of the Bureau Issues Association. He was general manager of the Washington office of the Westinghouse Corporation, which held a contract for the maintenance of the electric motors on the BEP printing presses. In this position, he was a frequent visitor to the Bureau and made many contacts there. In many instances he acted as a philatelic adviser to the Bureau, and it has been reported that he was instrumental in arranging many of the special groupings of stamps and proofs that were presented to President Franklin D. Roosevelt in the 1930s. He was also said to have traded items in his extensive personal collection to the Post Office Department in return for surplus proofs, in addition to receiving many items for his unpaid services [15].

It is a matter of record that two sets (possibly not complete) of the Panama-Pacific proofs were in his possession at the time of his death in 1940. These passed into the hands of Brazer, who wrote several articles concerning them and advertised them for sale. Brazer was an adviser for the proof section of the Scott U.S. specialized catalog at that time, and the information contained in the catalog derives from his personal knowledge of these examples of the 1915 proofs. Brazer later revised his notes and stated that there were three sets in the Southgate holdings.

One set was purchased by Chester A. Smeltzer and in turn acquired by Julian F. Gros. Gros presented this set to the Collectors Club of New York as a gift in 1965. The Collectors Club later sold the set, and it was acquired by Rudolf Wunderlich and then by Jack Rosenthal, in whose possession it still resided in 1988. Selected items from the Rosenthal collection were loaned to Bruns at the Smithsonian so that scientific tests could be conducted on the differences between them and the Smithsonian copies. None was found.

At the end of his seven-part report [15, Part VII, April 1989], Bruns made a series of concluding assumptions. With his kind permission, applicable sections of these assumptions are reproduced here:

"CONCLUDING ASSUMPTIONS

Based upon the information presented in this serialization, and from other associated research presented in the *U.S. Specialist*, a number of assumptions can be made about the scarcity of 1915 Panama-Pacific proofs. These include:

1. As is evident from the work done by R.H. White, . . . sophisticated testing procedures exist using scanning electron micrographs which enable accurate separation of 1903 Roosevelt proofs from those of the 1915 printing.

2. Non-destructive scientific analysis utilizing element x-ray data enable the accurate comparison of suspected 1915 proofs with those in the complete set held by the Smithsonian Institution, as was evident from the test results . . .

3. Under simple visual examination, discernible differences can be easily detected concerning the paper and ink colors of 1903, 1915 and various other proof issues.

4. All of the 1915 specimens in philatelic hands probably were considered as 'seconds.' While they were indeed produced at the same time as the two sets delivered in fulfillment of Bureau of Engraving and Printing order Q-38-A, and under the same circumstances and conditions, for whatever reason, the remaining proofs were perhaps considered to be slightly inferior to the two specimens of each type distributed in 1915.

5. The only remaining intact set is held by the Smithsonian Institution's National Philatelic Collection.

6. The Smithsonian's Panama-Pacific set should not be considered when describing scarcity in catalog listings, since it will never come on the market. Nor should the Postal Service's original set be counted with respect to the number of 1915 proof specimens available to private collections since this set cannot be found. In all likelihood it probably ceased to exist long ago.

7. Over the years there obviously has been more rhetoric than reality concerning the number of impressions which exist for each of the 413 specimens in the complete set.

8. More 1915 proof specimens than the 'two copies only' reportedly given to Hugh Southgate in the 1930's appear to have gotten out of the Bureau of Engraving and Printing under the table. While the impressions Hugh Southgate was given may never have been complete sets, there does appear to be many more than two of many of the 413 small die proofs. A correct count is critical in order to establish the level of scarcity. Many specimens will probably be found to be more scarce than others . . ."

It appears that, at least for some of the varieties, more than three copies may be in philatelic hands. An accurate census of examples known to be in private hands has never been completed, and in spite of Bruns request at the end of his series of articles for the reporting of copies, the response was minimal, and the question of absolute scarcity is still unanswered. In a recent communication from Bruns, he stated that two copies of the 1¢ Panama-Pacific proof in light blue and one in the dark blue shade were reported to him. These, of course, do not include the copies in the National Collection. In addition to the copies listed by Bruns, the author has seen one additional example in light blue that was offered in a Matthew Bennett auction in January of 1995.

The extremely infrequent appearance of these proofs in the philatelic market is a good indicator that the estimates of three to a maximum of six copies existing for each color of the 1861 1¢ Panama-Pacific die proof is reasonable.

References

1. Luff, John N. *Postage Stamps of the United States.* Quarterman Publications. 1981. (Reprinted from the original 1902 publication by Scott Stamp and Coin Company.)

2. Chase, Carroll. *The 3¢ Stamp of the United States 1851-1857 Issue.* Quarterman Publications. 1975.

3. Brookman, Lester G. *The United States Stamps of the 19th Century.* Vol. III. H.L. Lindquist Publications Inc. 1967.

4. Chapin, John C. *A Census of United States Classic Plate Blocks.* The Collectors Club of New York. 1982.

5. Friedman, Howard S. The Atlanta Expositions and United States Philately. *Essay-Proof Journal* No. 127. Summer 1975.

6. Friedman, Howard S. The United States Plate Proofs on Cardboard. *Essay-Proof Journal* No. 119-120. 1973.

7. Friedman, Howard S. The Die and Plate Proofs of the United States Stamp Designs, Part VIII. *Strictly U.S.* Winter 1980. Donna Von Stein. Dunedin, Florida. (This is one of an 11-part series, published in *Strictly U.S.* from October 1978 to Winter 1981.)

8. Brazer, Charles W. Atlantic Trial Colors. *Essay-Proof Journal* No. 2. 1944.

9. Graham, Richard B. Private communication. 1993.

10. Bierman, Stanley M. *World's Greatest Stamp Collectors.* Linn's Stamp News, Sidney, Ohio. 1990.

11. Brazer, Charles W. U.S. Proofs in Ackerman Collection. *Essay-Proof Journal* No. 47. 1955.

12. Meyersburg, Robert B. "Lost and Found Department." *Chronicle.* May 1982. U.S. Classics Society.

13. Burns, Ronald A. A Study of the Production Records for the 1903 and 1914-15 Printings of the "Roosevelt" and "Panama-Pacific" Small Die Proofs. *BIA Research Paper* No. 7. Bureau Issues Association. August 1994.

14. *S.P.A. Journal.* September 1981.

15. Bruns, James H. The Scarcity of Panama-Pacific Proofs. *United States Specialist.* Bureau Issues Association Inc. 1988-1989.

16. McCall, Francis J. United States Gems of Proofdom. *Philatelic Congress Book.* American Philatelic Congress Inc. 1956.

17. Friedman, Howard S. The Die and Plate Proofs of the United States Stamp Designs. Part XI. *Strictly U.S.* Donna Von Stein. Dunedin, Florida. Fall 1980.

CHAPTER 6

Summary of Postal Rates and Procedures

Introduction

The postal rates and fees charged for mail services, and the rules used by the Post Office Department to process and move the mails, are of vital interest to philatelic students and collectors. In this chapter, a summary of the domestic rates and fees in use during the decade of the 1860s will be presented, and some of the procedures used in the conduct of Post Office business will be explored. Many of the topics will be covered more thoroughly in later chapters, along with examples of uses.

The *Laws and Regulations of the Post Office Department*, as compiled in 1859 [1], form the initial source for the description of the fees and procedures presented here. That compilation included all of the applicable laws and regulations in effect as of that time.

Changes to fees and procedures due to new laws and regulations, and the issuance of additional postal instructions and orders, will be introduced as required.

Postmaster General Montgomery Blair summarized the regulatory situation in the following "Notice to Postmasters" that he included in an 1862 Post Office publication, *List of Post Offices in the United States* [2].

> "The laws and regulations attached to the List of Post Offices, published in 1859, are still in force, except such portions thereof as may have been amended, modified or superseded by the acts approved April 3, 1860, June 15, 1860, and February 27, 1861.
>
> The regulations predicated on the acts of April 3, 1860, and June 15, 1860, were published under date of July 23, 1860, and furnished to postmasters generally, and should be on file in their respective offices.
>
> The act of February 27, 1861, was printed in pamphlet form, under date of May 1, 1861, and furnished to postmasters. This pamphlet should also be on file in each post office, with such circulars as may have been furnished, from time to time, by the department, and should be preserved for future reference."

Of major impact was the following year's "Act to Amend the Laws of the Post Office Department" approved on March 3, 1863, to become effective on July 1, 1863. This was the most important postal act of the decade, and contained many innovative changes that had been proposed by Postmaster General Blair. It also repealed all previous postal laws and regulations that were inconsistent with the provisions of this act. Those not in conflict with the new laws and regulations remained in force.

Blair had noted in his 1861 postmaster general's annual report that it would be advisable to publish a revised code of Postal Laws. In the postmaster general report of 1862, he commented on the fact that the expected publication of a list of post offices had been delayed, and that the revised laws and regulations would be published at the end of the current congressional session. It appears that Blair then directed the compilation of an updated version of the Postal Laws and Regulations (PL&Rs) in anticipation of the procedures that Congress would authorize, and had it printed. Unfortunately, it contained provisions for the free forwarding of mail that Blair had requested of Congress but that were not provided for in the comprehensive Act of March 3, 1863. As a consequence, the revised PL&R was not a legal document, and the planned distribution of copies never took place [3:1-2]. Evidently, most copies were destroyed, but a small number were retained and became the source of the philatelic rumor that a PL&R for 1863 existed.

Instead of the comprehensive revision that he wanted, Blair was only able to distribute a small pamphlet that contained the new postal legislation enacted by Congress on March 3, 1863, and instructions for compliance. Extracts, covering the most relevant items from the pamphlet were also published in issues of the *U.S. Mail and Post Office Assistant* for June and July of 1863

Although Blair, in his 1863 report, asked Congress to reconsider his requests for legislation, they were not acted upon, and free forwarding did not become law until June 12, 1866, during Postmaster General William Dennison's tenure. In 1866 the Post Office Department finally published an updated Postal Laws and Regulations [4]. This compilation unfortunately contains a number of errors and conflicts. The compiler, Joseph A. Ware, to be sure he did not omit anything, included nearly every law that had been on the books, along with reference to its enabling act, including some that had long been abolished. This resulted in the reprinting of some outmoded laws, but the compilation does provide an excellent directory to the student for determining the sources of many of the early laws.

Acts that provided additions and changes to the postal laws were passed throughout the 1860-70 period, and one of the major sources for information to the philatelic researcher concerning these changes is the *U.S. Mail and Post Office Assistant* (USM&POA) [5]. This monthly semiofficial publication was subscribed to by many postmasters and contained information important to the conduct of their duties. New laws and regulations, and instructions for carrying them out, were included along with extensive information on foreign mails and post office procedures. The editor, J. Holbrook, was a special agent for the Post Office Department, and all instructional information contained in the publication had the approval of the postmaster general. In addition to the official aspects, many letters and articles describing problems and solutions of interest to postmasters, along with developments in the technology of processing and delivering the mail were included.

The perusal of a few issues of this publication provides a factual and intimate look at the postal system of the 1860s, and is highly recommended for all collectors interested in this period.

Only those provisions of the various PL&Rs that are of primary importance to collectors will be discussed here. The many details with respect to record-keeping, contracting regulations and many other types of information that are of less pertinence to the majority of postal students will not be included. Domestic mail only will be considered in this chapter. The rate structure and procedures for handling mail to and from foreign countries are somewhat complex because of the many countries, postal conventions and routes involved, and cannot be easily summarized. Chapter 17 is devoted to that subject, and many foreign destinations and rates are discussed and illustrated. Detailed information can be found in currently available literature such as Hargest's *History of Letter Communication Between United States and Europe* [6], and Starnes' work on *United States Letter Rates to Foreign Destinations* [7]. Both of these volumes should be part of the reference library of any serious student of this era.

Principal sources for rate and procedural information in this chapter include the PL&Rs, postal bulletins, official announcements, annual reports by the postmaster general [8], references from postal historians and the USM&POA. These sources are listed in the chapter bibliography and should be consulted if additional details are required.

For ease of reference, the subject matter in this chapter, as listed below, is arranged in alphabetical order. The chapter concludes with a table of rates and fees for the period.

 Advertised Mail
 Books
 Branch Post Offices
 Canceling
 Carriers
 Circulars
 Classes of Mail
 Collect/Underpaid
 Dead Letters
 Drop and Local Letters
 Forwarding
 Franked and Other Free Mail
 Letters
 Money Orders
 Newspapers
 Pamphlets
 Registered Mail
 Ship, Steamship and Steamboat Letters
 Soldiers' and Sailors' Mail
 Stamped Envelopes
 Supplementary Mail
 Transient Mail
 Way Letters

Note: The Postal Act of March 3, 1863, effective July 1, 1863, contained many provisions for change. For convenience and brevity, this postal law will be referred to as the PL of 1863, and the abbreviations PL for Postal Law, PR for Postal Regulation, PB for Postal Bulletin, PI for Postal Instruction, and § for section will be used.

Advertised Mail

Letters that were not called for were to be advertised in local newspapers. A 1¢ fee per insertion was paid to the paper, and this fee was, in turn, collected from the recipient upon delivery. Drop letters or box mail, circulars and refused mail were not to be advertised. Advertised mail was normally marked as "advertised" and with a due rating. Small offices could advertise by posting lists (1859 PL§56, PR§181-184).

Instructions for §7 of the 1863 PL enlarged on the types of letters that were not to be advertised, and included in this category those showing instructions to return to sender or to hold for a specific period [2:4-5].

The Act of March 3, 1865, and Postal Instructions (§4) from Postmaster General Dennison, dated May 1, 1865, provided that the rates paid to newspapers for advertising would be increased to 2¢, and that recipients would be so charged [2:1].

Additional instructions, dated July 1, 1866, restricted the use of paid advertising in newspapers to first-class post offices. All others were to post lists of unclaimed letters. §361 of the 1866 PR added the proviso that only offices where the salary of the postmaster exceeded $500 could advertise letters. These were to collect no more than 1¢ for the service. This certainly conflicts with the PL referenced in the previous paragraph and is indicative of some of the difficulties that may arise from relying too much on the contents of the 1866 compendium of PL&Rs.

Books

The Act of August 30, 1852, §2, provided that

books, bound and unbound, not weighing over 4 pounds were deemed mailable matter and were assessed postage at the rate of 1¢ per ounce for distances less than 3,000 miles, and 2¢ per ounce for distances greater than 3,000 miles [1:43].

PL§12 of February 27, 1861, effective May 1, 1861, revised the book rate to 1¢ per ounce for distances under 1,500 miles and 2¢ per ounce over 1,500 miles [2:2].

The 1863 PL, §34, again revised the book rate to be 4¢ for each 4 ounces of weight. No distance limitations were applied. No extra charge was to be made for a corner card printed or stamped on the wrapper or envelope [2:11].

Branch Post Offices

The Act of March 3, 1847, §10, first established the authorization for branch post offices, and at that time no additional postage fee or postage was authorized [1:28].

The Act of April 16, 1862, §1, provided for an additional charge of 1¢ for each letter deposited at a branch office to be entered into the mails at the principal office, and 1¢ for each letter delivered from the principal office to the branch office. Such payments were to be prepaid by stamp [4:17]. In response to the free-carrier provisions contained in the PL of 1863, the branch post office fee was eliminated on July 1, 1863.

Canceling

Directives provided that stamps were to be canceled with printer's ink. If the proper ink was not available, the canceling was to be effected by broad strokes across the postage stamp by a pen with black writing ink.

The 1859 PR, §397, prohibited the use of the office dating or postmarking stamp for canceling unless it was used with black printer's ink [1:118]. The following year, First Assistant Postmaster General Holt issued an order on July 23, 1860, further restricting their use by prohibiting the use of town/date postmarkings to cancel stamps, and specifically requiring a "distinct canceller device to be used" [9:177]. This requirement was frequently ignored, particularly for local letters and printed matter.

Again, on May 1, 1865, Postal Instructions from Postmaster General Dennison stated that the provisions of the 1859 PR, §397, related to using a postmarking device as a canceler were repealed. The use of office-rating or postmarking stamps as canceling instruments was positively prohibited, and failure to comply with this directive was grounds for dismissal [2:3]. In spite of all of these regulations and orders, the practice of canceling stamps with a town-dating or postmarking device was never completely eliminated.

Carriers

(For an extended discussion, see Chapter 10.) Carriers were first authorized by the Acts of 1825, §36, and 1836, §41. The fee allowed for this service was a maximum of 2¢ for delivery and collection of letters and ½¢ for pamphlets and newspapers [1:27].

The Act of June 15, 1860, effective July 1, 1860, reduced the fee for carrier service to a maximum of 1¢ [10:249].

PL§4, approved February 27, 1861, reinforced earlier laws by once again prohibiting the operation of any private post on any post roads in any city or town [2:4]. This law and some increased efficiency of the government carrier services effectively stopped the competition for mail delivery by many of the private post firms that had been in operation for many years in the larger cities. Private carriers, such as steamboats and expresses, continued to transport mail in many of the western states and other regions where the Post Office had not yet established adequate postal routes. Many companies were engaged in the transport of mail, and after 1852, it was legal for private carriers to carry mail if the letters were enclosed in government-issued embossed envelopes with the proper postage. The sender was charged an additional fee by the expresses for this service.

The PL of 1863, §10, required that letter carriers be employed at such post offices that the postmaster general directs, and that the carriers were to be postal employees and paid a salary. This is a departure from earlier practices that paid the carriers with respect to the number of letters that were handled. §13 of the same law again authorized the establishment of branch post offices and mail-collection boxes as required. §23 provided that all letters requiring carrier delivery or collection would be provided that service free, and that no additional postage or fee would be required. The rate for local and drop letters at all post offices was concurrently increased to 2¢ to be prepaid in stamps.

The PL of July 1, 1864, §15, made further changes to the carrier system. Realizing the inequity of charging 2¢ for drop and local letters where there was no free delivery or collection, the rate was reduced to 1¢ at those post offices. The law also stipulated that a system for free delivery would be established wherever the population was 50,000 or more, and other such places as the postmaster general directed. Postal Instructions for this section stated that postmasters where free delivery did not exist could arrange for the employment of Pennypost men. These individuals would receive no compensation except for 1¢ per letter from the recipient from whom they would collect the fee (presumably in cash). No mention of collection of letters to the mails was made in this instruction with respect to Pennypost men. This author has never seen a cover that had any markings that would indicate that this PI was actually put into use.

Circulars

(For an extended discussion of this type of mail, please refer to Chapter 12.) To qualify for the circular rate, the mailed item must be printed matter only, with no manuscript notations other than the address. If enclosed in an envelope, the cover must be unsealed.

§138 of the 1847 PR established a rate of 3¢ per sheet and required the postage to be prepaid. This predated by almost a decade the general requirement for prepaying letter postage.

Per the 1859 PR, §13, based on the 1852 PL effective July 1, 1852, the rate for circulars became 1¢ for each circular not exceeding 3 ounces and 1¢ additional for each ounce in excess. The printing of a business card on the cover of a circular subjected it to letter postage. (This provision was not vigorously enforced) [1:75].

§111 of the 1859 PR also lists the domestic rates for printed matter in more general terms. Under its provisions, it includes any article of printed matter (excluding books) within the same classification and rate as circulars. Although very few examples of enclosures for printed matter such as forms or preprinted envelopes have survived, scarce examples do show this use.

§34 of the PL of 1863 revised the rate of postage for circulars. Up to three circulars, with a total weight not exceeding 4 ounces, enclosed in a single unsealed envelope and mailed to one address, were charged at the rate of 2¢. No extra charge was to be made for a corner (business) card on the wrapper or envelope [2:11].

A provision was inserted into the PL of March 25, 1864, §4, that set a special rate for the mailing of all printed matter in the territory between the western boundary of Kansas and the eastern boundary of California to be equal to the letter rate. Newspapers and periodicals sent to bona fide subscribers were exempted from this increased rate [4:63]. This unusual provision became necessary because eastern publishers took advantage of the extremely low postage rates for printed matter, and mailed vast amounts of newspapers and other publications to news agents on the West Coast. This overburdened the stagecoach and wagon transport of the overland mail contractors who, in retaliation, frequently dumped the printed matter by the side of the road to make room for more remunerative cargo, or passengers. The low rates for printed matter were retained for mail to the West Coast via Panama, and this was an incentive for publishers to send their bulk mailings by ship.

The rate was again changed by the PL effective June 8, 1872, and became 1¢ per 2 ounces, or 1¢ each if delivered by carrier [11:43].

Classes of Mail

Three classes of mail were established by law. Letter postage, later to be referred to as "first-class mail," covered all correspondence, wholly or partly in writing, except for manuscripts and proof sheets, which were considered to be miscellaneous matter. Printed newspapers and magazines (second class) included all mailable matter exclusively in print and regularly issued and mailed from the office of publication. Miscellaneous mail (third class) included all other mailable matter. This encompassed circulars, transient mail, books, seeds, engravings, photographs, maps, engravings, plant scions, phonographic paper, envelopes and printed forms [2:2]. Other mailable matter, although not specifically enumerated, was most probably included under miscellaneous matter at the discretion of the postmaster accepting the item.

The PL of 1863, §19, provided that mailable matter be divided into three numbered classes: first, letters; second, regular printed matter; third, miscellaneous matter. This is no real change from earlier laws but is the most concise statement of the contents of the classes [5:8].

Many of the postal acts contained provisions that items other than those listed as mailable matter with specific rates, if entered into the mails, would be charged postage at the letter or first-class rate.

Very early pre-stamp regulations provided no weight limits on postal matter, and some abuses of the system occurred as a result. The PL of 1847 established a weight limit of 3 pounds for mailable matter, and by the time of the Civil War this had been raised to 4 pounds, where it remained for the balance of this period. There was no "parcel post" for merchandise as we know it today, although by the mid-1860s the Post Office Department was investigating the advisability of adding local small-package delivery to the scope of a carrier's responsibility.

Collect/Underpaid

§102 of the 1859 PR required that when unpaid domestic letters were received in a post office, the postmaster should advise the addressee of the letter and request payment of postage prior to delivery. If no response to this request was received within one month, the letter was sent to the Dead Letter Office (DLO) [1:71]. §106 of the same PR states that letters part paid were to be dispatched with the additional postage due at the prepaid rate, except when the underpayment was known to be intentional. In that case the letter was treated as unpaid.

On October 8, 1860, Postmaster General Holt issued a Post Office Order, effective November 1, 1860, requiring that all underpaid and unpaid letters be sent to the Dead Letter Office, and that the practice of notifying the addressee of postage due be discontinued.

The number of dead letters under this procedure soon overloaded the DLO, and on November 28, 1861, Postmaster General Blair, in a subsequent Post Office Order, rescinded Holt's order and directed a return to the procedures in effect under §102 of the 1859 PR.

The 1863 PL, §26, provided that if any mail requiring prepayment arrived at its destination without being properly paid, double the prepaid rate would be charged and collected upon delivery. The PI for this section added that if the postage was partially prepaid, the unpaid postage would be charged at double rates. Postmasters were authorized to use leniency in forwarding unpaid letters if it was thought that the underpayment was accidental.

§27 of the same law provided for the mailing of letters from noncommissioned soldiers, sailors and marines without prepayment. Ordinary postage was to be collected from the recipient upon delivery (see Soldier's and Sailor's Letters).

Postal Instructions from Postmaster General Dennison, dated May 1, 1865, referring to §1 of the Act of March 3, 1865, stated in subsection (b) that partially paid letters were to be forwarded to their destinations, charged with the amount of postage due. This was a change from earlier regulations that assessed a penalty for underpayment. An exception to this was provided for letters that included a return request. These letters were to be marked "Held for postage" and immediately returned to the writer (for both unpaid and underpaid cases). A further subsection (d) of this same PI stated that "All domestic letters upon which less than one full rate of postage is prepaid, must be treated as if wholly unpaid; the stamps must not be canceled" [2:1]. Unpaid letters were to be treated as dead letters, unless a return request and address was endorsed on the envelope.

Dead Letters

Per the 1859 PR, §185-186, "dead letters" were defined as those letters that had not been called for, had been advertised, and remained uncollected after a period of three months. In addition, letters that were refused or could not be delivered, unpaid letters (if not attended to), or illegally mailed were considered dead letters after a period of one month [1:93].

The subject of dead letters was of great importance to the Post Office Department, and procedures were established to ensure that all mail that was deliverable arrived at its destination or was returned to the sender if at all possible. The amount of mail in this category was substantial, and numbers of two to three million dead letters per year were common for this period. The postmaster general reported to Congress each year on details of this operation.

Changes to the law, effective on February 27, 1861, required a sliding scale for required dates for return of uncalled-for advertised letters, ranging from weekly for the larger offices to once every two months for the small offices [2:9-12].

The PL of 1863, §7, decreased the maximum time for holding letters to one month. Domestic circulars and newspapers were not returned to the DLO [2:5].

Dead letters, if the sender or addressee could be located, were returned at normal letter rates. If the letter was registered as valuable, a double letter rate applied. These fees varied over the period, and in 1866 they were abolished for ordinary letters. Valuable letters continued to require the payment of postage for return.

Drop and Local Letters

(For a more complete discussion, refer to Chapter 10.) At the beginning of the 1860s, letters and other classes of mail handed to the post office for local delivery at the same post office, either to be placed in post office boxes (box mail) or for general delivery at the post office window, were to be charged postage at the rate of 1¢ per item. (They were not charged by weight.) Prepayment was optional (1859 PR. §91,94) [1:70]. These letters, if delivered or collected by a carrier, were subject to an additional fee of 1¢ to 2¢.

The PL of February 27, 1861, §14, per U.S. Post Office Department bulletin, dated May 1, 1861, revised the above to require that all drop letters be prepaid by postage stamps [2:3].

The PL of 1863, §23, again revised the drop or local letter rate to 2¢ per ½ ounce, prepaid by stamp, but no additional fee was charged for collection or delivery.

On May 1, 1865, per PL§14, of March 3, 1865, the rate for drop and local letters at post offices where there was no delivery service was reduced to 1¢ per half ounce. This eliminated the inequity that had existed since 1863, where local letters were essentially charged for a carrier service that was not provided [2:2].

Forwarding

Note: Some caution should be exercised with reference to the meaning of the word "forward." The Post Office refers to letters normally entered into the mails as being "forwarded" or "mailed" when sent to their destination. In this section's discussion, "forward" will be used only to specifically describe those letters that when undeliverable at the original address were sent to another location where the addressee could be expected to be found.

The 1847 PR, §196 and §197, provided that letters could be forwarded if the addressee is known to be at another address, or if instructions have been left for forwarding to another address. Additional postage, at the normal rate, was charged for this service. Letters that were misdirected to the wrong address because of a post office error were not charged extra [12:29]. This provision was repeated in the 1863 PL, §30.

The 1863 PL, §28, also added a provision that letters that had written instructions on the cover, requesting a return of the letter to the sender if not delivered, were to be returned and charged the letter rate for this service. The written or printed instructions usually noted a specific number of days that the letter should be held before return. Such letters were given the name of "request letters" [11:66].

The PL of July 1, 1864, §10, amended previous laws by providing that undelivered letters returned as a result of a "return to sender" request on the envelope must be accepted by the writer and postage paid for their return. Failure to do this resulted in the assessment of a penalty of $10 [2:2].

Letters addressed to members of the armed forces were forwarded free of charge if the addressee had been transferred or had moved in response to official orders (Act of July 24, 1861, §1). Senders of mail to the armed forces often endorsed their letters with "Follow the Regiment," to emphasize this privilege.

The PL of June 12, 1866, §1, contained an authorization, effective July 1, 1866, to forward first-class letters at no additional charge. It was stipulated that a written request for this service must be on file at the post office. This free forwarding was also extended to the return of unclaimed "request letters" and letters forwarded from the DLO [11:67].

The Act of July 27, 1868, §15, further liberalized the law and stated that uncalled-for letters would be returned without additional postage to the writer if endorsed on the outside of the envelope with a name and address. No specific request to return needed to be stated.

Franked and Other Free Mail

In the early years of the postal service, the franking privilege was extended to a large number of people including the president and vice president, Cabinet members, senators and congressmen, every postmaster (with a ½-ounce limit), and many of the heads of government offices. Most Official mail was free. While most "free" letters do not have stamps attached and are therefore not of particular interest to this study, carrier service was not included with the franking privilege and required postage. Stamps were applied to these otherwise free letters to pay for this additional service, and interesting covers showing this use can be found.

In 1847, because of widespread abuse of the franking privilege, further restrictions were applied. For example, the franking privilege for postmasters was restricted only to those postmasters whose annual compensation did not exceed $200. This franking privilege also applied to personal letters to or from these low-income postmasters.

Mail to and from all postmasters in the conduct of official business remained free of postage, and was to be marked "Post Office Business" and signed by the postmaster. To pay for the vast amount of free mail that was generated by all of the franking privileges, the Post Office Department was reimbursed by the Treasury in the amount of $500,000 per year (Act of March 3, §8) [1:22-27,97-98]. Later laws increased this amount.

The PL of 1863, §42, made major changes in the franking privilege and again reduced it substantially. Persons writing to executive government offices had to prepay these letters. Of major philatelic interest, the franking privilege of postmasters for private correspondence was eliminated and applied only to letters on post office business. Each free letter was to be inscribed "official business" on the envelope and signed by the postmaster. A limit of 4 ounces was placed on these letters or packets [2:13].

During the Civil War years, the volume of free mail increased tremendously. Almost all official military correspondence from Washington that was carried by the mails was done so under the free-franking privilege, and the few official covers that are found with stamps are usually the result of carrier service.

Letters

The Act of March 3, 1855, §1, effective April 1, 1855, provided that the rate for letter postage, per ½ ounce, was to be 3¢ for letters to destinations less than 3,000 miles, and 10¢ for destinations in excess of this distance. Further, it required that all domestic letter postage be prepaid, and as of January 1, 1856, postmasters were required to place postage stamps on letters to provide for the correct franking if such had not already been accomplished by the sender. (This eliminated the practice of collecting postage in cash and marking the letter "paid.") [1:42-43]

The Act of February 27, 1861, §14, revised the above act to require a 10¢ rate of postage to be prepaid on letters that crossed the Rocky Mountains in either direction, regardless of distance. This was in addition to the 3,000-mile limit.

The 1863 PL, §22, established the domestic letter rate at a uniform 3¢ per ½ ounce, regardless of distance, and eliminated the 10¢ rate for crossing the Rocky Mountains.

Money Orders

The Act of May 17, 1864, §1, first authorized the issuing of money orders by the Post Office Department. Postmaster General Blair had recommended it to Congress to provide a safe way to transmit small sums of money through the mails. He was of the opinion that removing cash from letters would decrease the temptation for mail theft. At the beginning, only the larger post offices had this service (141 offices by November of 1864). It was to be extended to larger offices as rapidly as possible. The limit on the amount for which a money order would be issued was $30 [8:797]. Some envelopes from the period bear a notation of "Money Order Business," or the initials MOB.

Newspapers

Regularly published newspapers were normally transmitted through the mails to their subscribers without stamps, and the postal fees for the service were paid in advance by the publisher. It is of interest to note that weekly newspapers could be mailed free of charge to subscribers who resided in the same county as the place of publication. The regulations covering newspapers mailed by the publisher are lengthy and are not of particular interest to most collectors since the newspaper rates were paid in money and postage stamps were not applied. However, when newspapers were mailed by individuals other than the publisher, the circular rate authorized by the Act of 1852 was applied (1¢ per newspaper, up to 3 ounces, with 1¢ more for each additional ounce) [4:72]. §34 of the PL of 1863 increased the allowable weight per rate unit to 4 ounces and the rate to 2¢. Transient mail rates applied here, and the most common examples seen are wrappers that probably contained newspapers (see Transient Mail, Chapter 12).

Pamphlets

The PL&Rs are never completely clear on the precise definition of a pamphlet. It seems to be a small printed, but unbound, publication that meets specific criteria. It was not a periodical and should have been on a subject of general or local interest of a temporary nature, such as a local event or public address, or appropriate to some particular occasion. It could not exceed 16 octavo pages in length, and could be mailed at a rate of 1¢ per pamphlet, when mailed from the office of publication to subscribers. If mailed from other points, pamphlets were treated as ordinary printed matter and rated at third-class or circular rates.

Registered Mail

The Act of March 3, 1855, §3, effective July 1, 1855, provided for registration of letters for a prepaid fee of 5¢ to be paid in cash, in addition to postage. No insurance or notification of delivery to the sender was included [1:45]. Registered letters were to be marked with the registration number in the upper-left-hand corner of the envelope, and careful accounting of the handling of the letter at each point in the route to destination was made. Registration was possible to a limited number of foreign destinations [1:88].

The PL of 1863, §32, provided for an increase in the registration fee to 20¢. No insurance was included or available, but the Post Office Department furnished a signed receipt of delivery to the sender at no additional cost. In addition to the registration number, Postal Instructions that accompanied this law required that the word "Registered" be plainly written or stamped on the face of the envelope. The fee was still required to be paid in cash, and the postage was to be prepaid by stamps [2:10]. Although the registration fee for domestic letters had increased four-fold, the fee to Germany, Great Britain and British North America remained at 5¢ as a consequence of existing postal treaties with those entities.

The *U.S. Mail and Post Office Assistant* for May 1867 advised postmasters that revisions to the registry system had been made, and that from June 1, 1867, the registry fee of 20¢ was to be paid in stamps [5:317].

On January 1, 1869, the registry fee was reduced to 15¢ [5:398], and on January 1, 1874, further reduced to 8¢. On July 1, 1875, it was increased to 10¢.

Ship, Steamship and Steamboat Letters

(See also, Chapter 13, Special Services)

Per the 1859 PR, §164, the terms ship letters and packets denoted items brought into the United States from foreign countries or carried from one port in the United States to another in any private ship or vessel. The word "private" in this definition referred to ships that were not owned or leased by the United States, or under contract to carry U.S. mail. The master of the vessel was to deliver to the nearest post office, immediately upon arriving at a port, all letters and packets entrusted to him for mailing.

Ship letters were to be charged a fee of 6¢ each when delivered by the post office to an addressee at the port of arrival. When forwarded by mail to other post offices for delivery, they were charged a 2¢ ship fee plus the normal rate of postage. (This regulation resulted in the curious circumstance that it could cost more to send a letter to someone at the port of arrival than it did to a person who was many miles from the port.) Each letter received was to be marked "SHIP," and the master of the vessel was paid a fee of 2¢ for each letter. An exception to this was for vessels of foreign ownership. In that case, no fee was paid to the master, although he was required to immediately deliver his ship letters to the postmaster, who put the letters in the mail at the normal postal rate plus the ship fee, which was retained by the Post Office.

The PL of February 27, 1861, §9, revised the fee for ship letters delivered locally at the port of arrival from 6¢ down to 5¢, and added the condition that letters whose destination was beyond the Rocky Mountains would be treated as "over 3,000 mile" letters and charged with a 2¢ ship fee plus the postage rate of 10¢ per ½ ounce [2:1].

The PL of 1863, §31, again revised the rate and conditions, and provided for a ship-letter rate equal to double the normal postage, i.e., 4¢ if addressed locally and 6¢ if mailed beyond the port where deposited (regardless of distance). Vessels from a foreign port could be paid 2¢ per letter, and vessels traveling from one domestic port to another were paid 1¢ per letter. No mention of the nationality of ship ownership was made [2:10].

Steamship letters are those letters that were put aboard a scheduled U.S. Mail contract vessel at a foreign port, for transport outside the mails to the United States. The letters could be sent collect or prepaid. Upon arrival at a U.S. port, the letter was entered into the mail, marked with a STEAMSHIP handstamp, and assessed postage due if appropriate. Most of this type of mail originated at Caribbean or Mexican/Central-American coastal ports. The rate for this service was 10¢ for letters that traveled less than 2,500 miles, and a double rate for larger distances. By §8 of the Act of July 1, 1864, this rate was revised to standardize the amount at 10¢, regardless of distance. While this was not precisely a domestic rate, it serviced many citizens who were located along the steamer routes connecting the western and eastern parts of the United States.

Steamboat letters is the term for letters carried outside the mails aboard steamboats on the inland and coastal bay waterways of the United States. If the letters were prepaid, the master of the vessel was entitled to a fee of 2¢. If the letter was not prepaid, it was to be rated as a ship letter. Letters put aboard mail-contract steamboats en route could be treated as way letters (see Way Letters).

Soldiers' and Sailors' Mail

The Act of July 22, 1861, §11, provided that letters written by noncommissioned soldiers in the service of the United States could be mailed without prepayment in money or stamps, and that the normal rate of postage would be collected from the addressee upon delivery. Each letter had to be clearly marked on the outside that it was a soldier's letter, with a certificate on the letter so attesting and signed by a designated commissioned officer (or equivalent).

The PL of January 21, 1862, §1, extended this privilege to sailors and marines on the same basis as a soldier's letters [4:61].

Per the PL of July 24, 1861, §1, letters addressed to members of the armed forces were forwarded free if the addressee had moved under orders or had been transferred to a new location. Such letters were at times endorsed "Follow the Regiment" to ensure that letters were forwarded as required [11:66].

Stamped Envelopes (Postal Stationery)

Envelopes were to be sold by post offices for the

cost of the envelope plus the value of the imprinted postage stamp. They were valid for postal use and could be used to convey letters outside the mails without penalty if franked by the correct postage. This interesting provision (Act of August 31, 1852, §8) provided a means to transmit mail by private carriers [1:36]. The major reason for the introduction of these government envelopes was the large amount of mail that was being carried outside the mail on noncontract steamboats. After the rapid growth of the large western express carriers, such as Wells, Fargo, they became the largest users of government envelopes. Of course, fees required by the carrier would have to be paid in addition to the postage. Interestingly, the permission to carry letters outside the mails did not apply to plain envelopes to which adhesive postage stamps had been applied. They were still prohibited from being transported except by the Post Office Department or postal-contract carriers.

The PL of February 27, 1861, §2, provided for the production of stamped lettersheets for the first time. In addition, §3 of the same law made it illegal to use for postage any stamp that had been cut from a stamped envelope, wrapper or lettersheet [2:14].

Supplementary Mail

(See also Chapter 13, Special Services)

This was a service that provided for the deposit of letters into the mail after the normal mails had been made up and dispatched. It was normally used for foreign mail and was first authorized in New York City on July 7, 1853. Special bags were left open and transmitted to the ship just before sailing time. The service was usually performed at the wharf where the mail ship was docked. A fee equal to the normal postage was charged in addition to the postage, and the letter was marked with a special "supplementary mail" marking.

Chicago also had a supplementary-mail service with a special cancellation, but no fee was charged. The service was operated out of the Chicago Post Office and was to provide late mailers with connections to outgoing trains to major cities. A few other cities, such as San Francisco, provided a supplementary service for a cash fee, but no markings were used [13:97-112].

Transient Mail

(See also Chapter 12, Transient Mail)

Transient mail is defined as printed matter regularly published and mailed from locations other than the point of publication. It usually refers to newspapers and magazines. Newspapers and other publications mailed from the publisher to subscribers are covered under the topic title "Newspapers." The most prevalent use of transient mail was the mailing of a wrapper-enclosed newspaper from one person to another. Special postal stationery wrappers for this use were available at post offices.

The 1859 PR, §111, provided for transient-mail rates of 1¢ per newspaper, up to 3 ounces, with 1¢ more for each additional ounce [1:72].

§33 and §34 of the PL of 1863 provided for a maximum of 4 ounces for the single rate for printed matter and for third-class miscellaneous mailable matter, including transient mail but not including books and circulars. The single rate was 2¢ for each 4 ounces. No extra charge was to be made for a corner card on the wrapper or envelope [2:11].

Way Letters

The Act of March 3, 1825, §20, provided for "way" letters. Mail carriers, if more than one mile from a post office, were required to accept letters for deposit at the next post office on the carrier's route. The carrier was allowed a fee of 1¢ for this service, which could be collected in cash or received from the postmaster at the post office of deposit, who would then add the 1¢ collect to the postage of the letter [1:42]. Way letters were to be marked "way" on the envelope by the post office receiving the letter to be mailed. Route agents on rail and steamboat routes were also required to accept prepaid way letters, but no way fee was charged [1:96]. The major source of covers with handstamped "way" markings in the decades preceding 1863 were the noncontract steamboats, particularly from routes on the Mississippi River and its tributaries.

The PL of 1863, §31, prohibited any fees being paid for letters collected by a carrier on a mail route [2:10], and this effectively eliminated the category of way letters.

Note

A word of caution: The Postal Laws, and the regulations, instructions and bulletins that derived from them, are occasionally contradictory and ambiguously worded. Postmasters and postal clerks made mistakes based on their interpretation of the guidelines, and at times ignored them. While an knowledge of the postal regulations is of great benefit to collectors and postal historians, uses and procedures at variance to these laws and regulations are to be expected.

Domestic Postal Rates & Fees 1860 to 1870

Effective dates (*Approved dates)		Authority
	Letter Rates (per half ounce) GENERAL LETTERS:	
January 1, 1856	Prepayment by stamp compulsory. 3¢ to 3,000 miles, 10¢ over 3,000 miles.	§1 Act of March 3, 1855
May 1, 1861	10¢ if Rocky Mountains are crossed, regardless of distance.	§14 Act of February 27, 1861
July 1, 1863	3¢ for any distance.	§22 Act of March 3, 1863
	DROP LETTERS:	
March 3, 1851*	1¢ fee. Weight not a factor. Prepayment optional. If delivered to a local address, carrier fee was added.	§1 Act of March 3, 1851
February 27, 1861	Above revised to require prepayment by stamps on all drop letters.	§14 Act of February 2, 1861
July 1, 1863	2¢ per ½ oz. Increase included free carrier delivery if available.	§23 Act of March 3, 1863
May 1, 1865	1¢ per ½ oz. if posted at an office without free delivery, and 2¢ at offices with carrier service.	§15 Act of March 3, 1865
	SHIP LETTERS:	
March 3, 1825*	6¢, if delivered at the port of entry. Regular letter rate plus 2¢ if delivered elsewhere.	§5 Act of March 3, 1825
May 1, 1861	5¢, if delivered at the port of entry. Regular letter rate plus 2¢ if delivered elsewhere, except if over 3,000 miles or transited the Rocky Mountains, the rate was 12¢.	§9 Act of February 27, 1861
July 1, 1863	Established a uniform rate of double the normal letter rate for all ship letters to any domestic destination.	§31 Act of March 3, 1863
	Advertising Fee	
July 1, 1851	1¢ fee to be charged for each advertised letter.	§5 Act of March 3, 1851
May 1, 1865	2¢ fee for each advertised letter.	§4 Act of March 3, 1865
	Post Office Department Carrier Fee	
July 2, 1836*	2¢ for letter carrier delivery, ½¢ for newspapers.	Act of July 2, 1836
July 1, 1860	1¢ for carrier delivery or collection to the post office.	§2 Act of June 15, 1860
April 16, 1862*	1¢ for carrier service to or from branch post offices.	§1 Act of April 16, 1862
July 1, 1863	Carrier service to be free, wherever available.	§23 Act of March 3, 1863
	Forwarding Fee	
April 25, 1847	An additional fee equal to the letter postage is assessed. No fee if letter is missent by Post Office error.	§196 PR of 1847
July 1, 1866	Forwarded free upon request.	§1 Act of June 12, 1866
	Registry Fee	
July 1, 1855	5¢ fee to be prepaid in money in addition to postage.	§3 Act of March 1855
July 1, 1863	20¢ fee to be prepaid in money in addition to postage.	§32 Act of March 1863
June 1, 1867	Fee to be paid in stamps.	PI of May 1867
January 1, 1869	Fee reduced to 15¢.	----------

Summary of Postal Rates and Procedures

Effective dates (*Approved dates)		Authority
July 1, 1855	**Unpaid or Part-paid** Part-paid letters dispatched with underpayment collected on delivery. Addressee notified of unpaid letter. If no payment, treated as dead letter.	§106 PR of 1959
November 1, 1860	All part-paid and unpaid letters treated as dead letters.	P.O. Order, October 8, 1860
November 26, 1861	Return to July 1, 1855, procedures.	P.O. Order, November 26, 1861
July 1, 1863	Unpaid letters, if dispatched, are charged double the prepaid rate. Part-paid letters are assessed a fee equal to double the underpayment.	§26 Act of March 3, 1863
May 1, 1865	Part-paid letters forwarded to destination and charged with postage due. Unpaid letters sent to DLO.	§1 Act of March 3, 1865
August 30, 1852*	**Book Rates** Books, bound and unbound, with a 4-pound limit, were charged a rate of 1¢ per ounce under 3,000 miles and 2¢ per ounce over 3,000 miles.	§2 Act of August 30, 1852
May 1, 1861	1¢ per ounce under 1,500 miles and 2¢ per ounce over 1,500 miles.	§12 Act of February 27, 1861
July 1, 1863	4¢ per each 4 ounces, up to 4 pounds. No limit on distance.	§34 Act of March 3, 1863
September 30, 1852	**Circular Rates** Must be prepaid and unsealed. 1¢ per circular, not to exceed 3 ounces, 1¢ for each additional ounce.	§1 Act of August 30, 1852
July 1, 1863	Must be prepaid by stamp and unsealed. 2¢ for up to three circulars to one address (third-class mail).	§34 Act of March 3, 1863
September 30, 1852	**Newspaper Rates** When mailed to subscribers from the office of publication, stamps were not normally used, and the postage was paid to the POD by the mailer for specific periods of time, usually annually (second-class mail). In all other cases, newspapers were classed as transient printed matter, and charged at circular rates: 1¢ up to 3 ounces, with 1¢ for each ounce over.	§1 Act of August 30, 1852
July 1, 1863	2¢ per 4 ounces.	§34 Act of March 3, 1863
	Third-class (Miscellaneous) Rates Includes all listed mailable matter not otherwise provided for. Weight limit of 4 pounds (cannot contain any writing of a first-class nature).	
May 1, 1861	1¢ per ounce under 1,500 miles, and 2¢ per ounce over 1,500 miles.	§13 Act of February 27, 1861
July 1, 1863	One package to one address, 2¢ for each 4 ounces, any distance.	§34 Act of March 3, 1863

References

1. Leech, Daniel D.T., Compiler. *List of Post Offices in the United States, and Postal Laws and Regulations of the Post Office Department.* Published by John C. Rives, Washington, D.C. 1859.

2. *List of Post Offices in the United States, 1862, including Various Postal Laws and Instructions of 1861, 1863, 1864 and 1865.* Reprint from original sources. Theron Wierenga. Holland, Michigan. 1981.

3. Simpson, Tracy W., Ed. *U.S. 1851-'60 Chronicle.* No. 39.

4. Ware, Joseph A., Compiler. *Postal Laws and Regulations of the United States of America 1866.* Government Printing Office, Washington, D.C. 1866. Reprint by Theron Wierenga. Holland, Michigan. 1981.

5. *United States Mail and Post Office Assistant, 1860-1872.* Reprinted by the Collectors Club of Chicago. 1975.

6. Hargest, George E. *History of Letter Post Communication Between the United States and Europe 1845-1875.* Second Edition, 1975. Quarterman Publications. Lawrence, Mass.

7. Starnes, Charles J. *United States Rates to Foreign Destinations, 1847 to GPU-UPU.* Revised Edition. 1989. Leonard J. Hartmann. Louisville, Kentucky.

8. *Reports of the Postmaster General.* 1861 through 1870. A series of reprints from official sources, published by Theron Wierenga. Holland, Michigan. 1977-1978.

9. Graham, Richard B. "The Beginnings of the Duplex Style Handstamps, 1869-62." *Chronicle.* August 1991.

10. Kohlhepp, John. "The Carrier Service: Final Years of the Fee- Based System." *Chronicle.* November 1981.

11. Graham, Richard B. *United States Postal History Sampler.* Published by Linn's Stamp News, Handbook Series. Sidney, Ohio. 1992.

12. *Postal Laws and Regulations of the United States of America, 1847.* Reprints from official sources. Theron Wierenga. Holland, Michigan. 1980.

13. Stolnitz, Henry. "N. Y. Supplementary Mail Markings." *The Congress Book.* 1976. American Philatelic Congress Inc.

CHAPTER 7

Postal Markings

Introduction

In this chapter, the subject of postal markings will be considered. For the purposes of this discussion, postal markings are defined as those markings applied to mail at a post office to indicate date and place of origin, and other notations that provided special information concerning the postal item, such as DUE, ADVERTISED and so on. These last are also known as "auxiliary markings." Other markings indicating that a special service was performed, such as REGISTERED or SUPPLEMENTARY MAIL, as well as markings associated with foreign mails and cancellations will be addressed in later chapters devoted to those subjects.

The reader is advised that there is intentional repetition of background information in various sections of this chapter. It is the author's intent that the descriptions of each of the markings and the reasons for their use be self-contained so that users of this work can reference the markings individually and still be provided with all the necessary information.

There will be no attempt to exhaustively cover the field of postal markings. But a basic knowledge of types and uses is not only interesting but extremely important in investigating the postal history aspects of a philatelic item. It is also invaluable in determining authenticity.

There are a number of excellent reference works that cover these subjects comprehensively and in-depth. Among those that are recommended for further information is the outstanding Simpson/Alexander work, *U.S. Postal Markings, 1851-61* [1]. Although most of the material in Simpson/Alexander is for the decade preceding the years of interest for this book, many of the markings continued to be used through the 1860s and even later. Most of what the collector of the 1861-67 issues needs to know about postal markings can be found in this volume. Books on cancellations, such as the Herst/Sampson compendium of fancy cancellations [2], and the more recent and very complete cancellation book by Skinner/Eno [3], also devote chapters to postal markings in addition to their listing of cancellations. Specialized studies, of which there are many for individual states and towns, such as the Blake/Davis book on Boston postmarks [4] and Baker's two-volume definitive work on the postal history of Indiana [5], give even greater depth in their more limited areas. The problem with information on postal markings is not a lack of material, but rather that the thousands of articles and monographs and dozens of books that cover the subject stretch the assimilation capacity and library space of most collectors. The subject is interesting and important, and consequently is well-represented in the literature.

At the beginning of the stamp period, in 1847, the majority of towns used manuscript notations for both canceling and postal markings. This was primarily because the Post Office Department issued marking devices only to the larger offices, and the postmasters of small offices, who were not willing to pay for commercially manufactured handstamps to mark their mail, used pen and ink.

In 1857, post offices with annual postal receipts of $1,000 or more were provided with steel marking devices at government expense. Those with $500 or more were to receive devices made of iron, and those with at least $100 were furnished with markers engraved from wood. Those with less than $100 in receipts were required to purchase their own markers if they wanted them. Postmasters of all but the largest cities were paid on a commission basis, depending on the amount of stamps they canceled in their offices and fees derived from other activities such as a commission on "free letters" and newspapers. The commission structure was involved and changed from time to time, but for example: In 1861 the quarterly commission included 60 percent of the value of the first $100 of stamps canceled (note that commissions were paid on the amount of mail processed through an office, not by the amount of postage sold), 50 percent of the next $300, 40 percent of the next $2,000 and 15 percent of all amounts over $2,400. No postmaster could receive compensation from commissions in excess of $500 for any quarter. In addition, postmasters were reimbursed for some allowable expenses, but this reimbursement was limited in amount and applied to only a few items. The commission paid during the 1860s to postmasters at the majority of post offices amounted to less than $100 per year. Excellent sets of marking devices, including ink, could be purchased for amounts of $1 to $3, but even these small costs were an unaffordable luxury for most offices.

The problem of a proliferation of nonstandard marking devices and the use of inferior inks continued to bother the Post Office Department, but it was unable to persuade Congress to provide the necessary additional appropriations to correct the problem. Nothing much was done to alleviate the situation until the 1870s, when the 1873 Postal Laws and Regulations (PL&R) provided that offices with more than $50 per annum would receive wooden handstamps; over $75 would get wooden handstamps plus a letter balance; over $100 would add paper and twine; over $500, an iron marking stamp. For others over $1,000, a steel duplex marking device would be included.

The following year the Post Office Department began to classify postmasters for the first time and designated all postmasters whose annual compensation (exclusive of money-order commissions) was less than $1,000 as fourth-class postmasters, and their offices received the same designation. Fourth-class post offices received no issued supplies or reimbursement for privately purchased items. In 1882, Congress finally appropriated $35,000 to furnish necessary supplies, including markers, to all post offices. It was not a sufficient amount to supply all of the approximately 10,000 fourth-class offices, but the Post Office Department supplemented the appropriation with funds from its other operations. For all practical purposes, every post office was, from that time, supplied with equipment or funds for reimbursement, and the use of manuscript notations and non-standard marking devices began to diminish [6:6-9].

While it is true that most of the post offices in the 1860s did not have marking devices, the total amount of mail processed by these offices was small compared to that of the larger offices, so the net result was that most mail did receive markings made from commercial stamping devices. Town and date markers required a degree of skill to engrave, but a canceling device could be a piece of cork or wood with a simple pattern etched with a penknife. For this reason, many of the small offices used homemade killers for canceling and manuscript notations for all other purposes.

Town and Date Markings

Regulations required that the office where mail was posted endorse or stamp each piece with the name of the post office and the day and month of mailing. The year date was not required, but manuscript postmarks and canceling devices frequently did include the year. Local drop mail often had no indication of origin or date of mailing. Since the letter did not leave the office until delivery, it was not considered to be necessary to mark the letter, other than to cancel the stamp. This practice was not unusual, particularly in the smaller offices.

Most of the stock town and date stamps that were supplied by the Post Office Department, or were privately ordered from government suppliers, are of two basic types: single- and double-circle markings containing the

Figure 7-1. Stock circular town and date marking in common use in the early 1860s.

name of the town and state, with the date in the center. They are called circular datestamps and are normally referred to by the initials, "CDS" or "cds." Of course, there are many other types, including straightline markings and fancy designs that were produced by private manufacturers of marking devices or by local printing firms. Again, because of the preponderance of mail at the larger offices, better than 75 percent of the letters processed in the United States will show one of the standard stock types of CDS.

Figure 7-1 illustrates the most common type used in the early part of the 1860s. It is a double concentric-circle CDS that was used in many towns. It is about 26mm in diameter (measurements of marking devices are usually given in millimeters and are measured between the centers of lines) for the outer circle and about 13mm for the inner circle. The illustrated Boston red CDS is a well-known example. Depending on the degree of wear and the way a mark was applied, there can be variations of as much as 10 percent in the measurements of a specific design. Richard B. Graham in his excellent article on "Town Datestamps" [7:13-26] mentions that at the time these devices were specified, the metric system was not used, and that the measurements were to be 1 inch for the outer circle and ½ inch for the inner circle. The inner circle of the marker contained the "logo," which printed the date with removable type that could be changed as necessary. This town mark is also found with the year included. Markers with the year date usually use slightly smaller type for the year in order to fit another line into the inner circle. While the town and state lettering is sans-serif, the date logo usually has serifs, and probably was assembled from a font of movable metal type. These stock cancels were in use at the beginning of the 1861-69 era and continued in use throughout the period.

Larger double-circle stock devices, with outer circle diameters of 28mm and 30mm, came into use in 1863. These markers were duplex devices that had the town marking and killer both mounted on the same stamping instru-

Figure 7-2. An early duplex town and date marker includes the canceling marker on the same device.

ment (**Figure 7-2**). The duplex markers were the result of Postmaster General Joseph Holt's regulation, effective July 23, 1860, that prohibited the use of town and date markers for canceling stamps. This meant that each piece of mail had to be struck twice, once with the town and datestamp and once with a canceling device. To avoid the extra time this required, the use of a duplex marking device, originally developed by Marcus P. Norton, became a common practice. More will be said about the Norton device in a later section on patent cancels. Preempting the issuance of the government duplex marker, the postmasters of both New York and Cleveland, and some other larger cities, designed their own markers.

John A. Dix was the postmaster of New York City at the time that the Holt order prohibiting the uses of town markers for canceling went into effect. Noting the extra labor that was required to cancel stamps, he wrote to Horatio King, the first assistant postmaster general, as follows:

"Post Office, New York, August 8, 1860

Sir: The order of the Postmaster General of the 23rd ultimo, prohibiting the canceling of postage stamps by the dotting [dating?] or post-marking stamps, and requiring the work to be done by a separate instrument, could not be executed in this office without an increase of our clerical force. We were compelled, a few days ago, to keep back a mail nearly half an hour in order that the postage stamps on the letters to be transmitted by it might be properly canceled.

When the letters amount to tens of thousands, the duplication of the work of canceling and post-marking is a very serious matter. On Monday our carriers and messengers brought to this office 11,985 letters for the mails. In this extremity, and with an extreme reluctance to augment the clerical force of the office for the purpose of doing the work, I have hit upon an expedient which answers the purpose perfectly. It occurred to me that the "separate instrument" required by the department might be attached to the post-marking stamp, and I sent for the stamp-maker and gave him my idea, which he has carried out very well.

The canceling stamp is soldered on to the other, so that one handle answers for both, and the double operation is performed with one blow. There is, therefore, no increase of work.

I send you a specimen of the work on the enclosed envelope.

Respectfully yours,
JOHN A. DIX"

Two days later, the acting first assistant postmaster general answered this letter and informed Dix that although the idea was excellent and would save much labor, it had been thought of before and had been patented. He warned that use of the device might subject the New York office to a heavy charge or lawsuit [8:178-81].

Postmaster Dix then made arrangements with Marcus Norton, who held the patent, for 10 of the duplex handstamps to be furnished to the New York Post Office. Only one of these Norton-type handstamps from New York, dated January 30, 1862, has been identified on cover with the 1¢ Franklin, and an illustration of this item is shown in the following chapter as Figure 8-38, with the discussion of patent cancels.

Examples of a New York and Cleveland duplex marking on cover are shown in **Figures 7-3** and **7-4**. The postmarks from the two cities are similar in size and lettering; however, the Cleveland device does not show the year. Various killers were attached to the town markers, and a wide variety of designs for the cancelers were used. These early duplex cancels are seen frequently and were used for some years.

Toward the end of the Civil War, a new design of town marker was issued by the Post Office Department and consisted of a single circle, about 24mm in diameter, containing the town and state names with a date, but no year, duplexed with a killer. **Figure 7-5** shows an example of this type of marking.

In addition to the somewhat limited variations in

Figure 7-3. An example of an early (July 4, 1863) duplex marking from New York City. The unusual 5¢ rate is possibly the result of a prepaid ship's letter entering the mails at the New York port.

The United States 1¢ Franklin 1861-67

Figure 7-4. Cleveland, Ohio, duplex marker, similar to the type shown in Figure 7-3, but without the year date. Marked "Due 2," this cover is franked with a single 1¢ Franklin and was probably mailed subsequent to the 1863 increase in the drop rate to 2¢. The letter was consequently assessed double the short-paid amount, as required by regulation. (James Lee collection)

Figure 7-5. A smaller duplex CDS that came into use subsequent to the previously illustrated devices. Serif lettering was no longer used on these stock markers.

the stock cancels, there were a tremendous variety of town and date markers that were procured by the individual post offices from commercial sources. During this period, several wood and metal engraving firms advertised and circularized small-town postmasters with offers of postal-marking sets with many different designs of CDSs and killers. In addition, many local printing establishments provided custom devices for their post offices. Some printers and engravers were also postmasters and,

from this fortunate combination, issued some of the more imaginative of the markings. One of the best known of these manufacturers was Edmond S. Zevely of Pleasant Grove and Cumberland, Maryland. Zevely was also a postmaster and was able to use his free-franking privileges to inexpensively contact many of his fellow postmasters.

One of the most unusual of the circular town and date marks of the era is to be found from a marker used in December 1862 at Washington, D.C. This marking, known as the Washington balloon town mark, is exceptionally large with a diameter of 36.5mm and is duplexed with a five-ring target killer. However, the most unusual aspect of the mark is that the lettering is not concentric with the outer circle. A photograph of a cover with three 1¢ Franklins and an indistinct strike of the balloon marking is shown in **Figure 7-6**. Also shown is a tracing from the cover that more clearly illustrates the marking. The last digit of the year-date marking is missing, as is the case in all of the known examples.

The actual year of use was unknown for many years

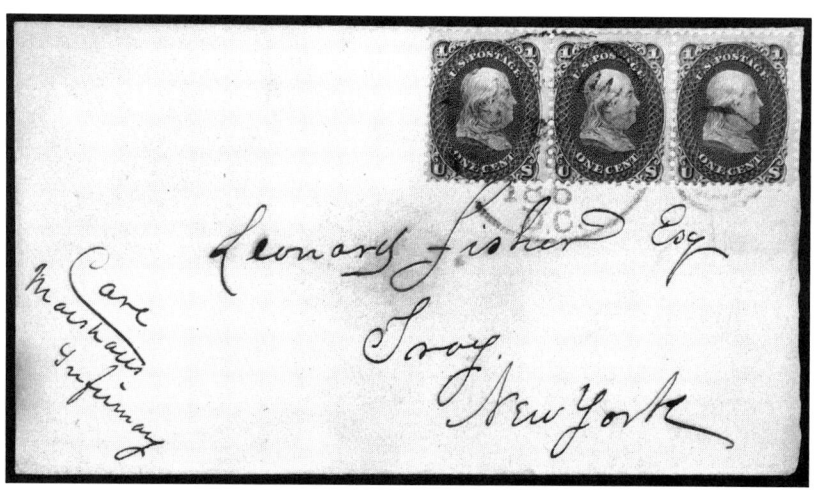

Figure 7-6. Scarce Washington, D.C., balloon town and date marker on a December 8, 1862, envelope, addressed to Troy, New York. Accompanying the cover illustration is a full-size tracing of the indistinct town mark and duplexed cancel. (Courtesy of Richard B. Graham)

Figure 7-7. Fancy blue town and date marker from Stony Creek, Connecticut, an example of the 3¢ letter rate. Note the interesting address endorsement, "please send by Freight Train to the care of John Lewis — Depot Master. Stonington."

until the cover illustrated in Figure 7-6 was reported in 1986. The cover contained an enclosure dated December 8, 1862, and consequently identified the year. The marking was used for a very short period and is relatively scarce. Richard B. Graham reported that the approximately 20 copies that he has seen were all used in the early part of December, probably 1862. He surmised that the short period of use may have been because the appropriate piece of type was not available to insert the missing year-date digit [9:194-5].

The PL&R of the era did not require a specific color of ink be used with the town and date marking devices, but the preponderance of markings are in black. Blue is the next common color and was used by many towns. Chicago, Cincinnati and Baltimore are three large towns where this was a favorite color for the application of markings. Red town cancels and datestamps are found for a limited number of towns. Boston, in the early part of the 1860s, combined a red CDS with a black killer on the majority of its outgoing mail. Green is a scarce color and was used only by a few towns. No other colors have been seen by the author, although some red markings tend toward the magenta, and some have faded to an orange color. Black ink was cheaper, easier to procure and did a better job of printing the necessary information compared to other colors. It was the choice for most users.

Although many of the markings look as if they could have been made with a rubber stamp, that is not the case. Rubber stamping devices did not come into use until the middle 1870s and were not common until the following decade. All town and date markers during the 1861-67 era were made of metal or wood, with possibly a very few being made from cork.

Privately procured town and date markers range from simple straight lines of letters to elaborate and framed designs. Both of these extremes are relatively scarce and avidly sought after. **Figure 7-7** shows a cover from Stony Creek, Connecticut, with a fancy town marking. In this case the town date marker was also used to cancel the stamp. For clarity, a tracing of the marking is also shown in the inset. The interesting endorsement on the letter, "please Send by Freight Train to the care of John Lewis - Depot Master. Stonington." is an indication that this cover may have been carried by other than the regular mail train to its destination.

Straightline town marks, or combined town and date straightline markings, were the earliest town-mark stamps to be used, but by the time of the 1860s, they had been mostly replaced by circular designs and were no longer common. Only a relatively few examples of uses of the 1¢ Franklin with straightline town markings have been recorded. These towns include Shed's Corners, New York, where the town marker was accompanied by an attractive star killer. An example of this use on piece is illustrated in **Figure 7-8**. Another attractive and scarce straightline town mark is from East Groveland, New York, and is shown in **Figure 7-9**. This marking is used additionally as a killer,

Figure 7-8. Straightline Shed's Corners, New York, on piece. This marking was usually accompanied by the fancy star killers as shown on this cover. The date was added in manuscript.

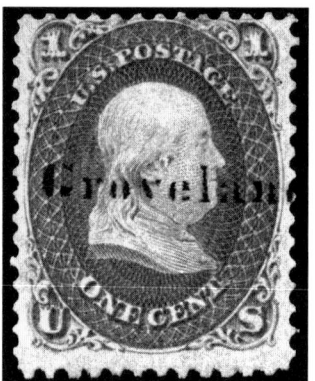

Figure 7-9. East Groveland, New York, straightline town mark in stencil lettering. The date was added in manuscript. This marking usually did double-duty as a cancel. The tracing below shows the actual size of the complete town mark.

East Groveland N.Y.

with the date added in manuscript. The author has also seen covers from Chattanooga, Tennessee, with a boxed straightline marking and franked with the 1¢ 1861, and a rare straightline from Churubusco, Indiana. It is probable that other examples exist, but they are not in the author's records. The simple, unspectacular straightline stamped town mark is probably the scarcest of all of the types of postmarks on covers with the 1861 1¢ stamp.

Received Markings

Postal regulations did not require the destination post offices to mark incoming mail with the place and date of arrival until 1879. This regulation applied to all offices except first-class offices, and in 1886 first-class offices were also included in the requirement for all letters to be backstamped with a receiving mark.

However, there are many earlier examples of received markings on covers during the 1861-70 time period. Boston used a small 19mm single-circle receiving mark from 1861-63 [4:297]. These are normally found on the face of the envelope and usually include the full date (**Figure 7-10**). A similar marking, but with a double circle and slightly larger at 21mm, used on cover in 1868 at Alton, Illinois, was illustrated as Figure 3-9 in Chapter 3.

Receiving marks, giving full information concerning place and date, were standard with most foreign post offices. Additionally, transit markings were applied at points along the route. It is unfortunate that the United States did not use similar procedures. The information would help answer a lot of philatelic questions.

Later receiving marks were similar to the standard 26mm single-circle stock town and date markings, but with the words "RECEIVED" or "REC'D" added. They were usually found on the reverse of the cover. It should be emphasized that received markings are to be found on only a very small percentage of domestic covers during the 1861-70 period.

Railroad Postmarks

Railway markings are found only on mail posted on the trains or at rail stations and, in rare cases, where the route agent applied his postmark to mail that had not been properly canceled by the originating post office. These markings appeared on only a very small percentage of the total volume of mail with the result that philatelic material with railroad markings is scarce. In particular, railway covers also showing the use of the 1¢ Franklin are very difficult to obtain. Compounding this scarcity is the fact that for some unknown reason, the use of railroad markings decreased substantially during the 1860-70 period in relation to both the earlier and later decades, where covers with railroad markings exist in larger numbers. This anomaly has been investigated by researchers

Figure 7-10. A local Boston cover with a small (18mm) receiving marking used in the early 1860s. The marking is normally placed on the front of the cover.
(James Lee collection)

in the field, but to date no satisfactory explanation has been found [10:XVI].

Railroad markings have been the subject of a number of excellent reference books. Charles Remele was one of the early pioneers in this research, and his text on the markings from 1837 to 1861 [11] remains the definitive study for that period. Charles Towle and Henry Meyer followed this up with a comprehensive treatment of the 1861-86 era [12], and Towle, in 1986, further enlarged and updated parts of this work to produce the currently most complete reference for railroad and waterway route agent and station markings of the 1861-86 period [10].

The U.S. mails and the railroads shared in the explosive growth of commerce and technology that took place during the 19th century, and the story of the tremendous impact that fast and safe rail transportation of mail had on communications is both fascinating and philatelically important. By 1861, the rail system had grown from 1,000 miles of track in 1838 to more than 20,000 miles of scheduled rail service. Congress had declared all railroads to be "post roads," which prevented any agency other than the Post Office Department from transporting mail on the rail cars. The Post Office contracted individually with railroad companies to carry the mail and provided postal employees, called "route agents," to accompany the mail.

Route agents were assigned to railroad mail or baggage cars to oversee the transport of through mail bags, and to receive, sort and deliver mail between local points on the route. If mail was received from station mail boxes, or given to them at stations, the route agent normally sorted these letters and applied a distinctive cancellation denoting the route and railroad. Route agents were also assigned to ships and steamboats on the waterway contract routes, where they performed the same functions.

Route agents were first used in 1837 and, with the expansion of the railway system, had an ever-increasing role over the years in the handling of mail. Although route agents did not have the duty of sorting or directing mail to destinations beyond the terminus of their routes, it was recognized in the early 1860s that the addition of this responsibility would expedite the transmittal of the mails. The normal way of directing mail was for the originating post office to sort and deliver mail for the local area, and also to forward mail addressed to offices on the route to the "distributing post office" (DPO). Mail addressed to distant locations was packaged and forwarded to the distributing post office to handle. DPOs were usually large post offices where a volume of mail was sorted and directed to post offices in their areas for further delivery or, if the mail was addressed to more distant points, to forward it to the appropriate distributing post office.

The postmasters of these distributing post offices received a commission for each piece of mail that was handled, and as a result, there was financial incentive to process and reprocess mail without regard for efficiency. It became common practice for each DPO to forward distant mail to the next DPO up the line, instead of determining the location of the correct regional distributing post office for final delivery and sending the mail directly there. This caused resorting and handling at each DPO with a resulting loss of time, and caused additional commissions to be paid. As early as 1850, the problems of cost and delay were recognized by the postmaster general's office, which reported that by the time some letters reached their destinations, so much money had been deducted from the postage revenue to pay postmaster commissions that there was little left for Post Office Department expenses [1:XLII]. In 1862 Postmaster General Mongomery Blair recommended the establishment of a railway post office system, where much of the sorting and directing work of the DPOs could be done by postal clerks on the trains. Such a system was soon initiated, and postal clerks began to replace the route agents, especially on the larger railroads.

Also in 1862 a successful trial of a mobile post office was conducted, and by 1864 the first permanent mobile post office was established on the Chicago & Northwestern Railroad. The offices were given the name "railway post offices," and the clerks performed the functions of the earlier route agents. In addition, they discharged many of the duties of a regular post office by sorting and routing mail, not only for the local traffic along the route but also for mails to destinations beyond the termination of the route. In this respect, they also replaced much of the work that had been done by the DPOs.

The system was very effective, and resulted in a faster and more efficient mail-distribution system at a lower cost. It was rapidly expanded to other rail lines, and by 1882, the postmaster general directed that all postal rail transport facilities were to be designated as railway post offices and the employees as railway postal clerks. This change was phased in over an extended period, and route-agent markings can be found on mail well into the 1890s.

The railway postal clerks were trained postal employees of the Post Office and were responsible for the operation of the railway post offices. All routes had special postmark devices for the use of the clerks, and these devices normally included the initials RPO to indicate that the marking had been applied at a railway post office [10:VII].

There are four basic categories of railway markings. The first group is the transit markings applied by a

Figure 7-11. A cover transported by the New York & New Haven Railroad. The railway marking is indistinct, and an enhanced tracing is shown at right. The cover carries 1¢ in postage for a probable carrier pick-up in New York plus 3¢ for the letter rate. There is no evidence that the letter passed through the New York post office, so it is possible that the carrier posted it at the train, where it was marked by the route agent. The same device was used to cancel the stamp, producing a deep impression in the 3¢ value, and breaking the fibers of the paper.

route agent. These include markings showing the name of the railway, markings that show only the names of the terminals at the beginning and termination of the route, and markings that add "AGT," "AG'T" or other similar terminology to indicate that a route agent had made the marking. Although route agents had been applying the handstamps since the early years, the word "agent" or equivalent did not appear in the marker until about 1875 and is rare after 1890. It is possible that this identification was added to the marker to definitely distinguish the agent marking from the railway post office marking. This author has never seen one of these markings used with a 1¢ Franklin, although such a use is possible.

Figures 7-11 and **7-12** illustrate two covers with railway name markings applied by route agents. In these examples the markings show the name of the railroad rather than the terminals of the agent's route. These covers both show a 4¢ rate, with the 1¢ stamps evidently paying for carrier service. In New York and Philadelphia, and likely in other large post offices with carrier service, mail that had been collected by the carriers and that was destined for another large office was put together, canceled and bagged at the carrier office of the originating post office. It was then delivered to a railway car by the carrier section and turned over to the route agent. The two illustrated covers probably were received in the originating post office after the bags were closed, and were carried along with the bags for subsequent canceling by the route agent. Examples of such use are rare. Although there is no way of absolutely determining the point of

Figure 7-12. The Morris & Essex Railroad was a 40-mile line running between New York City and Washington, New Jersey, where it connected with the Delaware, Lackawanna & Western Railroad. New York City and Philadelphia are the only cities on these routes with carrier service, so it is possible that the cover was posted at the train station in Philadelphia with the 1¢ to pay for carrier collection.
(C.W. Christian collection)

origin on the two covers shown, the routes of the railroads suggest that the cover in Figure 7-11 originated in New York City, and that the cover in Figure 7-12 was mailed in Philadelphia.

The second group of markings are those applied by the railway post offices and include the abbreviation R.P.O. An example of this type of marking is shown in **Figure 7-13**. Corner-card envelopes with railway markings are very scarce, and the "Stone Cutter" corner-card on the canary-yellow envelope also adds to its desirability. This interesting late-use cover also is an example of the reduction of the first-class rate to 2¢, which became effective on October 1, 1883. The cover is backstamped with a receiving mark dated December 22, 1886, which verifies the proper period of use for the reduced rate.

The third category is station markings. These are markings that show the name of a railroad and the name of a station on the route, together with the date. It is

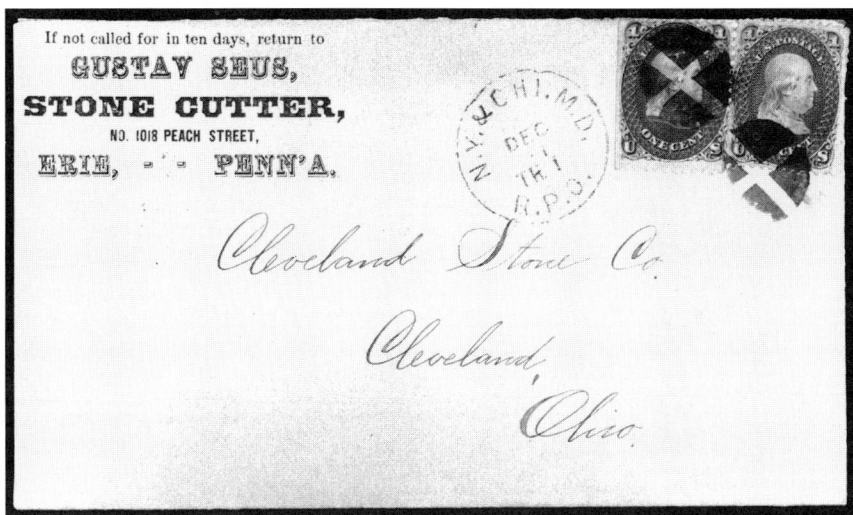

Figure 7-13. A very late use, showing the payment of 2¢ for the first-class rate that became effective in 1883. Postmarked with the R.P.O. marking for the Middle Division (M.D.) of the New York-to-Chicago route. The cover is dated December 21, with TR 1 for Track One. It is backstamped with a Cleveland, Ohio, receiving mark dated December 22, 1886, 3 AM, which makes it the latest regular postal use of the 1861 1¢ Franklin for which the author has a record.

Figure 7-14. Ilchester Station marking applied in lieu of a town marking at Ilchester Mills, Maryland. The letter rate is paid by three 1¢ stamps. (R.A. Siegel auction photo)

accepted that these markings were made with handstamps that were normally used by the railway station agent for stamping tickets and so on. They are usually found from small towns, and in many cases, both the postmaster and railway station agent have been identified to have been the same person. These markers were infrequently used as a canceling device, and all station markings are scarce and desirable philatelic items [13:80]. These are the rarest of the railway markings, and the largest number of examples is from from the Baltimore & Ohio Railroad during the war years. One of these markings, from Ilchester Mills, Maryland, on an 1863 cover franked with three 1¢ stamps, is illustrated in **Figure 7-14**. Another B&O Railroad marking, from Monrovia, Maryland, has been recorded. A photo of the marking, from a David G. Phillips' auction catalog, is shown in **Figure 7-15**. Both of these items may be unique with respect to use with the 1¢ stamp.

The last group of railway markings includes those markings that do not readily fall into one of the other three categories. An example is the interesting cover shown in **Figure 7-16**. This cover, with a Railroad Business (R.R.B.) corner card, was probably carried outside the mails on the railroad and entered into the mail at Warren, Ohio, where the stamp was applied to pay for local delivery. The question of whether a railroad could carry railroad-business correspondence without postage was never clear, and some post offices allowed free transit for this type of mail, while others required that postage be paid. On the cover shown, it is most likely that the postage stamp was added at the post office at Warren to pay for local delivery since the railway marking is not that of a route agent but rather the type that would be used by a railroad employee.

Of the thousands of railway markings that were applied from 1860 to 1870, only a limited number have been preserved. Of those, just a small fraction were used with examples of the 1¢ Franklin. Most railway markings were poorly struck and are difficult to read, so it is still

Figure 7-15. A cover showing a Monrovia, Maryland, station marking. Three 1¢ Franklins pay the domestic letter rate. The photo is cropped at bottom. (D.G. Phillips auction photo)

Figure 7-16. This railroad-business letter (R.R.B.) bears an Atlantic & Great Western Railroad, June 4, 1863, marking. The meaning of the 315 is not known, but may indicate the train or route number. The stamp pays the 1¢ drop rate at Warren, Ohio.

possible for the observant collector to find some of these gems in dealers' stocks where they have not yet been identified and are mixed with common town markings.

Auxiliary Postal Markings

These markings include a large number of types of handstamps that were used to convey rate information, status of the postal item or explanatory notices. Most of these markers are simple in design, but some examples with complex and attractive designs can be found. Many of these were briefly discussed in Chapter 6 with regard to the rates and fees involved.

Auxiliary markings can be divided into three general categories: markings that resulted from undelivery or delay in delivery, such as UNCLAIMED; markings that are related to the postal rate of the mail, such as DUE or FREE; and markings associated with a special service provided by the post office, such as REGISTERED. This last category will be covered in a later chapter. During the Civil War, special procedures were used for mail to and from the armed forces. Many of the following provisions were not applicable to soldiers' and sailors' mail, which is discussed in Chapter 14.

Delayed-delivery Markings

Every effort was made by the Post Office Department to deliver mail promptly to the addressee. Improper payment, incorrect addresses, illegible handwriting and uncollected mail were all problems that the post offices dealt with daily. Some covers show evidence of great effort expended by the postmasters and postal clerks to assure delivery. The service in 1861 was a far cry from the limited efforts that are currently provided for undelivered mail. Extensive regulations were written that covered every aspect of mail that was delayed or could not be delivered. Even mail that was sent to the Dead Letter Office (DLO) was carefully examined and returned to the sender or addressee if at all possible.

Outgoing mail markings include HOLD FOR POSTAGE, which was usually applied on mail where the prepayment of postage was omitted or underpaid, or where demonetized stamps were used. The practice of depositing unfranked mail with the post office was a carryover from the many years during which postage did not have to be prepaid. The Act of March 3, 1855, for the first time required prepayment for all letters except drop letters, and provided that lists of unpaid letters posted. If the writers of the letters did not pay the required postage within one month, the letter was to be sent to the DLO. In 1857 this practice was amended to require that the addressee be notified that an unpaid letter was being held and would be forwarded upon receipt of postage.

Figure 7-17 shows a reproduction of the type of notice that was sent to addressees to inform them a letter was being held for additional postage. The notice was enclosed in a "free" Post Office business envelope, but required the addressee to pay the return postage for the "held" letter.

Part-paid letters were treated differently. They were to be dispatched to their destination with the unpaid portion of the rate to be collected upon delivery (except where the underpayment was deemed to be intentional, when they were treated as being completely unpaid).

Attempts to contact the senders or recipients of unpaid or underpaid letters was very time-consuming and caused more expense to the Post Office than it gained in additional income. In his report to Congress, dated December 1, 1860, Postmaster General Holt commented on this fact and stated that the practice of notification of underpayment had been discontinued, and that all unpaid or underpaid letters would be sent at once to the DLO. He considered that this somewhat Draconian action would result in better compliance with the laws for proper prepayment of postage [14:213]. This procedure was codified in §16 of the Act of February 27, 1861, and returns of all letters "held for postage" were to be made at least once a week to the DLO.

Negligible improvement resulted from this change, and the DLO was soon inundated with unpaid or underpaid letters. Holt's replacement, Montgomery Blair, rescinded Holt's order and, on November 28, 1861, directed a return to the earlier procedure of notifying addressees of postage due.

The Act of March 3, 1863 (effective July 1, 1863) again amended some provisions of the prepayment law, and stated that underpaid letters were to be sent to their destination with double the amount of unpaid postage to be collected upon delivery. Totally unpaid letters, where the lack of payment was considered to be from neglect or accident, and where the writer could not be advised, could also be sent forward and charged with double postage. The previous policy of notifying the addressee was com-

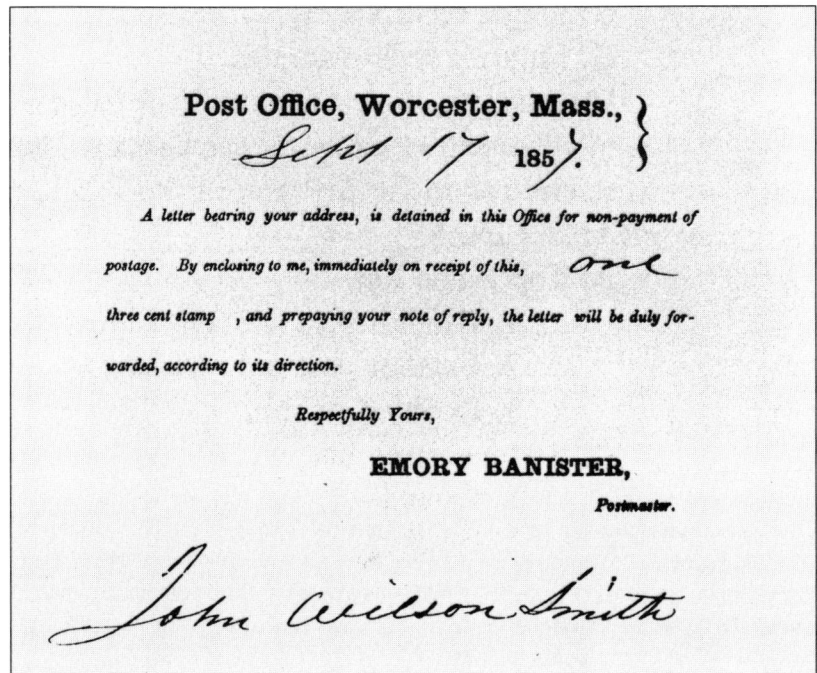

Figure 7-17. Standard form used by post offices to advise addressees that a letter to them was being held pending payment of additional postage.

Figure 7-18. A February 12, 1863, cover from Chicago, Illinois, with attempted use of a demonetized 1¢ 1857 stamp together with two valid 1861 1¢ Franklins to make up the 3¢ letter rate. The letter was held for payment, and later entered into the mails on February 15 with an additional 1¢ 1861 stamp added. HELD FOR POSTAGE, as shown on the tracing below, was stamped on the reverse. All markings are in blue. The manuscript "1070" is a file number applied at the post office to assist in locating the "held" letter.

pletely abolished.

In 1865, effective May 1, Postmaster General Dennison added to the regulations the requirement that if a letter with less than one full rate of postage was deposited, and the letter had upon it a request for return if not delivered, the letter would be returned to the sender and the stamps not canceled. The following year it was further required that deposited letters with less than a single full rate of postage and no return request be treated as held-for-postage letters and returned to the DLO.

With the many changes made in procedures and regulations over a limited period of time, it is not surprising to find many examples of letters whose handling did not precisely follow the regulations in force at any given time. A certain amount of leeway was afforded the postmasters and clerks in processing mail that did not meet the letter of the law with regard to prepayment. The underlying principles that were applied seem to be the intent of the sender, and the likelihood of achieving delivery and collection of any amounts due.

Letters being held in a post office pending payment of postage were usually postmarked with the date of original receipt and marked HELD FOR POSTAGE. When the money or postage was received, the necessary postage was applied to the letter, which was again postmarked and then entered into the mails.

Examples of this postal marking are quite scarce on covers with the 1¢ franking, and good complete strikes are difficult to find. The most prevalent use of the HELD FOR POSTAGE marking was the result of attempts to use demonetized stamps for postage during the early years of the Civil War. Several types of markings are known, usually with the words "held for postage" in a straightline marking or contained in an oval border. **Figure 7-18** shows a cover where an example of these markings was used.

This cover is of particular interest since it shows evidence of the procedure used to collect the underpayment. Post offices were furnished blanks to be sent to addressees, advising them that mail was being held pending payment of postage. In Chicago, a file system was evidently kept with a number assigned to both the advisory blank and the letter. The illustrated cover shows a manuscript "1070" in the upper left, and supposedly when the correct postage was received from the addressee along with the numbered blank, the proper letter was retrieved from the files, stamped, postmarked and sent on its way to the addressee.

Undelivered Mail

This includes mail not called for or where the addressee could not be found or, rarely, where the mail was refused by the addressee. In general, mail that was not delivered or picked up would be listed or advertised and, after a specified time, sent to the DLO. Exceptions to this general procedure existed and will also be discussed in this section.

Undelivered mail was the subject of many postal laws and regulations. In 1861, if a letter was uncalled for or the addressee not found at the given address, with no forwarding or return address available, the letter was to be advertised. Postmasters were instructed to contract with the local newspaper having the largest circulation for the printing of lists of letters that were being held at the post office for delivery. The newspapers were to be paid at the rate of 1¢ per name. If there was no local newspaper, which was true for many small offices, manuscript lists of undelivered letters were to be posted in public places.

The time that a letter was to be held before being advertised varied with the size of the office, from six weeks for offices with low revenues to once per week for the larger offices. Certain letters were excepted from the requirement for advertising. These included refused letters and drop or box letters. Advertised letters were charged a fee of 1¢ upon delivery to recoup the cost of the listing. If the letter had not been picked up within two months of the advertising, it was to be sent to the DLO in Washington. All letters returned to the DLO were required by regulation to be marked with the reason for nondelivery. These markings included UNCALLED FOR, NOT FOUND, NOT CALLED FOR and other similar wordings either alone or in combination. These notations provide much philatelic information concerning a cover, and an assemblage of the various markings on cover can add substantial interest to a collection. Examples of some of these markings are shown in **Figures 7-19** through **7-21**.

The postmasters kept careful accounts of letters returned to the DLO and were credited for them by the Post Office as processed letters in their annual compensation.

The Postal Law of 1860, for the first time, made provisions for the direct return of undelivered letters to the sender. If a letter was endorsed (handwritten) with the name and address of the writer, and there were no directions as to when an undelivered letter was to be returned, it was returned after the expiration of 30 days. If a request indicating a specific time for return was included, the request was honored. This type of letter came to be known as a "request letter." Printed corner cards did not require a return unless the printing specifically so stated. Additional postage at the usual rate was charged to the sender upon the return of a request letter.

Examples of this service are shown in **Figures 7-22** and **7-23**. A revision to this law was included in the postal law, approved July 1, 1864. It required that the originator of a "request letter" must accept the letter if returned and

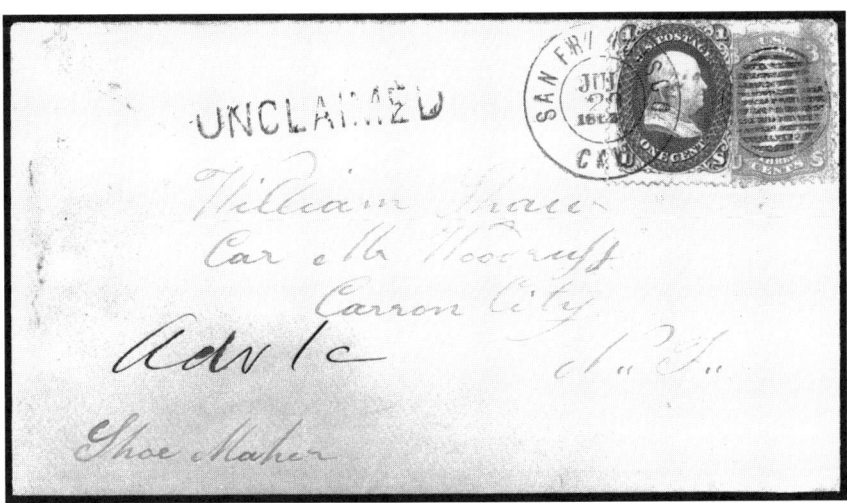

Figure 7-19. San Francisco, July 29, 1863, cover addressed to a "Shoe Maker" at Carson City, N.T. (Nevada Territory). The letter was advertised and marked "Adv 1c," but evidently never claimed. The cover is handstamped UNCLAIMED and backstamped "Carson City/Oct/1/1863/Nev T," for transmission to the DLO. It is franked with a 1¢ plus 3¢ for a 1¢ overpayment of the letter rate. Overpayment is possibly due to some public confusion about rates that resulted from the changes that became effective July 1, 1863.

Figure 7-20. An interesting cover with multiple auxiliary markings, from Buffalo, New York, May 7, 1893. It was received at Geneva, New York, on May 8, marked NOT CALLED FOR and ADVERTISED on May 16. Upon receiving the new location of the addressee, the postmaster forwarded the letter with the mark, FORWARDED 3, to Albany. The cover was backstamped Albany, July 6. The three 1¢ stamps paid the letter postage, and 3¢ for forwarding was to be collected upon delivery.
(James Lee collection)

Figure 7-21. Fancy advertised handstamp used at New York City. The letter was posted at Philadelphia on February 19, 1862, with the letter rate paid by three 1¢ stamps. The cover was held for delivery at the New York Post Office until March 16, 1862, when it was advertised, and then finally delivered.
(C.W. Christian collection)

Figure 7-22. A 1¢ drop letter retained by the postmaster at Dubuque, Iowa, for 49 days before returning to the sender in accordance with the printed instructions on the corner card. It was marked with a boxed RETURNED TO WRITER.
(James Lee collection)

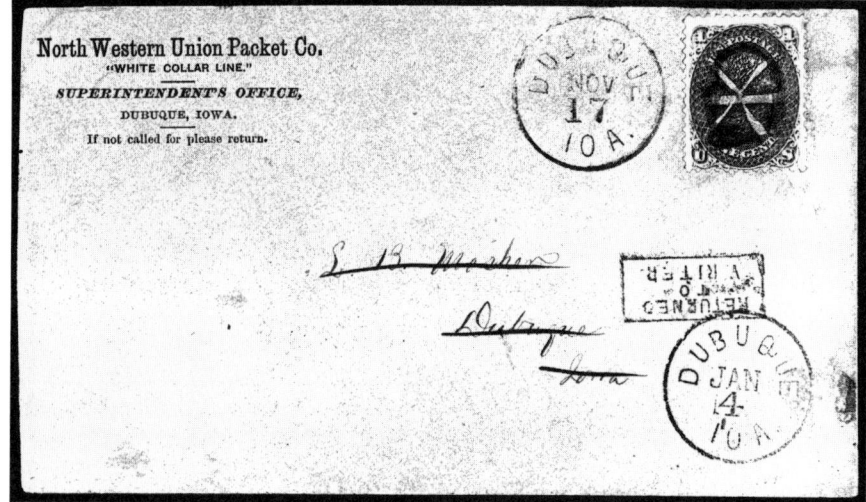

pay the additional postage required. Failure to do this could result in a $10 fine. **Figure 7-24** illustrates a drop letter where the sender requested a return if not delivered. The letter was stamped NOT FOUND, and returned. It is not clear in the regulations about a return fee being charged for properly paid mail on local letters that never left the post office, but there is no evidence on this cover of a return fee being assessed.

The omnibus revision to the postal laws, effective July 1, 1863, and the regulations accompanying them, made many changes in the way that undelivered mail was handled. It reduced the maximum time that a letter should be held before advertising from six weeks to one month, exempted letters sent to hotels from advertising, required that unclaimed and advertised letters be returned by small offices to the DLO one month after the date of advertising if still not delivered, and that such letters in the larger offices were to be sent to the DLO on a weekly basis.

Postmasters were given the authority to waive these requirements if they were reasonably assured that delivery could be accomplished at some later date. An example of this might be where an addressee was absent, but was expected to return after some extended period.

Instructions published by Postmaster General William Dennison on May 1, 1865, increased the advertising charge to be paid to newspapers and the charge to recipients of these letters to 2¢ [15:3] This increase was probably due to the inflationary pressures of the Civil War.

Forwarded Mail

Mail that was undelivered but where the addressee could be expected to be found at another place is usually denoted as "forwarded mail." Anthony Wawrukiewicz, in a *La Posta* monograph on the subject [16], made an argument for denoting this as "redirected mail," since the term

Figure 7-23. A late use mixed-issue franking with a 2¢ 1869 and a 1¢ 1861 making up the domestic letter rate from Albany, New York, April 2, to San Francisco, where it was marked RETURN TO WRITER on April 21 as requested by the writer's endorsement. The enclosure is dated April 1, 1875, after free forwarding went into effect, so there would be no fee collected for this returned letter.
(James Lee collection)

Figure 7-24. January 16, 1863, Rockford, Illinois, local 1¢ drop letter with endorsed request, "If not taken from post office, to be returned. (signed) Burnah S. Harvey." It is marked NOT FOUND and backstamped with the town marking on January 17 (the probable date of return to sender).
(C.W. Christian collection)

"forwarded" was used by the Post Office Department for many other procedures in transmitting mail. However, for the purpose of this discussion the time-honored term of "forwarded" is preferred.

In a constant attempt to improve delivery of the mails, many changes were made to the forwarding system over the years. In 1861 the regulations provided for a postmaster, if he had information concerning the new location of the addressee of an undelivered letter, to forward the letter to the new address and to charge the letter with additional postage at the normal rate to be collected upon delivery. An example is shown in **Figure 7-25**.

Postal regulations effective July 1, 1866, further liberalized the system with an authorization to forward first-class letters at no additional charge. It was stipulated that a written request for this service must be on file at the post office. This free forwarding was also extended to the return of unclaimed "request letters" and letters forwarded from the DLO. However, letters that were taken out of the post office, readdressed and then remailed were required to be franked with another full rate of postage. This was not changed until the late 1870s, when a readdressed letter, if promptly remailed, could be forwarded free of charge [7:67].

The Act of July 27, 1868, Section 15, further changed the law and stated that uncalled for letters would be returned without additional postage to the writer if they were endorsed on the outside with a name and address. No specific request to return needed to be stated. These procedures for forwarding mail continued without major change and are essentially those in effect today.

Missent Mail

Mail that could not be delivered because of an error on the part of the Post Office Department was considered to be missent. Examples of this would include mail sent to a city of the same name but in the wrong state, or to the wrong city. When this occurred, the letter was marked "missent" and forwarded to the correct destina-

Figure 7-25. Carrier-to-the-mails cover franked with 1¢+3¢, from New York to a doctor at the USA Hospital, Mansion House, Alexandria, Virginia. Forwarded on April 10, 1862, to a new address in Washington, D.C., the cover is marked with FORWARDED and DUE 3 for collection upon delivery.
(James Lee collection)

Figure 7-26. Boston, February 14, 1863, cover addressed to the Lincoln post office in Wabashaw County, Minnesota, with letter rate paid by three 1¢ stamps. By error, it was directed to Lincoln, Illinois, where it was marked "Missent" and forwarded at no charge to the proper destination.

Figure 7-27. An unsealed circular mailed at Boston, February 12, 1862, to Whitneyville (no state). The 1¢ paid the circular rate. The town was misread, and the letter was routed to Whitinsville, Massachusetts, where the mistake was noted, and the proper state (Connecticut) added to the address. No charge was made.
(James Lee collection)

tion at no additional charge. A cover showing this type of marking is illustrated in **Figure 7-26**. Another example is shown in **Figure 7-27**. Because the sender did not include the state in the address, the cover was delivered to a town with a similar but different name, and the postmaster forwarded it to the correct destination without assessing an additional fee. The hand-printed FORWARDED notation on the cover may be a later addition by some collector or dealer.

Dead Letter Office

In keeping with the Post Office Department's continued efforts to assure delivery of most letters to their proper destination, great emphasis was placed on following up on every undelivered letter. An intricate system was put into effect to accomplish this, and the postmaster general reported to Congress each year on the number of undelivered letters returned to the DLO and the number that were then put back into the mails after additional information concerning their writers or addressees had been determined. More space in postal laws and regulations was devoted to the subject of dead letters than almost any other consideration. Changes and refinements in the PL&Rs were constantly being made through the 1850-70 period to improve the efficiency and effectiveness of the system.

The DLO was located in Washington, D.C., during the period covered by this book. Branches had previously been maintained for short periods in San Francisco, St. Louis and Philadelphia, but had been discontinued.

The procedures for handling an undelivered letter were relatively straightforward, but the paperwork and packaging that accompanied the effort was extensive and time-consuming. For details concerning these, the PL&R effective July 1, 1863, provides extensive information in Sections 7 through 10 [17:5-7].

There were three basic classes of mail in the returns to the DLO: registered and valuable mail, unmailable letters and regular undelivered letters. These were all treated differently, with the regular undelivered mail sent directly to the DLO, while the other two classes were sent to the third assistant postmaster general for his consideration and subsequent forwarding to the DLO. Each of the classes of dead-letter mail had to be packaged separately, and within each class, there were further divisions and requirements for separate packaging. Valuable letters were to be registered at this time, even if this had not been done by the sender. Letter bills with exhaustive detail on the returned items had to accompany each of these. Each piece of mail was to be specifically marked in writing or stamped with the postmark of the returning office, together with the date of return on the sealed side of the envelope. The front was to be marked with the date of advertising (if applicable) and the specific reason for the return to the DLO.

An example of a letter returned to the DLO is shown in **Figure 7-28**. The letter was mailed with carrier pickup in Philadelphia on May 18, 1863, to its destination at Norristown, Pennsylvania. It was not called for by the addressee, and was advertised. With no response to the listing, it was then marked "Not Called for," backstamped Norristown, Pennsylvania, July 31, 1963, and finally sent to the DLO. It eventually must have been redirected or returned to the sender; otherwise, it would have been destroyed by the DLO.

Another cover illustrating this type of treatment is shown in **Figure 7-29**. It was mailed from Forrestville, New York, on December 22 to Olean, New York, with a corner card from the writer, who did not request return. The postmaster at Olean, therefore, advertised the letter, noting the date of advertising in manuscript. When there was no response to the advertisement, the postmaster noted "not called for," backstamped the cover, "Olean, Jan [indistinct date] N.Y.," and probably forwarded it to the DLO, where it was then returned to the sender. It

Figure 7-28. Philadelphia, May 18, 1863, cover with 1¢ carrier+3¢ postage paid. The cover was not called for at Norristown, Pennsylvania, and was advertised. It was backstamped July 31, 1863, for forwarding to the DLO and marked in manuscript with the reason for non-delivery. It was stamped with a large DLO marking for probable return to sender on October 10, 1863. (James Lee collection)

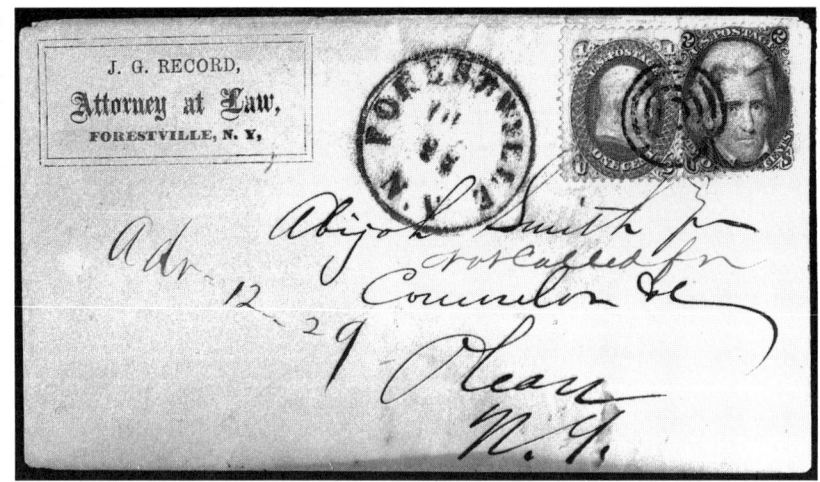

Figure 7-29. This cover was sent from Forrestville, New York, to Olean, New York. It was backstamped "Olean NY, Jan (?) 1864." It bears the manuscript notations, "Adv-12-29" and "Not Called for."

would have saved a lot of time and trouble if regulations had allowed the postmaster at Olean to directly return the letter to the sender with a "3¢ Due" notation instead of having it processed through the DLO since the return address was known. This needed change to the law was enacted in 1868.

Upon arrival at the DLO, mail was opened and read for clues to assist in redirecting the letters. There was a staff of nine clerks in the DLO in 1861, and these individuals were the only people who, under the law, could open mail addressed to others. Postmaster General Montgomery Blair reported to Congress that in fiscal year 1861 approximately 2,500,000 letters were handled by the DLO, and about 10 percent were redirected and returned with the single-rate postage due for the return of regular mail, and double rate for valuable letters. Of these, about 20,000 were valuable or registered letters. Of the number returned, over 90 percent successfully found their destination. Funds accruing from valuable mail that could not be returned, and that became the property of the Post Office after a period of time, financed the operation, usually at a slight profit.

In the annual report referred to above, Postmaster General Blair also recommended that because of the time-consuming operations that dead letters required, the fee for returning dead letters should be increased to double rate for regular mail and treble rate for valuable mail. This was put into effect in 1862, but had the unfortunate result that many recipients of dead letters, when found, refused to pay the higher fees and would not accept the letters. The incidence of refused letters increased, and the postmaster general in his 1862 report recommended that the DLO return fee for mail other than valuable mail be lowered to previous levels. This became effective on July 1, 1863, and the fee was reduced to a single rate for ordinary mail and a double rate for valuable mail.

By 1864 the amount of mail handled by the DLO increased to more than 3,500,000, and the amount of valuable mail even more in proportion. This was due primarily to war-related causes. The number of recipients who could not be found because of dislocations due to the war and the number of improperly mailed items increased tremendously. In addition, more valuable letters were being mailed by soldiers. Letters containing photographs or daguerreotypes were considered valuable letters, and many of these were being sent. The manning of the DLO was increased to 27 clerks and continued to operate at a small profit.

Although not intrinsically valuable, many letters originating from the armed forces in the field had great personal value. Third Assistant Postmaster General A.N. Zevely specifically instructed the DLO to reprocess soldiers' letters, and to send them again to the destination post office for another attempt at delivery without extra charge. It was realized that many of these letters may have been the last letters from soldiers or sailors who later died or were killed, and Zevely wanted every effort made to effect delivery.

Finally, in the act approved June 12, 1866, the fee for returning dead letters was abolished and letters were returned in FREE-franked envelopes. An example of a dead letter and the DLO return envelope is shown in **Figure 7-30**, where an unclaimed local letter to a Mr. Cunningham was returned to the sender.

Due Markings

Due markings are the most common of the auxiliary postal markings. Failure to affix sufficient postage on a mailed item, fees for forwarding or return of letters, fees for advertising, use of illegal stamps and collection fees on soldiers' letters were all possible candidates for due markings. Prior to 1855, when mail did not have to be

Figure 7-30. The upper illustration shows an unclaimed local letter posted at Charleston South Carolina, on January 1, 1869, and franked with a 1¢ E-grill. After an extended waiting period, it was backstamped with a FEB 6 postmark and sent to the DLO. The contents were a request for payment and identified the sender. On February 17, 1869, the letter was returned free by the DLO in the envelope pictured in the lower illustration.
(James Lee collection)

prepaid, markings with many different values were needed, and some of the markers were very elaborate and artistic. By the 1860s, with the requirement for prepayment in force, most of the high-denomination markers no longer were used, with the exception of occasional use as canceling devices. Markers with denominations of 1¢ through 6¢ were still needed, with the lower values being the most commonly used. There is certainly the possibility of a higher-denomination marking being used, but this author has never seen one used with the 1¢ Franklin. Manuscript due markings are more common than stamped impressions, and fancy designs are scarce.

Postal regulations in effect in 1861 required that underpaid letters were to be dispatched to their destination with the additional postage due at the prepaid rate (**Figure 7-31**), except when the underpayment was considered to be intentional. In that case the letter was treated as wholly unpaid and held for postage before dispatching.

On July 1, 1863, the new postal laws changed the above to require that if mail should arrive at its destination without having been properly franked, double the prepaid rate was to be charged and collected upon delivery. If the postage was partially paid, only the unpaid postage was to be charged at double rates (**Figure 7-32**). The penalty for intentional underpayment remained in force.

In May of 1865, these regulations were further amended to return to the earlier requirement that partially paid letters were to be forwarded to their destinations with postage due to be collected only for the unpaid portion of the postage. These regulatory changes and distinctions, depending on the intent of the sender, resulted in different interpretations of the laws and a resulting variety of charges. There was evidently a lot of individual discretion used by the postmasters and clerks in marking the amounts due, and the letter of the law was not always applied.

An interesting Boston carrier cover with an incorrect due marking is pictured in **Figure 7-33**.

Two different treatments of postage due where illegal stamps were used are pictured in **Figures 7-34** and **7-**

Figure 7-31. An October 31, 1862, letter from Amherst, Massachusetts, to Meriden, New Hampshire, franked with two 1¢ Franklins for the 3¢ letter rate. The cover was underpaid 1¢ and marked "Due 1" for collection.
(C.W. Christian collection)

Figure 7-32. January 1864 Hudson, Michigan, drop letter. The sender underpaid 1¢ of the 2¢ required rate, so double the underpayment was charged, and a "Due 3" marker was used with a manuscript correction to 2¢.
(C.W. Christian collection)

Figure 7-33. A March 5 (no year date) Boston letter with 4¢ prepaid was dispatched to Mount Morris, New York, where it was marked in manuscript, "Due 2." It is likely that the letter was posted with 1¢ for the carrier fee and 3¢ for domestic postage. The receiving post office may have determined that it was a double-weight letter and marked it "Due 2," mistakenly giving credit for the carrier fee as postage.

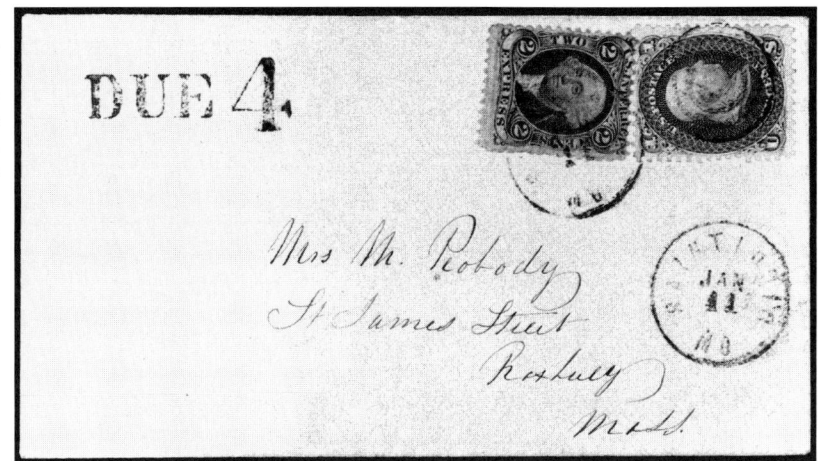

Figure 7-34. Illegal use of a 2¢ revenue stamp (Scott R9) with a 1¢ Franklin to make up the 3¢ letter rate resulted in a 4¢ penalty, equal to twice the underpayment, being assessed. (C.W. Christian collection)

Figure 7-35. February 16, 1864, illegal use of a revenue stamp (Scott R9) as in Figure 7-34. This time the underpayment was deemed to be intentional, and a double-rate penalty was assessed with no credit for the 1¢ partial payment.

35. The first cover, from St. Louis, shows the penalty being assessed as double the underpayment with the use of the illegal revenue stamp considered to be unintentional. The second cover gives no credit for the partial payment and doubles the normal postage rate as a penalty.

Leominster Labels

The Leominster, Massachusetts, adhesive labels are unusual enough to deserve special mention in this discussion of markings. Charles Colburn, the postmaster at Leominster, used adhesive labels to indicate postage due and other postal information such as advertised, registered, forwarded and missent [18:849-53]. These labels were used from the mid-1850s to the 1870s, and included a period subsequent to Colburn's tenure as postmaster.

From an examination of the labels on cover, it appears that they were made by applying a metal handstamp with the appropriate wording to a sheet of colored and gummed paper. The labels were cut from the sheets with scissors and applied to envelopes as needed. Space was left on specific types of labels to apply a stamp showing an amount or number, which might vary from cover to cover. A spectacular example, and one of the most prized of the Leominster label covers, is shown in **Figure 7-36**. This letter was written by a soldier on July 16, 1862, at "Camp near Harrison's Landing" (additional information concerning the date and origin was determined from a long letter enclosed in the cover). It was postmarked the same day at Old Point Comfort, Virginia, and dispatched to Leominster. The Leominster postmaster determined that the cover was overweight and should be double-rated. In addition, the addressee had moved to Northboro, Massachusetts, and the letter was to be forwarded. These circumstances caused the postmaster to affix two labels, one to note the underpayment and the other to establish the forwarding fee. Both labels were stamped with black ink on red glazed paper. A note in manuscript indicated that the letter was "Due 9 cts" upon delivery. It was then readdressed, marked with a red Leominster CDS dated July 21, and sent on its way to Northboro, where presum-

Figure 7-36. A spectacular example of use of the Leominster, Massachusetts, adhesive labels. This overweight letter was posted at Old Comfort, Virginia, on July 16, 1862. It was underpaid with only three 1¢ stamps. The cover was received at Leominster, Massachusetts, on July 21, where it was charged 3¢ for underpayment and also assessed 6¢ for the forwarding of the double-weight letter to Northboro, Massachusetts. (Wolffers' auction photo)

ably the postage due was paid and the letter delivered.

The large "3," shown on its side, is a well-known Leominster marking and was also used as a canceling device. The original metal handstamp is on display in the Leominster Library museum [18:852] and has been the subject of several articles. Labels are known on different colors of paper, and the numerical stamps also are found in colors. While a significant number of examples of the Leominster labels exist, those used with 1861 1¢ stamp are truly rare.

Free

The franking privilege, which allowed specific individuals and agencies to use the mails without charge, was another area where many laws and regulations were written and frequently revised. The free-franking system in the early 1800s was extremely generous. It allowed most senior government officials, military leaders, executive agencies and postmasters to mark their letters "free" and to not only send but also to receive letters free of postage. The loss of revenue to the Post Office Department and the widespread abuse of the franking privilege caused substantial restrictions to be written into the laws to curtail the number of people and agencies allowed to use franks, and the conditions under which mail could be sent free of charge.

Richard B. Graham, in an excellent and informative article on free mail [7:163], defines free-franked covers as "covers bearing the signature of a public official, where the signature serves in lieu of a postage stamp." While this definition covers the case where a letter is sent under the franking privilege, it does not cover the many cases where it was proper to send a letter to a public individual or agency without payment of postage. In these cases, the sender endorsed the letter as being "free" and "on official business."

Postmasters were normally granted special provisions under the franking laws. Laws in effect in 1861 provided that personal correspondence of low-income (less than $200 per year) postmasters could be sent free of charge, subject to a half-ounce weight restriction, and applied to mail being received or sent. This generous franking privilege was further limited in 1863, and postmasters could only send free mail after July 1, 1863, if it was official business and so endorsed. Reception of free mail was no longer provided for under the new statutes.

The Civil War substantially increased the amount of free mail, and almost all official military and naval mail was carried without charge. **Figure 7-37** shows an example of a war-time official letter franked by Admiral Foote, chief of the Bureau of Equipment and Recruiting at Washington, D.C. The cover departed Washington on December 2, 1862, as postmarked and with the postage paid by the free frank. The addressee, the captain of a ship that was being refitted at Philadelphia, had left for Washington before the letter arrived. The letter was readdressed at destination and sent back to Washington with the addition of a 1¢ stamp to pay the carrier-collection fee at Philadelphia. It was postmarked at Philadelphia on December 10 by three strikes of the octagonal Philadelphia U.S. PENNY MAIL carrier postmark, and received a boxed FREE handstamp to indicate that the postage for the return trip was also paid by Admiral Foote's free frank.

The Post Office Department was reimbursed by the Treasury for the costs of transporting free mail matter, and for 1863 this amounted to the sum of $700,000, which was about 6 percent of the entire annual budget for the Post Office, and consequently an item of considerable

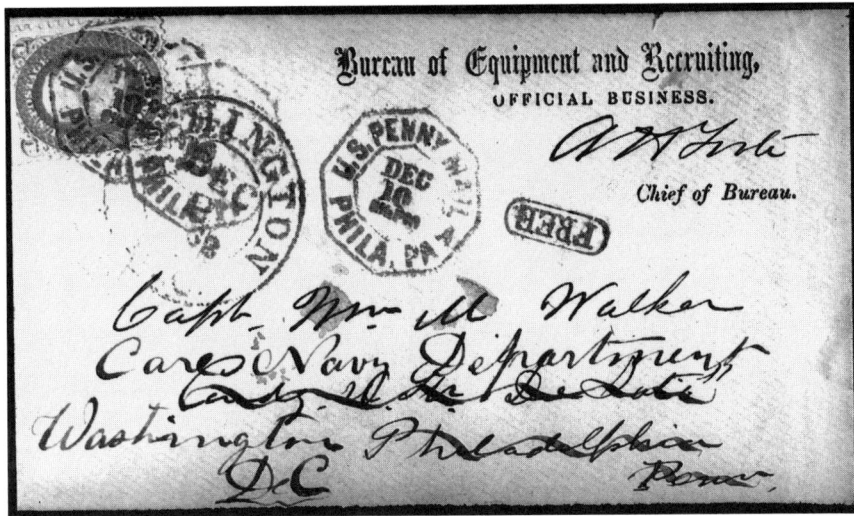

Figure 7-37. Official wartime correspondence mailed under the free frank of the chief of the Bureau of Equipment and Recruiting, postmarked DEC 2 1862 at Washington. The cover was addressed to Philadelphia. It was readdressed back to Washington with the addition of a 1¢ stamp to pay the carrier collection fee. It bears Philadelphia carrier postmarks dated DEC 10. The "Free" handstamp shows that forwarding postage was paid by the frank.
(Richard B. Graham collection)

Figure 7-38. Illegal use of a previously used 3¢ 1861 stamp on a January 22, 1863, mourning cover from Philadelphia to Woodbury, New Jersey. The valid 1¢ Franklin paid for carrier pick-up. "Free Service" was authorized by postmaster's franking.
(Photo courtesy of Richard B. Graham)

importance.

A most unusual mourning cover showing an unauthorized use of free service was brought to the author's attention by Richard B. Graham and is shown in **Figure 7-38**. This letter was posted in Philadelphia for carrier collection and addressed to Woodbury, New Jersey. The 1¢ stamp paying the carrier fee was proper, but the 3¢ stamp for payment of the postage rate had been previously used. It had been cut from its original envelope and then pasted on the cover. It is also possible, according to Graham, that since the stamp is composed of two torn halves that are pasted on the cover, it may have been reconstructed from the uncanceled parts of two previously used stamps. This illegal use of the stamp was obviously recognized, but a postmaster (location unknown), being unusually generous for a postal employee, applied a manuscript notation stating "Free Service, H.M.B., P.M." This allowed the letter to be delivered to its destination without a penalty or postage due charge.

The black border on the envelope, indicating that it was probably a letter of condolence to someone in mourning, may have resulted in this rare approval of illegal use.

Most letters sent or received under the free-mail privileges do not have any postage applied to them, and therefore are not appropriate to this text. The free-mail provisions, however, did not authorize the payment of carrier fees, and in some cases did not allow for overweight mail. Mail that fell into these categories had to have postage stamps applied, and the presently available "free" covers that show examples of the 1¢ Franklin are almost all covers where carrier use required payment.

Figures 7-39 and **7-40** show two examples of free letters mailed to postmasters with carrier service used for delivery to the mails, and **Figure 7-41** illustrates the personal franking privilege of a former vice president of the United States.

A cover with the free frank of former President Martin Van Buren is shown in **Figure 7-42**. Van Buren

Figure 7-39. August 26, 1862, cover from Philadelphia to the postmaster at Kirk's Mills, Pennsylvania. The 1¢ stamp paid for the carrier service to the post office in Philadelphia, where the cover was marked FREE, and dispatched.

Figure 7-40. New York City cover to the Cutchogue, Long Island, New York, postmaster. The 1¢ postage paid the carrier fee. The cover was endorsed "Free" and struck with a New York, May 7, FREE circular date marking.
(James Lee collection)

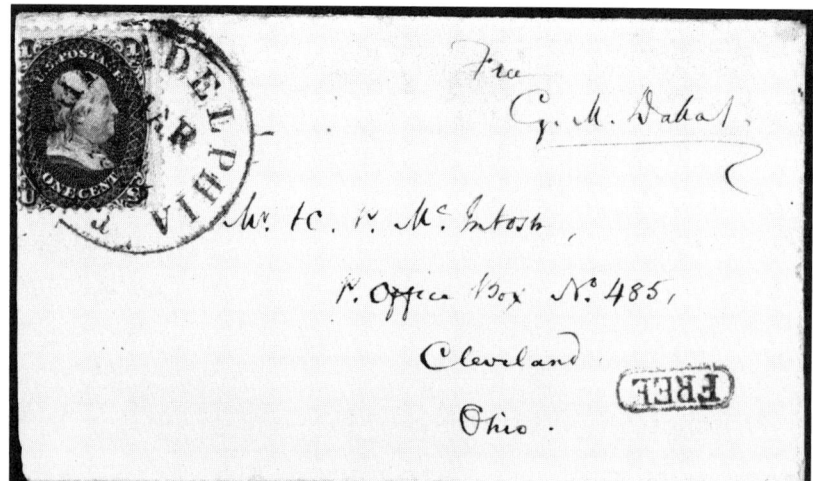

Figure 7-41. This cover was free-franked by George M. Dallas, who had been vice president under Polk, and who was entitled to life-time franking privileges. The 1¢ stamp paid for carrier service.
(James Lee collection)

Figure 7-42. Martin Van Buren, eighth president of the United States (1836-1840), franked this letter just two months prior to his death on July 24, 1862. The 1¢ Franklin paid for the carrier collection at New York.
(Richard B. Graham photo)

resided in New York in his later years, and frequently used the carrier service to mail his letters. This provided a number of free-franked covers with the 1¢ Franklin for today's collectors. While not rare, they are scarce and command premium prices. This particular cover was written two months before Van Buren's death on July 24, 1862, and is one of the last letters that he wrote.

A series of increasingly restrictive measures continued to be written into the postal laws and regulations with the intent of both decreasing the abuses of the system and the amount of mail that could be sent free of charge. In 1873 the free mails were discontinued, and the Official stamps of the United States were issued to take their place, with the hope that they would provide better accountability. These were also found to be unsatisfactory and were discontinued after a few years to be replaced by penalty-clause envelopes. In spite of the many changes made in both laws and procedures, the problem of free mail is still with us today, and is exemplified by the huge amounts of mostly self-serving mail sent out from Congress daily.

References

1. Alexander, Thomas J., ed. *Simpson's U. S. Postal Markings*. U.S. Philatelic Classics Society Inc. 1979.

2. Herst and Sampson. *Fancy Cancellations on Nineteenth Century United States Postage Stamps*. Herman Herst Jr. 1963.

3. Skinner, H.C. and Eno, Amos. *United States Cancellations, 1845-1869*. American Philatelic Society. 1980.

4. Blake, Maurice C. and Wilbur W. Davis. *Boston Postmarks to 1890*. Quarterman Publications reprint. 1974.

5. Baker, J. David. *The Postal History of Indiana*. 1976.

6. Stehle, Randy. "20th Century Non-Standard Postmarking Devices." *La Posta*. May 1990.

7. Graham, Richard B. *United States Postal History Sampler*. Linn's Handbook Series. Linn's Stamp News. Sidney, Ohio. 1992.

8. Graham, Richard B. "Beginnings of the Duplex-Style Handstamps, 1859-62." *Chronicle*. August 1991.

9. Graham, Richard B. "The Washington Balloon Town Mark of Civil War Days." *Chronicle*, August, 1986.

10. Towle, Charles L. *U.S. Route and Station Agent Postmarks*. Mobile Post Office Society. 1986.

11. Remele, Charles W. *United States Railroad Postmarks 1837-1861*. American Philatelic Society Unit 11 (U.S. Philatelic Classics Society). 1958.

12. Towle, Charles L. and Meyer, Henry A. *Railroad Postmarks of the United States 1861 to 1886*. U.S. Philatelic Classics Society. 1968.

13. Towle, Charles L. "Baltimore and Ohio Railroad Station Markings." *Thirty-third American Philatelic Congress Book*. 1967.

14. Norona, Delf, ed. *Cyclopedia of United States Postmarks and Postal History*. Quarterman Publications reprint. 1975.

15. *Reports of the Postmaster General for 1861, 1862, 1863 and 1864*. Reprints from official sources. Theron Wierenga. Holland, Michigan. 1977.

16. Wawrukiewicz, Anthony S. *Redirected Mail. La Posta* Monograph Series, Volume 9. 1993.

17. *List of Post Offices in the United States, 1862, including Various Postal Laws and Instructions of 1861, 1863, 1864 and 1865*. Reprint from original sources. Theron Wierenga. Holland, Michigan. 1981.

18. Jarrett, David L. "Leominster, Massachusetts Adhesive Labels." *American Philatelist*. September, 1978.

CHAPTER 8

Cancellations

Introduction

The many and varied cancellations affixed to postal items of the Civil War period have furnished collectors with some of the more interesting examples of contemporary postmasters' art as well as information concerning the origins, dates and services that were provided for these items.

While town markings had been used for many years, it was not until the advent in the United States of the adhesive postage stamp in the early 1840s that cancellations became a necessity. Cancellations have been recorded on the stamps of the City Despatch Post as early as 1842, and the 13-bar red grid of the New York City Post Office is known on the New York City provisionals prior to the first general issue of the U.S. postage stamps in 1847. However, it was this issue that initiated the need for canceling devices throughout the country.

A brief review of some of the postal regulations that covered the subject of canceling stamps is of some interest, even though these regulations were not rigorously followed in all cases. The individual postmasters of the era used a great deal of originality in their cancellation procedures, and the results left philately a legacy of interesting, and sometimes extremely attractive, designs and markings. These can be an important complement to any collection of classic U.S. stamps.

The first mention of cancellations appeared in the 1847 "Regulations for the Government of the Post Office Department" under the order of Postmaster General Cave Johnson. The regulations reiterated a standing requirement that all letters were to be marked with the date and place of origin, and in Section 501, stated the following:

> "Stamps so affixed are to be immediately canceled in the office in which the letter or packet may be deposited, with an instrument to be furnished to certain of the post offices for that purpose. In post offices not so furnished, the stamps must be canceled by making a cross X on each with a pen. If the canceling has been omitted on the mailing of the letter, the Postmaster delivering it will cancel the stamp in the manner directed, and immediately report the postmaster who may have been delinquent to the Department [1:70]."

As implied in the regulation, only the larger post offices were supplied with canceling devices. The smaller post offices followed the instructions for manuscript canceling or more often purchased or devised their own canceling instruments. The postal-marking devices from the pre-stamp period, such as "PAID," "5" and so on, were often used, as were designs cut from wood or cork. In the better-financed offices, there were often a variety of commercial canceling devices that could be purchased by the postmasters with their personal funds.

Substantial fines and penalties were assessed for the reuse of a postage stamp or a stamped envelope. This fraudulent action could result in a fine of $50, and the regulations of 1857 stated that stamps cut from stamped envelopes lost their legal value and could not be used to frank mail.

Section 336 of the above postal regulation enlarged on the regulations of 1847 by stating:

> "All postage stamps affixed to letters, packets, or parcels of any description, and all stamped envelopes must be immediately and effectually canceled . . . The cancellation should be effected by the use of black printer's ink whenever that material can be obtained; and where it cannot, the operation should be performed by making several heavy crosses or parallel lines upon each stamp with a pen dipped in good writing ink."

Section 338 added:

> "The use of the office dating or postmarking stamp as a canceling instrument is prohibited unless it be used with black printer's ink, and in such manner as thoroughly to effect the object [2:84]."

While it is obvious that the Post Office was concerned about the canceling process, the instructions did not provide for many alternative methods, and the lack of instructions did not deter many of the offices from canceling by their own favorite method. As long as the stamp or envelope was satisfactorily canceled so it could not be reused, it was sufficient for most postmasters and postal clerks.

Of course, reuse is almost always possible if the proper materials and procedures are used to remove the original cancel. The Post Office Department was ever sensitive to possible loss of income, and the potential of revenue being lost by the reuse of postage stamps seems to have been a constant worry. The experimental printings covered in Chapter 4 and the patent cancels that will be later discussed in this chapter were part of the effort to eliminate any illegal use of postage stamps. Postal stationery or stamped envelopes were not as much of a problem since it was usually easy to determine if the envelope had been previously used or if the stamp had been cut out and pasted on another envelope (which was, and is now, illegal).

Most of the types of cancellations of the era can be found on the 1861 1¢ Franklin, and there will be no attempt to describe or illustrate all of these varieties. A representative selection of cancellations will be discussed, and a few that are known only on the 1¢ value. In general, the scarcity of individual cancels on the 1861 1¢ denomination as compared to the 3¢ value is about 1 to 150. This is a result of the difference in numbers produced and used of each value, and the fact that many of the 1¢ stamps were used for circulars and local mail where the application of proper cancellations was frequently omitted.

Most canceling designs were made from wood or cork, and a few were made of metal. The metal types were normally used at the larger offices where constant use required resistance to wear. Cancels can be found in many shapes and patterns, and these variations produced a treasure trove of desirable philatelic items. Among the most sought-after cancels are those in the "fancy cancel" category. A fancy cancel, as the name implies, is a relatively complex design, usually cut into a cork or wood canceler. Although some were purchased from canceling-device manufacturers, particularly in the later years of the era, most were made by postmasters or postal clerks. The imagination and artistry of these individuals produced the many designs that decorated the stamps of the classic period.

Cork was one of the easiest materials to carve and was used for many of the fancy cancelers. However, it had the disadvantage of wearing rapidly and breaking easily. The resulting cancel impressions varied in appearance over their lifetime, and normally were used for only a short time before being replaced with another similar carving or an entirely new design. Wooden cancelers lasted longer but also showed distinct signs of wear over their lifetime.

Several good reference texts have been published on the subject of cancellations of the classic stamp era. A recommended source for information is *United States Cancellations 1845-1869* by Hubert C. Skinner and Amos Eno [3]. This text should be a part of the reference library of contemporary collectors of classic stamps. A new cancellation reference book by James Cole, covering the 1870-94 period, has recently been published by the U.S. Philatelic Classics Society [4]. Although the Cole book covers a later period, the 1861 and 1867 issues continued to be used during the early 1870s and occasionally at later dates.

In this chapter the subjects of fancy cancellations, patent cancels, colored and manuscript cancels, precan-

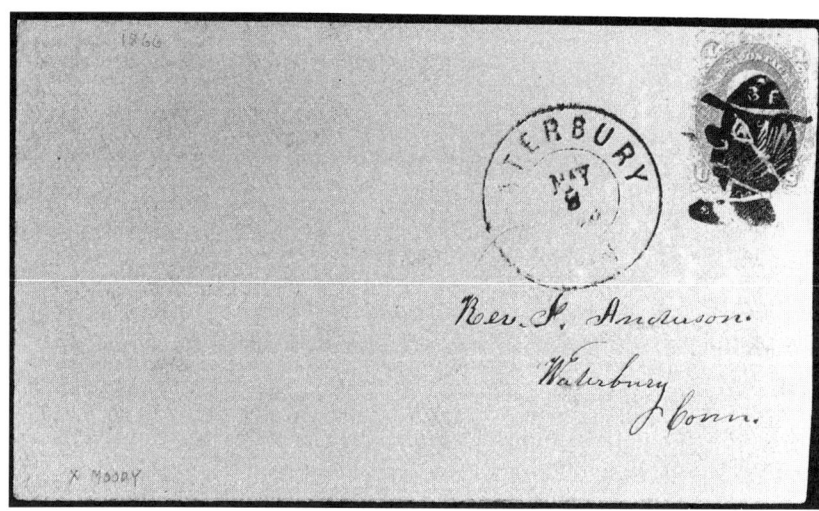

Figure 8-1. Waterbury, Connecticut, "Bridgeport Fireman" on yellow cover dated May 8, 1866. The 1¢ Franklin pays the local rate. The cover is annotated "X Moody." (Kelleher auction photo)

cels and postal markings used as cancellations will be covered. Selected examples of each type will be illustrated.

Fancy Cancellations

The most outstanding series of fancy cancels were a product of the Waterbury, Connecticut, Post Office. Over a period of 25 years, from 1865 to 1890, a large variety of figures were carved and used at this office. The cancels are known for their workmanship and the originality of their designs. Some were made to commemorate a special occurrence in the town, such as the carving of the "Bridgeport Fireman" shown in **Figure 8-1**. This marked the visit to Waterbury by members of the Bridgeport, Connecticut, fire brigade in April 1866. Others probably had no special significance other than a reflection of the whittler's whimsy of the moment. In general, the Waterbury cancels command a substantial premium, and the most valuable example has realized a six-figure price.

The talented hand that carved most of these attractive designs belonged to John W. Hill (**Figure 8-2**) who was known locally for his artistry with a penknife. Hill had been a regimental postmaster during the Civil War and, at the end of hostilities in 1865, joined the Waterbury Post Office as a postal clerk. He immediately put his flair for whittling to work, and over the following years produced dozens of distinctive cancellations. He was promoted to postmaster in 1869, and although he still carved an occasional cancel, the majority of his more elaborate and famous designs were made prior to this time.

The major current philatelic reference work on this subject is *The Waterbury Cancellations* by the late Paul

Figure 8-2. John W. Hill, postmaster of Waterbury, Connecticut (1869-86), who carved the majority of the fancy designs used in that city in the post-Civil War years.

Figure 8-3. "Congress gaiter," a type of shoe with an elastic side-opening. This cancel was used at Waterbury, March 19-27, 1870.

Figure 8-4. "Woman in Snood," on piece, used on a grilled 1867 stamp, and dated February 15, possibly 1870. (Richard B. Graham photo).

C. Rohloff. Much of the information in this section was derived from that source. Other earlier works were also consulted, and there is no doubt the "Waterburys" are the most heavily researched and publicized of all fancy cancellations. According to Rohloff, Hill carved his designs in cork and was afforded an opportunity by the local drug store to inspect each new shipment of corks that it received to select the best specimens for use in his cancels [5:3].

For a half-century after they were used, the Waterbury cancellations received little attention by collectors. Then, in 1919, Ray Sanborne, a Waterbury resident who had some of the strikes in his collection, attempted to find out more about them. He was able to establish the identity of the originator and had the opportunity to meet with Postmaster Hill, who was then retired. Another Waterbury resident, J.P. Elton, also began studying the cancels and wrote several articles in early philatelic journals. As a result of these pioneering efforts, the Waterbury cancels began to gain recognition and value.

Although it had been presumed that many of the designs were used in some type of sequence, Hill said that as they were carved, they were tossed in a drawer and removed at random when needed. Exceptions to this practice occurred for cancels for a special date, such as the Bridgeport firemen's parade previously mentioned. When a carving became worn, it was tossed in the pot-bellied stove, and another design from the drawer put in its place. Unfortunately, the Waterbury Post Office burned to the ground in 1902, and any records or examples of the devices were destroyed.

In spite of the many designs that were produced, and the output of a reasonably large post office, the number of Waterburys that can be found on the 1¢ Franklin is relatively small. Of course, the use of the 1¢ Franklin diminished rapidly after 1870, so the main period for use with the 1¢ was only about five years. There are probably only a dozen or so examples of the more artistic designs recorded on the 1¢ 1861, and the majority of these are off-cover and rarely show a complete strike. An off-cover example of a unique design, the "Congress gaiter," is pictured in **Figure 8-3**. This particular cancellation is known to have been used at Waterbury from March 19-27, 1870.

Another striking representation, on piece, called "Woman in Snood" is shown in **Figure 8-4**. Waterbury pictorials on patriotic covers are very rare, and an outstanding specimen showing the "Man Wearing Hat" cancel is illustrated in **Figure 8-5.**

A listing and drawings of the designs found on the 1¢ has been compiled by C.W. Christian from various sources, and an adaptation of his work is shown in **Figure 8-6**. The drawings are not life-size. The code with each design is from the Rohloff identification system, and the rarity values are Rohloff's estimates of the scarcity of the strike. These rarity values were established by including strikes found on all the stamps from the different issues during the 1865-90 period. Waterbury fancy cancellations on the 1¢ Franklin are significantly more scarce than the numbers in these estimates. The listing is not complete, and there are other Waterbury designs to be found on the 1¢, particularly geometric, leaf, rosette and letter motifs, which are less spectacular than the pictorial designs.

Figure 8-5. Waterbury "Man Wearing Hat" on patriotic cover dated April 21, 1866. The 1¢ Franklin pays the local drop rate.
(Kelleher auction photo)

Figure 8-6. Selected Waterbury cancellations recorded on 1¢ 1861-67 stamps.
(C.W. Christian)

A-4. Dog
1866 (<9)

E-3. Soldier's Head
1866 (<9)

E-5. Man with Hat
1866 (<6)

E-6. Brideport Fireman
1866-69 (<9)

E-12. Woman in Snood
1870 (<6)

F-13. Shamrock
1865 (<6)

G-1. Pumpkin
1868-69 (<15)

H-19. Circular Grill
1867-69 (<9)

J-8. Circle of Hearts
1869 (<9)

J-9. Hearts & Diamonds
1867 (<6)

K-1. Letter A
1866 (<9)

K-15. Letter W
1866 (<15)

L-2. 3-sectioned Leaf
1866 (<15)

O-6. Mortar & Pestle II
1869 (<6)

O-7. Mortar & Pestle III
1869 (<6)

O-10. Congress Gaiter
1870 (<6)

P-28. Rosette
1869 (<9)

R-1. Skull & Crossbones
1866 (<6)

R-5. Andrew Johnson
1869 (<6)

S-2. Star
1865 (<15)

Cancels similar in appearance to this last group are common to many post offices, and establishing that a particular off-cover design of this group originated at Waterbury can be extremely difficult and, at times, impossible. Hubert Skinner has informed this writer that he has a Waterbury "barrel" on a 1¢ Franklin. It is on piece and was used on November 9, 1867. It is listed as design "PO-Bb 5" in the Skinner-Eno book. This is an addition to the designs found on the 1¢ Franklin that was shown in Figure 8-6.

An outstanding Waterbury cover was offered in September 1993 by Christie's of New York. This particular item is illustrated in **Figure 8-7**. The cover was part of the Ishikawa collection and sold for an auction realization in the five-figure range.

Figure 8-7. Waterbury "Skull and Crossbones" cancel on a bright blue 1¢ Franklin for local delivery. Ex-Jackson and Ishikawa.
(Christie's New York auction photo)

The post office at Waterbury was the most prolific of the offices that produced fancy canceling designs, but it was not alone. Thousands of fancy cancels were hand-carved or purchased from commercial die makers and used by the clerks and the postmasters of the period, with many of the designs exceeding those of Waterbury in beauty and complexity. Pictorial designs such as the Corry, Pennsylvania, "eagle" and the Hockanum, Connecticut, "fox" are very rare on the 1861 1¢. This is probably because pictorial cancels are very scarce on any stamp, and the majority of examples are to be found on the more common 3¢ value.

A few representative cancellations will be illustrated and described here as a sampling of the many attractive fancies that can be found on the 1¢ Franklin. All cancellations are in black unless noted otherwise.

Figure 8-8 shows a fancy geometric design of the type that was used at the New York City Post Office on foreign mails during 1861-70. These designs were never duplexed with a postmarking device and, because of the frequency of use, wore out quickly and were replaced with succeeding designs. This particular cancel is known to have been used in 1868. Similar designs in duplex markers were used on domestic mail. New York City used a large number of complex geometrics during this period, and because of the volume of mail that was processed through the office, a significant number of covers and stamps with these attractive designs are currently available.

Figure 8-9 illustrates a very desirable deep-ultramarine stamp with unusually large margins and a fancy segmented-circle cancellation. Stamps with wide margins,

Figure 8-8. New York City fancy geometric used at New York City in 1868. Scarce on 1¢ Franklin.

Figure 8-9. Segmented circle-within-a-circle cancel. Origin unknown.
(Steve Ivy auction photo)

fine color and an attractive cancel are very difficult to locate and are very much in demand. The origin of this cancellation is unknown. Tracking down the origin of specific designs is one of the interesting challenges of collecting fancy cancellations, and there are still a significant number of attractive or unusual designs for which the source has never been identified.

Figure 8-10 illustrates two cancellations that are both unlisted. It should be noted that just because a cancellation has not been recorded in one of the cancellation studies, it is not necessarily rare. Of course, the fact that it has not been previously recorded is usually an

Figure 8-10. Fancy cancellations.

Figure 8-11. Fancy monogram cancels.

Figure 8-12. Hand-carved "K D." Origin unknown.

Figure 8-13. Chicago "double K." (Christie's New York auction photo)

Figure 8-14. Fancy geometric cancel. (Courtesy of Ventura Stamp Company)

Figure 8-15. Rutland, Vermont, Masonic "Open Book" cancel.

indication that it is not particularly common. The cancellation on the left, the tic-tac-toe cancel, is obviously hand-carved, probably in cork, while the star-in-star cancel on the right shows the fine detail and straight lines that are found on commercial devices made from wood or metal.

Two monogram cancels are shown in **Figure 8-11**. The letter "R" is from Rockville, Connecticut, and the inverted strike of the Old English "G" is from Greenfield, Massachusetts. Both of these cancelers appear to be metal devices made principally for uses other than canceling stamps and adapted for use as killers. Skinner reports that he has only seen the "G" cancel on the 1861 1¢ Franklin, and he has two copies of it. This raises an interesting question concerning its origin. Normally, a canceling device in general use at a post office would be found on about 100 3¢ values for each one found on the 1¢ value. Is it possible that this canceler was used to pre-cancel a pane of 1¢ stamps, and that was the only time it was used? Of course, there is no way of answering the question. Possibly, an example on another denomination will turn up.

Figure 8-12 illustrates a hand-carved cancellation with the initials "K D." The meaning of the initials is unknown, but possibly may be those of a postal clerk or postmaster.

Figure 8-13 shows the well-known "double K" from Chicago on an 1867 E grill. This particular item was part of the Grunin holding and then appeared in the Ishikawa collection, from which it was offered in a September 1993 Christie's auction.

Figure 8-14 illustrates an almost perfectly centered strike of a fancy geometric pattern. The origin is unknown.

Fraternal organizations, particularly the Masonic Order, were frequent subjects for cancel designs. **Figure 8-15** shows a Masonic open-book symbol from Rutland, Vermont.

Another star, this one probably hand-carved, is illustrated in **Figure 8-16**. Stars were a favorite design since they reflected the patriotic sentiments of the times and also because they were relatively easy to make.

A number of anchor designs exist, and Figure **8-17** shows a somewhat crude design from East Greenwich, Rhode Island.

Rockford, Illinois, produced a graceful and most attractive cancellation in its "bluebird" design, shown in **Figure 8-18**. A light-blue ink was used both for the can-

Cancellations

Figure 8-16. Hand-carved star with enclosed Old English "C" or "G." Possibly Masonic.

Figure 8-17. East Greenwich, Rhode Island, "Anchor."

Figure 8-18. Rockford, Illinois, "bluebird" cancel in light blue.

Figure 8-19. A circular arrangement of holes.
(C.W. Christian collection)

cel and for the postmark.

An unusual cancellation is shown in **Figure 8-19.** The device appears to be made from a broom-handle section with a number of round holes drilled or impressed into the surface. It is similar to the "telephone dial" cancel of West Eau Clair, Wisconsin, but the circles are all the same size and irregularly placed.

Examples of fancy cancellations on cover are more scarce but much in demand because they almost always show the complete design. A representation of good strikes on a cover is shown in **Figure 8-20** with the well-known and fairly common "New Haven star."

While fancy cancellations have always attracted the most attention from collectors, there are many other types of cancels that are also extremely interesting.

Manuscript Cancellations

Many postmasters of small offices exercised their option to cancel stamps by marking them with pen and ink. In these cases, the town marking frequently was also in manuscript. It must be remembered that the annual income for a significant number of these small offices was less than $50. The purchase of commercial marking devices and inks was an expenditure that could not easily be justified for the small number of letters that were processed. While postal regulations dictated that stamps be canceled with an X or several broad strokes of a pen, many postmasters were more imaginative and produced some interesting manuscript designs.

Figure 8-21 illustrates the work of a postmaster who definitely had money on his mind. This cover is from West Epping, New Hampshire, to the "School for Feeble

Figure 8-20. "New Haven Star" from New Haven, Connecticut. Three strikes on three 1¢ Franklins, paying the letter rate to New Canaan, Conn.
(C.W. Christian collection)

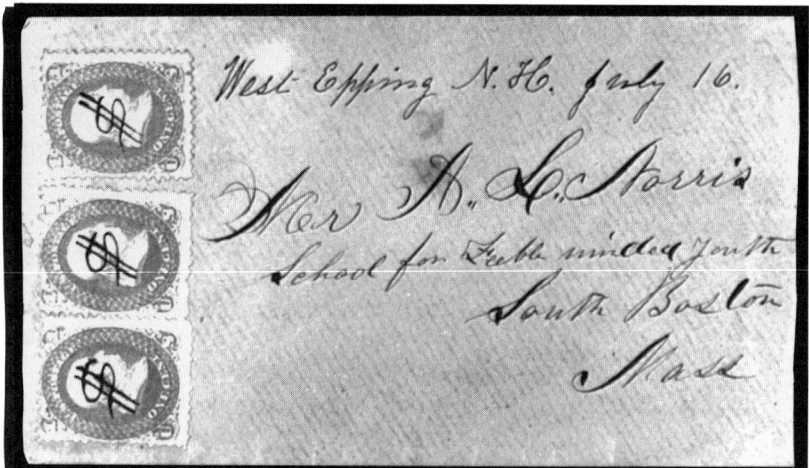

Figure 8-21. Manuscript "$$$" from West Epping, New Hampshire. 3¢ letter rate to South Boston, Massachusetts.

Figure 8-22. Manuscript "SSS" from North Tewksbury, Massachussets. 3¢ letter rate to Salem, Massachusetts.

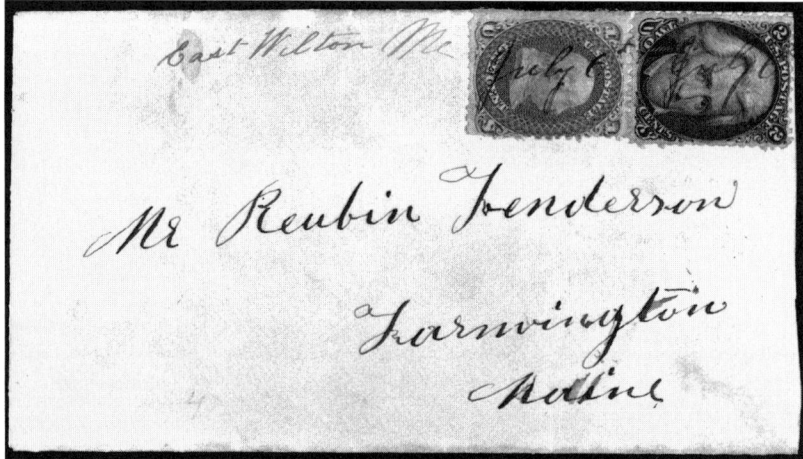

Figure 8-23. Domestic letter with 1863 2¢ Jackson plus an 1861 1¢ Franklin making up the rate. Manuscript date (July 6th) used as cancellations.

Cancellations

Figure 8-24. Boston "boxed PAID" cancellation on 1¢ stamp for local mail. The cover also bears a red circular datestamp.

Minded Youth" in South Boston, with manuscript "$" signs as killers, and a manuscript town and date marking. It is possible that the envelope may have contained money, and the cancels were a way of indicating that it was a valuable letter. Another simple manuscript killer and town marking from North Tewksbury, Mississippi, to Salem, Massachusetts, is shown in **Figure 8-22**.

A cover with combination use of the 1¢ Franklin and the 2¢ Jackson from East Wilton to Farmington, Maine, and manuscript canceled by writing the date "July 6th" on each stamp, is pictured in **Figure 8-23**.

While all three of the manuscript covers illustrated show both written town and date markings together with manuscript cancellations, this is not always the case. At times a cover may have a commercially prepared circular datestamp on the envelope and a pen cancel on the postage stamp. This could have been the result of the postmaster not having a canceler available, and rigorously following the postal instructions, which forbade the use of the town mark as a killer, or possibly from canceling an incoming town-marked letter that had slipped through without the stamp being canceled by the originating post office.

Manuscript cancels provide some of the most interesting cancels since they are almost always from small towns with limited postal volume and represent many of the scarcer origins for postal historians.

Postmarks Used as Cancels

The use of discontinued marking devices, or markers designed for other uses, provides a special class of cancellations.

In the early classic period there were a number of marking devices used to indicate that letters were prepaid. Typically amounts were written or handstamped on the cover to indicate the amount of prepayment or amount due. After the introduction of postage stamps, many of these earlier markers continued to be used, but as cancelers. In addition, special markers such as FREE, MOB and STEAMBOAT, or altered markers from the stampless period, were frequently put into use as killers.

The most common example of this type of use is the boxed PAID marking from Boston, Massachusetts. An example is illustrated in **Figure 8-24**. This was the normal cancel used at Boston during the early 1860s, and was accompanied by a double-circle CDS struck in red.

PAID markings were a favorite for use in canceling. George Linn, the founder of *Linn's Stamp News*, was an early specialist in these cancels, and in 1955 he published a booklet about them showing more than 100 varieties that had been used on the 3¢ denomination of the 1861 issue. These PAID cancel varieties are also found on the 1¢ value. After the 1860s, the frequency of use rapidly declined, and by 1890 their use was extremely rare [6:9]. Some of the PAID designs are quite elaborate and make excellent additions to a collection. Though most are in black, some were struck in shades of red and blue. **Figure 8-25** shows a PAID 3 in circle, neatly struck on a 1¢ Franklin.

Rate markers also were frequently used, and most of the values are represented on the 1¢ Franklin as a cancel. **Figure 8-26** illustrates the use of a 2¢ rate marker, and **Figure 8-27** shows a patriotic cover with three cancellations by a 3¢ marker. **Figures 8-28** and **8-29** show two types of 5¢ markers, and **Figure 8-30** demonstrates

Figure 8-25. PAID 3 in circle. This commercial marker was used in several towns.

135

Figure 8-26. A 2¢ rate marker used as canceler.

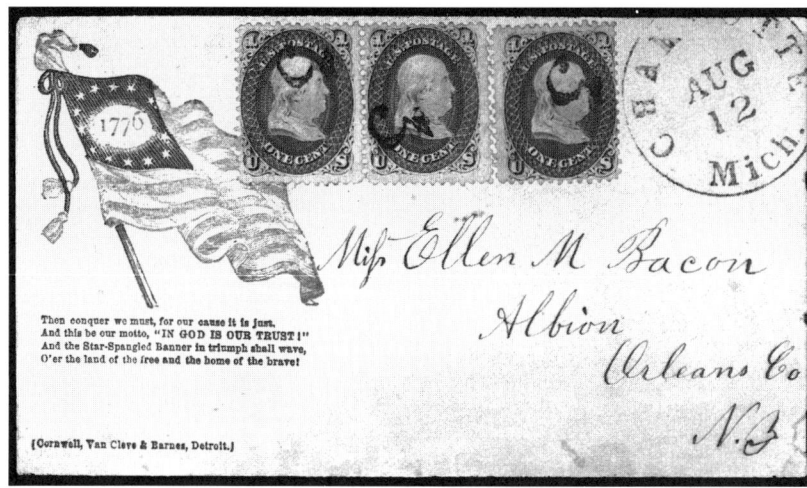

Figure 8-27. A 3¢ rate marker used as canceler on three 1¢ stamps paying the letter rate for patriotic cover from Charlotte, Michigan, to Albion, New York.

the use of a 24¢ rate marker as a cancel on a circular. High-denomination rate marks are seldom used as cancels on domestic mail, and examples are quite scarce. This cover has a manuscript town marking and no date. Both circular and drop mail was frequently given less attention than the regulations required, and the town and date marking was frequently omitted. While regulations required the post office and date to be applied to letters, it did not specifically state that the requirement also included drop and circular mail. Postal employees, taking advantage of this ambiguity, took the easier route of the fewer markings the better.

It is not unusual to find a rate-marking cancel where the original marker has been altered in some way before use. **Figure 8-31** shows an example where a 10¢ marker has had the "1" removed and the remaining "0" used for the cancel. One of the most attractive and well-known of the altered rate-marking cancels is the "C in circle" from Springwater, New York. It is illustrated in **Figure 8-32**. This cancel was made by removing the top bar from a "5 in circle" rate marker. The originating post office used the rate marker to cancel one of the stamps and the town date marker for canceling the other two.

Auxiliary markings were also used as cancels. Ex-

Figure 8-28. A 5¢ commercial rate marker used as a canceler.

Figure 8-29. A 5-in-circle rate-marking cancel.
(C.W. Christian collection)

amples of SHIP and STEAMBOAT, as well as REGISTERED, are known. They command a premium because of their comparative scarcity, particularly examples of good strikes. These auxiliary markings did double duty as a cancel and also to denote the postal service. **Figure 8-33** shows a partial strike of an MOB in circle. This was a money-order business marking, and although there is no way to confirm it with this off-cover stamp, it was probably attached to a money-order envelope. The author has a stamp in his collection showing TOO from the aux-

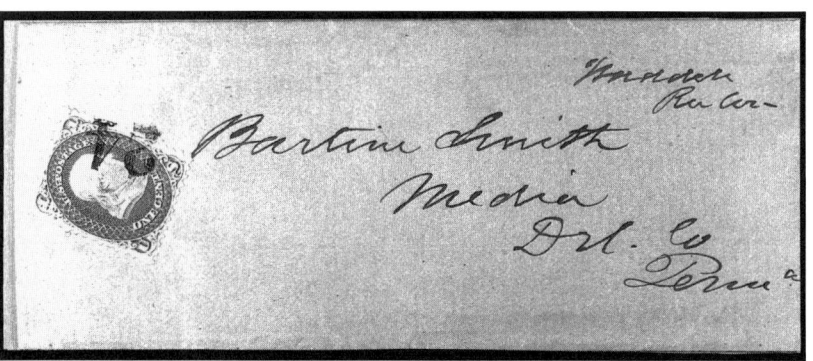

Figure 8-30. Circular with 24¢ rate-marking cancel. The 1861 Franklin payed the 1¢ rate. The origin is indecipherable.
(C.W. Christian collection)

Figure 8-31. Allegheny, Pennsylvania, cover with an altered 10¢ rate-marking cancellation on three 1¢ stamps making up the letter rate.

iliary marker TOO LATE. This marker was used to indicate that the letter had been received too late to go into a pouch for the required mail. The marking was used when there was some inscription on the envelope that requested a particular carrier or route, and the request could not be honored because of time constraints.

The thrifty habits of the period resulted in the retention of many obsolete devices for use as cancelers. Also, the convenience of using an auxiliary marker as a canceler expedited processing. Their use consequently provided a selection of attractive and unusual cancellations for the modern collector.

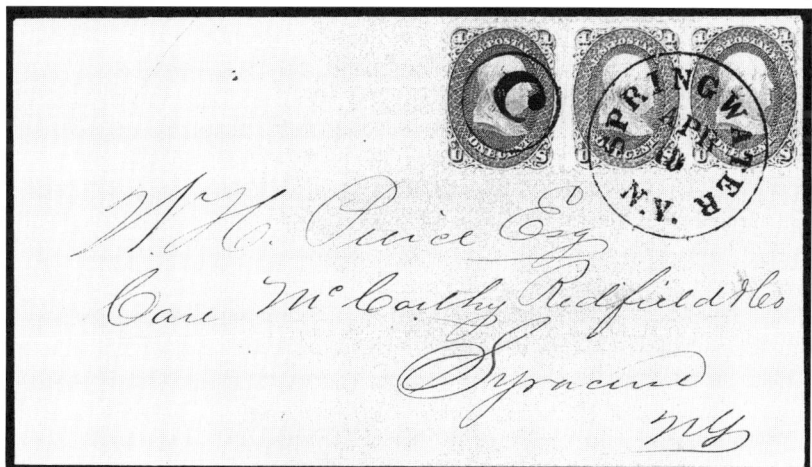

Figure 8-32. Altered 5¢ rate marker to make a "C" cancel. Springwater, New York, 3¢ rate to Syracuse, New York.
(James Lee collection)

Precancels

Precancels on classic stamps are rare. As far as this writer is aware, there are only two towns with cancellations that fit the definition of a precancel, examples of which can be found on the 1¢ Franklin. These are Weston, Massachusetts, and Cumberland, Maine.

The Weston W is an extremely attractive cancel and is a large script "W" applied in black ink with a broad quill pen. An example is shown in **Figure 8-34**. Dr. Guy Dillaway, a prominent philatelist who resides in the town of Weston, has made an in-depth study of these cancels. He has determined that some sheets of stamps were precanceled with the manuscript "W," and others were pen canceled with the script "W" after being affixed to the covers. The number precanceled was about equal to the number pen canceled after being placed on the covers.

Figure 8-33. MOB in circle. Money-order business postal marking used as cancel.

Figure 8-34. "Weston W" provisional precancel from Weston, Massachusetts.

The writer accepts Dillaway's conclusions, which classify the marking as a provisional precancel.

George W. Cutting was appointed postmaster of Weston on December 7, 1859, and served in that position until 1916. He started using the large script "W" as a cancel in 1861 and continued the practice at least until 1885. Weston was a very small community during the early years, with a limited volume of mail. In spite of this, the long period over which the cancellation was used resulted in a reasonable number of examples for collectors. Finding it on the 1¢ Franklin is a much more difficult task, and a collector may have to search for some time to find a good copy.

Figure 8-35. Off-cover Cumberland, Maine precancel. (From R.M. Hooper)

The printed postmark from Cumberland, Maine, which is also known on the 1¢ stamp, has been classified as a precancel because it was press-printed directly on the franked envelopes by the postmaster after the adhesive stamps were affixed to the cover (see **Figure 8-35**). This precancel is truly scarce, and only a few copies are known on the 1¢ Franklin, probably no more than three or four.

This set of circumstances resulted from the fact that the postmaster of Cumberland (1853-70) was David Gray, who also operated a print shop on the same premises with the post office. Gray printed envelopes and enclosures advertising his wares for mailing to prospective customers such as school committees and the boards of selectmen. His procedure in handling the envelopes gave rise to the precancel situation. Stamps were first applied to the envelopes, and then the town mark and a partial address were printed on them. The stamp was placed so the printed town mark would cancel it. Figure 8-35 shows an off-cover example that resulted from this operation.

In addition to envelopes that he prepared for his own personal mailing, Gray is also known to have printed circulars and envelopes for other clients. Ashbrook records an 1859 cover with a 1¢ 1857 stamp with printed cancellation and a printed flyer enclosure from Sanborne & Carter, who was evidently a customer [7:11-13].

In some cases, though the postmark is press-printed, the date is inserted in manuscript and the stamp is canceled by pen marks (see **Fig-ures 8-36** and **8-37**). Such examples cannot be verified as precancels. Some collectors have, however, accepted both of these covers as precancels and affirm that the pen cancels were applied before the envelope was filled. Such examples are in great demand and have had auction realizations in the four-figure bracket.

In this author's opinion, there is no way of knowing whether the stamps were applied before the printing and insertion of the enclosure, or afterward, and there is no absolute knowledge of when the pen cancel and date was applied. This lack of information seems to cast some doubt on the propriety of listing these items as precancels. However, it is certainly possible that since the user and the postmaster were the same person, the pen-and-ink addition to the printed address, post date, and cancel were all applied at the same time. Then, wearing his other hat, Gray dropped them in the mail bag.

The Pennsylvania legislature post office at Harrisburg also precanceled stamps during the 1860s. To the author's knowledge, these have only been found on covers franked by the 2¢ or 3¢ denominations from 1865 to 1867. Letters written by state senators or representatives were signed by them on the upper right of the envelope, and then placed in the mail at the legislative post office, where a precanceled stamp was affixed, generally in the upper-left corner. Various cancelers were used, including pen strokes and a blue line, as well as different cork cancels [8:204-207]. The precancels are distinguished by the fact that although the cancel design should extend beyond the boundaries of the stamps, no part of the cancel appears on the envelope.

Figure 8-36. March 26, 1862, Cumberland, Maine, precancel on an unsealed circular to Pittstown, Maine. The circular rate is paid by a 1¢ Franklin. (Christie's New York auction photo)

Other offices undoubtedly precanceled stamps on occasion during the 1860-70 period because of the convenience in so doing, but it was not done to the extent that actual examples of the practice can be confirmed.

Patent Cancels

The many patent cancelers of the period provide a gold mine of interesting philatelic information and examples of their impressions. A dozen or so patents were granted for such devices, and about 150 different cancels are known on stamps and covers of the period between 1860 and 1880. The philatelic definition of a patent cancel is a cancellation made by a device that includes some means of cutting or disfiguring the stamp to prevent reuse. In addition to marring the stamp, most patent cancelers also applied a canceling ink that penetrated into the broken fibers of the stamp and consequently was very difficult to remove. There were other patented techniques for the prevention of stamp reuse, such as the fugitive inks discussed in Chapter 4, but the term patent cancel is applied by collectors only to those that were intended to cut or destroy at least part of the stamp.

One of the early reports on patent cancelers was made by John W. Scott, the pioneer dealer and founder of the Scott catalog, at a meeting of the Philatelic Society of New York on March 19, 1900. Some excerpts from his presentation are presented here, both for their interesting content and as a historical footnote to philately of almost a century ago.

> ". . . The various governments and their employees have been trying to make postage stamps that could not be used a second time, while the dishonest among the population have constantly been trying to have their letters carried free by getting the best of the postage stamps. Some of the most curious and interesting of the essays to which I shall call your attention are the invention of cranks, men with just brains enough to devise some curious combination which they warrant cannot be beaten (and they were nearly always correct) without stopping to think if the scheme could be put into practical operation . . ."

One of the many specific schemes that Scott described is amusing, and follows:

> "The plan of this inventor was to put a few grains of fulminate of mercury on the back of each stamp; this was covered by a disk of white paper, gummed as usual and stuck on the letter or document. All the postmaster had to do was to hit the stamp with a hammer — the fulminate of mercury did the rest, for it promptly blew the center out of the stamp. It is stated that a large quantity of these stamps were prepared and sent to New Orleans for trial use. As the story goes the expressman, with the usual care taken by these gentlemen in making a delivery, threw the case on the sidewalk in front of the office, and thus saved the officials the use of their little hammers, for the whole case went up in a cloud of glory — or smoke; at any rate that was the last seen or heard of explosive stamps except the few that have been saved by a divine providence to gladden the hearts of stamp collectors [9:9-11]."

Unfortunately for 1¢ Franklin collectors, this type of cancel was never used on the 1861 issues.

Many patent cancels are based on a type of device first patented by Marcus P. Norton in 1859. Norton submitted his patent application for a marker that contained a series of type-wheels that could be rotated to set the required day and month for the datestamp without the need to remove and replace individual type slugs as was normally done. Also described in the application was an attached canceler with sharp-edged projections designed to cut into the surface of the stamp and promote the penetration of the ink. His patent, with respect to the movable type wheels, was rejected because of an earlier patent with the same features that had been granted in 1857 to a T.J.W. Robertson. A patent was, however, granted to Norton for the idea of duplexing the killer with the town-date marking. At the time, this was not a particularly important feature since the July 23, 1860, ban by Postmaster General Holt against canceling stamps with the town-marking stamp had not yet been issued. As has been discussed in the previous chapter, the new requirement for applying a separate killer to the stamp resulted in almost doubling the canceling workload. This was of

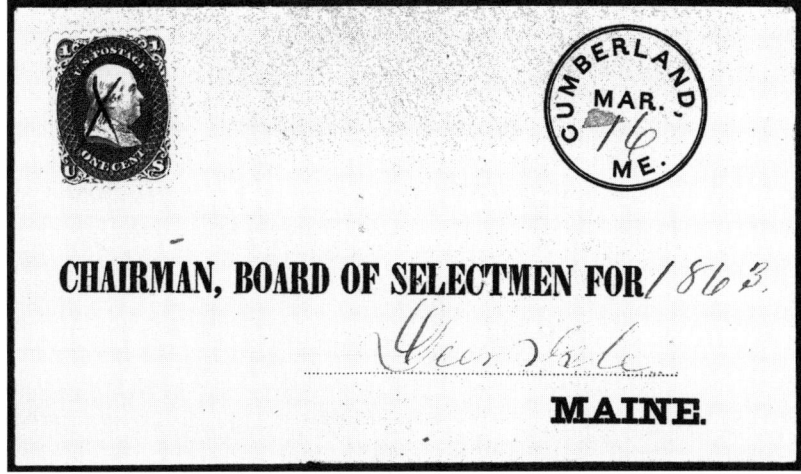

Figure 8-37. March 16, 1863, precanceled circular. Note small differences from Figure 8-36, and the reversal of the positions of the stamp and town-date mark. (James Lee collection)

Figure 8-38. Scarce example of the use of a Norton patent canceling device on a cover at New York City, January 30, 1862. This is the latest use on cover recorded for a Norton patent cancel with the "lazy date." The 3¢+1¢ franking pays the carrier and letter rate. (Courtesy of Richard B. Graham)

major importance in post offices with large volumes of mail, and the postmasters took steps to alleviate the problem.

During the period that he was applying for his patent in 1859, Norton had received permission from the Post Office Department to conduct a test of his device on mail at the Troy, New York, post office. These tests were completed in the spring of 1859, and a few examples of canceled 3¢ 1857 stamps on cover from these tests have been identified.

Whether from a knowledge of Norton's devices, or from seeing duplexed cancels used by British post offices, or from innate ingenuity, the postmaster of New York City, John A. Dix, requested his marking-device contractor to provide him with duplexed town markers and canceling markers. After being advised that these devices possibly infringed on the Norton patent, Dix arranged for Norton to provide 10 devices for the use of the New York Post Office. It is probable that these cancelers were not too successful since the number of surviving covers from these devices is very limited. According to Richard B. Graham, fewer than two dozen are known (Skinner suggests that this number may be closer to 50 covers), and all of these except two covers are from the period between January and March of 1861. The two exceptions, fortunately for the 1¢ Franklin collector, are both carrier-service covers. Each is dated January 30, 1862. The fact that these covers were both canceled on the same day, and no covers seem to have been found from the previous nine months, suggests that at least one of the Norton canceling devices was resurrected, possibly for a very short period and then removed from use. An example of one of these two covers with the latest-known use of a Norton "lazy date" patent cancel on cover is shown in **Figure 8-38**. **Figure 8-39** shows a tracing of

Figure 8-39. Tracing of the cancel and town mark from the patent marker used on the cover in Figure 8-38. (Courtesy of Richard B. Graham)

the marking, to better illustrate the arrangement of the date logo, which is almost illegible on the cover. Norton's early cancels are easily identified by the use of a "lazy" year date. To save space on the device, the rotating cylinder that held the dates for the years had the numbers placed at right angles to those for the month and day. A duplexed canceler with a 15mm circular pattern of 12 narrow lines was attached to the marker. Although the lines appear to have been produced by blades, there is no evidence that they penetrated the paper of the postage stamp.

One of the problems with the marker may have been that the duplexed canceler was only attached to the town marker and handle with a screw, and may not have been rugged enough to handle the incessant pounding that such instruments received in a large office. The duplex marker that Postmaster Dix had earlier devised had the sections soldered together, and this probably resulted in a more satisfactory product since thousands of examples of their use are known.

Patent cancels, because of their relative scarcity and the uniqueness of their characteristics, have long interested collectors, and most of the famous students of stamps and postal history have written to some extent about these interesting cancels. One of the early researchers was Fred Schmalzriedt, who wrote a series of articles on the subject in 1932 for the *Collectors Club Philatelist*. This was followed in 1933 with his "Patent Cancellations (1847 to 1887)" published as a section in Delf Norona's *Cyclopedia* [8:142-169]. He based his findings on 10 years of research, and his listing of all of the patent cancels known at that time is still a most comprehensive source for information. As with any compilation that is over a half-century old, additional facts and examples have come to light over the years that add to, and in some cases, contradict Schmalzriedt's conclusions. A more recent survey of more limited scope in time, but extremely complete and carefully researched, as well as being exceptionally interesting and readable, is Graham's series of articles in the *Chronicle* [10] concerning the patent cancels of the 1860s, with particular emphasis on the Norton patents. Much of the information contained here is based on the work of Graham and Schmalzriedt.

A problem common to all patent cancelers using sharp projections or knives to scarify or cut the postage stamp was the need for careful adjustment so that the blades would not cut too deeply and damage the contents of the letter. An opposite type of problem was that constant use soon dulled the sharp edges of the device so that the impression failed to cut the stamp at all.

In spite of these drawbacks, patent cancelers were used in many cities during the 1860-70 period, and some very interesting examples of their use on the 1¢ Franklin can be found.

Returning to the saga of Norton and his patent cancels: After Postmaster Dix tried the patent cancelers provided by Norton in 1861, probably with limited success, the New York Post Office evidently continued the use of duplex cancelers of the type that Dix had designed and described in his 1860 letter to the Post Office Department. These markers were manufactured by Edmund Hoole, who had the contract for supplying the Post Office Department with marking devices and who also coincidentally manufactured the patent devices for Norton. Hoole provided duplex markers (without any cutting device) not only to New York, but also to other large cities such as Cleveland and Chicago. Examples of some of these markings were shown in the previous chapter as Figures 7-3 and 7-4. In testimony during hearings regarding the Norton patents during 1864-65, Hoole stated that he had provided the Post Office Department with 500 of the duplex markers as of January 1865. There is no indication that Hoole considered that these devices constituted any infringement on the Norton patent at that time, but he did obtain a license to use the Norton patent subsequent to losing a patent infringement suit brought against him by Norton's assignees.

In 1863, Abram Wakeman, postmaster of New York City, reported to A.N. Zevely, the third assistant postmaster general, concerning his experiments with a Norton canceling device [10: *Chronicle* 157. p. 39]. The contents of this letter are quoted in part, and explain the reason for the New York City patent cancels that are to be found from late 1862.

"Post Office, New York
January 3, 1863.
Sir: Some time since you requested that I should test the utility of Norton's double post-marking and canceling stamping iron, and report my opinion thereon. It was in use in this office when I first entered upon my duties. Since then the canceling part has been changed in various forms. We have tried the cutter thoroughly. This is the most complete method of cancellation; but it is liable, even if used with the greatest care, to injure the contents of the envelope, especially if the enclosures are cards, photographs and the like. We have also used cork, by inserting it in the cylinder of the canceler. This has proved successful, and our cancellation is now performed in this way.

I am confident no office in the country performs cancellation more thoroughly. The design of Mr. Norton is indispensable to us. Indeed, unless I should nearly double the stamping force, we could not dispense with its use. I am satisfied the interests of the Department would be subserved by securing its general use . . .
Very respectfully, your obedient servant,
ABRAM WAKEMAN, Postmaster.
Per Secretary."

The trials of the "cutter" mentioned in the letter probably resulted in the New York patent-cancel covers dated during October and November of 1862. Schmalzriedt reports three types of cutters being used in October. Each consisted of an open circle of approximately 25mm in diameter with parallel knife blades. The first type contains 13 blades and was used October 10-21. The second type had nine blades and saw use October 15-21. The third type contained 10 blades and was used October 20-29. Tracings of of the nine- and 10-blade types, from the Schmalzriedt report [8:150], are reproduced as **Figure 8-40**. Skinner [3:249] reports the 1862 use at New York of this type of cancel for seven, eight, nine, 10 and 13 blades.

Figure 8-41 illustrates an interesting cover from these trials with a 10-blade cancel. The cover is postmarked October 21, 1862, and the blades of the canceling device completely cut through the stamps, envelope and contents. Another example of this cancel is shown in **Figure 8-42** with an October 29 date that corresponds with Schmalzriedt's last reported date of use. He recorded 10 examples of use on the 1¢ value.

An off-cover stamp with an eight-blade patent cancel is illustrated in **Figure 8-43**. Its use has been confirmed on a 3¢ cover from New York City during the 1862

Figure 8-40. Tracings of Norton-type patent cancellations used during test period at New York during October 1862.

Backstamped

Figure 8-41. Ten-blade Norton-type patent cancel. This New York patriotic cover was evidently mailed without the carrier fee being paid. Not visible but under the 1¢ stamp is a black "Due 1," and the cover is backstamped with a straightline "Held For Postage" with an October 21, 1862, postmark as shown in the tracing. Additional payment was made with a 1¢ Franklin, making up the required amount, and the cover was dispatched on October 24. The patent knife cancel completely cuts through the stamps and the envelope.

Figure 8-42. Ten-blade Norton-type cancel on an October 29, 1862, 3¢+1¢ carrier cover to Troy, New York. The cancel penetrates the stamp, but does not cut the envelope. The "OCT 30" handstamp applied at the Troy Post Office indicates the date that the cover was advertised.

trial period.

Examples of the 13-blade cancel on the 1¢ Franklin have not been seen by this writer nor were any reported by Schmalzriedt, who recorded it on 100 3¢ (and one 5¢) 1861 stamps. With this many recorded uses, it is quite possible that a 1¢ use exists.

Another entirely different type of Norton cancel was used on the 1¢ during the same test period. This cancel had 10 rows of dots or short dashes, and appears to have been made from a 10-blade canceler by filing grooves at right angles to the blades. **Figure 8-44** shows an October 25 cover with this cancel. The dots dent the stamp, but do not cut through the paper. According to Schmalzriedt, these were used from October 21-26, 1862, and 20 examples were recorded by him.

In November a new type of cancel design was tested. This design consisted of a circle of eight triangular sections with an open area in the center with four very small triangles that caused a deep impression into the canceled postage stamp and envelope. A tracing of this design is shown in **Figure 8-45**. Schmalzriedt records a single use on cover with the 1¢, and no examples have been seen by this writer.

Because of the short period of use, all of these Norton-type patent cancels from New York are relatively scarce. The numbers that exist are somewhat greater than those first reported by Schmalzriedt, who based his census primarily on his specialized holding of patent cancels in about 1930. His comprehensive collection, which probably contained examples of most of the patent cancel that were known at that time, has remained intact and has

Figure 8-43. Off-cover example of an eight-blade Norton-type cancel.
(C.W. Christian collection)

consistently been added to over the years. Presently it is housed in six large volumes, and according to Skinner, to whom the collection now belongs, not many new types have been discovered during the 65 years that have passed since Schmalzriedt first wrote about these unusual cancels. However, it has been possible to identify the previously unknown origin of many of the types from covers that have been subsequently located.

Philadelphia also used a variation of the Norton knife cancel between March and June of 1863. This cancel had 12 blades and was somewhat smaller than the New York type with a diameter of about 16mm. The end blades were slightly thicker and curved, as can be seen in the actual-size tracing accompanying the June 1, 1863, mourning cover shown in **Figure 8-46**. Schmalzriedt mentions that during the early Philadelphia use of this device, the knife blades were sharp and cut into the stamps, but were dulled by use. The later examples appear like a normal grid cancel. Skinner reports that from late March to early May, the blades were sharp enough to cut into the stamp. Schmalzriedt records 10 examples on the 1¢ Franklin.

Schmalzriedt also reported patent-knife cancels used on the 1¢ from Oberlin, Ohio (10 blades, 1861); an eight-blade device used on an off-cover block of four from an unknown origin; a device with arc-shaped blades used at New York; and a grid of short blades and dots used at Fall River, Massachusetts (device cuts into stamp). None of these examples has been seen by this author. Skinner reports, concerning these items, that the eight-blade block of four is still in the collection, along with two off-cover singles. The reported New York arc-shaped can-

Figure 8-44. Norton-type patent cancel with 10 rows of dots, used at New York City during the 1862 trial period.

Figure 8-45. Tracing of a Norton-type cancel used in the latter part of the 1862 trial period. Design has small triangular cutters surrounded by a cork killer, and is distinctively different than those used during the previous month.

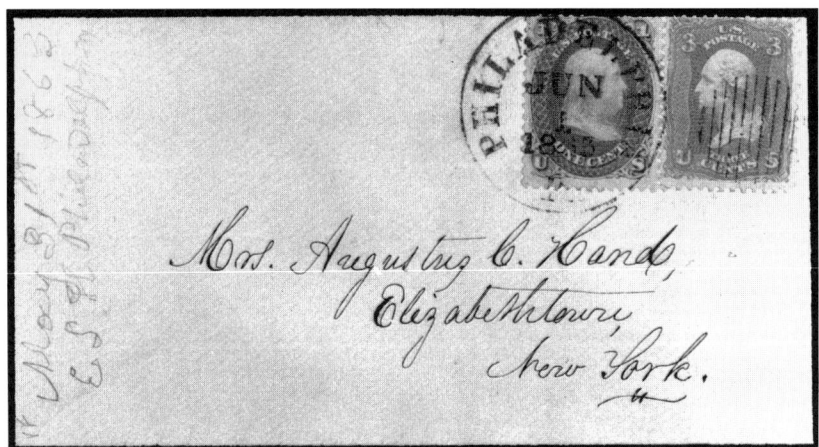

Figure 8-46. Norton-type 12-blade cancel, used at Philadelphia on a black-bordered mourning cover. Carrier fee and letter rate are paid by 1¢+3¢ stamps. The tracing of the markings is actual size.

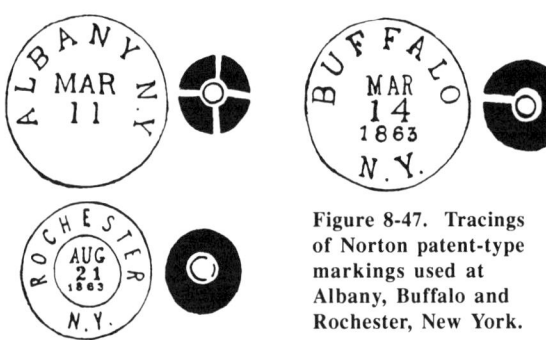

Figure 8-47. Tracings of Norton patent-type markings used at Albany, Buffalo and Rochester, New York.

cels are actually on an earlier stamp issue.

Norton continued to apply for new patents with alleged improvements to his original device. One of his devices contained a metal tube in the center of the attached duplex canceler. The end of the tube was sharpened, and resulted in a round punchlike ¼-inch circular cut in the stamp. The tube was surrounded by an annular cork ring that was used to ink the cancel.

Cancels from these duplexed devices are known from upstate New York at Albany, Buffalo and Rochester, with those from Rochester being the scarcest. Simple cuts were carved into the cork rings, and these serve to differentiate the cancels at the various locations. **Figure 8-47** illustrates tracings from Schmalzriedt of these designs. **Figure 8-48** shows an April 21, 1863, drop letter illustrating the characteristic Buffalo, New York, ring cancel with one opening and a center "cookie cutter" impression, which in this case barely cuts the paper. This type of cancel is known to have been used between February 1863 and November 1865.

Figure 8-49 shows a cover with the same cancel, dated July 11, 1863. This was posted soon after the increase in the drop-letter fee to 2¢ on July 1, 1863, and is a good example of how duplexed cancelers could be used to cancel more than one stamp without duplicating the town mark. One normal strike with the duplex marker was made to cancel the stamp on the left, and then the marker was rotated so that only the canceling half contacted the envelope on the second strike to cancel the stamp on the right. Well-defined and sharp strikes such as shown in Figure 8-48 are the exception rather than the rule.

The center "cookie cutter" punch of the Rochester cancel (Figure 8-47) is reported to always show slight breaks in the circle. This is probably the result of some damage to the end of the sharpened tube, and indicates that probably only one canceling device was used for all of the known impressions. Examples also show the cork ring to be slightly oval in shape. These designs were used during 1863 and 1864.

Albany used the quartered design shown in Figure 8-47. The town mark that was duplexed with this cancel did not have a year date. Albany patent cancels are difficult to find on the 1¢ stamp and are quite scarce with good strikes. The reported period of use was less than a year, December 1862 to November 1863. An off-cover example of this cancellation is shown in **Figure 8-50**.

Buffalo used two new and different designs in June and July of 1865. Tracings of these designs are pictured in **Figure 8-51**, and an off-cover example of the design shown in the tracing of the July 10, 1865, cancel is illustrated in **Figure 8-52**.

One other cancel with the circular punch in the center has been reported on the 1¢ Franklin. This is a square made up of four triangles surrounding the central punch. It has been recorded as having been used in New York during November 20-21, 1863. This writer has never seen an example of this particular cancel, but a tracing is pictured in **Figure 8-53**. Skinner confirms its existence, but only off cover on the 3¢ 1861.

Norton, or various assignees of his patents, were almost continuously involved in suits against the gov-

Cancellations

Figure 8-48. Buffalo, New York, drop cover dated April 21, 1863, with characteristic broken-ring Norton-type cancel.

Figure 8-49. Buffalo, New York, drop cover dated July 11, 1863, with two 1¢ Franklins to pay the increase to 2¢ for the drop rate, effective July 1, 1863. Double strike of Norton-type patent cancel.

Figure 8-50. Norton-type cancel used in Albany, New York.

Figure 8-51. Tracings of Norton-type markings used on Buffalo covers in mid-1865.

Figure 8-52. Off-cover example of 1865-era Buffalo, New York, Norton-type cancel.

Figure 8-53. Tracing of cancel reported to have been used at New York City, November 20-21, 1863.

ernment or manufacturers of markers for infringement on his various patents for producing cancels. These suits began with the previously mentioned successful action against Edmund Hoole in 1864, and continued through the years until final action was taken in 1881 by the Supreme Court to dismiss the filed suits as being without validity. The litigation did not stop with this decision. In fact, the suits and attempts to obtain compensation from the government continued for more than 100 years [11:188-192]. The patented feature that was the basis for these claims was the duplex nature of the canceling device. The sharp knives or cutting attachments were evidently not considered to be of enough utility to request payment for their use.

The Post Office Department, in 1866, had offered to settle claims requesting compensation for the use of the duplexed canceler for the sum of $20,000 plus $12,282.70 for development costs and interest. Shaver & Corse, the assignees of the Norton patent refused the offer and asked for $125,000. This counteroffer was not approved, and the legal controversy continued.

An interesting aspect of the case was the introduction of fraudulent documents by Norton into the files of the U.S. Patent Office. It seems that in about 1864 he surreptitiously placed documents falsely dated 10 years earlier (August 7, 1854) into the files. These documents described his invention of the duplex canceler, and effectively predated other developers of the duplex concept. The success of the suit against Hoole in 1864 was probably due to these false documents. His illegal actions were later discovered and contributed to the Supreme Court's final decision in the case, as well as resulting in his disbarment from access to the Patent Office records as a patent attorney.

Richard B. Graham's account of Norton's legal problems and machinations [10:November 1993] is very interesting, and is recommended for additional reading concerning the people and facts surrounding the Norton patent disputes.

During 1861-70, a large number of patent cancels of different designs were used in various cities. With the advent of grilled stamps, the frequency of use diminished rapidly, but some examples of use from as late as the 1880s have been discovered.

The Skinner and Eno book on cancellations [10] contains an entire chapter on patent cancels used prior to 1870. Tracings of 88 different designs are shown and identified as to origin, when known. It is an excellent reference work and, in conjunction with the Schmalzriedt articles, provides most of the available information on

Figure 8-54. Patent cancel with Charleston, South Carolina, as reported origin.

types of patent cancels.

Baker [12:258] mentions another type of patent cancel to be found on the 1¢ Franklin. **Figure 8-54** shows an example of this from the author's collection. According to Baker, this was used at Charleston, South Carolina. The source of his information is not known, and this writer has never seen it recorded on cover. Since Charleston was occupied by Confederate forces until early 1865, it seems somewhat strange that this "Yankee" type of killer would be used in that city. Nine examples of this cancellation are reported by Schmalzriedt on the 1¢, and one on the 1861 3¢ denomination. All his reported examples were off cover, and he listed the origin as unknown. It is an attractive cancel, and the design is quite different from most patent cancels. The blades of the device were evidently quite sharp because the impression cuts through the paper of the stamp. Both Skinner and Graham doubt that Charleston is the city of origin.

While many devices with cutting or abrading characteristics were used to cancel and prevent reuse of postage stamps, none of them achieved a high degree of success, and their use was limited. Contemporary opinions of their effectiveness varied and excerpts from the writings of two postmasters general of the period are quoted as follows:

From Postmaster General Montgomery Blair's report to Congress, dated October 31, 1863:

"It is not believed that the department has ever suffered any considerable loss from the use of washed or restored stamps, yet there has been a constant endeavor, either by the introduction of some effectual method of cancellation, or by a peculiar process in the manufacture of the stamps, to render impossible a second use thereof for the payment of postage. No improvement of this nature has yet been perfected, though much attention has been given to the subject, and many ingenious devices for this purpose invented. Instruments for cancellation, with cutting or abrading edges, have been submitted by various parties and upon being thoroughly tested were found to be inherently defective, owing to their liability to injure, or be injured by, the contents of letters or packets. These instruments furthermore, speedily became dull or disarranged by ordinary use, requiring frequent sharpening or adjusting."

A contrary opinion from Blair's successor, Postmaster General Dennison, was included in a letter that he submitted on March 1, 1865, to the U.S. Senate Committee on Post Offices. Dennison stated in part as follows:

"This stamp [marking device] is an invention of importance to the postal service, particularly at our large post offices; it is also an effectual instrument for canceling postage stamps; and it diminishes the chances of cleansing postage stamps and using them a second time [8:143]."

It is reasonable to assume, based on the collected knowledge of the limited use of the patent cancelers, that the "importance" referred to by Postmaster General Dennison applied more to the duplex feature of the markers rather than the sharp-bladed cancelers.

The search went on for the ideal canceler, and still continues to this day, but with less emphasis on avoidance of fraud as opposed to efficiency of use.

Colored Cancels

More than 95 percent of the cancels to be found on the 1¢ Franklin are in black. Other colors, in order of frequency of use, are blue, red, green and violet.

Colored inks were generally more costly, easier to remove from the stamp and provided less obliteration than black ink. For these reasons, plus the fact that many post office regulations and advisories advocated the use of black inks, the number of colored cancels is relatively small.

Some large cities, including Cincinnati, Chicago and Baltimore, used blue ink for the majority of their town markings. When duplex markers were used, the blue color also appeared on the cancellations.

Boston was a principal user of red town marks, but most of the cancels were in black. By the time duplex markers were generally used, both the Boston town mark and the cancel appeared in black.

New York City used red "city delivery" combination town and carrier-service markings as cancels on local mail during the period from 1856 to 1864. These cancels are also known in black. Illustrations of these interesting cancels are shown in the chapter on carrier use.

The most spectacular of the colored cancels are to be found with large red or vermilion designs. (An example is pictured in the color section.) These, as is the case with most outstanding colored cancels, are extremely difficult to obtain on cover. It is the writer's opinion that early collectors, before a high degree of interest in covers and postal history developed, removed the brilliantly colored examples from their original envelopes and mounted the items as interesting additions to their collections. This was done in spite of the fact that the cancellations frequently obscured much of the design and therefore were not preferred candidates for general philatelic acquisition. The practice undoubtedly saved many of these attractive specimens from destruction.

Skinner reports a large red outline heart cancel on the 1¢ Franklin. This design was used on New York City foreign mail in December 1862. Though known in black, it

Figure 8-55. Richmond, Virginia, deep-green, negative shamrock cancel. The tracing of the cancellation is actual size. Also illustrated in the color section.

was most commonly struck in bright red. It is the earliest fancy or elaborate design from New York City that he has recorded for either domestic or foreign use.

Examples of the 1¢ with green cancels are scarce. The author has seen fewer than a dozen with distinctly green cancels, although a large number of blue-green or gray-green examples do exist. These are probably the result of blue canceling ink that has been contaminated or changed slightly by the environment over the years. Caution should be exercised when purchasing "green" markings on yellow or cream covers. These are frequently blue inks that appear green because of the combination of colors.

A deep green cancel was used by Richmond, Virginia, from 1861 to 1866. It is rare on the 1¢ since for most of this period Richmond was in Confederate hands. A example of this cancel is shown in **Figure 8-55** and also illustrated in the color photo section.

An irregular star in green is a well-known cancel from Sharon, Vermont, and examples are known on the 1¢ Franklin.

A distinctive cancel consisting of seven parallel bars surrounded by a rectangular frame is known in green from Columbus, Ohio. It is frequently called the "prison bar" cancel, but has no connection with Camp Chase, the nearby prisoner-of-war facility. The same cancel was also struck in blue and black.

The Ishikawa sale by Christie's in September 1993 offered a 1¢ 1861 with a circle of eight wedges in an olive-green color. No information regarding its origin is known.

Violet or shades of purple seem to be the rarest canceling color for the period. Although purple became very common in the succeeding decades when coal-tar dye pigments became available, it remains extremely difficult to find on the 1¢ 1861. To date, this writer has only seen a single example of a cancel in the purple category, and that is an off-cover stamp canceled with a violet star (see **Figure 8-56** and color section).

A few yellow and brown cancellations have been

Figure 8-56. Examples of outstanding colored cancellations on the 1¢ 1861. A carved cork geometric cancel in deep red is shown on the left, and a rare violet star on the right. Also shown in color section.

seen an example of use on the 1¢ Franklin. Clyde Jennings, who has collected colored cancellations on classic U.S. stamps for many years, reported to the author that he has a true orange, nine-bar grid in a closed ¾-inch circle, on the 1861 1¢.

Many different shades of red exist, from a bright crimson to pink and magenta. Shades of blue, from bluish-black to blue-green and ultramarine, are also to be found. No attempt has been made to classify the many variations of the basic colors, and probably little information of importance would be gained from such a listing.

In concluding this chapter, it can be noted that unusual cancellations have added a great deal of spice and interest to otherwise commonplace stamps, and the pursuit and study of these specimens continues to provide challenges and enjoyment to all collectors.

References

1. *Postal Laws and Regulations of the United States of America, 1847*. Reprints from official sources. Theron Wierenga. Holland, Michigan. 1980.

2. Leech, Daniel D.T. *List of Post Offices and Postal Laws and Regulations of the United States of America 1857*. 1980 reprint by Theron Wierenga. Holland, Michigan.

3. Skinner, Hubert C. and Eno, Amos. *United States Cancellations, 1845-1869*. American Philatelic Society. 1980.

4. Cole, James M. *Cancellations and Killers of the Bank Note Era, 1870-1894*. U.S. Philatelic Classics Society Inc. 1995.

5. Rohloff, Paul C. *The Waterbury Cancellations 1860-1890*. Collectors Club of Chicago. 1979.

6. Linn, George W. *The PAID Markings on the 3¢ U.S. Stamp of 1861*. George W. Linn Company, Sidney, Ohio. 1955.

7. Hooper, R. Malcolm. *A Historical Survey of Pre-cancels*. Cardinal Spellman Philatelic Museum. 1979.

8. Norona, Delf, ed. *Cyclopedia of United States Postmarks and Postal History*. Quarterman Publications. 1975.

9. Scott, J. W. "The Birth of a Postage Stamp." *Essay-Proof Journal*. No. 145. Winter. 1980.

10. Graham, Richard B. "Norton Patent Duplexed Postmarks of the 1860s." *Chronicle* No. 126, May 1985. A two part series with the title "The Beginnings of the Duplex Style Handstamps, 1859-62." *Chronicle* Nos. 151 and 152, 1991. A three part series titled "Duplex Handstamps, Marcus P. Norton and Patent Cancels of the 1860s." *Chronicle* Nos.156, 157, 158, 160, November 1992 through November 1993.

11. Skinner, Hubert C. "Patents and Philately During the 1860s." *Chronicle*. No. 163, August 1994.

12. Baker, Hugh J. and J. David Baker. *Baker's U.S. Classics*. U.S. Philatelic Classics Society. 1985.

CHAPTER 9

The Demonetization Period and First Uses

Demonetization

Demonetization of U.S. postage stamps is a rare occurrence, and it has only happened twice. The first postal issue of 1847 was demonetized on July 1, 1851, at the time the 1851 series of stamps was issued. The reason for this action has never been absolutely determined; however, Elliott Perry [1:115] surmised that a possible reason was the first issue had the words "U.S. POST OFFICE" printed on the stamps. It may have been deemed appropriate to replace this with "U.S. POSTAGE," since there was no such entity as a U.S. Post Office.

Richard Graham [2] advances another plausible theory: that the Post Office Department did not have possession of the plates for the 1847 issue. This observation, however, seems to conflict with the letter proposal by Rawdon, Wright, Hatch & Edson [3:145] that stated in part: "... The stamps are to be executed in the best style of line engraving, and the dies and plates to belong to, and to be held for the exclusive use of the Post Office Department..."

The second demonetization occurred in 1861 and effectively made illegal the use of all previously issued stamps and stamped envelopes (with two exceptions that will be discussed later). Thousands of dollars worth of postage stamps were in the possession of Southern postmasters at the outbreak of the Civil War, and there was great concern that these would be smuggled into the Northern states, where they could be sold and the proceeds used to further the rebel cause.

The contract for printing the 1851-57 series of stamps by Toppan, Carpenter & Company was due to expire on June 10, 1861. This fact, plus the desire to demonetize the issue and replace it with different designs, led to the advertisement on March 27, 1861, for bids for new postage stamps (as was discussed in Chapter 1). National Bank Note Company was selected to provide the new issue, with initial distribution scheduled for August 1, 1861.

Postmaster General Blair, in his annual report in December 1861, explained the situation and proposed actions as follows: At the beginning of the second quarter of 1861, shipments of stamps and supplies to the postmasters in states that had claimed to have "seceded" were discontinued until it was determined that individual postmasters would accept responsibility for these items. Circulars were sent to 1,200 postmasters requesting that they reaffirm their commitments. Nine hundred replies were received; all except 20 stated their intention to remain responsible to the United States for all revenues, and their regrets for the actions of their state authorities. Stamps continued to be supplied to the postmasters who had affirmatively replied until June 1, 1861, when it appeared that the postal service could no longer be safely continued. The balance of stamps and stamped envelopes that remained unaccounted for in the hands of postmasters in the disloyal states on October 1, 1861, amounted to $207,000.

In his report, Blair continued as quoted below:

> "The contract for the manufacture of postage stamps having expired on the 10th of June, 1861, a new one was entered into with the National Bank Note Company, of New York, upon terms very advantageous to the department, from which there will result an annual saving of more than thirty per cent, in the cost of the stamps.
>
> In order to prevent the fraudulent use of the large quantity of stamps remaining unaccounted for, in the hands of postmasters in disloyal States, it was deemed advisable to change the design and the color of those manufactured under the new contract, and also to modify the design of the stamp upon the stamped envelopes, and to substitute as soon as possible the new for the old issues. It was the design of the Department that the distribution of the new stamps and envelopes should commence on the first of August, but from unavoidable delays, that of the latter did not take place until the 15th of the month."

The above statement contains a couple of minor errors. Primarily because of difficulties in producing a satisfactory color for the 3¢ denomination, the new stamps were not available for initial distribution until August 16. Distribution of the stamped envelopes began about a week earlier.

The number of stamps available in August was not sufficient to simultaneously replace all of the earlier issue throughout the loyal states. There was a desire to demonetize the old issue and to replace it as rapidly as possible to minimize any possible loss from illegal use by the South. To accomplish this with the limited number of new stamps available, a somewhat complicated system for demonetization and replacing the old stamps was proposed.

The proposed plan provided that the distribution of the new stamps would take place in three zones. Each zone contained a number of states. The demonetization and replacement actions would take place in a particular zone over a period of three or four weeks, and then distribution in the next zone would commence. The entire demonetization was to be completed by November 1, 1861.

Because of the probability that most illegal sales of the 1857 postage stamps from the South would take place

149

in the border states, the first zone that was to be supplied with the new stamps covered the states of Kentucky, Missouri, Illinois, Indiana, Ohio, Maryland and Pennsylvania. Demonetization in this zone was to be completed before September 10, 1861. The next zone included all other loyal states and territories east of the Rocky Mountains, with demonetization to be completed by October 1, 1861. The third and final zone included those states and territories in the far west and on the Pacific Coast, with completion of the demonetization and distribution of new stamps by November 1, 1861.

If the new stamps had been available in sufficient quantities on August 1 as scheduled, it is possible that the plan could have been executed as proposed. However, the stamps were not available, and the carefully orchestrated scheme was never put into practice. Instead, deliveries were first made to the large Eastern cities, and as more stamps were printed, the distribution extended to more distant locations and smaller post offices. Another factor that made it difficult to supply an adequate number of stamps was the unexpected large surge in demand for stamps that was caused by the activities of the Civil War. In addition to increased commercial and government communications, many thousands of soldiers and sailors, who previously had little reason to use the mails, were now regularly writing to and receiving letters from home. This increased demand was compounded by the fact that the Post Office Department for some time had deliberately reduced shipments of the 1857 stamps to individual post offices in anticipation of the new issue. This was to minimize the number of stamps that would have to be exchanged later.

The letters of instructions that were sent to the postmasters to explain the distribution and demonetization plan are of considerable interest and contain much pertinent information. They evidently accompanied shipments of the new stamps to individual post offices. These documents have been the subject of considerable philatelic research over the years, and articles concerning them have been published by many authors, including Tiffany, Luff, Ashbrook, Chase, Perry and most recently, Graham. Several slightly different notices were sent out. Large offices had different instructions than small ones, and as the delays in stamp production continued, the proposed dates for the completion of demonetization were moved back.

A copy, from an article by Graham [4:118], of the text of one of the notices of the type sent to smaller offices, and which contained the later dates for demonetization completion, is reproduced in **Figure 9-1**:

An item from *The U.S. Mail and Post Office Assistant* for August 1861 [4:121], added some information to the demonetization notices:

> "The instructions to the larger class of post offices vary somewhat. They are directed to exchange new for old stamps and envelopes, on application from the smaller offices. They will also retain all the old styles in their possession, until a Special Agent calls to count and destroy them, and furnish a certificate of the quantity so disposed of."

Another interesting and illuminating circular was reproduced by Perry in his *Pat Paragraphs* [5:117]. It reads:

> "Old Postage Stamps to be Continued in use.
>
> The following important document is to be forwarded to every postmaster in the loyal States:—
>
> Post Office Department,
> Finance Office, Sept.—, 18
>
> Sir— It is found to be impossible to supply at the present the demand for postage stamps of the new style. Every effort will be made to increase the amount manufactured daily, but under the most favorable conditions, the distribution of these stamps to all post offices in the loyal States,

Post Office Department,

Finance Office, 1861.

Postmaster

Sir:

You will receive herewith a supply of Postage Stamps, which, you will observe, are of a new style, differing both in design and in color from those hitherto used, and having the letters U. S. in the lower corners of each stamp, and its respective denomination indicated by figures as well as by letters.

You will immediately give public notice, through the newspapers and otherwise, that you are prepared to exchange stamps of the new style, for an equivalent amount of the old issue, during a period of six days from the date of the notice, and that the latter will not thereafter be received in payment of postage on letters sent from your office.

You will satisfy yourself, by personal inspection, that stamps offered in exchange, have not been used through the mails or otherwise ; and if, in any case, you have good grounds for suspecting that stamps presented to you for exchange were sent from any of the disloyal States, you will not receive them without due investigation.

Immediately after the expiration of the above period of six days, you will return to the Third Assistant Postmaster General all stamps of the old style in your possession, including such as you may obtain by exchange, placing them in a secure package, which *must be carefully registered in the manner prescribed by Chapter* (39) *of the Regulations of this Department.*

Be careful also to write legibly the name of your office, as well as that of your county and State.

A strict compliance with the foregoing instructions is absolutely necessary, that you may not fail to obtain credit for the amount of stamps returned.

Instead of sending the old stamps to the Department, you can, if convenient, exchange them for new ones at some city post-office, where large supplies are to be found.

It being impossible to supply all offices with new stamps at once, you will deliver letters received from Kentucky, Missouri, Illinois, Indiana, Ohio, Maryland and Pennsylvania, prepaid by stamps of the old issue, until November 1st ; those from other loyal States east of the Rocky Mountains, until the 1st of December ; and those from the States of California and Oregon, and from the Territories of New Mexico, Utah and Washington, until the 1st January, 1862.

I am, respectfully, your obedient servant,

A. N. ZEVELY,
Third Assistant P. M. General.

Figure 9-1. Notices similar to this were sent to smaller post offices. They contained later dates for demonetization completion.

cannot be effected within the period contemplated by the department. Under these circumstances notice is hereby given to all postmasters who have not received new stamps, to continue the sale of the old issue, and, of course, to mail all letters brought to their offices prepaid by stamps of the old style. With each supply of new stamps postmasters will be directed how to dispose of the old, A strict compliance with the foregoing instructions is required by the Postmaster General.

I am, respectfully, your obedient servant,
A. N. Zevely, Third Assistant P. M. Gen."

With the many and somewhat conflicting instructions that were sent out, and the many newspaper articles that were published concerning the new stamps and the demonetization of the old, there was a certain amount of confusion in the minds of the public and many of the postmasters. The unevenness of distribution and the time-phased periods of demonetization resulted in many interesting and rare philatelic items, and some examples of these will be discussed in this chapter.

In the letter of instructions sent to the postmasters with the distribution of the stamps, there were two main elements that governed the acceptance of the old style of stamps and envelopes. The first was the six-day exchange period. This was to be put into effect upon the receipt of the new stamps by each post office. Notices were to be published or posted, allowing six days for the exchange of old stamps for new, after which, the old stamps would not be accepted for postage. This instruction was rigorously followed by most post offices (with some significant exceptions).

The second element was that subsequent to a specified date, letters franked with the old stamps from particular zones would not be accepted for delivery by receiving post offices. This requirement was added to provide the Post Office Department with a second opportunity to detect illegal use of the demonetized stamps at the destination point. Because of the inability of the Post Office to distribute the new issue according to plan, there was no reasonable way for a receiving postmaster to determine the validity of the original posting, and consequently this element of the instructions was never really put into practice and was officially deleted by the Post Office Department in September 1861. Very few covers that indicate they were considered by the receiving postmaster to be an illegal posting have been recorded.

Contrary to the original plan, the new postage stamps were evidently distributed without regard to geographical location of the post offices. The stamp agent at the New York City office of the National Bank Note Company seems to have filled orders for some of the large Eastern cities first, and followed that distribution with shipments to other post offices, possibly in the order of their requisitions for stamps.

Because of the continuing limited supply of new stamps in the initial month or two, it was necessary at times to send additional supplies of the old stamps to post offices that had exhausted their supplies of the new issue. In those cases, advertising and exchange periods had to be reaccomplished. This added to the confusion, but the results of the entire demonetization period, from the perspective of philately, resulted in one of the most interesting of all periods in the history of the U.S. mails.

In his continuing quest for irrefutable evidence that the so-called premieres gravures of the 1861 issue had not been regularly issued and used, as some early scholars contended, Perry began a countrywide search for newspaper advertisements that reflected the dates of the initial distributions and exchange periods. His search began in 1931 and went on for about 10 years, aided by the many readers of his *Pat Paragraphs*. The result was literally hundreds of advertisements, excerpted from old newspaper files all over the country. These give a reasonably complete picture of the time-phasing of the introduction of the new stamps at most of the larger post offices.

Perry published copies of these advertisements in his *Pat Paragraphs*, and they make extremely interesting and informative reading. New finds of additional advertisements continue to be made to this day and are reported in the philatelic literature.

Forming a specialized collection that contained examples of the first day of use for the 1861 issue at all the various post offices where the date could be ascertained would be a challenging and philatelically valuable endeavor. Of course, completeness would be probably unattainable since no examples may remain from many of the towns, but the search for and acquisition of those that do still exist would be a stimulating experience. To date, advertisements or notices for the exchange of stamps have been located for only about 1 percent of the post offices in operation at that time, so there remains a lot of philatelic detective work still to be done.

One of the strange situations that occurred because of the somewhat haphazard distribution of the new issue was where two towns separated by only a few miles may have had their demonetization periods differ by a month or more. For example, Rutland, Vermont, a county seat, placed the new issue on sale on August 22. West Rutland, which is only five miles away, did not sell its stamps until October 19, almost two months later, and Center Rutland, which is half way between the other two Rutlands, did not issue the new stamps until another week later on October 26, 1861 [5:143].

Similar situations occurred in many locations all over the country. Another example is Northampton, Massachusetts, which began distributing the new issue on

August 20, while its neighbor, Hadley, Massachusetts, which was just four miles away across the Connecticut River, did not have the stamps available until October 4.

While the requirement to make all earlier issues of stamps and envelopes invalid for use is clearly made in all official notices, the situation with regard to envelopes was modified to some extent. The 1¢ star-die envelope, which had been issued the previous year in 1860, was never demonetized. Although no documentation to this effect has ever been located, there is no doubt this was the case. It was believed that so few, if any, of these envelopes were in the hands of the Confederacy that any possible loss would have been very small and much less than the cost of exchanging and replacing all of the 1¢ star-die envelopes in the loyal states. The same situation was true of the 1¢ star-die wrappers, which were issued in October 1861 with the same design as the 1860 envelopes. Another envelope that escaped the demonetization ax was the "compound envelope" (Scott U28-29), which had been issued in December of 1860 to pay both the carrier fee and single-weight postage. This envelope had the 1¢ blue star die and the 3¢ red star die embossed upon it. The 3¢ star die on an envelope by itself was demonetized, but in combination with the 1¢ remained valid for postage. This fact is validated by a notice in the *U.S. Mail & Post Office Assistant* for July of 1862. Almost all of the combination envelopes were sold in New York City. Other origins are scarce.

The lack of documented authorization in this matter has caused much confusion for postal historians and stamp collectors through the years, but the fact remains that specific types of postal stationery of the old designs continued legally in use and can still be used to this day.

In a compendium such as this volume, it is impossible to delve into all relevant subjects to the depth where all of the interesting aspects are covered and explained. The demonetization period is an excellent example of this type of situation. Much has been previously written and a lot of information is available. Interested readers are urged to sample some of the articles and books referenced in this chapter, particularly the writings on the subject by Perry and Graham.

First Uses of the 1¢ Franklin of 1861

According to the records of the National Bank Note Company [5:103], the first delivery, "Order No. 1," was delivered to the government stamp agent, Daniel M. Boyd, on August 16, 1861. This order contained a total of over 5 million stamps for all eight denominations (and probably contained the total output from production for several days previously). About 1.5 million 1¢ and over 3 million 3¢ stamps were included in the delivery.

Baltimore, Maryland, received the first shipment of the new 1861 stamps in time to place them on sale on Saturday, August 17, 1861, and an advertisement appeared in the Baltimore paper on that day announcing their arrival and the exchange procedures and demonetization date for the old stamps.

Perry's *Pat Paragraphs* [5:123] records that two advertisements and a reading notice were published in the *American and Commercial Advertiser*. The initial advertisement on Saturday, August 17, contained the following wording:

"Post Office Notice
The public are hereby notified that the Postmaster at Baltimore will be prepared from this date to Exchange ENVELOPES and STAMPS of the new style for an equivalent amount of the old issue, up to THURSDAY, the 22nd instant, after which the old issue will not be received in payment of letters mailed at this office.
WM.PURNELL,
Postmaster, Baltimore, Md."

The ad ran again on Monday, August 19, with the addition of another paragraph stating:

"The smaller Post Offices in the neighborhood can exchange their stamps up to September 17, 1861."

It was, of course, understood that any of the smaller post offices that availed themselves with the opportunity to exchange their old stamps for new ones were required to notify their customers of their availability and to initiate an exchange period of six days following the notification.

For some weeks, the newspapers of the country had been publishing articles on the new stamps that were being prepared for distribution, and the interest of the public was extremely high. A news item in the Baltimore paper for Monday, August 19, reflects this situation:

"EXCHANGE OF POST OFFICE STAMPS.— On Saturday the stamp department of the Baltimore Post Office was literally besieged with crowds of persons anxious to exchange the old style stamps for the new ones now issuing by the Department. Several extra clerks were required to attend to the demands, as some of the claimants had large quantities of stamps with them. All persons holding them should have them promptly exchanged, otherwise they may lose their value. Mr. Purnell, by way of accommodation has extended the time of exchange for the smaller post offices to the 17th of September."

Only one example of use of the 1861 1¢ Franklin on August 17, 1861, has been recorded. This is an off-cover stamp with a Baltimore, Maryland, August 17, 1861, CDS clearly showing the city and date. A photograph of this rarity is shown in **Figure 9-2**. It was discovered in a small collection in 1938 by Warren DuBois, a Los Angeles dealer, who widely publicized his find and exhibited it at the Treasure Island Golden Gate 1939 International Exhibition [3:240]. The stamp is reported to be the "dot-in-U" variety from plate number 9, the first plate to be printed, which would be correct for this early use. The stamp was subsequently purchased by L.S. Fisher and remained in his spectacular collection of early uses until May 30, 1996, when it was offered by Christie's New York at auction.

With the initial delivery to the stamp agent being on August 16, 1861, at New York City, the only probability for use earlier than August 17 would have been at that city. However, it is known that the anticipated demand for very large numbers of stamps delayed the New York sale of the new issue for an extended period until the post office was assured of an adequate supply. In fact, it was a month later, on September 15, 1861, before the notice of new stamps was published at New York City.

Figure 9-2. Earliest-known use of the 1¢ 1861, Baltimore, Maryland, August 17, 1861.
(Christie's New York auction photo)

The earliest-known use (EKU) on cover is dated August 21, 1861. Four examples of this early use have been recorded, the most spectacular of which is the patriotic cover illustrated in **Figure 9-3**. Tudor Gross, a pioneer collector of the 1¢ 1861, wrote in 1941 that he was aware of two covers, dated August 21, 1861, one of which was in his collection. He did not describe these covers further, and no photos are available, so it is impossible to identify the covers to which he referred.

Two 1¢ 1861 EKU covers were offered in the May 30, 1996, Christie's New York auction of the outstanding L.S. Fisher collection of first-day and earliest-known uses of U.S. stamps. One was postmarked at Pittsburgh, Pennsylvania, with indistinct double postmarks dated August 21, 1861, tying three 1¢ Franklins to an overall printed pink background envelope with a Commission Merchant's corner card. The cover is docketed 1860, in error.

The other cover is clearly postmarked "Philadelphia, Pa., August/21/1861," with 3¢+1¢ postage to pay for carrier pickup to the mail and letter postage to Academia, Pennsylvania. The stamps are canceled with two strikes of an 11-bar circular grid.

Later in 1996, the Unicover Corporation Museum's collection of first-day and EKU covers was auctioned at a September 26 postal-history sale by Shreves Philatelic Galleries. The coincidence of two similarly specialized holdings, with scarce material that had not been on the market for decades, being sold in the same year is remarkable.

The Unicover collection also contained a 1¢ 1861 EKU cover. This cover is a companion piece to the cover to Academia, which was described above. Both are dated August 21, 1861, with a double-line octagonal postmark and have 3¢ and 1¢ stamps of the 1861 issue to pay the letter postage and carrier fee at Philadelphia. Each stamp is canceled by an 11-bar circular grid. Both covers are addressed in the same handwriting and to the same person. The existence of two almost identical covers representing a rare EKU is another remarkable occurrence.

Returning to the superb EKU cover pictured in Figure 9-3, this was first reported by Simmy's Stamp Company of Boston in 1976, and its origin was not disclosed. Whether it is one of the covers referred to by Gross is unknown, but because of its unusual philatelic excellence, it is unlikely he would have seen this item and not described it in some detail.

Figure 9-3. An outstanding example of earliest-known use of the 1¢ on cover. It was posted for carrier collection at Philadelphia, Pennsylvania, on August 18, 1861, with a 3¢ 1857 Washington to pay the letter rate. Because of failure to prepay 1¢ for carrier pickup, the letter was delayed at the post office until the additional postage was paid. The 1861 1¢ Franklin was added on August 21, and the letter entered the mails on that date.
(John Kauffman Inc.)

The cover has a patriotic design in red and blue with a heading for Colonel Friedman's Cameron Regiment Dragoons. It is franked with an 1857 3¢ stamp and an accompanying Philadelphia octagonal town and date marking dated AUG 18 1861. A 1¢ blue 1861 stamp is on the upper-right corner of the cover, adjacent to another Philadelphia octagonal town marking dated AUG 21 1861. Both stamps are canceled with identical syncopated or dashed grids. On the left side of the cover are two REC'D handstamp markings in fancy borders, both dated AUG 19.

The order of application of these markings is of utmost importance in establishing the mailing date of this cover and its bona fides as an earliest-known use of the 1¢ 1861. While there is no absolute way of determining this, a logical sequence can be deduced from the postal requirements of the day. It is most probable that the cover was franked by the writer with the 1857 stamp and dropped into a carrier collection box. The letter was picked up, transported to the post office where it was canceled, and the octagonal AUG 18 1861 marking applied. This would have been on a Sunday. Since the cover was short paid, having not paid the carrier fee, it was held for postage. The writer was advised of the short payment (by advertisement or notice), and this date was probably documented with the AUG 19 received stamp. On August 21, the writer provided the additional postage, the 1¢ 1861 stamp was applied and canceled, and the cover marked with the AUG 21 1861 octagonal town datestamp and sent on its way.

Upon its discovery, the cover was widely publicized, and articles describing it appeared in the Baker column, the *Pennsylvania Postal History Society Journal*, the *Chronicle* and the *American Philatelist*. It was sold in the spring of 1976 at a Simmy's Stamp Company auction, and again in 1979 in a John Kaufmann auction, where it realized a five-figure price.

Figure 9-4. Early use cover from Hartford, Connecticut, posted on August 22, during the local exchange period from August 19-25, 1861, when both the 1857 and 1861 issues were valid for postage.
(James Lee collection)

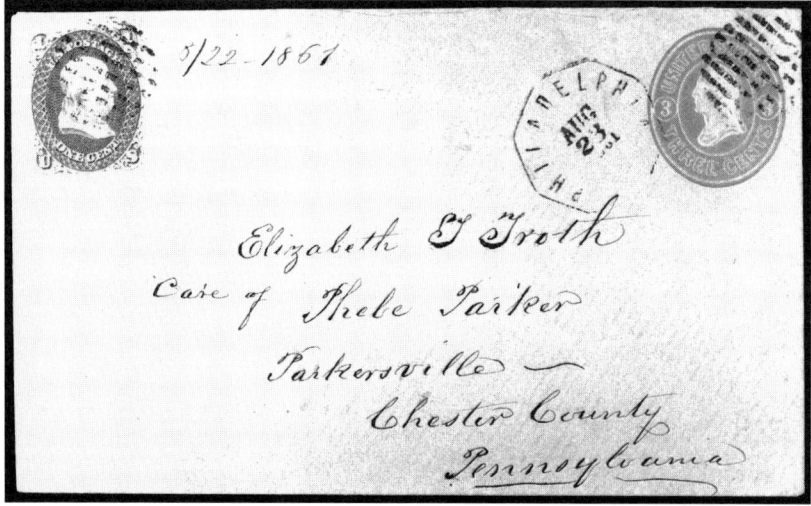

Figure 9-5. Philadelphia, Pennsylvania, August 23, 1861, cover. Both the stamped envelope (Scott U34) and the adhesive stamp (Scott 63) are from the new issues. The envelopes were put on sale at Philadelphia on August 8, 1861, and the postage stamps were available on August 19, with a six-day exchange period.
(C.W. Christian collection)

In the author's opinion, this is the most desirable cover for a specialized 1861 1¢ blue collection because of its uniqueness, philatelic beauty and because, as an earliest-known cover, it provides a foundation for all of the postal history to follow.

After the initial order on August 16, the first week of distribution through Saturday, August 24, 1861, saw five more orders delivered by National Bank Note Company to the resident stamp agent at New York for a total of more than 6 million additional stamps (including all denominations). One and a half million of these were of the 1¢ value. The stamps were rapidly distributed to post offices in the East, and as far west as Minnesota and Kansas. All of the border states with the South were supplied, at least at a main post office, and this satisfied one of the objectives of the original distribution plan.

Figure 9-6. Early use of the 1¢ 1861 Franklin to pay the local drop-letter rate, postmarked August 23, 1861, Canandaigua, New York, and mailed within the legal exchange period for the area.

As stated previously, when supplies of the new stamps were delivered to a post office, they notified their patrons of the fact and established a period for exchange of old stamps for new, which was directed by the Post Office Department to be six days from the date of the notice. Because of the slight ambiguity caused by the word "from," and the occasional inclusion of a Sunday in the period (many, but not all, post offices were open on Sundays, usually with shortened hours), the actual period of exchange varied from six to seven days, and in rare circumstances individual postmasters, upon their own initiative, varied the exchange period.

The Louisville, Kentucky, postmaster placed a notice in the *Louisville Democrat* stating that the old stamps could be exchanged for the new for a period of three days, commencing August 22 [5:122]. This short period for the exchange was an unusual departure from the normal period of six days.

During the advertised exchange periods, it was perfectly legal to use stamps from the 1851-57 issues, alone or in combination with the new 1861 stamps. Some examples of early use of the 1861 1¢ are illustrated. **Figure 9-4** shows a cover, dated August 22, 1861, from Hartford, Connecticut. The cover is franked by two 1¢ values from the new 1861 issue and a single 1¢ stamp from the 1857 issue, making up the normal 3¢ rate. Hartford placed the new issue on sale on August 19, and the old issue was valid until August 25.

Figure 9-5 illustrates a Philadelphia cover dated August 23, 1861. The new 1¢ stamp is used to pay the carrier fee on a 3¢ government envelope, also of the new 1861 issue. The envelopes were first sold at Philadelphia on August 8, and the stamps became available on August 19, a Monday. The rush to exchange stamps was so great that the Philadelphia postmaster, C.A. Walborn, found it necessary to temporarily secure additional space, and to staff it with a full force of clerks to handle all of the business [5:141].

The search for first-day-of-use covers, dated August 17, 1861, has continued, and only one so far has been found for the 1861 series of stamps. This cover is franked with a single 3¢ stamp and was mailed at Baltimore, Maryland. Coincidentally, the addressee of this unique early cover, Elizabeth T. Troth, is the same person to whom the cover illustrated in Figure 9-4 was addressed.

Another August 23 cover is shown in **Figure 9-6** on a local drop letter at Canandaigua, New York. While the dates of exchange for Canandaigua have not been determined, Rochester, New York, which is the nearest large post office (23 miles), advertised its exchange period beginning August 21, 1861. Stamps for sale at Canandaigua may have been obtained from this source.

Figure 9-7 shows an interesting exchange-period cover, dated October 1, 1861, at Huntingdon, Pennsylvania, a small county-seat post office in the central part of the state. Huntingdon advertised the new issue on October 1, so this cover is an example of a first day of use for that city. The cover is franked with two 1861 Franklins and a 10¢ from the 1857 issue. The oversize envelope was marked as containing election blanks and could have been sent at the third-class rate for printed matter.

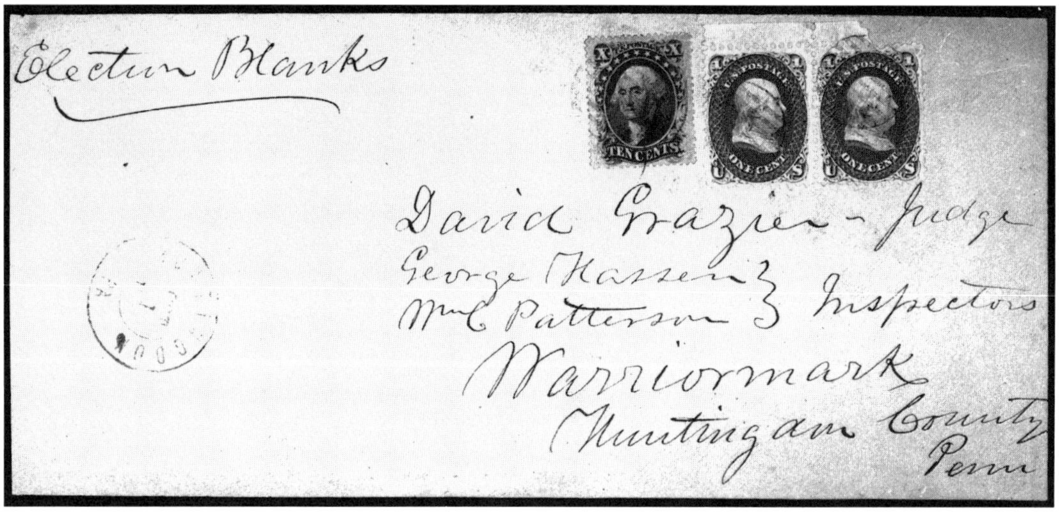

Figure 9-7. Huntingdon, Pennsylvania, to Warriormark, Pennsylvania, October 1, 1861. Large cover containing election blanks, and possibly mailed as printed matter. Unusual example of an 1857 10¢ value in combination with two 1861 1¢ stamps. The cover was posted during the exchange period. The 12¢ postage would pay for 13 ounces of election blanks at the rate for printed matter.

Demonetization Across the United States

As fast as the stamps could be produced, they were delivered to post offices, and the exchange periods initiated. As previously stated, the end of the first week saw stamps from the new issue in the hands of postmasters in at least one major post office in each of the eastern and border states. In the days that followed, distribution was made to more distant post offices and to the smaller post offices in the eastern part of the country. Distribution to the smaller post offices was accomplished by shipping orders directly to them, or by the small post offices obtaining their supplies from nearby major post offices. This drain on the stamp inventories of the large post offices meant that they frequently had to be resupplied with additional shipments.

The production capacity of the National Bank Note Company was strained to the utmost, and in spite of seven-day and almost 24-hour operation, the demand for the new stamps exceeded the supply for the first several months. The confusion resulted in many extremely interesting letters and newspaper articles. Keeping the public up to date on the situation required continuing notices in many cases, and the opinion, held by many, that the government had no right to deny its citizens the right to use something they had purchased and owned, led to some heated editorials and refusals to abide by the demonetization regulations.

The postmaster of New York City, William B. Taylor, dragged his feet in complying with the demonetization edict, at least with respect to stamps. New York, however, was the first office in the country, on August 7, to advertise the new envelopes for sale. Postmaster Taylor stated publicly that the new stamps would not be put on sale until he had a sufficient amount in his possession to meet all his anticipated needs. This seemed to take a particularly long period, considering that he probably was the recipient of a considerable number of stamps by the time the second National Bank Note Company shipment on August 17, 1861, was distributed.

Reading between the lines of his personal letters, notices and articles, it is not difficult to deduce that Postmaster Taylor was pressured by public opinion or personally thought that the demonetization action was improper. Of course, as an appointed government official, he could not officially say so or directly contradict the orders of the Post Office Department. Some of the contents of the newspaper articles and Taylor's letters are repeated here because they are indicative of the state of affairs in New York City and lay the groundwork for the interesting fact that only one cover mailed at New York City, even long after the exchange period had expired, has ever been found where demonetized stamps were not accepted for postage.

The late Morris Fortgang made a study of New York City's reaction to demonetization, and in an 1956 article [6:337] he made a strong argument for the theory that Postmaster Taylor explicitly allowed the use of the demonetized stamps. Fortgang also stated that he had never seen a New York City cover franked by the old stamps that had not been accepted for postage. His search continued as long as he lived without success, and it is

Figure 9-8. Only known cover from New York City showing refusal to recognize demonetized stamps. The sender originally placed a 3¢ 1857 and a 1¢ 1861 on the letter to pay the carrier fee plus postage. After being held at the post office for additional postage, the sender added two 1¢ 1861 stamps, and the letter was accepted. (James Lee collection)

only recently that one has been found.

In an excellent series of articles on carriers, John Kohlhepp [7:194] pictures and describes this cover (see **Figure 9-8**). It was mailed at New York City in 1862 with a 3¢ 1857 stamp paying the postage and a 1¢ 1861 paying the carrier-collection fee. The old stamp was not recognized, and the cover was marked "Held For Postage." After notification, the sender paid an additional 2¢, and two more 1¢ 1861 stamps were added. Obviously, by only assessing additional postage in the amount of 2¢, the postal clerk erred and gave postage credit for the 1¢ 1861 that had been affixed to pay the carrier fee. The cover was originally postmarked on July 19, 1862. After the additional two stamps were added, partially covering the original postmark and the "Held For Postage" marking, the cover was postmarked again on July 23, 1863, and entered into the mails.

While this cover terminates the search instituted by Fortgang, it does not invalidate his conclusions. To have found only one example among the surviving thousands of covers that traversed the New York City Post Office in the 1862-63 period indicates that this particular cover is an anomaly, and that in general demonetized covers were accepted.

A *New York Times* article dated August 25 follows [5:135]:

> "POSTAGE STAMPS — The new stamps will be ready for delivery on or about Sept. 1, after which time six days are to be allowed for exchange. The Postmaster received a large number of the new stamps a week since; but as his supply was thought to be insufficient, it was deemed prudent to wait until the printers might be able to produce three millions for the New-York office, and then publish the fact of his readiness to adopt the new postal token."

The large number of new stamps referred to must have been from one or both of the first shipments on August 16 and 17, so the many references in the literature that state that New York City did not receive any of the new stamps until later are in error. The following day (August 26), the New York *Tribune* noted that the postmaster had received a large but insufficient supply of the new postage stamps, and if there were 3 million of them at the New York Post Office as expected on September 1, they would be issued at that time.

On September 1, 1861, the *Times* stated [5:135]:

> "THE NEW POSTAGE STAMPS
> New York has barely a million stamps as her share of the new stamps, and the postmaster desires to begin with at least three millions. Consequently, notwithstanding the printers are very busy, new stamps cannot be exchanged before the end of the week. Meantime the public should not forget that the stamps that are now in use will be worthless in a week from the time when the Postmaster sends forth the first stamp of the new design. It is scarcely necessary to add that the new stamp will be worthless in the rebel States."

On September 16, the New York Post Office inserted a notice in the *Times*, as follows:

> "The new style of Government Postage Stamps is now ready, and for sale at this office. Exchange will be made of the new style for an equivalent amount of the old issue during a period of
> SIX DAYS
> from the date of this notice, after which stamps of the old issue will not be received in payment of postage on letters sent from this office.
> Wm. B. Taylor, P. M."

Finally New York had its stamps, but the public was not very happy with the idea that six days later any old stamps that they still possessed would be without value. Editorials appeared in the New York papers requesting that the government extend indefinitely the time for exchange. One of these editorials from the *Times*, dated September 21, 1861, is quoted [5:136]:

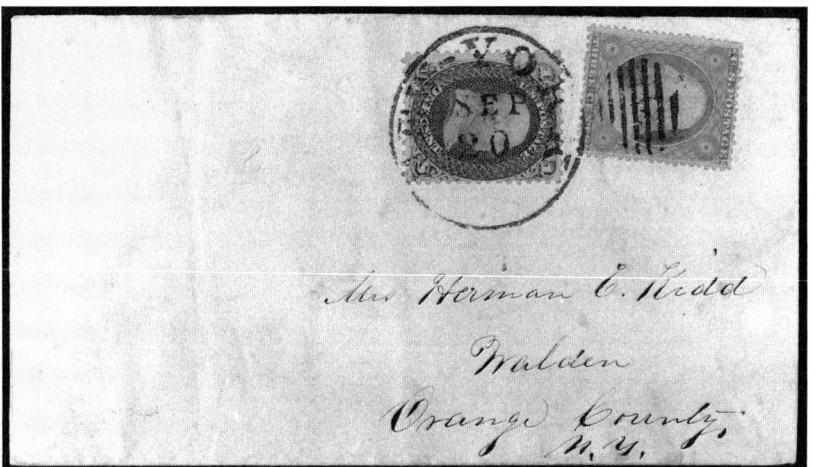

Figure 9-9. New York City, September 20. Mixed issue use with an 1857 3¢ and an 1861 1¢ to pay the 3¢+1¢ letter rate and carrier fee. If the year of mailing was 1861, this fell within the exchange period that ended for New York City on September 28, 1861.

"Exchanging Postage Stamps

According to the notice issued by Postmaster Taylor, the time allowed for the exchange of stamps expires today. The people have unanimously acquiesced in the necessity of rendering useless the stamps scattered through the rebel States and have done their utmost to comply with the conditions declared indispensable to this end; but the cue attached to the cashier's window at the Postoffice yesterday evening, was twice as long as that formed there on Monday, and this fact alone shows how ludicrously short was the time fixed for the transaction of such an amount of business as this exchange of stamps involved.

Undoubtedly, any holder of a stamp, whether it represents one, three, or twenty-four cents, can oblige the Government to accept it in payment of postage or to refund its value, for issues of this kind can be repudiated with no more justice than could the Treasury Notes now in circulation because it was thought best to change the tint of the ink in which they were hereafter to be printed. The community is not disposed to stand on such points as these, however, and the Government should exhibit a corresponding spirit of accommodation.

The time for completing the exchange should be extended for a fortnight at least, and supplies of the new stamps should be deposited in all the branch Post Offices. Such arrangements are positively necessary if justice is to be done to the thousands through the City who still hold stamps of the old issue, very many of whom can neither afford to lose the small values which they represent nor the time involved in a visit to the General Post Office. The Government does not intend to act meanly in this matter, and it could not afford to do so if it had the inclination. We trust that Postmaster Taylor will immediately persuade Mr. Blair to authorize him to make the arrangements at which we have hinted."

While it is unlikely that Taylor changed Blair's mind in any way, the newspaper articles and editorials certainly made an impression on the New York postmaster. He repeated the announcement a week later and extended the exchange period to September 28. This action was repeated again for a final time on October 2, 1861 [3:224].

Figure 9-9 shows an example of concurrent use of the old and new issues. This carrier-fee cover was mailed at New York City on September 20. Unfortunately, there is no way to determine the year of use since the standard New York City CDS of the period did not contain a year date, and as previously mentioned, illegal use of the old issues never deterred New York mail from being processed and sent on its way. Of course, if the year was 1861, this cover illustrates a legal exchange-period use.

The search for more illegal-use covers that were not recognized at New York City still goes on, but with diminishing chance of success. Of course, some years after the end of the Civil War, the memories of the demonetization regulations faded, and the use of stamps from the 1851-60 issues usually passed without comment through many post offices. Examples of these have been recorded.

Vermont postmasters maintained their state's reputation for individuality and opposition to government control by also declining to penalize their patrons for using demonetized stamps. Although they gave lip service to the regulations, and posted all the necessary notices and advertisements, they apparently never failed to recognize the use of old stamps as legal for postage. Graham remarked in a *Chronicle* article that George Slawson, an expert in Vermont postal history, had stated that acceptance of old stamps was normal, and that he had never seen a cover bearing demonetized stamps that was not accepted by a Vermont postmaster.

It should be mentioned that, although it would not become a separate state for another two years, western Virginia remained loyal, and the post offices in that part of Virginia were supplied with the new stamps. Wheeling, (West) Virginia, advertised the new stamps for sale on August 26, 1861.

Documentation of the distribution of the new stamps in the territories and along the Pacific Coast is relatively sparse. The Denver Post Office, in Colorado

Territory, inserted advertisements in the September 20 and 30 issues of the *Rocky Mountain News* regarding the new issues. They departed significantly from the usual format so are worth repeating here.

> (September 20, 1861)
> "All letters enclosed in stamped envelopes of old issue will be retained for postage on and after this date. Letters with old stamps may be mailed until further notice.
> J.S. Fillmore, Dep. P.M."

> (September 30, 1861)
> "The old postage stamps are no longer received at this office for postage; they may be exchanged for the new style stamps until the evening of Monday, October 7th.
> SAM'L S. CURTIS, P.M."

Although there was a seven-day exchange period, the postmaster did not allow any period for the continued use of the old stamps after the new ones were available. It might be wondered how he handled the situation where a customer deposited a letter during the exchange period with an old-style stamp on it. Since the stamp was glued to the envelope, he certainly could not exchange it for a new one, and if a new stamp were gratuitously pasted over the old one, the postmaster would have no old stamp to turn in for credit. It is possible that the notice erred in its wording, and that Denver used the same procedures of dual use during the exchange period as did the other post offices.

On the Pacific Coast, San Francisco was probably the first office to receive new stamps, and on October 9, 1861, advertised their sale. In the notice, the hours of exchange were restricted to between 10 and 12 each day. This is unusual and is the only example that the writer has noted where such a restriction applied.

The new stamps arrived in Steilacoom City, Washington Territory, on December 4, 1861, as proclaimed in an announcement in the *Puget Sound Herald* on the following day. Steilacoom is a small village about five miles south of Tacoma, so it is probable that Tacoma also had the new issues by that time.

The actual pattern of distribution that seems to emerge from a study of the places and dates where the new stamps were put on sale throughout the country shows that most of the major post offices in the eastern half of the United States received some supplies in the last two weeks of August. September shipments appear to have been used to restock supplies at these major post offices, and to initiate shipments to some of the major offices in the West. Then in late-September and October, deliveries began to smaller post offices, and it was early in 1862 before distribution was finally completed to all U.S. post offices.

For approximately six months, the public and the postmasters had to deal with a combination of legal and illegal stamps, and with old stamps, at particular times and places, being relegalized for brief periods. It was a postally confusing and philatelically fascinating period.

'Old Stamps Not Recognized'

The most sought-after postal history covers from the period are those covers franked with the old stamps and used after they were demonetized. A significant number of these scarce and desirable covers were used in combination with the 1861 1¢ Franklin, and examples of this type of use will be discussed in this section.

Their scarcity, to a large degree, is due to the October 8, 1860, regulation that required mail with illegal franking to be immediately forwarded to the Dead Letter Office. Subsequent to the exchange periods, many letters were still being posted with the old stamps and, in accordance with regulations, were dispatched to the DLO. Failure by the DLO to obtain the required additional postage resulted in many of the letters being destroyed.

The additional work and congestion in the DLO due to demonetization caused this regulation to be amended after a short period, and the following notice was issued:

> "POST OFFICE DEPARTMENT, Nov 26
> In view of the increased number of letters held for postage and returned to the dead letter office, it is ordered that the the order of this department dated Oct. 8, 1860, be rescinded and the prior practice be restored. Postmasters will therefore notify the person addressed that such letter is held for postage, and that upon his writing and prepayment of the postage on his letter and enclosing a stamp to be placed on the letter held for postage, the same will be forwarded to his address.
> By order of the Post Master General
> (signed) JOHN A. KASSON
> 1st Assistant Postmaster General."

This change in regulations set the stage for some of the interesting "not recognized" covers that resulted following the end of legal use for the old stamps.

The gems of the "not recognized" covers are those where a postal marking such as OLD STAMPS NOT RECOGNIZED was applied. These are truly scarce. A patriotic carrier-use cover is shown in **Figure 9-10**. This cover originated at Philadelphia and was postmarked on September 26, 1862. It was marked with the OLD STAMPS NOT RECOGNIZED device and also with a "Due 3." Since a new 3¢ stamp was not added to replace the illegal 3¢ on the cover, it most likely was forwarded to the addressee and the postage due collected at that point. This example is probably the most spectacular of the covers showing the Philadelphia "Old Stamps" marking, and has resided in many famous collections including those of Kimmel,

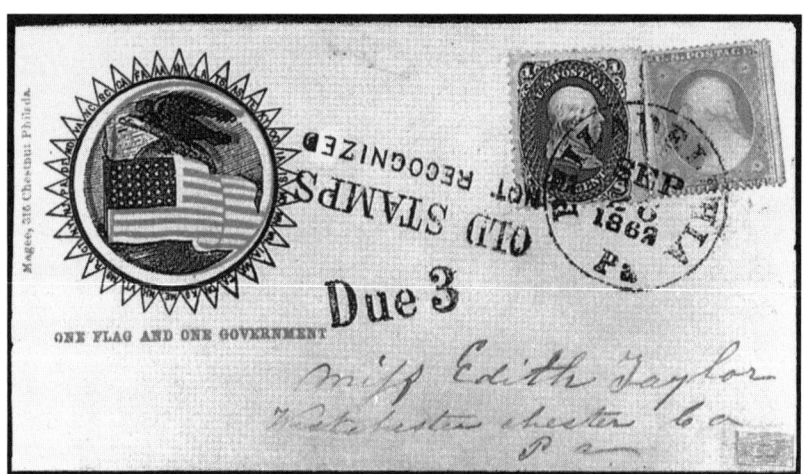

Figure 9-10. Philadelphia, Pennsylvania, September 26, 1862, carrier use with mixed franking, including a demonetized 3¢ 1857. The cover is marked with OLD STAMPS/NOT RECOGNIZED and "Due 3" for collection at destination.
(R.A. Siegel Auction Galleries)

Figure 9-11. Philadelphia, Pennsylvania, November 10, 1862. Use of a single 1¢ 1857 with two 1¢ 1861 stamps to make up the 3¢ letter rate. The cover is marked OLD STAMPS NOT RECOGNIZED and "Due 1 Ct" for collection.
(Christie's New York)

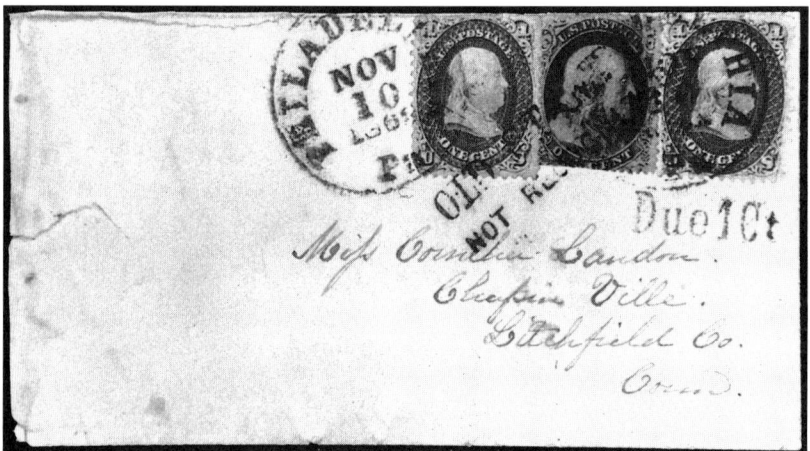

Figure 9-12. Cover posted at Chicago, Illinois, on February 12, 1863, with attempted use of the demonetized 1¢ 1857 stamp. The letter was held for payment, and later entered into the mails on February 15 with an additional 1¢ 1861 stamp added to make up the 3¢ letter rate. HELD FOR POSTAGE was stamped on the reverse. All markings are in blue. The manuscript "1070" is a file number applied at the post office to assist in locating the "held" letter.

Haas, Paliafito and Wunderlich. It was offered by Harvey Warm at Ameripex 1986, and again in a Robert A. Siegel auction in 1993, where it realized $20,000.

A similar cover with the same handstamp, but in this case marked "Due 1 Ct," is shown in **Figure 9-11**. The letter with a single 1¢ 1857 stamp, which was not recognized, and two legal 1861 1¢ stamps was postmarked at Philadelphia on November 10, 1862. This cover was part of the Ishikawa collection and was also sold in 1993 for a price considerably less than the previous example.

This same Philadelphia marking has been reported as used on August 26, 1861 (with an 1857 3¢ stamp). This was posted on a Monday, the second day after the end of the exchange period, and may qualify it for listing as the earliest-known use of the OLD STAMPS NOT RECOGNIZED marking.

Similar markings are also known from Chicago and Harrisburg, and include an ILLEGAL STAMP marking from New Orleans, Lousiana. No covers from these origins are known to be franked with the 1¢ 1861 stamp [8:28].

An excellent example of non-recognition of the old issue is illustrated in **Figure 9-12**. In the case of this February 12, 1863, Chicago cover franked by two 1861 1¢ stamps and a single 1857 1¢, the letter was marked on the back HELD FOR POSTAGE and inscribed on the front with a file number "1070" (probably for ease of later retrieval). The sender was notified of the short payment, and when the 1¢ due was received, a stamp was added and the letter postmarked with a February 15 CDS and entered into the mails.

It is strange, but no advertisements were found from Chicago during Perry's long search. However, Richard McP. Cabeen stated in an August 5, 1961, article in *Stamps,* as reported by Graham [9:30], that the exchange period for Chicago was printed in the *Chicago Tribune* to be from August 21 to 27, 1861.

Since in the 1861 period the most common way to mail a letter was to hand it to the postmaster, the illegal use of demonetized stamps was usually detected at that point. The postmaster normally requested additional payment from the sender to compensate for any use of old stamps, and affixed new stamps over the old. A well-known cover from the J. David Baker collection [3:225] that illustrates this procedure is shown in **Figure 9-13**.

This October 14 (year not known) patriotic cover from South Manchester, Connecticut, was posted with three 1857 1¢ stamps (incidentally, these were vertically double-perforated) to pay the postage. The old stamps were not accepted, and the sender paid an additional 3¢ and applied the new stamps over the unused strip of three. The postmaster canceled the stamps with PAID markings, postmarked the cover and sent it on its way. In the illustration of this cover in **Figure 9-13**, the 1¢ strip has been lifted from its original position and hinged in place so that the underlying unused

Figure 9-13. South Manchester, Connecticut, October 14. Strip of three 1861 1¢ stamps pasted over the original demonetized 1857 stamps. (Baker collection)

strip of three can be seen. The cover is signed by Ashbrook and contains his analysis on the reverse side.

Another similar use is pictured in **Figure 9-14**. This Lancaster, Ohio, January 8, 1862, cover to Prairieford, Illinois, was posted with three of the demonetized 1857 1¢ stamps. The postmaster did not accept the old stamps and required the sender to pay an additional 3¢. A vertical strip of three 1861 1¢ stamps were affixed over the uncanceled old stamps, which are clearly visible.

Covers from this period should be carefully examined. One or more demonetized stamps may be lurking beneath the visible postage, and can transform an ordinary cover into a scarce and desirable item.

Figure 9-14. Lancaster, Ohio, January 8, 1862. Old stamps not accepted and a vertical strip of three 1861 1¢ stamps affixed over the original postage paid by three 1¢ stamps of the 1857 issue. (James Lee collection)

Figure 9-15. Cincinnati, Ohio, July 14. Old 1857 1¢ stamp accepted with the two 1¢ 1861 stamps for letter delivery to destination at Freedom, Ohio, without penalty.
(James Lee collection)

Old Stamps Accepted

A number of covers showing franking with stamps of the 1857 issue after the end of the demonetization grace period are to be found in the category "old stamps accepted." In addition to the actions of Vermont and New York City postmasters who passed all mail regardless of the use of old stamps, there are many examples of other covers that went through the mails with illegal stamps. Some of these, undoubtedly, just slipped through undetected. Some were mailed years after the demonetization action, and the postal clerks didn't know or possibly didn't care that the stamps were not legal. Others probably reflected the opinion of individual postmasters who felt that people should not be penalized for using a stamp they had already purchased from the government in good faith.

Some uses originated in the South where, subsequent to 1865, Southerners attempted to use old stamps that were still in their possession. Most of these letters were detected. The postmasters in the South during the post-war period probably were particularly watchful for these attempts at fraudulent use.

Figure 9-15 shows a patriotic cover from Cincinnati, Ohio, used on July 14. Although the year date is not shown, it obviously was mailed after completion of the demonetization exchange period. The illegal 1¢ 1857 stamp was accepted without question and the letter sent to its destination at Freedom, Ohio.

By the beginning of 1862, the demonetization furor had subsided substantially, and the Civil War furnished many more serious problems for the populace to consider. However, the legacy left by the postal authorities in attempting to exchange one small piece of paper for another of equal value has provided a great challenge to students and a delight to the collectors of the scarce philatelic artifacts surviving from these actions.

References

1. Norona, Delf, ed. *Cyclopedia of United States Postmarks and Postal History*. Quarterman Publications. 1975.

2. Graham, Richard B. "Demonetization of the Stamps of 1851-61." *Linn's Stamp News*. May 27, 1991.

3. Baker, Hugh J. and J. David Baker. *Baker's U.S. Classics*. U. S. Philatelic Classics Society. 1985.

4. Graham, Richard B. "Demonetization and Replacement of Stamps in 1861; The Instructional Letters." *Chronicle*. May 1984.

5. Perry, Eliott. *Pat Paragraphs*. Bureau Issues Association Inc. 1981.

6. Fortgang, Morris. "Old Stamps Recognized at New York." *Stamps*. December 1, 1956.

7. Kohlhepp, John. "The Carrier Service: Final Years of the Fee-Based System." *Chronicle* No. 115. August 1982.

8. Graham, Richard B. "Demonetization of the U. S. 1851-60 stamps." *Linn's Stamp News*. October 25, 1993.

9. Graham, Richard B. "U.S. Civil War: 'Old stamps not recognized.'" *Linn's Stamp News*. March 28, 1994.

CHAPTER 10

City Carrier Collection and Delivery

Introduction

The collection and delivery of mail by local carrier services during the 19th century provides one of the most interesting areas for collecting and philatelic inquiry. The subject has been thoroughly investigated, and hundreds of articles have been written about the private carriers and the government-operated local delivery systems. From this vast amount of information, an attempt has been made to present here a condensed version of the story of the carrier mails in the early 1860s.

In 1861, most towns and villages did not provide any carrier service to their postal patrons. Of the approximately 20,000 post offices (not counting the 9,000 in the South), only about 50 offices offered carrier service. These offices were mainly located in the populous northeastern states, and in the majority of these offices, the carrier service was paid for in cash and not by stamps. As a result, covers showing postal carrier service are not particularly common.

In most post offices throughout the country, the mail-collection and delivery system was very simple. If a letter or packet was to be mailed to an out-of-town destination, it was presented at the post office where, if the postage stamp or stamps had not already been affixed, postage was paid, and the item stamped and entered into the mails. Incoming mail was called for at the post office, where it was received at the counter or from a rented post office box.

Mail deposited for local delivery was called drop mail. It was deposited at the post office with postage paid for by stamps, and subsequently delivered at the counter to the addressee or placed in the addressee's box.

While this system adequately served the needs of small and rural communities, it did not meet the requirements of the rapidly growing large cities. As early as 1825 and 1836, laws had been enacted that provided for the delivery and collection of mail by post office carriers. The laws authorized the postmaster general to employ carriers to deliver and collect mail for a fee, not to exceed 2¢ for each letter and ½¢ for each newspaper or pamphlet. It was stated in the 1836 statute that delivery was to be at the option of the addressee. This was a fundamental part of the original statute, and all amendments and revisions to the law. If a person wanted his mail to be delivered by carrier, it was necessary to notify the post office in writing to that effect, except in New York City and some other large cities, where the mail would be delivered by carrier unless the individual had notified the post office that he did not want his mail delivered. In either case, it was the decision of the recipient that governed the carrier delivery of mail.

In the more populous cities where private carrier services were prospering in the early years, intense competition and rivalry existed between the government and the private posts for the business of local mail delivery. By 1851, the Post Office Department was engaged in a concerted attempt to eliminate the private operators. By the time the 1861 series of stamps was issued, in August of 1861, the colorful and turbulent era of the private carrier posts in the large cities was drawing to a close. Legislative actions by the government in response to requests from the postmaster general were effectively putting most of the privately owned mail carriers out of business.

All competition was finally eliminated in the early part of 1862, when Blood's, the last operating local private post that was competing with the post office, closed its doors in Philadelphia.

The period of time between the first use of the 1861 1¢ Franklin and the end of operations of the private local posts in the cities with government carrier service was less than a year. Few posts were still in business during this period. The result is that covers showing concurrent use of a private local-post stamp and the 1¢ 1861 stamp are extremely scarce. **Figure 10-1** shows a rare example of an October 22, 1861, letter handled by Blood's Penny Post in Philadelphia. The letter, franked by three 1¢ stamps, was probably deposited at a Blood's collection point, where the private carrier fee of 1¢ was paid and the Blood's adhesive label and distinctive postmarking applied. It was carried to the post office on the same day. There the Philadelphia CDS was applied and the letter entered into the mails. This date is less than three months prior to the end of business by Blood's on January 11, 1862.

During the more than a quarter of a century the government carrier service was being developed, the fee charged for the service varied with respect to both location and time. The upper limit to be charged was fixed at 2¢ per letter by law, but the actual fee depended on the level of competition from private posts in each city. The final determination of the amount to be charged for each type of carrier service in a specific city was made by the postmaster general, based on recommendations by the local postmaster.

Generally, the fee for carrier collection or delivery was set at the maximum of 2¢ in those towns where there

Figure 10-1. Rare use of Blood's Philadelphia Penny Post stamp with three 1861 1¢ stamps to pay for collection to the mails. The cover shows a faint double-line 23mm Blood's circular datestamp. (C.W. Christian collection)

was little or no competition from private carriers. Where competition was strong, the fees were reduced.

Since the Post Office Department had a monopoly on the delivery of incoming mail, it normally charged 2¢, the maximum allowable, for this service. Concurrently in some large cities such as Boston, New York and Philadelphia, collection of letters to the mails at times was free. This effectively undercut the private competition.

The varying and uneven rate structure finally came to an end with the passage of the Act of June 15, 1860, effective July 1, 1860, which set a nondiscretionary rate of 1¢ for carrier service in those cities where a fee-carrier system was operating.

The 1¢ paid the carrier fee for delivery of incoming mail to the addressee, or paid the collection fee for mail deposited in boxes or handed to the carriers or other postal employees for transmission to the post office, or paid for both collection and delivery of local mail. The drop-letter postage of 1¢ was eliminated for local letters delivered by carrier, and the 1¢ was instead paid to the carriers. Drop letters that were both deposited and picked up at the post office continued to be charged 1¢ for the drop-letter service.

This rate structure remained in effect until July 1, 1863, when all fees for carrier service were abolished.

The Post Office Carrier System

With authorization from the postmaster general, the postmasters of selected cities instituted systems for collection of mail for delivery to the post office, and for delivery of mail from the post office to the public. In addition, the systems provided for the collection and delivery of local letters and packets that did not enter the mails.

The carrier system was manned primarily by nonsalaried employees of the post office. They were hired and directed by the postmaster or his representative and were bonded. These carriers were known as "penny-postmen," which was probably a carryover from the days of colonial rule by Great Britain, where the carriers collected one penny (2¢) per letter for their services.

The revenue for their services was derived entirely from the cash fees that were collected and from the payment by the public for stamps used to pay for carrier service. Normally, the collected fees were placed in a common fund, and the proceeds divided among the carriers to equalize reimbursement for the different jobs within the carrier service. Regulations required that the carrier services be self-supporting, and careful records were kept of the number of letters handled and amounts collected and paid.

Carriers were debited for each letter they received from the post office for delivery, and were required to return the collected fee to the post office or to return the letter for credit if the addressee could not be found or refused the letter.

Since the payment of carriers was the responsibility of the individual postmasters, it was necessary for their post office accounts to be reimbursed by the Post Office Department for stamps purchased and used by the public to prepay the carrier-collection fee. The number of cities that allowed prepayment of the carrier-collection fee in stamps was limited, and these cities will be discussed later in some detail.

In a large city, such as New York, the carrier-service area was divided into sections, and each section contained a carrier station. Within each section was a network of collection boxes mounted on lamp posts or placed strategically in stores. Collecting carriers made the rounds of these boxes three to six times daily and carried the contents to the carrier stations. At the station, the mail was sorted. Out-of-town letters were forwarded to the main post office, while local mail was sorted for delivery from the appropriate carrier station. Carrier runs between the stations and between the stations and the main post office were conducted at frequent intervals. Each carrier station also received incoming out-of-town mail from the main post office for delivery.

The carriers delivered all mail and collected the delivery fee of 1¢ from the addressee. While making his rounds, the carrier also picked up items for the mails and for local delivery, receiving 1¢ for each one not prepaid by a stamp. Letters deposited in boxes were picked up by "collecting carriers," whose primary job was to visit each of the boxes in his section several times each day and to carry the collected mail to the section station.

It should be emphasized at this point that the delivery fee for mail arriving from out of town had to be paid in cash upon delivery. There was no way for the sender to prepay this fee. More will be said about this later in the chapter. The carrier fee for local letters or for mail directed out of town had to be prepaid by postage stamps. The single exception to this requirement was in Washington, D.C., where the 1¢ Eagle carrier stamp (Scott LO2) was still available. It had not been demonetized along with the other 1851 issues and could legally be used to pay carrier fees. Examples of this use are scarce.

In addition to being available at the post office and carrier stations, postage stamps could be purchased from many of the stores where collection boxes were located. Establishments vied to provide space for the collection boxes since the presence of the boxes was an incentive for the public to patronize the stores.

While the fees were generally to be paid in stamps or cash, there was a permitted deviation from this requirement for companies or individuals who had established accounts with the carriers or post offices. In these cases the fees were recorded and collected at stated intervals.

Identifying and collecting covers that show carrier handling requires, among other things, a knowledge of which cities and towns had carrier services provided by their post offices. All of the carrier cities do not seem to be listed in the reports of the postmaster general for the years prior to 1863. For example, the listing contained in the 1861 annual report of Postmaster General Montgomery Blair for the fiscal year ending June 30, 1861 [1:650], is reproduced here, at right. This gives some information concerning the number and identification of the cities with operating carrier systems. It is, however, not complete since it is known that carriers were operating contemporaneously in other cities that are not listed, such as Brooklyn, New York, and New Bedford, Massachusetts.

It is the author's opinion that in this listing the only cities that normally used postage stamps for prepayment of the carrier-collection fee were New York City, Philadelphia, Boston, Baltimore and Washington. Although not listed, Brooklyn, New York, also used postage stamps for prepayment.

Although covers are known from other cities where the franking suggests that prepayment of the collection fee by stamp was intended and possibly accepted, this writer believes that these examples are due to errors or lack of knowledge on the part of the senders. This interesting aspect of the carrier mails will be discussed more fully in context with the descriptions of the services in the major cities. This writer's opinion in this matter is not universally shared by all philatelic students of the carrier systems. Unfortunately, as of this writing, there does not seem to be a sufficient weight of evidence on either side to completely settle the question of general acceptance of stamps as a means of prepayment.

In the postmaster general's report for 1862, the list of carrier cities decreased from 12 to 11, with the loss of Kensington, Pennsylvania, and Roxbury, Massachusetts, and the addition of Kingston, Massachusetts. Although lost as a separate post office, Kensington was incorporated into the Philadelphia system as a sub-post office, and continued to operate. The reader is cautioned not to consider these lists to be complete. The reason for not including some of the known carrier cities is not known to this writer. Elliott Perry suggested that many of the post offices with carrier services (such as Cincinnati) did not always report their carrier activities to the Post Office Department, and as a result, information in the annual report was frequently incomplete [2:228].

This sounds like a reasonable assumption. There were no fiscal interactions between the carrier services

---

REPORT OF THE POSTMASTER GENERAL.

No. 5.

Statement of the number of letters, circulars, newspapers, and pamphlets, received and delivered by carriers, and the amount received and paid out for carriage, in the cities mentioned below, for the year ending June 30, 1861.

Cities.	Number of letters.	Number of circulars.	Number of newspapers and pamphlets.	Total number of letters, circulars, &c.	Amount received and paid out for carriers.
New York, N. Y.	6,935,410	2,071,531	559,898	9,566,839	$92,868 90
Philadelphia, Pa.	2,093,020	49,713	331,504	2,474,231	23,320 38
Baltimore, Md º	660,170	----------	147,412	813,572	7,398 71
Boston, Mass.	1,595,684	46,841	129,628	1,772,153	17,073 39
Washington, D.C.†	240,741	----------	79,202	319,943	2,803 38
Providence, R. I.‡	178,227	----------	19,826	198,053	1,881 50
Kensington, Pa.	128,044	----------	20,521	148,565	1,382 99
Harrisburg, Pa.	43,801	----------	9,285	53,056	484 42
Lowell, Mass §	80,878	----------	9,733	90,611	857 45
St. Louis, Mo	54,858	605	1,613	57,076	562 66
Roxbury, Mass ‖	7,086	----------	977	8,063	75 74
Manchester, N. H.	35,271	----------	2,278	37,549	364 10
Total	12,059,190	2,168,690	1,311,877	15,539,711	149,073 62

º Returns for second quarter of 1861 not received.
† Returns for first quarter of 1861 not received.
‡ Returns for fourth quarter of 1860 not received.
§ Returns for first quarter of 1861 not received.
‖ Returns for third quarter of 1860 only received.

G. ADAMS, *Auditor.*
OFFICE OF THE AUDITOR OF THE TREASURY FOR THE
POST OFFICE DEPARTMENT, *November* 13, 1861.

and the Post Office Department except in cities where postage stamps could be used to prepay carrier fees. Conversely, the postmaster general's reports listed many cities as having carriers where the use of stamps for carrier fees is not known.

On July 1, 1863, when the fee-carrier system came to an end, the report of the postmaster general for fiscal 1863 stated that there were 49 cities with carrier service, and listed them together with the number of carriers and their income. In the same report Postmaster General Blair commented on the subject as follows [3:4]:

> LETTER-CARRIERS.
>
> The law authorizing the free delivery of mail matter by carriers took effect on the first day of July last. About that time the system was put in operation at 49 of the larger offices, with a competent corps of carriers to each, numbering in the aggregate 449, at an aggregate annual compensation of $300,680.
>
> Our own experience and that of Europe demonstrates that correspondence increases with every facility for its conduct, and free delivery in the principal towns and cities has been proved in the mother country to be a facility attended with very remarkable results. Further time is required to prove whether it will operate in the same way here, but, as far as ascertained, the results are highly satisfactory.
>
> In the city of New York there are now, daily, five deliveries from the office, and six collections of letters for the mails from the depositories in the various parts of the city. During the quarter ending September 30, 1863, there were delivered by carriers 2,069,418 letters, and 1,810,717 collected for the mails and city delivery, being an increase of 968,825 letters (about 25 per cent.) over the preceding and last quarter under the old system. Returns from other offices indicate results equally flattering.
>
> A table exhibiting the offices at which the new system is in operation, the number of carriers at each, with their aggregate compensation, appears in the Appendix, No. 3.

Appendix 3, to which he refers, has been reproduced in many publications. The following was compiled by Perry, who alphabetized the list and added footnotes [4:197].

**CITIES WITH FREE DELIVERY
JULY 1, 1863**

When free city delivery service was begun on July 1, 1863, the service was initiated in 49 cities. Elliott Perry in *Pat Paragraphs* No. 31 furnished a list of the cities, together with the number of carriers employed in each city and their aggregate salaries. The list is reproduced here.

Office	Aggregate of carriers	Aggregate of pay	Office	Aggregate of carriers	Aggregate of pay
Albany, N.Y.	5	$ 3,500	Newark, N.J.	7	3,500
Allegheny, Pa.	1	500	New Bedford, Mass.	4	1,620
Baltimore, Md.	22	15,900	Newburyport, Mass.	1	400
Bath, Me.	1	300	New Haven, Conn.	3	1,500
Boston, Mass.	32	22,360	Newport, R.I.	2	750
Brooklyn, N.Y.	18	12,600	New York, N.Y.	137	103,600
Cambridgeport, Mass. (a)	1	500	Norristown, Pa.	1	450
			Paterson, N.J.	2	800
Charlestown, Mass. (b)	3	1,500	Philadelphia, Pa.	119	79,700
Chelsea, Mass.	1	500	Pittsburg, Pa.	3	1,700
Cincinnati, O.	12	8,400	Poughkeepsie, N.Y.	1	300
Cleveland, O.	2	1,500	Providence, R.I.	5	3,000
Fall River, Mass.	2	1,000	Reading, Pa.	1	450
Frederick, Md.	1	350	Roxbury, Mass. (b)	2	1,000
Germantown, Pa. (c)	2	900	Salem, Mass.	3	1,050
Hartford, Conn.	2	1,200	St. Louis, Mo.	7	4,400
Hoboken, N.J.	1	300	Syracuse, N.Y.	1	400
Jersey City, N.J.	2	1,000	Trenton, N.J.	2	800
Lancaster, Pa.	1	500	Troy, N.Y.	2	1,200
Lawrence, Mass.	2	800	Utica, N.Y.	1	600
Louisville, Ky.	3	2,100	Washington, D.C.	11	7,700
Lowell, Mass.	3	1,350	Williamsburg, N.Y. (d)	6	4,200
Manchester, N.H.	2	900	Wilmington, Del.	2	1,000
Marblehead, Mass.	1	200	Worcester, Mass.	3	1,800
Nashua, N.H.	1	500	York, Pa.	1	300

(a) Separate from Cambridge at that date.
(b) Separate from Boston at that date.
(c) Separate from Philadelphia at that date.
(d) Separate from Brooklyn at that date.

It is interesting to note, of the seven cities with the largest number of carriers, six are cities for which a substantial number of covers showing carrier payment by stamp can be found. Cincinnati, Ohio, is the only exception. While the volume of mail would certainly be a major reason why these cities are well-represented in today's inventories of carrier covers with stamps, it does not explain why such covers should be be so extremely scarce from other relatively populous cities, such as Cincinnati and St. Louis. A reasonable explanation would be that those cities did not normally use postage stamps to pay for the carrier fee. This further substantiates the author's contention that covers showing stamp payment of carrier fees from these other cities reflect only use that was contrary to normal procedures.

In the following sections, the carrier systems in the major cities will be described, along with their carrier markings and examples of carrier use for both local delivery and collection to the mails.

New York City

The New York City carrier system handled more letters, circulars and newspapers than all other carrier cities combined. The postmaster general's report for the fiscal year ending June 30, 1862 [5:216], listed the New York City total number of carrier letters for the year at 7,671,500. The number of circulars handled was 2,003,936, and 476,528 newspapers and pamphlets were delivered. This impressive total indicates why examples of carrier mail from New York are not particularly difficult to obtain.

In 1860, the government carrier operation was operating successfully in New York, having started and stopped on several occasions during the previous decades. By the late 1850s, Postmaster John A. Dix was directing a fairly complex and satisfactory carrier system. Under the authority of the Act of 1851, the streets and roads of New York City, south of 55th Street, had been declared as post roads, and delivery of mail was legally the sole province of the post office. While this did not completely deter all competition, it did reduce the number of private posts in operation.

In a report to the postmaster general, Dix described the system in great detail [6:28]. Information from this report provides a good picture of the salient aspects of the New York service. In 1857, there were six carrier substations, identified by the letters A through F, in addition to the carrier operation handled from a carrier station in the main post office. Some time later, substation G was added. The supervisor of the carrier operation was John H. Hallett. From the stations and the principal office, the carriers made four deliveries each day. Eighty-nine carriers were employed.

At the main post office, a corps of clerks sorted all incoming letters that were intended for carrier delivery. These were sent in wagons by mail messengers seven times per day to the carrier stations for subsequent delivery. A force of 28 collecting carriers made the rounds four times per day to 574 cast-iron boxes affixed to lamp posts.

The area for carrier delivery was Manhattan Island between the Hudson and East rivers, bounded on the south by the Battery, and on the north by 55th Street. Plans were in place for an extension to the north as the density of the population increased. However, in 1857, letters addressed to locations north of 55th Street and to other suburban locations outside the carrier-service area were generally handled by local post offices (such as Harlem or Washington Heights) as out-of-town mail at the normal 3¢ rate, even though they were within the New York City limits. At times, letters outside the carrier area, but not too distant, were delivered by the carriers for an additional fee. In the latter part of his report, Postmaster Dix made the suggestion that it would be advisable to provide free delivery to all parts of the city (requiring an additional annual appropriation from the Post Office for $100,000, increasing as the city expanded), and also to increase the frequency of delivery from four to six times daily, at a cost of another $30,000.

New York City used several postal markings that distinguish letters that were handled by the carrier department. These handstamps were applied on letters that remained within the carrier system and did not enter the regular mails. Incoming letters were delivered and fees collected with no markings to that effect, except in very rare cases where some manuscript notation regarding carrier delivery might be found on the envelope. Letters collected for transmission to the mails show carrier handling only by the presence of a 1¢ stamp in addition to the normal postage.

Carrier Markings and Local Service

Nine different carrier-related markings have been reported as being used at New York City during the 1861-63 period. These markings are illustrated, together with examples of some uses on stamps and covers. Unfortunately, the carrier markings at New York are generally poorly struck, and it is very difficult to obtain good examples.

The drawings in **Figure 10-2** are adapted from those shown in Skinner/Eno [7:337]. While most of these markings have been seen by the author, the marking shown as **Figure 10-2b** may not exist on a cover with the 1¢ 1861 issue. This marking was used in the latter half of the 1850s and then evidently was discontinued when the carrier rate was reduced in 1860 to 1¢. It seems to have resurfaced in 1864, subsequent to the carrier-fee increase to 2¢ in 1863. The Skinner/Eno book reports use of this marking. Maryette Lane also reports use on a 2¢ 1861 Black Jack [8:102]. There is no reason that this marking could not also be found on a cover with the 1¢ 1861 stamp, but it would undoubtedly be scarce.

Figure 10-3 shows a 1¢ 1861 Franklin with a carrier marking in bright red. A drawing of the marking (**Figure 10-2a**) is shown in the right frame.

Figure 10-4 illustrates the use of a collection marking (Figure 10-2h) in red together with a boxed delivery marking (Figure 10-2d) in black. This collection marking is the most common of the carrier markings and is always

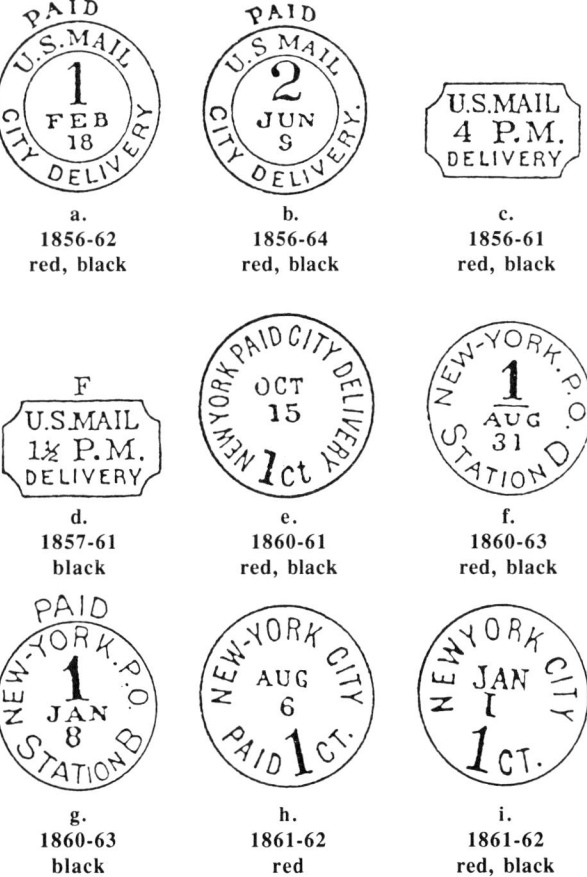

Figure 10-2. Markings used by the carrier department of the New York City Post Office. All circular markings are approximately 23mm in diameter.
(Courtesy of Hubert C. Skinner)

Figure 10-3. New York City carrier marking in red. Enlarged drawing of the marking at right.

Figure 10-4. New York City local delivery. Red carrier postmark in red on 1¢ Franklin. Boxed carrier delivery marking in black.

Figure 10-5. New York City Station B collection mark in red. 1¢ local delivery fee. Station C delivery marking in black.

struck in red.

The addressee of the letter, Alexander T. Stewart, was a well-known merchant whose dry-goods business occupied the entire block bounded by Broadway and Fourth Avenue between Ninth and Tenth streets. It was the largest business of its kind in the world, and in 1862 the store employed 2,000 people. Although close-fisted with his employees and in business dealings, he was known for his many philanthropic gifts to causes and organized charities. This reputation brought him thousands of letters from individuals requesting his financial help. Many of these letters were evidently filed, and have furnished collectors with examples of interesting and sometimes very sad tales of the times. Upon his death, the business was sold to John Wanamaker. It continued to prosper under that name.

Figure 10-5 shows a December 6 (year unknown) letter that remained entirely within the substation carrier system. It was collected by Station B, which applied the circular marking (Figure 10-2g) in black, and then was transferred to Station C, where the delivery marking in black was applied. On the next delivery, it was sent by

City Carrier Collection and Delivery

Figure 10-6. Unusual use of a PAID cancellation with a boxed carrier mark for local delivery.

Figure 10-7. Station B collection marking with suburban delivery outside of the normal carrier routes. Marked "Due 2" as a fee for special service to be collected from the addressee.
(Robert B. Meyersburg collection)

carrier to the addressee. By 1861, as noted, there were seven stations, identified by the letters A through G.

Figure 10-6 shows a scarce set of markings for New York City carrier use. This local letter, with an embossed corner card from "Williams College, Class of 62," contains an invitation to an evening of debate on the subject, "Should Foreign Colonization be a Condition of Emancipation?" The cover has a standard boxed delivery marking (the station identification is blurred, but is possibly "C") and the unusual use, for New York City, of a PAID marking in black to cancel the stamp.

Figure 10-7 illustrates the situation that arose when a local letter was addressed to a recipient who resided within the city limits of New York, but outside the carrier-service area. In this case, the letter was collected by Station B on January 8, 1863, and the stamp canceled with its marking (Figure 10-2g). The address on 61st Street was determined to be outside the carrier area, which, at that time, only extended north to 55th Street.

There were two ways this letter could have been delivered. It could have been carried to the main post office and held for additional postage, then put into the mails to be delivered to a post office that served the addressee's area. In 1863 there were five post offices on Manhattan Island in addition to the main New York City Post Office and its carrier stations. These were Yorkville, Manhattanville, Harlem, Washington Heights and King's Bridge at the northern extremity of the island. All of these post offices were within the city limits of New York City. If this had been the method used for this example, there would have been an additional 3¢ in stamps added, along with the name of the destination post office.

The other method, and undoubtedly the way this letter was handled, would be for the carrier office at Station B to transfer the letter to the main post office where the January 10, 1863, CDS was applied and the letter routed to the carrier station closest to the address. The "Due 2" was applied to indicate that there would be an additional

169

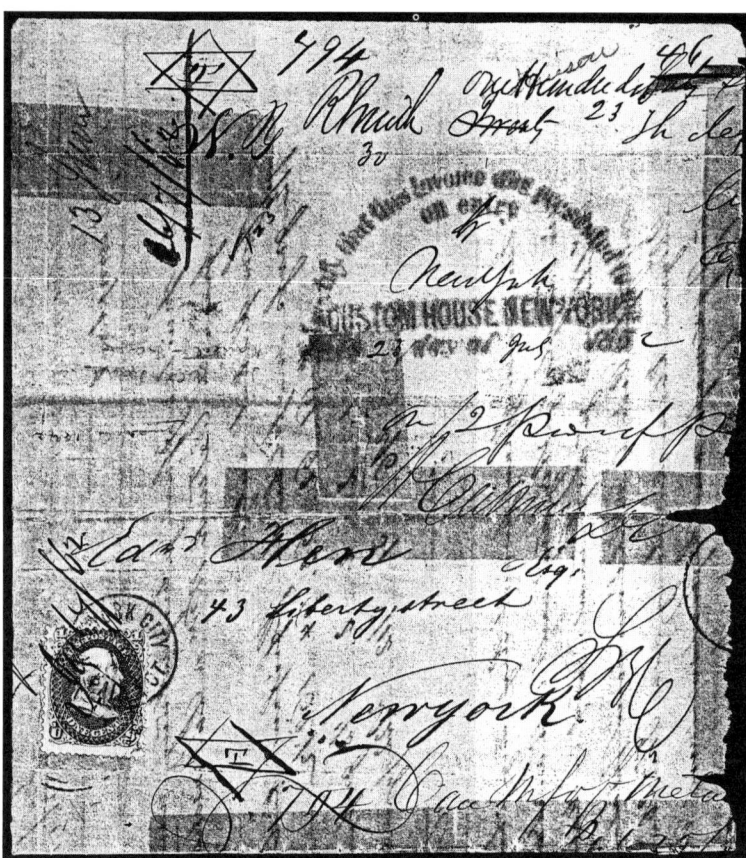

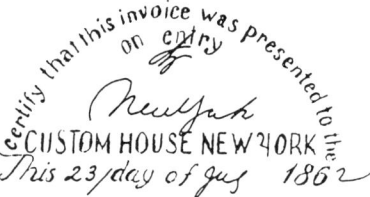

Figure 10-8. Invoice carried from Germany outside the mails and entered into the mails at New York City on June 13, 1862. The 1¢ Franklin pays for carrier delivery. The cover also bears a shipper's mark in dark blue ink and a Custom House handstamp in red. The invoice is partially unfolded to show some of the special markings of the shipper and customs.

charge for delivery by a carrier outside his normal area. It is probable that there was a standard surcharge for the additional service, and that it was limited to addresses reasonably close to the normal service areas.

Provisions for this type of service were contained in Section 11 of the Act of February 27, 1860, which stated the postmaster general was authorized "to establish a daily or semi-daily delivery of letters and newspapers by carriers, throughout a circuit of nine miles from the City Hall, in the city of New York, under the supervision of the postmaster of New York, whenever, in his judgement, the revenue from such service shall defray the expense thereof [4:196]." The 61st Street address was approximately five miles from City Hall. How the additional fee of 2¢ that was charged in this case was justified is not known in light of the act effective July 1, 1860, which established a standard carrier fee of 1¢.

One of the scarcest prepaid carrier uses is on incoming letters from foreign countries. This can only occur where a letter or other mailable item is brought into the United States outside the mails, and then stamped and entered into the carrier system for collection and, possibly, delivery. **Figure 10-8** shows a somewhat tattered, but very interesting, folded invoice of foreign origin that was collected and delivered by carrier in New York City.

The invoice, dated June 13, 1862, accompanied a shipment of goods from Germany to the merchant, Edward Hen, at New York. In accordance with regulations in effect at that time, documents that related to the cargo of a ship could be carried outside the mails without postage. After arrival at New York, the shipment was held in bond at customs, and the invoice was stamped and mailed via postal carrier to the receiver of the merchandise. The date of the red carrier postmark (Figure 10-2h) is July 15. Evidently, the invoice was then presented to the New York Custom House on July 23, 1862, and stayed with the shipment throughout a comprehensive inspection and determination of import duties. This is attested to by many dates on the document and more than a dozen initials and signatures of custom officials.

Another example of a similar use is shown in **Figure 10-9**. This is a folded-letter cover sheet without the enclosure. It probably contained some sort of manifest or invoice, as suggested by the commercial handstamps and address to a New York company. The folded letter sheet is dated July 20, 1862, which is evidently the day it was written at Havana, Cuba. It is endorsed "Koenigian Au-

Figure 10-9. Folded letter sheet carried outside the mails from Havana, Cuba, to New York, where it was entered into the mails for carrier service in August (1862). Overpaid 1¢. The folded letter sheet is datelined July 20, 1862, and endorsed for transport aboard the *Koenigian Augusta*. Forwarding agent and originator's oval handstamps were applied. (James Lee collection)

Figure 10-10. Illegal "bootleg" folded letter sheet, datelined July 21, 1862, and originating at Mannheim, Germany. The letter was carried outside the mails to New York City, where it was franked with a 1¢ Franklin and deposited in the mails for carrier service. (James Lee collection)

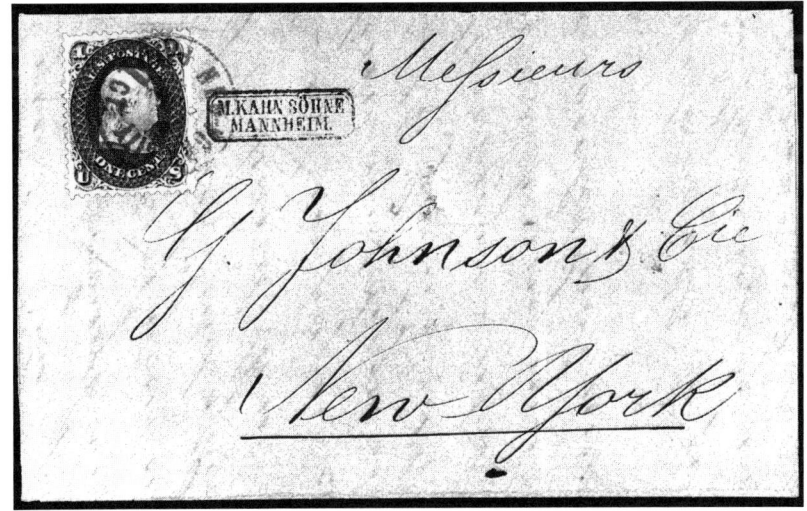

gusta," probably the name of the ship that was to carry the document to New York. The folded letter sheet was placed aboard the ship by a Havana forwarding agent, and has the handstamp "Runge Balbiani & Co." on its front. It entered the mails at New York City, where it received New York carrier cancels, dated in August (day undecipherable). It is paid by two 1¢ Franklins, a 1¢ overpayment of the carrier fee.

Examples also exist of foreign incoming mail that was illegally carried outside the mails. In the philatelic lexicon, these are frequently referred to as "bootleg" covers. This situation occurred when a letter was carried with the personal possessions of a traveler, and not entered into the mail until a destination port was reached. This was against postal regulations but was probably not too uncommon an occurrence. Some postage could be saved in this manner, but it was used mostly as a convenience. At the destination port, the document would be deposited in the mails with enough postage to pay the domestic rate or fee.

Figure 10-10 is an example of such illegal use. This July 21, 1862, folded letter sheet originated in Mannheim, Germany, and is a hand-written reply to a query regarding merchandise prices. It was carried outside the mails to New York, where the 1¢ Franklin received a carrier postmark as a cancellation, and the folded letter sheet was entered into the carrier system for delivery.

Collection for Delivery to the Mails

Letters with normal postage plus an additional 1¢ for carrier collection to the mails are the most common carrier uses to be found. As previously mentioned, there

Figure 10-11. May 18, 1863, carrier to the mails with a striking "circle-of-wedges" cancellation. New York City to Fort Ethan Allen, Virginia, via a Washington, D.C., post office box. The 1¢+3¢ franking paid for carrier service and letter postage.

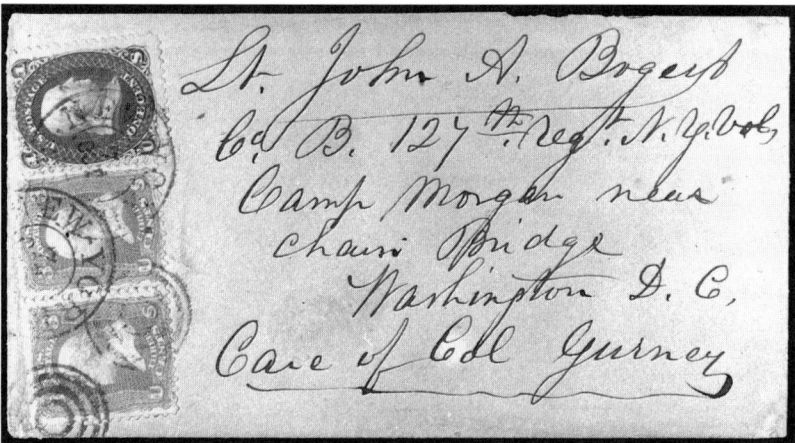

Figure 10-12. Double-weight letter with carrier collection to the mails. The 1¢ paid for the carrier fee and 6¢ for 2x3¢ letter postage. The letter is addressed to a lieutenant in Colonel Gurney's regiment at Camp Morgan, which was evidently bivouacked near Chain Bridge, Washington, D.C.

is no way to determine that this type of mail was handled by the carrier system except for the presence of the additional postage.

Figure 10-11 shows a New York carrier cover mailed on May 18, 1863, and addressed to a captain at Fort Ethan Allen in Virginia, via a Washington, D.C., post office box. Military units that were stationed in the vicinity frequently had mail sent to a Washington post office box, where it was collected by the unit mail clerk for distribution to the addressees. The cover illustrates the standard 3¢+1¢ franking for carrier collection.

Figure 10-12 shows an October 7 double-weight letter mailed to an officer in Colonel Gurney's regiment. This cover illustrates the fact that carrier fees were not subject to weight penalties. Although the postage was doubled for the overweight letter, the carrier fee remained the same at 1¢.

Figure 10-13 shows a September 3 New York use of the compound 3¢+1¢ envelope that was issued in December 1860. This envelope was designed to pay both the carrier-collection fee and single-weight postage. It was never demonetized even though both embossed stamps were of the star-die variety. However, the 3¢ value, when appearing alone on an envelope, was demonetized in 1861. Existing examples of compound envelopes are relatively scarce; almost all were used at New York City. It is possible that all the envelopes were sold there, and the few that exist from other cities were purchased in New York City and carried to these other towns by individuals prior to mailing.

One of the most interesting uses of the prepaid carrier fee to the mails is for foreign destinations. These may be found on unpaid letters with just the 1¢ Franklin to pay the carrier fee, or the 1¢ for the fee plus prepaid postage to destination. **Figure 10-14** shows an example of the carrier fee only to Strasbourg, France, at the 15¢ rate. It is addressed to a maker of musical instruments and is endorsed to be routed via Liverpool, England. In France, the letter received the distinctive red octagon-and-circle marking of the Paris exchange office used from 1861 to 1866 for mail arriving via Calais.

Figure 10-15 shows another carrier cover of the

Figure 10-13. Use of the combination 3¢+1¢ (Scott U28) government envelope to pay for carrier collection to the mails and postage from New York City to Lincoln, Massachusetts. Used examples of this combination envelope are scarce.

Figure 10-14. New York City, March 8, 1862, prepaid carrier collection to the mails for an unpaid letter to Strasbourg, France, per American contract steamer *Etna* of the Inman Line. the steamer arrived at Liverpool, England, on March 21. The Paris exchange office marked 8 decimes (15¢) on the cover for collection. The cover is backstamped Paris March 23 and Strasbourg March 23, 1862.

Carrier fee	1¢
U.S. inland	3¢
Sea	6¢
British Transit	2¢
French inland	4¢
	16¢

 Paris Exchange marking, denoting American packet via England

 New York Exchange marking, 9¢ debit to France

same type, to Darmstadt, Germany, via the Hamburg-American Line (HAPAG). At the time of the mailing of this letter, HAPAG had a contract to carry U.S. mail, and the 5¢ debit to Hamburg paid for the U.S. internal postage part of the total 15¢ rate to Germany. An interesting feature is shown by the "1" in the lower middle of the cover. This charge was in addition to the 22 kreuzer due, and probably was for a carrier-delivery fee to the address. This type of fee was imposed in many of the German states prior to 1862, when its use began to be phased out. In 1864 the delivery fee was discontinued except for rural delivery.

The U.S. internal rate for letters to foreign destinations was either 3¢ or 5¢, depending on the country to which the letter was addressed. The internal rate was established by the individual postal treaties. For example, the U.S. internal rate for a letter to Hamburg or Great Britain was 5¢, but a letter to France was only charged 3¢. This dichotomy in rates for the same service seems strange by today's standards but was the result of the mail treaties being negotiated in different years. The treaty with Great Britain reflected the internal U.S. rate of 5¢ in effect in 1848 when it was negotiated, while the French treaty was signed in 1856, after the U.S. postage had been reduced to 3¢.

A fully prepaid carrier-collection cover to Liverpool, England, is shown in **Figure 10-16**. This letter was entered into the mails on January 3, 1863, at New York City,

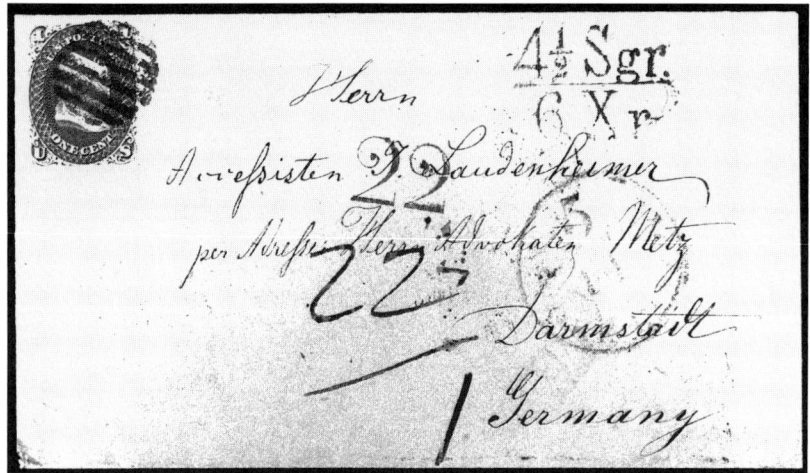

Figure 10-15. Unpaid except for U.S. carrier fee. The Hamburg packet *Saxonia* departed New York City, June 14, 1862, arriving at Hamburg on June 28, then overland to Darmstadt via Thurn and Taxis Post, arriving July 1, 1862. The cover was backstamped at Hamburg, Frankfurt and Darmstadt.

5¢ debit to Hamburg

Hamburg exchange office. Dividing the 22-kreuzer (15¢) collection fee into 4½ silbergroschen (10¢) to be credited to Hamburg, and 6 kreuzer to the Thurn and Taxis Post for delivery to Darmstadt.

Figure 10-16. Prepaid 1¢ carrier fee and 24¢ (Scott 70) postage to Liverpool, England. The cover departed New York City January 3, 1863, aboard the contract mail steamer *Etna* of the Inman Line. It arrived in Liverpool, January 14, 1863. (C.W. Christian collection)

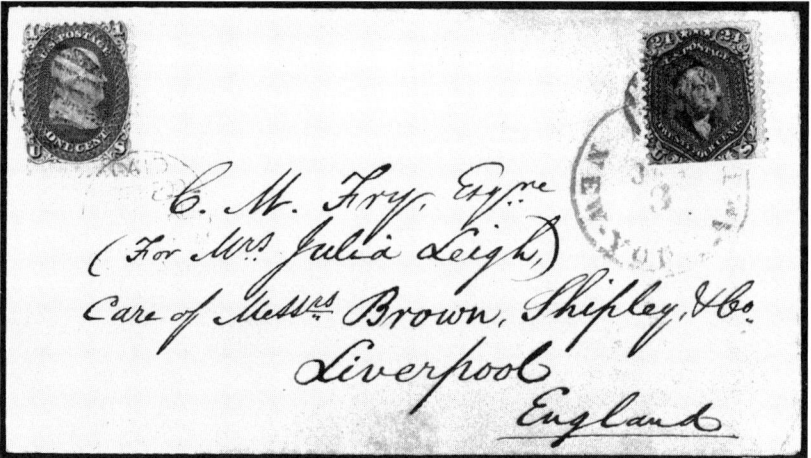

Figure 10-17. Scarce combination of foreign and U.S. stamps. The 1¢ 1861 paid for the carrier collection. The cover was forwarded from the original Liverpool destination by Brown, Shipley and Co. to Paris with the payment of 8 pence by two Great Britain 4d stamps in additional postage. The New York exchange marking is dated March 8 (1862), with a debit of 21¢ to Great Britain. The manuscript due marking of 1 shilling (24¢) was applied at Liverpool and evidently collected at the original address. The PD in circle is a London marking to alert French postal clerks that the letter was prepaid. (James Lee collection)

where the exchange office postmarked the cover indicating sea transit by American packet. The 24¢ stamp paid the first-class rate for up to ½ ounce to England, and the 1¢ stamp paid for the carrier collection. The letter was addressed to a forwarding agent, Brown, Shipley & Co., to be sent on to the recipient.

An exceptionally scarce example of carrier collection to the mails with a foreign destination and with foreign franking is illustrated in **Figure 10-17**. This cover was sent unpaid by the Inman Line's steamer *Etna* under American mail contract to Liverpool, England, where Brown, Shipley & Co., the same agent as shown on the previously illustrated cover, paid the 1 shilling due and affixed the forwarding postage of two 4 pence British stamps. Combinations of the 1861 Franklin and foreign stamps are extremely scarce.

Figure 10-18. Brooklyn, New York. November 25 carrier to the mails. The cover bears a large 32mm circular postmark.

Brooklyn, New York

Although just across the East River from New York City, Brooklyn in the 1860s was a separate city with an independent post office system.

In 1863, Brooklyn had 18 carriers (compared with 137 for New York City) and was a thriving post office. With approximately 700,000 letters reported to have been handled by the carrier service in the previous year [9:161], it would appear that carrier covers from Brooklyn should be easy to locate, but this is not the case. They are relatively much more difficult to obtain than those of New York City. Numerically, it should be possible to find one Brooklyn carrier cover for approximately every 13 New York covers on the market, but they are scarcer than these statistics predict.

The carrier-service operation in Brooklyn was typical for the large cities of the period; no special markings were struck to indicate carrier service. The three cities that had special carrier markings were New York City, Philadelphia and New Orleans. Because of the lack of carrier postmarks, it is difficult to determine if local Brooklyn letters, franked with a single 1¢ stamp, were drop letters or carrier-delivered letters.

No cover showing a single 1¢ 1861 for drop or carrier delivery in Brooklyn is available for illustration. However, such covers should not be more difficult to locate than covers showing carrier pickup to the mails. This latter category is easily identified by the presence of a 1¢ stamp in addition to the required postage.

An example of such use is shown in **Figure 10-18**. This caricature patriotic cover shows the state of Virginia as an old bent-over lady with the early battles of the Civil War raging over her back. The caption above the figure reads, "SOUTHERN CHIVALRY! 'You may plant your seeds in peace, for Virginia will have to bear the brunt of the battle.'—— Gov. Pickens." This 1861 or possibly 1862 cover was printed by H. Ropes and Co.

Figure 10-19 illustrates a double-weight letter with carrier collection to the mails, dated November 10, 1862, and postmarked with a double-circle 27mm CDS. This smaller marking shows the use of the newer type of CDS, but this and the previous type in Figure 10-18 were used concurrently for much of the period.

Philadelphia

At the end of the fee period, Philadelphia's carrier service was the second largest in the country with 119 carriers and a volume of more than 3,500,000 letters and circulars delivered in the fiscal year ending June 30, 1863. Just 18 months earlier, in January 1862, there were only 32 carriers employed by the Philadelphia Post Office. The rapid increase in carrier personnel was required by the new carrier business generated by the previous customers of the now-defunct private carriers, the expansion of the carrier service into the Philadelphia suburbs and a general increase in mail volume due to the Civil War. During the following year, the number of carriers continued its increase to 127, and the volume of carrier deliveries increased to about 7,000,000 pieces.

Figure 10-19. Double-weight letter from Brooklyn, New York, November 10 to Westborough, Massachussets. The 1¢ stamp paid the carrier fee to the mails.

The history of the government carrier service in Philadelphia is exceptionally interesting, and most of the facts about the service have been well-documented by postal historians. **Figure 10-20** illustrates a typical scene of the period with a lady depositing mail in a lamp-post collection box. This picture was taken from an old print that presently is in the collection of the Library Company of Philadelphia. The idea of combining a letter box and a lamp post was patented, according to the wording on the print, by Albert Potts of Philadelphia on March 9, 1858.

The government carrier service had competed against the private posts, generally without much success, until the early part of 1862. Blood's Penny Post (also known as Blood's Despatch), from 1842 until its demise on January 12, 1862, had enjoyed the majority of the local delivery business. This continued in spite of incentives by the post office (such as free collection to the mails) to induce the public to use the government service. The public took advantage, to a limited extent, of the free collection, but had to pay the delivery fee to the post office carriers for incoming letters from other towns, since this was the only way they could get them delivered.

Local mail was predominantly handled by Blood's. From a review of the records, it is easy to understand why the public preferred Blood's. It offered more frequent deliveries and collections, with many more collection boxes than the government service. In addition, Blood's had a history of good service for many years, in contrast to the post office carrier service, which seemed frequently to be in a state of starting, discontinuing or reorganizing.

By 1860, the U.S. government, in the person of the postmaster general, was firmly committed to eliminating all competition from the private carrier services in large cities where it was felt revenue was being lost to competition.

In July of 1860, Postmaster General Holt declared that all the streets and roads of New York City (south of 55th Street), Philadelphia and Boston were post roads, and that it would be illegal for any private post to transport mail over these routes. This pronouncement was based on laws enacted in 1827, 1845 and 1851, which declared certain roads to be post roads that could be used only by the Post Office for the transport of mail.

Figure 10-20. Typical downtown Philadelphia scene, circa 1860. The lady is depositing a letter in a patented collection box. The letter box is inscribed "Philada P.O./U.S.M./LETTER BOX/G.G. Westcott, P.M."
(Courtesy of the Library Company of Philadelphia and Robert B. Stets)

The New York private carriers shut down in response to this order, but Blood's continued to collect and deliver letters as if the order had never been issued. The government then brought court action against Blood's proprietor, Charles Kochersberger, requesting an injunction against further operation. In a landmark decision, the court found for Blood's, with some reservations. The court judged that the post roads referred to in the Acts of 1827 and 1845 were those roads between main post offices, and that the Act of 1851 referred only to routes between a city post office and its subordinate stations. The postmaster general's order of July 1860 was therefore issued without proper authority [10:240].

One of the reservations mentioned above is important. Until 1854, Philadelphia was a small city of approximately 2 square miles, surrounded by many populous areas, such as Spring Garden, Germantown and Northern Liberties. These suburban areas were autonomous and contained separate post offices that operated independently of Philadelphia. In 1854 the Pennsylvania legislature declared that all areas in Philadelphia County would henceforth be a part of the City of Philadelphia. By a stroke of the pen, the area of the city was increased from 2 to 129 square miles. In 1860, many of the suburban Philadelphia post offices outside the limits of the former city were still operating independently, and these areas were also being served by Blood's carriers. The court ruled that streets and highways to these post offices were post roads, and therefore closed to private carriers. This did not, however, enjoin Blood's from operating in any areas then served by the main Philadelphia post office.

Although damaged by this decision and faced with the loss of considerable revenue, Blood's continued to do business. The final blow was delivered in the following year. Montgomery Blair had become postmaster general, and he persuaded Congress to pass a new postal law that declared all streets of a city or town with carrier service to be post roads.

Blood's Despatch finally realized it had lost. The business declined through 1861 and was finally terminated on January 11, 1862. The proprietors announced in a local newspaper that they were acquiescing to the law, that arrangements had been made with the Philadelphia Post Office and Postmaster Walborn for the transfer of many of its personnel to government service, and that the carrier delivery of mail would be as satisfactory in the future as it had been under its control.

Few carrier covers are found from the period of February to April 1862, and it may be surmised that the government carrier service was undergoing intensive reorganization during this period, during which service was substantially curtailed.

As mentioned earlier in this chapter, the chances of finding a cover with both a Blood's Penny Post stamp and a 1¢ 1861 is extremely small. Blood's stamps would be found on a letter collected by private carrier to the mails with an additional 3¢ postage, and this 3¢ would be paid by the 3¢ 1861, only rarely by 1¢ stamps. The period for this use would be restricted to dates between August 19, 1861, and January 11, 1862. These facts, coupled with the declining business of Blood's, make this use a genuine rarity (see Figure 10-1).

A curious cover showing the combination of a Blood's Penny Post stamp and an 1861 1¢ Franklin is shown in **Figure 10-21**. This cover is dated July 23 and most probably was mailed in 1862. This is over six months after the termination of Blood's Despatch Penny Post, and in this case, the 1¢ 1861 stamp alone would have been sufficient to obtain delivery in Kensington. The former independent Kensington post office was closed on March 13, 1862, and the area was subsequently serviced from a Philadelphia sub-post office. Both collection and delivery of letters between Philadelphia and Kensington would be handled by the Philadelphia carrier system, and the total fee would have been 1¢. It should

Figure 10-21. Unnecessary use of a private post stamp on a July 23 (1862) carrier collection in Philadelphia for delivery in Kensington, a suburb. Letters to Kensington were delivered by the Philadelphia system at no additional cost.

be noted that Blood's Despatch is also at times referred to as Blood's Dispatch. These different spellings were both used by Blood's with "Despatch" being predominant over the years.

The reason for the Blood's adhesive appearing on this cover cannot be absolutely determined, but a possible scenario could be constructed as follows. An individual with a Blood's stamp in his possession, not knowing that Blood's was out of business, places the adhesive on an envelope and takes it to the usual Blood's collection point. Some of the same collection stations probably continued to be used as government carrier stations by the post office after the demise of Blood's. The individual was informed that the adhesive was no longer valid, and that a 1¢ U.S. postage stamp would have to be used. The sender bought and applied the stamp. It was canceled by the carrier station and sent on its way to Kensington, resulting in an unusual cover for a fortunate collector.

Following the 1854 annexation of the suburban areas, the main post office did not immediately increase its operations to cover the entire city. In fact it was August 1867 before the last group of the 26 previously independent post offices was integrated into the Philadelphia postal system. In the interim, the cost to mail a letter from one part of the city to another could vary from 1¢ to 4¢, depending on where and when it was mailed and delivered. For example, in 1862, if a letter was collected and delivered within the area serviced by the Philadelphia carrier department, the total fee would be 1¢. If a letter was mailed from the main Philadelphia post office to the post office at Germantown (which was now incorporated into the city of Philadelphia), the letter required the normal postage rate of 3¢ for transport between the post offices. In the case where the letter was collected by a carrier to the mails, another penny would be charged for a total of 4¢.

This situation shows another way in which Blood's had offered a better deal to its customers than did the post office. Blood's, through the years, had extended its operations into the heavily populated suburbs surrounding the central city, and would happily collect and deliver letters between the areas for a penny. This gave it the advantage of lower prices in addition to better service.

At the time of the issue of the 1861 stamps, the Philadelphia postal operation was well-equipped for a rapid expansion of its volume and revenue from its carrier operation. It had eliminated all competition from private posts, had organized its delivery system to provide better service and was extending its service area farther into the surrounding suburbs. The large volume of mail and the distinctive carrier markings have provided many interesting covers for contemporary collections.

Two carrier markings were used during the fee-carrier period between 1860 and 1863. **Figures 10-22** and **10-23** show these special markings as adapted from drawings by Robert J. Stets [11:24]. Figure 10-22 is known as the U.S.P.O. DISPATCH octagon, and the second marking in Figure 10-23 is the U.S. PENNY MAIL octagon.

Figure 10-22. U.S.P.O. DISPATCH. Known use: May 1860 to April 1862.

Figure 10-23. U.S. PENNY MAIL. Known use: April 1862 to August 1863.

Early conclusions formed by Elliott Perry, and stated in his notes, indicated that the two markings were used at the same time. Later investigations by Stets show that this is incorrect. The DISPATCH octagon was used first, and is known from as early as May 1860 to as late as April 1862, while use of the PENNY MAIL octagon is recorded from April 1862 to August 1863. No cover indicating an overlap in the period of use has been found.

It seems probable that the DISPATCH design was used as the carrier marking until the time of the reorganization of the carrier department upon the cessation of operations by Blood's. Postmaster Walborn, aware of the excellent reputation of Blood's Penny Post, decided to capitalize on this reputation and renamed his U.S.P.O. Dispatch carrier service the U.S. Penny Mail. This, of course, required new markers, and as soon as they became available, they replaced the old DISPATCH octagons.

A cover illustrating the use of the U.S.P.O. DISPATCH carrier marking is shown in **Figure 10-24**. The marking is usually struck twice on the front of the cover, once to cancel the stamp and once as a carrier postmark.

Examples of this carrier marking on covers with the 1¢ 1861 Franklin seem to be relatively scarce. Of course, the period of possible use spanned only eight months from August 1861 to April 1862. Many of the covers known to the author are to the same destination, "Bank Penn Township," and addressed in the same handwriting, with dates in October or November (1861). An exception to this is the local cover shown in **Figure 10-25** from the collection of Stets.

In this particular example, the letter was evidently posted at the main post office as a local letter and post-

Figure 10-24. U.S.P.O. DISPATCH marking. Local carrier collection and delivery, Philadelphia. November 7 (1861). Use with the 1861 issue has been reported only between August 1861 and April 1862.

Figure 10-25. This cover was posted as a drop letter and delivered by carrier. After April 3, 1860, the drop charge of 1¢ was waived on local letters delivered by carrier. Note the CDS of September 2, 1861, and the carrier marking of September 3.
(Elliott Perry photo file. Courtesy of Robert J. Stets)

marked on September 2, 1861. The following day, a carrier marking was applied for delivery, and the stamp was canceled with another strike of the same marker.

This cover also illustrates the unusual rate structure for a drop letter that was delivered by the carrier service. In the Act of April 1860, the rate for a drop letter was established at 1¢. In the same act, the fee for carrier collection or delivery was also fixed at 1¢. In accordance with this, a drop letter that was subsequently delivered by carrier should cost 2¢. Since this would be obviously an unfair rate, the drop-letter charge was waived by regulation, and the 1¢ stamp was credited to the carrier fund.

Year-dating covers with the U.S.P.O. DISPATCH marking depends on the existence of docketing or dated enclosures, and most of the surviving examples unfortunately do not have either of these attributes. This marking is known with four different hours of delivery: 8 AM, 11 AM, 2½ PM and 5 PM. It was usually not used for letters addressed to other towns that had been collected by carriers for delivery to the mails. These letters were generally postmarked with the standard Philadelphia CDS.

Covers with the U.S. PENNY MAIL octagon carrier marking are somewhat easier to find. The period of use was longer, and also the volume of carrier mail had increased considerably. Unfortunately, this new marker also lacked a year date and, therefore, continued the problem of precisely dating covers. It was usually struck twice on the front of local letters in the same manner as the previous marking, once to cancel the stamp and once again as a postmark.

Figure 10-26 shows the earliest-known use of the U.S. PENNY MAIL octagonal marking. The cover was postmarked at the Philadelphia post office on April 10, 1862, with the carrier marking added the following day. The letter was addressed to a suburb of Philadelphia, but at that time there was no carrier service to Germantown, which was still operating its own post office. The 2¢ due marking is to make up the first-class rate between post

Figure 10-26. Earliest-reported use of the U.S. PENNY MAIL carrier marking. The cover is postmarked April 10, 1862. The octagon carrier mark is dated April 11, 1862. The cover is marked "DUE 2" for collection from addressee. (Elliott Perry photo file, courtesy of Robert B. Meyersburg)

Figure 10-27. October 29 (1862), 11½ AM, Philadelphia city delivery. U.S. PENNY MAIL with letter "A" carrier marking.

offices, to be collected from the addressee.

A typical example of the use of the PENNY MAIL marking is shown in **Figure 10-27**. The purpose of the letter that follows the word MAIL in the marking (in this case, an "A") has been the subject of some controversy. Perry believed that it identified the station or sub-post office at which a cover was mailed. Stets refuted this hypothesis by showing that the letter "E" was used on covers dated a year prior to the opening of Station E. He also determined that at the time the PENNY MAIL marking was in use, the sub-post offices or stations were not known by letters, but rather were identified by names such as Western, Northwest and 24th Ward. These stations were not assigned letters for identification until about July 1, 1863.

It is now believed that specific handstamps were assigned to stations, but that there was no correlation between the letters on the markers and the later assigned letter names of the stations or sub-post offices. The letter "A" is significantly more common in a survey of examples of the markings. This might indicate that "A" was as-

signed to the main post office carrier section, which would probably handle more letters than any of the individual stations. Letters A, B, C, D, E and U have been reported, and eight different delivery times have been found on the markings. All of the times are on the half-hour.

Figure 10-28 is a scarce local use of the U.S. PENNY MAIL carrier marking after the end of the carrier fee period on July 1, 1863. This also shows the rare use of a triple strike, which resulted from canceling each of the 1¢ stamps individually and once again to add the postmark. Stets has recorded six uses of the marking subsequent to July 1, 1863, and one of these, the latest recorded, was on a 2¢ Black Jack with a date of August 10 [11:28]. It seems probable that instructions were given at the end of the fee system to stop using the carrier marking. After that time, all carriers were paid a salary by the Post Office Department, and there would be no need to specially mark carrier letters so that records could be maintained for reimbursement.

The collection of letters by carriers to be carried to the post office for destinations outside the city consti-

COLOR PLATES

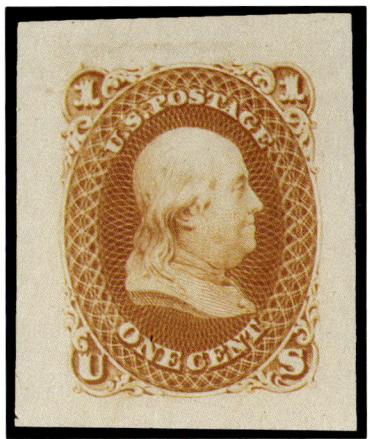  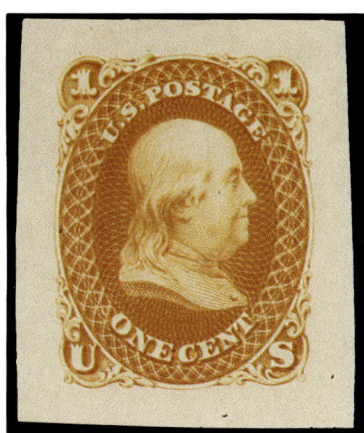

Figure 2-9. Small die trial color proofs of the issued design.

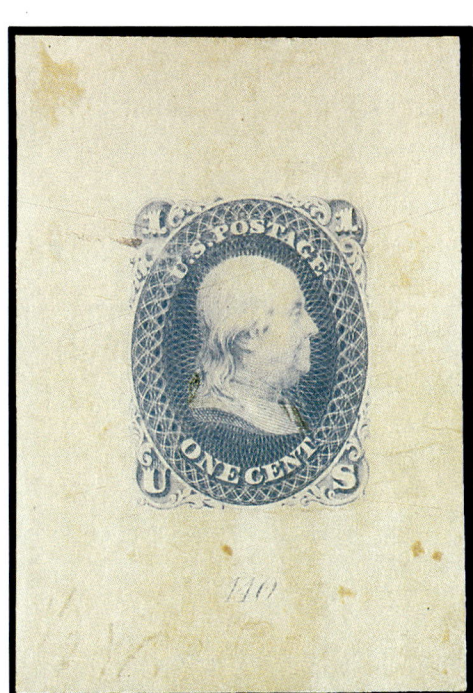

Figure 2-18. Large die premiere-gravure India proof in ultramarine (rare).

Figure 4-3. Bowlsby patent large die color proof on India, die sunk and printed in apple green.

Figure 4-9. Wyckoff patent experimental printing in brown water-soluble ink.

Figure 4-12. Gibson patent overprint in red fugitive ink. This is known as the "bedspring" overprint.

Figure 5-7. Red control-number overprint.

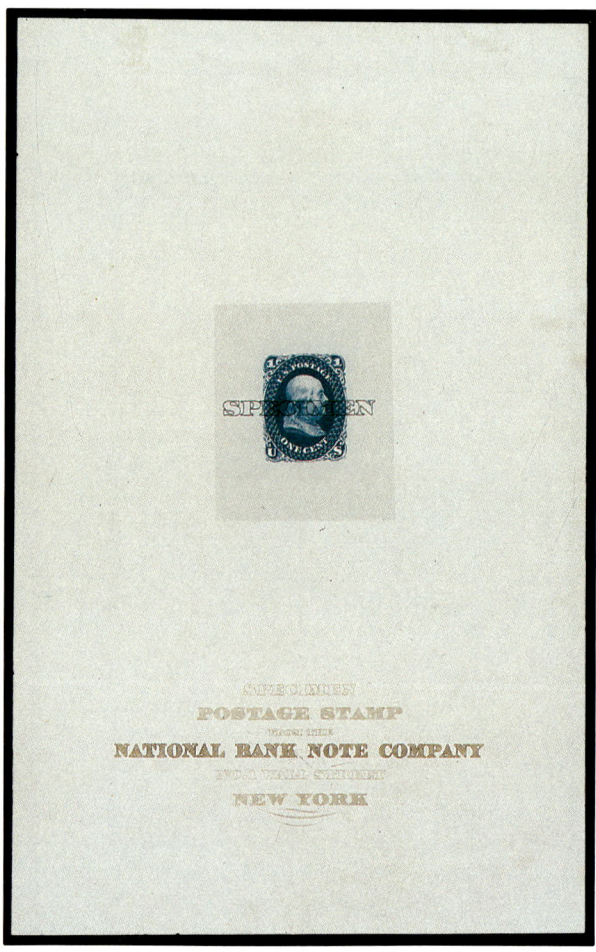

Figure 5-5. Page from a salesman's sample book showing a die proof on India paper with a large outlined block-letter "Specimen" overprint.

Figure 5-16. Color proofs from the 1881 printing for the
International Cotton Exposition at Atlanta, Georgia.

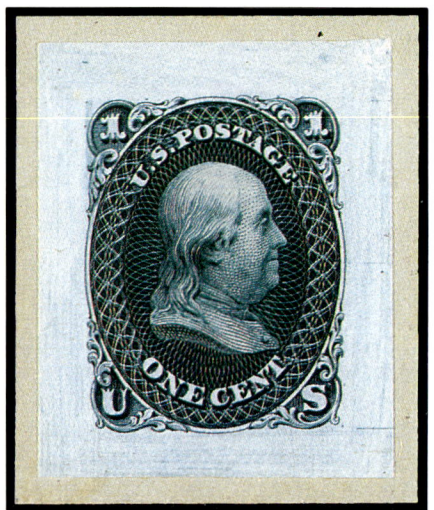 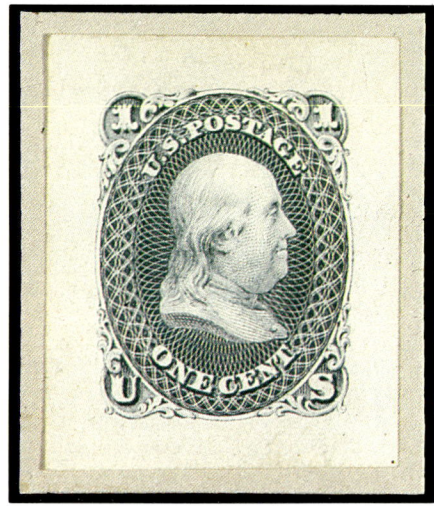

Figure 5-22. Examples of the 1¢ 1861. The dark blue printing on the left was to simulate the indigo premiere gravure, and the gray-blue printing on the right was for the issued stamp.

 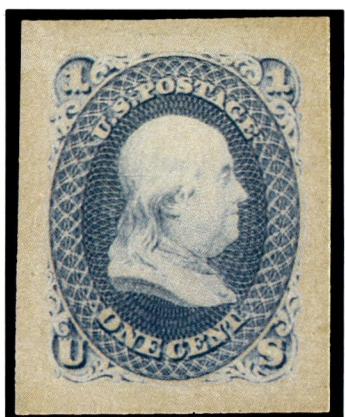

Figure 5-23. Rare small die proofs, printed for exhibition at the 1915 Pan-Pacific Exhibition in San Francisco, California. The two shades simulate the premiere-gravure and issued-stamp colors.

Figure 8-55. Negative shamrock cancellation in green from Richmond, Virginia.

Figure 8-56. Colored cancels in red and the rare violet shade.

Figure 10-30. Colorful woodcut illustration of a civilian volunteer-operated hospital for Civil War casualties.

Figure 10-31. Illustrated corner card for the Knickerbocker Ice Company, Philadelphia.

Figure 14-19. A scarce franking from Port Royal, South Carolina, to Germany, via Prussian Closed Mail.

Figure 14-34. Patriotic cover showing the 1847 assault by U.S. forces on the fortifications at Churubusco, Mexico.

Figure 14-46. Scarce naval design on a New York carrier cover. The cover commemorates the November 1861 battle at Hilton Head, South Carolina.

Figure 14-51. Unusual Philadelphia carrier patriotic cover. The design was accidentally printed on both sides.

Figure 14-56. Colorful and scarce Philadelphia carrier patriotic cover, homemade by pasting cut-out pictures on an envelope.

Figure 15-2. Local Philadelphia carrier use showing an advertising corner card of the Manhattan Life Insurance Company.

Figure 15-22. Large patriotic valentine showing Washington, D.C., carrier use. Also shown are two views of the enclosure. Without question, the most desirable patriotic valentine of the Civil War period.

tuted a large percentage of the carrier business. As mentioned in the introduction to this chapter, for some years prior to 1860 letters were carried to the post office without charge. This free service was offered primarily to undercut the private carriers who were charging a 1¢ fee for collection to the mails. The Post Office charged 2¢ for each letter that was delivered from the mails by carriers since it had a monopoly on this business. This higher fee reimbursed the Post Office to some extent for the loss that it experienced from the free collection to the mails.

The Act of June 15, 1860, effective July 1, 1860, changed all of this. The law removed the authority of the postmaster general to fix carrier fees at his discretion within the 2¢ limit. The new law stated that the charge for delivery of letters would not exceed 1¢ each. This did not meet with Postmaster General Holt's expectations with respect to recommendations he had made concerning rate changes. He was faced with a considerable reduction in revenue from carrier operations.

His response was to reinstitute a charge for collecting letters to the mails. Since the law did not specify the type of delivery, this was perfectly proper, but it did require that the collection fees to the mails be prepaid. This caused a problem because the public in cities such as New York, Philadelphia, Boston and possibly some others had become accustomed to dropping their out-of-town mail in collection boxes with only the postage affixed and no stamp for the carrier fee. As can be imagined, in spite of notices and newspaper announcements about the new requirements, many people forgot or refused to add the additional amount, and the letters ended up at the post office short-paid.

The practice of holding a letter with insufficient postage at the originating office, and informing the addressee of the deficiency, had been in effect since 1855 with limited results. The additional labor required of the clerks, and the large number of requests for payment that were ignored, made it an undesirable procedure. At that time most mail did not include a return address, so it was difficult to contact the writers except by notices, which were not too effective in larger cities. While this provision had previously only applied to postage charges and not carrier fees, Postmaster General Holt, in his 1860 annual report, stated that because of the large number of letters with unpaid carrier fees, he was also applying the "hold for postage" to carrier fees.

At first, after the collection charge to the mail was reinstituted, some of the short-paid letters were marked with 1¢ DUE and forwarded to their destination, where the carrier fee was to be collected from the addressee. This also caused problems. The collecting carrier in the city of origin had been credited with 1¢ for his fee. The city then had to debit the Post Office Department to recover this amount, and the destination city or town that collected the fee had to remit it to the Post Office Department, which then credited it to the originating office. While cumbersome, this system could work. However, in the case where the letter was not delivered and the amount due not paid, the debits and credits did not balance, and the carrier system of the originating city was no longer self-supporting, as required by law. This limited practice of collecting the underpayment from the recipient was discontinued in October 1860 at Philadelphia and Boston, and probably at other major cities [4:43]. It is possible that at about this time was instituted the systemwide decision of Postmaster General Holt to hold short-paid carrier letters for payment before putting them in the mail.

The practice of charging 1¢ for collection of letters to the post office had been in effect for over a year by the time the 1861 stamps were distributed to post offices. It would seem that the public by this time would have become accustomed to paying the fee, which was to be prepaid by the sender, but a significant number of short-paid letters were still arriving from the collection boxes. Some interesting covers have resulted from this failure to prepay the carrier fee, and **Figure 10-29** shows an outstanding example. This cover was illustrated in Chapter 9 (Figure 9-2) as an earliest-known use and demonetization cover, but is certainly worthy of a repeat appearance as a "held for carrier fee payment" example from Philadelphia. On this cover, the ornate framed REC'D marking evidently takes the place of the "Held For Postage" marking that was applied in New York and some other cities. Stets reported that the REC'D marking was used at Philadelphia beginning about November 9, 1860 [11:254].

Collection-to-the-mails use is the most common of

Figure 10-28. Scarce example of the use of the U.S. PENNY MAIL carrier marking after the end of the fee carrier period. Mailed on July 14, 1863, as attested by docketing on the cover, this item reflects the increase in local mail rate to 2¢ as of July 1, 1863.
(C.W. Christian collection)

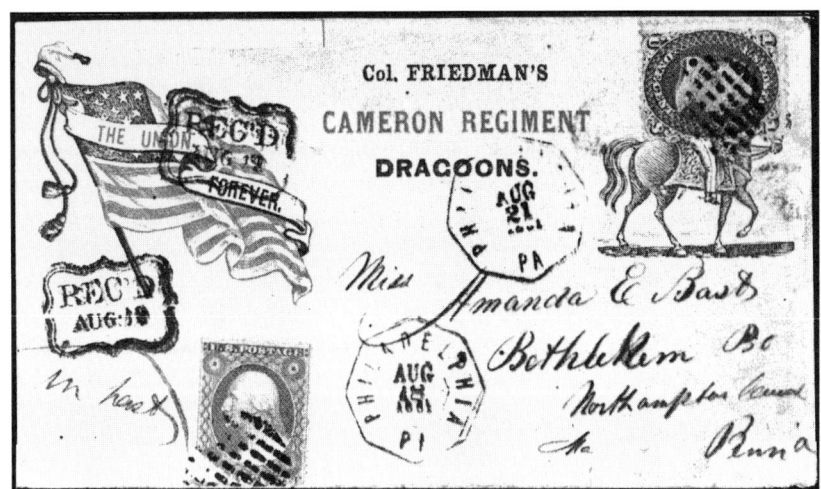

Figure 10-29. An outstanding example of earliest-known day of use of the 1¢ on cover. It was posted for carrier collection at Philadelphia, Pennsylvania, on August 18, 1861, with a 3¢ 1857 Washington to pay the letter rate. Because of failure to prepay 1¢ for carrier pickup, the letter was delayed at the post office until the additional postage was paid. The 1861 1¢ Franklin was added on August 21, and the letter entered the mails on that date.
(John Kauffman Inc.)

Figure 10-30. Colorful woodcut illustration of a civilian volunteer-operated hospital for Civil War casualties. Note patient on stretcher being carried in. Early use of the 1861 1¢ paying carrier collection to the mails, and a 3¢ for letter postage. Also shown in color section.

the Philadelphia carrier uses, and some interesting covers and uses can be illustrated. **Figure 10-30** shows a November 11, 1861, letter with a picture of a "Volunteer Hospital." Establishments such as this were organized and operated by private groups during the Civil War for the care of military personnel. While some of them were medical facilities, most were welfare, recreation and morale installations similar to the Red Cross and USO establishments of today. This particular facility was operated by the Volunteer Refreshment Committee.

Figure 10-31 illustrates a March 25, 1862, use with an ornate embossed corner-card advertisement for a Philadelphia ice company.

Shown in **Figure 10-32** is an example of the normal carrier-to-the-mails franking on an unusual patriotic cover. The cover is from Henry Simons, U.S. National Wagon Works of Philadelphia. Patriotic covers with business corner cards are quite scarce.

Figure 10-33 shows a scarce carrier cover dated June 27, 1862, with an octagonal PENNY POST carrier marking on the front together with the normally seen Philadelphia CDS. Covers with 1¢+3¢ franking and this marking arrangement have been reported only from May 6, 1862, to June 27, 1862. Subsequent to this short period, the octagonal marking was placed on the reverse side of carrier collection-to-the-mails covers.

While the carrier-to-the-mails franking normally consisted of a combination of the 1¢ and 3¢ denominations, examples of other combinations are not too difficult to obtain. **Figure 10-34** illustrates an unusually symmetric arrangement of stamps where a 1¢ Franklin is placed on each corner of the envelope.

Figure 10-35 shows the use of a single 1¢ stamp to pay the collection fee to the mails. In this case the postage was waived because of the free-franking privilege accorded to postmasters. The carrier fee, as is always the case, must be paid even though the letter is "free."

A very unusual situation has been recorded for

Figure 10-31. Red embossed advertisement for the Knickerbocker Ice Company on a March 25, 1862, collection-to-the-mails cover. Also illustrated in color section.
(C.W. Christian collection)

Figure 10-32. September 24 (illegible year date) carrier to the mails. This design was known to have been used in 1861 and reflects the somewhat benevolent feeling between the North and the South that existed in the early years of the war.

Figure 10-33. Latest-recorded example (June 27, 1862) of the use of a Philadelphia octagon carrier marking on the front of nonlocal mail.

The United States 1¢ Franklin 1861-67

Figure 10-34. March 31, 1862, Philadelphia carrier collection to Fort Delaware, Delaware. Standard usage, but interesting arrangement of stamps.

Figure 10-35. FREE letter to postmaster at Kirks Mills, Pennsylvania. The cover required a 1¢ stamp to pay for the carrier-to-the-mails service.

Figure 10-36. Early example of a Philadelphia reduced-contract carrier rate for delivering circulars. The normal rate for this date was 2¢. The single-circle CDS is dated December 6, 1863.

184

Figure 10-37. A more common type, but still scarce, Philadelphia contract-carrier cover dated February 17, 1866, with a double-circle CDS. The contract rate was paid by a 1¢ Franklin.

Philadelphia. The postal law establishing free carrier delivery also provided that the local postmaster could contract with publishers of newspapers, periodicals and circulars for delivery by carrier, within his district, at agreed upon rates, subject to approval of the postmaster general (§15, Act of March 3, 1863). Examples of items delivered under this provision are scarce and, to the author's knowledge, have only been seen from Philadelphia between 1863 and 1866.

During this period, the normal fee for local delivery was 2¢ for circulars and printed matter at all cities that provided carrier service. All covers discussed here are unsealed, including one wrapper, indicating that the enclosure was probably a circular or other printed matter, and each has a single 1¢ stamp to pay the special contract carrier fee.

Nine of the 12 items that the author has recorded were delivered between 1864 and 1866, are unsealed covers that probably contained circulars, and are marked with a double-circle PHILADELPHIA/POST OFFICE town marking [12:184]. The three recorded exceptions to this are a single-circle Philadelphia CDS, dated in December of 1863 (**Figure 10-36**); a Sanitary Fair cover (not illustrated) with a large undated PHILADELPHIA/1/PA. in oval cancel of a type used for circular mail; and a wrapper (not illustrated) that may have contained a periodical. This later item is the only example known to the author of use of a wrapper under this special-fee provision. The stamp is canceled with a double-circle PHILADELPHIA/POST OFFICE town marking, unfortunately with an illegible year date. This unusual item was brought to the attention of the writer by Richard F. Winter, in whose collection it now resides.

Figure 10-37 illustrates the type of postmark that is found on most of the examples. Three of these are Sanitary Fair covers, all dated in 1864. All of the Sanitary Fair covers showing this special fee were part of the outstanding Alvin and Marjorie Kantor collection of Sanitary Fair covers.

An unusual example of a letter carried outside the mails from a foreign port to Philadelphia is shown in **Figure 10-38**. This interesting folded-letter cover is endorsed "p Canada." indicating expected passage aboard the Cunard steamship *Canada*. The letter is sealed with a wax wafer and, on the reverse, is docketed "1863/Liverpool 13 June/Rec 27 do/ans 20 Jul." The *Canada* was a mail packet and departed Liverpool on June 13, 1863, arriving at Boston on June 26, 1863. These sailing dates correspond with the docketing and substantiate the convey-

Figure 10-38. Carrier delivery at Philadelphia of a folded letter that originated in Liverpool, England, carried outside the mail on the Cunard mail ship *Canada*. The letter was docketed as being written June 13, 1863, and arriving at its destination on June 27, 1863. The 1¢ carrier fee was paid by stamp.
(Photo courtesy of Robert B. Meyersburg)

ance of the letter aboard the *Canada*. It obviously was carried outside the mails since there are no English postal markings or stamps. The letter was probably carried by a passenger on the *Canada*. After arrival in Boston, the passenger carried it to Philadelphia by train. At that point, a 1¢ stamp was added to pay the carrier fee, and the letter was dropped into a local collection box. This private conveyance of mail, of course, was illegal under the statutes.

Boston

The Boston carrier service was the third largest carrier operation in the country. During the 1860s, it had a delivery volume of about one-fifth that of New York City. There were no special handstamps used to indicate local carrier delivery, and such covers can only tentatively be identified by the fact that street addresses are included. Infrequently, examples can be found where manuscript notations on the cover refer to carrier delivery. Collection-to-the-mails carrier service, of course, is easily identifiable by the inclusion of a stamp to pay the carrier fee in addition to the postage.

In comparison to New York and Philadelphia, the carrier history of Boston is relatively uneventful. Government carrier service was initiated as early as 1846 with five "penny post" carriers. Some competitive private carrier operations were attempted over the years, but none of them was particularly long-lived or successful, and the post office carrier service was never seriously challenged.

At the end of the fee-carrier period on July 1, 1863, Boston had 32 carriers employed and was handling about 1,300,000 pieces of mail per year. This volume of mail was not significantly different than that reported two years earlier for 1861. For some reason, Boston does not seem to have shared in the rapid increase of carrier deliveries that was experienced by New York and Philadelphia during the same period.

An interesting excerpt from Ashbrook's *Special Service* is included here [13:26]. This is from an article that was copied from the *Boston Chronicle* and that appeared in the July 1862 issue of *U.S. Mail & Post Office Assistant*.

> "THE PENNY POST — We copy the following from the *Boston Chronicle*. Although written for that locality, which it is admitted is blessed with a penny-post system, as perfect, to say the least, as in any other of our large cities, is still applicable to the penny-postman everywhere, as are the wholesome suggestions to those whose servant he is; 'Our Penny Post-man.' There are thousands of our citizens who are served daily by the penny-postman, and served very faithfully too, who are unaware that by a very little attention on their part they could greatly relieve them of a portion of their most disagreeable duties. A few sugges-
tions may be advantageous. Every letter taken from the Post Office for delivery is charged to the postman, and on his return to the office from his route he must either pay for it or return it. How unfair, then, is it to blame him, because he will not trust or change a bill to take from it one or two cents . . ."

The above quotation adds information on how the carrier-fee collections were handled and recorded, and describes problems in dealing with the public that have not changed much in the past 130 years.

Figure 10-39 shows an example of a probable carrier delivery of local mail. As is true with most carrier covers recorded by this writer for this period, the cover is postmarked with a Boston red double-circle town and date marking with no year date, and the stamp is canceled with a black PAID marking. This marking is usually boxed, as in this case, but also is occasionally seen without the box as a plain PAID.

Illustrated in **Figure 10-40** is an outstanding patriotic cover from the collection of Robert B. Meyersburg. It shows the normal franking and markings of a carrier-to-the-mails use. The letter was mailed April 16 (1862), and the design pictures the origins and history of the U.S. flag from the early St. George's Cross of England to the current (1861) U.S. flag.

Another carrier to the mails example is shown in **Figure 10-41**. This August 29 cover shows the relatively scarce Boston use of the unboxed PAID cancel. The M.V.M. in the upper-left corner probably stands for the Massachusetts Volunteer Militia, and the drawing pictures a soldier dressed in a uniform of the Mexican War of 1845. While this was inappropriate for the Civil War period, a number of early patriotic covers can be found with old stock cuts that bore some resemblance to a patriotic theme. There was a great urgency by the printing establishments to cash in on the patriotic fever, and cuts from files of stock illustrations were used to get something on envelopes as rapidly as possible.

Figure 10-42 illustrates the rare use of a block of four of the 1861 1¢ stamp to pay the postage plus carrier fee. There are only three blocks known to have been used (on the front of a cover), and this is reported to be the finest example.

Another scarce carrier-to-the-mails use is illustrated in **Figure 10-43**. This shows the use of the short-lived and seldom-used 3¢ letter sheet that was issued in August 1861. It did not achieve popularity for some reason and was withdrawn from use in 1864.

Figure 10-44 shows the combination use of the 10¢ 1861 with the 1¢ to pay for the transcontinental rate of 10¢ plus the 1¢ carrier fee. This combination is also seen on covers to Canada.

An unusual "bootleg" item is illustrated in **Figure**

City Carrier Collection and Delivery

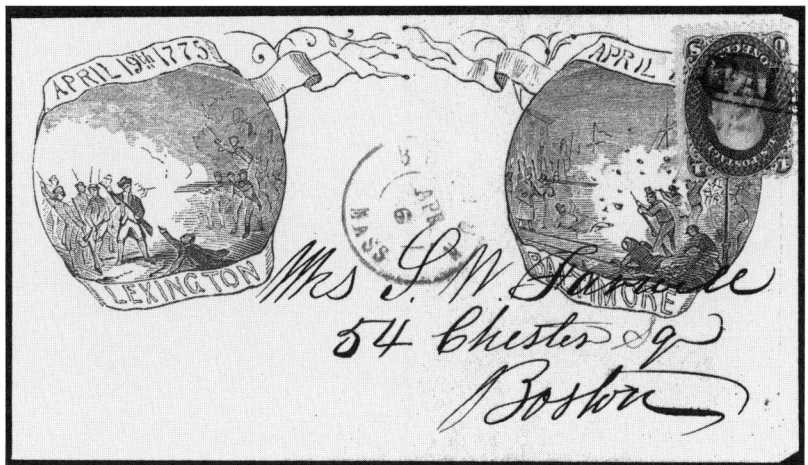

Figure 10-39. Local Boston carrier use. The 1¢ stamp paid the carrier fee. The patriotic cover illustrates two battles fought on April 19: the battle at Lexington, Massachusetts, in 1775 between the patriots and the British, and the Baltimore Riot in 1861 between the Federal Army and Southern civilian sympathizers. The cover was printed in mauve by Samuel C. Upham of Philadelphia.

Figure 10-40. Colorful red, white and blue Boston patriotic cover illustrating a carrier-collection fee to the mail. Dated April 16 (1862). (Robert B. Meyersburg collection)

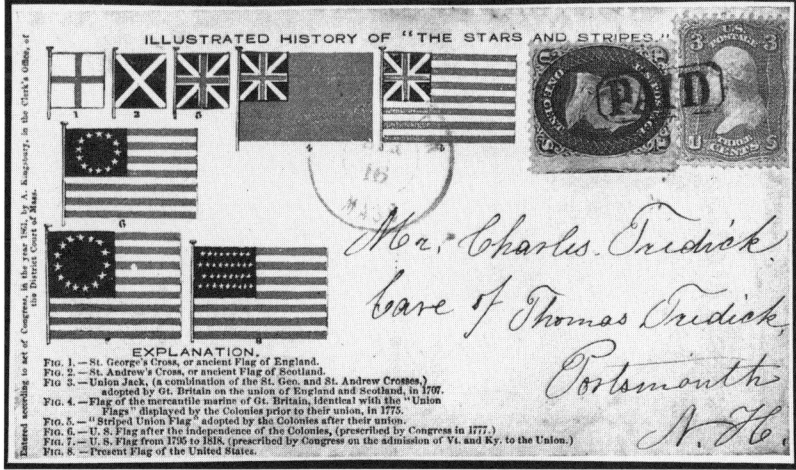

Figure 10-41. Boston carrier use, dated August 29 (possibly 1861). Early use is denoted by the "dot-in-U" variety of the 1¢ stamp from plate 9, the first plate, and the use of a rose-pink 3¢ denomination. The stamps are canceled by an unboxed PAID handstamp.

The United States 1¢ Franklin 1861-67

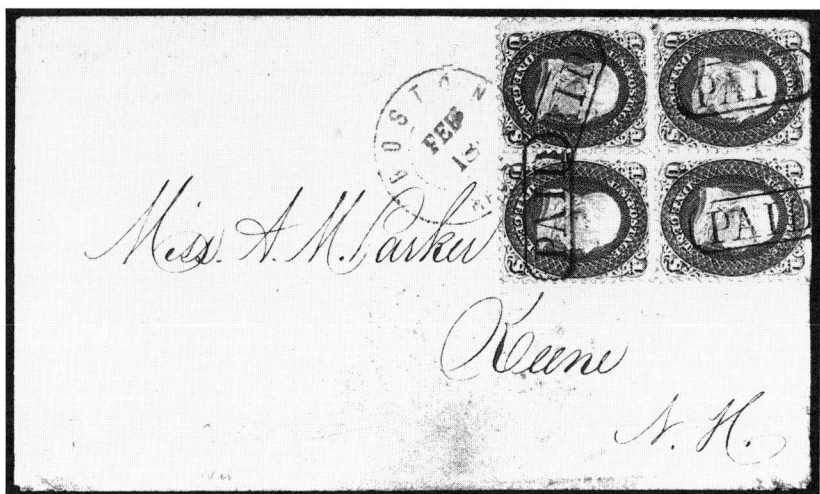

Figure 10-42. Scarce on-cover block of four of the 1¢ 1861 issue, paying both the carrier fee and postage from Boston to Keene, New Hampshire.
(James Lee collection)

Figure 10-43. Rare carrier-to-the-mails use of an 1861 letter sheet (Scott U36). The 3¢ embossed stamp is printed in pink on a watermarked blue laid-paper letter sheet and pays the letter rate from Boston to Cohasset, Massachussets. The 1¢ Franklin pays the carrier fee. Both stamps are canceled with a single boxed **PAID** canceler.

Figure 10-44. Boston carrier-to-the-mails cover with a 10¢ 1861 paying the transcontinental rate to San Francisco and the 1¢ stamp paying for carrier delivery to the post office.
(James Lee collection)

City Carrier Collection and Delivery

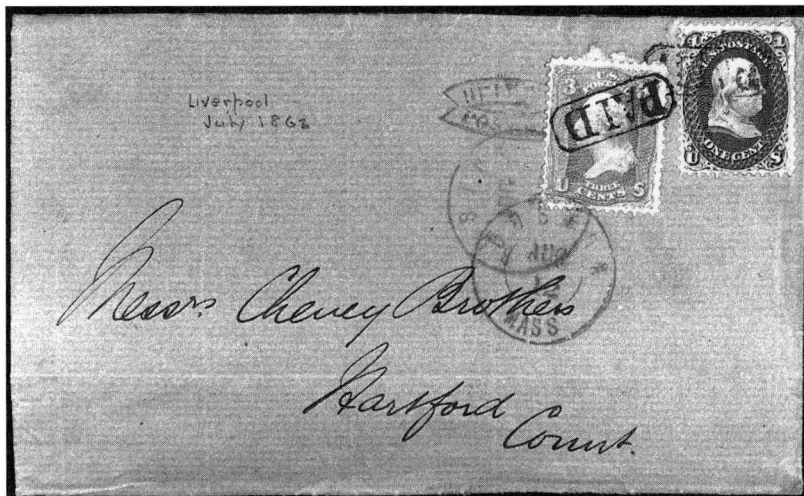

Figure 10-45. Underpaid, and possibly "bootleg" use. The folded letter sheet originated at Liverpool, England, and is datelined July 22, 1862. It was entered into the mails for carrier collection at Boston on August 5. The nonlocal destination required additional postage. The letter sheet was marked "Held For Postage." The 3¢ stamp was applied on August 12, and the letter sheet was entered into the mails.
(James Lee collection)

Figure 10-46. Local Baltimore cover with typical blue CDS cancel. Carrier delivery is indicated by the presence of a street address.

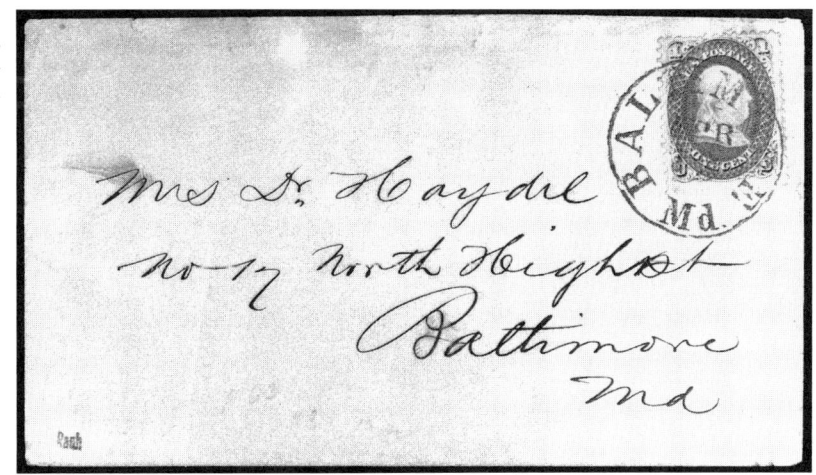

10-45. This sealed folded letter sheet is datelined "Liverpool, England, July 22, 1862," and was carried illegally outside the mails from Liverpool to Boston. It was then deposited for carrier collection to the mails and franked with only a single 1¢ Franklin for delivery to Hartford, Connecticut. The folded letter sheet received an August 5 postmark, and the 1¢ stamp was canceled. Because of the out-of-town destination, additional letter-rate postage was required, so it was marked with a "held for postage" handstamp, and the addressee was notified of the short payment. After the necessary postage was received from the addressee, a 3¢ stamp was affixed to the folded letter sheet. It was postmarked August 12.

Baltimore and Washington, D.C.

These two neighboring cities complete the roster of towns with carrier service where a postage stamp was normally used to pay the carrier fee. Baltimore carriers delivered approximately 1,000,000 letters for the year ending June 30, 1863, with a staff of 22 carriers. For the same period, Washington D.C., delivered about 750,000 letters with a carrier force of 18.

Examples of covers showing carrier service from either of these towns are considerably more difficult to obtain than those from the larger cities, and it is particularly difficult to find covers with clear and readable postmarks. There were no special carrier markings.

Baltimore used a large bright-blue 31mm CDS showing the month and day, but not the year. The CDS was consistently used to cancel the stamps and was not generally struck separately as a town marking.

Figure 10-46 shows a typical local Baltimore use with carrier delivery suggested by the presence of a street address.

A Baltimore carrier collection-to-the-mails cover is shown in **Figure 10-47**. This October 9 (probably 1861) patriotic cover commemorates the death of Colonel

189

Figure 10-47. Baltimore, Maryland, to Lincoln, Maine, patriotic cover dated October 9 (1861?). Early use is indicated by the "dot-in-U" 1¢ variety and the rose-pink shade of the 3¢. Cover illustrates carrier collection to the mails.

Figure 10-48. Washington, D.C., carrier collection to the mail to Machias, Maine. Date of mailing is unreadable, but probable early use is indicated by the use of four 1¢ stamps from plate number 9, the first plate.

Ellsworth, one of the earliest casualties of the war. He died at the hands of an irate Southern citizen on May 24, 1861, after removing a Confederate flag from an Alexandria, Virginia, rooftop. He was known for his well-publicized recruitment and organizing of a Zouave regiment. At the age of 24, he became a national hero and martyr.

Washington, D.C., is one of the earlier cities to establish government carrier operations. Documentation indicates that a letter carrier was employed in Washington as early as 1799 [14h:239]. Washington was also a principal user of the U.S. eagle carrier stamp of 1851. The use of that stamp to pay the carrier fee has been recorded on an 1863 cover with an accompanying 3¢ of the 1861 issue. This late use suggests that the eagle carrier stamp may not have been specifically demonetized along with all the other pre-1861 stamps. The eagle carrier stamp seems to have been used exclusively between 1853 and 1861 to pay the carrier fee, and is frequently seen canceled in manuscript with the initials of a carrier. Ten carriers were employed when the fee system ended in 1863.

A large amount of mail was handled by the Washington post office during the last years of the fee system as a result of the war, and the number of letters delivered by carriers increased by 25 percent between 1861 and 1863. Nonetheless, examples of carrier use are relatively difficult to find. **Figure 10-48** shows an example on a patriotic cover with four 1¢ stamps being used to pay the carrier-collection fee plus postage.

Because of the large amount of government mail originating or directed to Washington, it is not too unusual to find examples of free-franked mail with a 1¢ stamp affixed for a carrier fee. The postal regulations were quite specific in limiting the number of individuals who could use the free-franking privilege. However, during the Civil War most official and military mail seems to have qualified for free postage. **Figure 10-49** illustrates an example of such use. If this had been a local drop letter, it could have been handled without charge as "official business."

The presence of the 1¢ stamp indicates carrier collection.

The cover illustrated in **Figure 10-50** is also paid with a single 1¢ stamp for the carrier fee, but in this case, the letter was postage free because it was addressed to a postmaster, and postmasters of small towns were given the privilege of free mail service. Carrier service in this example was for delivery to the mails.

Carrier Service in Other Cities

Of the 49 cities that were reported by the postmaster general to have carrier services at the end of the carrier-fee period, the six that consistently used postage stamps in the payment of these fees have been discussed. The majority of the remaining 43 were smaller offices with fewer than five carriers employed. They evidently operated on a strictly cash-or-charge basis.

There are some exceptions to this general observation. For example, Cincinnati had a large carrier operation, comparable with that of Washington, D.C., but did not use postage stamps for payment of the carrier fee. This somewhat anomalous situation may have come about from the practice in Cincinnati in prior years where only cash or the U.S. eagle carrier stamp was accepted for payment. When the eagle carrier stamp was no longer available, the Cincinnati postal officials evidently did not replace it with an acceptance of postage stamps for the carrier fee. Only the cash-or-charge payment option remained.

A very few examples of attempts to use postage stamps in some of these other carrier cities have been recorded. They are quite scarce and have sparked much discussion concerning their validity for actually paying a carrier fee. In this writer's opinion, as previously stated, these examples were "accidental uses." The stamp was probably placed on the letter to pay for carrier service by individuals who were transient to the area or relatively new arrivals, and who had had experience in other cities where carrier service was paid by postage stamps. Know-

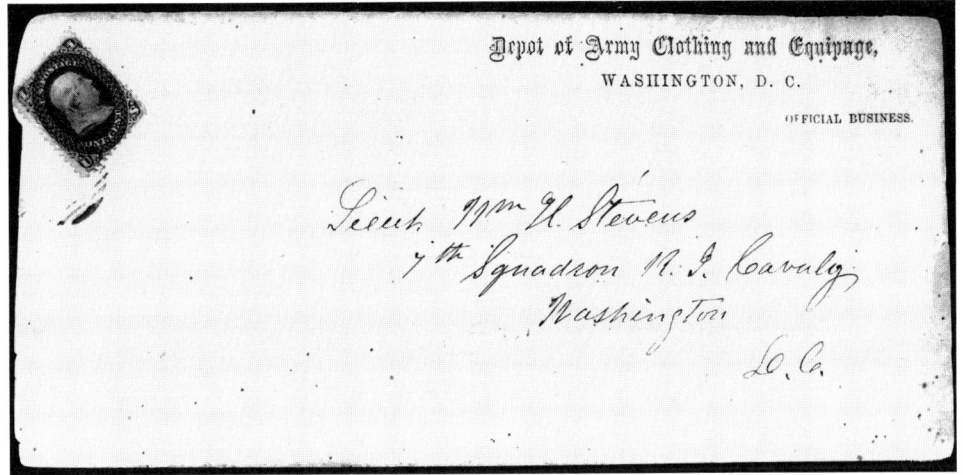

Figure 10-49. Local carrier collection and delivery of an OFFICIAL BUSINESS letter from the Depot of Army Clothing and Equipage at Washington, D.C., to a lieutenant in the cavalry.

Figure 10-50. Washington, D.C., May 16, 1863, carrier collection to the mail, paid for by a 1¢ Franklin. Addressed to Rowlandsville, Maryland, Postmaster. The cover was mailed without postage under the provision for free franking of mail to or from postmasters of small offices.

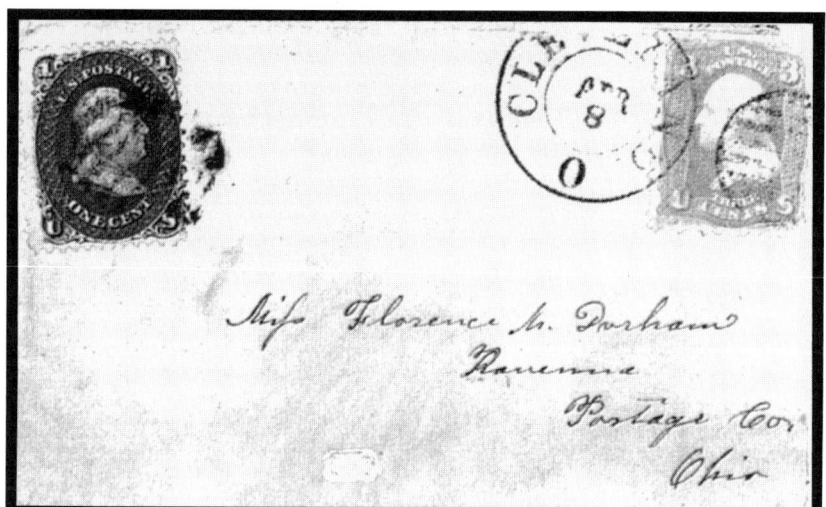

Figure 10-51. Scarce Cleveland, Ohio, carrier cover dated April 8 (year unknown). It shows prepaid carrier collection to the mails by the use of the 1¢ Franklin in addition to the 3¢ for letter postage.
(Richard J. Frajola photograph)

Figure 10-52. St. Louis, Missouri, to Cincinnati, Ohio, dated May 17?, 1862. This is a rare example of the carrier fee paid by stamp from this city. The cover is marked "Due 3" to be collected on a double-weight, short-paid letter.
(Robert B. Meyersburg collection)

ing that a carrier system existed in the city, this individual might reasonably assume that a similar procedure was in effect.

This conclusion is based on several observations. Even for relatively large cities, such as St. Louis, which in 1863 employed seven carriers and probably delivered over 100,000 pieces of carrier mail, the existence of covers showing carrier-fee payment by stamp is rare. If payment by stamp had been an authorized or even an acceptable method of payment, it seems there would be many more examples of this use than actually exist.

In addition, if a stamp was used for payment, it would be incumbent upon the local post office to bill the Post Office Department for reimbursement to avoid a loss on the transaction since a payment of 1¢ would have been made to the carrier, but no money collected. While the larger cities maintained strict accounting and reporting for this kind of service, reports of carrier activities from the smaller carrier cities are frequently missing from the Post Office Department reports. This substantiates the premise that such use was not a recognized practice at these cities. It is also possible that payment by stamp was accepted on the few occasions that it occurred, and that the local post office just absorbed the loss. It is known from the few examples of covers where the carrier fee was paid by stamp that these letters were not "held for postage" or marked for collection from the addressee.

Finally, there have been no reported instances of any notices in newspapers or other documentation from these cities that support, or even discuss, the use of postage stamps to pay carrier fees. Although, as in most conclusions, these facts do not prohibit alternate interpretations, it seems that the weight of evidence supports accidental use.

In the following paragraphs, some of the existing carrier covers showing the use of the 1¢ 1861 stamp from other towns and cities will be illustrated and discussed. These scarce and sometimes rare examples are items to be searched for. Their inclusion in any collection is definitely a challenge.

Cleveland, Ohio, instituted a government-sponsored carrier service as early as January 1854, when Henry S. Bishop was contracted with to operate a penny post service for the city. Bishop's City Post was short-lived. By July 1854, Bishop was employed directly by the Post Office as a carrier. From that period on, the local delivery of mail was done by government carriers. By July 1, 1863, three carriers were employed.

For some reason, there appear to be more examples of carrier covers with the fee paid by 1¢ 1861 stamps from Cleveland than other small carrier cities. Thomas F. Allen [15:231] has reported eight examples between 1862 and 1863, and this probably accounts for the majority that still exist.

Figure 10-51 illustrates one of these covers. Addressed to Ravenna, Ohio, with an April 8 double-circle Cleveland postmark, this shows the use of an additional 1¢ stamp to pay the carrier fee to the mails.

Figure 10-52 is an example of prepaid carrier use from St. Louis. Three similar covers, all from the same correspondence and all short-paid, have been recorded.

New Bedford, Massachusetts, was a medium-size carrier town with four carriers in 1863. **Figure 10-53** shows an example of a probable local carrier delivery paid for by stamp. Although this example could be a drop cover, the fact that New Bedford had carrier service and a street name is included in the address indicates possible carrier service. This small cover is postmarked with the typical orange-red, large and distinctive New Bedford/Paid CDS, and is canceled with a bold, black, fancy geometric design. The purpose of the black PAID handstamp is not known. Possibly it was to alert the carrier to the fact that the delivery fee had been prepaid.

A similar New Bedford cover (not illustrated) in the Robert B. Meyersburg collection, dated June 22 and paid by 3¢+1¢ 1861 stamps, is addressed to San Francisco and represents payment by stamp of the collection fee to the post office.

Examples of this type of carrier payment are known from a few other small carrier towns, but unfortunately are not available for listing or illustration at this time. Covers on which the carrier payment was made with the 1851-57 series of stamps are known from more locations, but descriptions of those are not relevant to this volume.

Figure 10-53. Lady's cover illustrating possible local carrier service, paid for by stamp, at New Bedford, Massachusetts. The cover is dated February 16 and postmarked with an orange-red CDS.

The few examples discussed here are indicative of the paid-by-stamp carrier covers that can be found from the smaller offices. It should be emphasized, though, that this type of use is genuinely scarce, and sharp eyes and good fortune are needed to discover them among the many ordinary covers originating from these towns.

Another rare use of the 1¢ 1861 stamp on a carrier cover is illustrated in **Figure 10-54**. This exceptional cover shows the use of a blue Floyd's Penny Post stamp, which paid for the collection fee to the post office by private carrier, and the three 1¢ Franklins, which paid the first-class postage to destination. Chicago was one of the few major cities where private posts continued to operate during this period. Chicago did not establish its own government carrier operation until 1864. Although no year date is contained in the CDS, the cover must have been mailed in 1862 or 1863.

Branch Post Offices

In in his *Report of the Postmaster General* for 1861, Montgomery Blair requested Congress to amend existing law, which authorized the establishment of branch post offices. The then-current law allowed branch post offices, but prohibited the charging of fees for branch post office service. The postmaster general requested that a fee of 1¢ per letter be authorized to meet operational costs. Postmasters from several cities had asked Blair to establish branch offices for the receipt and delivery of letters auxiliary to the city post office, but he was unwilling to accommodate these requests without some additional income to offset the expense.

Figure 10-54. Rare use of a private carrier and the 1¢ 1861 on a Chicago, Illinois, June 28 cover to St. Louis, Missouri. The cover bears a blue Floyd's Penny Post stamp with black carrier cancel to pay the collection fee. It is postmarked with a typical Chicago CDS, and stamps canceled with a blue cork killer.
(Courtesy of Richard C. Frajola)

Figure 10-55. Scarce example of Chicago branch office mail with a duplex CDS in blue, dated February 6, 1863. Chicago had no carrier service at this time, and the 1¢ stamp paid for sending the mail from the branch post office to the main post office.

Figure 10-56. A probably unique example of Chicago North Branch Post Office use on a compound envelope (Scott U28). The cover is dated January 26, 1863, and addressed to the Smithsonian Institute in Washington City, D.C. The use of the 1¢+3¢ envelope is scarce outside New York City.
(Courtesy of Richard C. Frajola)

The Act of April 16, 1862, effective July 1, 1862, again provided for the establishment of branch post offices and, in addition, stated that a fee of 1¢ per letter would be charged to carry mail between the main post office and a branch office. The branch offices were to collect and deliver letters and other postal matter, and to sell stamps. Other services, such as registration, would be accomplished only at the main post office. While these offices did not provide carrier collection and delivery at residences, such as has been discussed throughout this chapter, their business was reported to the Post Office as part of the carrier operation.

It does not appear that many cities took advantage of this law, at least in the period between July 1, 1862, and July 1, 1863, when the carrier fee was legislated out of existence. For one thing, the sub-post offices and carrier stations that had been established in most of the larger carrier cities already performed most of the functions of a branch post office. Their biggest advantage would be in a city where a comprehensive carrier system was not yet in operation.

Only Cleveland and Chicago have been recorded as operating branch post offices during this period. The Cleveland *Morning Leader* for October 3, 1862, carried the following announcement:

"BRANCH POST OFFICE FOR THE WEST SIDE
The application of Postmaster Cowles to the Postoffice Department, for authority to establish a branch Postoffice on the West Side having been granted, he has appointed M.Y. Hutten, to act as branch Postmaster. He will open his office at No. 149, Detroit Street, a few doors from Pearl.
Citizens on the West Side wishing their mail matter sent to the branch office, will please leave directions to that effect with Mr. Hutten or at the Postoffice. All letters mailed at the branch office will require a penny stamp in addition to the three-cent stamp. All letters delivered will be charged 1¢ additional postage, which will be collected by the branch postmaster. Newspapers, periodical and circulars will be received without any additional postage . . . [15:230]"

While it may be assumed that patrons took advantage of the new Cleveland branch post office, no covers to attest to this fact are known. Unfortunately, letters collected at the branch office for delivery to the mails at the main post office would be indistinguishable from any letters collected at carrier stations for the mail unless some specific notation was written on the envelope. To date, none has been found.

A more fortunate situation, from a philatelic point of view, exists with the Chicago branch offices. Since Chicago did not have a carrier service until 1864, any cover with a 1¢ stamp in addition to the postage and mailed between July 1, 1862, and July 1, 1863, is very likely to be a branch carrier cover.

Figure 10-55 shows an outstanding example of this rare use. This yellow cover is struck twice with a blue Chicago CDS and duplexed canceler, and dated February 6, 1863. It is addressed to Saratoga Springs, New York, and docketed, "J. Atkinson Feb 8." Since there was no carrier service at this time, the extra 1¢ stamp can be assumed to be for payment of the branch post office fee. The only other possibility is for this to be a way cover, most improbable for a city like Chicago.

James Lee, who has researched this usage, estimates that five or six of these covers are known.

Because the Chicago branch post office covers carry the same postage as carrier collection-to-the-mails covers from other cities, they can easily be mistaken for the more common type carrier covers. While the number of recorded Chicago branch examples is very small, it is certainly possible that a significant number of these interesting and scarce covers are residing in collections with their true identity unknown.

An even rarer branch office cover is shown in **Figure 10-56**. This outstanding cover is scarce in three different ways. It is a compound 1¢+3¢ envelope used from a city other than New York. It is a Chicago branch post office carrier use, and it has a rare "North Branch/Post Office" marking. It is reported to be a unique use of the compound envelope from Chicago. The exact purpose and origin of the marking is not certain. From the inscription "Direct To," it is possible that it was applied by the sender as a notice of how replies should be addressed. It is also possible that this marking was applied by the North Branch post office to the outgoing mail of individuals who had requested delivery of their mail to the branch post office. As with many rare usages, it is impossible to make a distinction between alternate explanations.

Another, more conventional branch marking from the Chicago North Branch Post Office is shown in **Figure 10-57**. This example was mailed after the 1¢ fee for branch office mailing was eliminated on July 1, 1863. The 3¢ postage paid for the standard domestic letter rate. The cover is postmarked SEP 28 with a double-circle Chicago marking in blue. The postmark has the letters RA at the top of the date slug. The inclusion of letters in Chicago postmarks during a short period in the fall of 1863 has piqued the interest of philatelic students for many years. Richard McP. Cabeen [16:54] and Richard B. Graham [17:118] both have written interesting articles discussing this unusual use.

For some reason, on or about September 13, 1863, the previously used handstamps at Chicago were discarded, and a new set was placed in use. These were double-circle duplex handstamps with an attached cut-cork killer. The postmark is larger with a diameter of 30mm, as contrasted with 26mm for the previous double-circle

Figure 10-57. Chicago Branch Post Office use with a double strike of the oval NORTH BRANCH P.O. handstamp. The cover is dated September 28 (1863), subsequent to the end of the special 1¢ fee for branch post office mailing. The postmark shows the initials "R.A."
(James Lee collection)

Figure 10-58. Chicago use on a star-die envelope (Scott U19), showing carrier delivery and the "Chicago City" postmark used for local letters. The postmark contains the initial "T" and is dated August 25. A 1¢ Franklin in addition to the 1¢ envelope make up the 2¢ local rate.
(James Lee collection)

Figure 10-59. Interesting and scarce Chicago, Illinois, cover mailed on January 18, 1864, after the end of the carrier-fee period but before carriers were established in this city. This shows mailing at the West Branch Post Office. The 3¢ letter rate was paid by 2¢ Jackson (Scott 73) and a 1¢ Franklin stamp.
(James Lee collection)

handstamp. Each of the new handstamps had one or two letters or initials placed in the top row of the date slug, and the year date that had previously been shown was no longer included.

These handstamps were used for all mail directed out of town from September 11 until November 13, 1863, when they were taken out of service as suddenly as they appeared. It seems that some sort of controlled test regarding the handling of mail may have been in progress. RA is the most common of the initials to be found. Postmarks with GA, SB, and X are also known. For many years, it was surmised that these initials might identify postal clerks or carriers involved in handling the mail, but recent investigations show this is probably not the case.

A new and comprehensive study by Leonard Piszkiewicz, titled "Chicago Postmarks of 1863 with Initials," was published in the August, 1996 edition of the *Chronicle* (pages 167-79). Piskiewicz examined more than 100 examples of the Chicago initial cancellations, and made some interesting discoveries. A new initial, "U," was added to the list, and a strong correlation was found to exist between the initials and the destinations of the covers, as well as with the trains that would have probably been used for their transport out of Chicago. The conclusion reached from these relationships is that the initials in the cancels most likely refer to specific train stations for outgoing mail routes, and the initials assisted in the sorting of the mail.

Evidently, the experiment was not very successful, for at the end of the test period in November of 1863, the initials were removed from the cancelers, and a two-digit year date, preceded by an apostrophe, was added to the date slug in the bottom row.

Local mail was usually canceled with a single-circle "Chicago City" postmark, and these local postmarks have also been recorded with about a dozen different one- and two-letter initials. The use of these local canceling devices covered the same general period as the special double-circle postmarks, and probably were part of the same test. A local-mail example with the earliest reported use of an initial postmark is shown in **Figure 10-58**. This postmark, with the letter "T," was applied to a 1¢ star-die envelope that had a single 1¢ Franklin added to make up the 2¢ city delivery rate. The stamp was canceled with a cut-cork killer, but the embossed star-die was not canceled. While the lack of the second cancel is unusual, the act of postmarking a government envelope essentially canceled it so it could not be used again. As previously discussed in Chapter 9, the 1¢ star-die was not demonetized, unlike the other star-die denominations, which were demonetized. While this is not a branch post office use, it seems appropriate to include it at this point to complete the discussion of initial postmarks at Chicago.

Another Chicago branch office cover, also mailed after the end of the carrier-fee period, is illustrated in **Figure 10-59**. This cover shows the oval marking of the West Branch Post Office and is dated January 18, 1864. Of course, no fee could be charged at that time to carry the letter from the branch office to the main office, so the 2¢ Black Jack and the 1¢ Franklin completely paid the intercity postage to the destination at Lancaster, Wisconsin. The blue postmark now shows the addition of the year date. Examples showing any evidence of branch post office use from Chicago are scarce.

In the ensuing years, branch post offices were rapidly established as needed in the larger cities throughout the country. In most cases, no special markings were used, and philatelic interest in this part of the postal operation consequently decreased as these offices replaced the more colorful carrier stations of the past.

Prepayment of Carrier Delivery Fee

For many years, discussions have continued regarding the possibility of prepaying the carrier fee for delivery in another city. The two outstanding U.S. postal historians of the mid-1900s, Stanley B. Ashbrook (**Figure 10-60**) and Elliott Perry (**Figure 10-61**), aligned themselves on opposite sides of the question and did battle in print for an extended period without a mutual resolution of their disagreement.

Ashbrook contended that it was a perfectly legal and accepted practice to place a 1¢ stamp on a letter in addition to the postage to pay in advance for the delivery carrier fee at destination. In support of his thesis, he produced some covers with 3¢+1¢ stamps that had been sent from a noncarrier town to a town or city with a carrier service. He also showed covers with 3¢+1¢+1¢ franking

Figure 10-60. Stanley B. Ashbrook. Philatelic scholar and expert on U.S. classic postal history, whose writings and research still constitute the basis for many philatelic opinions. It is not unusual to find an interesting cover where Ashbrook's analysis and comments still remain in manuscript on the reverse side.

from one carrier city to another. These, he contended, certainly indicated an attempt to prepay a carrier delivery fee.

His arguments also included a quotation from Postmaster General Holt, who in his 1860 report stated that one of the purposes of the compound 3¢+1¢ envelope, issued in December 1860, was to make it more convenient for the public to prepay the carrier delivery fee. An excerpt from his report on this subject follows:

> "This envelope will also be used by those who, when addressing their city correspondents, desire to relieve them from the payment of the carrier's fee for delivering their letters at their domicil [18:292]."

These arguments and examples afforded good substantiation for Ashbrook's position, and he was joined in support of his premise by other notable philatelic figures, including E. Tudor Gross, the pre-eminent pioneer collector and early student of the 1¢ 1861 Franklin.

In this author's opinion, one of the main problems with Ashbrook's contention is that if prepayment was authorized and generally used, why aren't there many more examples to be found showing this type of use?

On the other side of the fence was Perry, who argued long and eloquently on the difficulty of putting the principle of carrier-delivery prepayment into practice and

Figure 10-61. Elliott Perry: 1884-1972. Philatelist, scholar, dealer and writer whose excellent research and original discoveries have added much information to the philatelic world.

cited many references written by postal officials where prepayment of the collection fee was discussed, but where the possibility of prepaying the delivery fee was never mentioned.

Over the half-century since these debates started, the weight of philatelic thinking has accumulated on the side of Perry. Today, prepayment of carrier-delivery fees normally paid at destination for intercity mail is regarded as a nonstandard and in most instances an unacceptable procedure.

Meyersburg reported in a conversation with this writer that he had engaged in an extended correspondence and in many discussions with Perry on this subject, and at one meeting, also attended by George B. Sloane, a consensus was reached that "acceptance of the prepaid carrier fee for delivery in another town was the prerogative of the postmaster and clerks at the town of delivery." Since there were no postal regulations or laws that covered prepayment for out-of-town delivery, this is an entirely reasonable conclusion. The lack of definitive regulations and instructions to the public concerning these procedures resulted in some confusion and dissatisfaction. This was particularly true when postal patrons, acting on the publicly advertised statements of Postmaster General Holt, prepaid the fee for carrier delivery at the destination city, and then had their letters assessed an additional penny upon delivery.

Ashbrook produced a number of covers in defense of his thesis. They all had one feature in common. They were franked with a 1¢ stamp in addition to the amount that might be required for postage including, where appropriate, the fee for carrier collection. There is no doubt these 4¢ and 5¢ covers exist in limited numbers, but for each one of them an alternate explanation, other than prepayment of the delivery fee, can be offered.

Figure 10-62 illustrates a lady's small patriotic cover. (Patriotic designs are seldom found on reduced-size envelopes.) This letter, mailed in Dedham, Massachusetts, for delivery to a street address in neighboring Boston, is overpaid by 1¢. Dedham did not have a carrier system, and it may be surmised that the sender attempted to pay for the carrier-delivery fee at destination. There is no way to know if this cover was delivered free or if an additional penny was collected from the addressee. It is also possible that the 1¢ could have been paid as a way fee. Way fees will be discussed later in Chapter 13. Five-cent covers with port city postmarks could also be prepaid ship letters. This type of use will be also discussed in Chapter 13.

On Perry's side of the debate, logic is the primary consideration. As was discussed in the previous section, cities with carrier systems that did not normally use stamps to pay for the service would have to bill the Post Office for reimbursement of money that they paid to a carrier for delivery of a prepaid fee-prepaid letter. This could be done, but most smaller carrier towns apparently did not appear to engage in this type of accounting.

A more telling indictment against the Ashbrook theory is the case where a person in a large carrier city, for instance, Boston, sent a letter to another carrier city such as New York City, by depositing it at the main Boston post office, franked with 4¢ in postage. Since Boston applied no special markings for carrier service, the post office at New York would have absolutely no way of knowing whether the additional 1¢ was to pay for the carrier delivery at New York, or whether it had been affixed to pay for carrier collection in Boston.

This situation can be predicated for mail between other carrier cities and, in this writer's opinion, is sufficient evidence to assert that prepayment for collection fees at a destination city was not a valid procedure.

A later word on this controversy was contained in a 1989 article by Richard B. Graham [19:183]. While reviewing some early editions of the *U.S. Mail & Post Office Assistant*, he discovered a short notice, dated August 1862, which discussed prepayment of carrier fees. This notice is quoted as follows:

> "The Four-cent Rate. — There is a somewhat prevalent impression that the affixing of a penny stamp to an otherwise prepaid letter, designed to be forwarded by mail, will pay the carrier's fee when it arrives at the place of destination, and many letters, thus prepaid, are received at New York and other offices employing carriers. The impression is entirely erroneous. When a mail letter is deposited in a U.S. lamp-post box or other receptacle provided by Government, to be carried from thence to the post office, the extra penny is then requisite to pay the carrier's fee for delivering to the office. In all other cases, any prepayment of a penny beyond the regular rate, is simply thrown away."

The critical element in this notice is contained in the phrase, "forwarded by mail." This essentially eliminates all letters except local letters from the provision for prepayment of carrier delivery. It should be understood that local letters were not considered by the Post Office Department to be part of the "mail."

While this may not be the last word on the subject, it summarizes the situation from a semiofficial view, and seems to reflect the general procedures in effect during this period.

Epilogue

With the end of the carrier-fee period, the more colorful and philatelically interesting aspects of the government city carrier systems began to diminish. In the years immediately following the historic establishment of free-carrier service, the volume of local mail in the carrier cities increased rapidly, as did the number of carriers employed. Additional cities initiated carrier service for their patrons, and some discontinued service. It is surprising, but by 1870 a net increase of only four towns is found in the reported list of carrier cities.

The Post Office remained committed to providing free collection and delivery wherever feasible and directed its postmasters to give the best possible service. Instructions for Section 14 of the act approved July 1, 1864, gives a good insight into the policy and goals of the Post Office Department, and is quoted as follows:

> "SEC. 14. Letter-carriers will be appointed and their salaries fixed by the Postmaster General as heretofore.
>
> Where letter-carriers are already appointed, their duty is to deliver all letters concerning which there is no positive direction to the contrary.
>
> It is the special duty of postmasters to provide that all letters are regularly, frequently, and promptly delivered by the carriers, so that citizens may have no excuse for clinging to the old custom of calling at the post office. The purpose of the law, providing for a free delivery of letters at the houses of owners, is to promote the public convenience and at the same time reduce the labor in post offices. Postmasters will especially discourage the use of private boxes, and steadily aim at reducing them to the lowest number possible.
>
> In order to facilitate the carriers' work, citizens must be induced to provide letter-boxes at their houses or places of business.
>
> Where carriers are not yet employed, postmasters should immediately recommend one or more for appointment—selecting only young, vigorous, and reliable men in whom the people can fully confide."

Figure 10-62. Dedham, Massachussets, September 10, cover directed to Boston, Massachussets. Dedham did not have a carrier service, so the letter is overpaid 1¢. This was possibly an attempt by the writer to pay the carrier-collection fee at Boston in addition to the 3¢ letter rate.

All carriers had to be bonded and were to receive a salary not to exceed $800 annually, which could be increased from time to time with evidence of good performance to a maximum of $1,000. This was a good income for that time, and there was active competition for the positions.

Although the door had closed on the penny-postman, it was opened again slightly in 1865. The Act of March 3 of that year provided that in towns and cities where a free delivery system was not in operation, and where it was deemed beneficial to institute such a service, the postmasters could apply to the first assistant postmaster general for permission to employ penny-postmen. All of the Postal Laws & Regulations relating to carriers would apply, with the exception of compensation of carriers. They would be paid only from the fees they received for delivering letters, and the fees could not exceed 1¢ per letter.

It is not known if this provision of the law was ever used to again establish a local carrier-fee system. No covers showing evidence of this type of operation have ever been found. It is, of course, quite possible that penny-postmen were active in many communities, but since all business was done on a cash basis, there would be no way of determining from a cover that it had been delivered by the last survivors of a special breed of postal servant.

Much of the information contained in this chapter has been obtained from the works of the many postal historians and scholars mentioned in the preceding sections. The most notable of experts in this area was Perry. During his lifetime, Perry accumulated a vast store of knowledge concerning all aspects of the carrier services with particular attention to the many private local posts of the era. His goal of publishing a definitive work on the subject was unfortunately not achieved before his death, but his meticulous notes have provided information for many later articles. He was the author of a particularly comprehensive chapter on carriers, which appeared in Ashbrook's work on the 1857 1¢ stamp [20], and numerous facts relative to carriers have been published in Perry's *Pat Paragraphs* [2].

Some of his notes have been carefully put in order and published in the *Chronicle* in a series of articles between 1982 and 1986, by Robert B. Meyersburg, editor of the U.S. carriers section of the journal [14]. Meyersburg is one of the leading contemporary experts and authors in the field. Other acknowledged students of the carrier system include John Kohlhepp, whose extremely interesting story of the final years of the fee-based carrier system was also published in the *Chronicle* [4], and Robert J. Stets, whose expertise is focused on the postal system of the Philadelphia area. Stets' account of the Philadelphia carriers from 1860 to 1863, also published in the *Chronicle* [11], is outstanding.

Another very interesting account of the carrier system was written by the late Henry A. Meyer in the September 1963 *S.P.A. Journal* under the title "Good-by, Penny Post!" Meyer's reputation as a distinguished postal historian is reflected in the careful research and exceptional style that make this account a pleasure to read.

The limited scope of this volume does not allow for the comprehensive treatment the author would like to give to carrier operations from the early 1800s to the end of the fee-based system on July 1, 1863. The story is fascinating, and the reader is strongly urged to sample some of the given references to complete a picture of early commercial entrepreneurship and government service that can only be outlined in these pages.

References

1. *Report of the Postmaster General for 1861*. Reprints from official sources. Theron Wierenga. Holland, Michigan. 1977.

2. Perry, Elliott. *Pat Paragraphs*, Compiled and Arranged by George T. Turner and Thomas E. Stanton. Bureau Issues Association Inc. 1981.

3. *Report of the Postmaster General for 1863*. Reprints from official sources. Theron Wierenga. Holland, Michigan. 1977.

4. Kohlhepp, John. "The Carrier Service: Final Years of the Fee-Based System." *Chronicle* 113-115. February-August 1982.

5. *Report of the Postmaster General for 1862*. Reprints from official sources. Theron Wierenga. Holland, Michigan. 1977.

6. Meyersburg, Robert B. "New York: An Overview of Its Carrier Operations Between 1825 and June 30, 1863." *Chronicle* 141. February 1989.

7. Skinner, Hubert C. and Eno, Amos. *United States Cancellations, 1845-1869*. American Philatelic Society. 1980.

8. Lane, Maryette B. *The Harry F. Allen Collection of Black Jacks*. APS Handbook Series. 1969.

9. Meyersburg, Robert B. "Brooklyn." *Chronicle* 139. August 1990.

10. Harvey, Edward T. "Blood's Despatch." *Chronicle* 144. November 1989.

11. Stets, Robert J. Sr. "Government Carriers at Philadelphia: 1860-1863, An Epilogue." *Chronicle* 128-129. November 1985 and February 1986.

12. Shachat, Norman. "1¢ Circular Carrier Contract Rate at Philadelphia During the Mid 1860s." *Chronicle* 135. August 1987.

13. Ashbrook, Stanley B. *19th Century U.S. Postal History, A Special Service prepared by Stanley B. Ashbrook*. Vol. I. 1951. Privately printed.

14. Perry, Elliott. Edited by Robert Meyersburg. "The Carrier Stamps of the United States."
    a. St. Louis. *Chronicle* 113:16. February 1982.
    b. Cleveland, Ohio. *Chronicle* 114:104. May 1982.
    c. Philadelphia. *Chronicle* 115:173. August 1982.
    d. Philadelphia. *Chronicle* 116:240. November 1982.
    e. Philadelphia. *Chronicle* 117:16. February 1983
    f. Philadelphia. *Chronicle* 118:94. May 1983
    g. Philadelphia. *Chronicle* 119:168. August 1983.
    h. Washington (City),D.C. *Chronicle* 120:239. November 1983.
    i. Washington (City),D.C. *Chronicle* 121:26. February 1984.

15. Allen, Thomas F. "Carriers: Private, Semi-Private and Government." *Chronicle* 148. November 1990.

16. Karlen, Harvey M., Editor. *Chicago Postal History*. The Collectors Club of Chicago. 1970.

17. Graham, Richard B. "Chicago in the 1860s." *Chronicle* 130. May 1986.

18. Ashbrook, Stanley B. "Exceptional Uses of U.S. Covers of the Period 1851-1863 Inclusive." *American Philatelist*. February 1943.

19. Graham, Richard B. "1860-1863 Three Cents Plus 1¢ Plus 1¢." *Chronicle* 143. August 1989.

20. Ashbrook, Stanley B. *The United States Stamp of 1851-1857*. Vol. 2. 1938.

The United States 1¢ Franklin 1861-67

CHAPTER 11

Drop Letters

A drop letter is a letter that is deposited in a local post office by the sender for local delivery. It is also occasionally referred to as a "box letter," possibly because many local letters were addressed to individuals who maintained a box at the post office for their mail.

The terms "drop letter" and "local letter" are not quite synonymous and may have slightly different meanings. Most often, a drop letter is deposited at a post office and delivered to the addressee at the same office. If the post office is located in a town with carrier delivery, it is possible for the drop letter to be delivered locally by the carrier service. In this sense it is also a local letter. However, a letter that is collected by a carrier and carrier-delivered to a local address is also a local letter, but it is not a drop letter

Drop letters for delivery at the post office are a category of mail that embodies the simplest of all of the postal services. Examples are relatively common, and many are available for research and collecting. They are also of particular interest to collectors of the 1¢ Franklin, since paying the drop fee was one of the primary uses of this stamp from 1861 to 1870.

Even as late as 1875, more than 99 percent of the post offices in the United States had no carrier collection or delivery service. Any letters intended for local addresses had to be both deposited and picked up at the post office. It should be emphasized that these local letters were not considered to have entered the mails. The money or stamps that paid for the service was a fee rather than a rate (at least until July 1, 1863).

The distinction between these two terms is frequently overlooked in various books and articles, and should be explained. A rate is the postage charged for the transmission in the mails of a letter or packet. The rate of postage is a function of the weight and (until 1863) the distance carried. A fee is the charge for a service by, or under the auspices of, the Post Office Department where the fee charged is not a function of weight or distance. Fees are charged for items both in and outside the mails. For example, registry service is paid by a fee, and the registered item usually enters into the mails. Ship letters delivered at the port of entry never pass through the mails but are charged a fee for the service of local delivery.

During the period of interest to this book, new postal laws and regulations made significant changes in the fees and procedures for handling local drop letters.

Commencing July 1, 1851, the fee for a drop letter was reduced from the previous 2¢ to 1¢ per article. This fee remained constant until it was revised on July 1, 1863, to become a rate of 2¢ per ½ ounce. During this 12-year period, other changes were also made to procedures and requirements pertinent to drop mail [1:40].

The Act of March 3, 1855, effective April 1, 1855, required for the first time that the postage on letters must be prepaid, but did not specifically mention drop letters. Section 77 of the Postal Regulations of 1857 cleared up any uncertainty by stating that prepayment of drop letters was optional. This procedure remained in place until the Act of February 27, 1861, where Section 14 specified that the drop-letter fee was to be prepaid by stamps. The effective date is not known to the author. However, it was announced in a Post Office bulletin issued May 1, 1861.

Until 1860, local letters deposited in the post offices of cities with carrier service could be delivered to a street address for an additional fee. The April 3, 1860 Postal Act, Section 2, changed this by fixing the total fee for a carrier-delivered drop letter at 1¢. The normal drop fee was not charged in this case, and the 1¢ was credited to the carrier as his payment.

Among the many changes made in rates, fees and procedures by the comprehensive Act of March 3, 1863, effective July 1, 1863, was a provision in Section 23 to the effect that drop letters would henceforth be rated with regard to weight, and the rate would be 2¢ postage per ½ ounce, paid in advance by stamps. Carrier collection or delivery (when available) would be free.

This immediately established the inequitable situation where the inhabitants of the approximately 20,000 cities without carriers paid the same drop-letter rate as those in cities with free carrier pickup and delivery. This was corrected by the Act of March 3, 1865, and announced in Section 15 of the Post Office bulletin of May 1, 1865. The change reduced the drop rate to 1¢ per ½ ounce in towns and cities where carrier service was not available, but retained the 2¢ rate for all carrier cities.

A consequence of the drop-letter rate structure during this interval was that between July 1863 and May 1865 there was no rate or fee that required the use of a single 1¢ stamp.

Another interesting feature of the Act of March 3, 1863, was contained in Postmaster General Montgomery Blair's Instructions for Section 14. Blair stated that the purpose of free delivery was for the convenience of the public and to reduce the labor in the post offices to the effect that ". . . citizens may have no excuse for clinging to the old custom of calling at the post office. Postmas-

Figure 11-1. Southold, Long Island, New York. 1¢ Franklin paying the drop letter rate, dated November 14. Shows scarce use of old-type DROP/ct marker. (C.W. Christian collection)

ably would never come under the scrutiny of postal inspectors or other postmasters, contributed to a general laxity in the observance of regulations. A great many drop letters were canceled with the town/date marker, and some, although correctly canceled, do not have a town mark. In almost all cases, there are no special markings that denote drop use.

Figure 11-1 shows an exception to this statement. This lady's envelope is addressed locally at Southold, Long Island, and in addition to the bull's-eye killer and CDS, is stamped with a circular DROP/ct marking. This marking was possibly left over from the period prior to February 27, 1861, where it was used to show that the drop-letter fee had not been prepaid. The amount written in the handstamped marking was to be collected from the addressee.

Figure 11-2 shows another example of a drop-letter marking. On this Stroudsburg, Pennsylvania, cover, the postmaster has canceled the stamp with the manuscript notation "Drop Letter/Jan 15/ . . ." (balance of notation is unreadable).

Frequently, drop use showed only the killer on the stamp with no date or town marking. **Figure 11-3** illustrates an embossed lady's cover with a PAID cancel and a town-only address.

A cover with an absolutely minimal address is

ters will especially discourage the use of private boxes, and steadily aim at reducing them to the lowest number possible."

The problem of overwork in handling box mail was primarily confined to the larger cities. Incoming mail frequently was addressed by name and city only. There was no box number or street address. In some cities, clerks were required to commit to memory the names and associated box numbers of thousands of patrons so mail could be expeditiously sorted and placed in the proper receptacle or relegated to the general-delivery section. In addition, those individuals desiring carrier service needed to be identified, even when there was no street address on the letter. This was truly a formidable task.

Drop letters can at times be difficult to identify as such. The postal rate for circular and transient mail was at times the same as that for drop letters, and these various types of service cannot always be unambiguously separated. Circular and transient mail will be discussed in detail in Chapter 12. The basic identifying features of drop letters are postage of 1¢ or 2¢ (depending on the date and location), a sealed envelope and a local address.

Although regulations required that drop letters be postmarked and also canceled with a separate canceling device, the fact that the letter never left the post office, and prob-

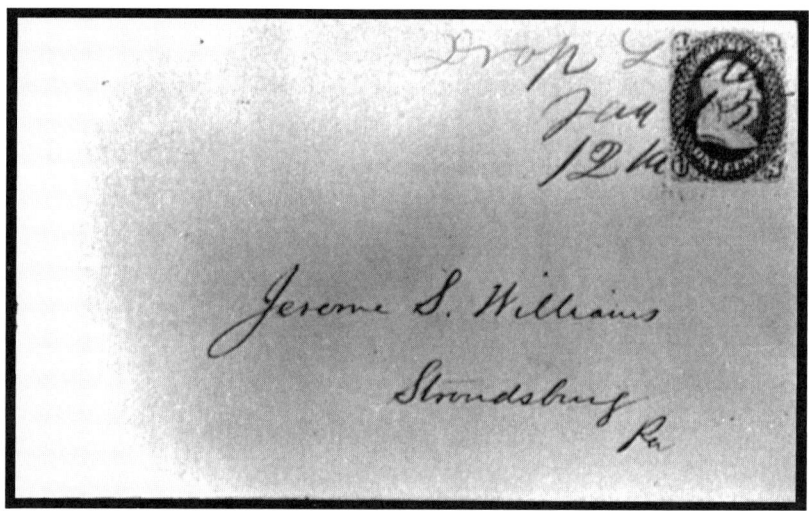

Figure 11-2. Stroudsburg, Pennsylvania, drop use with manuscript cancel, reading "Drop Letter/Jan 15/ . . ." (Courtesy of Dr. James W. Milgram)

shown in **Figure 11-4**. This January 4, Dedham, Massachusetts, letter is canceled with an elaborate stars-and-bars PAID marking and has only a printed name for the address and the docketing notation "Masonic" on the cover. It is likely that this letter was a return response from a multiple mailing by the addressee, Fred D. Ely, who had enclosed preprinted return envelopes in his original mailing. The Masonic notation suggests that this may have been a solicitation to members from a local Masonic lodge.

Figure 11-5 shows an elaborate overall illustrated cover from the Home Insurance Company of New Haven, Connecticut. New Haven had carriers, so the 1¢ postage means that the date of use was prior to July 1, 1863. The fact that it does not have a street address indicates it was probably picked up by the addressee at the post office as a drop letter.

The procedure of using a town/date marker to cancel the stamp on drop mail was frequently used. This allowed the postmaster who did not have the luxury of

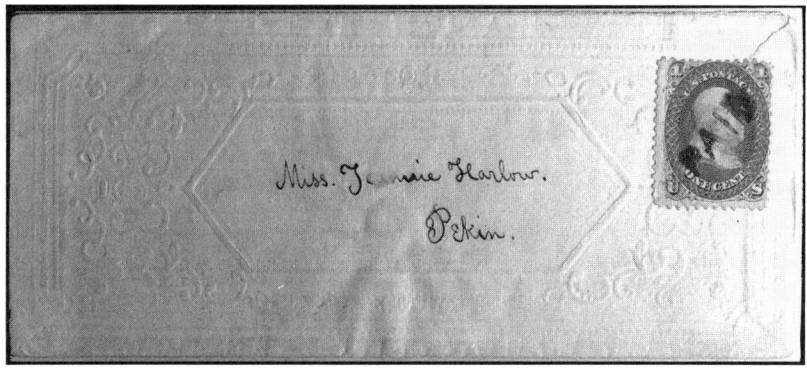

Figure 11-3. Embossed lady's cover showing drop use at Pekin (state unknown). The stamp is canceled with a PAID killer.

Figure 11-4. Dedham, Massachusetts, January 4 letter. Unusual drop use of a preprinted addressee name. Fancy Dedham cancellation, as shown in the drawing.
(C.W. Christian collection)

Figure 11-5. Drop usage at New Haven, Connecticut, CDS dated DEC 13. 1¢ postage indicates pre-July 1863 use since carrier service was available.

Figure 11-6. Interesting drop cover from Fort Edward, New York, canceled with a CDS dated in June of 186(3). The use of "Present" in the address is analogous to writing "City."

Figure 11-7. Terre Haute, Indiana, June 8, 1863. Drop letter with an exceptionally fine printed patriotic design. Patriotic illustrations are seldom seen on local mail.
(Courtesy of John Becker. Photo by Richard B. Graham)

Figure 11-8. Scarce example of a Lincoln campaign cover, showing one of the "beardless Lincoln" portraits. Drop letter use from North Brookfield, Massachusetts.
(C.W. Christian collection)

possessing a duplex town marker and canceler to process the stamp with a single marking. While not responsive to the regulations, it saved a lot of the effort that using two marking devices would have required. The cover shown in **Figure 11-6**, used at Fort Edward, New York, illustrates such a procedure. Also in this example the word "Present" is used for the address. This type of address is reported to have been used for the mailing of invitations or alternatively just to denote a local address, similar to the use of the word "city."

Patriotic illustrations are scarce on local covers. **Figure 11-7** shows an unusually well-executed patriotic design on a June 8, 1863, drop letter at

Figure 11-9. Holmes' Hole (now, Vineyard Haven), Tisbury County, Massachussets, located on the island of Martha's Vineyard. The folded notice, dated February 2, 1862, originated at New Bedford, Massachusetts. Evidently, it was hand-carried to the Holmes' Hole Post Office and mailed as a drop letter. The contents are reproduced below.

Terre Haute, Indiana.

Figure 11-8 shows a drop letter from North Brookfield, Massachusetts. While this is a normal drop use, the "beardless Lincoln" presidential campaign illustration on the cover makes it a scarce and desirable item.

An example of a printed folded notice, which was probably carried outside the mails, is shown in **Figure 11-9**. It appears that it originated at the Wamsutta Mills in New Bedford, Massachusetts, and was hand-carried to Martha's Vineyard. It was there deposited at the Holmes' Hole post office in Tisbury County, with a 1¢ stamp paying the drop rate for pickup by the addressee. The savings of 2¢ from the letter rate would not seem to be of particular importance here, and it may have been hand-carried as a matter of convenience or to expedite its delivery.

After the rate increase of July 1, 1863, 2¢ covers made their appearance. Shown in **Figure 11-10** is a probable drop cover. The street address indicates that it possibly was delivered by the carrier service available in Hartford at that time. Of course, the letter could have also been collected by a carrier instead of being deposited at the post office, which would make it a carrier cover rather than a drop cover. There is no way to absolutely determine how the letter was handled.

Figure 11-11 illustrates an unquestionable drop letter at the higher rate. The letter is postmarked at Buffalo, New York, on July 11, 1863, shortly after the new rate came into being. The cover was sealed, and the content is a written letter. Buffalo had no carrier service until 1864, so it can definitely be identified as a 2¢ drop-

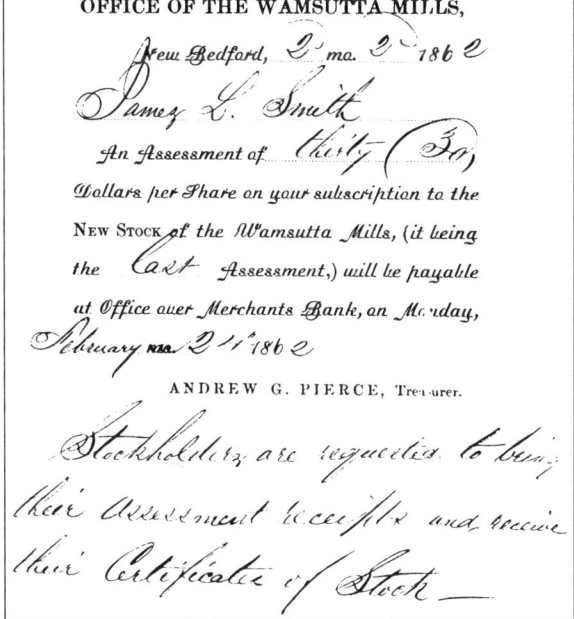

Figure 11-10. Local use at Hartford, Connecticut. The cover is dated December 8, 1863, and reflects the increase in rate to 2¢, which became effective the previous July. Shows three strikes of a Hartford CDS: one to cancel each of the two 1¢ stamps, and one used as a town and date marking.

Figure 11-11. Buffalo, New York. July 11, 1863. Drop usage showing the increased rate for local mail. Stamps canceled with a Norton-type patent cancel.

rate use.

Figure 11-12 shows an example of use after May 1, 1865, when the rate for local mail in cities without carrier service was reduced to 1¢. The F grill used on this advertising cover from Florence, Massachusetts, definitely establishes the use as post-1867. The cover is also docketed "S. Strong/Nov 30/68." At that time, Florence had no carrier service.

Another example from the same period is illustrated in **Figure 11-13**. This tax notice was mailed from Concord, New Hampshire, on February 7, 1870, as a drop letter at the 1¢ rate. On the reverse of this small folded notice is space to provide the tax-return information. The recipient duly filled out the form and evidently returned it to the tax office by hand or never returned it, since there is no evidence of it going through the mails a second time.

The occupation of Confederate cities by federal troops during the Civil War produced some examples of drop letters, but covers showing this use are very scarce. Richard B. Graham has provided photos of two excellent examples, shown in **Figures 11-14** and **11-15**.

Figure 11-14 is a photo of a drop letter originating from the *USS Richmond* on December 15, 1862. It was deposited the same day in the New Orleans post office, where it received a New Orleans CDS as a cancel and was subsequently delivered.

Figure 11-15 shows an occupation cover from Alexandria, Virginia. This official-business drop letter was posted on December 20, probably 1861 or 1862. The

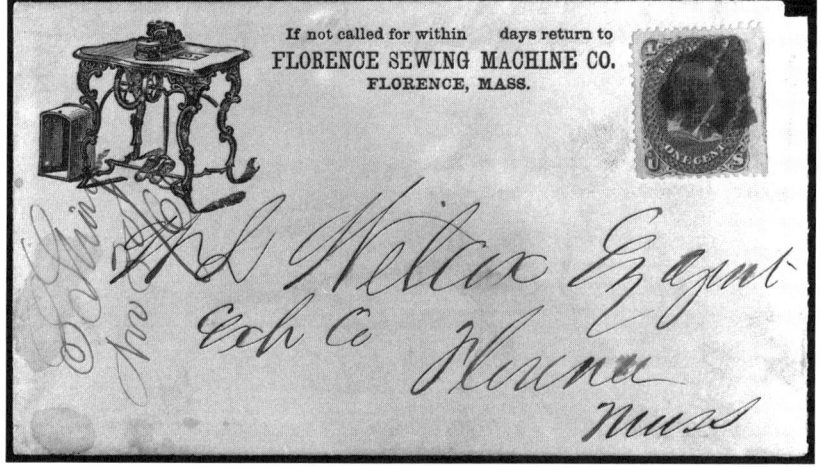

Figure 11-12. Local drop use at Florence, Massachusetts. Docketed November 10, 1868. Paid with a 1¢ F grill for the reduced noncarrier city rate.

datestamp is indistinct. It was picked up at the post office by a military courier and delivered to the addressee at some nearby encampment. Federal forces occupied Alexandria shortly after the beginning of hostilities and retained control throughout the war. Alexandria was part of the defense perimeter of Washington, and a large number of federal troops were constantly on duty in the vicinity.

These described and illustrated uses show most of the variations that can be found in drop letters during the period covered by this book. Drop letters are relatively abundant and usually carry little in the way of postal markings. Drop letters that are in great demand possess additional features such as scarce cancels or postmarks, patriotic illustrations or other unusual characteristics.

Locally addressed circular or transient mail could also have the same franking as drop letters. This poses

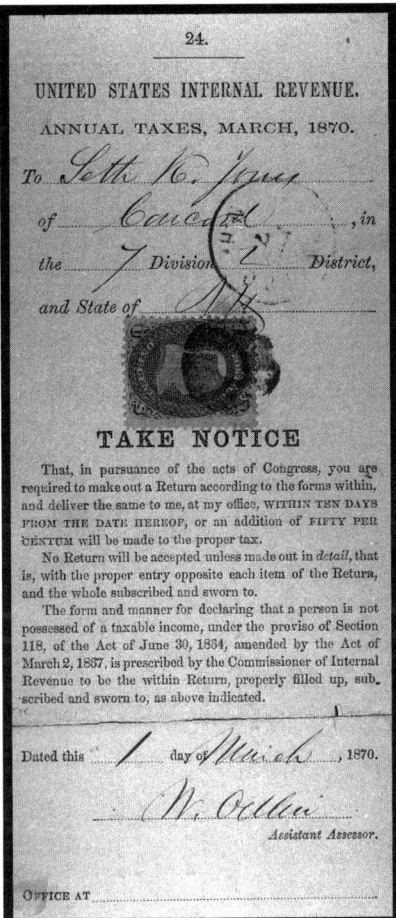

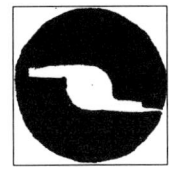

Figure 11-13. Printed tax notice, mailed as a drop letter at Concord, New Hampshire, on February 7, 1870. Paid with a 1¢ F grill (Scott 92) for the reduced noncarrier city rate. The drawing to the right of the notice illustrates, in actual size, the unusual cancel on the stamp.

Figure 11-14. Scarce drop-letter use at an occupation post office. The letter originated from the *USS Richmond* and was deposited in the New Orleans, Louisiania, post office. It received a CDS dated December 15, 1862, which was also used to cancel the stamp.
(Courtesy of Richard B. Graham)

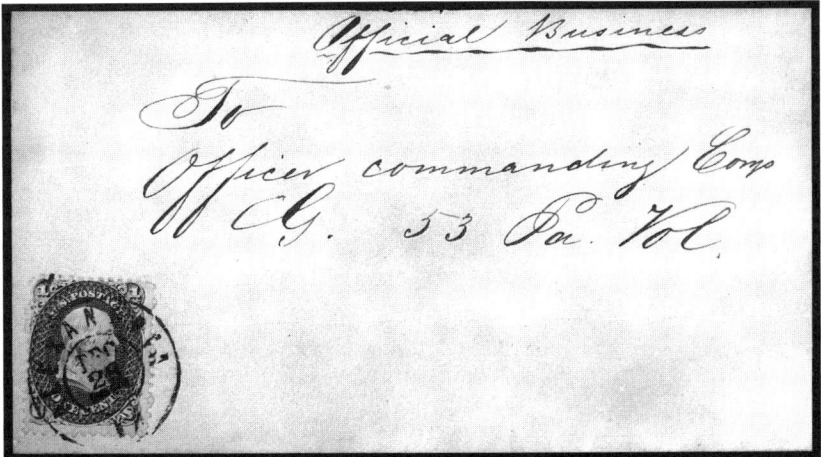

Figure 11-15. Official-business drop letter, deposited at the Alexandria, Virginia, post office. December 20 (year uncertain) CDS. Although endorsed as "official business," this cover did not receive free service, possibly because there was no franking signature or official corner card.
(Courtesy of Richard B. Graham)

LIST OF PEDLERS

Who hold Licenses to Sell Foreign Goods in the State of New York, May 10th, 1868.

STATE OF NEW-YORK,
OFFICE OF THE SECRETARY OF STATE, } ss.

I CERTIFY, That pursuant to the Fourth Title of Chapter 17, of the First Part of the Revised Statutes, and of the act entitled "An Act in relation to Hawkers and Pedlers," passed March 23, 1840, the persons hereinafter named (the terms of whose Licenses have not expired), have been licensed to travel and trade as Pedlers within this State, and to sell and expose to sale any goods, wares or merchandise, of the growth, produce or manufacture of any foreign country, at the date in the mode and for the term set opposite to their respective names, viz:

NAME OF PEDLER.	DATE OF LICENSE.	MODE OF TRAVELING.	TERM OF LICENSE

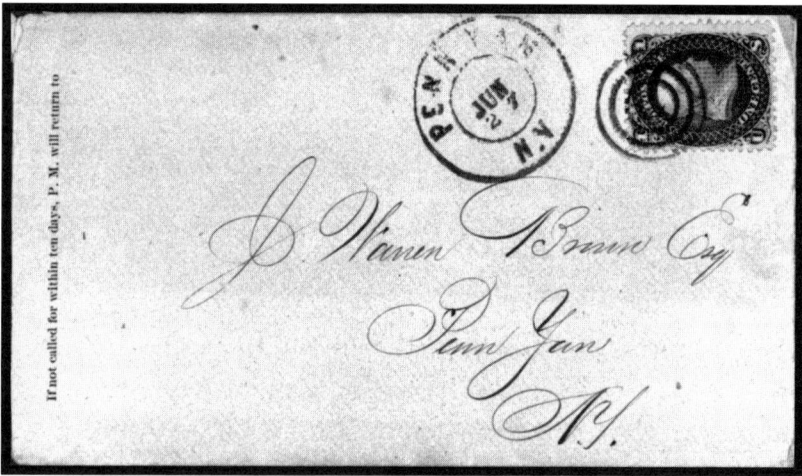

Figure 11-16. Mailed as a reduced-rate drop letter on June 27, 1868, at Penn Yan, New York. A portion of the contents, as illustrated above, show a printed *List of Pedlers*. The cover is sealed and was mailed as a drop letter rather than a circular, realizing a savings of 1¢.
(James Lee collection)

an interesting question. Is a circular or piece of transient mail that was deposited in a local post office for local delivery classified as drop mail or circular/transient mail? Essentially it is both. The only difference would be that circulars and transient mail were required to be unsealed so that the contents could be checked to ensure that no first-class enclosures were present. However, if the item was sealed, it would be handled as first-class drop mail. This dichotomy, while normally of little importance, does allow for a method of saving money on some mailings of circulars after May 1, 1865. When the local drop rate was reduced from 2¢ to 1¢ in towns without carrier service, the circular rate remained at 2¢. It was, therefore, less expensive to mail a local circular or transient newspaper as a drop letter, providing it did not weigh over ½ ounce.

An example of this use is shown in **Figure 11-16**. A locally addressed circular was sealed and deposited in the Penn Yan, New York, post office. The date is June 27, 1868, where the year is determined from the printed enclo-

sure. The use of the E-grill 1¢ stamp also ensures that the use is post-1867. During this period, the circular rate was 2¢, and the drop rate was 1¢ at a noncarrier city. By sealing the envelope the originator was able to cut his postage bill by 50 percent. It is unlikely that many examples of the 2¢ rate exist for local circular use in towns without carriers since it certainly was a simple and legal expedient to mail an item first class and thereby save half the postage. While this writer has seen nothing in the regulations or postal notices that discusses this situation, it seems entirely reasonable to assume that postmasters in cities without carriers would rate all single-weight local items at 1¢, no matter what the class of mail might be.

One interesting but very elusive type of drop letter is a letter carried outside the mails from a distant location and placed in the mail at the destination post office for delivery to the addressee. This practice, in general, is illegal, and at times is referred to as "bootlegging." Ship and steamboat letters are examples of legal carriage out-

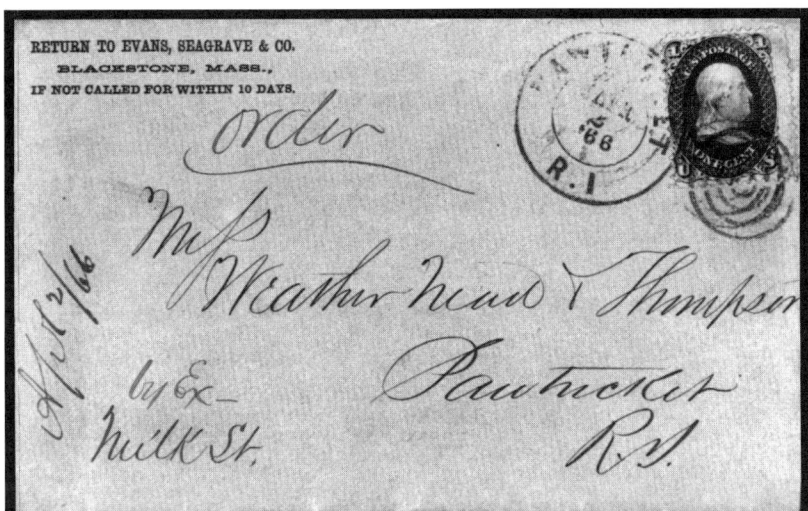

Figure 11-17. Unusual example of a commercial letter being carried by an express company, outside the mails, and being deposited as a prepaid drop letter. The cover originated in Blackstone, Massachusetts, and was delivered in Pawtucket, Rhode Island, on April 2, 1866. The large seal of the Earle Express Co., shown in the reduced photograph below, was placed on the reverse of the cover. (James Lee collection)

side the mail, but many instances of individuals doing a favor by personally carrying letters for favor occurred, and that was illegal under a strict interpretation of the postal laws. While it may have been unlawful, it is likely that the laws were written to deter private mail services for a fee, and the occasional "free" carrying of a letter for a friend or acquaintance was benignly tolerated.

These casual drop letters are very difficult to identify. Normally there are no markings on the cover that show its origin, only the CDS of the destination post office. In rare cases there may be a notation that identifies where it was written, but usually the only clue is in the contents of the envelope, and these usually are missing from old letters. The practice of bootlegging was not uncommon and occurred most frequently with letters being brought in from foreign countries. For example, consider a person who was returning to the United States at the end of a visit to England. A friend asked him to carry a letter for an address in New York City and to post it upon his arrival. The request was granted, and the letter arrived at its destination, looking just like thousands of other drop letters, and at a cost that was only a small fraction of the legal postage.

Such personal mail service could be a tremendous help in those instances where the normal postal service from a foreign country was irregular or very slow. Clues to watch for in discovering these interesting and hard-to-identify covers are corner cards or return addresses and other notations from locations different than the destination, indications suggesting that the letter may have been aboard a ship, or contents that clearly show the origin.

A very interesting domestic example of a drop letter carried outside the mails is shown in **Figure 11-17**. In this case, the letter originated at Blackstone, Massachu-

setts, and was carried to Pawtucket, Rhode Island, a distance of about 15 miles. The letter was carried by the Earle Express Co., as attested by a seal on the back of the envelope. It was deposited in the Pawtucket post office as a prepaid drop letter, where it was canceled and postmarked on April 2, 1866. By regulation (Section 19, Act of March 3, 1865), such service was illegal unless the letter was enclosed in a government stamped envelope. Evidently there was some understanding with the post office, for there was certainly no attempt to hide the fact that the letter was carried by an express company. There is even a manuscript notation on the front of the cover, "by Ex—/Milk St."

While drop letters may not generally be exotic, there are gems to be found among them, and every collection of postal history of this period needs a representative group of drop letters for completeness.

References

1. Graham, Richard B. "Special Rate Services," Chapter 4. *United States Postal History Sampler.* Linn's Handbook Series. Linn's Stamp News, Sidney, Ohio. 1992.

CHAPTER 12

Circular and Transient Mail

Introduction

Little has been published that comprehensively covers the subject of circular and transient mail for the period of the mid-1800s. The information that has been written, although very informative, is scattered throughout many philatelic journals and books, or published in official government documents and publications sanctioned by the Post Office Department. Unfortunately, these sources are not always easily available to collectors who are interested in furthering their knowlege in the field. This chapter covers many aspects of the subject and should provide a convenient reference.

Circular and transient mail are both part of a more general class of mail that includes all printed matter. Early postal laws stated that the purpose of the mails was to transmit intelligence. To that end, the regulations provided for letter mail, which was to include all correspondence, and printed matter, which included newspapers, pamphlets, circulars and other items entirely in print.

Before proceding further, it will be advantageous to present definitions of the different terms used in referring to printed matter in the mails. When reference is made to regulations, it should be noted that the regulations cited are the ones in effect for the use in question and during the period of use of the 1¢ Franklin.

NEWSPAPER: Per regulations: "A newspaper is a printed publication issued in numbers and published at short stated intervals of not more than a month, conveying intelligence of passing events." (Section 143, 1859 Postal Regulations)

Newspapers mailed from the office of publication to bona fide subscribers received very beneficial rates of postage. The postage on those mailings was paid quarterly in money to the Post Office Department. Stamps were not affixed to the newspapers. This type of mailing has negligible philatelic interest, and the fees and procedures will not be discussed here.

Newspapers not mailed to subscribers from the office of publication or sent from one person to another were considered to be transient newspapers. This is the type of newspaper mail of philatelic interest.

TRANSIENT MATTER: Printed matter whose content is transient in nature. That is, the information contained is not likely to be of permanent interest.

Within this category are circulars, advertisements, business cards and all other transient printed matter, with the exception of books.

CIRCULAR: Although not specifically defined in the PL&Rs, circulars are referred to by name in the postal regulations and appear to encompass a subcategory of transient matter that was subject to a special rate structure. The term is well-known and understood by the philatelic community to mean the following: A circular is a notice or advertisement, entirely in print and intended for mass distribution. To qualify for the reduced circular postal rate, the item cannot be sealed and must be addressed to a single address.

PAMPHLET: Per regulations: "A pamphlet is a printed, but unbound publication, relating solely to some subject of local ephemeral, or temporary interest or importance . . . under 16 pages." (Section 142, 1859 Postal Regulations)

PRICES CURRENT: A term used to specify a printed notice published at frequent intervals, sometimes daily, by merchants who wished their customers to remain informed of the latest prices for the sale and purchase of commodities. These were mailed in substantial numbers to domestic and foreign destinations. Prices current were considered to be within the category of circulars.

BUSINESS CARDS: Again, this is a term referred to in the postal regulations, but not specifically described or defined. A business card is generally regarded to be a printed announcement on the front of a piece of mail that gives the name and location of the sender, and sometimes includes an advertisement or statement of the type of business. It is normally located at the upper left of the cover and is usually referred to by philatelists as a "corner card." Until July 1, 1863, the presence of a business card required the item to be rated as a letter.

BOOKS: Books, although within the definition of printed matter, were treated as a different category and with a different rate structure for mailing. Books were to be sent unwrapped or in wrappers that could be opened for inspection. Books were first authorized as mailable matter in 1851. Book wrappers from the mid-1800s that have survived to the present day are very scarce. The wrappers would generally be fairly large, which would preclude many of them being saved. The various postage rates and distance and weight limitations for books were discussed in Chapter 6 and will not be repeated here.

Although not postally defined in the PL&Rs, books are generally considered to be a number of printed pages fastened together. A book may be bound or unbound, and the content is usually thought to be of relatively

213

permanent interest.

The writers of the PL&Rs possibly considered that everyone knew what a book was, so there was no need to define it.

The preceding definitions include most of the terms used in this chapter that may cause some confusion to the reader. While it is possible to assign specific definitions, it can be seen that these are not always mutually exclusive. A particular piece of mail matter might fall under more than one definition. This caused some difficulty for postal clerks, and presents difficulty for modern-day postal historians. Misrated items are not unusual.

In general, circular and transient mail included a lot of what we would today call junk mail. It was charged at a lower rate than normal correspondence, and from the frequent lack of postmarks, it appears to have been processed with less care than letter mail. This is not surprising. Examples suggest that mass mailings were often made in the larger cities, and it is to be expected that they would be processed as conveniently as possible.

Interest in circular and transient mail generally ranks below that for letter mail with collectors and philatelic students, mostly because of its usual lack of exotic destinations, high-value stamps or interesting postal markings. Although they seem to have been mailed in large numbers, relatively few of these items were saved to become a part of today's philatelic inventory. In 1860, stamp collecting was in its infancy. The public generally retained things because of their interest or intrinsic value, and stamps were not of particular interest. It is indeed fortunate that at least some of these early postal items have survived through the years to grace albums and to provide material for study.

Restrictions were placed on transient and circular mail. To qualify for the reduced rate, the mailed matter could not contain any handwritten information, and if covered, it was to be enclosed in an unsealed envelope, or in wrappers for newspapers and magazines. These wrappers were to be "narrow bands" with the ends left open so that the contents could be easily removed for examination without damage. The sender was allowed to underline or mark items in newspapers or magazines to call them to the attention of the reader, but that was the limit of additional information that could be included.

It should be noted that mailable matter during the mid-1800s was carefully enumerated with respect to what could be mailed. General merchandise, as we know it today, was not included. However, correspondence and printed items, maps, photographs, plant cuttings, seeds and engravings were considered to be mailable in addition to correspondence and printed items.

Town and date markings do not seem to have been required on printed matter. Richard Graham noted this in one of his excellent articles on the subject of transient mail. This author attempted to find some justification for the statement in the PL&Rs but was unsuccessful. When asked about the source of his information, Graham replied with a most cogent and convincing argument.

Graham points out that while the PL&Rs definitely required that letter mail be marked with the date and origin of mailing, nothing was specifically said about other types of mail except that all stamps were to be canceled. Marking mail was a laborious and repetitious task that most postmasters and clerks would want to get out of the way as rapidly as possible and with the least effort. By only canceling the stamp, the labor could be substantially decreased. Even the use of duplex markers required more time and care than just hitting the stamp with a killer. In some of the larger cities, there were squads of postal clerks whose sole duty was to affix markings to the mail, and these large cities were the origin of most of the circular and transient mail. It is most reasonable to assume that the minimum marking specifically required by the regulations would be the procedure that was followed.

In canceling circular and transient mail, the stamps were frequently canceled by the use of a town and date marker. While not strictly legal, this procedure was used so often that it appears to have had at least unofficial approval.

Although circular and general transient mail had common features and frequently were handled with the same procedures and at identical rates, they were distinctly different types of mail and will be discussed separately in this chapter.

Domestic Circular Mail

In order to be classified as a circular, certain restrictions, earlier mentioned, had to be met. There could be no manuscript markings on the contents, and if an envelope was used, it was not to be sealed. Many circulars were simply folded printed notices. The presence of a business card on the outside subjected the mailing to letter postage. This last restriction was not generally enforced, and many early circulars with corner cards can be found with payment at the circular rate. The advantage of having a return address or name on the mail was eventually recognized, and this restriction was rescinded on July 1, 1863.

Many circulars have the historical advantage of consisting of folded printed sheets, mailed without envelopes. This means the contents are an intrinsic part of the item and were not thrown away separately. These no-

Circular and Transient Mail

Figure 12-1. Folded printed notice at the 1¢ circular rate from Boston, Massachusetts, to Chicago, Illinois. The notice is dated August 8, 1861, and is franked with the "dot-in-U" variety of the 1¢ Franklin and tied with a Boston CDS with an illegible date.

tices, advertisements and prices current provide a gold mine of interesting information concerning the commerce and culture of the mid-1860s.

During the very early years, circulars could be sent collect. This resulted in advertisements being paid for by the addressee. This, understandably, created much resentment and a frequent refusal to accept delivery. The law was soon changed, and circular mail in 1847 became one of the first types of mail (along with transient newspapers) on which prepayment of postage was required. Until 1852, the rate structure for circulars was at times quite complex, with rates varying with both weight and distance. On September 30, 1852, the system was simplified. The rate became 1¢ per unsealed circular not weighing more than 3 ounces, prepaid to anywhere in the United States, with 1¢ for each additional ounce over 3 ounces [1:42].

This rate remained in force until July 1, 1863, when it was changed to 2¢ for up to three unsealed circulars to a single address. No weight limitation was stated. Postage was to be prepaid, and for the first time mail was divided into classes. Circulars were included in third-class mail.

The classes of mail that were established were: first class, letters and correspondence; second class, all mailable matter exclusively in print, regularly issued at stated intervals; third class, all other specified mailable matter, including circulars, pamphlets and books.

Items in the mail that were not included in the above were considered to be miscellaneous matter and were charged at first-class rates.

No further changes in the domestic rate for circulars occurred until 1872, when it became 1¢ per 2 ounces, or 1¢ each if delivered locally by carrier [1:43].

Figure 12-1 shows early circular use of the 1¢ Franklin on a folded notice. Unfortunately, the Boston CDS that cancels the stamp is poorly struck, and only a "2" can be identified in the date marking. The notice is from the Massachusetts Historical Society and is a request for material that may be used to document the causes and progress of the Civil War. The printed date of the notice is August 8, 1861, and that leads to the major reason that the illegibility of the cancel date is really unfortunate. It is reasonable to assume that the notice was mailed shortly after the date printed on it, and the 1861 1¢ Franklin was first offered for sale at Boston on August 21, 1868. If the cover date were August 2(1), 1861, it would be a companion for the Philadelphia earliest-known day of use for the stamp on cover.

Figure 12-2 is a beautifully illustrated cover from the adjutant general's office for the state of Maine. This type of cover, featuring the coat of arms of a state, is known from most of the Northern states. This example is an unsealed envelope mailed at the circular rate, prior to July 1, 1863.

Bulk mailings of circulars frequently occurred. **Figure 12-3** shows an example of an unsealed circular from

Figure 12-2. Augusta, Maine, to Durham, Maine. Circular use of an all-over illustrated cover. 1¢ postage canceled with an "Augusta Me./PAID" CDS.

215

The United States 1¢ Franklin 1861-67

Figure 12-3. Circular at 1¢ rate to Winchester, New Hampshire. Date and origin unknown, but possibly from New York City.

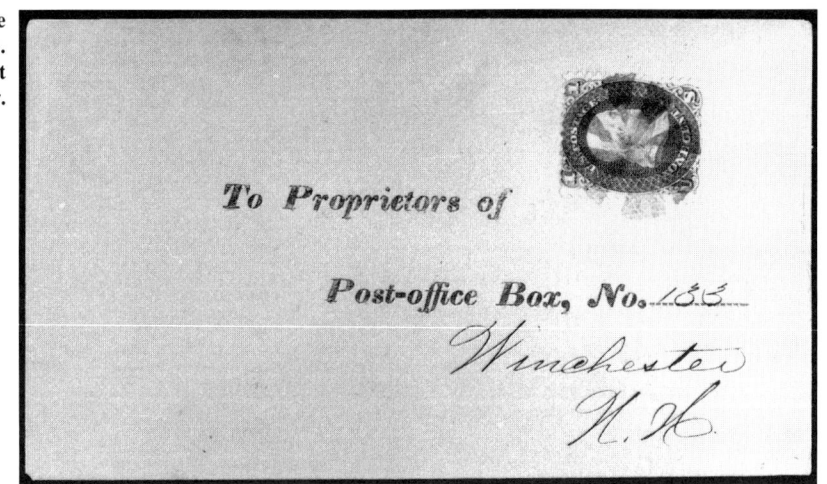

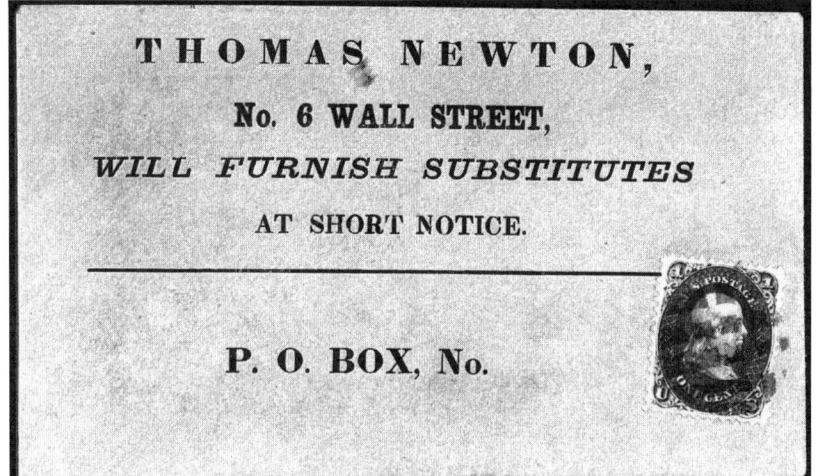

Figure 12-4. Interesting circular advertisement, probably bulk mailed at the New York City Post Office. Lack of the box number in the address suggests that all box-holders were recipients of the notice.
(James Lee collection)

Figure 12-5. Circular use at the 1¢ rate from New London to Litchfield, New Hampshire, with an indistinct date marking (probably February 20, 1863). The circular has a corner card, which legally classified this item as a letter with postage underpaid by 2¢.

216

an unknown origin with a partially printed address to a post office box. The address was completed in manuscript, possibly from a mailing list.

Another bulk-mailing circular is shown in **Figure 12-4**. This example is a forerunner to the present "to Occupant" type of address. Evidently this advertisement was to be placed in all of the boxes at the post office of mailing since no box number was indicated. The Wall Street return address and the New York-style block grid cancel suggest that the origin was New York City. If so, this mailing could have consisted of several thousand circulars. The circular features an offer to provide substitutes for individuals who had been drafted into service for the Civil War. The fact that a "business card" is printed on the outside of the envelope legally subjects it to letter postage, and it is possible that this circular was mailed as a drop letter at the 1¢ drop rate.

Another example of circular use, prior to the increase in rate, is shown in **Figure 12-5**. This early 1863 unsealed notice is from a school at New London, New Hampshire, and mailed to Litchfield in the same state. It also has an informative corner card on the envelope and correctly should have been rated with letter postage.

A circular posted at the increased rate, effective July 1, 1863, is illustrated in **Figure 12-6**. This unsealed cover was mailed on January 1, (1864?), and postage was paid by two 1¢ Franklins. Presence of a corner card no longer required letter-rate postage since that restriction was lifted concurrent with the rate increase.

Figure 12-6. Brookline to Marblehead, Massachusetts. January 1 circular use showing the increased rate of 2¢. The cover bears a fancy embossed corner card.

A preprinted and unsealed envelope that was used by the Wells, Fargo express company in San Francisco to inform addressees that a package had been received is shown in **Figure 12-7**. This example has several features of interest. The notice is printed on the front of a 1¢ government stamped envelope. The printing was probably done before the increase in the circular rate, and the 1¢ Franklin added to make up the circular postage required at the date of mailing (August 26, 1864). Since all of the information is printed on the outside of the envelope, it is a kind of precursor to the government postal card, which was not authorized until almost a decade later.

Figure 12-8 shows a spectacular 16-page, two-color 1867 advertising circular that was probably mailed at the less expensive drop rate. The circular weighs ex-

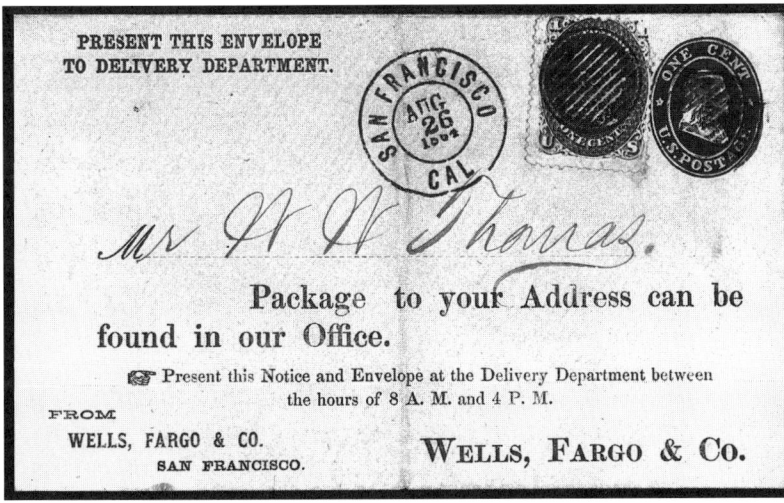

Figure 12-7. San Francisco, California. August 26, 1864. Preprinted government stamped envelope (Scott U19) used for a local notice. The 1¢ stamp was added to make up the required 2¢ drop or circular rate. Although this stamped envelope has the pre-1861 star-die indicia, it was never demonetized since none of the envelopes had been issued to Southern post offices.
(James Lee collection)

actly ½ ounce, and therefore could be mailed as a drop letter for 1¢ since Pottsville had no carrier service. The circular was published by the Pottsville, Pennsylvania, *Miner's Journal* newspaper and distributed without charge. In addition to the philatelic interest of this item, the many descriptive advertisements provide an informative and entertaining look at the commerce of a thriving small town during the 1860s.

Circulars to Foreign Destinations

The gems of circular mail are most frequently found among those examples of use to foreign countries. Although a large number of these circulars were undoubtedly mailed, very few of them have survived. The subject matter of these circulars was usually of very little permanent interest. Prices current and similar information quickly became obsolete, and the circulars were generally discarded soon after receipt. Examples are truly scarce.

Foreign circulars are also of special interest to the 1861 1¢ Franklin specialist since it is one of the three foreign uses where the 1¢ stamp can make up the complete prepayment without the addition of other denominations. The other two are the transient newspaper rate and the carrier collection fee for unpaid foreign letters.

In the PL&R listings for the rates of foreign postage, printed matter is divided into two categories: newspapers and pamphlets. It would seem that circulars would best fit under the pamphlet classification, but existing examples of circulars to foreign destinations seem to indicate that they were classed as newspapers. This seems to hold until at least the latter part of the 1860s. Foreign newspaper rates were generally more than the corresponding pamphlet rate, and this may have been the reason for the anomaly

The newpaper rate to most of the common European countries was 2¢, while that for pamphlets and printed matter was 1¢ per ounce. The writer has never seen a transoceanic circular mailed during the 1860s that was rated at 1¢ (circulars to Canadian North America could be mailed for 1¢).

Single-weight circulars usually required the prepayment of 2¢, which paid for internal U.S. postage and delivery to the first foreign post office in transit to the destination. Amounts for subsequent transits through countries and the internal postage of the destination country were to be collected from the addressee. These transit fees varied by country, route and date. For many foreign circulars, the analysis of the rates charged and the meaning of the added printed and manuscript markings can be an interesting challenge.

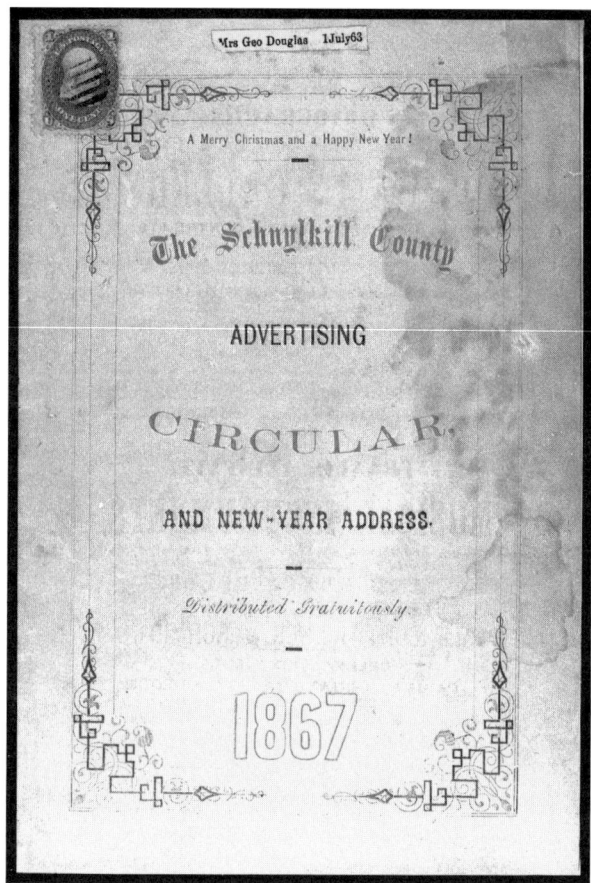

Figure 12-8. Sixteen-page 1867 advertising circular mailed by the Pottsville, Pennsylvania, *Miner's Journal* newspaper. Postage of 1¢ paid, taking advantage of the lower 1¢ rate for local drop mail as compared with 2¢ for circular mail.

The author is deeply indebted to Richard F. Winter for his valuable assistance in deciphering the routes and rate structure for many of the circulars that will be discussed in this section. In addition to his personal expertise, his published work on the sailings of mail steamships to Europe [2] has been invaluable.

Figure 12-9 shows a folded circular from New York City to Genoa, Italy, sent under the British Mail Convention through France. The addressee must have been a steady recipient of these circulars for this writer has seen several similar covers to the same person, all dated during 1862 and 1863. The 2¢ pays the U.S. circular rate, and the collection marking in black of 15 centesimi (about 3¢) is for the foreign postage to be collected at Genoa.

The "Per Africa" at the upper left of the cover refers to the name of the mail ship that the sender wished to use. Post Office Department policy during this period requested that the originators of foreign mail annotate their envelopes with the desired route and carrier. The

Figure 12-9. New York City, March 11, 1863, to Genoa, Italy. The circular departed New York on the Cunard steamer *Africa* on March 11 and arrived at Queenstown, Ireland, on March 22, 1863. It reached Genoa on March 26, where it was backstamped with a bright red receiving mark.

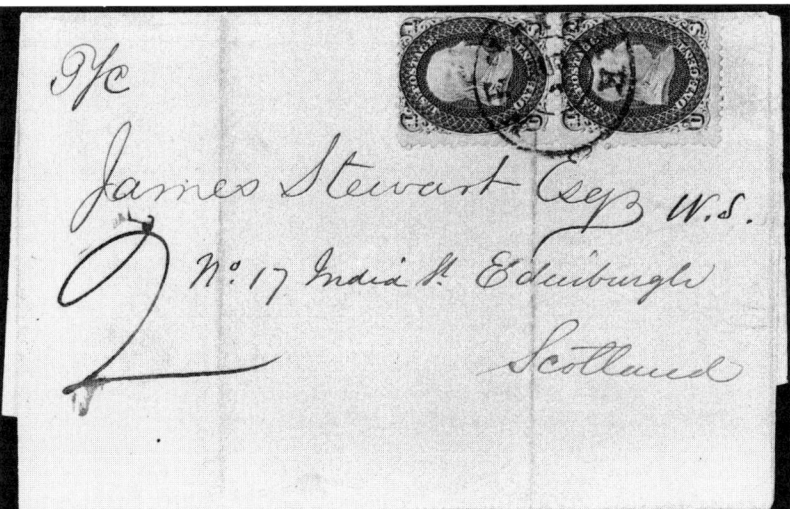

Figure 12-9b. Folded printed circular from New York, June 2, 1862, to Edinburgh, Scotland. Two 1¢ Franklins pay the U.S. portion of the circular postage. The manuscript "P/C" in the upper-left corner is to advise that the content is a printed circular. The circular is marked "2" for collection. Circulars to Scotland from the U.S. are scarce.

reason for this was that many destinations could be reached via different routes and mail systems. The postage and the time in transit could vary significantly, and the postal clerks in the Foreign Mail office requested guidance to process the mail as the sender desired.

A scarce example of a folded circular from New York City to Edinburgh, Scotland, is shown in **Figure 12-9b**. This circular announces the retirement of a member of a New York brokerage firm, and the concurrent opening of his own firm. A fancy manuscript notation "P/C" is written on the envelope, probably to indicate to postal authorities that the content is a printed circular. The circular is marked "2" for collection upon delivery.

Figure 12-10 shows an 1862 price list from a New York barrel-stave manufacturer to Cadiz, Spain, by British Mail via France. The circular rate was paid with two 1¢ Franklins. Surprisingly, there are no foreign markings on the circular other than a red transit mark applied at London, England. In spite of the lack of due markings, it is likely that additional postage was collected at Cadiz. Other examples of circulars to Spain for this period indicate that the postage due amount was usually ½ reale. Many U.S. Mail contract steamers departed for Europe from New York. Tables in reference [2] list the ships and their departure and arrival dates. These tables can be of help in determining the routing and carriers for transatlantic mail when there are no endorsements on the covers.

A printed prices current from New York to Bremen, via French mail, is illustrated in **Figure 12-11**. Although the year in the New York datestamp of March 28 is not legible, it can be determined to be 1863 from the French entry marking dated "10 Avril 63," applied by the Calais-to-Paris railway post office. French entry markings can provide a substantial amount of information concerning

Figure 12-10. New York City to Cadiz, Spain. The circular departed New York on October 11, 1862, aboard the Inman steamship *City of Baltimore*. It arrived at Liverpool October 23 and was forwarded to Spain via London (receiving mark) and France. There are no Spanish markings on the circular and no postage due markings.

Figure 12-11. New York to Bremen circular, March 28, 1863. The circular was carried aboard the Inman steamer *Edinburgh* under U.S. Mail contract, via French mails. U.S. postage of 2¢ was prepaid. The circular bears a Bremen postage due marking in blue of 4 grote (23 French centimes), of which 14 centimes went to France for transit.

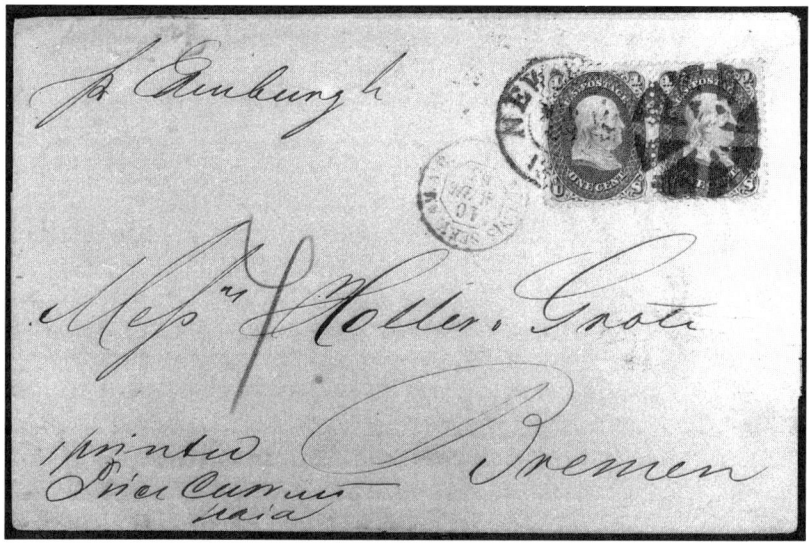

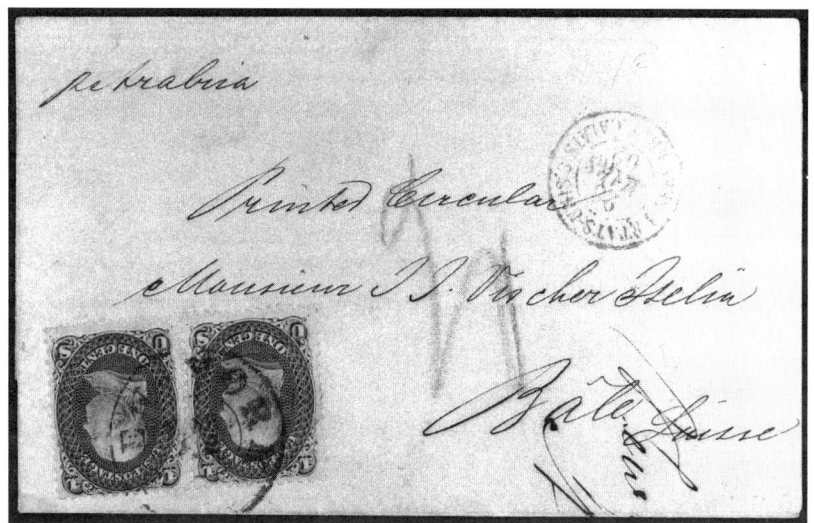

Figure 12-12. This circular departed New York City on March 12, 1862, per Cunard steamship *Arabia*, via England and France, to Basel, Switzerland. A Basel receiving mark on reverse is dated March 27, 1862.

Figure 12-13. 1862 circular mailed from Baltimore to Amsterdam, Netherlands, via French mail. The circular departed Boston by Cunard mail steamer *Niagara* and arrived at Paris on January 21, 1862. It is marked 12½ to be collected. The circular carries a reverse marking of "19" in blue crayon and "25" in black.
(C.W. Christian collection)

a piece of mail. The various types of markings and information provided is discussed in Chapter 17.

The blue collection mark of 4 grote was applied at Bremen. Bremen currency of 4 grote equals approximately 23 French centimes, or 5½¢ U.S. Under the French/Thurn and Taxis Convention of 1862, the French received 14 centimes of this amount. Since the mails were accounted for by bulk, markings showing the division of the due amount are not made on the cover. This circular is marked on the reverse with a Thurn and Taxis (German mail system) receiving mark at Bremen. The date is not legible.

Figure 12-12 shows a circular, departing New York on March 12, 1862, and addressed to Basel, Switzerland. This particular item was carried to Queenstown, Ireland, by the British Cunard steamer *Arabia*. From Queenstown, it went via London and Paris, where it received a red French marking showing entry at Calais. At Basel, it was marked in red crayon for 20 centimes collection. The collection fee was divided up, with probably 15 centimes going to France and the balance to Switzerland. The circular is backstamped with a Basel receiving mark dated March 27, 1862.

The majority of recorded circular covers to foreign destinations originated at New York City. This is not surprising since New York in the 1860s was the site of most of the larger commercial enterprises. Foreign circulars from other cities are relatively scarce. **Figure 12-13** illustrates one of these uses. This cover to Amsterdam, Holland, was mailed from Baltimore, Maryland. The date of mailing is illegible in the poorly struck CDS, but the probable departure date from the United States can be deduced by working back from a French entry mark, which was applied at Paris on January 21, 1862. The mark also shows that the circular was carried by a British mail ship. The Cunard steamship *Niagara* arrived off Queenstown, Ireland, on January 19, 1862, and that is about the right date for mail to arrive in Paris on the 21st. The *Niagara* departed from Boston on January 8, 1862.

From this information, the likely itinerary of this cover can be assumed to be a mailing at Baltimore during the first week of 1862, followed by forwarding to the Foreign Exchange Office at New York City. There it was bagged with other mail being sent via the French mails for ocean transport by British ship. Since the next British steamer would be leaving from Boston (Cunard alternated its weekly departures between New York and Boston), the bags were sent to Boston to be added to their mails for Europe.

The circular is franked with two 1¢ stamps that paid for the U.S. portion of the rate, and is marked on the front with a large "12½." This represents 12½¢ (Dutch), equal to about 5¢ U.S., and is the rate for a printed circular weighing no more than 25 grams, from the United States to Holland via England. The marking was probably applied at the border office at Breda, Holland. On the reverse is a large "19" in blue crayon and a stamped ½-inch circle containing a "25`" in black. The "25`" is the mark of the postman who delivered the circular, and the "19" represented the amount, in Dutch cents, collected from the addressee. The additional 6½¢ probably paid for collect postage that was due on other mail to the addressee that was delivered at the same time. It was the practice of several European countries to total a number of postal charges and mark the due amount on one letter.

A scarce and interesting printed freight report to Moss, Norway, is illustrated in **Figure 12-14.** This report was mailed at New York City on March 1, 1863. It was carried aboard the *Borussia* of the Hamburg-American

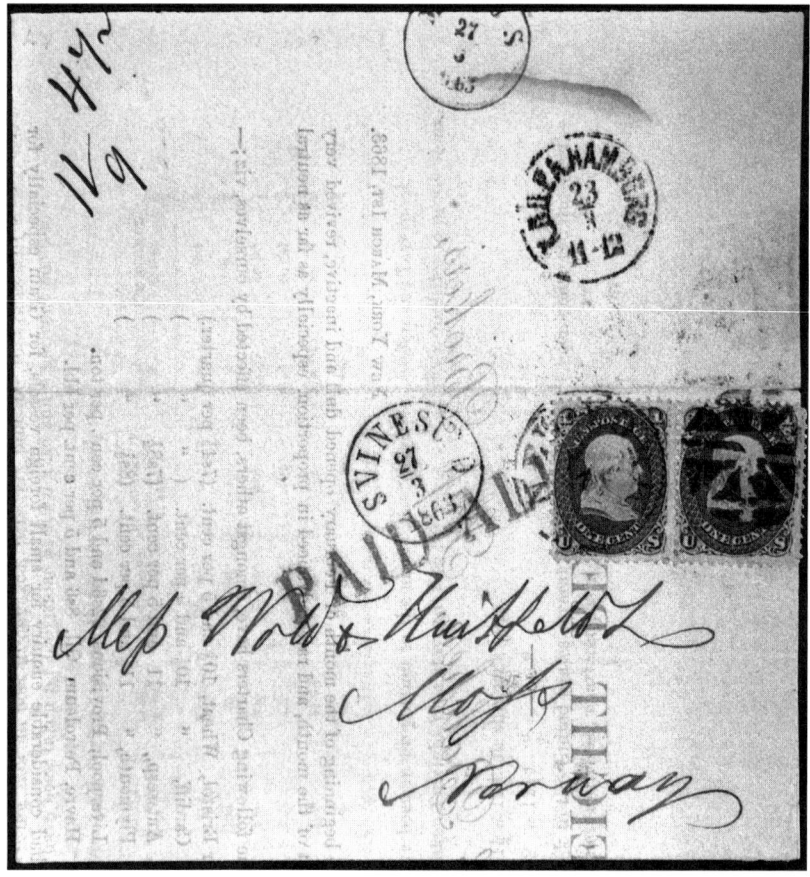

Figure 12-14. Scarce use to Moss, Norway, dated March 1, 1863, at New York. This printed freight report was carried by HAPAG steamer *Borussia* via Hamburg and Sweden. It is marked 4½ on the reverse for collection. The folded sheet is opened to show markings. (James Lee collection)

Line (HAPAG), a German steamship line with a U.S. mail contract. The *Borussia* departed New York on March 8, one week after the notice was mailed. The cover arrived at Hamburg on March 22 and was transferred to the Danish postal service where it received a K.D.P.O.A.(Royal Danish Post Office) Hamburg backstamp on the following day. A SVENSUND transit marking was subsequently applied to the front to show that the notice went though Sweden on its way to Norway (winter ice prevented direct transit), and a backstamped receiving mark at Moss, Norway, shows arrival on March 27, 1863.

The notice also has the manuscript notation "11/9 4½~" on the reverse. This notation is particularly important in deciphering the rate structure. According to Richard Winter, most Norwegian covers of this period had the rating marks on the back. The actual postage due, as indicated by these markings, is 4½ (which looks like 47) skilling speciedaler, equal to about 4¢. The 11/9 marking is thought to show the two Norwegian post office identification numbers under which the postal accounting was accomplished. The number "11" was the list number at Moss, Norway, and the number "9" the list number for the nearby town of Soon, Norway, where the addressed company was actually located.

The large black PAID ALL handstamp on the front of the notice does not mean that postage is paid to destination. It was used at New York for circulars mailed under the German postal treaties to indicate that the postage was paid to Hamburg. From that point on, postage was to be collected from the addressee. The two 1¢ stamps paid for U.S. internal postage and sea transport to Hamburg.

The above discussed items comprise a representative selection from the circular-type uses to Europe that the author has recorded. All of these uses are from the period between fall of 1862 and spring of 1863. It seems reasonable that there should be examples to be found from both earlier and later dates with the 1¢ Franklin making up the postage. Of course, after July 1, 1863, the 2¢ Jackson became available and probably was the stamp of choice for this type of use.

Circulars to non-European destinations are extremely scarce, with the exception of those to Canada. Under the provisions of the postal agreement between the United States and Canada, effective April 6, 1851, postage was to be paid by the sender for transmission to the border. The receiving country would receive its post-

Circular and Transient Mail

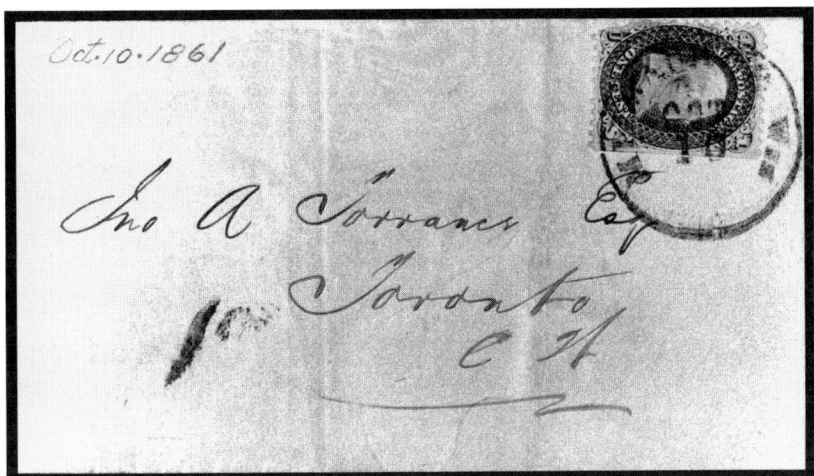

Figure 12-15. Milwaukee, Wisconsin, to Toronto, Canada West. The 1¢ 1861 Franklin pays for internal U.S. circular postage to the Canadian border. The folded circular is dated October 10, 1861, and marked "1 ct" for collection of the Canadian portion of rate. The folded circular contains information on the grain market. A portion of the contents are reproduced below.

age by collection from the recipient [3:223]. Under these arrangements, prior to July 1, 1863, a 1¢ stamp paid postage to a Canadian exchange office where the circular was marked for 1¢ to be collected upon delivery (1859 PL&R, Section 150). Canada had the same weight limitations as the United States: 1¢ for a circular up to 3 ounces.

Figure 12-15 illustrates an early use of the 1¢ Franklin on a folded commercial circular from Milwaukee, Wisconsin, to Toronto, Canada. The cover is marked for 1¢ collection. The contents show that the circular was published daily, describing the latest status of the grain market.

Newspapers

The founding fathers of the United States took very seriously their commitment to ensure that the citizens of the country were well-informed. To this end, they authorized extremely beneficial rates for the mailing of newspapers. In many ways, it amounted to a government subsidy for the education of the public. Weekly newspapers could be sent free of charge to subscribers who lived in the county of publication. Newspapers that were printed more frequently were charged only a small amount for mailing. Even newspapers that were sent long distances were charged insignificant amounts. A weekly newspaper could be sent from the East Coast to subscribers in California for less than 1½¢ per copy. This was much less than the cost of transportation. Postmaster General Blair mentioned in his Annual Report for 1861 that reports had been received of bags of newspapers being thrown off stages en route to the West in order to make room for passengers. Normally, newspapers were transported by sea to California, but if the mail load for stagecoaches did not make up the poundage agreed upon in the contract, the letter mail was supplemented with magazines and newspapers. The stagecoach drivers evidently felt they could put the space to better use.

Although the logistics and procedures for handling the regular distribution of newspapers is interesting in a postal history sense, the lack of stamps or markings on the papers makes them philatelic noncollectibles. Postage was normally paid quarterly in cash and no stamps were used. The newspapers that were mailed to nonsubscribers or mailed between individuals are the "transient newspapers" of interest. Regulations required that these mailings be treated as transient printed matter and the postage prepaid by stamps.

The domestic rate for transient newspapers in 1861 was the same as that for circulars and all other matter in print (except books), 1¢ up to 3 ounces and an additional 1¢ for each ounce over 3. This rate paid for transmittal to any place in the United States.

On July 1, 1863, the transient rate was increased to

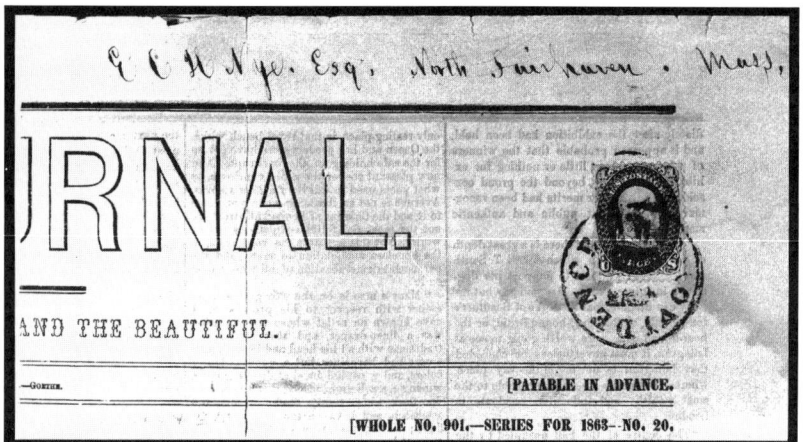

Figure 12-16. Providence, Rhode Island, *Home Journal* newspaper for the week ending May 16, 1863. It was mailed at the 1¢ rate for transient newspapers.

2¢ for papers up to 4 ounces, with an additional rate of 2¢ for each additional 4 ounces.

Transient newspapers were to be wrapped with narrow bands so the contents could be easily removed and inspected. Wrappers for this purpose were sold in stationery stores, but most of the wrappers that exist today were made from scraps of paper or opened envelopes. All wrappers are scarce. They are not the kind of item that is normally put away and saved.

Transient newspapers with addresses and stamps directly on them can also be found but are even more scarce than wrappers. Because of size and lack of enduring value, they were usually quickly discarded. Of those that remain, most are specialty newspapers with weekly or longer intervals of publication and a limited number of subscribers. Rarely, a regular newspaper that seems to have been mailed without a wrapper is found.

Figure 12-16 shows an example of such a mailing. This folded piece is from the front page of the Providence, Rhode Island, *Home Journal* newspaper for the week ending Saturday, May 16, 1863. It is addressed to the recipient at Fairhaven, Massachusetts. Postage is paid by a 1¢ stamp attached to the paper and canceled with a Providence, Rhode Island, town marking.

Figure 12-17 shows a weekly medical journal that was mailed locally to a street address at a special rate. The date of the mailing at Philadelphia is March 24, 1866. Postal regulations effective at that time required 2¢ postage if mailed as a transient printed publication. This particular item was probably delivered by a Philadelphia city carrier. Laws effective on July 1, 1863, authorized bulk mailers to contract for carrier delivery at negotiated prices. Philadelphia is the only city where examples of this practice have been recorded (see discussion in Chapter 10 under Philadelphia), and the cancel used on this example is consistent with other recorded contract-carrier items. Therefore, although an obvious newspaper or transient printed item, it was not rated under those categories.

Wrappers come in all sizes and shapes. Since the majority were handmade, the choice of paper and dimensions were dictated by the material available and the size of the item to be wrapped. Wrappers were primarily used for newspapers and magazines but could be used to transmit any piece of bulky printed matter.

Figure 12-18 shows a somewhat tattered example that seems to be made from an old piece of brown wrapping paper. This wrapper was mailed at Boston, Massa-

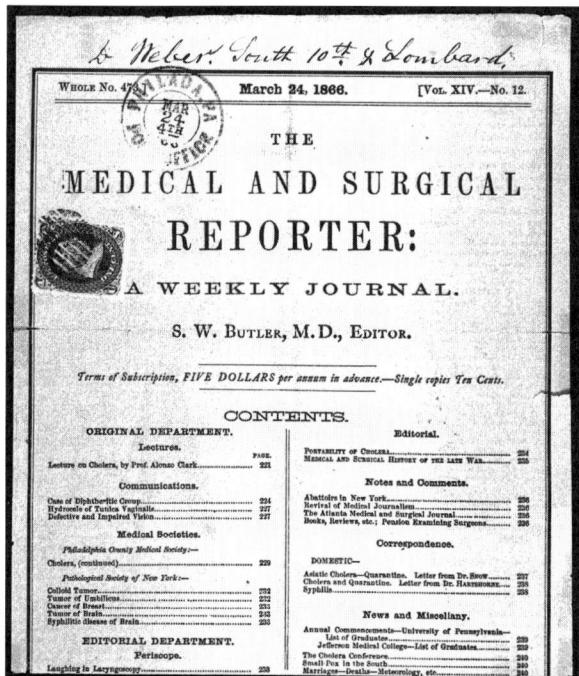

Figure 12-17. Weekly medical journal mailed locally at Philadelphia, Pennsylvania, on March 24, 1866. The 1¢ postage indicated probable carrier delivery under a special contract rate.
(James Lee collection)

Figure 12-18. Homemade wrapper from Boston, Massachusetts, to Newbern, North Carolina, dated May 5 (1862). The 1¢ transient rate was paid by a 1¢ Franklin. The wrapper was probably transported to Newbern by military dispatch ship from a Northern port.

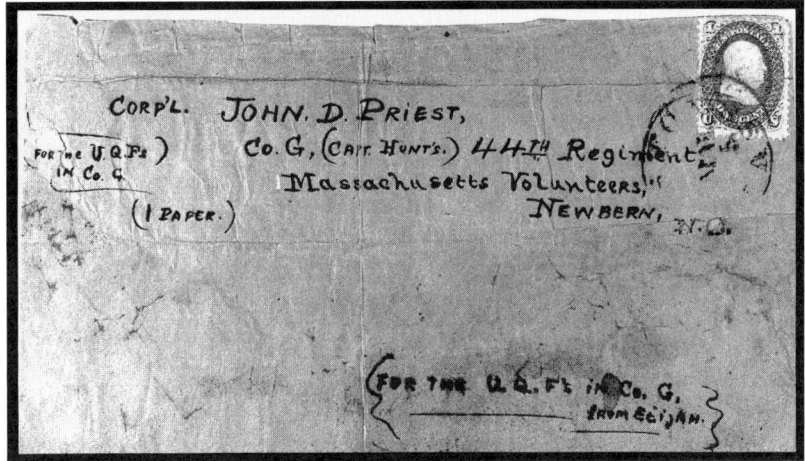

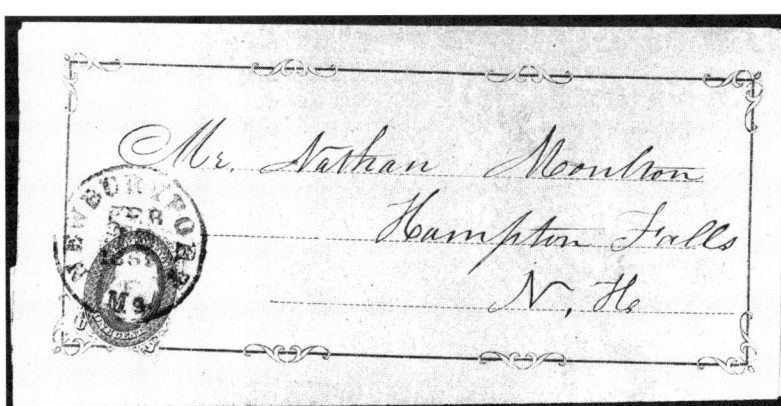

Figure 12-19. Commercially manufactured wrapper, mailed at Newburyport, Massachusetts, to Hampton Falls, New Hampshire. The rate is correct at 1¢, and the stamp is canceled with a Newburyport CDS, dated February 10, 1862.
(C.W. Christian collection)

chusetts, on May 5. No year date is included in the town and date marking. It is addressed to an army corporal at Newbern, North Carolina. Newbern was captured by Union troops under the command of General Burnside on March 14, 1862, and information from Richard B. Graham fixes the arrival in Newbern of the 44th Massachusetts Volunteers as October 1862. The date of mailing is therefore most likely May 5, 1863, and it was probably carried by an Army or Navy dispatch steamer from Boston, or some other Northern port, to its destination. Manuscript notations on the wrapper state that it is "For the U.Q.F's in Co. G." The meaning of this notation is unknown to the writer.

A commercially prepared wrapper is shown in **Figure 12-19**. This type of wrapper could be obtained in most of the stationery stores of the period, but examples are difficult to find. It is likely that the senders preferred to make their own as a matter of convenience or to save the small cost of a purchased wrapper.

Figure 12-20 shows a stamped government wrapper, produced specially for use with transient printed matter. These wrappers were franked with the 1¢ star-die design of 1860 and were issued in 1861. They were never demonetized since no supplies had been delivered to Southern post offices. They were never popular, and examples are extremely difficult to find. This particular wrapper has a 1¢ stamp added to make up the 2¢ rate for transient matter mailed subsequent to the rate increase of 1863. The Post Office Department stopped issuing the wrappers on October 14, 1864. Postmaster General Dennison in his annual report explained that they had been discontinued because the contract cost had "suffered an enormous advance" and also because parties other than the manufacturer were claiming to be the patentee of newspaper wrappers.

A rare example of a multiple-rate wrapper is illustrated in **Figure 12-21**. This wrapper was mailed from Concord, New Hampshire, on May 25, 1863, to Penfield, New York. The government wrapper with 1¢ embossed stamp was augmented with two 1¢ and one 3¢ stamps for a total of 6¢. This would pay the transient rate for an unusually heavy 8-ounce newspaper. It is also possible, and very likely, that this wrapper had an enclosure weighing between ½ and 1 ounce, but too large to be contained in a regular envelope. If the material contained any writ-

Figure 12-20. Government postal stationery wrapper (Scott W20). Wadham's Mills, New York, to Lewis, New York. The wrapper was mailed on March 18. The year of mailing is post-1863, as attested by the added 1¢ stamp which made up the increased 2¢ rate for transient mail.

Figure 12-21. Concord, New Hampshire, May 25, 1863, government wrapper (Scott W20) to Penfield, New York. Total postage of 6¢ with the addition of two 1¢ and one 3¢ stamps indicated either that the enclosure was transient matter weighing over 8 ounces, or contents weighing ½ to 1 ounce, with the wrapper mailed at the double-letter rate.
(C.W. Christian collection)

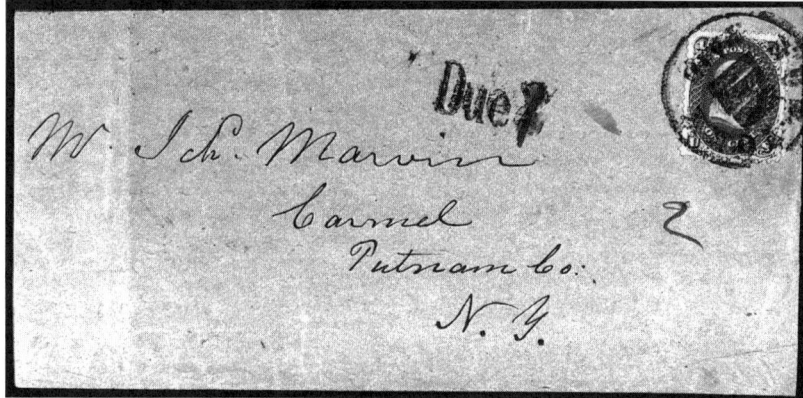

Figure 12-22. New York City to Carmel, New York. Date unknown. The wrapper is marked for collection.
(James Lee collection)

ing, it would not qualify for the transient rate, and regular letter rates would have to be paid. In either case, it is an interesting example of a seldom-seen usage.

Auxiliary postal markings are rarely seen on newspaper wrappers. **Figure 12-22** shows a wrapper originating at New York City and marked with a "Due 2." The "2" is marked over with a manuscript "1," and there is another manuscript "2" on the wrapper. The date is un-

known since the circular town mark that cancels the stamp has a slug in place of a date marker. Exactly what rate was charged and why is not certain. The wrapper may have been mailed after the rate was increased to 2¢, and the "Due 2" was marked to collect under the provision that underpaid letters were to be handled as completely unpaid. It is also possible that the "Due 2¢" was to show the correct rate and then marked over with the manuscript

Circular and Transient Mail

Figure 12-23. Newspaper wrapper from Boston, Massachusetts, to Sanbornton, New Hampshire, dated July 23, 1868. Two 1¢ stamps pay the transient mail rate. (James Lee collection)

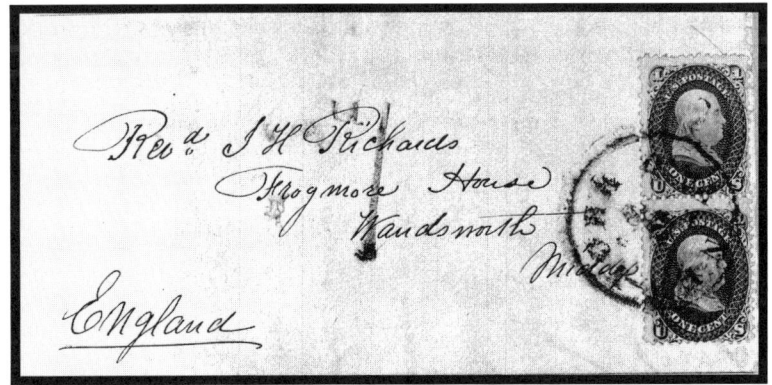

Figure 12-24. New York City to Wadsworth (a suburb of London), England. Date unknown. The wrapper is canceled with a New York PAID CDS and marked 1d for collection.

"1" to give credit for the partial payment. It was also possible for an underpaid newspaper to be debited for only the amount of underpayment. The manuscript "2" is anyone's guess. This is an example of one of those postal history items that frequently appear where there is not enough information to make a definite decision regarding procedures and rates, and where the number of similar examples is so limited that there is no common-use information available.

For some reason, wrappers mailed after the increase in rates in 1863 seem to be less common. **Figure 12-23** shows a wrapper, dated July 23, 1868, with the increased rate of 2¢ paid in postage.

The difficulty in classifying all the different types of printed matter to arrive at the correct rate of postage was recognized by the Post Office Department, and the Post Office invited postmasters, via notices in the *U.S. Mail and Post Office Assistant*, to submit any questionable items to the Department for a determination of rates and procedures.

Newspapers and Periodicals to Foreign Destinations

As should be expected, examples of use to foreign countries are more difficult to find. Newspaper rates to the various countries varied substantially from 2¢ to 10¢ each, depending on routing and postal agreements with the countries. For the more commonly addressed destinations in Europe, the rate was 2¢, to be paid in advance by stamps. This paid for delivery to the destination country, which, in turn, collected its own newspaper rate upon delivery. Each country retained the postage that it collected, and there was no accounting between countries with respect to amounts.

Figure 12-24 shows a wrapper to England, 2¢ postage paid, and mailed from New York. It is marked in black for 1 penny (2¢) to be collected upon delivery. This wrapper was made from a used sheet of letter paper and contains a portion of the original letter on the inside of the wrapper. For that reason, strict interpretation of the regulations would have required letter postage, but the illegal transmission of information was overlooked or ignored and the wrapper rated for collection at the British news-

227

Figure 12-25. Wrapper to England dated April 4 by a red Winchendon, Massachusetts, CDS. It was marked "2" at London for collection upon local delivery to the addressee.

Figure 12-26. Wrapper from New York to Bordeaux, France. Marked 30 centimes (double rate) for collection. (James Lee collection)

paper rate. The date is illegible and the wrapper provides no information regarding when it was sent.

Figure 12-25 illustrates a wrapper, mailed on April 14 (no year date) from Winchendon, Massachusetts, to London, England. This small wrapper is marked with a black "2" for collection. Why this is not the normal 1-penny collection amount is not known.

Figure 12-26 shows a wrapper to Bordeaux, France. It was mailed from New York City (illegible date) and is backstamped with a receiving mark at Bordeaux, dated December 11, 186? Newspapers to France could be sent either direct or via England. Agreements in force with Great Britain as of 1859 provided for printed matter to be routed through England to France, and to other countries, such as Egypt, where France had established post offices. There is no indication on this wrapper that would identify the route. The U.S. newspaper rate to the French border was 2¢, paid in advance. France collected 15 centimes per 40 grams of weight for its portion of the postage. In this case, the large "30" marked in red on the front of the wrapper is for 2x15=30 centimes postage due. This would pay for a newspaper weighing between 40 and 80 grams (about 1½ to 3 ounces).

Newspaper rates to countries in the German Postal Union (GPU) were 6¢ per paper if sent via Prussian closed mail. This paid for the postage to final destination. If the newspaper was sent by Bremen or Hamburg mail, the postage was only 3¢, and this also paid all of the costs to destination (1859 PL&R, Section 149-150).

Examples of wrappers to these countries are quite rare. **Figure 12-27** shows a wrapper, mailed in New York (date illegible) and addressed to Jedesheim near Illertissen, Bavaria, via Hamburg. The required 3¢ postage rate was underpaid by 1¢, and the wrapper was marked with a manuscript "6" for 6 kreuzer (about 4¢) to be collected. The wrapper was probably considered to be paid only to Hamburg, and the 6 kreuzer was for postage to destination.

Postage rates for transient mail to countries all over the world are listed in the postal regulations, even for

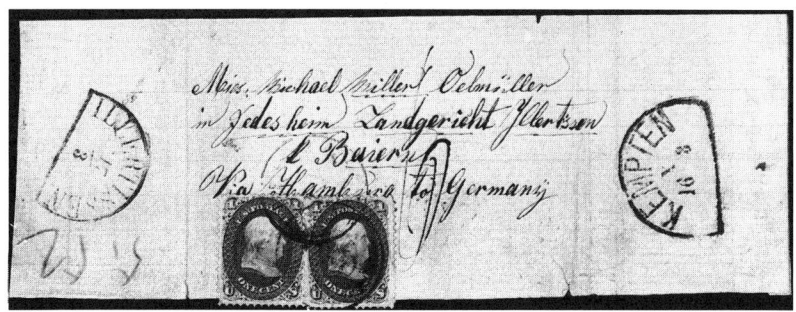

Figure 12-27. Wrapper to Bavaria via Hamburg. The 3¢ paid-all rate was underpaid by 1¢. The wrapper is marked with a manuscript 6 (kreuzer) for collection. Part of the enclosed newspaper, printed in German, is stuck to the inside of the wrapper. This item was handstamped at Kempten, Bavaria, on March 16 and at Illertissen, Bavaria, on March 17. (James Lee collection)

unlikely destinations such as Borneo (10¢). However, the author has not recorded any examples from the 1860-70 time period of non-European use, other than Canada, where postage included the 1¢ 1861 Franklin. Any such use can be considered to be very rare and a great asset to any collection.

The analysis of the rates and routes for printed matter can be frustrating at times and certainly a challenge to any philatelic student. More needs to be published on these scarce and somewhat neglected postal history stepchildren. Hopefully, a better general documentation of the regulations and procedures, particularly for foreign usage, will eventually be available.

References

1. Graham, Richard B. "Special Rate Services," Chapter 4. *United States Postal History Sampler*. Linn's Handbook Series. Linn's Stamp News, Sidney, Ohio. 1992.

2. Hubbard, Walter and Richard F. Winter. *North Atlantic Mail Sailings 1840-75*. U.S. Philatelic Classics Society. 1988.

3. McDonald, Susan M. "The Cover Corner." *Chronicle* No. 76. November 1972.

The United States 1¢ Franklin 1861-67

CHAPTER 13

Special Services

In this chapter some of the special services that were provided for postal patrons will be discussed. These services are registered mail; ship, steamship and steamboat mail; way letters; and supplementary mail.

Registry Service

For a number of years prior to the official beginning of the registry service in 1855, some postmasters provided an unofficial service whereby important or valuable letters could be "recorded." This provided the record of mailing that was required by the Post Office Department before any search for a lost-in-the-mails letter would be initiated, and it could be used as an official record of the mailing for other purposes [1:42]. These letters were usually marked with a manuscript or handstamped letter "R." While this service was unofficial, it definitely was with the consent of the Post Office Department, and there is evidence that it was encouraged by the Post Office. The availability of this service was limited to a few cities, most notable the post offices at Philadelphia and New Orleans [2:29]. No fees were charged, and it did appear to provide a more careful handling of the mail and, in some cases receipts of delivery which were retained by the destination post office.

These unofficial systems were popular with the legal profession and commercial postal patrons. However, the extra effort required to handle and process these quasi-registered letters was time-consuming and expensive to the individual post offices, and the postmasters requested that they be allowed to charge for the service [1:42].

Great Britain had instituted a registry system in 1841, and there was an increasing desire in the United States for something comparable that would assist in the tracing of lost correspondence, as well as serve as a proof of mailing. In his annual report for 1854, Postmaster General Campbell recommended such a system to Congress for adoption [3:180].

The registration of postal items became an official service to postal patrons on July 1, 1855. Section 3 of the Act of March 3, 1855, authorized the postmaster general to establish a uniform plan for the registration of valuable letters for transmission in the U.S. mails upon the application of the person posting the item. The act further stipulated that the registration fee was to be 5¢, and it was to be prepaid, with prepayment also required for the postage on the item. This was in accordance with another stipulation of the act, effective April 1, 1855, which required prepayment of all domestic postage.

The Act of March 3, 1855, also stated that registration was not to be compulsory, and that the Post Office Department would not be liable for any loss that occurred. The regulations implementing this act added that no mark of any kind was to be made on the envelope that would indicate that it contained a valuable enclosure. This requirement was at times ignored, and the word "registered" was frequently stamped or written on the cover. Some examples exist of the old unofficial "R" for a "recorded" letter being used along with a registry number. Certainly, the majority of registered letters probably carried a registry number to facilitate the identification and specific accounting for these letters.

Section 386 of the postal regulations for 1857 recognized the need for the registry number to be on the letter and added the requirement that each registered letter "be marked on its upper-left-hand corner with the number corresponding to it on the receipt book."

These arrangements were still in effect in 1861. In the regulations, which specified the procedures to be followed in the transmission and storage of registered mail, emphasis was placed on the security of the items with recording and accountability maintained at each post office where the item was handled. Registered mail was enclosed in separate envelopes together with the letter bills for the items. More than one registered item could be included in the special envelope if they were all going to the same destination. A receipt for the registered item was to be signed by the recipient, and his identity was to be established to the satisfaction of the postal clerk or postmaster.

Registration was available only to a few foreign destinations with fees as provided for in postal treaties with those countries. The postal regulations in effect in 1859, Section 155, provided that:

> "VALUABLE LETTERS, addressed to Germany, or any part of the German-Austrian Postal Union, by the Bremen line via New York, or by the Prussian closed mail via New York and Boston, as also letters addressed to Great Britain and Canada, will be registered on the application of the person posting the same . . ."

Full postage to destination plus a registration fee of 5¢ on each letter was to be prepaid.

Although the above countries were the only ones included in the provisions for registered mail according to the regulations of 1859, an agreement between the

231

United States and Canada had been in effect since October of 1856. The agreement provided for the exchange of registered mail between the two countries for a fee of 5¢.

According to the USM&POA for August 1861, Great Britain was also included in the countries with which registered mail could be exchanged. Again, the fee was 5¢.

In his Annual Report of the Postmaster General for 1862, Montgomery Blair proposed a meeting in Europe to establish uniform postal practices between all nations. He included recommendations for many changes that he thought would be beneficial, and among them was the suggestion that a "uniform international system of registration of letters and postal charges therefor" be established. This suggestion for a conference eventually resulted in the Universal Postal Union and the simple and economical system of international mails that we now enjoy.

The use of the registry system by the general public was not extensive during this early period. The fact that the sender received no receipt that proved delivery decreased its usefulness to a considerable extent. Postmaster General Blair noted this shortcoming, and in his Annual Report to the President, dated December 1, 1862, proposed three changes to the postal laws pertaining to the registration of letters and packets. It was Blair's contention that losses due to theft in the transmission of mail were primarily the result of the temptation provided by sending cash in letters. He proposed (1) the adoption of a money-order system to reduce the need for sending cash by mail, (2) to substantially increase the fee charged for registration to an amount that would be commensurate with the amounts charged by other parties who engaged in the transportation of packages of money (which at that time was 25¢, or more), and (3) to require that all letters known to contain money be registered.

He felt that the small fee of 5¢ that was currently being charged did not pay for the expenses to the Post Office Department of the registry system, and as previously mentioned, the fact that the sender received no information concerning the delivery of the registered item were both defects of the system. Blair proposed that when an item was presented for registration, the postmaster would execute duplicate receipts, one to be given to the sender and the other to be transmitted with the registered item to the recipient, who would be required to sign it. The receipt would then be returned to the sender by return mail and would provide proof of delivery. He also recommended that the registry fee be increased to 20¢.

These suggestions (with the exception of the requirement that all money letters be registered) were included in the many changes to postal procedures made by the Act of March 3, 1863, which became effective on July 1, 1863. The new law provided for a fee not to exceed 20¢ and made it a requirement that a return receipt be provided to the sender, and that this receipt would be received by the courts as prima facie evidence of delivery. Regulations required that in addition to the registered number in the upper-left-hand corner of the letter, the word "Registered" should be plainly stamped on the face of the envelope.

The previous requirement for prepayment of the registration fee and postage remained in force, with the stipulation that the postage would be paid for by stamps, but the registration fee was to be paid for in money. This is the first time the method for payment of the fee had been stated, and for many years, philatelic scholars were unsure if payment of the fee by stamps had been authorized during the period from 1855 to 1863. Three examples of covers showing the fee paid for by stamps are known, but it is now believed that these examples were due to errors on the part of the initiating postmaster, and that prepayment in money had always been a requirement [3:185].

The registration fee to the United Kingdom of Great Britain and Ireland was also raised to 20¢ on July 1, 1863; however, the previous agreement with Canada remained in force with the same 5¢ registration fee [4:147]. The 5¢ fee for the Prussian and Bremen treaties also remained unchanged.

An incentive to promote the use of the registry service was provided in the regulations of 1863 by increasing the amount to be paid to postmasters for each registry fee received at their offices. The commission rate was set at 50 percent. Earlier regulations, as noted by the well-known philatelic student and author Barbara Mueller, had provided for a commission to be paid at the rate of 80 percent of the registration fee [2:30]. Although the percentage was previously higher, the associated registration fee was lower, so the new commission rate actually increased the commission on each registered article from 4¢ to 10¢. It had been observed that the use of the registry system actually declined over the first five years following its inception, and the commission increase may have been an inducement for the postmasters to more vigorously promote the sale of this service for valuable mail.

Postmaster General Blair also urged his postmasters to promote the use of money orders and to reduce the number of money letters to a minimum. This seems to conflict with the desire to increase the use of the registry service. Perhaps the goal was to reduce the number of money letters and the consequent inducement to theft, but at the same time to increase the use of registered mail for other types of valuable mail, such as depositions, deeds and contracts.

Registered covers from the decade of the 1860s are

Figure 13-1. Registered letter from Philadelphia, Pennsylvania, to Boston, Massachusetts, April 17, 1863. The cover was printed in colors by Edward Cogan of Philadelphia, showing *The Arms of the Keystone State*. This is probably the most attractive example of the 1¢ Franklin on a registered cover for this period. The three 1¢ stamps pay the letter rate and are canceled by four strikes of a straightline REGISTERED marking. The 5¢ registry fee was paid in cash.
(Kelleher auction photo)

relatively scarce, and those exhibiting the use of the 1¢ Franklin are even more difficult to find. In spite of the requirement, beginning on July 1, 1863, to stamp or mark registered mail with the word "Registered," this was not always done, and many covers can be identified only by the presence of the registry number.

Care must be taken in identification, since numbers on the fronts of envelopes were also used for other purposes. Mail held for insufficient postage sometimes was marked by the post office with a file number, and some recipients of correspondence marked their letters with numbers to indicate their order of arrival or as a reference notation.

Figure 13-1 illustrates a cover mailed in 1863 shortly before the fee was increased to 20¢. This spectacular Philadelphia letter shows the registry number "683" and has the three 1¢ stamps canceled by multiple strikes of a REGISTERED marker.

Registry numbers were usually applied consecutively. Small offices might start their numbering sequence at the beginning of each year, while larger offices would begin to renumber several times per year to keep the numbers from getting too large.

Figure 13-2 shows an 1864 registered transcontinental letter with the 20¢ fee paid in cash and double-rate postage of 6¢ paid in stamps. Two manuscript numbers are on the front. The "1226" is probably the registry number at San Francisco since it is placed at the upper left of the cover per regulations, and the "6262" may be a file number at New Bedford, or other nonpostal notation.

While most registry covers are from intercity mail,

Figure 13-2. Use after the fee increase to 20¢. Double-weight letter, with 6¢ in stamps paying the postage only. San Francisco, California, to New Bedford, Massachusetts. The letter, dated February 11, 1864, shows the registry number 1226, in manuscript. The registry fee was paid in cash per regulations.

the author has recorded one example of a drop-letter registered cover at Providence, Rhode Island, dated May 23, 1866. This letter is paid by a 1¢ Franklin with a manuscript cancellation and a red CDS. It is marked REGISTERED and has a manuscript "250." It is a scarce use.

One of the most outstanding examples of registry use with the 1¢ Franklin also has the largest number of the 1¢ stamps known to have been used on cover. This cover is illustrated in **Figure 13-3** and was in the collection of Henry Novak for many years.

No other changes in the registration procedures were put into effect until 1867. However, the compilation of the Postal Laws and Regulations that was published in 1866 (this was the first published compilation of all of the laws since 1859) expanded the number of countries with whom registered mail could be exchanged. It included any part of the German-Austrian Postal Union (GPU),

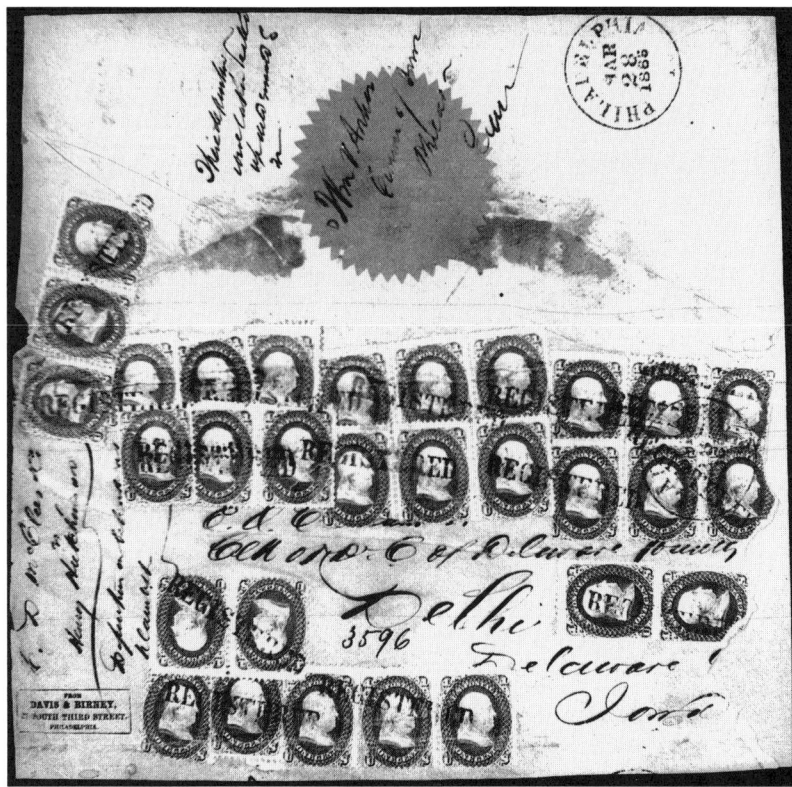

Figure 13-3. March 28, 1865. Philadelphia, Pennsylvania, to a county court clerk at Delhi, Iowa. This is the largest number of 1¢ stamps of the 1861 issue known to have been used on a single cover. Thirty copies are canceled by 16 strikes of the REGISTERED marker. Photo shows the standard legal-size cover, opened to illustrate both sides. It contained a deposition and was closed with a large red seal. The 30¢ in stamps paid for 10x3¢ postage, and the 20¢ registry fee was paid in cash.
(From the Henry Nowak collection; photo courtesy of Richard B. Graham)

Figure 13-4. Reduced legal-size registered envelope from Columbia, South Carolina, to Augusta, Georgia, dated April 23 (no year date). Total payment affixed is 59¢ for 20¢ registry fee, paid in stamps, and 13x3¢ for the overweight postage. Use of 10¢ E grill (Scott 89) suggests 1868 for year of use. Scarce domestic use of 24¢ stamps (Scott 78a).

provided that the letters were forwarded by Bremen or Hamburg line via New York, or by the Prussian closed mail via New York and Boston. Five cents was still the fee for these letters per existing treaty stipulations. The 1866 regulations also specified the procedure whereby registered mail could be forwarded. The addressee was required to request such forwarding in writing. No additional registration fee was needed. The provisions requiring prepayment of postage and fees were retained.

In 1867 a major change was made in the provisions for handling registered mail. The *U.S. Mail and Post Office Assistant* for May of 1867 advised postmasters of changes to the regulations as follows. Effective June 1, 1867, registration fees were to be paid in stamps (attached to the letter and canceled) instead of money as previously required [5:193]. This applied to all registry fees, the 20¢ fee on letters to any part of the United States, England, Ireland, Scotland, Wales and the Island of Jamaica, or the 5¢ fee on letters to Canada or Germany [1:26].

According to Roger B. Cotting who studied some

Figure 13-5. Late use of the 1¢ Franklin on a registered cover. Registered markings in pale blue on front and reverse of cover as shown in drawings. New York City to Rochester, New York, August 28, 1878. The 10¢ registry fee and 3¢ postage was paid by a 1¢ Franklin plus a 12¢ (Scott 117). Note the five-digit registration number.

**REGISTERED
AUG 28 1878
NEW YORK N. Y.**

of the early examples of registry fees paid by stamps, there were about 100 registered letters per day processed at New York City in the latter months of 1867 [6:135]. In spite of this substantial volume, examples are scarce, and this writer has never seen an 1867 registered letter with the use of the 1¢ Franklin.

The reduced cover shown in **Figure 13-4** unfortunately does not provide any information specifying the year it was mailed. The 10¢ stamp is grilled, so the use must be post-1867. This registered cover shows an unusual boxed REGISTERED marking, and the cover is further enhanced by the very scarce use of the 1861 24¢ value on domestic mail. The total franking is correct for a 13x3¢ postage rate plus 20¢ for the registry fee making a total of 59¢, so it is likely that the year of mailing was 1868.

The next change in the fee structure became effective on January 1, 1869, when the fee was reduced to 15¢. It is thought that public displeasure with the high 20¢ rate contributed to the lowering of the fee. Covers showing this reduced fee and franked with the 1¢ 1861 stamp are extremely scarce. The author has seen only one, which was offered at a Henry M. Spelman auction in San Francisco about 1978. The registration fee on that particular cover was paid for by use of an 1866 black 15¢ stamp, with three 1¢ Franklins paying the postal rate. The 15¢ Lincoln in combination with the 1¢ Franklin on any domestic cover is a very scarce combination.

On January 1, 1874, the registration fee was reduced, this time to 8¢. This fee was relatively short-lived and was raised to 10¢ on July 1, 1875. For these later periods, registered covers showing the use of the 1¢ 1861 stamp are exceedingly hard to find.

Figure 13-5 shows an example of such use in combination with a 12¢ value of the 1869 issue. This cover,

dated August 28, 1878, has light-blue registered markings on both the front and reverse sides. The fee of 10¢ and postage of 3¢ make up the total payment in stamps of 13¢.

On January 1, 1893, the registry fee was again reduced to 8¢, and for the first time insurance, up to $10, was authorized. But according to Richard B. Graham [5:195] it was not made available to users until 1898.

For convenience, a table of the 19th-century registration fees and the dates of applicability follows. This table is adapted from a more complete listing contained in Graham's *United States Postal History Sampler*.

Domestic Registry Fees and Services			
Effective Period	Fee	Paid By	Services Provided
July 1, 1855 to June 30, 1863	5¢	cash	Registration with mailing receipt only. No insurance.
July 1, 1863 to May 31, 1867	20¢	cash	Registration with mailing and delivery receipts. No insurance.
June 1, 1867 to Dec. 31, 1868	20¢	stamps	Same
Jan. 1, 1869 to Dec. 31, 1873	15¢	stamps	Same
Jan. 1, 1874 to June 30, 1875	8¢	stamps	Same
July 1, 1875 to Dec. 31, 1892	10¢	stamps	Same
Jan. 1, 1893 to Oct. 31, 1909	8¢	stamps	Same, with insurance to $10 beginning in 1898.

Ship, Steamship, and Steamboat Mails

The mail categories of ship, steamship and steamboat letters have probably caused more problems to U.S. postal historians in the determination of rates and procedures than any other types of mail.

It should be emphasized that each of these three categories of mail was unique and subject to differing regulations. The titles, while suggesting a type of maritime vessel, were classes of mail, not types of ships. For example, a steamship letter could be transported aboard a sailing vessel or other kind of craft as well as aboard a steamship.

Examples of covers showing these types of use are relatively scarce, particularly after 1860. This scarcity, coupled with confusing, overlapping and changing postal laws and regulations on maritime and waterway mail, makes it extremely difficult to reconstruct the actual postal procedures and rating for many examples.

Determining the correct rating and postal handling is not only a problem for the present-day postal historian, but also affected the contemporary post office employees of the 1850s and 1860s who had to deal firsthand with the complicated and fragmented regulations. This is attested to by a substantial number of covers that have survived showing evidence of incorrect classification and ratings. A respected postal historian has remarked, "The only way to properly determine the actual methods of handling and the rates being used for any situation is to collect together a significant number of representative covers, put them in chronological sequence, and let them tell the story. Postal regulations and directives are not enough, for they were frequently poorly written, misunderstood or ignored." This is particularly true for maritime and waterway uses, but the shortage of representative covers unfortunately makes this a difficult recommendation to follow.

By the beginning of the 1860s, the number of ship and steamboat letters had begun to markedly decrease. The number of railroads carrying mail and the proliferation of contracts for the transportation of ocean mails had increased to the point where the earlier dependence upon steamboats and noncontract ships for moving the mails was greatly reduced. The Civil War also had a great deal to do with the disappearance of covers with the markings STEAM, STEAMBOAT, WAY, and route-agent markings of all kinds. Most of these markings originated along major rivers in the southern and the western part of the country. Much of that territory was lost to the Confederacy at the beginning of the war, along with the commerce and the accompanying correspondence between the North and the South. Many steamboats were converted to war use, and the once-flourishing river-mail traffic dwindled to a trickle.

In analyzing a maritime or waterway cover, the first step is to determine its classification. This was assigned by the postmaster or postal clerk where the cover first entered the mail. The classification, coupled with the date of mailing (which is extremely important because of major changes made during the 1860s), will determine the provisions of the PL&Rs that are applicable. Once a letter was given a classification or category, it remained unchanged until delivered. For example, if a cover was received from a ship coming in from a foreign port and marked as a ship letter, it cannot be considered to ever have been handled as a steamboat or steamship letter.

Briefly, the definitions and characteristics of the three categories of maritime and waterway mail for the mid-1800s are:

SHIP: Mails brought into domestic ports by private ships operating without a U.S. Post Office Department mail contract, and over routes that had not been designated as post roads. This usually consisted of mail of foreign origin, but could include mail picked up by a vessel at a domestic port.

STEAMBOAT (also includes covers marked STEAM, which was synonymous): Mail transported by private vessels, without mail contracts, plying inland and coastal bay waterways. This is considered nominally to be mail carried on domestic waterways but could include mail that was picked up at nearby coastal ports in Nova Scotia, New Brunswick or similar locations.

STEAMSHIP: Mails brought into the United States aboard regularly scheduled mail packets. These vessels had contracts to carry U.S. mail in closed pouches. Steamship mail was carried outside the regular mails. The term "outside the mails" denotes any mail carried without being officially locked in mail pouches.

Ship Letters

The ship letter is the oldest classification of maritime mail, and as defined in Section 164 of the Postal Regulations of 1859:

> "The terms ship letters and packets embrace the letters and packets brought into the United States from foreign countries, or carried from one port in the United States to another, in any private ship or vessel, before such letters have been mailed."

The key concept of this regulation is the requirement that the letters had not yet entered the mails prior to their delivery to the postmaster at the port of arrival of a vessel.

Figure 13-6. Scarce SHIP markings canceling an incoming ship-mail cover at Boston, Massachusetts, on August 7. This black-edged mourning cover was mailed under the 5¢ ship rate in effect from May 1, 1861, to July 1, 1863.
(James Lee collection)

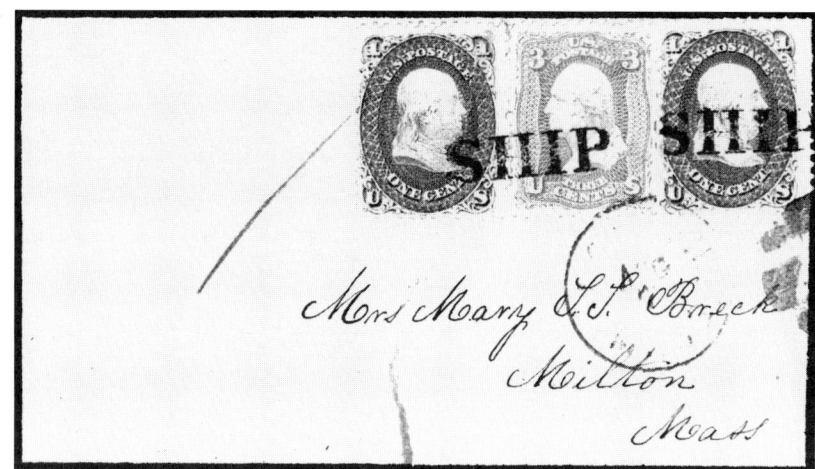

The definition is quite broad and obviously includes the category of what we are considering to be steamship letters. Other sections of the regulations make it clear that to be designated as a ship letter, the route of the vessel carrying the letter should not be over a "post road" (sea ways over which scheduled U.S. mail packets traveled were designated as post roads). With the initiation of subsidized mail routes between the East and West coasts via Panama during the 1840s, those sea routes, including stops at intermediate ports such as Havana and coastal towns in Mexico, were declared to be post roads.

Section 168 of the 1859 postal regulations set the postage rate for incoming ship letters and packets at 6¢ each when delivered locally from the office at which they are first received. It further stipulated that if the letter or packet was forwarded in the mail to other offices, the total charge would be 2¢ in addition to the ordinary rates of postage.

This rate structure set up the unusual situation that for a single-weight letter the charge at the 3¢ letter rate could be less for mail to a more distant destination, i.e., 2¢+3¢, than the 6¢ charged for a letter delivered locally at the port of arrival. Locally delivered ship mail was also not subject to weight limitations, thus, could be considered a special type of drop mail at a fee of 4¢ plus the ship fee of 2¢.

The masters of vessels of U.S. registry, which delivered ship letters to a port post office, were to be paid 2¢ for each letter. Letters deposited by masters of foreign flag packets would be accepted for the mails and charged postage at the ship rates, including the 2¢ fee, but the masters would not receive this fee for their service.

The laws and regulations were very firm in their requirements that each vessel from a foreign port carrying any letters or packets outside the mails deposit these with the postmaster at the port of entry.

To correct the inequity of having a ship letter to a local port address cost more than one addressed to another town, a change to the postal laws was enacted in 1861.

The Postal Act of February 27, 1861 (§9), effective May 1, 1861, reduced the incoming ship-letter charge to 5¢ for letters and packets if delivered locally at the port of arrival. If conveyed by post to other destinations, the total cost was to be 2¢ plus the ordinary rate of postage. This eliminated the previous higher charge for local port delivery compared to delivery beyond the port.

Upon being placed in the mails after arrival at a port, letters and packets were to be marked SHIP by the post office of deposit. However, this practice was not always followed. It appears that letters not prepaid were generally marked SHIP to show the reason for a postage-due charge, but that fully prepaid letters were often processed without any additional markings. This makes the finding of SHIP markings on covers franked with postage stamps less likely.

Almost all incoming ship letters were sent unpaid. While the covers were usually handstamped with the SHIP marking, the required postage in these cases was collected in cash from the recipient. No stamps appear on the covers, and this further decreases the odds of finding a legitimate ship cover with postage stamps affixed.

Prepaid examples marked with SHIP, of the 5¢ ship rate for local delivery or the 2¢+3¢ ship fee plus letter postage for domestic mail, although scarce, do offer a situation where the 1¢ Franklin could be used to make up the rate. **Figure 13-6** shows such a letter. While there is no indication of the origin of this mourning cover, it possibly was carried by a coastal steamer or from a more distant location such as the Caribbean, to Boston, where it was postmarked on August 7, and received the SHIP markings, which also served as cancellations. The year

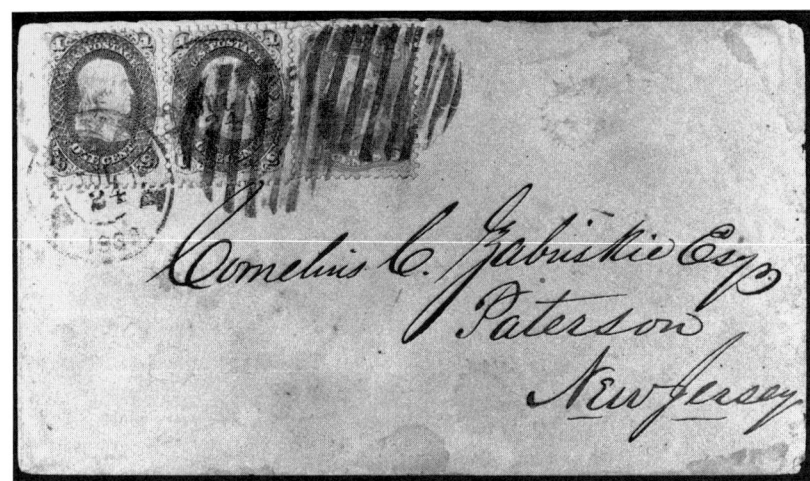

Figure 13-7. Example of a possible prepaid incoming ship letter, postmarked July 24, 1863. The 5¢ postage for the ship rate, paid by two 1¢ and a 3¢ stamp, is not correct for this date, but the letter is dated less than a month following the rate change. (See text for alternate explanation.)

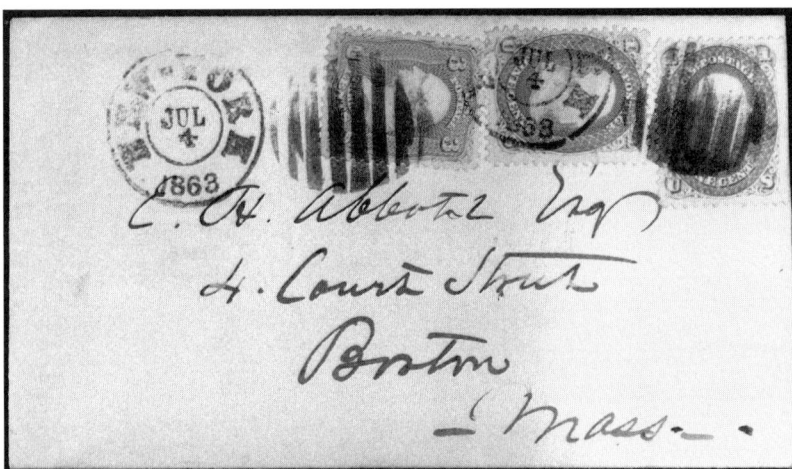

Figure 13-8. Another example of a possible incoming ship letter to New York City. It is dated July 4, 1863, just four days after the ship rate for a single letter had been raised to double the normal postage. If this is a ship letter, the two 1¢ plus one 3¢ stamps could have been affixed prior to the rate increase.

was probably 1862 or 1863. Although the ship rate had increased to 6¢ on July 1, 1863, some letters with 5¢ postage, which are suspected to be ship letters, are known from a short period following the change in rates. These will be discussed later in this section.

The Act of March 3, 1863 (§31), effective July 1, 1863, revised the ship and steamboat rates to make them less complicated and to bring them into agreement with the many other rate changes that were made by this act. The postmaster general was authorized to pay a sum, not to exceed 2¢ for each incoming letter conveyed by a vessel or steamboat, not under contract to carry mail, and deposited in the post office at the port of arrival. These letters, if for delivery in the United States, were to be charged double rates of postage. (This charge included the fee paid to the vessel.) This act also prohibited the payment of any way fees or other fees to persons carrying letters aboard contract mail vessels.

The regulations concerning this section of the act, further stipulated that the fee paid to noncontract vessels from a foreign port would be 2¢ for each letter addressed to a destination in the United States, and 1¢ for each letter arriving by inland waters or on coast routes from one domestic port to another. The provision denying payment to foreign flag vessels was no longer included in the law.

If the letters were unpaid, double-rate postage was to be collected from the addressee. If prepaid at the double rate, no additional charge would be made. Just why this last statement of the obvious was included is not known, but possibly it was to make it clear that the traditional 2¢ ship fee was not to be added. If a ship letter was partially prepaid, double the unpaid balance was to be collected upon delivery.

Stanley B. Ashbrook extensively researched the subject of prepaid ship covers and published his findings in articles in the *American Philatelist* [7:224-29] and in the privately printed *Ashbrook Special Service* he distributed to subscribers. In these writings, he also noted his opinion that SHIP marking were used as sort of a postage-due marking, and when the letter was completely prepaid, the marking was normally omitted.

A cover he specifically discussed is shown in **Figure 13-7**. This cover was postmarked on July 24, 1863, and has 5¢ in postage, prepaid by a 3¢ Washington and two 1¢ Franklins of 1861. Ashbrook was convinced that this was a prepaid letter, carried into New York outside the mails by ship with the 3¢ domestic postage plus the 2¢ ship fee paid with stamps. He also points out that the cover is dated 21 days after the July 1, 1863, revision in rates that increased the ship-letter rate to double the regular postage. His explanation of this discrepancy was that prepaid letters were for some time accepted at the lower rates, while unpaid or partially paid letters would be charged at the double rate. Ashbrook contended that while the law definitely provided for the double rate, it was intended only to apply to unpaid letters, and a loophole had been provided by the phrase "subject to such regulations as the Postmaster General may prescribe," which was included in the law [5:221]. Actually, that phrase, or similar wording, appears in most of the postal laws.

Ashbrook's reasoning, of course, is somewhat convoluted and is open to considerable debate, but it provides one explanation for use of 3¢-plus-2¢ postage on covers dated after the July 1, 1863, increase in rates.

Another cover that shows the same rate, but is dated earlier at New York on July 4, 1863, is shown in **Figure 13-8**. If this is actually a ship letter, the postage would probably have been applied before the increase in rates, and certainly under those circumstances, it would be expected that the post office would recognize the lower rate. These two examples could be used in support of Ashbrook's assumptions.

Another possible explanation for a cover with 5¢ in stamps would be an attempt by the sender to prepay both the letter postage and the new 2¢ local postage, not realizing that city carrier service was now included in the 3¢ postage rate at no additional cost. This change was widely publicized, but there are a number of covers that are franked with 5¢ in postage and postmarked shortly after the revision in rates went into effect on July 1, 1863.

The public announcements stated that the local delivery fee would be increased to 2¢, and this possibly led some readers to the conclusion that a letter sent to a town with carrier service would require 2¢ in addition to the 3¢ postage if it was desired to have the letter carrier-delivered to its destination. This theory was convincingly presented by John Kohlhepp in a *Chronicle* article [8:197], and this author is inclined to accept the explanation as very plausible. It has the advantage of being simple and straightforward. It is well-known that much confusion regarding drop and carrier fees resulted from the new regulations, and the dates of these 5¢-rate, possible ship-letter examples are from a period when misinterpretation of the new laws was very likely.

Other theories have been advanced to account for these and other unexplained covers with 5¢ postage. Another possible alternative answer is that for the uses in the first couple of months following the July 1, 1863, rate change, the Post Office Department accepted the short payment on ship letters during a grace period for those far away who desired to prepay their letters and who possibly were not yet aware of the postage increase.

However, without any special notations on the covers, there is no way to absolutely establish the facts concerning the intended purpose for this unusual rate during this particular period.

Steamship Mail

Steamship is another specified category of ocean mail and includes those letters of foreign origin that are brought into the United States aboard scheduled U.S. contract-mail vessels, but where the letters are not included in the locked pouch mail aboard the ship. These could be considered somewhat similar to way letters. The letter would be placed in the hands of a ship's officer at a foreign port-of-call and delivered to a post office at the U.S. destination port. Although prepayment was not required, the covers of interest to this compendium of uses of the 1¢ Franklin would necessarily be at least part-paid by stamps.

This class of mail was established by acts of Congress to authorize the handling of mail with countries where there were no postal treaties or agreements with the United States. However, the primary need and use for these directives was to provide procedures and rates for mail packets carrying letters outside the mails on the U.S. mail routes that came into being during the 1840s through the Caribbean and Gulf of Mexico to the Isthmus of Panama and from there to California.

The original rate for a ½-ounce letter carried less than 2,500 miles was 12½¢, and this was changed, effective July 1, 1851, to 10¢ for distances less than 2,500 miles and 20¢ for further distances. This steamship rate remained in force until 1864 and provided the rate structure during the early years of use of the 1861 1¢ Franklin.

It is interesting to note that the Post Office Department was meticulous in determining the exact distance that a letter was carried and assessing the proper rate. An official published announcement in December 1856 noted that the direct steamer distance between Panama (Aspinwall) and New York City was 2,345 miles. There-

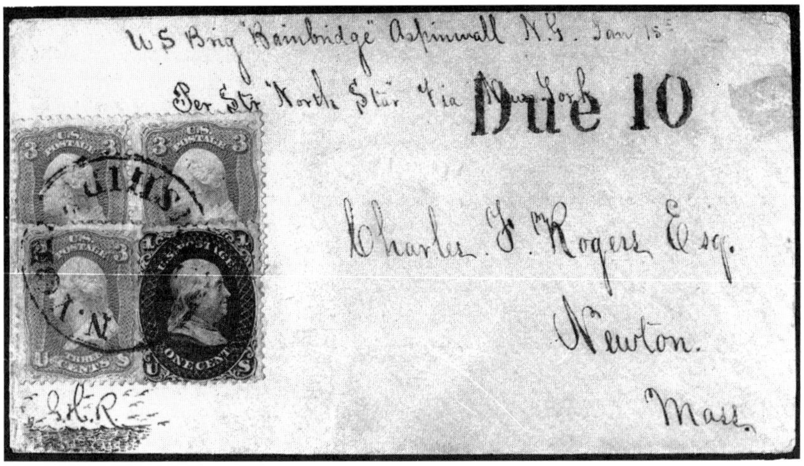

Figure 13-9. Underpaid letter originating on the U.S. brig *Bainbridge*, on January 15, at Aspinwall, New Granada. Endorsed "Per Str. 'North Star' Via New York," the cover was postmarked in New York as a steamship letter. It was franked at the 10¢ rate for distances less than 2,500 miles, but marked at New York "Due 10" because distance carried to Newton, Massachusetts, was over 2,500 miles.
(Richard B. Graham photo)

fore, the 10¢ steamship rate applied to all letters from Panama addressed to destinations that were no further than 155 miles from New York. Further destinations required 20¢ for the single rate.

Figure 13-9 shows a scarce cover that illustrates this point very well. This letter originated on the U.S. brig *Bainbridge* at Aspinwall, N.G. (New Granada), January 15 (1862 or 1863) with 10¢ prepaid by three 3¢ and a single 1¢ stamp. Aspinwall is now Colon, Panama, and the *Bainbridge* was stationed there to protect the Atlantic terminus of the route across the Isthmus of Panama. The letter was sent via the mail steamer *North Star* to New York, where it was postmarked with a circular N.Y. STEAMSHIP (no year date) handstamp, which also canceled the stamps. It was classed as a steamship letter and marked "Due 10" for collection upon delivery. The *North Star* was one of the contract-mail steamers of the New York-California route and operated on a regular monthly schedule between New York and Aspinwall.

For some years, philatelic opinion regarded the 10¢ due marking on this cover to have been required because the letter was overweight. However, current analysis suggests that the additional rate was assessed because the destination, Newton, Massachusetts, was about 200 miles from New York, and the letter was carried a total distance in excess of 2,500 miles.

Steamship covers bearing the 1¢ Franklin of 1861 are quite rare since the rate was 10¢ or multiples thereof, and in the cases where the letter was prepaid, it was usually paid with 10¢ stamps.

Prepayment on incoming letters is not common, but since many covers originated with U.S. citizens abroad who might possess stamps or have access to a supply, examples are not rare. These covers originated with individuals who were traveling or working at ports in foreign countries where there were no postal treaties with the United States, and where U.S. mail packets frequently docked. The simplest, and least expensive, way to send a letter home was to deposit it with an officer of a packet headed for the United States.

Much of the mail in this category had its inception in the Caribbean and Central American areas. U.S. mail ships were operating between the Isthmus of Panama and the United States on regular schedules. En route, the ships would put in at ports such as Havana or Vera Cruz. Letters destined for the United States could be put aboard in the care of the master or ship's purser and carried outside the mail until deposited in the post office at the destination port.

A major change to the steamship rate structure was made in 1864. Section 8 of the Act of 1864 (approved July 1, 1864, and effective the following month) established a uniform rate of 10¢ per ½ ounce, without reference to distance, for letters addressed to or received from foreign countries, when forwarded from or received in the United States by steamships or other vessels regularly employed in the transportation of the mails. This law did not apply in those instances where the United States had previously concluded a postal treaty with the originating or destination country. Prepayment was required for letters addressed to nontreaty countries, but could be prepaid or collected at destination on incoming letters. The 10¢ rate paid only for the U.S. postage.

Figure 13-10 illustrates an underpaid steamship cover. Although there is no indication of the point of origin on the cover, the cover's owner states that it was part of a large correspondence from the Caribbean, and that the paper is distinctive and matches other examples in the same correspondence that show Caribbean origin. This letter was part-paid with three 1¢ stamps. It was carried to New York outside the mails, and upon arrival it received the distinctive New York City N. YORK/STEAM-

Figure 13-10. Steamship letter to Hudson, New York. Unknown point of origin (probably Carribean area). The letter arrived in New York, by U.S. mail steamer, aboard which the cover had been carried outside the mails. It received a N.YORK/STEAMSHIP CDS, dated November 21 (year date indistinct). The letter was underpaid by three 1¢ stamps. It was marked "Due 7" to pay the balance of the 10¢ rate.
(James Lee collection)

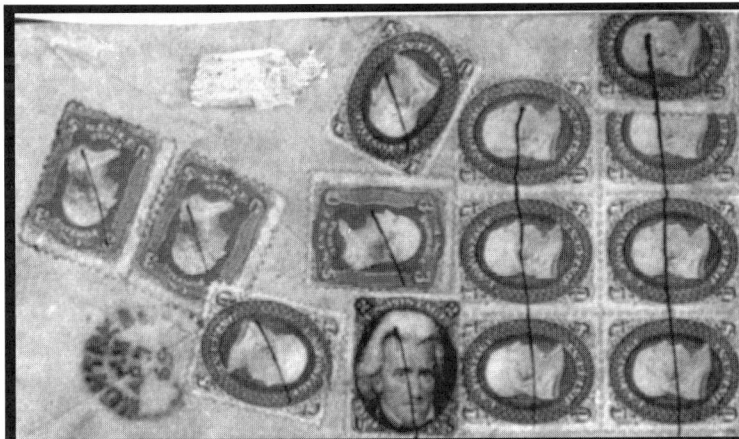

Figure 13-11. Steamship letter of unknown origin, addressed on the front side to Montreal, Canada, via New York. Postage totaling 20¢, made up of nine 1¢, one 2¢ (Scott 73) and three 3¢ stamps, is affixed to the reverse of the cover (pictured). The letter bears a Montreal receiving mark dated April 7, 1865. The front has a NewYork STEAMSHIP 10 in circle marking. A portion of the franking is provided by a scarce block of six of the 1¢ 1861.
(Courtesy of David G. Phillips)

SHIP marking with a manuscript "Due 7" added in ink to make up the required 10¢ rate. The STEAMSHIP CDS shows the date of November 21 with an indistinct year. The cover could have been mailed before or after the 1864 revision in rates since the distance from a Caribbean port to the destination at Hudson, New York, was less than 2,500 miles. The assigned 10¢ postage is correct for either the old or new rate structure. The New York post office recognized the 3¢ payment, and no penalty was assessed for the underpayment.

The reverse side of an interesting cover is shown in Figure 13-11. All of the stamps are on the back side of the cover, together with a Montreal, Canada, receiving mark dated April 7, 1865. The total of 20¢ in postage is prepaid by a combination of a rare block of six plus three single 1¢ Franklins, a 2¢ Jackson and three 3¢ Washingtons. All are pen canceled.

The front shows an address to a Lieutenant Colonel in the 60th Rifles, Montreal, Canada, with manuscript notations "Via New York" and "Recd April 7th 1865," together with a STEAMSHIP/10 in a circle marking (a tracing of which is shown with the illustration). This marking was usually used on letters that were totally unpaid and is known to have been used at New York City and other port cities as a postage-due marking.

The steamship rate of 10¢ paid for the postage to the United States. For letters that were to be forwarded to foreign countries, additional postage was required. During this period, the rate from the United States to Canada was 10¢ per ½ ounce. This accounted for the balance of the 20¢ postage that was prepaid.

The alternative analysis that the cover was overweight and a double-rate steamship postage assessed at New York can be discounted, for in that case Canada would have marked the cover for an additional 20¢ due for their 2x10¢ inland postage, which was not done.

Section 152 of the 1859 postal regulations listed ports on the Pacific coast of South America in Bolivia, Ecuador, Chile and Peru, and also in New Granada (Colombia), along with the postage rates to and from those countries. It was noted that for incoming letters to the United States, the rate was 10¢, which paid for U.S. postage only. This was to provide for letters from these ports that were transported by private or British ships (with British consular post office markings) to Panama or Aspinwall, where they were deposited with a U.S. mail packet on the California-New York route, and carried as steamship letters to the destination port.

In addition to the listings in the PL&R, the *U.S. Mail and Post Office Assistant*, which began regular monthly publication in October of 1860, carried a comprehensive and constantly updated record of foreign rates and handling procedures.

Mail to and from South American countries on the Atlantic coast were generally routed via England and the British mail system. However, it would have been possible, for example, to place a letter aboard a private vessel at Rio de Janiero, Brazil, prepaying a fee to the vessel for its delivery to Aspinwall and transfer to a U.S. packet. From there the letter would proceed to the New York post office, where it would be accepted as a steamship letter and marked at the 10¢ rate for postage due. While possible, covers showing such usage would be extremely scarce since the route via England would usually be much faster and certainly more reliable.

During the 1860s, frequent changes were made to the rates for foreign mails, but steamship mail remained fairly constant with regard to rates and routes. Postal agreements or treaties were made with a number of additional countries as the decade progressed, and scheduled packet services to Mexico, Brazil and others were instituted. As these services were established, the need for steamship letters decreased, and for the period from 1860 to 1870, the Caribbean was the main source of covers bearing STEAMSHIP markings.

Steamboat Letters

Covers carrying the markings STEAM or STEAMBOAT, and also those stamped WAY, originated with letters that were handed to the purser or deck officer of a steamboat at a landing or aboard the boat somewhere along a domestic waterway. Such routes were usually the navigable rivers of the United States, but lakes and coastal bays and routes were also included.

By regulation, such letters were to be deposited at the first landing of the vessel where there was a post office. However, this was not the general practice. Usually, to expedite the delivery of the letter, it was retained on board until the steamboat reached the post office to where the letter was addressed, or where it could be put into the mails for expeditious transmission to its final destination.

If the steamboat carrying the letter did not have a contract for carrying the mail, the vessel received from the post office 2¢ for each letter deposited (except for vessels plying the Great Lakes, who received 1¢ per letter). Upon receipt, the post office stamped each letter with STEAMBOAT or STEAM. Each of these markings meant exactly the same. The letter then became a steamboat letter as defined in the regulations.

If the steamboat carrying the letter had a mail contract with the Post Office Department, but no post office route agent aboard, the letter was carried as loose mail outside of the locked mail bags. When the steamboat reached the next post office, the letter was deposited and marked WAY by the postal clerk. For this service, the vessel was entitled to a fee of 1¢ for each way letter. Way fees only apply to situations where the letters are being transported by a contracted mail carrier. This special category of mail is further described in a later section.

In describing steamship mail, the 1859 Regulation (§178) recommended that all letters conveyed outside the mails by vessels not in the mail service (or vessels under contract and carrying mailbags with no route agent aboard) be prepaid. If prepaid, the master of the vessel, if under contract to carry the mail, could receive a 1¢ way fee, and if not under contract, the master was entitled to 2¢. These fees were not passed on to the addressee, but were absorbed by the Post Office Department in an unusually benevolent practice. If not prepaid, a letter aboard a noncontract vessel was to be treated as an unpaid ship letter: 6¢ if addressed to the port of arrival, and 2¢ plus regular postage if sent on by mail. This charge was changed on May 1, 1861, to 5¢ for local delivery at the port and 2¢ plus regular postage if forwarded on to another post office for delivery. On July 1, 1863, the rate was again changed to double the normal postage in accordance with the new ship rates effective as of that date.

It was also recommended that letters destined to be carried on vessels, outside the mails, be prepaid by government stamped envelopes, which could be carried by any carrier without restriction. Government envelopes with embossed franking were brought into existence primarily to ensure that the Post Office Department received proper postage on all letters that were transported, realizing that there were many places in the United States where the Department did not provide adequate service, and where private carriers such as express companies and steamboats were needed to carry the mail.

If a letter was posted aboard a mail steamboat carrying a postal route agent, it was required that the letter be prepaid, as was the case at any domestic post office. While the letter would be carried outside the mail as a loose letter under the care of the route agent, it would be

Figure 13-12. Carried by the steamer *Perry* from Newport to Providence, Rhode Island, where the three 1¢ stamps, paying the regular domestic postage rate, were canceled by a Providence CDS, dated August 4, 1862, and a black STEAM BOAT handstamp applied. The circular STEAMBOAT PERRY marking in red was applied aboard the steamboat. (James Lee collection)

deposited in the next post office the vessel reached, and there handled as a regular letter. The master of the vessel received no fee for carrying the letter.

The regulation also opened a loophole. After requiring in Section 176 of the 1859 regulations that mail-contract steamboat letters must be prepaid, it went on to state, "But should any chance to be unpaid they should be deposited by the route agent in the post office at or nearest the point at which they are received where the postmaster will treat them in all respects as other unpaid letters."

Effective May 1, 1861, the Act of February 27, 1861, and its accompanying regulations, made the charge for both prepaid and unpaid steamboat letters the same as the concurrent new ship charge: 5¢ to the port of arrival and 2¢ plus regular postage if sent on by mail. In an attempt to combine both ship and steamboat laws, the writers of the statute evidently did not realize that steamboat letters were normally prepaid, whereas ship letters were usually unpaid.

The provision requiring 2¢ plus the normal postage for steamboat letters was routinely disregarded, as is clearly demonstrated by the cover shown in **Figure 13-12**. This cover was posted in August of 1862, with the regular 3¢ domestic rate paid by three 1¢ Franklins. It bears the handstamped circular red purser's cachet of the Narragansett Bay steamer *Perry*. Such cachets were an advertisement of the boats, frequently applied to letters that were handed to the pursers or clerks aboard the steamboats of the 19th century.

The significant marking on the cover is the handstamp STEAM BOAT, which was applied at the Providence, Rhode Island, post office when the letter was deposited by the steamboat's clerk. This indicates the *Perry* was a noncontract boat at that time. Although the annual reports of the postmaster general during this period show mail contracts in effect to carry mail over a 28-mile route in Narragansett Bay between Providence and Newport, Rhode Island, it should be recognized that there were several steamboat companies operating on the bay in competition with each other. Although no data has been discovered on the subject, it may be assumed that the *Perry* was not one of the contract-mail carriers.

Another *Perry* cover, illustrated in **Figure 13-13**, verifies that the steamboat was on the Providence and Newport route. This cover bears a different STEAMBOAT marking, all one word, and was applied at Newport, on the other end of the line from the one shown in Figure 13-12. There was no CDS applied to this cover, and the stamps were canceled with the red steamer *Perry* cachet. The year of mailing cannot be definitely determined, but it is likely that it was before 1863 when the rates were revised.

On July 1, 1863, the rate was changed to double the regular postage, whether unpaid or prepaid, and this schedule of charges remained in force until 1882. Again, steamboat letters were considered exactly the same as ship letters under the new act. But in contrast with letters bearing the SHIP marking, very few, if any, unpaid letters with STEAM or STEAMBOAT are known, and no prepaid or partially paid covers posted after July 1, 1863, and bearing the 1¢ Franklin have been recorded.

It is interesting to note that, as far as the author is aware, ship and steamboat letters are the only examples of domestic mail subsequent to 1851 (other than drop mail) where a letter could be legally posted without prepayment and forwarded with postage collected upon delivery.

Figure 13-14 shows the only steamboat route-agent marking to be recorded to date with 1¢ Franklin stamps. This cover bears two strikes of the JUL 28/ ST. LOUIS & KEOKUK/ S.B. (S.B. for Steam Boat) handstamp,

Figure 13-13. Steamboat letter, carried on the outward-bound leg of the route, from Providence to Newport. Three cents in 1¢ stamps prepaid the letter rate. Stamps were canceled with the red STEAMBOAT PERRY in circle marking. Subsequently, three canceling strikes of the black STEAMBOAT handstamp, but no CDS, were applied at the Newport, Rhode Island, post office.

applied by the route agent to cancel the three 1¢ stamps paying the domestic postage. The year of mailing is established from manuscript docketing as being 1862. While route agents continued to postmark mail on most important Northern steamboat routes during the war, and covers showing these markings are available, much of this mail was in 3¢ government stamped envelopes, and practically all other letters were prepaid with 3¢ stamps. This rare cover was placed on board the steamboat, outside the mails, as a way letter in the care of the route agent. In accordance to Section 176 of the 1859 Postal Regulations, letters so deposited did not receive the 1¢ way fee.

Way Letters

A way letter is another specific category of mail. Its purpose was to establish procedures for handling mail that was picked up en route between post offices by a Post Office Department employee or contracted mail carrier. The mail carrier, as considered here, should not be confused with the letter carriers operating in large cities. The carriers that are relevant to this discussion are the mail carriers who regularly traversed long routes between post offices by means of wagons, stages, horseback, steamboats or, in some instances, on foot.

The method of transport does not enter into the determination of the classification. To be classed as a way letter, it must have been presented to a mail carrier on a regular mail route, and carried as a loose letter outside the mails to be posted at the next post office. These carriers normally carried locked bags of mail plus an unlocked container in which way mail could be temporarily deposited.

It is important to keep in mind the following distinction. If postal route agents were aboard the transport, they accepted the letter, postmarked it with their route-agent marker and placed it in a locked way bag to which they had a key. These letters were considered to be regular mail and were not classified as way letters. No fee for

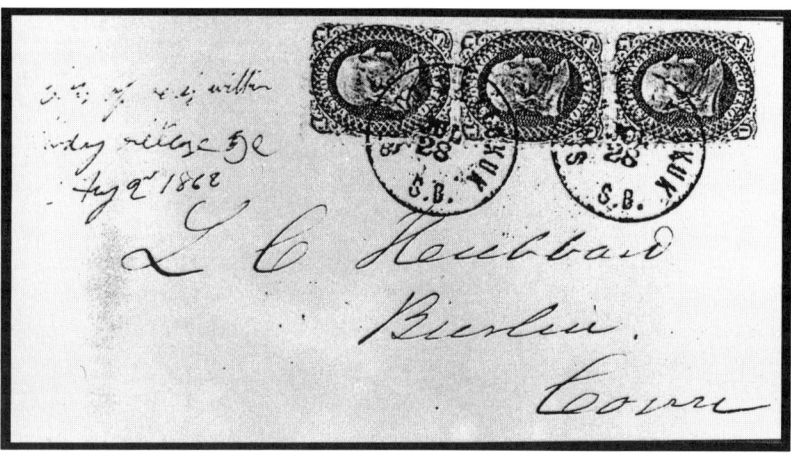

Figure 13-14. Scarce steamboat route-agent marking ST. LOUIS & KEOKUK/S.B. The cover is dated July 28, (1862), and addressed to Berlin, Connecticut. It was probably posted en route, with the letter rate of 3¢ prepaid.
(From a Henry A. Meyer photo)

the service was payable to the route agent.

By regulation, a mail carrier was required to accept mail that was given to him, providing he was at least a mile away from any post office on his route, and if not a route agent, he was authorized to receive reimbursement of 1¢ for this service.

Specifically, the PL&R of 1859 stated in Section 219 of the regulations:

> "Way letters are such letters as a mail carrier receives on his way between two post offices. The carrier will deliver them at the first post office at which he arrives. The postmaster will rate them with postage, writing against the rate the word 'way.' "

Section 222 further stipulated:

> "The postmaster will pay the mail carrier 1¢ if demanded for each way letter which he delivers to him, and add that cent to the ordinary postage on the letter."

The wording in sections 219 and 222, quoted above, is essentially the same as that found in earlier PL&Rs, dating back to 1825 and before. Way fees never were required to be prepaid, although as the 1860s approached, they frequently were. When the fee was not prepaid, the postmaster or clerk at the post office where the letter was turned in would rate the letter with 1¢ due, regardless of the amount of postage, and mark it WAY to explain the due charge. It should be noted that the way charge was a fee, independent of letter weight or distance to be sent.

Although way letters could originate from any type of mail transportation, the vast majority of them come from steamboats where, if not prepaid, a handstamped WAY identifies them.

Henry A. Meyer, a noted postal historian and specialist on inland waterway mails, remarked that he "had never seen a handstamped WAY marking that was not on a steamboat cover." The few manuscript WAY markings that are recorded generally originated from mail carriers not traveling on waterways.

Way covers where the fee was prepaid by stamp or cash were normally not given any special markings. When a 1¢ stamp was applied in addition to the regular postage to prepay a way fee, the 4¢ franking was the same as that required for city letter-carrier collection-to-the-mails service. This results in many possible way covers being misidentified as the more common city-carrier type.

The true way cover from the 1860s is a scarce item. As discussed in the previous section, steamboat mail decreased significantly with the beginning of the Civil War, and in 1863, new laws were passed eliminating the way fee. This meant there was only a short time between August 1861 and July 1863 when the 1861 stamps could be used on a way-for-fee letter. This combination of circumstances resulted in a relatively small number of covers with WAY markings being generated during the period.

Way letters showing use of the 1¢ Franklin are usually found on prepaid covers, without a WAY marking and with 3¢+1¢ franking. The postage plus way fee could, of course, be paid with four 1¢ stamps, but none has been recorded. In 1861 the great majority of post offices were still small offices and often some distance away from many of their patrons. The convenience of being able to hand a letter to a postal carrier along the road or river could save a trip to town and in many cases was well worth the extra penny that it cost.

Because of this convenience, it could be expected that a large number of way letters would have been handled, and a significant number would still be in existence. The contrary is true. They are difficult to find and, without WAY markings, almost impossible to identify without some reservations. This writer has never seen a 1¢ 1861 Franklin on a cover with a WAY marking.

Figure 13-15 illustrates a probable prepaid way cover. This interesting cover is postmarked at Hill, New Hampshire, on August 19, year unknown, but probably 1862, and addressed to Boscawen, New Hampshire. It carries the requisite 1¢ stamp in addition to the 3¢ domestic postage, and both the originating town and destination are small post offices without city carrier service. The towns are about 15 miles apart, and both are situated on the banks of the Merrimack River, with a post road connecting them. This cover can be classed as a way letter with a high degree of confidence.

The cover shown in **Figure 13-16** is a prepaid way letter to Canada. Originating at Toddsville, New York, a small post office in Otswego County, it is addressed to Ottawa, C.W. (Canada West). Three 3¢ and two 1¢ stamps were affixed by the postmaster, with some overlapping to get them all on the envelope, after applying the manuscript postmark, "Toddsville, N.Y., Dec. 26, 1862." This shows that the letter was originally stampless and was probably handed to a mail carrier on his way to Toddsville. Eleven cents was given to the carrier, which was turned in with the letter when the carrier reached the post office. It was rated for 10¢ postage for the ½-ounce postage to Canada, and 1¢ was credited to the carrier as his way fee.

While, in accordance with the Canadian/U.S. postal agreement, the 10¢ postage could be either prepaid or collect, with no partial payments being accepted and each country retaining all it collected, the way fee had to be prepaid. There were no provisions for it to be collected from the addressee and then returned to the United States.

The cover is backstamped "City of Ottawa/U.C./ DE 31/1862." The U.C. stands for Upper Canada and was synonymous with Canada West. This difference in geographical description results from an older practice of

Figure 13-15. A probable way cover from Hill, New Hampshire, to Boscawen, New Hampshire. The town and month marking is in a striking apple-green color with a black manuscript day of the month. The 1¢ stamp pays the way fee, and the 3¢ stamp pays the letter-rate postage.

Figure 13-16. Prepaid way cover to Canada. The cover bears a manuscript town mark, dated December 26, 1862, from Toddsville, New York. It is backstamped "City of Ottawa/U.C./DE 31/1862." The 11¢ in postage pays the 10¢ rate to Canada, plus the way fee of 1¢.
(Collection of Richard B. Graham)

using the upper and lower parts of the St. Lawrence River as a reference instead of the eastern and western parts of Canada. In either case, the dividing line was between Montreal and Quebec.

Figure 13-17 shows a cover considered by Ashbrook to have been a prepaid waterways way letter. The cover still retains Ashbrook's distinctive notation from 40 years ago. Franked with a 3¢ Washington and a 1¢ Franklin, it entered the mails at Dubuque, Iowa, where it was postmarked on February 18, 1862. It is most likely that this cover was delivered to the Dubuque post office from a steamboat plying the Mississippi.

Although way service by mail carriers continued for many years after the July 1, 1863, elimination of the way fee, the covers are generally indistinguishable from a standard letter, unless the contents or some marking or notation on the cover give some indication of an origin other than that indicated by the postmark.

Figure 13-18 shows a very unusual post-way-fee cover with a steamboat purser's marking. It is prepaid with three 1¢ stamps for the domestic rate and carries the circular handstamp cachet of the steamboat *Gladiator*. Applied directly over the purser's handstamp is a New Orleans CDS. The letter was placed in the mails at New Orleans on November 26, 1863, as a loose letter carried aboard a steamboat. No STEAMBOAT marking was applied to the cover at New Orleans, which indicates that no fee was paid to the boat. While the *Gladiator* did not have a mail-carrying contract, it also was not operating as a private vessel. For most of the war, it was under contract as a U.S. Army transport on the Mississippi River and its tributaries. This probably gave it a status similar to that of a mail-contract boat. The *Gladiator* was operating on the Mississippi north of Vicksburg until that strategic point and Port Hudson fell to the Union in July of 1863. The date on this cover indicates that the *Gladiator* must have been one of the early steamers to pass down the Mississippi to New Orleans after the river was reopened.

The above information suggests that this cover

may actually have been treated as a post-July 1, 1863, way letter, picked up en route by a vessel engaged in carrying the mails under military supervision. The September 1863 issue of the USM&POA published an order regarding mails on the Mississippi that included a directive that all mails for New Orleans, except those from Atlantic ports, were to be sent via Cairo, Illinois, and the Mississippi River.

Supplementary Mail

The scarce supplementary-mail postal markings of New York and Chicago present an interesting area of philatelic research and in the past have sparked considerable controversy.

Supplementary mail was a special service provided by the Post Office Department for dispatching mail after the regular mail had closed. Its use was limited to a few port cities within the United States for the dispatch of foreign mails, and to the city of Chicago for domestic mail (plus a special service to Canada).

Supplementary-mail service was available at New York City, San Francisco and San Pedro, California; Seattle, Washington; and at Chicago. But only New York City and Chicago provided special markings on the letters to show that such a service had been provided.

NEW YORK: The supplementary-mail service was initially authorized for New York City by the postmaster general in 1853 to provide special handling of mail to foreign destinations so that letters could be deposited almost up to the time of actual sailing of the mail vessel. There have been no published laws or regulations that contain authorization for this service, and as a result, early philatelists, at least until the first part of this century, did not evidence a great deal of interest in them. This changed in 1923 with Dr. W.L. Babcock's first published research on this interesting special service, and since that time, collectors have assiduously searched for covers and stamps showing supplementary mail processing.

A letter from the postmaster general, James

Figure 13-17. Probable way usage from Dubuque, Iowa, February 18, 1862, to Des Moines, Iowa, with 1¢ for the way fee, and 3¢ for the letter rate. Ashbrook's notations appear on the cover.
(Robert B. Meyersburg collection)

Figure 13-18. Carried aboard the steamboat *Gladiator* with 3¢ letter postage prepaid by three 1¢ Franklins, the cover shows the steamboat's circular handstamp. It entered into the mails at New Orleans on August 26, 1863, with the postmark applied directly over the boat's purser marking. The cover is addressed to Baltimore, Maryland.
(From the Henry Nowak collection, courtesy of David G. Phillips)

Campbell, dated July 7, 1853, to Isaac V. Fowler, the postmaster at New York City, is quoted as follows:

"Sir:
Your suggestions of yesterday's date, with reference to the plan proposed in my letter to you of the 2nd inst., for receiving letters up to the moment of sailing of the European steamers, at double rates of postage, are approved, and you will proceed to carry them into effect.
In conversation here, some weeks since, Mr. Riggs, one of the Directors of the New York and Liverpool U.S.M. St. Ship Company, remarked that he thought their company would be willing to provide, free of expense, a room to make up the mails in their office upon the wharf." [9:549]

The fee for the service was to be equal to, and in addition to, the normal postage. The service was primarily established as a result of the requests of merchants who wanted their mailed communications, price lists, and so on, to foreign destinations to be available for revision or mailing up until the last possible moment.

Schedules of the departure of mail-carrying vessels and their destinations, and the times when the mail for each vessel would be closed prior to the sailing, were published daily. Because of the time needed to process the mail and to bag and deliver it to the dock prior to the ship's departure, the closing of the normal mail preceded the sailing substantially. By leaving a mail bag open, and by specially processing mail that arrived later than the published closing time, it was possible to accommodate later arrivals. Initially, this service was thought by philatelic scholars to have been available only at the main post office, where the patron by paying the additional fee could obtain the special processing and the letter would be carried to the ship just before departure. Later research has established that service at the wharf was available from the very beginning.

A notice that appeared in the July 9, 1853, New York *Commercial Advertiser* clearly shows that to be the case [10:7].

"Post-Office, New York — Notice 9 July 1853
Letters for Europe, (excepting Spain and Portugal) per steamers from this port, will be received at a convenient point on the wharf from which the steamer sails, by Clerks from this office. The time for the reception of such correspondence, will be from 11:15 AM to 11:50 AM. No newspapers taken. Postages must be pre-paid in all cases as follows:

For Great Britain,	Am. Steamer,	48¢ per 1/2 oz.
Do do	Br. Steamer,	48¢ per 1/2 oz.
For Cont. Letters,	Am. Steamer,	42¢ per 1/2 oz.
Do do	Br. Steamer,	25¢ per 1/2 oz
July 8 1853	Isaac V. Fowler P.M."	

When the letter was given to the mail postal clerk along with the supplementary fee, it was rated and marked per regulations for foreign mail, postage affixed, if not previously applied, and bagged for last minute transport to the ship.

Figure 13-19. Off-cover example of the New York City SUPPLEMENTARY MAIL marking on the 1861 1¢ Franklin. This marking is aways in red.

The distinctive red marking (type A) illustrated in **Figure 13-19** was first recorded as being used on May 14, 1859, and the latest recorded use is June 1873 [9:112]. The fact that there have been no examples found for the period between the authorization of the supplementary-mail service in 1853 and 1859 was considered by Ashbrook to be because in the early years all of the supplementary mail was handled at the main post office and that no hand marking was used. He suggested also that the pier service did not begin until later, possibly 1859, and at that time a special marking was provided to identify the letters receiving this additional service. There is no confirmation for this theory, and in light of the postmaster general's supposition in 1853 that wharf space could be made available, and the newspaper notice concerning the pier service, it appears that Ashbrook was in error. However, it is a fact that no examples of covers with supplementary service have been identified from those years, so it is most likely that the type A handstamp was not used anywhere until 1859, and that early supplementary letters were processed without any special markings. Without some notation for identification, it would be impossible to distinguish a supplementary letter from a normal double-weight letter since the rate would be the same.

Use of the supplementary-mailing service was heavy at New York, and the vast majority of the letters were mailed at the wharf, as compared to the number deposited for supplementary service in the downtown post offices. The volume of supplementary mailings continued to increase, and by the early 1900s reached several thousand supplementary-mail letters to Europe for each steamship sailing. At that time, the supplementary post offices at the piers were opened an hour and a half before sailing time, and closed 10 minutes before the ship's departure. As many as five clerks were detailed to process the mails for some of the vessels [9:552].

The latest recorded supplementary-mail cover with a type A marking is dated April 18, 1872, and is addressed to Rome, Italy.

Beginning in 1873, a series of different markings were sequentially put into use until the supplementary-mail service was discontinued in 1939. These later markings are designated by Scott as types E, F and G, and are illustrated in the Scott U.S. specialized.

As previously mentioned, the pioneering philatelic research into the subject of supplementary-mail service was done by Babcock. In November of 1923, he published his original findings on the New York service in an *American Philatelist* article. He continued his investigations and also began the study of the Chicago supplementary-mail service. In 1939 he privately published a monograph titled, *Supplementary Mail Markings including Notes on Chicago, San Francisco, San Juan, P.R., and Honolulu*. This monograph essentially presented most of the information that was available on the subject to that time. Concurrently, Ashbrook had become interested in the area and submitted a manuscript on the subject to H.L. Lindquist, to be published in Lindquist's, *The Stamp Specialist*, Volume 5, 1941 (Orange Book). Lindquist accepted the manuscript but, before publishing it, forwarded it to Babcock for comments. These comments and a rebuttal to the comments by Ashbrook were included in the final publication and documented the substantial disagreements that existed between Ashbrook and Babcock.

The supplementary fee was paid in cash during the first three decades of this service. The reason for requiring payment by cash rather than stamps has long been debated.

Ashbrook was of the opinion that the fee was to be paid in cash instead of stamps to avoid any misinterpretation by the receiving post offices that might result from suspected overpayment. For example, the original postal treaty of 1848 with Great Britain established 24¢ as the rate for a single-weight letter. If a prepaid letter had its supplementary fee paid in stamps, the franking on the letter would amount to 48¢, with foreign-exchange markings that might only account for 24¢ of the total. This could possibly lead to some confusion at the post office in Great Britain. It seems reasonable that the U.S. Post Office Department would recognize this as a possible problem and easily avoid the possibility by requiring that the fee be paid in cash. Babcock disagreed with Ashbrook's hypothesis with respect to the reason for the cash payment, but did agree that it was paid in cash. Babcock felt it was analogous to the cash payments that were required for registry service, and that there was no specific motive for requiring that the payment be made in cash [9].

In 1868 some postal treaties were concluded that eliminated the cumbersome debiting and crediting between countries for each international letter. Subsequently, covers have been recorded that show double postage and that seem to be single-weight letters. These covers were most likely serviced as supplementary mail, although they do not have any markings that would indicate such service. When the fee was paid in stamps, there would be no requirement to use any other indication to show receipt of the additional fee.

Supplementary-mail covers with the type A marking are quite scarce. As of 1976, only 55 had been recorded, most of these to England. Ashbrook pointed out that the number of off-cover stamps that showed the type A marking as a cancellation was substantially greater than the number of recorded covers with the marking. On the covers, the supplementary-mail markings seldom touched the stamp. In addition, he had seen off-cover examples with original gum.

Ashbrook's explanation for this unusual situation was that when the supplementary fee was paid, the sender was presented with a stamp of equal value canceled with the type A marking as a receipt for the cash fee. This was an ingenious hypothesis, and to date, it still remains a likely possibility, neither proved nor verified [9:537]. Babcock again disagreed with this explanation and suggested that the lack of supplementary covers compared to off-cover examples was just a result of the European practice during the past century of removing all stamps from covers, because at that time the postal history value of covers had not yet been realized, and off-cover stamps were easier to handle.

The author tends toward Ashbrook's theory. The fact that almost all of the recorded covers show the supplementary marking on the cover without touching the stamp, and that most off-cover examples show the marking reasonably centered on the stamp, gives credence to the possibility that many of these off-cover examples could have been given to patrons of the service as a receipt. Such a practice also would have assisted in accounting for the fees collected by the post office clerks at the wharf.

Although more plentiful than covers, single stamps showing the type A supplementary marking are also scarce. The author has never seen a cover bearing the 1¢ 1861 stamp and a New York supplementary marking. Only three off-cover examples of markings on the 1¢ Franklin are known to the author, including the one shown in Figure 13-19, but there may be a small but significant additional number of these off-cover Franklins residing in collections around the world.

CHICAGO: Covers showing the Chicago supplementary-mail markings are also scarce. There are only about five such covers recorded that also include franking by the 1¢ Franklin.

Figure 13-20. Scarce example of a Chicago supplementary-mail cancel, with two strikes on three 1¢ stamps paying the letter rate on a cover to a destination to the west of Chicago, Illinois. Markings are in the typical bright blue used in Chicago.

The Chicago service differed from that of New York in two important aspects: No additional fee was paid for the service, and it was evidently limited to domestic mail and letters to Canada.

In 1939, Babcock wrote a short article, for inclusion in Norona's *Cyclopedia*, on the Chicago supplementary service. The article summarized the information known at that time and listed the known covers [11:65-69]. The reason for the supplementary service was still a subject for discussion, and two hypotheses were suggested: (1) a final or late bag of unsorted mail to be delivered to the train just before leaving, and which was to be sorted at the next distribution office, or (2) a sealed bag containing sorted mail received after the closing of the regular mail, and which was to be placed on trains to specific post offices. The latter hypothesis is the more likely theory, as later evidence shows.

The Chicago Post Office published a notice in the *Chicago Press and Tribune* on January 23, 1860, as follows:

"Supplementary letter mails will be hereafter, made up in the evening only, for Toledo, Cleveland, Erie, Buffalo, Washington City and all principal Eastern cities, thirty minutes after the advertised closing of the evening mails at this office.

A supplementary letter mail will be made up at the same time for Cincinnati and the same arrangement will also extend to Canada . . .
I. Cook, P.M. [12:106]"

In the early 1860s, railway post offices had not yet come into being, and the mail was sorted before being placed aboard the trains in sealed sacks. (A small amount of mail sorting and processing was sometimes done by route agents on the trains, but this was limited, as is attested by the scarcity of route-agent covers.)

Chicago was a distribution center and sorted much of the mail coming into it. Evidently, some of the fast eastbound trains departed for the eastern cities soon after the close of the mails for the day, and the Chicago postmaster arranged to put late-posted letters aboard these trains as a service to the public at no extra charge. It is suspected that this service only applied to letters for eastern cities, and for many years no examples of supplementary-mail letters were found with destinations to the south or west of Chicago.

Subsequently, a few letters have surfaced addressed to cities to the south or west. **Figure 13-20** shows an example of a letter mailed to Galena, Illinois, which is in the northwest corner of the state. Covers to these non-eastern cities are considered to have been accidentally processed as supplementary-mail letters.

The supplementary-mail cancellations of the Chicago Post Office were used from about 1857 to 1866. On most recorded examples, the handstamps served as both a town/date marking and cancellation. Only two types of

Type CA (Babcock)   Type CB (Babcock)
C (Scott)   B (Scott)

Figure 13-21. Chicago supplementary-mail markings. Type CA was used from 1857 to 1864 and almost always is struck in blue. Type CB was used from 1862 to 1866 and usually is struck in black. A variation of type CB also exists with the bar (cradle) under the day replaced by the last two digits of the year date.
(Drawings adapted from W.L. Babcock)

Special Services

Figure 13-22. Only recorded Chicago supplementary-mail marking to Canada. The cover is addressed to Belleville (Ontario), Canada West and is franked with three 3¢ and a single 1¢ to pay the 10¢ letter rate to Canada. It is marked with a red U. STATES/10 PAID handstamp.
(Courtesy Robert A. Siegel Auction Galleries)

Figure 13-23. Domestic use of the Chicago supplementary-mail service to Williamstown, Massachusetts. The cover is dated May 25. The stamps are canceled in blue.
(James Lee collection)

markings are known. These are illustrated in **Figure 13-21**. Type CA (Babcock), also identified as type C (Scott), is the earlier-used marking and is known from 1857 to 1864. Type CB (Babcock) or type B (Scott) was used between 1862 and 1866. No covers with CB-type markings are known used with the 1¢ Franklin. All of the recorded CA-type markings are in blue (with one exception in black), and the majority of the recorded CB-type markings are in black.

Figure 13-22 illustrates a rare use to Canada, and **Figure 13-23** shows a domestic use to Massachusetts.

To date the listing of Chicago supplementary-mail covers with the use of the 1¢ 1861 Franklin is:

1. three 1¢	Jan. 8	To Providence, Rhode Island
2. three 1¢	? 23	Galena, Illinois
3. three 1¢	March 25	Williamstown, Mass.
4. 1¢ + 2¢	Sept. 29 (63)	Baltimore, Maryland with a North Branch marking
5. 1¢ + three 3¢	Sept. 28	Belleville, Canada

References

1. Mueller, Barbara R. "U.S. — Pre-1855 Registry System." *The Congress Book*. 1963. Twenty-Ninth American Philatelic Congress.

2. Mueller, Barbara R. "U.S. Registry Fees, 1855-1955." *The Congress Book*. 1955. Twenty-First American Philatelic Congress.

3. Alexander, Thomas J. "Registration." *Chronicle* 139-140. August-November 1988.

4. Reprint of *United States Mail and Post Office Assistant*. Collectors Club of Chicago edition. 1975.

5. Graham, Richard B. "Registration of Letters, 1861-1869." *Chronicle* 139-140. August-November 1988.

6. Graham, Richard B. "The 1861-69 Period." *Chronicle* 53, 1966.

7. Ashbrook, Stanley B. "Exceptional Uses of U.S. Covers of the Period 1851-1863 Inclusive." *American Philatelist*. February 1943.

8. Kohlhepp, John. "The Carrier Service: Final Years of the Fee-Based System." *Chronicle* 115. August 1982.

9. Ashbrook, Stanley B. "The New York Supplementary Mails." *American Philatelic Miscellany, Selections from the Stamp Specialist*, Susan M. MacDonald, Editor. Quarterman Publications. 1976.

10. Hubbard, Walter and Richard F. Winter. *North Atlantic Mail Sailings, 1840-75*. U.S. Philatelic Classics Society Inc. 1988.

11. Babcock, W. L. "Supplementary Mail Cancels of the Chicago Post Office (1861-1865)." *Cyclopedia of United States Postmarks and Postal History*. Edited by Delf Norona. Quarterman reprint. 1975.

12. Karlen, Harvey M. "Chicago Supplementary Mail Cancellations." *Chicago Postal History*. Collectors Club of Chicago. 1971.

CHAPTER 14

Armed Forces and War-related Mails

The story of the Civil War military mails is a fascinating philatelic subject, and one whose breadth and depth is greater than the space allotted in this book can accommodate. The war had a profound effect on postal communications, and the covers that have survived provide a particularly rewarding field for collecting and study.

The designator "Armed Forces Mail" is used to describe mail that was handled both by the U.S. Post Office Department and the Army or Navy postal systems. This includes official military letters, and much of the personal mail of soldiers and sailors and their correspondents.

"War-related mail" is the mail handled only by the U.S. Post Office Department, and where the covers show some indication of Civil War relevance. These items include patriotic covers, advertising covers with a patriotic theme and covers from Sanitary Fair organizations. Some special philatelic items, such as "Mails Suspended" handstamps and "Old Stamps Not Recognized" markings, which fall within this classification, have been discussed in previous chapters.

It was only a month after the disastrous first Battle of Bull Run when the new issue of 1861 stamps was initially distributed, and the philately associated with this issue reflects the momentous events that occurred during the war years. In 1861, Postmaster General Montgomery Blair was faced with the challenge of not only providing an effective postal service to a country that was divided by war, but also to a large armed force that grew in size hourly and was constantly on the move.

Fortunately, the United States had in Blair a man of uncommon ability and initiative. During his tenure of office, between 1861 and 1864, he improved the entire postal system, introducing many innovations that provided better service to the public. His guidance and support to the army in the early years of the Civil War was crucial to the military-run postal system that provided the collection and delivery of mails within the army units. The military postal system operated separately from the Post Office Department. Army postal clerks were not, in general, authorized to perform many of the normal civilian postal functions such as issuing money orders, canceling letters or officially stocking and selling stamps.

Obviously, with large armies, often operating in Southern territory, transferring the mail between civilian and military jurisdictions posed a tremendous logistical problem. Close cooperation was needed, and Postmaster General Blair and his staff were instrumental in advising and working with the military to establish a system that successfully distributed and moved the mails during this difficult period.

The amount of mail increased rapidly during the early years of the Civil War. Many young men, who had never previously had the occasion to write a letter, now found themselves a long way from home, and the only contact was by mail. In turn, these soldiers and sailors received letters from their families and friends. All of this personal correspondence added significantly to the burden of the postal service. In addition, tremendous increases in commercial mail and official correspondence resulted from the war effort. In spite of losing almost a third of the postal system to the Confederacy, the total revenue of the Post Office Department increased each year.

In the early months of the war, a system of handling armed forces mail was developed for the federal Armies in the east. Shortly after hostilities began, large numbers of troops were brought to Washington to protect it from attack by the Confederacy. The number of military units in the vicinity of Washington, and the fact that it was the central headquarters for all military operations, made it a logical choice to be the major initial distribution center for mail to the military. Most of the mail to military units east of the Alleghenies was distributed from Washington, D.C. To expedite the operation, a military department or section was established at the Washington post office.

Mails addressed to soldiers and naval personnel in care of their organizations were sent from the post offices of origin to Washington where they were sorted and placed in containers to be given to authorized military agents who then transmitted them to the proper military units. Lists of the units to be serviced from the Washington post office were provided by the military. These units numbered as many as 800 regiments and batteries, whose locations ranged from New Orleans to units along the entire eastern seaboard, and included most of the Shenandoah Valley area. The postmaster at Washington, Sayles J. Bowen, reported that the Washington post office received and sent an average of 250,000 military letters per day [1:70].

Military mail to western and outlying organizations was handled primarily by the Post Office Department. It was forwarded to the post office nearest to the location of the unit, and there was turned over to the military for delivery. As the western armies grew, St. Louis, Missouri; Cairo, Illinois; Wheeling, Virginia (West Virginia); Louisville, Kentucky; and a few other post offices performed a regional distribution function similar to that of Washington, D.C., but on a smaller scale.

In addition to devising a workable system to deliver the military mails, Blair was faced with the loss of more than 8,000 post offices to the Confederacy and disruptions to the entire civilian mail system as a result of the war.

Early in 1861, the idea of a violent and long-lasting war was not widely held. It was thought that the Southern states would quickly come to their senses, and that after limited conflict, things would return to normal. Even after the formal secession of many of these states, the postmaster general directed that mail service be continued in them. He was the target of much criticism for this action and defended his position by outlining the advantage of open communications. He pointed out that such communications provided insurance that the South would receive objective news from the North that had not been distorted by propaganda. Open communications also provided information from Northern sympathizers in the South concerning the military and political actions, and maintenance of the important commercial ties between the North and the South.

In March of 1861, John H. Reagan was appointed Confederate postmaster general. He rapidly took over control of the federal post offices and routes that were located in the South. It appears that Reagan and Blair remained in contact for some time and attempted to provide order in the changes that were taking place. Reagan directed his postmasters to close their accounts with Washington, to return all unsold stamps and envelopes, and to pay all accounts due. This was to be done by May 31, 1861. Subsequent to that date, mail operations in the South were to be exclusively the province of the Confederate Post Office Department [2:164]. History shows that the majority of Southern postmasters did not follow these orders. Blair reported that as of October 1, 1861, $207,000 worth of stamps and stamped envelopes remained unaccounted for in the hands of postmasters in the disloyal states [1:571]. By today's standards, this does not seem like enough money to justify demonetizing the old issue. However, the dollar was worth a lot more then, and also there was much less tolerance for embezzlement. Debts were to be paid regardless of circumstances. Morever, every dollar that the South could raise would strengthen its war effort.

At the beginning of April, Blair petitioned postmasters in the South to affirm their willingness to assume personal responsibility for stamps and supplies they had in hand or would be sent to them. About 1,200 of these requests were sent out, and about 900 returned. There were only 20 replies refusing the request. Blair continued to supply the 880 offices with stamps and envelopes until June 1, 1861, when it appeared that the postal service to the South could no longer be maintained [3:571].

Blair issued a directive on May 27, 1861, to the effect that mail service to the Confederacy would be suspended "from and after the 31st instant." This action was discussed in some detail in Chapter 1. Tennessee was not included in the directive since it had not yet seceded. Service to "Western Virginia" via Wheeling was also maintained. It is important to note at this point that although service to the South was discontinued, there was no prohibition of receiving mail from or sending mail to the Confederacy. For about a week, until Tennessee seceded on June 8, 1861, there was an open route for mail between the federal post offices at Nashville and Memphis, Tennessee, and the Confederate post office at Louisville. Several private carriers, of whom the Adams Express Company is the best known, conveyed private and commercial mail between these points. Although it is estimated that thousands of letters were handled by these private carriers, examples from this short period are extremely scarce.

Considerable mail to foreign destinations from the South was routed in this manner since the federal blockade of the Eastern seaboard, and the lack of Confederate postal conventions with foreign countries, precluded effective direct mail transmission. The federal government was less than pleased at the amount of mail arriving from the South, paid for by U.S. postage stamps that Southern postmasters had sold but not accounted for. The postmaster at Louisville was instructed on June 24, 1861, to remove all stamps from Southern mail and forward them as unpaid. Letters to foreign destinations for which prepayment was compulsory were to be sent to the Dead Letter Office. The task of removing stamps from thousands of letters without damaging the contents was formidable, and the Louisville postmaster compromised by stamping each of these letters as SOUTH^N LETTER/UNPAID [2:168].

These actions predated the issue of the 1861 stamps by about two months, but they are of particular interest to this discussion for they provided the first instances of the demonetization of the 1857 stamps. Naturally there are no examples showing franking by the 1861 1¢ Franklin, but some examples of the 1861 issue used on envelopes with an Adams Express Company corner card have been recorded.

The situation regarding mail between the Union and the Confederacy was finalized by President Lincoln's proclamation of August 10, 1861. This required the cessation of all open commercial intercourse with the South, effective August 16, 1861. Coincidentally, this was the date the new 1861 issue of stamps was first delivered to the U.S. Post Office Department by the National Bank Note Company.

Subsequently, on August 26, 1861, Blair issued the following order [2:170]:

> "The President of the United States directs that his proclamation for the 16th, interdicting commercial intercourse with the South, shall be applied to correspondence.
>
> Officers and agents of the Post Office Department will, without further instructions, lose no time in putting an end to the written intercourse with these states by causing the arrest of any express agent or other person who shall after this order, receive letters for transmission to or from said states, and will seize such letters and forward them to this department.
>
> (signed) M. Blair,
> Postmaster General"

The only legal mail after this directive between the North and the South consisted of correspondence with prisoners of war, a few special-case civilian letters and necessary official interchanges. These were transmitted under controlled conditions via "Flag of Truce" exchange points.

Armed Forces Mail

One of the problems that soldiers had in posting mail was their frequent lack of postage stamps. Stamps were seldom available for purchase in the encampments, particularly during the early part of the war. Even when available, a large number of soldiers had no funds with which to buy the stamps. To remedy this situation, §11 of the Act of July 22, 1861 (Mustering Act) provided that soldiers' letters could be mailed without prepayment. Postage at the normal rate would be collected upon delivery. To qualify for this handling, the letter was to be endorsed "soldier's letter," marked with the sender's military unit and certified by the signature of a staff or other specified officer. This provision was reaffirmed by §27 of the Postal Act, effective July 1, 1863.

All commissioned officers were required to prepay their postage. It was probably considered that they would have an easier time obtaining and purchasing the necessary stamps. These acts (§1, PL July 24, 1861) also provided for the free forwarding of letters addressed to soldiers or sailors, including commissioned officers who had been transferred under orders. This resulted in many covers being endorsed "Follow the Regiment," which reminded postmasters not to charge the additional forwarding rate that would normally have been assessed.

The difficulty in getting stamps to individual soldiers could have been prevented to some degree if the prohibition against selling stamps at a profit (§2, Act of March 3, 1855) had been relaxed. Civilian "sutlers" were present in many Army units, and most soldiers had contact with them. The sutlers operated a sort of mobile predecessor to today's post exchanges and provided necessities to the troops such as soap and tobacco. If they had been able to sell stamps at a reasonable profit, the problem of prepaying postage would have diminished. Provisions were made (§9, Act of July 1, 1864) for stamps to be sold to anyone at a discount of 5 percent in amounts of $100 or more, and also a 5-percent discount for stamped envelopes in quantities of 500 envelopes or more. But the law prohibited the buyer from reselling the stamps at a profit. A small change in the law could have made a lot of difference. Of course, the fact that individual soldiers were frequently without funds and welcomed the opportunity to send a letter "collect" should not be overlooked.

The Act of 1861, granting the privilege of posting mail without prepayment, did not include the Naval and Marine forces. This oversight was corrected, in accordance with a suggestion by Blair in his report for 1861, by the Act of January 21, 1862, §1, which specifically extended the privilege to sailors and marines [4:261].

Another special privilege was granted to the armed services in 1864. By the provisions of §1 of the Act of January 22, 1864, articles of clothing not exceeding 2 pounds in weight could be sent to any private or non-commissioned officer in the armies of the United States at a rate of 8¢ per 4 ounces, or fraction thereof. The Navy and Marines again seem to have been overlooked, but it is likely that they also shared in this benefit.

A precedent for special mailing privileges for the armed services had been established during the Mexican War. All mail (up to 1 ounce) addressed to officers, privates and musicians of the U.S. Army stationed on the border, or in Mexico, was entitled to be received free of charge. Mail was to be endorsed "belonging to the army." The law remained in force for the duration of the Mexican War and for three months after its termination. It should be noted that this occurred before the mandatory prepayment of postage, so most mail was sent collect. Mail from soldiers required postage to be paid by the recipient.

Examples of covers marked "soldier's letter" from the Civil War period are not particularly scarce. However, since the great majority of them have no stamps attached, they have been of primary interest to postal historians and have not been sought after by most stamp collectors. "Soldiers' letter" covers where some sort of postage has been prepaid by stamps are genuinely scarce. These usually originated from postage being paid by an intermediate agency such as the Sanitary Commission organizations, or where the sender had only enough postage to partially pay the rate, or where a preprinted soldier's-letter envelope was used as a convenience by an officer,

Figure 14-1. Preprinted "Soldier's Letter" envelope. Camp Van Buren, Tennessee. The letter entered the mails at Louisville, Kentucky, on April 3, 1862, and was postmarked with a dark-blue duplex canceler. This is an example of the 10¢ transcontinental letter rate to Sacramento, California.

Figure 14-2. Scarce prepaid soldier's letter addressed to Bethlehem, Pennsylvania, with 5¢ paid for the ship rate in effect from 1861 to 1863. This possibly originated at a coastal Army post and was carried by private vessel to Old Point Comfort, Virginia, where it entered the mails and was postmarked on November 22 (probably 1862).

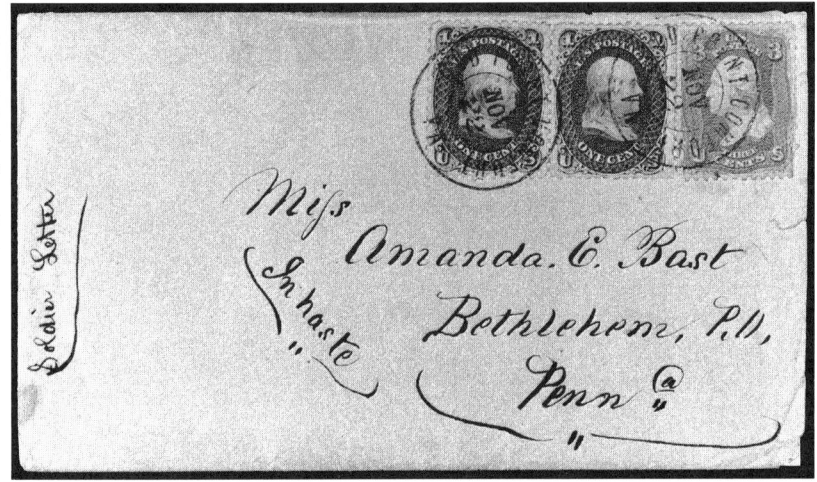

and postage affixed.

With the large amounts of soldiers' mail originating from many organizations, it was not long before specially printed envelopes were made to include all of the information for certification except the certifying officer's signature. An example of one of these envelopes from the 10th Regiment, Wisconsin Volunteers, is shown in **Figure 14-1**. This particular envelope was not used for an unpaid soldier's letter, but was prepaid, probably by a commissioned officer, at the 10¢ transcontinental rate to California. The sender marked the cover as originating at Camp Van Buren, Tennessee. It entered the mails on April 3, 1862, at Louisville, Kentucky.

As the war progressed, empathy for the soldiers, both officially and by the public, increased. Much leeway was given to soldiers' mail. Covers that did not meet all of the criteria for special handling were often transmitted without penalty. Efforts were made to ensure that soldiers' mail, even when not specifically endorsed as such and ending up in the Dead Letter Office, was forwarded to the destination without penalty. Third Assistant Postmaster General A.N. Zevely specifically instructed the DLO to reprocess soldiers' letters and to send them to the destination post office for another attempt at delivery without extra charge. It was realized that many of these letters may have been the last letters from soldiers who later died or were killed, and Zevely wanted every effort made to deliver them.

Figure 14-2 illustrates a rare example of a prepaid soldier's letter. The cover carries the endorsement "Soldier Letter," and it also has the distinction of being a ship letter with a prepayment of the 5¢ ship postage rate. As noted in Chapter 13, the postal law of February 27, 1861, provided that letters carried outside the mail on private vessels be delivered to a post office at the first port of call and charged with 5¢ postage. Two cents of this amount was to be paid to the master of the vessel as his reimbursement for carrying the letter.

Armed Forces and War-related Mails

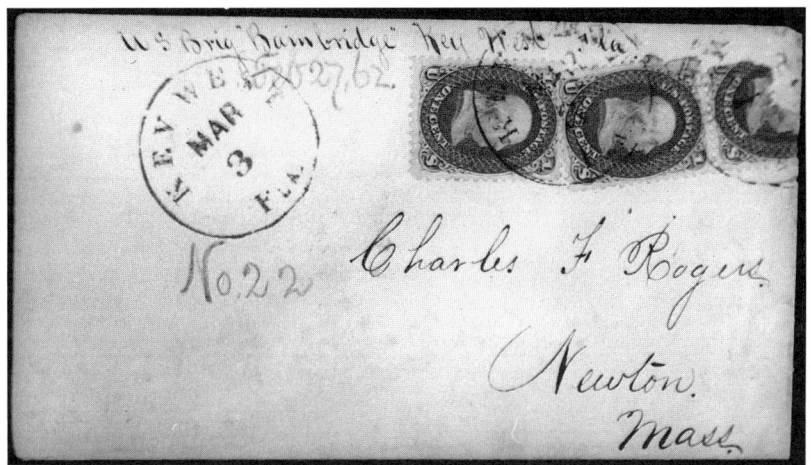

Figure 14-3. Naval letter originating on the U.S. brig *Bainbridge*, entered into the mails at Key West, Florida, on March 3 (1862). Domestic postage was paid with three 1¢ stamps. Manuscript "No. 22" and "Feb 27, 62" docketing is on the cover. (Richard B. Graham photo)

It might be surmised that this cover was written by a soldier stationed somewhere along the Eastern seaboard or Gulf Coast at one of the Army installations where there was no U.S. post office. He was in a hurry to get the letter posted and did not want to wait until the next Navy mail packet or supply ship picked up his organization's mail. The address suggests that the addressee may have been a lady friend, and the sender did not want it to be a collect letter. He therefore affixed 5¢ in postage and handed the letter to one of the officers of a private vessel that was in the local harbor, to be mailed at their next port of call. The vessel put in at Fortress Monroe, and the letter was deposited at the Old Point Comfort post office, where it received a 22 NOV postmark and was sent on its way via the regular mails.

The reason for the "Soldier Letter" endorsement may be that the writer originally intended to send the letter as an unpaid soldier's letter and then changed his mind.

Other than soldiers' letters, prepaid covers to and from military personnel are plentiful. Many historical and interesting examples showing the use of the 1¢ Franklin can be found.

Letters to and from naval addresses are much scarcer than their army counterparts. The number of individuals serving in the naval units was only a small fraction of those in the Army, and naval covers are relatively difficult to obtain. A substantial percentage of the few surviving covers addressed to naval personnel seem to have been addressed to individuals aboard ships of the blockading squadrons. The federal blockade of Southern ports and coastal waters was conducted by five squadrons, the North and South Atlantic, the East and West Gulf, and the West India blockading squadrons. The cat-and-mouse tactics and confrontations between the Northern blockaders and the Southern blockade runners provide some of the most interesting and exciting tales of the Civil War, and a lot of history is represented by the covers to and from these ships.

Three outstanding naval covers from the collection of Richard B. Graham are illustrated in Figures 14-3 through 14-5. **Figure 14-3** shows a letter, paid by three 1¢ stamps at the domestic rate. This cover originated aboard the U.S. brig *Bainbridge* early in 1862, while the *Bainbridge* was engaged in blockade duty in the Gulf of Mexico. It was a successful tour, and two schooners attempting to run the blockade were captured.

The cover entered the mails at Key West on March 3, 1862. The year date is ascertained by pencil docketing, "Feb 27, 62," and "No. 22." on the cover, probably by the addressee at Newton, Massachusetts. These notations probably refer to the date that the contents were written and the number of the letter. During the Civil War, it was not unusual for correspondents to track their letters by assigning them sequential numbers.

Key West, off the southern tip of Florida, was an important strategic base for the Union. It never was under Confederate control and was protected by Army troops plus a substantial fort with twin bastions. These, and the continued presence and superiority of the federal Navy, prevented any serious occupation threat from the South. Its location was almost in the center of the area monitored by the Eastern Gulf Blockading Squadron, and it provided a convenient port where blockading and other Union ships could put in and be supplied. Although the Key West Post Office was in operation throughout the entire conflict, war-period covers with a Key West CDS are scarce, and those franked with the 1¢ Franklin are rare.

Figure 14-4 shows a cover from a famous blockade ship, the *USS Santiago de Cuba*. During its tours in the South Atlantic and West Indian Blockading Squad-

The United States 1¢ Franklin 1861-67

Figure 14-4. Scarce multiple-rate Naval cover. The cover originated on the *USS Santiago de Cuba* and entered the mails at Baltimore on May 19 (1863). It is addressed to Philadelphia. The cover is handstamped with two strikes of a distinctive ship's marking and franked with 15¢ postage to pay the 5x3¢ rate for an overweight letter.
(Richard B. Graham photo)

rons, this ship amassed more than $1,500,000 in prize money, which was shared by the crew. This was the largest amount for any of the blockading ships during the war. The circular handstamp with the enclosed ship's name and seven-point star was probably applied by the paymaster's clerk. Naval ships during the Civil War usually assigned the responsibility of handling the mail to the paymaster's office. The cover was postmarked at Baltimore on May 19. From records of the ship's locations, it is likely that the year of use was 1863. During April and May of that year, the *Santiago de Cuba* was on blockade duty in the West Indies. The presence of the ship's handstamps indicate that the letter was written on board sometime during this period and posted with the ship's

paymaster. It can be assumed that the paymaster in his duties as a naval postmaster could provide stamps for letters. Since the letter entered the mails at Baltimore, it was subjected to the normal domestic rate. It is a large cover and evidently had contents that weighed between 2 and 2½ ounces to require the quintuple rate of 15¢.

Figure 14-5 shows a spectacular two-color pre-printed envelope used for mail addressed to the *USS Mercedita*. This cover front is the only example of an illustrated naval letter with a list of the crew that the author has ever seen. The printed name of the addressee, John W. Mead Jr., is heavily crossed out, and Charles B. Wilder written above it. Wilder is listed as an acting master on the crew list, but Mead is not listed. This raises the

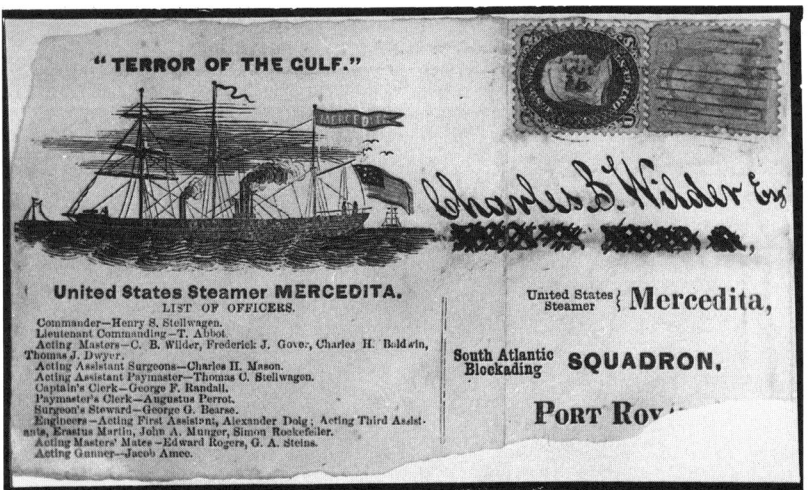

Figure 14-5. Carrier use from New York, October 15 (1862). The cover front is printed in black, red and blue, and addressed to the U.S. steamer *Mercedita*, South Atlantic Blockading Squadron, Port Royal, South Carolina.
(Richard B. Graham photo)

Figure 14-6. Double-weight plus carrier fee required 7¢ postage on this cover to the *USS San Jacinto* of the Eastern Gulf Blockading Squadron at Key West, South Florida. The cover was mailed at Philadelphia on July 18, 1862, and endorsed "Via New York." Below: Drawing of Confederate commissioners being removed from the British mail steamer *Trent* to the *USS San Jacinto*. (From the sketch book of Captain J.S. Mitchell, courtesy of Richard B. Graham)

curious question of why Mead went to the expense of having these special envelopes printed with his name and address when he was evidently not a member of the crew.

The letter was mailed at New York as a carrier letter to the *Mercedita*'s base at Port Royal, South Carolina. The 1¢ and 3¢ stamps are canceled with a patent duplex marker dated October 15 (probably 1862). The knives of the patent canceler penetrate deeply and even cut through the envelope beneath the 3¢ stamp. This type of canceler is known to have been used in New York in the fall of 1862 (see Chapter 8). Other examples of envelopes sent from that ship showing varying illustrations of the *Mercedita* are known. These other examples have the printed message SHIP'S LETTER/USS MERCEDITA on the upper right of the cover, and obviously were printed for the crew to use in their personal correspondence [5:41].

Figure 14-6 shows another blockade cover. This is addressed to a Dr. Horner, who was a "fleet surgeon" assigned to a flagship, but who evidently also went from vessel to vessel overseeing the activities of the assistant surgeons attached to each ship. Several covers addressed to him at different ships have been recorded. The particular cover in Figure 14-6 was addressed to Dr. Horner on the *USS San Jacinto* at Key West, Florida.

The *San Jacinto* is one of the more famous ships of the blockading fleets. On November 8, 1861, while cruising north of Cuba, the *San Jacinto* intercepted the British mail ship *Trent* to inspect it for contraband cargo that might be intended for delivery to the South. On board were two Confederate commissioners, John Slidell and James M. Mason, who were en route to England and France seeking to obtain more positive support from those countries for the Confederacy. At that time, Napoleon III was hoping for setbacks to the Union, which objected to his sponsorship of Maximilian as the emperor of Mexico.

The British public was also very sympathetic to the Confederate cause. It was an opportune time for the Confederacy to attempt to move both the English and the French from their position of neutrality to one that actively supported the South.

The captain of the *San Jacinto* removed Mason and Slidell from the ship and returned them to the United States. Union citizens were jubilant. This was a victory of sorts for the North after a long series of defeats to the South. In addition, the citizenry thought it was only fitting that Great Britain be given some of the same medicine it had so often meted out during the early part of the century when its press gangs abducted U.S. sailors from the high seas. The British were incensed. There was talk in England of declaring war on the United States. Fortunately, the "Trent Affair" cooled down, and by order of President Lincoln, Mason and Slidell were returned to England. Instrumental in Lincoln's decision was Postmaster General Blair's arguments, in opposition to most of the president's Cabinet, that the seizure violated international law, and that holding them was not worth chancing the possibility of war with Great Britain.

Getting back to the description of the cover in Figure 14-6, it is docketed "From wife/July 17th & 18-1862/ Rec. Aug 9th (1862)." The letter was mailed at Philadelphia

Figure 14-7. New York carrier cover, dated June 13. To the "U.S. Steamer Patroon," at St. Johns River, Florida. South Atlantic Blockading Squadron.

Figure 14-8. Carrier cover, postmarked with a red Boston CDS dated May 13, to the "U.S.A. Stemer (sic) Hendric Hudson/Easters (sic) Gulf Blockading Squadron/Key West Fla." (with misspellings as written on the cover). A photo of the *Hendrick Hudson*, courtesy of Richard B. Graham, is shown below. The black squares are gunports.

on July 18, 1862, at the double-weight rate plus 1¢ carrier fee. The letter was endorsed to be sent "Via New York" and was probably carried from there by a Navy ship to Key West, where the *San Jacinto* was based. Seven covers from this same correspondence have been seen by this author, dating from mid-1861 to December 1862.

Figure 14-7 shows another blockade cover. This is a carrier cover, mailed at New York on June 13, year not shown. The cover is addressed to L.G. Hayton, master's mate of the *USS Patroon*, at St. Johns River, Florida. The St. Johns River flows into the Atlantic near Jacksonville, at present-day Fort George. According to Richard B. Graham, the year had to be 1862 since the *USS Patroon* was not placed in service until March 18, 1862. The ship began its station off St. Johns River in May of 1862. In November of 1862, it was sent north, where it was decommissioned (it apparently leaked like a sieve) and sold out of the Navy.

The letter is endorsed "If found elsewhere/please forward." The cover has also been marked with a large manuscript "30." This is possibly docketing written by

the recipient who numbered his letters in order of reception. Such markings are occasionally seen, and alternatively were often applied to a cover by the sender to alert the recipient in case a letter had gone astray. A missing number in the sequence meant a missing letter.

Figure 14-8 shows a Boston carrier cover, dated May 19, addressed to the *Hendrick Hudson*. Figure 14-8 also includes a rare photo of the *Hendrick Hudson*. This was a blockading ship of the Eastern Gulf Blockading Squadron, operating out of Key West. The *Hendrick*

Figure 14-9. Picturesque corner card for the Buffalo Boys of 21st Regiment N.Y.S.V., commanded by Colonel William F. Rogers. Washington, D.C., to Buffalo, New York (illegible date). Envelope printed by Young Lockwood & Co.'s Printers of Buffalo.
(James Lee collection)

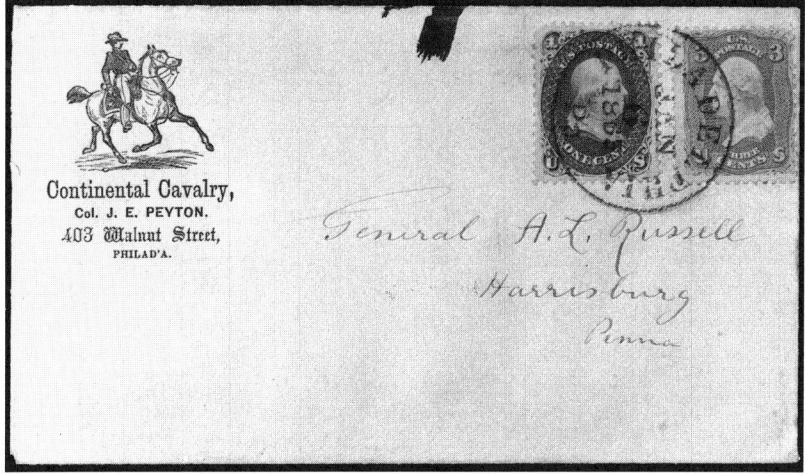

Figure 14-10. Personal printed return address corner card. Carrier cover mailed at Philadelphia, January 6, 1863, to Harrisburg, Pennsylvania.

Hudson was originally the Confederate steamer, *Florida*, captured by the Union on April 6, 1862. It was refitted for blockade duty and renamed the *Hendrick Hudson* in December of 1862. This was a relatively small ship of 429 tons, not to be confused with a larger Confederate raider, also named the *Florida*. This larger vessel was built in Liverpool, England, leaving there on March 22, 1862, for service as a blockade runner. It was a very successful blockade runner and raider and destroyed much federal shipping.

Preprinted address and corner-card return envelopes for use by Army units are frequently found. They seem to be more common for militia and volunteer organizations than for the regular Army units. The volunteer organizations from the various states had a great deal of local and organizational pride, and publicized their identities whenever possible. Examples of some of these preprinted envelopes are illustrated in the following figures.

Figure 14-9 shows a preprinted envelope for the 21st Regiment of the New York State Volunteers, the "Buffalo Boys." The cover also has a preprinted partial address, "_____/Buffalo/N.Y." Evidently, it was expected that much of the correspondence from the Volunteers would be to inhabitants of their hometown. The cover was mailed at Washington, D.C., and addressed to the B&E R.R. Freight Agent at Buffalo.

Figure 14-10 illustrates a printed personal return corner card for a Colonel J.E. Peyton of the Continental Cavalry. Mailed as a carrier letter at Philadelphia on January 6, 1863, and addressed to General A.L. Russell at Harrisburg, Pennsylvania.

Figure 14-11 shows an example of an addressed envelope with a patriotic illustration. The design and address are printed in red, with space left to fill in the name and company of the addressee. The cover was mailed at Tomhannock, New York, with a CDS of November 18. It is addressed to Colonel Carr's regiment of the New York Volunteers at Old Point Comfort, Virginia.

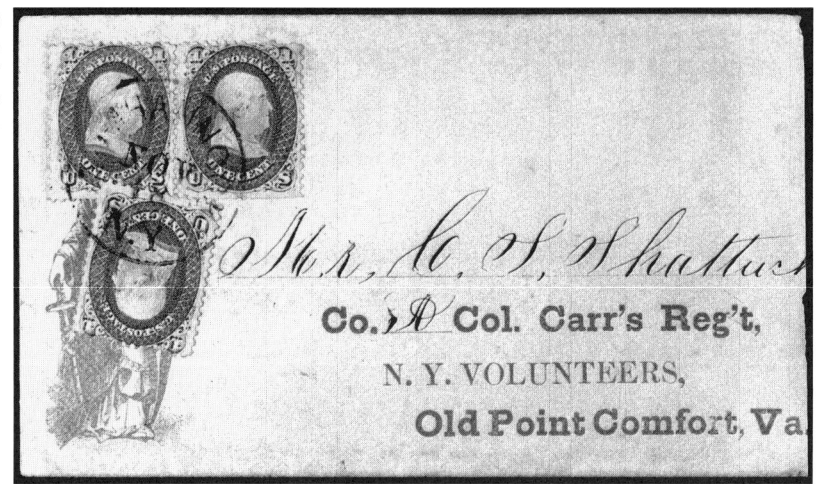

Figure 14-11. Preprinted address patriotic envelope. Mailed at the 3¢ letter rate to Tomhannock, New York, on Nov. 18 (no year date) to Old Point Comfort, Virginia.

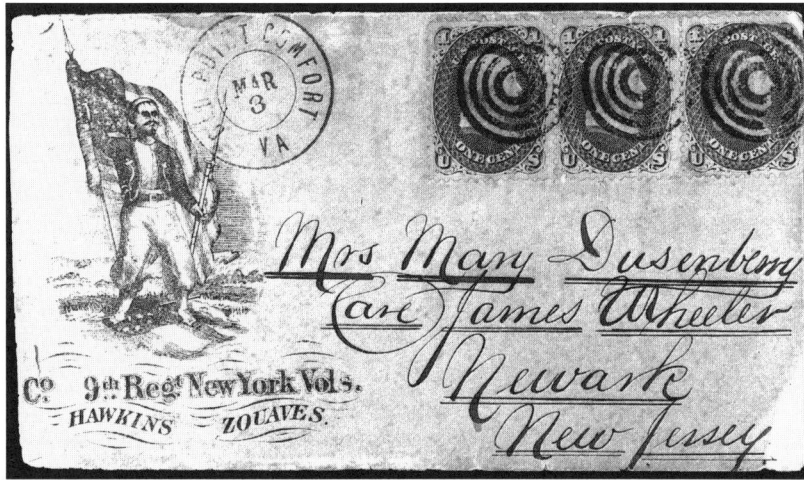

Figure 14-12. Old Point Comfort, Virginia. Dated March 3 (1863), this patriotic preprinted envelope is franked by three ultramarine 1¢ stamps of the "dot-in-U" variety. This is an example of early use of the bull's-eye killer at this post office.

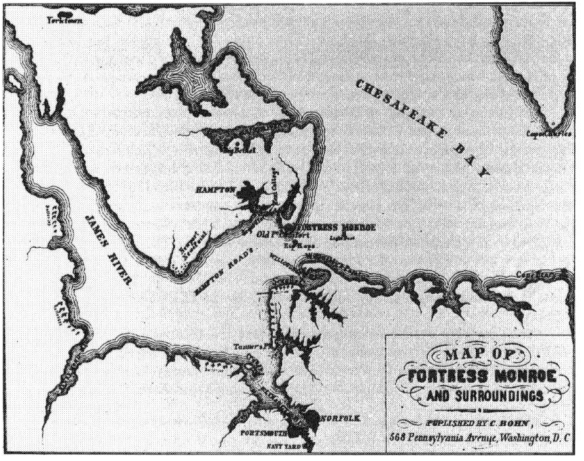

Figure 14-13. Upper woodcut shows Fort Monroe and the adjacent village of Old Point Comfort, Virginia. The map shows the relative positions of Fortress Monroe and the City of Norfolk, which was under Confederate control at that time. Between the two are the "Rip Raps," low rocky shoals that were the location of a small Union fortification (Fort Wool) that further controlled access to Hampton Roads. Map and woodcut published by C. Bohn, Washington, D.C., in 1861.
(Courtesy of Richard F. Winter)

A letter mailed from Old Point Comfort is illustrated in **Figure 14-12**. This attractive patriotic cover shows a soldier in the Zouave uniform and the legend, "9th Reg^t New York Vols./ Hawkins' Zouaves." This regiment was organized by Rush Hawkins in New York, one of many volunteer regiments early in the war modeled and named after the famed Algerian light-infantry troops who fought with the French colonial army. The volunteers wore colorful and spectacular uniforms, and were usually outstanding in their ability to drill and parade. As the war progressed, the bright uniforms and fancy drill gave way to the more mundane blue and battle drill, but these troops continued to demonstrate competence throughout the war.

This cover is paid with a strip of three of the "dot-in-U" variety of the 1¢ Franklin in the scarce ultramarine shade. The cover is docketed on the reverse in pencil "Mch 2 1863." Canceling of stamps with a separate bull's-eye killer at Old Point Comfort commenced in February of 1863. Before that time, letters were canceled with the CDS, and by March of 1864, cork killers were in use [6:560].

The post office at Old Point Comfort deserves special discussion as a receiving and distribution point for mail to many naval and military units. The location of the post office was near the walls of Fort Monroe. Fort Monroe (called "Fortress Monroe" by many) was situated at the tip of a peninsula of land between the James and the York rivers in southern Virginia. It was just across the bay from Norfolk, and controlled the sea entrances to both Richmond and the Chesapeake Bay and Washington, D.C. Because of its location, it was of great strategic importance throughout the war, and was also used as a base and supply point for many blockading and other naval vessels. Mail to and from these vessels was frequently processed at the Old Point Comfort Post Office. The postmaster was Alanson Crane, who was appointed on May 29, 1861, and remained in that position through the war [6:558].

Figure 14-13 shows an 1861 woodcut of Fort Monroe and the adjoining village of Old Point Comfort with a large resort hotel. The fort occupies the high ground of the spit of land, surrounded by the hotel, beaches and houses of the village. The accompanying map shows the location of Fort Monroe and its important position for controlling the naval traffic of the Hampton Roads and surrounding waterways [7:133].

Fort Monroe was considered to be the most impregnable fort on the coast. Well-supplied and well-manned, it remained in federal hands throughout the war. At the beginning of the conflict, it was the most important Union military installation in the South. It was the "Flag of Truce" exchange point with the Confederacy for the eastern part of the country. In addition to mail, prisoners of war were exchanged, and such business conducted as was necessary between the warring factions.

An early commander of Fort Monroe was Major General John A. Dix, who had been the successful and innovative postmaster of New York City in 1860-61 and secretary of the treasury under James Buchanan for a short two months at the end of Buchanan's presidential term. Dix had great capabilities and even in this short time gained the confidence of the nation's bankers and business leaders in the policies of the government. While secretary of the treasury, Dix sent his famous, and often quoted, telegram to a Treasury officer in New Orleans, "If anyone attempts to haul down the American flag, shoot him on the spot."

Dix was appointed by Lincoln as a major general in May of 1861. Later, Fort Monroe came under his command. While there, he issued orders that established rules and guidelines to be followed by individuals who wished to send letters from the North to the South. In the North, these were published in the *National Intelligencer* and the June 1863 issue of the *U.S. Mail and Post Office Assistant*. In the South, they were announced in the Richmond, Virginia, *Daily Examiner* on May 18, 1863 [8:129].

The main points were: Letters were to be sent in two envelopes with the outer one addressed to the commanding general of the Department of Virginia at Fort Monroe. The outer envelope postage was to be prepaid with stamps of the sending area (Confederate or Union). The inner envelope, addressed to the destination, was to contain a letter of no more than one page, unsealed so that it could be censored. The content was to be restricted to domestic matters. Postage for the transmission from Fort Monroe to destination was to be enclosed. This was to be 5¢ for letters addressed to Richmond, Virginia, and 10¢ for destinations beyond. General Dix emphasized the point that the notice was not to be construed to authorize correspondence, and that at times it might be "inexpedient" to transmit letters. Any letter that did not meet all of the required conditions would be sent to the Dead Letter Office. Prisoner-of-war letters were dealt with more leniently and were usually forwarded even though they did not meet all of the requirements.

Although many letters entered the mails at Old Point Comfort, it should be remembered that most of these actually originated from distant encampments and ships that may have been hundreds of miles away (or more) at the time the letters were actually written.

"Flag of Truce" and prisoner-of-war letters are highly prized by collectors. **Figure 14-14** shows one of these. This particular cover, of unknown origin, is addressed to Confederate Virginia. It appears to be a civil-

Figure 14-14. Rare North-to-South civilian letter, via Fort Monroe. It was examined and forwarded to destination by "Flag of Truce." The cover was canceled and postmarked at Old Point Comfort and Norfolk, Virginia (CSA). It was marked "5" for collection of postage due.
(C.W. Christian collection)
Below: Portrait of Major General John A. Dix, commander of the Seventh Corps.

ian cover directed to Fort Monroe, where it was censored and the manuscript endorsement "Ex/Ebie Mary" applied. It was then probably sent by "Flag of Truce" boat across the Hampton Roads to Norfolk, Virginia, where it was postmarked and entered into the Confederate mail system. A "5" marking also was applied for collection of postage due from the addressee at Sussex Court House, Virginia (about 50 miles south of Richmond).

The sender evidently complied with the required procedure to enclose this cover in a second stamped envelope addressed to the commander at Fort Monroe. However, the ambiguous wording of the regulations did not specify that the postage to final destination on the enclosed letter was to be furnished in cash or loose stamps not affixed to the envelopes, and the sender tried to pay the 5¢ for Confederate postage with attached U.S. stamps. Upon arrival at Fort Monroe, the unsuable stamps were canceled (to prevent reuse) by almost illegible strikes of the early single-circle Old Point Comfort postmark.

This is the only cover the writer has seen with a Confederate postmark and a 1¢ Franklin included in the postage, It is exceedingly rare, if not unique.

Figure 14-15 illustrates a spectacular example of a South-to-North letter to Gallatin, Missouri. Endorsed "By Flag of Truce/Via Little Rock," this cover is postmarked at Little Rock, Arkansas, on October 29, 1864. It is further endorsed "Ex^d & App'd/By order of/Maj Gen F. Steele." Below this is a handstamped signature "W. D. Green" (probably a member of Steele's staff). Part of this signature ties the 1¢ Franklin to the cover. An additional endorsement (Confederate?) is at the left side and reads "Ex^d & app^d" with a signature. The cover is also stamped

Figure 14-15. Rare example of a South-to-North letter, franked by the 1861 1¢ Franklin and 2¢ Jackson, which paid the letter rate, and transmitted through the lines by "Flag of Truce." The letter entered the mails at Little Rock, Arkansas, on October 29, 1864. It is addressed to Gallatin, Missouri. The origin of the "DUE/4" handstamp or its meaning is not known to the author.
(Courtesy of Joseph F. Rorke)

Armed Forces and War-related Mails

Figure 14-16. Probable prisoner-of-war letter. The red provost marshall's examining handstamp was used at the Old Capitol Prison (pictured below) in Washington, D.C. The letter was postmarked at Washington on January 6, with the 3¢ letter rate paid by three 1¢ Franklins, and addressed to Baltimore, Maryland.
(C.W. Christian collection)

with a DUE/4 in a circle. Major General Frederick Steele was commander of the Army of Arkansas and was instrumental in the capture of Little Rock, which he used as his headquarters during this period.

Figure 14-16 shows an example of a letter from a prisoner who was confined in the Old Capitol Prison in Washington, D.C. This particular prison was primarily used for the confinement of high-ranking prisoners of war, suspected spies, deserters and persons awaiting trial. Some Confederate generals were incarcerated here, along with prominent civilian prisoners such as Rose Greenhow, the notorious Confederate spy.

The prison was housed in a hastily constructed building that had served as the temporary U.S. Capitol while the original building was rebuilt after being burned by the British in 1812. The cover is postmarked at Washington on January 6 (no year date) and addressed to Baltimore, Maryland. It shows a red Washington, D.C., provost marshall handstamp known to be used at the Old Capitol Prison, and the signature of the examining officer.

Figure 14-17 shows a cover from Fort Warren, a

federal prison located in Boston Harbor. It is endorsed with a manuscript "Fort Warren/No 64 - May/16th - 1862" and addressed to a Miss Wallis at Baltimore, Maryland. S. Teackly Wallis, who sent the cover, was a Maryland state legislator who was imprisoned at the fort for his proclaimed Southern sympathies and most likely was the writer of this cover. The number 64 probably refers to the chronological order of letters that were mailed to this addressee. No examiner's mark or endorsement is present on the cover, which was hand carried from the prison and

Figure 14-17. Civilian prisoner-of-war letter. Originating at Fort Warren, a federal prison in Boston Harbor, the letter was postmarked at Boston on May 17 (1862) with a red CDS, to Baltimore, Maryland. It is franked with three 1¢ stamps, each canceled with a boxed PAID killer.
(James Lee collection)

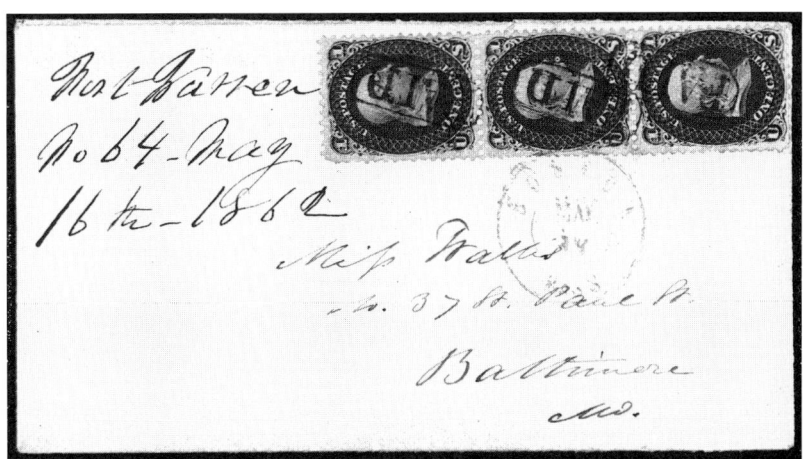

265

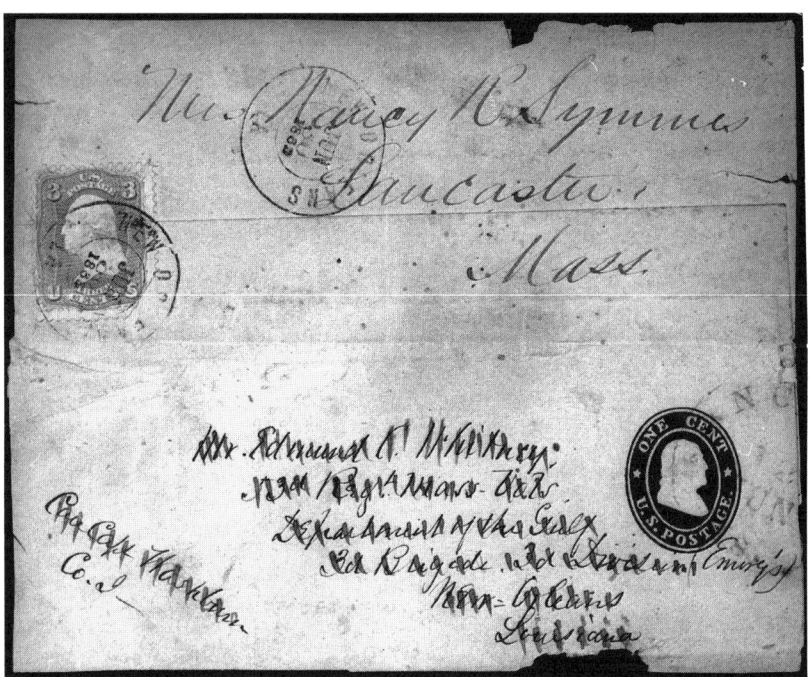

Figure 14-18. Government wrapper (Scott W20) mailed at the 1¢ transient newspaper rate from Lancaster, Massachusetts, June 12, 1863, to a soldier in Emory's Division of the Department of the Gulf at New Orleans. The wrapper was reused as a cover for a letter and entered back in the mail at New Orleans on June 30, 1863, prepaid at 3¢.
(Richard B. Graham photo)

entered the mails at Boston on May 17, 1862.

Occupation Covers

"Occupation covers" comprise a particular philatelic category of Civil War covers. These are letters that were mailed during the war from federal post offices that had been established in occupied Confederate territory. Some of these post offices, such as the one in Alexandria, Virginia, which was occupied on May 24, 1861, were under Confederate control for only a very short time, and so for most of the war were U.S. post offices. Others were established as occupied areas under federal control. Most of these U.S. post offices were at first staffed by military personnel under the supervision of Post Office special agents or a combination of military and civilian postal workers. Until an area was deemed secure, mail service was not available to local residents, though a few censored covers are known. Regular civilian post offices were established when safe civilian transportation for mail became available. It was the practice initially to reopen post offices only at county seats.

The corps of special agents commissioned by the Post Office Department had great responsibilities in re-establishing these post offices and ensuring that they were properly staffed. The post offices were primarily intended to act as distributing offices for military mail. At many of the post offices, civilians who lived in the vicinity and who could have contact with persons or elements in the Confederacy were not provided service.

Covers from many occupation post offices are scarce and much sought-after. A few post offices in the South were never lost to the Confederacy. Old Point Comfort and Key West are two examples. Letters from these locations are easier to obtain, but remain extremely desirable philatelic material.

An interesting, and possibly unique, twice-used government stamped wrapper with the 1¢ Franklin star die is shown in **Figure 14-18**. The wrapper was originally mailed from Lancaster, Massachusetts, on June 12, 1863, via New Orleans, to a soldier in the 53rd Regiment, Massachusetts Volunteers. At that time, the regiment was a part of Brigadier General Emory's 3rd Division, participating in the siege of Port Hudson, Mississippi. The recipient crossed out his name and address and used the wrapper as a cover for a return letter to Lancaster, which he paid with a 3¢ 1861 stamp. This letter was carried by military mail back to New Orleans, where it entered the U.S. mails on June 30, 1863.

New Orleans was captured on April 25, 1862 by federal forces under the command of Admiral David G. Farragut and General Benjamin F. Butler. It remained in Union hands for the balance of the war and became a major distribution point for military mail. General Butler was initially in charge of the occupation of New Orleans and wanted John Parker as the new postmaster. Parker, who coincidentally, or maybe not coincidentally, was Butler's brother-in-law, accompanied him from Boston when Butler sailed south with his division in the latter

Figure 14-19. Port Royal, South Carolina, double-circle CDS dated December 2, 1862. Forwarded via New York, where it was postmarked December 17 for Prussian closed mail with a 23¢ debit. Sea post by British ship *China*. Arrived at Aachen December 30 and at Hildburghausen, Germany on December 31. Also shown in color section.

Debit to Prussia for 23¢ (5¢ for local U.S. inland and 18¢ for the British packet fee).

Marked 45 kreuzer with a 1-pfennige surcharge for delivery.

part of 1861. Most of the invading force was disembarked at Ship Island, a small island at the mouth of the Mississippi River. Butler pulled strings to have Parker appointed as the postmaster at Ship Island, and after the occupation of New Orleans on May 1, 1862, he transferred him to New Orleans to take over the postmaster duties. Butler had no authority to appoint Parker as postmaster of New Orleans, but it appears that Parker acted in that capacity until an official appointment was made [9:184].

In Washington, announcements were made on May 2, 1862, that mail could again be sent to New Orleans, and the first mail departed from New York aboard the Navy dispatch and supply steamer *USS Connecticut* on May 14, 1862. Commercial mail steamers would soon reopen their routes, and military and naval dispatch steamers had begun to use New Orleans as their base of operations in the Gulf.

Aboard the *Connecticut* was Major Scott, an official of the Post Office Department, under the direction of Postmaster General Blair. Upon arrival, he took charge of the New Orleans post office, and after satisfying himself about its operation, legally appointed Parker as a chief clerk and acting postmaster (pending presidential action to appoint a permanent postmaster) and then returned to the North. The agent had also brought new postmarking devices with him. The first-known use was on June 2, 1862 [10:44].

Another major Confederate port city occupied by Union forces was Port Royal, South Carolina. The combined forces of Admiral Samuel Du Pont and General Thomas W. Sherman captured the Confederate forts, Beauregard and Walker, at Port Royal Sound on November 7, 1861. This secured for the Union another strategic port for basing and supplying the blockading fleet, and created another occupation post office for philatelists.

An interesting cover, originating from the Port Royal post office, is shown in **Figure 14-19**. This cover is a part-paid letter to Germany with a patriotic illustration. Patriotic covers to foreign destinations are relatively scarce, and even more so from an occupation post office. The letter was mailed at Port Royal on December 2, 1862, for a destination at Hildburghausen in the German State of Thuringia. This cover is one of those special philatelic items containing many interesting and unusual features. In addition to being an attractive patriotic cover, it was posted at an occupation post office with incorrect partial payment and an unauthorized fee notation. It also shows evidence of a carrier delivery fee being added to the amount to be collected upon delivery. The presence of three 1¢ Franklins as the only postage makes this cover an extremely scarce example. While a single 1¢ stamp might be found on unpaid covers to foreign destinations where a carrier picked up the letter, or two 1¢ stamps for circulars and newspapers, finding a foreign cover with three of the 1¢ Franklins, and no other values, is rare.

Analysis of this cover indicates that when the letter was posted, the postmaster at Port Royal, realizing that partial payments on mail to most foreign destinations was not recognized, marked it with a black "Due" in boxed-oval and a bold 15¢ manuscript notation in blue. Postmasters by Post Office policy were not to mark short-paid or unpaid foreign letters with the amount due. This was to be done by the foreign exchange office where the rates were better understood. Many postmasters did not

Figure 14-20. Naval letter from the *USS Wabash*, prepaid by three 1¢ stamps for the domestic letter rate. The letter entered the mail at occupied Port Royal, South Carolina, on May 22 (1862), to Washington, D.C. Photo below shows the bow deck of the *Wabash*, with its famous Parrott gun and crew.
(Cover photo by Richard B. Graham)

follow this policy, and according to Richard F. Winter, the due amount may have been noted to show a preference for routing. The cost of a letter to a foreign destination could at times vary considerably as a function of the route and service used.

The Post Office Department, however, only recognized endorsements of the ship name and/or postal service desired, or indications of the preferred route as influencing their assignment of routes and rates. In this case, the rate for a ½-ounce letter to Germany was 15¢ via Bremen mail, and 30¢ via Prussian closed mail (PCM). The exchange office at New York chose the PCM option, ignored the 15¢ marking on the letter and marked it with a black circular New York exchange marking dated December 17, 1862, and showing sea transit via British mail packet with a debit to Prussia of 23¢. No credit was given for the 3¢ partial payment. The letter departed New York on December 17 aboard the British Cunard steamer *China* and proceeded by closed-mail bag through England and Belgium to Aachen, Prussia. It was there backstamped in red

on December 30 and marked on the front with a blue manuscript "13" for collection. This is for 13 silbergroschen and is equivalent to 30¢ U.S. The letter was then transported by the Thurn and Taxis Post to Hildburghausen, where it was backstamped on December 31 and marked with a large manuscript "45/1" in blue. This was for the postage due of 45 kreuzers (Southern Germany currency), which was equivalent to 13 silbergroschen (Northern German currency) and 1 kreuzer

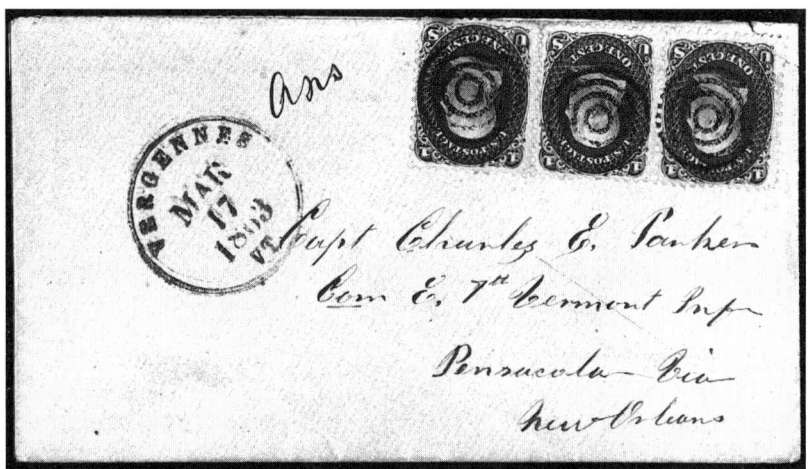

Figure 14-21. Vergennes, Vermont, to occupied Pensacola, Florida. Postmarked with a bold double-rim CDS dated March 17, 1863. The 3¢ paid the letter rate. The cover was addressed to be sent via New Orleans.
(James Lee collection)

Armed Forces and War-related Mails

Figure 14-22. Boston, Massachusetts, November 18 (1863) to Fort Totten at occupied New Bern, North Carolina. Cover is docketed November 25, 1863. Double-weight cover paid by an 1861 1¢ and a 5¢ (Scott 76) stamp. (James Lee collection)

for a delivery fee. The final destination, Hellingen, was a small town without a post office, and the delivery fee paid for transportation from Hildburghausen. The purpose and origin of the faint red crayon marking (between the shield and the left stamp) of "45/2" is unclear. It may be that Hildburghausen misrated the delivery fee, which depended on distance. It should have been 2 kreuzer, the correction being marked in red on the cover at delivery.

Another Port Royal cover is shown in **Figure 14-20**. This cover originated aboard the *USS Wabash*, the pride of the U.S. Navy at the outbreak of the Civil War. The *Wabash* was a steam frigate of more than 3,000 tons, one of the finest naval vessels in the world at that time. It served as the flagship of Admiral Du Pont, who was in command of the South Atlantic blockading squadron, and was captained by C.R.P. Rogers. The cover in Figure 14-20, addressed to Washington, D.C., entered the mails at Port Royal and was postmarked on May 22 (year unknown, but very probably 1862 from the type of postmark). A photograph of the famous forward pivot-gun of the *Wabash* is shown below the cover. This 200-pounder Parrott gun was used with great effect during the capture of Fort Fisher and its adjoining port at Wilmington, North Carolina, in January 1865. This was the last seaport remaining under Confederate control. Its loss sealed the fate of the South [11:259].

The mail to and from the members of the services tells a personal story of the conduct of the war and the great sacrifices of those who fought in it. While most surviving covers are missing their contents, much information can be deduced from an analysis of the cover itself, including information from regimental corner cards and docketing. In a few cases, the letters have remained with their original covers and provide graphic descriptions of the war years.

Fort Pickens, Florida, at the tip of Santa Rosa Island guarding Pensacola Bay, was one of the three Southern forts that remained in Union hands throughout the war. Pensacola Bay had one of the best harbors in the Gulf, and Fort Pickens denied this asset to the Confederacy. In May 1862, the Confederate fortifications on the mainland side of the bay were abandoned by the Southerners, and federal forces reoccupied these positions. Pensacola became headquarters for the Western Gulf Squadron and a major supply base for naval operations. **Figure 14-21** shows an 1863 cover addressed to a captain of the 7th Vermont Infantry at Pensacola, via New Orleans. The cover was most likely carried from New Orleans to Pensacola by naval dispatch steamer.

Figure 14-22 shows another occupation cover. This 1863 letter was addressed to Fort Totten at New Bern, North Carolina. New Bern was captured by Union forces on March 14, 1862, during General Burnside's expedition to North Carolina. It is situated at the south end of Pamlico Sound, and was accessible for resupply by water. New Bern remained under federal control for the balance of the war. The cover was overweight, and the 6¢ postage was paid by the relatively scarce combination of a 1¢ Franklin and the 5¢ 1861 Jefferson.

Major General Nathaniel Banks replaced Major General Ben Butler at New Orleans in October of 1862, and remained there until 1864. The cover shown in **Figure 14-23** was probably written in that period, during one of the two expeditions that Banks led against the Confederate forces along the Red River. The cover, addressed to a "Member of Band in the 47 Mass Regt/ Bankes Expedition Via New Orleans," is manuscript postmarked and canceled. The origin is difficult to decipher, but may be South Merrimack, New Hampshire, with a date of "Jun 6(?)."

269

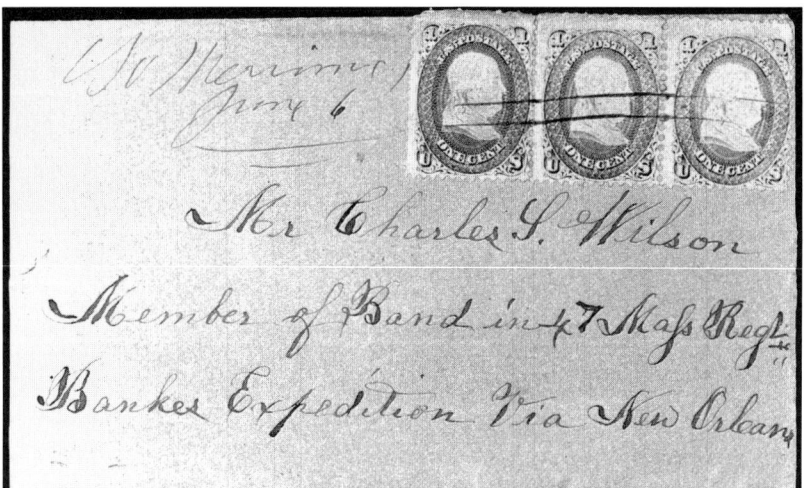

Figure 14-23. Letter to a soldier in occupied territory with manuscript postmark and cancel. The letter is dated June 6, with a possible origin of South Merrimack, New Hampshire. It was addressed via New Orleans to a member of a band in Banks' Expedition.

Figure 14-24. UNCLAIMED letter from Saegerstown, Pennsylvania, to a member of the 83d Regiment, Washington, D.C. The letter is dated April 27 (year unknown). The addressee is listed as wounded, but not in Washington hospitals.
(Richard B. Graham photo)

Letters written from General Banks' command are known with special markings that could be considered to be the forerunner of APO markings from later wars. Unfortunately, an example of these postmarks on a 1¢ Franklin cover is not available for illustration. There were two basic types of markings with variations. One consisted of the initials "G.B.D" (for General Banks' Division) and a date. The other was a CDS with the words BANKS' DIVISION and an accompanying date. These markings are found on covers from September 1861 to November 1862, and cover the period when Banks' division was a part of the Army of the Potomac. The marking is found in black during 1861 and in blue during 1862 [12:120-2].

Figure 14-24 shows a cover mailed at Saegerstown, Pennsylvania, to a soldier attached to a regiment that was served via the Washington, D.C., post office. The cover shows a manuscript notation on the reverse, "Sent to Hospital Washington/May 5th." On the front of the cover is noted "In Hospital/Washington/Wounded." It is further endorsed with "Not at Lincoln" and "Not at Finlay," and finally handstamped "UNCLAIMED." The evidence suggests the possible demise of the addressee. The only records that were kept concerning a soldier's location and condition were his regimental records and roster. If he was separated from his regiment due to circumstances other than a transfer, there was no official accounting of his whereabouts, and his death might be discovered only by the fact that he never returned home [1:72]. This particular cover was probably sent to the Dead Letter Office from where it was returned to the post office of origination, and eventually to the writer.

Figure 14-25 shows a cover with the scarce New York SHED'S CORNERS straightline town mark and accompanying star used as a cancel on a letter to a patient in the Mansion House Hospital at Alexandria, Virginia. Alexandria was an occupation post office by definition, but since it was taken by Union troops almost a month before the cessation of mail service to the Confederacy

Armed Forces and War-related Mails

Figure 14-25. Shed's Corners, New York, to Alexandria, Virginia, August 10 (1863). The cover is docketed as being received on August 15 and contains an enclosure dated August 9, 1863.
(James Lee collection)

Figure 14-26. "Follow the Regiment" letter. Philadelphia, January 25, 1863, to Columbus, Ohio, where the cover was re-addressed, postmarked on March 28, and forwarded without additional cost to Camp Dennison, Ohio.
(Richard B. Graham collection)

on May 31, 1861, mail to and from Alexandria was never subjected to the restrictions levied upon most occupation post offices. Alexandria was host to many Union hospitals and convalescent hotels, and many of the fine homes of the city were taken over for that purpose.

As earlier discussed, letters to soldiers and sailors who had changed location as a result of official orders had their mail forwarded without additional charge.

Figure 14-26 illustrates an example of such free forwarding, or "follow the regiment" use as it is frequently described. This cover originated at Philadelphia on January 25, 1863. It has a red patriotic label with white lettering at the upper right of the pale buff cover, and postage is paid by three 1¢ stamps located on the left side of the envelope. The addressee is a captain of the 15th Infantry at Columbus, Ohio. The cover is endorsed by the sender, "If not here will Postmaster please forward." Evidently the captain was not there, and the destination "Columbus" was marked out with red ink and replaced with "Camp Dennison," also in red ink, and the letter forwarded with

a Columbus, Ohio, CDS dated "Mar 28." Considering that over two months elapsed between the time the letter was sent and the time it was finally forwarded, it appears that considerable searching had to be done before a forwarding destination could be determined.

Figure 14-27 shows a cover to Captain C. Rodney Layton, a member of a prominent Delaware family. Captain Layton was evidently able to preserve much of his correspondence, and numerous examples have been offered in philatelic sales. This cover originated as a carrier letter at Philadelphia on October 1, 1862. It is addressed to Captain Layton via Washington, D.C., in the 11th Infantry, U.S.A., General Sykes' Division, "Army of the Potomac." This was just after the bloody engagements at 2nd Bull Run, and just before the costly battles for Fredericksburg, both of which were supported by General Sykes' Division, and where casualties were of the order of 15 percent.

"Official Business" covers comprise a special category of war-related mail. These covers, which usually

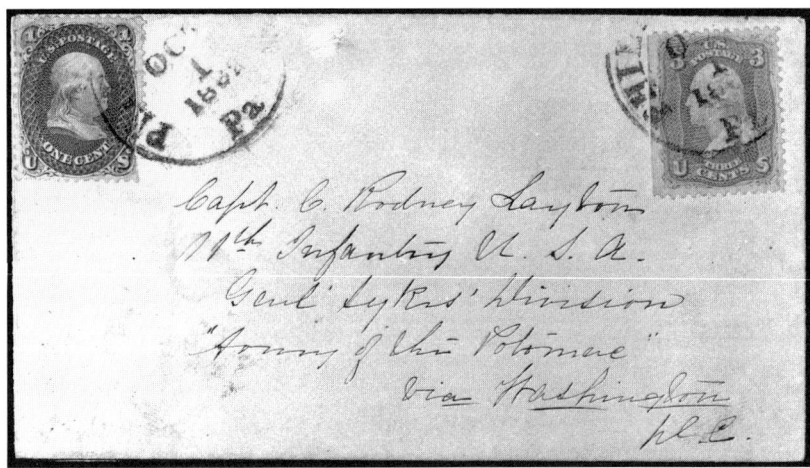

Figure 14-27. Carrier use, Philadelphia, October 1, 1862, to an officer in the 11th Infantry Regiment, 2nd Division, under Brigadier General Sykes.

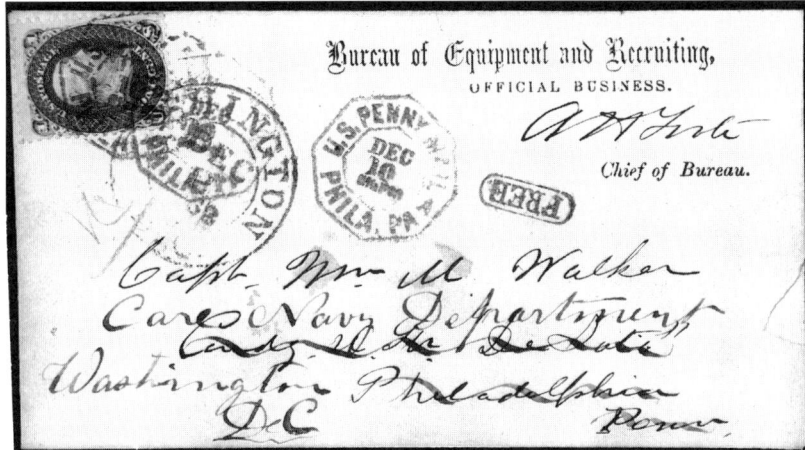

Figure 14-28. Bureau of Equipment and Recruiting, official-business cover from Washington, D.C., December 2, 1863, to Philadelphia, Pennsylvania. Mailed under the free frank of Admiral Foote to the captain of the *USS De Soto*, the cover was backstamped upon receipt at Philadelphia on December 10, 1863. It was forwarded back to Washington on the same day. The carrier fee, paid by a 1¢ Franklin, probably was applied aboard the ship for delivery back to the post office at Philadelphia. Engraving is of Admiral A.H. Foote. (Courtesy of Richard B. Graham)

were sent free from or into Washington under official franks, were mailed by the hundreds of thousands, if not millions, during the Civil War era. Few examples remain. The usual lack of stamps on the envelopes and the fact that the contents would generally be filed separately, mitigated against the covers being retained over the years. These covers have official imprints and often the signatures of the officials given the franking privilege by law. Such covers do not generally bear postage stamps aside from the rare occasion, prior to July 1, 1863, when a 1¢ Franklin was used to pay the carrier fee.

A rare example of a free official-business use with the addition of a 1¢ Franklin is illustrated in **Figure 14-28**. This cover was mailed free from Washington, D.C., on December 2, 1863, from the Bureau of Equipment and Recruiting under the frank of Rear Admiral Andrew Hull Foote. Admiral Foote was one of the most outstanding naval officers of the Civil War. He was seriously wounded during the Fort Donelson campaign and found it necessary to give up his command in June 1862 and to accept a desk job in Washington as chief of the Bureau of Equipment and Recruiting. A year later, he was chosen to replace Admiral Du Pont as commander of the fleet off Charleston harbor, but unfortunately died, at the age of 57, en route to his new post.

The cover is addressed to Captain William M. Walker of the *USS De Soto* at Philadelphia, where it was undergoing repairs. Captain Walker had left for Washington before the letter arrived, so the cover was readdressed at the ship and forwarded back to Washington with a 1¢ stamp to pay the carrier fee to the post office. The cover received three strikes of the Philadelphia "Penny Mail" marking, dated December 10, one of which canceled the stamp. It also received a boxed FREE mark-

Figure 14-29. Official-business Army letter originating at Springfield, Illinois, dated November 10 and addressed to the commander of the 59th Illinois Regiment at Danville, Kentucky. Double-rate postage was paid by a strip of six 1¢ Franklins.

ing to indicate that no postage was due. Forwarding was free under the franking privilege.

Figure 14-29 shows a cover from the Adjutant General's Office for the State of Illinois to a colonel commanding the 59th Illinois Infantry Regiment at Danville, Kentucky. The cover contains a letter with the heading "General Head Quarters, State of Illinois,/Adjutant General's Office." The letter is dated November 8, 1862, and the content refers to commissions being sent for Company H, and promotions for Company I. This is without doubt a true official-business military letter, and is so certified by the signature of the state adjutant general, A.C. Fuller. However, state adjutant generals were not authorized to frank mail. Consequently, a spectacular strip of six 1¢ Franklins was applied to pay the postage on this double-weight letter.

An official business cover with a single 1¢ stamp affixed was shown as Figure 10-54 in Chapter 10. That example was mailed for local delivery in Washington, D.C., and as is frequently the case with local mail, no CDS was applied so the date cannot be determined. Obviously, with the postage amounting to only 1¢, it must have been mailed prior to July 1, 1863. The 1¢ stamp could have paid either for carrier service or drop postage. Although pre-printed DEPOT OF ARMY CLOTHING AND EQUIPAGE/OFFICIAL BUSINESS, the envelope was not franked.

Patriotic Envelopes

Covers illustrated with patriotic themes form a special class of philatelic collectibles. Their attractive and historically significant illustrations have appealed to generations of philatelists. Many outstanding collections of patriotic covers have been developed over the years.

George Walcott, in the mid-1920s, formed what is probably the most comprehensive group of patriotic covers ever assembled. It contained more than 3,000 used Civil War patriotic covers and provided the material for Robert Laurence's 1934 book [13], which was actually the auction sale catalog describing the Walcott material. The book's listings are also a recognized source of identification numbers that have been widely used by philatelists to specify particular designs. In 1977 a follow-up to the Laurence book was produced by Robert W. Grant [14]. It extended the Laurence system for cataloging the designs and was intended to be the first of a series of handbooks that would attempt to list all of the known designs. Unfortunately, only the first volume was ever published, including only a small fraction of the known designs. It does, however, provide useful data concerning the printers and publishers of patriotic envelopes.

In 1995, William Weiss Jr. of Weiss Philatelics completed a comprehensive survey of the field and published an updated catalog of Union patriotic envelopes [15]. This work is an excellent reference for any collector who is interested in the subject. Weiss based his listing on a large number of covers acquired over a period of years and also included for the first time unused covers. This substantially increased the number of listed designs since many of the unused designs are not known on postally used Civil War-period covers.

The Weiss catalog lists more than 5,500 different designs with excellent illustrations of each design. This is approximately double the number previously cataloged. Weiss also introduced a new alpha-numeric numbering system that is simple and can be easily extended. It is possible that the Weiss numbers will become the standard for identifying Union patriotic covers.

The Weiss catalog also includes a useful cross-reference, listing all the covers alphabetically by the verse or legend that appears in the design. Although all patriotic illustrations do not have a text component, most do, and this feature of the catalog saves much time in locating a specific design. Weiss also cross-references all of his listings with the Walcott/Laurence catalog number.

Figure 14-30. "Angell" correspondence to Vienna, Austria. The red NEW YORK 12 BREM PK. 12 NOV 7 exchange CDS credited Bremen for 12¢. The cover was probably mailed in 1863 with sea transit aboard the NGL steamship *Bremen*. The 15¢ rate to Austria was paid with 1¢ (Scott 63), 2¢ (73) and 12¢ (69). The cover bears a blue AMERICA UBER BREMEN transit marking. The red fancy wreath design was produced by S.H. Zahm of Lancaster, Pennsylvania.
(Courtesy of Christie's New York)

The famous early collector, Judge R.S. Emerson, possessed a large selection of patriotic covers, including most of the spectacular "Angell" covers. These covers were from the Dr. Henry C. Angell correspondence and addressed to various European locations. Each cover featured one of the better designs of the period, with many printed by Charles Magnus or Frederick Kimmel. These individuals were two of the most outstanding engravers and manufacturers of fine patriotic envelopes. Their products are in great demand by philatelists. The foreign destinations of the Angell covers also resulted in the use of many of the higher-denomination and scarcer stamps of the period. Because of their beauty, rarity and philatelic significance, the Angell patriotics are the most highly priced and sought-after of the Civil War patriotics. Judge Emerson's holdings of these patriotics passed on to Katherine Matthies, another highly respected collector. They were exhibited both nationally and internationally and garnered many top awards. In 1969, the entire group was sold at a Robert A. Siegel auction. An example of one of the Angell covers is shown in **Figure 14-30**.

The historical impact of patriotic covers should not be overlooked. While many of the patriotic envelopes are works of art with beautiful engraving and printing, and many have philatelic significance that transcends the illustration, almost all present a window into the beliefs, sentiments and hopes of a country at war. Seen in this light, they provide a comprehensive view of what people thought and experienced. Postal history and Civil War history are inseparably interwoven in patriotic envelopes, and these covers have provided a wonderful philatelic legacy.

A representative assemblage of used patriotic covers is highly desired for any collection that includes Civil War postal history. If a patriotic cover has the additional philatelic merit of unusual markings or use, that is a bonus but need not be a requirement for collection or exhibition. Patriotic covers are not scarce. They were printed and sold in huge quantities. Their interesting designs resulted in a significant number surviving to this day. All command a substantial premium over nonpatriotic covers showing similar postal use.

In this volume, only a limited number of patriotic designs, and only those on covers where the 1¢ Franklin has been used, will be discussed. Most postally used patriotic covers were paid with the 1861 3¢ stamp. Use of the 1¢ stamp, singly or in combination, is estimated to represent less than 1 percent of the total number of available covers.

Patriotic covers began to appear in the early part of 1861. Within weeks of the April 12, 1861, bombardment of Fort Sumter, hundreds of patriotic designs became available on envelopes. Sentiments were running high, and the entrepreneurs of the printing and stationery shops were anxious to provide material to express those feelings, at a profit, of course.

At the beginning of the war, there were not many identifiable heroes or pictures of current battle scenes available to the print shops, so they improvised with what they had. Inventories of stock dies were searched for suitable topics. They did have one military leader to picture. General Winfield Scott (**Figure 14-31**), although 75 years old and in declining health, was still heading the Army. His outstanding record of military achievements, spanning the period from the War of 1812 to 1860, had earned him great public admiration. He was tapped to provide leadership in the new war, and his likeness soon found its way onto patriotic envelopes. George Washington, as the embodiment of the United States, was also pictured in many poses. There also remained illustrations from the Mexican War of 1846-48 that seemed marginally appropriate. Allegorical figures that looked even vaguely patriotic were pressed into service, and many of the early illustrations showed infantrymen and sailors in the outdated uniforms of earlier conflicts. Campaign covers from the previous election were reprinted, and the engravers and artists were busy producing new illustrations to satisfy the patriotic fever of the public. The first covers, with some exceptions, were relatively simple, but by the time the war ended, many magnificently engraved and colored masterpieces had been printed.

Collecting patriotic covers has not been confined to philatelists. As early as the spring of 1861, collecting of the envelopes had begun, and later, special albums were produced to hold them. Patriotic envelopes were often collected in unused condition. Many of the later and most spectacular printings were made primarily for the collectors' market. This is evident in some illustrations that left no room on the envelope for stamps or addresses. A small number of postally used examples of these overall designs have been recorded where the sender solved the problem by placing address and postage on the reverse side of the envelope. It is unfortunate that so many of the exquisite designs of those later years were never postally used. They would make wonderful acquisitions for a present-day philatelist. They are still available in unused condition, but in that form can only be considered as collateral material.

An interesting article was printed in the USA&POA for June of 1861 [8:33]. An excerpt follows:

> "The post office, too, is made the means of dissemination of sentiment, and envelopes with patriotic motto or device are much used in correspondence. A collection of such envelopes has been made at the New York Post Office by the Secretary Captain Morgan and it is really a curiosity. They are of every degree of workmanship as far as engraving is concerned — from the finest steel engraving to the coarsest wood — plain and colored, gay and grave, some all love and fervor and others threatening war and devastation . . ."

The use of patriotic covers continued to escalate during the initial years of the war, but when the realities and carnage of the conflict began to temper idealistic enthusiasm, their postal use diminished remarkably. They were still in vogue as an art form, but just were not used as much for letters. Over the period of the war, it is believed that more than 10,000 different designs were created.

Patriotic covers are generally divided into groups for cataloging. For example, all covers featuring generals and other officers will be in one category, while another grouping may show those covers with female figures, while another is for flag-related designs. In the discussion that follows, the covers will not necessarily be arranged by type. Instead, where applicable, they will be described in approximate chronological order with respect to the subject of the printed illustrations.

Figure 14-32 shows a scarce naval illustration. The sailor in the woodcut is wearing a uniform appropriate to the War of 1812 period or even earlier. Pictures denoting naval themes are relatively scarce, and those actually depicting Civil War events were not produced for some time following the outbreak of hostilities.

Another early woodcut is illustrated in **Figure 14-33**. This resurrected die shows an infantry officer in the uniform of the War of 1812, standing guard at a Washington encampment with the Capitol building in the background. It is printed in blue and red on a white envelope. The 1¢ stamp is a "dot-in-U" variety from the first plate to be used, plate 9. The date on the Cambridgeport, Massachusetts, CDS appears to be August 22, 1861. If this date is correct, the cover has the distinction of being mailed on the second day of known use for a cover bearing the 1¢ Franklin. A single earliest-known-use cover from Philadelphia is dated August 21, 1861. Cambridgeport was located near Boston, and Boston first received the new issue on August 21, 1861. (No cover from Boston for that

Figure 14-31. New York, November 11, carrier use to Nantucket, Massachusetts. Red, white, and blue illustration of Lieutenant General Winfield Scott, commander of the Union Forces at the outbreak of the Civil War and veteran of many major military engagements including the War of 1812 and the Mexican War.
(C.W. Christian collection)

Figure 14-32. Cover shows sailor with cannon, flag, shield and eagle. Mailed at the 3¢ letter rate at St. Clairsville, Ohio, on December 30 (no year date), to Parkersburg, (Western) Virginia. The design is printed in mauve on a light-yellow envelope.
(C.W. Christian collection)

Figure 14-33. Cambridgeport to North Attleboro, Massachusetts. The envelope is open at both ends and was mailed at the 1¢ newspaper rate. The cover is postmarked AUG 22/1861, and the stamp is from plate 9. Use on this date would make it the second day of known use for a cover with the 1¢ 1861 Franklin stamp.
(C.W. Christian collection)

Figure 14-34. Mexican War of 1847, battle for Churubusco. The patriotic cover was mailed at the 3¢ letter rate to Milton, Massachusetts. It bears an indistinct town mark, possibly Washington, D.C. The difficulty in addressing and postmarking an all-over design is clearly evident from this example. Also shown in color section.

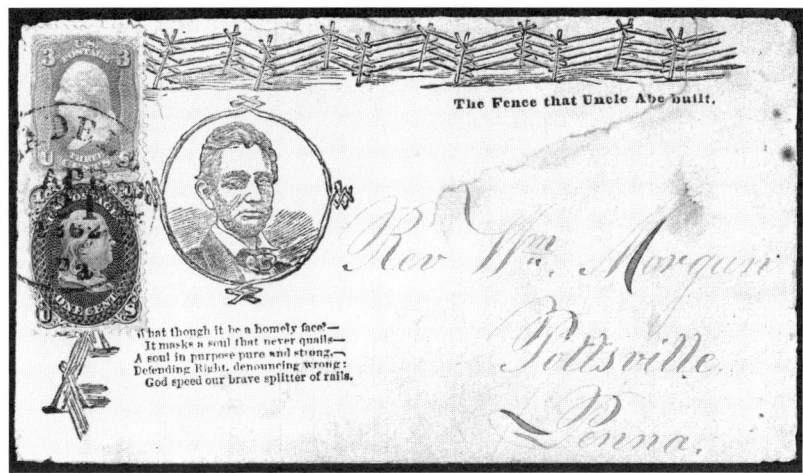

Figure 14-35. Civil War use of a Lincoln campaign cover. Philadelphia carrier use to Pottsville, Pennsylvania, dated April 11, 1862. The franking of 1¢+3¢ paid for the carrier fee plus letter postage.

date is known.) The cover is also open at both ends. It evidently was used as wrapper and mailed at the 1¢ newspaper rate. This possibly qualifies it as the EKU for the 1861 1¢ stamp on a wrapper. On the reverse of the cover is a signed authentication by Ashbrook, although he also was not sure of the date. He lists it as "Aug 2? 1861."

The spectacular overall battle scene pictured on the cover in **Figure 14-34** depicts an epic 1847 battle during the Mexican War. The convent at Churubusco, Mexico, had been heavily fortified and was defended by some of General Santa Ana's best troops. The woodcut shows the assault by U.S. infantrymen on a bridgehead leading to the fortress, and the defending Mexican force. No attempt was made to make the woodcut more representative of the Civil War, but that probably did not matter to the majority of the buying public. The envelope was produced by J.W. Bond of Baltimore, printed in red and blue.

The printers and artisans who produced the colorful and sometimes intricate patriotic envelopes of the Civil War are worthy of mention. While the origin of many of the designs is not known, some envelopes have the names of the printer or manufacturer or, at times, the stationer who sold the envelope. For many, the only clues are the style of engraving and printing. Woodcuts, lithographs and fine intaglio engraving can all be found. Many envelopes are multicolored. Some are printed with metallic inks in bronzes and golds, and a few of the most elaborate are handpainted. Some of the later efforts consisted of several parts, and some contained foldouts.

More than 275 different sources for Union patriotic envelopes have been reported by Robert Grant [14:4-5]. The printers and manufacturers were mostly concentrated in the large cities of the Northeast, but some were located as far west as San Francisco, California, and as far east as London, England. The output of some of the larger manufacturers could be as much as several hundred thousand envelopes per day. Millions were printed and used. Thankfully, a small percentage of those survived the years and are still available.

As previously mentioned, the two leading manufacturers, with respect to artistic quality, were Kimmel and Magnus. Both these firms were producing engraved prints of high quality before the war, and their products were considered to be among the best. Their designs are characterized by fine artistry and engraving. It seems that at times they must have used the same artists, since they produced very similar envelopes. Charles Magnus produced many more covers than did Frederick Kimmel, and his handpainted camp scenes and maps of cities and battlefields are among the most beautiful of the patriotic envelopes. Covers manufactured by either of these firms command high premiums in the marketplace and, when combined with a desired postal use, attain realizations in the low five-figure range. An informative survey of most of the known manufacturers and purveyors of patriotic envelopes is contained in the Grant book.

In the tumultuous election of 1860, Abraham Lincoln was opposed by the Democratic candidate, Stephen A. Douglas, and the Southern state's candidate, John C. Breckenridge. Illustrated campaign envelopes for each of the candidates were printed and used extensively during the campaign, and surviving covers are favorite items for collectors. A significant number of the Lincoln campaign envelopes were not used until the Civil War and may be identified by their "beardless" Lincoln portraits. **Figure 14-35** shows an example of one of these covers, used in 1862. The envelope was printed in black by James L. Magee of Philadelphia. Magee was very prolific and produced many of the cartoon and caricature designs that were common during the war.

A typical example of the use of a stock design is

Figure 14-36. Port Byron, Illinois, November 12 use to Normal University at Bloomington, Illinois. Rate paid by three 1¢ Franklins from plate 9.

shown in **Figure 14-36**. With the addition of the caption "Young America off for the War," the allegorical design was transformed into a not-very-appropriate Civil War patriotic motif. The design was printed in mauve on a pale-yellow envelope, and the combination makes this an unusual and attractive cover.

Figure 14-37 shows an interesting drawing of a raccoon and the caption "FLOYD, of the C.S.A." The raccoon was a symbol of theft and chicanery, and in the eyes of the Northern citizens, General Floyd fit the description perfectly. John B. Floyd, formerly governor of Virginia, had been President Buchanan's secretary of war from 1857 until his forced resignation on December 29, 1861. He was accused, among other things, of using his position to see that federal guns and ammunition were concentrated in Southern arsenals where they could be easily captured by the Confederates if hostilities broke out.

The charge was probably true, and Floyd was definitely on the side of the South. After leaving the government, he raised a brigade and was commissioned as a brigadier general in the Confederate Army. He was initially given command of the forces in the Kanawha section of Western Virginia. In 1862, he was second in command at Fort Donelson during Grant's attack on the fort. His superior, General Pillow, faced with defeat, turned over command to Floyd and escaped through the lines. Floyd evidently thought that was a pretty good idea, turned the command over to his subordinate, General Buckner, and followed in Pillow's footsteps. Buckner was forced to surrender to Grant, and this became the first significant victory of the war for the Union forces. For his less-than-courageous conduct, Floyd was relieved of command, as was Pillow. His earlier actions as secretary of war, possibly expedient with regard to the Confederacy, were a violation of trust and did not conform to the ideas of honesty and responsibility held by most citizens. Thus the raccoon became his alias.

The cover in Figure 14-37 is from the extensive "Farewell" correspondence. All of these covers that the author has seen are local, probably carrier, letters mailed at Boston. Each carries a patriotic illustration. Another cover to the same addressee was pictured in Chapter 10 as Figure 10-40. All letters are addressed in the same hand and postmarked with a normal red Boston CDS.

By the late spring of 1861, the war was rapidly heating up. General Ben Butler was in command of Fort Monroe, and on May 23, three escaped slaves sought refuge in the fort. Their owner, a Confederate colonel, demanded their return under the Fugitive Slave Acts, which were still in force. General Butler refused, and stated that the runaway slaves were property that could be used by the Confederacy in prosecuting the war; therefore, they were "contraband of war" and could be confiscated. This interpretation of the law caused much controversy. At that time, the war was still in its infancy, and the government's goal was to bring the seceding states back into the Union, not to foment a war.

Butler's proclamation was finally endorsed by Lincoln's Cabinet after much dissension. Postmaster General Blair strongly supported the action. The term "contraband" continued through the war to be a synonym for fugitive slaves. From that date, the flow of escaped slaves across the lines steadily increased.

The patriotic caricature cover shown in **Figure 14-38** commemorates this incident and depicts a number of slaves running to Fort Monroe while their Simon Legree-type master unsuccessfully calls for their return. The woodcut design is printed in blue.

Figure 14-39 shows a woodcut design honoring Colonel Elmer Ellsworth, the first authentic hero of the Civil War. Ellsworth was only 24 years old when he was killed, but he was very well-known. He was famous before the war for organizing the Chicago Zouaves and presenting spectacular exhibitions of precision marching and drills throughout the country. He was also a favorite of President Lincoln and accompanied him during part of the 1860 campaign. Ellsworth and his group of Zouaves would put on exhibitions at the campaign stops and set

Armed Forces and War-related Mails

Figure 14-37. Floyd, of the C.S.A. design. Boston 1¢ local usage with indistinct red Boston CDS. The stamp is canceled with the standard boxed PAID. Design printed in blue.

Figure 14-38. Fort Monroe design with carrier fee of 1¢ and letter postage of 3¢ paid at Philadelphia, April 23, 1862, to Avondale, Pennsylvania.

Figure 14-39. Early patriotic woodcut. Allen's Grove, Wisconsin, November 21, to Corfu, New York. 3¢ domestic letter rate. The cover bears an unusual rimless postmark in blue, with the manuscript day in place of the day-of-the-month slug.

Figure 14-40. Springfield, Illinois, 3¢ letter rate, to Butler, Illinois, dated October 3, 1861.
(C.W. Christian collection)

Figure 14-41. Local carrier use from New York City, dated January 18. Two 1¢ Franklins pay the increased local delivery rate effective July 1, 1863. The cover shows Lincoln's Cabinet and the commander of his army.
(John Kaufmann auction photo)

the stage for the speeches that followed.

At the outbreak of the war, Ellsworth recruited a group of volunteers in New York, the 11th New York, also known as the Fire Zouaves, and took them to Washington to help protect that endangered city. Shortly thereafter he was ordered to move his regiment across the Potomac to Alexandria, Virginia, and to secure that city. Upon his arrival, Ellsworth noted a Confederate flag flying from the roof of a local tavern, and with great zeal and drawn sword, he bounded up a stairway to cut it down. The proprietor of the tavern was a staunch secessionist, and felled Ellsworth with a shotgun blast at short range.

The incident fanned the war fervor of the North. Ellsworth's body was returned to Washington where it laid in state in the White House. Thousands of patriotic envelopes bearing Ellsworth designs were quickly printed and sold. The cover in Figure 14-39 was printed in red and blue on a white envelope. It shows Colonel Ellsworth standing on a Confederate flag. The cover originated at Allen's Grove, Wisconsin, and has an unusual and scarce rimless CDS in blue ink with a manuscript day of the month in black.

The patriotic cover shown in **Figure 14-40** is illustrative of the sentimental and frequently optimistic feelings that were prevalent during the first year of the war. This cover shows two antagonists, both wearing breeches and probably from a Revolutionary War design, engaged in swordplay. They are each wearing strange-looking hats, possibly tricorns, with a feather cockade. An angel is watching over two sleeping children with the caption "God Watches over Them." Also in the design are the words, "As it is — as it will be," a somewhat fatalistic sentiment for those patriotic days. This envelope was printed by Berlin & Jones of New York City.

Figure 14-41 shows the original Lincoln Cabinet, with the addition of General Winfield Scott to round out the roster of early leaders. The portraits on the envelope were printed in black with the rest of the design in red and blue. The cover was printed by Samuel C. Upham of Philadelphia.

The portraits, clockwise from one o'clock, are General Winfield Scott, commander of the Army; Simon Cameron, secretary of war; Salmon P. Chase, secretary of the treasury; Gideon Welles (name misspelled on portrait), secretary of the Navy; William Henry Seward, secretary of state; Edward Bates, attorney general; Caleb B. Smith, secretary of the interior; Montgomery Blair, postmaster general; and Abraham Lincoln, president.

Simon Cameron was not Lincoln's preferred choice as secretary of war. He was appointed to satisfy a promise made by one of Lincoln's campaign managers to secure nomination support from the Pennsylvania Republican Party machine. Poor performance and scandals marred his brief tenure, and he was replaced in January of 1862 by Edwin Stanton.

Figure 14-42 shows another cover from the Farwell correspondence. This exceptionally attractive and well-executed cover has an overall background of pale greenish gray with the words "OUR ZOUAVES." The portraits, in black, are of three regimental colonels of the Pennsylvania militia. These regiments followed the example, popularized by Colonel Ellsworth, of adopting the Zouave uniforms of the French colonial forces. There were many regiments of militia that used the Zouave type of uniform. The baggy pants and colorful short jackets and caps made quite a show at parades, and appealed to the new volunteers. The envelope was printed by S.C. Upham of Philadelphia.

Colonel David Bell Birney had recruited the 23rd Pennsylvania, largely at his own expense. He achieved an excellent war record and was a major general by the time he died of malaria in 1864. Colonel DeWitt Clinton Baxter commanded the 72nd Pennsylvania Regiment and was breveted as a brigadier general at Gettysburg.

Portraits of colonels are usually seen only on the earlier patriotic covers. Pictures of known military figures were scarce, and no general, other than Scott, had yet made a name for himself. By the latter part of 1861, enough campaigns had been waged and battles fought that many generals achieved prominence and displaced the lower-ranking colonels from the envelopes.

General George McClellan was one of the first outstanding generals. With a successful military background, including West Point and the Mexican War, McClellan was made a major general early in the war and given command of the Division of the Potomac. Shortly thereafter, he replaced Scott as commander-in-chief of the Armies. Lack of success in the Peninsular campaigns and at Antietam resulted in his being replaced. He was greatly admired by many and disliked by some. In 1864, he ran as a presidential candidate against Lincoln. After the war, he became governor of New Jersey.

Figure 14-43 shows a cover that honors McClellan. The caption reads, "The right man in the right place." The sender, or someone else at a later time, crossed this out and wrote in pencil, "The wrong man in the wrong place." The envelope illustration features the portrait of McClellan in blue, surrounded by flags, cannons and guns in red and blue. The manufacturers were King and Baird of Philadelphia.

The cover is addressed to R.C. Hale, quartermaster general at Harrisburg, Pennsylvania. A fine engraving of Brigadier General Reuben C. Hale is shown along with the cover.

Another general to gain early prominence was Major General Nathaniel P. Banks. A former governor of Massachusetts, General Banks headed Banks' Division and was active early in the war in the Shenandoah Valley campaigns. His division is also known philatelically for its special postmarks, discussed earlier in this chapter.

Figure 14-42. A 1¢ Franklin pays for local Boston carrier collection and delivery. The cover is postmarked with a red CDS, illegible date, and the stamp is canceled with a boxed PAID.
(C.W. Christian collection)

Figure 14-43. Patriotic envelope, dated September 27, from Christiana, Pennsylvania, honoring Major General George B. McClellan. Addressed to Harrisburg, Pennsylvania, with 3¢ paying the letter rate. The portrait below shows an engraving of Brigadier General Reuben C. Hale, the addressee, as quartermaster general at Harrisburg.

Figure 14-44 shows an example of a patriotic cover honoring General Banks and printed by Charles Magnus. The fine work on the portrait and map are illustrative of the excellence of a Magnus product. The map shows the areas around Harper's Ferry and the Shenandoah Valley, localities where operations commanded by General Banks were conducted.

Figure 14-45 shows an outstanding Magnus design with a statue of General George Washington on horseback and a map of the District of Columbia. This beautiful cover is executed in pale blue, pink and beige. The overall design leaves no room for a stamp and addresses, and is somewhat typical of the later production, which was aimed primarily at patriotic-cover collectors. This particular cover was part of the Ishikawa sale by Christie's, New York in 1993, and achieved an auction realization of $9,200, which reflects the high prices that have become standard for better Magnus covers.

One of the earlier battles to be pictured on patriotic covers was the combined sea and land assault on Fort Royal on November 7, 1861. **Figure 14-46** shows a colorful design in blue and red that commemorates that engagement. Although the arrangement of the design seems to be perfectly appropriate for the Hilton Head/Port Royal battle, the female figure appears to be dressed in the style of the 17th century and was probably adapted from an old print. This envelope was printed by J.R. Hawley of Cincinnati. Naval themes on patriotic covers are hard to find, and only a few dozen different designs have been recorded.

Caricature illustrations were favorites with the public, and the designs ranged from the morbid and macabre to somewhat light-hearted and comic scenes. Caricature and cartoon designs were produced by many of the Civil War printers, but James L. Magee of Philadelphia was probably the most prolific [14:4-26].

Figure 14-47 illustrates one of the more grisly designs. This 1862 cover depicts a monument composed of a pile of human skulls, with a statue of Jefferson Davis as an armed skeleton standing on top. The caption reads, "Monument to the memory of Jeff Davis." As president of the Confederacy and a symbol of the South, Davis was a favorite sub-

Figure 14-44. Magnus cover. New York local carrier collection and delivery at the 1¢ fee. Black "Station D" carrier postmark, dated 2 DEC. Printed in mauve. (James Lee collection)

Armed Forces and War-related Mails

Figure 14-45. Magnus patriotic cover to Keene, New Hampshire. Letter postage paid by a 1¢ (Scott 63) and a 2¢ (73).
(Christie's, New York auction photo)

Figure 14-46. Naval patriotic cover with carrier use from New York City to Bristol, Maine. Also shown in color section.

Figure 14-47. Caricature patriotic originating at New York with 1¢ for carrier fee and 3¢ for letter postage, dated June 25, 1862. Uncalled for at destination, and advertised. Marked at Bordentown, New Jersey, with a boxed "ADVERTISED," and a "1" in a circle for collection of the 1¢ advertising fee. Forwarded from Bordentown to Harrisburg, Pennsylvania, with no forwarding fee noted.
(Robert A. Siegel auction photo)

ject of the cartoonists, and was pictured in many undesirable and humiliating situations.

The cover is addressed to Mr. John Wyman at Bordentown, New Jersey. It was unclaimed, advertised and forwarded to Harrisburg, Pennsylvania, with an advertising fee of 1¢ marked. The Wyman correspondence is another rich source of fine patriotic covers. Wyman was a professional entertainer who put on shows in many

The United States 1¢ Franklin 1861-67

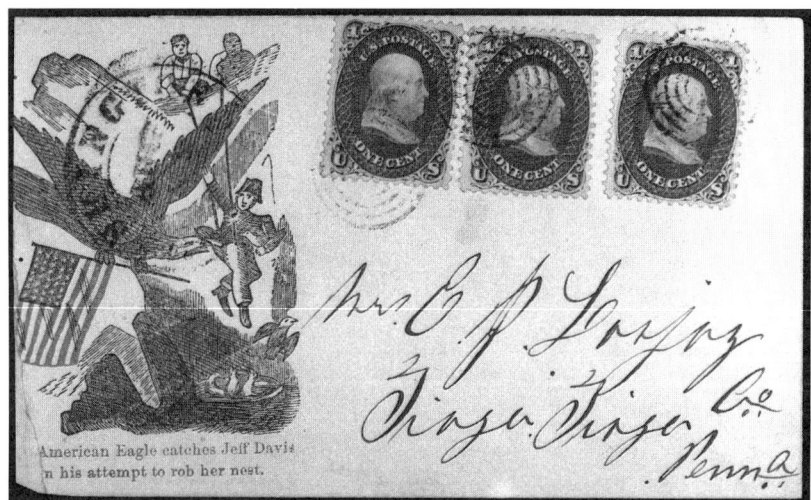

Figure 14-48. Cartoon patriotic showing a large double-circle Washington, D.C., town mark, with three 1¢ Franklins paying the letter postage. Addressed to Tioga, Pennsylvania.

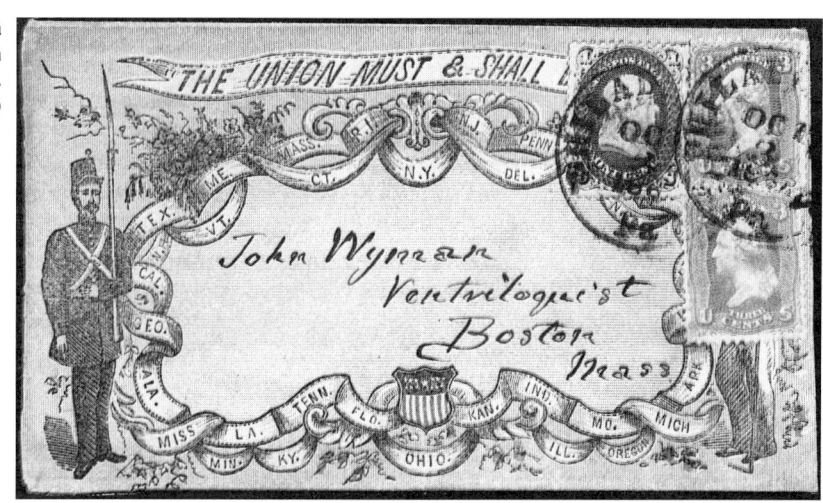

Figure 14-49. Philadelphia double-weight letter with carrier collection to Boston. (James Lee collection)

Figure 14-50. Philadelphia carrier use to Washington, D.C., at the normal 3¢+1¢ postage.

Armed Forces and War-related Mails

Figure 14-51. Unusual printed-both-sides patriotic cover. This attractive cover, with 1¢ to pay the carrier-collection fee and 3¢ for the letter postage from Philadelphia to John Wyman at Barnum's Aquarial Gardens in Boston, has a partial design imprint in blue only on the inside of the envelope. Scarce error. Reverse has an octagonal Philadelphia Penny Mail carrier postmark. Also shown in the color section.

Figure 14-52. Local carrier use with 1¢ paying for carrier collection and delivery at Boston. Faint red CDS, and canceled with a boxed PAID. (C.W. Christian collection)

of the principal Eastern cities. Covers addressed to him at these cities frequently are addressed as "Wyman the Magician," "Wyman the Ventriloquist" or some similar title. Evidently his act included demonstrations of legerdemain and ventriloquism. Most, but not all, of the correspondence originates in Philadelphia, and each is embellished with a patriotic design.

Figure 14-48 shows a more comical design. Jefferson Davis is being lowered from a cliff-top into an eagles' nest. The caption reads, "American Eagle catches Jeff Davis in his attempt to rob her nest." The illustration is done in red and blue, with the caption in red, on a buff cover.

Another interesting cover from the Wyman correspondence is illustrated in **Figure 14-49**. This design was probably conceived early in the conflict. It shows a soldier and sailor in pre-Civil War uniforms, with a central ornate border containing the names of all of the states, including the secessionist states, on an unbroken ribbon. Above is a banner proclaiming THE UNION MUST AND SHALL BE PRESERVED. The overall design is printed in blue on a white envelope.

Figure 14-50 shows another Wyman cover with the popular design motif of an eagle, flag and shield. Many of the surviving patriotic covers contain these three design elements in various combinations. Of the three, a representation of the flag is the most common and is frequently seen as the only element in a design. The patriotic illustration is printed in red and blue on a buff envelope.

A very attractive and unusual cover is illustrated in **Figure 14-51**. This red, white and blue patriotic cover shows a naval warship with a background of an Army barracks and cannon. It is addressed to John Wyman at Barnum's Aquarial Gardens in Boston, and has the unusual feature that the inside of the envelope has another printing of the design in blue without the red color. This is the only example of this type of error that this writer has seen on a patriotic cover. The printing on the reverse can be faintly seen through the paper in the illustration

285

Figure 14-53. New York City carrier use 1¢ paying for carrier collection and 3¢ for letter postage to Gardiner, Maine. The CDS is dated July 28, 1862. The 3¢ stamp (Scott 63) is in the scarce plum shade (unlisted in Scott).
(C.W. Christian collection)

Figure 14-54. Local use with 1¢ paid for carrier collection and delivery at Philadelphia. Double postmarked with the octagonal Philadelphia carrier marking, one strike used as a cancellation.

presented here.

Figure 14-52 illustrates a classic design of the period. These "Loyal to the Union" envelopes were made in large quantities for each of the states in the Union, and were very popular. The design was the same for each state, with only the name of the state and the representation of the state seal being different. This State of Massachusetts design was produced by John G. Wells of New York City. Other designs of similar nature were printed by Samuel Upham of Philadelphia and Reagles and Co. of New York. The latter company was possibly the most prolific producer of this type of envelope.

The illustration is in pink, red and blue, with an overall background of light blue. This is another cover from the Farwell correspondence.

Figure 14-53 shows an unusual flag illustration. This particular design has a finely executed picture of an eagle printed in blue, carrying a crude representation of the American flag in its beak. Obviously a stock die was altered to add the flag. The envelope was printed by J.G. Wells at New York City. The unusual boldness of the flag design, which is the only part of the design in black, adds emphasis to the illustration. A somewhat melodramatic poem is printed below the design:

"Woe, woe, to the traitorous children of Mars,
Who challenge this bird, with his banner of stars;
We will teach them this lesson, that truth and the right,
Are ever Triumphant, and must win the fight."

Another striking flag patriotic is illustrated in **Figure 14-54**. The cover shows a representation of both the Union flag and the "palm tree and serpent" flag of the secessionists. The banner on the serpent flag reads, SOUTHERN RIGHTS AT ALL HAZARDS. The cover is printed in red and blue, and shows a stanza from a song of the period, "Down with the Serpent Flag." In very small print along the side and top left is a notice that the song was published and sold with piano accompaniment by Judson Higgins, Chicago. The writer noted in manuscript above the Union banner, "Good Old Flag."

A rare flag patriotic is shown in **Figure 14-55**. Only two examples of this particular design have been reported. It depicts the Irish "harp flag" in an attractive shade of emerald green. The combination of the green flag with a red Boston CDS and a blue 1¢ Franklin make this an outstandingly beautiful cover. Below the flag, printed in green, is the poem,

"Erin, O Erin, though long in the shade,
Thy Star will shine out when the problems shall fade."

While not exactly a Civil War sentiment, it was known by the producers of patriotic envelopes that Irish theme covers could be big sellers with the large Irish populations of Boston and some other cities, and the volunteer Irish Brigades, such as the 60th Corcoran Brigade, had been formed. This cover may have been printed by Frederick Kimmel, who is known to have produced at least one other Irish design [14:4-23].

The final patriotic cover to be discussed in this section is a homemade design and is a favorite of this author. Its colorful and unique design, while not approaching the artistic excellence of many of the commercial covers, gives a feeling of personal involvement by the sender. **Figure 14-56** shows this cover. The illustration was evidently cut from a book or poster and pasted on the envelope. The shield at the upper right of the design is tied to the cover by the Philadelphia carrier handstamp. The picture depicts a Revolutionary War scene with George Washington on horseback, accompanied by American troops. They may be advancing in a battle, for there is a recumbent, and possibly wounded, soldier in the forefront. The design is printed in blue, red and black. Hand-drawn patriotic designs showing the work of artistic mailers are also recorded, but they are very scarce.

With the cessation of hostilities, general interest in patriotic envelopes practically disappeared. Hundreds of thousands of unused envelopes remained unsold, and those that could not be disposed of at bargain prices

Figure 14-55. Local carrier use at Boston with 1¢ paid for carrier collection and delivery, dated February 28 and canceled with a boxed PAID. (C.W. Christian collection)

Figure 14-56. Homemade patriotic design. Carrier use with 1¢ to pay the carrier collection fee and 3¢ for the letter postage from Philadelphia to Columbia, Pennsylvania. Canceled by a balloon Philadelphia town mark dated June 3, 1862, and additionally marked with a JUN 3/ 5½ PM carrier handstamp. The picture was probably cut from a publication of some sort and pasted on the envelope. Also shown in color section.

were stored in warehouses. Some of these were resurrected for the Spanish-American War and offered again to the public. Civil War theme covers from the later conflict are scarce. A large number of surplus covers surfaced at various times over the years and can still be obtained at reasonable prices. The collector of used Civil War covers should use some caution when acquiring items to ensure that the use is authentic and not an unused cover with added stamps and postmarks.

Sanitary Commission Covers

Envelopes with illustrations or corner cards from the U.S. Sanitary Commission, and covers that bear handstamps showing that the postage had been paid by the commission, are a scarce and important subcategory of patriotic covers.

Just two weeks after the fall of Fort Sumter, a small group of ladies met on April 25, 1861, in New York City. These women wanted to be part of the war effort, and the meeting was held to decide how they could help. It turned out to be one of the most momentous meetings of the war, and resulted in the formation of the Sanitary Commission, an organization that saved thousands of lives and provided care and comfort to soldiers throughout the war. Over a four-year period, it raised more than $20 million in money and in supplies for the care of members of the armed services, and also provided hundreds of thousands of hours of service by volunteers.

The immediate result of the initial meeting was the formation of the Central Association of Relief. Looking for guidance on how to proceed, the group requested advice from Dr. Henry W. Bellows, a prominent New York clergyman. Bellows advised them to find out what the government would and could do with regard to the health and welfare of the individual soldiers, and then to attempt to do those things that the government felt it was unable to do. It was good advice.

At the beginning of the war, the federal government had a military medical service in place to care for the needs of the regular Army, but there were absolutely no government provisions made for the hundreds of volunteer and militia organizations that would soon arrive on the scene. Volunteer surgeons and medical personnel did accompany the new units, but they had little experience in ensuring sanitary conditions in the field encampments that came into being. The commanders of many of these units frequently were political or business leaders with meager or no experience in actual wartime conditions. They found themselves overwhelmed with the problems of a war command.

Congress had refused to appropriate any money for the enlargement of the federal medical system, so the recruits were forced to rely on their vounteer regiment's well-meaning, but inexperienced, medical and sanitation support. Even the well-informed and trained regimental surgeons had little in the way of equipment and supplies with which to work. Conditions in the militia and volunteer camps around Washington, D.C., were deplorable, an invitation to disease and sickness that could take more lives than secessionist guns.

Bellows became personally interested in the relief project, and journeyed to Washington to see what could be done. He met with strong initial opposition from the Army medical service, the War Department, and even from President Lincoln, who remarked that he thought it would be a "fifth wheel to the coach" [16:330]. Bellows persevered in his attempts to convince the government that it needed help, and finally won the support of the acting surgeon general who wrote to Simon Cameron, the secretary of war, requesting that an unpaid commission be formed to investigate and report on sanitary conditions in the camps and to offer advice to correct the problems. On June 13, 1861, the request was approved by President Lincoln, and the U.S. Sanitary Commission was established.

The charter of the commission rapidly expanded. In addition to having experienced physicians inspect the camps and advise commanders, the commission enacted a far-reaching campaign to collect funds. Although the top leaders and the Army surgeons of the commission were men, most of the thousands of volunteers who collected money and donated supplies, arranged fairs and bourses to raise funds, and who volunteered for every kind of support task, were women. The seeds planted in New York had flourished, and an organization devoted to medical and convalescent care, sanitation, morale, and every type of assistance to the troops, came into being.

There were other smaller relief groups such as the U.S. Christian Commission, which was formed by the YMCA, but the Sanitary Commission is the only one that produced any quantity of philatelic material.

At the large fairs that were organized to raise funds, special stamps or labels were sold by the Sanitary Commission to help raise money. These stamps could be placed on an envelope (usually an envelope purchased at the fair with a printed corner card of the commission) and addressed to a destination within the fairgrounds. The local letter would be delivered by Sanitary Fair volunteers. With the addition of proper U.S. postage, such letters could be addressed to any destination. The Post Office Department maintained a temporary post office at the fairs where postage stamps could be purchased and the souvenir letters mailed. Only one example of a cover

Figure 14-57. Very rare use of a green Brooklyn Sanitary Fair stamp with the 1¢ Franklin. The cover was mailed locally at the 1¢ fee for carrier delivery at Brooklyn, New York. It was postmarked in December, probably 1863.
(Courtesy of Alvin and Marjorie Kantor)

showing a fair label and also the use of the 1¢ Franklin has been recorded (**Figure 14-57**). The 1¢ stamp was accompanied with a green Brooklyn Sanitary Fair label. The cover is postmarked at Brooklyn, New York. The Brooklyn Fair was held from February 22 to March 8, 1864.

Sanitary Commission stamps used at these fairs are listed in the Scott specialized catalog, and collections of them have been formed. Nine different designs are listed. One of the most outstanding collections of these items has been formed by Alvin Kantor and his wife, Marjorie. In 1992, they published a specialized treatise on the subject [17]. This without a doubt is one of the most beautiful and well-produced philatelic books ever printed. The illustrations, type fonts, book design, informational content, and even the paper used, are all outstanding. The Kantors produced a superlative book that covers every aspect of the Sanitary Commission and its philatelic legacy. It is highly recommended for the library of any collector of Civil War postal history.

In addition to the covers produced for the fairs, illustrated envelopes were printed that portrayed some of the other benevolent activities of the commission. Figure 10-30 in Chapter 10 showed a Volunteer Hospital that was maintained in Philadelphia. This November 11, 1861, cover is one of the earlier examples publicizing the Sanitary Commission efforts. The illustration is printed in blue and red, and a legend in small type at the left side of the cover reads, "Volunteer Refreshment Committee, foot of Washington St. Phila."

Another view of the same installation is shown in **Figure 14-58**. This drawing is printed in pale blue on a white envelope and is most attractive. The illustration shows the volunteer refreshment saloon, with a large number of visiting troops, some of them in formation. On the side of the building a sign proclaims, "Hot Coffee and Refreshments for Union Volunteers." In the foreground are two railway cars with a column of soldiers going on-board. Troops passing through Philadelphia evidently were frequent users of the facility, and troop trains made a special stop for the convenience of the soldiers in transit. At the bottom of the illustration is the legend, "W. Boell, Lithographer and Printer, Walnut St. Ph."

A special series of envelopes was printed for the "Great Central Fair for the Sanitary Commission" that was held in Philadelphia from June 7 to June 28, 1864. An example of one of these covers is shown in **Figure 14-59**. The design depicts a recumbent, wounded soldier being attended, presumably by medics. In the background is a covered wagon with "U.S. Sanitary Commission" written on the side. This design was printed in black, violet, purple, brown, maroon, red, blue and possibly green [17:142]. Some of the envelopes have only the illustration with the wording GREAT CENTRAL FAIR for the SANITARY COMMISSION. Others show additional return legends and addresses. The cover in Figure 14-59 is unsealed and was posted at Philadelphia at the 2¢ circular rate. The stamps are canceled with a worn octagonal Philadelphia postmark. This is the last year of use for this marking. The cover is docketed in pencil "4/26/1864." Most of these covers have postmark dates that preceded the opening of the fair. It is presumed that they contained brochures advertising and describing the coming event.

Figure 14-60 shows a similar item. This cover is printed in red and has additional return-address lettering. It was mailed at Philadelphia for unsealed circular delivery. The normal rate in 1864 for local mail was 2¢. The 1¢ charge is another example of the previously discussed special rates where mailers of circulars could contract with the Philadelphia post office for a special reduced carrier-delivery charge. The 1¢ stamp has been scissor-cut at the top and bottom. It appears that horizontal strips were cut from the panes to reduce the job of applying

Figure 14-58. Sanitary Commission cover from Philadelphia, dated February 18, 1862, with 1¢+3¢ for carrier fee and letter postage to Washington, D.C. A similar cover dated 10 days earlier is shown in the color section.
(Courtesy of Alvin and Marjorie Kantor)

Figure 14-59. Sanitary Commission. Unsealed circular use at the 2¢ rate from Philadelphia to Coudersport, Pennsylvania. Stamps canceled with late use of an octagonal carrier marking. Cover docketed in pencil 4/26/1864.

Figure 14-60. Sanitary Commission. Unsealed local circular use at Philadelphia. Postmarked on April 12, 1864, with the distinctive PHILADA/POST OFFICE mark that was frequently used on cover for contract circular delivery at the reduced rate of 1¢.
(John Kaufmann auction photo)

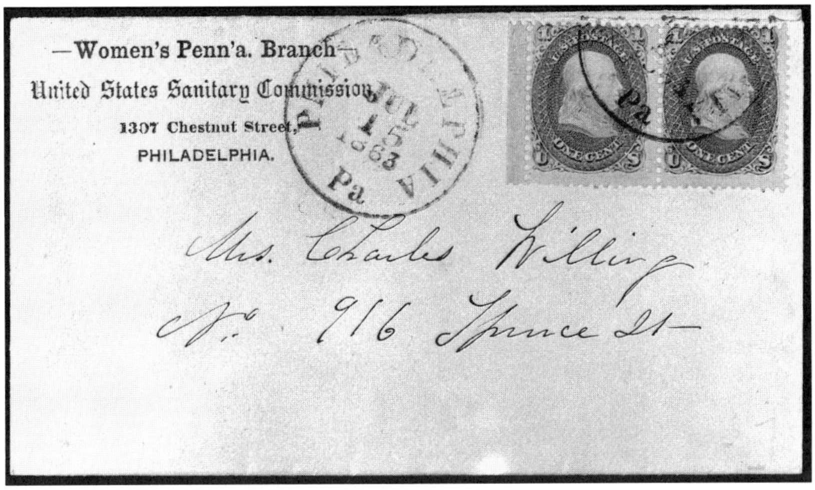

Figure 14-61. Women's Branch of the Sanitary Commission. Philadelphia, July 15, 1863. Local cover with postage paid by a pair of light-blue 1¢ Franklins.

stamps to a large number of envelopes.

Phildelphia seems to have had the largest group in the Sanitary Commission organizations, or at least it is the best represented by correspondence that has survived to the present day. **Figure 14-61** illustrates a local cover, dated July 15, 1863, at Philadelphia, with two 1¢ Franklins paying the new 2¢ local rate with free carrier delivery. This particular cover has a corner card from the "Women's Penn'a. Branch" of the Sanitary Commission, which evidently had its office on the same street near the Sanitary Commission office address on the cover in Figure 14-60.

The headquarters of the commission was located in Washington. **Figure 14-62** shows a corner-card cover. The cover was mailed in New York on May 3 (year not shown). The cover is franked by the signature of Anson P. Morrill, who was a congressman from Readfield, Maine, and a 1¢ stamp was applied to pay for the carrier collection at New York. The cover is addressed to Roxbury, Massachusetts. On the surface, this seems to be a strange set of circumstances: A congressman from Maine franks a Washington return-address cover mailed in New York to a Massachusetts destination.

Actually, this is not too unusual. Some congressmen, evidently to support the Sanitary Commission work, affixed their frank to a significant number of envelopes that were then used for commission correspondence. This saved the commission postage and possibly provided the congressman with some feeling of contributing to the effort. The practice, of course, was not legal, since the letters were not the personal or legislative correspondence of the congressman. Evidently this was widely tolerated. Congressional free franks are also found on soldiers' mail.

In 1864, the Sanitary Commission also entered the picture with regard to the delivery of mails. This was a much more important postal function than the production of illustrated envelopes, but unfortunately did not result in any artifacts bearing 1¢ stamps. Postal regulations adequately took care of the problem of a soldier who wanted to mail a letter but had no stamp. All he had to do was to write "soldier's letter" on it and get it signed by a certifying officer. The postage would be collected from the addressee. This was fine for mail being sent to civilian addresses, but when the recipient was also a soldier in the field, the situation frequently was unmanageable.

Mail addressed from one field location to another was collected by the military postal clerk from the sender for deposit in the U.S. mail. It was then delivered to a post office as near the destination as possible. At that point, the mail returned to the military system where it was carried to the addressee.

The problem arose when there was postage due on a letter. The civilian postmaster was not allowed to release any unpaid mail to the military. Therefore, it was necessary to list the unpaid letters and amounts due and have the military mail service try to contact the addressee, collect the amount due and turn the money over to the civilian postmaster, who would then release the letter. Obviously, this was cumbersome. Often the request for payment never caught up with the addressee, or he didn't have the money to pay the charge.

Huge amounts of collect mail were piling up in forward-area post offices such as Nashville and Louisville. On May 20, 1864, a Post Office Department special agent, who had been inspecting the postal operations at Nashville and Chattanooga, wrote to the Sanitary commissioner at Louisville concerning this undelivered mail. He suggested that the Sanitary Commission might want to add a

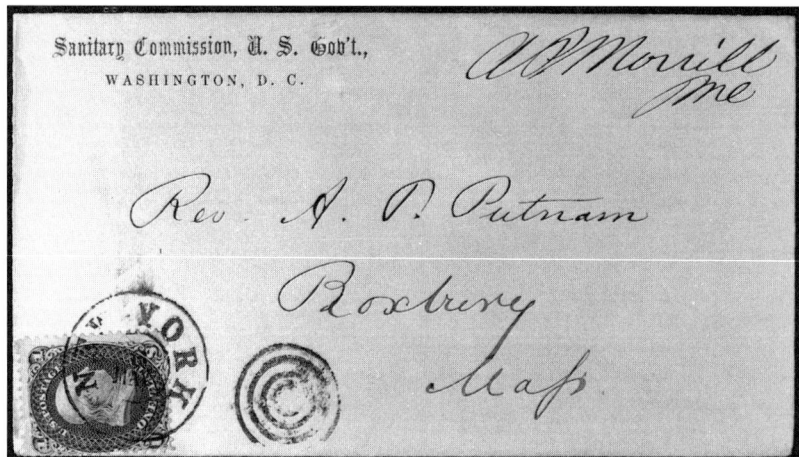

Figure 14-62. Free-franked Sanitary Commission cover, dated May 3, at New York. It carries the franking signature of A.P. Morill. The 1¢ stamp pays the carrier-collection fee to the mails for postage-free transmission to Roxbury, Massachusetts.

service to its many others, paying the postage due on these letters so they could continue on to their destination. The suggestion was favorably acted upon and the ransom was paid. Each cover was marked with a distinctive handstamp "Paid By the U.S. Sanitary Commission," and the letters were released to be delivered [18:252].

Many letters also originated from soldiers at hospitals or other Sanitary Commission relief centers. Frequently the soldiers could not provide stamps and were in no position to have their mail certified by regimental officers. The commission provided stamps for these soldiers, as well as writing materials. Stamped covers can be found with a manuscript notation, "Paid by the Sanitary Commission." The payments could have been made at any location where a stamp from the commission would help send a letter on its way. Most all of these examples are paid with the 3¢ 1861 stamp. The volunteers from the commission who were engaged in this work normally had an adequate supply of 3¢ stamps for their purpose, and didn't have to resort to affixing three 1¢ Franklins.

An account of the many charitable and humanitarian achievements of the commission would fill a large book. It raised money to equip hospital boats, built huge convalescent homes, sent hundreds of thousands of boxes of clothes and needed items to troops in the field, and after the end of the war, supported the veterans in many ways. The country and its soldiers and sailors owed a great debt of gratitude to this magnificent organization.

References

1. Graham, Richard B. "Washington During the Civil War." *Chronicle*. May 1966.

2. Graham, Richard B. "North-South Mail Ends." *S.P.A. Journal*. November 1963.

3. *Report of the Postmaster General for 1861*. Reprints of the original documents. Theron Wierenga. Holland, Michigan. 1977.

4. Graham, Richard B. "Federal Soldiers' and Naval Letters." *Chronicle*. No. 116. November 1982.

5. Graham, Richard B. "Mercedita Revisited." *Chronicle*. No. 149. February 1991.

6. Graham, Richard B. "Old Point Comfort." *S.P.A. Journal*. April 1965.

7. Winter, Richard F. "Havana to London - Unusual Civil War Routing." *Chronicle*. No.150. May 1991.

8. *United States Mail and Post Office Assistant*. Reprinted by the Collectors Club of Chicago. 1975.

9. Graham, Richard B. "Ship Island, Mississippi." *Chronicle*. No. 127. August 1985.

10. McGee, M. Clinton. "Re-establishment of Federal Postal System in New Orleans." *Chronicle*. No. 129. February 1986.

11. Barnes, James. "The Navies." *The Photographic History of the Civil War*. Volume VI. Review of Reviews Co. 1911.

12. Graham, Richard B. "Armed Forces Mail." *United States Postal History Sampler*. Linn's Handbook Series No. 2. Linn's Stamp News, Sidney, Ohio. 1992.

13. Laurence, Robert. *The George Walcott Collection of Used Civil War Patriotic Covers.* Privately published. 1934.

14. Grant, Robert W. *The Handbook of Civil War Patriotic Envelopes and Postal History.* Vol I. 1977.

15. Weiss, William R., Jr. *The Catalog of Union Civil War Patriotic Covers.* Weiss Philatelics. Bethlehem, Pennsylvania. 1995.

16. Thompson, Holland. "The Sanitary Commission and Other Relief Agencies." *The Photographic History of the Civil War.* Volume VII. Review of Reviews Co. 1911.

17. Kantor, Alvin R. and Marjorie S. *Sanitary Fairs.* Amos Philatelics Inc. 1992.

18. Graham, Richard B. "Paid by the Sanitary Commission." *Chronicle.* No. 124. November 1984.

The United States 1¢ Franklin 1861-67

CHAPTER 15

Illustrated Covers

Introduction

Illustrated envelopes began to appear about the same time as the first U.S. postage stamps. Prior to 1845, postage was charged on the basis of how many sheets were contained in a letter and how far it was to be sent. An extra cover sheet or envelope was an unnecessary extravagance, and not many were used. The Acts of 1845 changed the basis for assessing postage to weight and distance, and letters began to take on a somewhat different appearance. The paper was generally thinner and lighter, and the sheets were smaller. Envelopes began to be used frequently, and advertisements and fancy corner cards were printed on some of them. By the mid-1850s these illustrations were starting to appear in quantity, and by the outbreak of the Civil War many designs were in use.

During the Civil War, the rate of increase of new commercial designs slowed due to other commitments to the war. Of course the thousands of designs that appeared on patriotic covers more than compensated for the reduction in commercial illustrations. After the war, the volume of commercial and specialty designs again increased, reaching a peak somewhere around the turn of the century.

Illustrated covers have for many years been a philatelic stepchild. Other than patriotic covers, which were discussed in the preceding chapter, few significant general collections of illustrated covers have been assembled until recently. Starting about 1970, John R. Biddle began acquiring illustrated covers of the 19th and early 20th centuries. Over the following 11 years, he accumulated about 13,000 different covers and stated that he had inspected more than 750,000 items in his search for outstanding material [1].

The Biddle collection was placed at auction in 1981, and the David G. Phillips Co. of North Miami, Florida, prepared a color catalog of the collection. This is the first major cataloging of illustrated covers to become available since the sale of the Edward S. Knapp collections in 1941-42.

Illustrated covers fall into several major, and somewhat arbitrary, categories. There are the advertising covers, which is the largest group. Then come the patriotic covers, followed by smaller selections of local and state government designs, fancy corner cards and logos, valentines and love letters, and envelopes that advocate various causes, such as the well-known "temperance covers." All of these may be collected primarily because of the design. To the collector of illustrated covers, stamps and postal use are often of secondary importance.

Attractive or striking illustrations have always been of interest to philatelists. Covers combining special uses or scarce stamps along with an intriguing design have invariably commanded an additional premium. However, for many years only a few major collections were put together where the design on the cover was the important element. The rules and regulations for exhibiting also tended to discriminate against this type of showing. Fortunately, this is changing, and specialty categories in exhibiting now allow for presentations of illustrated covers where the designs contribute in a major way to the philatelic goal of the exhibit. In this writer's opinion, there is no way that the tremendous amount of historical and cultural information that resides in the designs of illustrated covers can be overlooked, or thought not to be important to philately. Of course, to be collectible in a philatelic sense, these covers must have been used postally.

For the Civil War era, patriotic designs open a window into the thoughts and patriotic sentiments of a nation. Advertising illustrations do the same thing for the commerce and trade that was being conducted during those years. Without understanding a little of how the people who wrote the letters thought and lived, the collecting of their postal history loses some of its depth and fascination.

Commerce was the life-blood of the nation. The Civil War was raging, but normal pursuits still occupied the majority of most lives in the North. One needs only to read some of the contemporary journals, such as *Harper's New Monthly Magazine*, to see that the majority of space was assigned to nonwar activities. Industry, fashion, literature and other normal activities continued to play a prominent part in everyday living.

In this chapter, a limited but representative selection of illustrated covers that include use of the 1¢ Franklin will be discussed. They provide small glimpses into mid-19th-century life.

Advertising Covers

The simplest of the advertising covers are those that show a corner card, usually in a single color, with varying intricacy of design. Most covers with printed designs give no indication of the manufacturer or printer

Figure 15-1. Embossed corner advertisement in red brown for a carpet merchant in New York City. The cover is postmarked June 8. Three 1¢ Franklins pay the domestic letter rate to Durham, Connecticut.

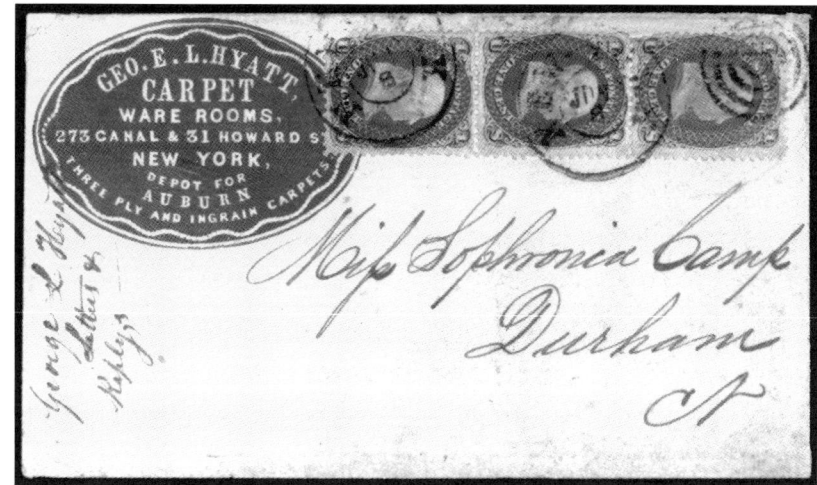

Figure 15-2. Embossed corner-card advertisement in dark blue for a Manhattan life insurance firm. The 1¢ fee paid for local carrier collection and delivery at Philadelphia. The cover is postmarked and the stamp canceled with two strikes of the Philadelphia octagonal carrier marking. Also shown in color section.
(C.W. Christian collection)

Figure 15-3. Corner illustration for a New York City hotel. The illustration is printed in dark blue. The 1¢ stamp paid the carrier-collection fee and the 3¢ paid the postage to Norwich, Chenango County, New York.

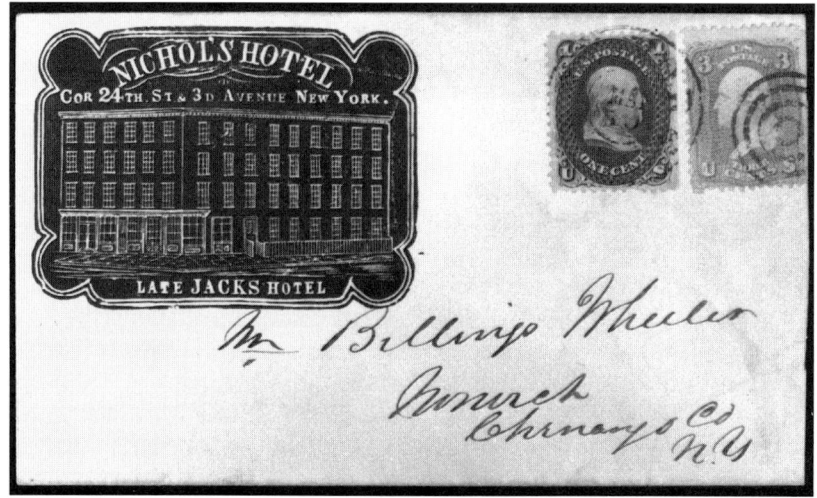

Figure 15-4. Corner illustration for a Montreal, Canada, telegraph firm. The cover was mailed at Watertown, New York, on August 20, 1863. Postage was paid to Cape Vincent, New York, with three 1¢ stamps.
(Richard B. Graham photo)

of the envelope, but it is likely that many printers of patriotic covers were also heavily involved in the production of illustrated envelopes for business customers.

The example shown in **Figure 15-1** is typical of the early type of fancy corner-card advertisement. These became popular during the 1850s and continued to be used through the following decade. The design on this cover is embossed and printed in a deep brownish red on a buff envelope, advertising a New York City carpet sales room. The docketing at the left side reads "George L. Hyatt/Letters &,/Replys—."

A colorful embossed corner advertisement of the Knickerbocker Ice Company of Philadelphia, showing a horse-drawn ice wagon and two icemen, is reproduced in Chapter 10 as Figure 10-31. This cover is also shown in the color section. The design is printed in a deep red on an orange cover. The combination of those colors with the 1¢ blue and 3¢ rose stamps is attractive. Additionally, the unusually elegant Spencerian script makes this cover particularly appealing.

Another embossed design is shown in **Figure 15-2**. This advertisement for the Manhattan Life Insurance Co. is printed in dark blue on a buff envelope. The advertisement lists the capital of the insurance firm as $100,000. That seems a bit small, even with the greater worth of the dollar in the 1860s.

Figure 15-3 shows an early hotel advertisement. The illustration is printed (not embossed) in dark blue on a buff envelope. The caption at the bottom of the design is interesting. "Late Jacks' Hotel" is a quaint way to refer to the previous name of the hotel, or proprietor, as the case may be. In most illustrations of buildings and installations, a bit of artistic license is taken. The artist's rendition generally shows the edifice as larger and more imposing than is actually the case – sort of like the architect's drawing of one's new home. Hotels continue to this day to be one of the principal users of illustrated corner-card envelopes.

A different type of corner illustration is shown in **Figure 15-4**. The picture shows an early telegraph machine, encircled with a belt as a frame. On the belt is the name of the firm, "Montreal Telegraph Co." The design is printed in black. The cover originated at Watertown, in northern New York state, and is addressed to Cape Vincent, a small town on the shore of the St. Lawrence River at the entrance to Lake Ontario. Cape Vincent is just a couple of miles from the Canadian border, so it is not surprising that a Canadian telegraph company would be operating in that area.

Another Philadelphia insurance company advertising cover is illustrated in **Figure 15-5**. The Connecticut Mutual Life Insurance Co. appears to be on a strong financial footing, with capitalization of $4.5 million. Along the top of the cover is a notice: "Dividends to policy holders of 50 per cent per annum." This seems to be a very high return. One wonders what was the basis of the 50-percent dividend.

Figure 15-6 shows a cover with an enclosure that reflects the inflationary pressures due to the Civil War. Johnson's "Union Washing Machine" had been offered at the price of $10 as noted in the advertisement on the envelope. An enclosure to the notice, dated January 17, 1863, announces that "Owing to the very great advance in the price of the various Materials used by us . . . as well as in the rate of wages, we are COMPELLED to raise the price . . . to $12 . . . Regretting the necessity and the cause of it." The design on this interesting cover is printed in black on a pale-yellow envelope.

Figure 15-7 shows a cover with an advertisement for a patented spring bed. John Putnam's store was located in Boston, and he was the sender of numerous letters to Samuel Putnam, a soldier with the 14th Massa-

297

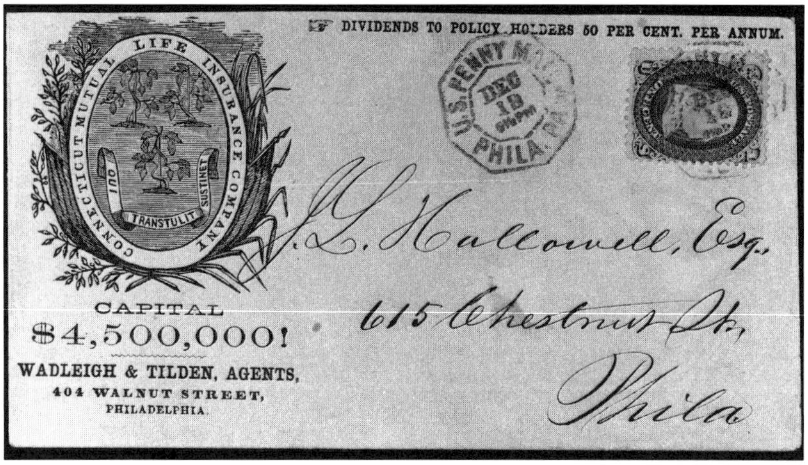

Figure 15-5. Insurance company advertisement. The 1¢ Franklin paid for local carrier collection and delivery at Philadelphia. The cover bears two strikes of the "Penny Mail" DEC 18 marking. The cover features an unusual fancy embossed return address on the envelope flap.
(C.W. Christian collection)

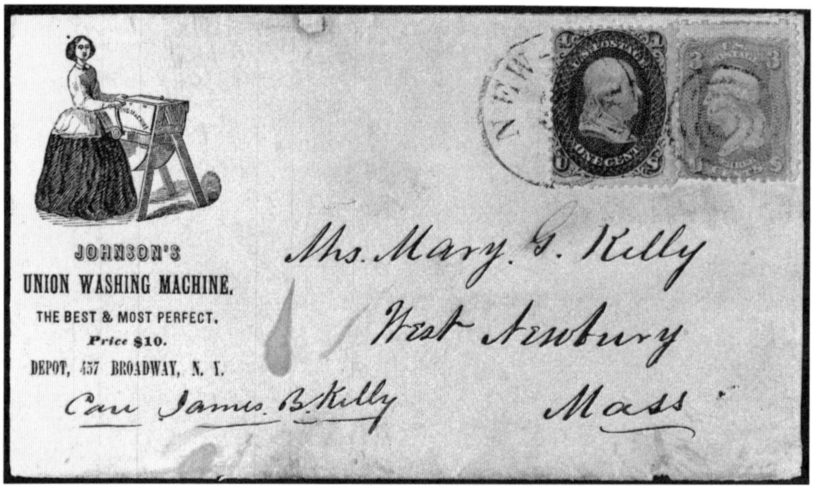

Figure 15-6. The advertisement for a clothes-washing equipment manufacturer is printed in black on a pale-yellow envelope. The stamps paid the New York City 1¢ carrier collection fee and 3¢ postage to West Newbury, Massachusetts, in 1863.

J. JOHNSON & CO.
No. 457 Broadway.
PROPRIETORS OF
Union Washing Machine, - - $12
Union Clothes Dryer, - - $3, 4 & 5
Union Wringer, - - - - - $8
We sell only for Cash and never Consign.

New York, Jan. 17th, 1863.

Dear Sir,

Owing to the very great advance in the price of the various Materials used by us, as well as in the rate of wages, we are COMPELLED to raise the price of our UNION WASHING MACHINE to $12, to take effect on 1st February, with the usual discount to Agents.

All orders sent to us previous to that date will be filled at present rates. Regretting this necessity and the cause of it,

We are, dear Sir,

Your obedient Servants,

J. JOHNSON & CO.

P. S. The price of our UNION WRINGER will, for the present, remain as heretofore.

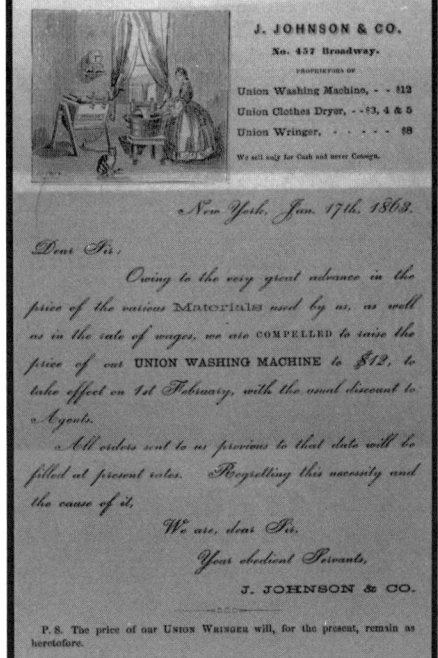

chusetts Volunteers. Many similar Putnam letters have survived the years, and their appearance at auctions is not unusual. The illustration here is printed in black on an orange cover, which makes a nice contrast with the blue stamp. On this particular cover, the 1¢ blue stamp, paying the carrier fee, is not canceled, apparently from an oversight.

The cover in **Figure 15-8** shows an unusually well-executed design. The illustration shows the J. Bigler & Co. shipyard on the shore of the Hudson River at Newburgh, New York. The design is printed in bright magenta on a white envelope. The drawing of the shipyard with the river in the background is quite artistic, creating one of the better advertising renditions that this author has seen. The cover has a private double-circle marking in blue with "J. Bigler & Co." and the date "25 JUL 1863." The postmark is dated July 27, and the letter is addressed to another shipbuilder at Nyack, New York, 30 miles down the Hudson.

Figure 15-9 shows a design that covers most of

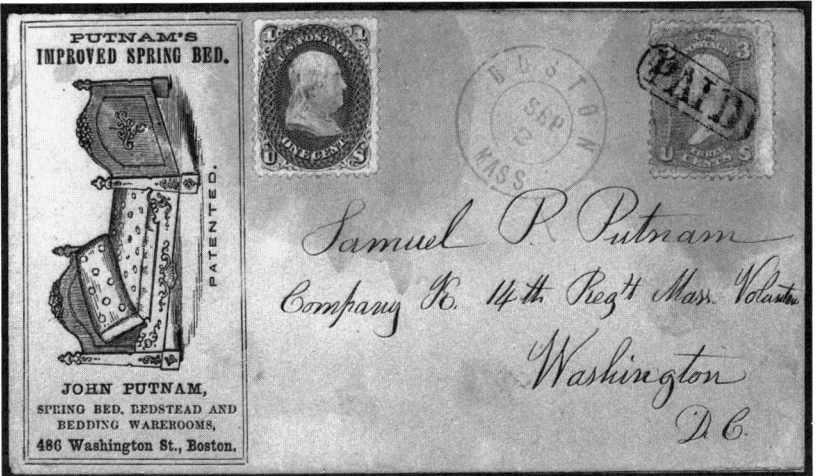

Figure 15-7. Advertisement for a purveyor of beds and bedding in Boston, Massachussets. The 1¢ stamp paid for carrier collection to the mails, and the 3¢ paid for postage. The cover is addressed to a soldier at Washington, D.C. The advertisement is printed in black on an orange envelope.

Figure 15-8. Advertisement for a Newburgh, New York, shipbuilder. The cover was mailed on July 27, 1863, to Nyack, New York, at the 3¢ letter rate. The origin of mailing is illegible. The illustration is printed in magenta on a white envelope. A blue double-circle private mailer's marking is at lower left.
(James Lee collection)

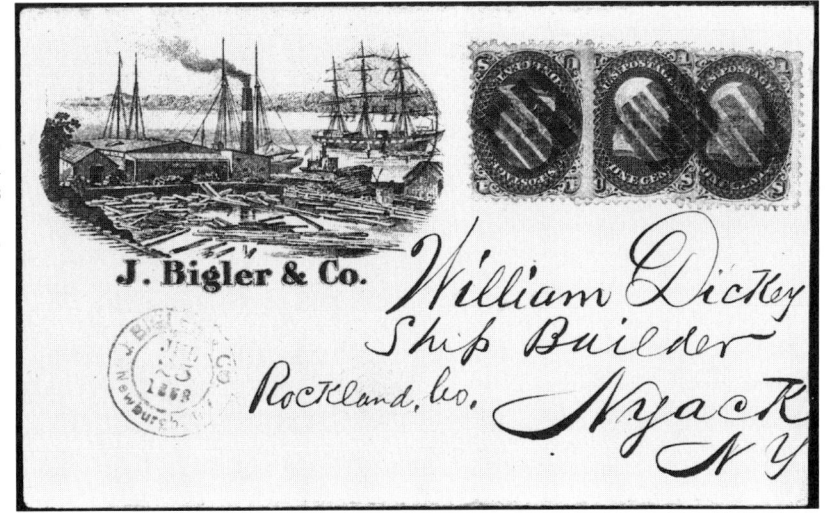

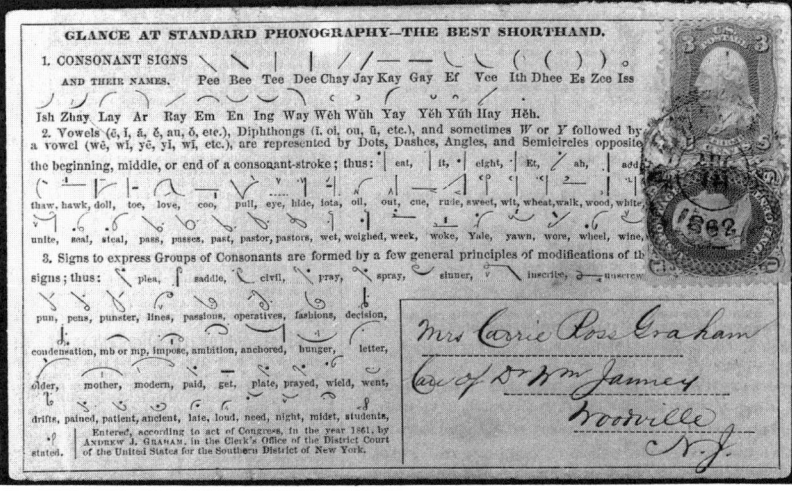

Figure 15-9. Phonography advertisement with 1¢ for carrier collection at New York City, on August 14, 1862, and 3¢ for postage to Woodville, New Jersey.
(Courtesy of Robert A. Siegel Inc.)

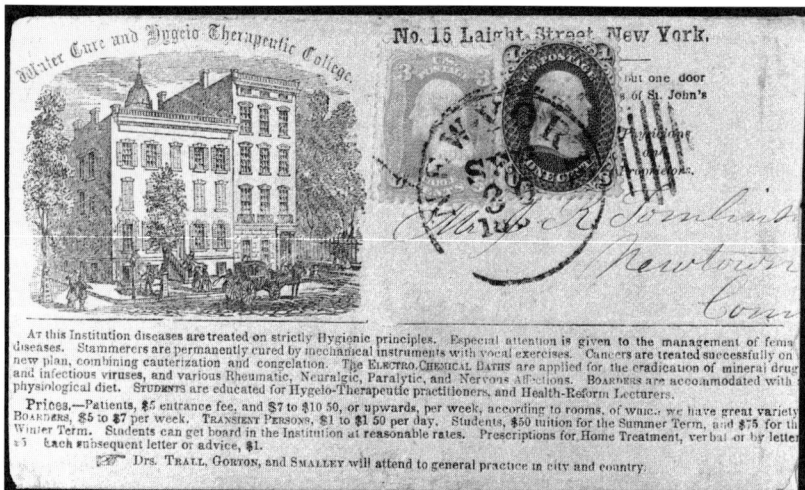

Figure 15-10. Advertisement for a New York City medical college that specialized in somewhat unconventional treatments. The cover originated in New York City with 1¢ for carrier collection to the mails on September 30 (probably 1861). A 3¢ rose-pink stamp (Scott 64a) paid the postage to Newtown, Connecticut.

Figure 15-11. Lithographed brewery advertisement, New York City, 1862. The 1¢ paid for the carrier-collection-to-the-mails fee, with 3¢ for postage to Rutland, Vermont. (Courtesy of Herb La Tuchie Auctions)

the front with a space left for the address but no room for postage stamps. This item is actually an 8-inch by 11-inch folded sheet, printed on both sides in small type with long descriptions and sales pitches for publications on the subject of "Standard Phonography." Phonography was essentially a method of shorthand. Standard phonography was described as being an improvement over the Pitman method. Different publications were listed along with varying prices, which depended on the binding. For example, the 800-page dictionary sold for $3 when bound in muslin and $4 when bound in Turkish-Morocco leather with marbled edges and gilt side-titles. This advertisement was folded and sealed with a wax wafer, and posted at New York on August 14, 1862. The author and publisher was Andrew J. Graham of New York City. Examples of phonography advertisements are scarce.

Figure 15-10 shows a particularly interesting advertisement. The illustration and wording cover most of the envelope, with just a small space left for an address.

The advertisement is for the "Water Cure and Hygeio-Therapeutic College," a New York institution that promised cures for many major ailments by the use of somewhat questionable medical procedures (at least by today's standards).

For instance, "Cancers are treated successfully . . . combining cauterization and congelation. The Electro-Chemical Baths are applied for the eradication of . . . infectious viruses." The cost of in-patient care was as low as $7.50 per week, and student tuition was only $50 to $75 for a full term. The design is printed in black on a buff envelope. The cover is paid by a 1¢ Franklin of the "dot-in-U" variety, and the 3¢ stamp is a rose-pink shade, Although the year date is not complete in the postmark, the early shades of the stamps suggest 1861.

A fabulous cover is shown in **Figure 15-11**. The quality of its color-lithography is outstanding for the period. A 1994 auction description of this item stated that it is considered to be the "finest advertising cover known,"

Illustrated Covers

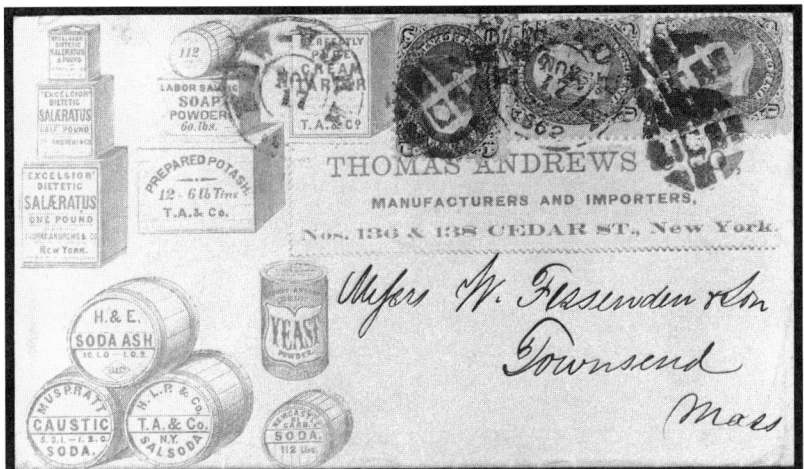

Figure 15-12. Advertisement for household chemicals on cover from New York City, November 17, 1862, to Townsend, Massachussets. Three 1¢ Franklins paid the letter rate.

and this may be correct. The price realized for the cover was $10,000 plus 10-percent buyer's premium. To this writer's knowledge this is by far the highest price ever paid for an advertising cover that did not have some additional philatelic value because of rare usage or scarce stamps.

The illustration shows two men holding up glasses of beer, with another gentleman, possibly the brewer, standing between. On the barrel is the wording "India Ale/Smith & Brother/Brewers/New York." The natural positions of the subjects, and the blending of color tones, are unusually lifelike and add to the artistry of the cover. In addition to the illustration, the cover has a light-gray moirelike background printing on both the front and the back. The cover was printed by Sarony, Major & Knapp, of New York, and their name appears at the bottom of the design. A contemporary advertisement for the firm stated that it occupied three floors at 449 Broadway and did work "better than any done in the country, equalling that done abroad" [2:4-24].

The company also printed many patriotic envelopes, and those covers showing the name of "Knapp" were manufactured by Sarony, Major & Knapp. Sarony was a pioneer in the new art of photography. Shortly after the war, he opened his own photographic studio and became world-famous for his work in that medium.

Figure 15-12 shows a graphic representation of a New York wholesale merchant's products. The design is in light blue on a white envelope with illustrations of saleratus (bicarbonate of soda) in boxes of different sizes, as well as containers of soap powder, yeast and so on. In the center is the advertiser's card. The color of the design is nicely complemented by the three blue 1¢ Franklins.

An overall printed design (probably a lithograph) is shown in **Figure 15-13**. The background consists of narrow horizontal lines printed in a pale-green color with negative lettering and design on a white envelope. The advertisement is for the "Young America Nursery," which fittingly is located at Young America, Illinois. The cover has an enclosed wholesale price list, dated 1868, with a selection of extraordinarily low-priced trees and shrubs. Osage orange (an ornamental tree) plants are offered for $2 per thousand, and 2-year-old, 5-foot apple trees sell for 10¢ each.

A well-designed advertising cover is pictured in **Figure 15-14**. The illustration on the cover is printed in light gray and shows types of machine tools manufactured by J.A. Fay & Co., Worcester, Massachusetts. The drawings show the results of the rapid advance in steam-powered machine-tool technology that took place in the 1850s and early 1860s. The arrangement of the design makes maximum use of the cover area for the advertisement, with just enough space left for the address and a postage stamp. Not too many of the early printers seemed to be concerned with the fact that the envelope would eventually be addressed and mailed. Frequently they covered every square inch of the envelope with a design.

City and State Illustrated Covers

Many states and a few of the larger cities adorned their official correspondence with preprinted illustrated envelopes.

Figure 15-15 shows a letter from the New York City mayor's office to a local fire station. The cover is lithographed with an overall design consisting of thin horizontal lines. The lines are printed in a light gray and do not obscure the written address. On the left is a replica of the seal of New York City. The letter was mailed for local carrier delivery, and the stamp is canceled with a red carrier CDS.

The city of Brandon adapted the state seal of Ver-

Figure 15-13. Advertisement for a wholesale nursery. The unsealed circular contained a price list, mailed at the 2¢ rate. The cover was mailed from Young America, Illinois, on June 5 (1868) to Oregon, Missouri.

Figure 15-14. Machinery advertisement. The local letter was mailed at Worcester, Massachusetts, at the 1¢ rate. The cover is undated, but evidently was mailed before the rate increase of 1863.

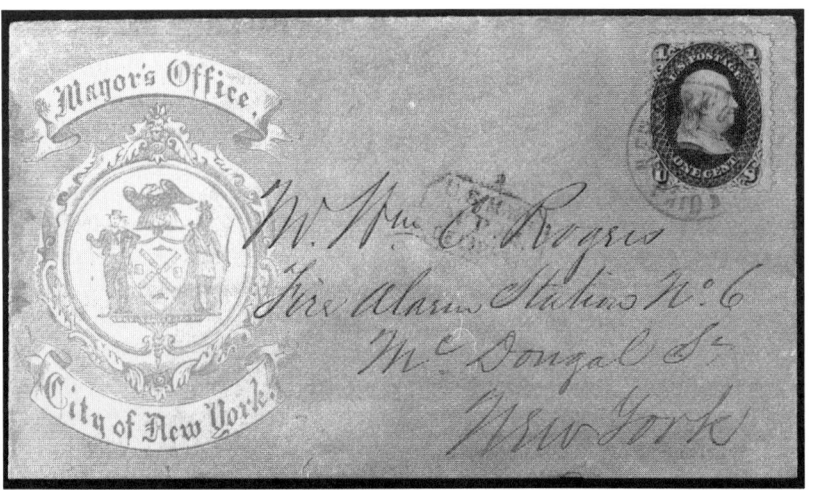

Figure 15-15. Seal of the City of New York. The 1¢ paid for local carrier service. The cover bears a New York City red carrier CDS, and boxed U.S. MAIL/4 P.M./DELIVERY marking in black.

Illustrated Covers

Figure 15-16. Seal of the state of Vermont. The unsealed cover was mailed from Brandon to West Braintree, Vermont. It bears a CDS dated November 28, 1862. This is an example of an unusual 2¢ rate, underpaid if contents were correspondence, overpaid if a printed circular was enclosed.

Figure 15-17. Seal of the state of Pennsylvania. This cover from Philadelphia is dated DEC 22. The stamps paid the 1¢ fee for carrier collection to the mails and 3¢ postage to Boston, Massachusetts.
(C.W. Christian collection)

mont for its illustrated corner card shown in **Figure 15-16** by adding BRANDON, VT. This would be an inexpensive way of customizing a stock die for local use. The design is printed in black on a buff cover. The 2¢ rate on this unsealed 1862 cover is curious. Circulars weighing up to 3 ounces were charged at the rate of 1¢ and an extra cent for each additional ounce. It is unlikely that this small envelope weighed more than 3 ounces. Docketing on the cover, in addition to the date, notes "Directions." Possibly the envelope contained two separate printed items, and each one was rated separately. This would be an unusual situation. Examples of multiple printed enclosures seen by this writer have all been charged at a single rate. However, the regulations of the period did specify that if more than one circular was printed on a page, each would require a single rate. This statement is somewhat ambiguous, and no confirmed examples of this rating are known to the author.

The Pennsylvania state emblem makes an attractive design on the cover in **Figure 15-17**. This particular envelope was manufactured by Magee of Philadelphia and is a good example of his excellent work. The illustration is printed in black, but this same design is also known in a three-color printing. Many designs taken from the official seals of the states were in use during the Civil War. Covers with illustrations such as Figure 15-17, where there is no design or text connection to the Civil War, should not necessarily be considered as patriotic covers. But they were popular with the general public and certainly were an expression of loyalty to a state. The multi-colored version of this particular design is listed by Weiss as a patriotic cover (ST-512).

The state of Maine used its seal on envelopes for many of the state's offices. The cover shown in **Figure 15-18** shows a use from the adjutant general's office, directed to the selectmen of the town of Kenduskeag. The attractive overall design is printed in light gray with a distinct moire pattern in the background

The enclosure is an order announcing that, by direction of the commander-in-chief, a state bounty will be

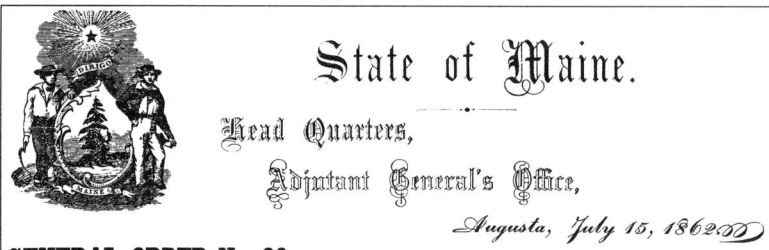

Figure 15-18. Seal of the state of Maine on a cover from the adjutant general's office. The cover bears an Augusta, Maine, CDS, dated November 3, 1862, to Kenduskeag, Maine. Illustrated above is the enclosure directing the payment of bounties for enlistment. This is an example of the unsealed circular rate of 1¢. (C.W. Christian collection)

paid for enlisting in current regiments or new regiments being formed. The amount of $30 or $35 would be added to the U.S. enlistment bounty of $40. During the Civil War, over $300 million was paid as enlistment bonuses. A large number of the many desertions were attributable to individuals enlisting, collecting a bounty, deserting, enlisting again under another name to obtain another bounty, and repeating the process as often as they could get away with it [3:266]. This practice not only cost the government a lot of money, but resulted in severe problems trying to sort out service records after the war.

Another illustrated cover with a wartime heritage is shown in **Figure 15-19**. This attractive and scarce cover carries a logo for the "U.S. Pension and Bounty Land Office," and indicates that the office was operated by an attorney who was also commissioner of the U.S. Court of Claims. In spite of its official-sounding name, this was a private organization. The 1¢ rate on the cover indicates mailing as a circular, prior to the rate increase on July 1, 1863. Unfortunately, the Auburn, New York, CDS does not contain a year date.

By the end of the Civil War, many such offices had been established to assist veterans in obtaining the pensions, bounties and land grants that were due as a consequence of their war service. Some of these offices were under the direction of the Sanitary Commission from the war and provided a very useful service for veterans. Other companies were run by shady individuals who collected high fees for marginal service.

Valentines and Love Letters

The last group of illustrated envelopes includes those unabashedly sentimental covers that carried expressions of love and affection. Special envelopes proclaimed by their design that they contained a letter with special sentiments.

The simplest of these envelopes were designed particularly for the use of young ladies, who in the fashion of the times carried on an affectionate correspondence with their friends and relatives. These envelopes

Figure 15-19. Ornate advertising design from Auburn, New York, to Susquehanna Depot, Pennsylvania, dated March 14 (year unknown). The cover was mailed at the circular rate of 1¢.

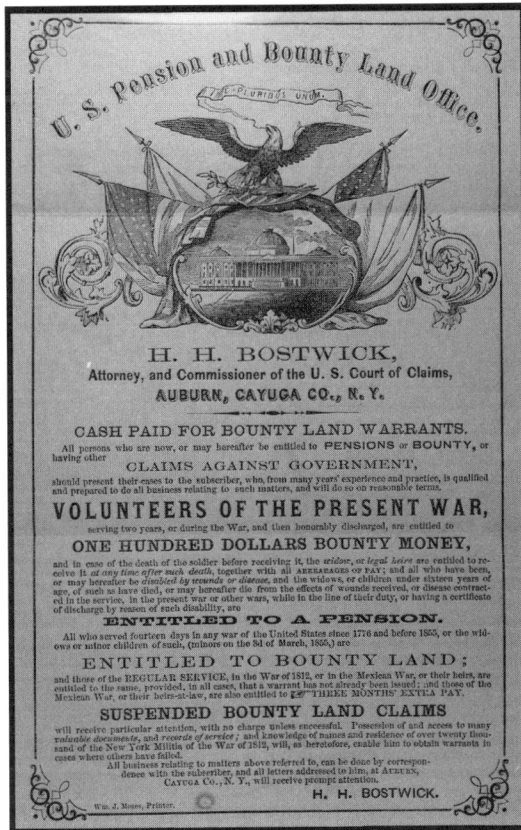

were sold in the small sizes that are known philatelically as lady's envelopes. This is an apt nomenclature. Almost all small covers that the author has seen, including those with no design, are addressed in a characteristically feminine hand.

Figure 15-20 shows the front and reverse of one of these dainty covers. The intricate design features a group of winged Cupids. On the front, they are building a fence whose rails provide the space for the address. On the reverse flap is a Cupid delivering letters. The envelope is printed in a pale gray, making it difficult to photograph the detail on this attractive local drop cover.

While the above-described type of cover was used throughout the year for special occasions, more elaborate envelopes with special enclosures were manufactured for primary use on Valentine's Day. Many of these envelopes were oversize, their intricate designs depicted by embossing or printing.

Figure 15-21 shows one of these large (4¾ inches by 7¼ inches) envelopes with a heavily embossed design. Although there is no valentine enclosure in the envelope, the Marion, Massachusetts, CDS with a FEB 14 date strongly supports the assumption that this was a valentine usage. The design scene, depicting children at play, suggests an affectionate rather than romantic valentine communication.

One of the most beautiful and spectacular of valentine covers in philately is imprinted with an overall design known as the "Soldier's Farewell," and originated at Washington, D.C. This large (5 inches by 7¼ inches) carrier cover, dated February 14, 1863, is illustrated in **Figure 15-22**, shown through the courtesy of Richard B. Graham [4:264], in whose collection it now resides. The envelope is printed in yellow orange. At times, examples of this design have been referred to as being in gold, but there is no metallic component to the ink that was used. The design depicts a soldier bidding goodbye to his lady in a lavishly decorated salon. Postage on this cover is paid by four 1¢ 1861 stamps, each placed at a corner: one stamp for the carrier fee to the post office and three for the postage. While 17 covers with this particular valentine design have been recorded, this is the only one showing the 1861 1¢ Franklin.

The cover, shown here and in the color section,

Figure 15-20. Ornate lady's cover, an example of the local 1¢ drop-rate use at Gloversville, New York. The illustration below shows the reverse of the cover.

Figure 15-21. Large embossed cover with Marion, Massachusetts, CDS dated FEB 14. An example of a local 1¢ drop-letter use.

contains an embossed valentine, which is pictured below the cover. The illustration at the left shows the design with the tent flaps closed, draped with flags in red, white and blue. On the right, the enclosure is pictured again, with the flaps folded back to reveal a soldier writing a letter at a folding camp table. The design in the interior of the tent is hand-colored in red, yellow and blue. Superimposed on the background is an image of the lady of his dreams, and below is a printed romantic message:

"I DREAM OF THEE
I long for tatoo, for sweet is my rest,
With vision of thee each hour is blest,
From beating of taps 'till reveille call,
Thine image my soul doth forever enthral."

Figure 15-22. Elaborate and beautiful patriotic valentine showing carrier use from Washington, D.C., to Barre, Vermont, dated February 14, 1863. Four symetrically placed 1¢ stamps paid the 1¢ carrier fee plus the 3¢ postage. Below are shown two views of the enclosure. On the left is a flag-draped tent with the tent flaps closed. On the right, the flaps are folded back and the interior of the tent is shown. Also shown in color section.
(Richard B. Graham collection and photos)

Figure 15-23. Earlier, nonpatriotic version of the the valentine cover design shown in Figure 15-22, printed in pale blue and red. Trowbridge, Michigan, to Centreville, Michigan. The date is undecipherable. The 1¢ Franklin short paid the required 3¢ rate. The cover shows a faint unreadable manuscript due marking. (Kukstis Auction photo)

Similar valentine covers, with what is called the "Romeo and Juliet" design, are also known. In the place of the soldier is a courtier of the renaissance period. It is believed that the "Soldier's Farewell" was adapted from this other, probably earlier, design. The "Romeo and Juliet" designs are printed in dark red and pale blue, with a skillful combining of these two colors to provide shades of brown. The covers generally contain valentines of a more conventional type than the "Soldier's Farewell." Fourteen of these have been recorded, but only one includes the use of the 1¢ Franklin [5:48]. This cover is shown in **Figure 15-23** and is a beautiful example of a multicolor printing. The Trowbrige, Michigan, CDS is faint, and the date is indeterminate. The cover is addressed to Centreville, Michigan, and it is paid by a single 1¢ Franklin. The rating for this use is 3¢, and a faint marking on the envelope shows an undecipherable postage-due marking. Valentines with collection fees are unusual. It certainly was not the best of manners to expect the recipient of one's valentine sentiments to pay for the postage.

The recorded dates for the use of the "Soldier's Farewell" design range from 1863 to a late use of no earlier than 1868, as indicated by the use of a 2¢ grilled Black Jack. The known dates of use for the "Romeo and Juliet" design include both 1862 and 1863. Graham notes that the detail in the "Romeo and Juliet" is greater and better executed than that in the "Soldier's Farewell," and that it is most probable that the patriotic design was copied on a new plate from the earlier "Romeo" envelope. This is in contrast to some other writers on the subject who contend that the new design was accomplished by altering the principal figures in the original plate. Graham makes a valid point here and is probably correct in his conclusion.

The use of fancy envelopes to enclose valentines increased dramatically with the 1845 repeal of the postal law that required an additional rate for an envelope. The complexity and beauty of the envelope designs increased too, probably reaching a peak during the 1850s and 1860s. Specialized collections have been made of these exceptionally beautiful covers and their enclosures. Subsequently, while the valentine enclosures continued to increase in complexity, the envelopes became plainer. Today, only a few valentine envelopes have any printed or embossed designs, and the enclosures lack the frills and furbelows of years past.

References

1. Phillips, David G. *American Illustrated Cover Catalog, The Collection of John R. Biddle.* David G. Phillips Co. 1981.

2. Grant, Robert W. *The Handbook of Civil War Patriotic Envelopes and Postal History.* Vol I. 1977.

3. Kantor, Alvin R. and Marjorie S. *Sanitary Fairs.* Amos Philatelics Inc. 1992.

4. Graham, Richard B. "Two Civil War Valentine Designs." *Chronicle* 128. November 1985.

5. Graham, Richard B. "Reports on 'Romeo and Juliet' and 'Soldier's Farewell' Civil War Era Designs." *Chronicle* 129. February 1986.

CHAPTER 16

Transcontinental and Western Mails

The development of the U.S. mail system in the western part of the country between 1840 and 1869 is one of the most colorful and interesting areas of postal history available to philatelic students. Facilities for the transmission of Western mail went from essentially nothing in 1840 to a fast and reliable daily delivery by rail across the continent by 1869.

The politicians, stage-line entrepreneurs, steamboat magnates, and the thousands of settlers in the West who needed and demanded a better mail system, provide a cast of characters for this drama. Their many brave to inglorious activities round out an unforgettable story. Only the last decade of this era falls within the dates of primary interest to this volume, but some understanding of the foundation on which the Western mail system of the 1860s was based is needed for a full appreciation of the postal history of the period.

Just a brief summary of the early years will be included here, but the reader is strongly urged to consult one or more of the excellent texts that have been published on the Western mails. One of the best, and an extremely interesting book on the California mails, is *Letters of Gold* by Jesse L. Coburn [1]. *The Overland Mail* by LeRoy R. Hafen [2] is another recommended and readable text. Many other fine publications are available, and any philatelist who owns or desires to own as much as a single Western cover owes it to himself to investigate this subject in depth. The rewards are guaranteed to please.

The Early Years

In the middle of the 19th century, the lines of communications that tied together the remote sections of the United States were essential to the Pacific coast and Western regions. Until 1848, there were no arrangements for the regular transmission of mail to and from the Pacific coast under the auspices of the Post Office Department. The small amount of mail that did make the journey was carried privately by individuals or as ship mail by the captains of private vessels.

The sparse populations of the Western states and territories at first did not warrant the establishment of a postal system, which could be put in place only by the expenditure of large amounts of money. The long distances, almost impassable mountain ranges and deserts, and the danger from Indians argued against providing a reliable and cost-effective system for the delivery of mail.

Beginning about 1840, emigration to the West began to rapidly increase. Private stage and express companies were organized to take care of transportation and communication requirements, and the U.S. government began to embrace the concept of Manifest Destiny. This idea carried with it the goal of acquiring all lands between the Atlantic and Pacific oceans, including parts of the British claims to the Oregon territories, and the Mexican claims to territories in the Southwest, including Texas and California. Mail routes that could provide the way for emigration routes to these distant areas along with a steady influx of settlers were recognized as being essential as the first step in establishing control and a U.S. presence. The old policy of making the Post Office Department pay its own way was reversed, and it was acknowledged that subsidies in great excess over the anticipated postal revenues would be necessary to induce mail contractors to establish the hazardous but necessary mail routes.

It was also recognized that the overland routes were extremely difficult, and that the volume of mail that could be transported overland was severely limited by the inhospitable terrain. Early attention was therefore focused on providing a scheduled mail and passenger service to the Pacific coast by steamship via the Isthmus of Panama.

In 1847, Congress authorized the postmaster general to enter a contract for the delivery of mail from Charleston, North Carolina, to Chagres (now Colón) at the Atlantic side of the Isthmus of Panama, across the isthmus to Panama City, and then by ship north to Astoria, Oregon. Trips were to be made every two months, and the contractor was to be paid $100,000 annually for his services. Bids were solicited, but there were no bidders at the price offered [2:38]. This lack of response was evidently anticipated, for Congress concurrently directed the Navy to construct a number of steamships that could be used for the mail service. They were to be operated by a civilian contractor, with a small naval detachment aboard each of them. The intent was to modernize and enlarge the fleet of the United States and at the same time to provide a means to establish a scheduled mail and passenger service to the Pacific coast. Title to the ships and the cost of maintenance remained with the government, and they could be reclaimed at any time by the Navy if the need arose [1:83].

The terminus of the route was originally to be Astoria, Oregon, because that is where the majority of American settlers were at that time. Oregon territory boasted an American population of more than 5,000 people, while fewer than 1,000 were in California. Contracts were let, and the United States Mail Steamship Company was formed to provide the service from New York to the Isthmus of Panama. The Pacific Mail Steamship Company, under the control of W.H. Aspinwall, was established for the Pacific part of the route, and the terminus was changed to San Francisco with a branch extension to Oregon Territory.

The *California* was the first mail ship to the Pacific coast. It departed with mail but no passengers from New York on October 6, 1848, as a part of the Pacific Mail Steamship Company. It left prior to the departure of the United States Mail Steamship Company's ships since it was necessary to make the long voyage around Cape Horn to be in place in the Pacific Ocean for the beginning of the two-way service.

Two coincident events turned the trickle of American emigration to California into a flood of new arrivals. These were the end of the Mexican War on February 2, 1848, with the ceding to the United States of California, Texas and the land between, and the discovery of gold just three weeks later at Sutter's Mill. The *California* had left New York before the news of the gold strike was

Figure 16-1. Map of steamship routes

general knowledge, but upon putting in at Callao, Peru, on the northern leg of her journey, 80 Peruvians, who had heard of the gold strike, awaited transportation to California. At Panama City there were another 700 gold-seekers clamoring for passage. The *California* was built to carry a little more than 100 passengers, but by the time she reached San Francisco there were about 400 crowded on board. As soon as the *California* docked, the crew jumped ship for the goldfields, leaving only the engineer to man the ship [2:40]. The two following ships of the Pacific Mail line, the *Oregon* and *Panama,* had similar experiences, and the amounts offered by eager gold-seekers for passage reached astronomical heights. The arriving captains now moored their vessels at San Francisco under the guns of a naval warship to prevent desertions. With crews intact, it was then possible to initiate a return mail service to the East. **Figure 16-1** is a map showing the principal sailing routes for mail service between the East and the Pacific coast.

By January of 1850, the population of California had soared to more than 107,000 [1:32], and the need for improved mail service had become the source of continuing complaints from the inhabitants. In the 1850s, additional ocean routes via Nicaragua and the Mexican isthmus at Tehuantepec were put in place, and the frequency of trips was increased. The great Butterfield mail route over the southern part of the country was established and began to handle a large part of the letter mail. A limited amount of mail was also sent overland via Salt Lake City on what was called the "central route."

On September 9, 1850, California was admitted to the Union, and John C. Frèmont and William M. Gwin were elected as U.S. senators. One of Gwin's goals was the development of a frequent and reliable overland mail service that would connect California to the rest of the nation. He worked unceasingly toward that end. There is little doubt the vast fortunes that would be made from the development of through routes and eventually a railroad was one of the driving forces for the establishment of these routes.

The political maneuvering and commercial wars to establish and maintain mail and express routes continued through the pivotal decade of the 1850s. Fortunes were made and lost, and in the process, a continual improvement in the overland and ocean mail service was effected.

Aaron V. Brown was appointed postmaster general on March 7, 1857. He was a strong believer in the concept of using the Post Office to advance the settlement of the West, and under his auspices a large number of new overland routes and services were established, as well as improvements to the ocean mail. He died while in office on March 8, 1859, and this set the stage for a temporary setback in the steady improvement of Western mail service. Joseph Holt, from Kentucky, was selected as his replacement on March 14, 1859. Holt was conservative in fiscal matters and felt that the postal service should be self-supporting without subsidies, if possible. There were also many members of Congress who had strong ideas concerning the profitability of the postal operation, and their contention was that routes that did not pay their own way should be cut back or canceled. This policy was not limited to the West, and postal services throughout the entire United States were curtailed. Holt reported, correctly, to Congress that revenues and costs of the Pacific mail were way out of balance. His annual report for 1859 included the following figures [2:135]. The total cost of the overland and ocean routes amounted to an annual expense of $2,184,697 with concurrent receipts of only $339,747, for a net loss of $1,844,950. The route over southern Mexico at Tehuantepec was a major loss. The annual cost was $250,000 and the receipts were just $5,276.

The public, particularly in the West, violently opposed the reductions. Congress had decreased the compensation for the mail contract via the Isthmus of Panama to the value of the postage transported. The steamship contractors refused to continue at that rate, and for a period of months, little mail was received on the West Coast.

The subsidized overland lines and the extended services were not without their champions. Among these, Senator Gwin of California was especially prominent. He spoke in the Senate [2:140].

"You begrudge the expense of transporting our letters to and from the Pacific Coast . . . You knew these plains and mountains, covered with perpetual snow existed when you so eagerly sought possessions on the Pacific Coast. After you got these possessions did you not intend to communicate with them for postal, military, commercial, and social purposes? Did you not intend to make us one people, part and parcel of you? Did the statesman who shaped that policy count the cost of conveying letters to these distant possessions when they risked war and engaged in war to get them at the cost of tens of millions?"

In spite of his eloquence, Gwin did not obtain the revocation of Holt's actions, but some relief later became effective. In the meantime, internecine warfare continued in Congress with one group supporting Holt's cost-cutting measures and the other wanting to rescind all of his decisions. No compromise was achieved, and Congress failed to pass the Postal Appropriation Act of 1859. The Post Office Department was faced with a lack of funds to support its operation. Many mail contractors suffered severe financial problems as a result.

The situation was now in place that existed at the beginning of the period of primary interest to this book. While many of the pioneering aspects of the routes had become history, there were still many problems to be solved. An increase in the number of Indian attacks resulted from the growing encroachment by settlers and miners on Indian land and hunting preserves. This caused mail to be delayed or lost. The outbreak of the Civil War meant that the southern overland routes were no longer feasible, and the mountains of the central route continued to be an obstacle to the new primary overland route. As the waves of emigrants and fortune-seekers spread out over the West, new mail routes had to be established, and the volume of mail continued to increase. More and more letters were written. Fortunately, some transcontinental and Western covers from the 1860-70 period have survived to the present time.

Transcontinental Mail by Steamship

By the summer of 1861, and the advent of the new issue of postage stamps, the steamer routes from New York to San Francisco were essentially under control of Commodore Cornelius Vanderbilt. He had successfully bought or forced out of business most of his many competitors on these lucrative routes.

The completion of the railroad across the Isthmus of Panama in 1855 had made passenger travel comparatively easy. Steamship was the preferred mode for individuals making the trip from the East Coast to California. By 1859, the volume of letter mail was about evenly divided between the overland and the ocean routes, but the majority of public documents and newspaper mail continued to be sent by ship.

The Postal Appropriation Act of June 15, 1859, had grave consequences for the ocean transportation of the mails. As previously mentioned, it restricted compensation for ocean mail to the amount of postage on the mails carried. The proponents of the law had meant for this provision to force the transcontinental mail to be carried overland, but had not realized the problems it would cause [2:201]. The 10-year contract for the Pacific mails expired in 1859, and the steamship companies refused to renew at the lower payments. Vanderbilt pointed out that the majority of mail carried via Panama consisted of newspapers at low postage rates and public documents, much of which was free-franked and therefore carried no postage. It was a losing proposition to carry mail for only the amount of the postage. The act also impacted the transmission of foreign mail. Those problems will be discussed in Chapter 17.

Postmaster General Holt advised Congress that because of the bulk of the total mail, it could not all be carried overland, and that some accommodation must be made with the steamship companies. Vanderbilt finally agreed to establish a three-times-a-month mail service via Panama for only the postage in return for a promise by Holt that a recommendation would be made to Congress at the next session for additional compensation. This promise was kept, and $350,000 for the service was appropriated [2:205].

During the period between 1849 and 1860, when they provided the primary means of transportation from one end of the country to the other, the steamship lines carried more than 450,000 people to California, and returned about $450 million worth of gold and silver bullion to the East. In 1859 alone, 2 million letters and 3 million newspapers were carried. In spite of these impressive numbers, philatelic items showing such use are scarce.

The year 1861 brought some major changes to the transcontinental mail situation. The Act of February 27, 1861, effective July 1, 1861, provided a daily overland mail via the central route (at an annual cost of $1 million) that would carry all letter mail and as much of the remaining mail as possible. The contractor was to have the option to send the remaining mail via Panama by steamship.

Figure 16-2. Biddeford, Maine, MAY 9, to San Francisco, California. This double-weight letter is endorsed "By Steamer, May 11th/63." Three 3¢, one 1¢, and a 10¢ paid the 2x10¢ transcontinental rate.
(C.W. Christian collection)

Figure 16-3. San Francisco, California, October 3, 1863, to New York City. The overweight item was mailed at the rare septuple first-class rate of 7x3¢ for 21¢ postage. The cover was endorsed, "pr 'Golden Age,' " for sea transit via Panama.

In March of 1861, a provision was added to the law requiring the southern Butterfield route be discontinued as of July 1, 1861. This, of course, was a consequence of the outbreak of the Civil War.

Postal regulations prior to July 1, 1861, required that letters be sent by sea unless they were specifically endorsed to be carried overland. Mails for the Pacific coast, South America and the Sandwich Islands were made up at New York and dispatched by steamship on the 1st, 11th and 21st of each month. Subsequent to July 1, 1861, letters were to be transmitted via the overland route unless endorsed for sea transport. Mails were made up daily (except Sunday) and dispatched overland via St. Joseph, Missouri [3:38]. The steamship schedule remained the same as before, three departures per month. In spite of the regulations, letter mail destined for overland transport at times had to be sent by ship. Overland mail was frequently delayed or lost due to weather, accidents or the Indian problem. Postmaster General Montgomery Blair in his annual reports cited several periods where the entire Pacific mails had to be transported by sea because of problems on the overland route [4:11].

Figure 16-2 shows a cover mailed from Biddeford, Maine, to San Francisco, California, on May 9, 1863. This was endorsed "Per Steamer, May 11th/63." and is rated as a double-weight letter at 20¢, paid by one 10¢, three 3¢ and a single 1¢ stamp. The sender was evidently aware of the sailing date of the next steamer to San Francisco and endorsed the cover with that date.

A fabulous cover is illustrated in **Figure 16-3**. This folded cover sheet was mailed from San Francisco on October 3, 1864, after the reduction of the transcontinental rate to 3¢. The 21¢ postage, paid for by a 1¢ Franklin and two 10¢ 1861 values, is the only septuple transcontinental rate that this author has seen with use of the 1¢. While the cover is not particularly large, it could have contained a heavy folded invoice or records. To require the 7x3¢ rate, the enclosure must have weighed between 3 and 3½ ounces.

The cover is docketed on the reverse, indicating that it was received on October 29, 1864, for a 26-day transmission. This is about right for the sailing times during this period. The cover is endorsed to be sent "pr 'Golden Age.' " The *Golden Age* was one of the fastest ships of the Vanderbilt line and had previously sailed under the flag of the Pacific Mail Steamship Line until that company came under the control of the Vanderbilt interests [2:41].

Figure 16-4 shows a San Francisco, California, to Cherryfield, Maine, cover endorsed "Per Steamer." No year date is shown, but the letter was obviously mailed at the single rate after the July 1, 1863, reduction.

The Overland Mail and Western Express Companies

While ship service was beginning in 1849 to transmit mail from the East Coast to San Francisco and return, there was almost no government mail service beyond the ports in the West, where the mail ships stopped. The need for internal mail delivery was overwhelming, but the Post Office Department did not have the necessary funds to establish even a rudimentary system. The Gold Rush had almost instantaneously created a large population of individuals who were separated from their families and willing to pay almost anything to send and receive mail. For the most part, these miners and tradesmen were located in small encampments and temporary towns. The only way to get mail to them was by individuals who realized the potential profits to be made, and consequently began to establish private postal routes. Such services came high. It could cost up to $5 to send a letter and an ounce of gold dust to receive one. Of course, with such

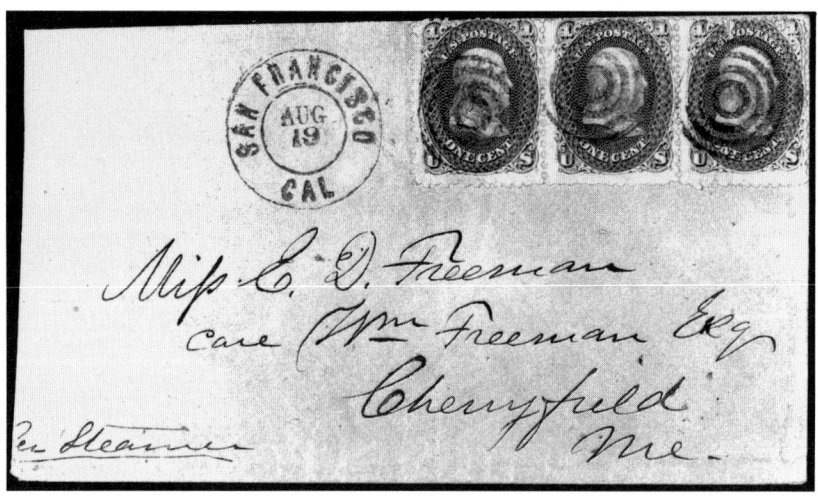

Figure 16-4. San Francisco, California, to Cherryfield, Maine. The double-circle San Francisco postmark is dated AUG 19. The cover was endorsed "Per Steamer," and mailed at the 3¢ transcontinental rate, effective July 1, 1863. The postage was paid by a strip of three 1¢ Franklins in the scarce ultramarine shade.

Figure 16-5. Unusual Wells, Fargo cover showing carrier service at New York. This double-weight cover originated in San Francisco. It was carried transcontinentally outside the mails in a government 10¢ stamped envelope (Scott U40) with an additional 10¢ stamp to pay the 2x10¢ rate, and delivered locally in New York by Wells, Fargo. The cover was forwarded by the U.S. Post Office to Westfield, Massachusetts, with carrier collection at New York. It was postmarked New York, February 27, 1862. Seven cents additional postage was added to pay for the forwarding and carrier collection fee.
(Robert B. Meyersburg collection)

high profits to be made, dozens of companies came into existence in 1849, to be followed by hundreds more in the next few years. In addition to letters, there was a need to carry gold dust from the miners to San Francisco, and eventually to the East. This gave birth to the express companies, which would transmit gold for a percentage of its value (usually 2 percent to 5 percent) along with letters.

The transmission of mail on post roads by private companies was forbidden by law, but the Post Office Department had no alternative service to offer, so the practice was never challenged. In order to protect its interests and to legalize a situation that could not be avoided, Congress, in the Act of August 31, 1852, provided that letters could legally be carried outside the mail if they were enclosed in sealed government stamped envelopes of a denomination sufficient to pay the required postage.

Adams & Co., which had been in business for many years in the East, initiated a branch operation in California and was soon doing a large part of the express and private post business. In 1852, Wells, Fargo & Co. began a successful operation and soon became known for its honesty and reliability. In 1855, a financial panic swept the country and caused many banks and companies to fail. The Eastern owners of Adams & Co. found it necessary to strip their Western subsidiary of all its assets in order to remain solvent. Wells, Fargo was the only major Western bank to meet all of its obligations. It immediately became the most respected financial institution in the West [1:152]. Wells, Fargo continued to expand conservatively and buy into competing organizations, and soon controlled the major part of the express operations.

The company purchased government stamped envelopes in large quantities and printed its distinctive trademark on them. The Wells, Fargo envelope became a common sight. The green letter-collection boxes of Wells,

Fargo stood beside the red Post Office boxes, and the Wells, Fargo boxes were the more frequently used. By 1859, the company was buying 500,000 3¢ stamped envelopes per year. In 1863, its purchases of envelopes in which to transmit the mail amounted to 2 million 3¢ envelopes, 15,000 of the 6¢ denomination and 30,000 with 10¢ and 12¢ denominations. In addition, it purchased thousands of adhesives of various denominations. Because of these large numbers, examples of Wells, Fargo service can be obtained at a reasonable price. However, covers with postage stamps applied to the government stamped envelope to make up the rate are more dificult to find. Those showing use of the 1¢ Franklin are even scarcer.

Figure 16-5 shows an example of a cover that was carried by Wells, Fargo, outside the mails, from San Francisco to New York. The letter was enclosed in a 10¢ government stamped envelope to pay the required transcontinental rate. The letter was evidently overweight, and an 1861 10¢ adhesive was added to the cover to make up the 20¢ rate. This did not exactly meet government regulations (§8, Act of August 31, 1852) which stipulated that only government envelopes with stamps printed or embossed on them of the correct rate were to be used to prepay the required postage. However, the exact rate was not always available in a stamped envelope, and regular postage stamps were affixed to the envelopes to make up the correct rate. The envelope and adhesive stamps were canceled with a blue San Francisco Wells, Fargo CDS and carried out of the mails to New York. During this period, Wells, Fargo sent much of its transcontinental mail via steamship to New York. Wells, Fargo agents accompanied the closed letter bags on the steamships, and the company essentially operated as a private postal system.

When this particular cover arrived in New York City, it was delivered to its destination by the local Wells, Fargo agent, without having been in the mails at any time. But the addressee had moved to Westfield, Massachusetts, so the letter was readdressed and 7¢ in postage stamps added to pay for the double-weight forwarding postage plus the 1¢ carrier-to-the-mail fee at New York, where it received a postmark dated 27 FEB 62. Thus the cover finished its journey in the hands of the Post Office.

A companion cover from the same correspondence is shown in **Figure 16-6**. This was a single-weight letter, and the 10¢ stamp applied by Wells, Fargo provided the correct postage. The stamp was canceled with a Wells, Fargo CDS, as required, and carried to New York. Evidently, no 10¢ entire (such as had been used in Figure 16-5) was available, and an ordinary nongovernment envelope was put into service. After delivery in New York, and the addition of 4¢ in stamps for carrier service and forwarding postage, the cover entered the mails and was sent to Westfield, Massachusetts. On this cover, New York applied a pen cancellation to the 10¢ stamp along with a March 26 CDS. The blue PAID in oval was probably added by Wells, Fargo.

The express company charged a fee for its service in addition to the cost of postage. What the fee was at the time of this mailing is not known to the author, but it was a modest amount and considered by the users to be well worth the added expense to ensure more rapid and safer delivery than that provided by the Post Office Department. The fee was usually collected as part of the cost of a Wells, Fargo imprinted government stamped envelope. These were available at the various Wells, Fargo offices and were used to enclose letters to be deposited at the offices or collection boxes for transmission.

When government stamped envelopes in the required denomination were not available at the express companies, they usually made up the rate by the addition of adhesive postage stamps, as previously discussed. Alternatively, in an effort to satisfy completely the postal

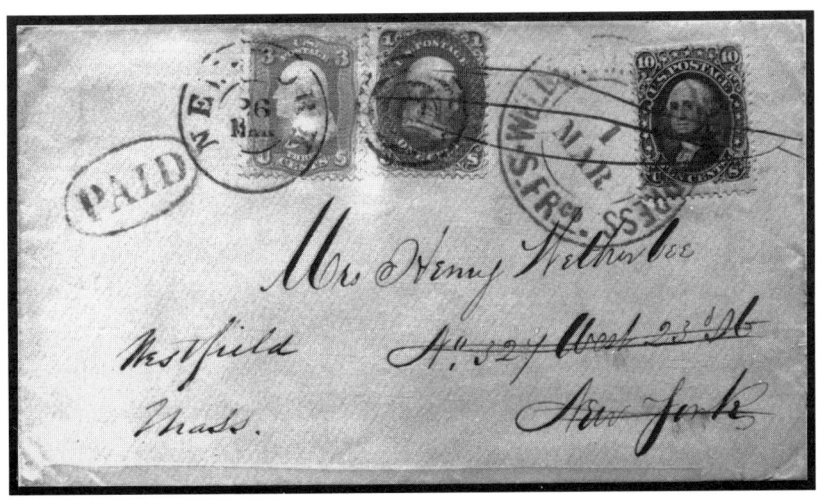

Figure 16-6. San Francisco to New York to Westfield, Massachusetts, cover from the same correspondence as Figure 16-5. The cover departed from San Francisco on March 1, as shown by the blue Wells, Fargo CDS. It is also marked with a blue PAID in oval. The cover was carried outside the mails by Wells, Fargo in an envelope paid by a single 10¢ adhesive. On March 26, it was forwarded by the Post Office to Westfield with the addition of 3¢+1¢ postage for the single rate forwarding plus carrier fee.
(Walter Cole collection)

Figure 16-7. A scarce example of a "pasteup" Wells, Fargo cover with the addition of a single 1¢ Franklin. The cover was carried outside the mails by Wells, Fargo from San Francisco to New York. It bears a Wells, Fargo, San Francisco oval marking dated JAN 10 and a straightline PAID marking. Three 3¢ government stamped envelopes (Scott U34) were pasted together to make up most of the 10¢ transcontinental rate. The 1¢ Franklin made up the difference. Upon arrival at New York, the cover was given to Boyd's Dispatch, which postmarked the cover FEB 1 186(3) and delivered it to the addressee. (James Lee collection)

Figure 16-8. Rare "Brents and Nelson's Express, John Day Mines, PAID. 10" corner card on Wells, Fargo & Co. envelope. The cover is postmarked with "The Dalles, Or. May 25" CDS and bears a red exchange office "Chicago Ill. Paid 15" in dateless circle. Canadian backstamps show 1863 use. The 15¢ rate was paid by a 3¢ embossed envelope (Scott U34) plus two 1¢ Franklins and a 10¢ green (Scott 68). (R.A. Siegel Auction Gallery photo)

regulations, pasteups were made. By pasting additional government entires onto the original envelope, a composite envelope was created that fulfilled the legal requirement that letters carried outside the mails must be enclosed in a government stamped envelope with the correct postage embossed. **Figure 16-7** illustrates an excellent example of a pasteup that doesn't quite meet all the requirements. This cover, opened up in the figure, shows three 3¢ entires pasted to the back of the envelope and a 1¢ Franklin affixed to the front to make up a total transcontinental single rate of 10¢. Wells, Fargo did not seem to stock 1¢ envelopes, and this combination was probably as close as it could come to satisfying the regulations. The cover carries four strikes of a JAN 10 San Francisco Wells, Fargo handstamp that effectively cancels all of the stamps. The cover was carried outside the mails to New York City, where it was given to Boyd's Dispatch, a private carrier, for delivery to the addressee.

The Boyd's handstamp shows a date of FEB 1, with a blurred year date that must be 1862 or 1863, for the same reasons as noted for the cover in Figure 16-6.

Figure 16-8 shows a rare and beautiful cover to Canada at the 15¢ rate. The normal 10¢ Canadian rate required an additional 5¢ if the distance from the point of mailing to the Canadian border was more than 3,000 miles, or if the origin was on the Pacific coast. Brents and Nelson's Express was a small company operating during 1862 and 1863 and providing service between the camps around the John Day Mines and the post office at The Dalles, Oregon (Oregon had become a state in 1859). The cover was carried by Brents and Nelson's in a Wells, Fargo 3¢ stamped envelope, and entered the mails at The Dalles on May 25. The year was 1863, as confirmed by multiple receiving marks on the reverse of the cover. The two 1¢ Franklins and the 10¢ adhesive were probably added by the postmaster at The Dalles and paid for by the express company. The letter was then carried by the Post Office, probably via the Central Overland Route, to the exchange office at Chicago, Illinois, where a "paid 15" circular Chicago marking in red was applied. It was forwarded to its Canadian destination. The 15¢ rate, effective April 9, 1851, was applicable to letters originating on the Pacific coast and addressed to the East. On April 1, 1855, the agreement with Canada was modified to require that all letters with transit distances of more than 3,000 miles from the origin to the Canadian border would require 15¢ postage per ½ ounce. The Pacific coast surcharge was also retained. This rate was effective until February 17, 1864, when a 10¢ rate was established for mail from any part of the United States to Canada.

Concurrent with the development of the stage routes and the private express mails, the Post Office Department began to establish subsidized mail routes across the continent. The decisions made regarding these routes were based on a complex amalgamation of interests, including politics, sectional concerns, the proposed transcontinental railroad and its financial windfalls, the opening up of a vast section of the country to settlement, influence peddling and chicanery to obtain lucrative contracts and, of course, the public demand for a better mail system. These many conflicting pressures, resulted in laws being passed and contracts being awarded that did not always reflect the best interests of the nation.

By 1850, the new state of California and its senators, Fremont and Gwin, pressed Congress for authorization for a transcontinental railroad. Such a venture was unthinkable to Congress at that time, but it did authorize a monthly mail service for a 1,150-mile route between the Missouri River and Salt Lake City at a cost of $14,000 per year. The results were unsatisfactory, and the schedule was never maintained, but the contract remained in force for four years.

In 1851, Congress established a connecting route between Salt Lake City and Sacramento. This was 990 miles, also on a monthly schedule, and at a contract fee of $14,000 per year. The High Sierras made this an extremely difficult route, and during the winter months, it was necessary to carry the mail by steamer to San Pedro, California, then by land over the old Mormon route to Salt Lake City.

In principle, a through mail service now existed from Sacramento to the railhead on the Missouri. But it never carried much mail and was not very reliable at any time. By 1856, the burgeoning population of California, and its significant contributions of bullion to the wealth of the nation, made it a voice to listen to. Californians presented a 75,000-name petition to Congress requesting the establishment of a reliable overland mail system. It was an election year, and Congress began to debate the matter seriously. The following year, in the Act of March 3, 1857, the postmaster general was authorized to establish a twice-weekly mail service from the Mississippi River to San Francisco at an annual fee of $600,000. In the act, the postmaster general was given the right to choose the contractor, who in turn would select the specific route.

This enabling clause caused unexpected results. The Northern congressmen, in supporting the measure, had assumed that the route would be along the central Oregon Trail route since that was the shortest and most direct. However, on March 7, 1857, Aaron Brown was appointed the new postmaster general, and as previously discussed, Brown had Southern origins and leanings. He immediately prescribed that the route was to originate from two points on the Mississippi River, one at St. Louis and the other at Memphis, Tennessee (which happened to be his hometown). These two routes were to merge at Fort Smith, Arkansas, and to proceed via Texas to Los Angeles, California, then north to San Francisco. This route was about 800 miles longer than the central route, but did have the advantage of better winter weather and the concurrent disadvantage of long stretches of desert to be traversed.

Figure 16-9 illustrates the major overland routes.

The contract was awarded to John Butterfield, who organized the Overland Mail Co. and immediately invested more than a million dollars in surveying the route, buying horses and equipment, and building stations [1:245]. The Great Butterfield Route, as it came to be called, was to carry passengers as well as mail, and Concord coaches, made in Concord, New Hampshire, were purchased. These vehicles were the Cadillacs of the day and carried from six to nine passengers inside in relative comfort and as many as could be accommodated on the roof of the coach.

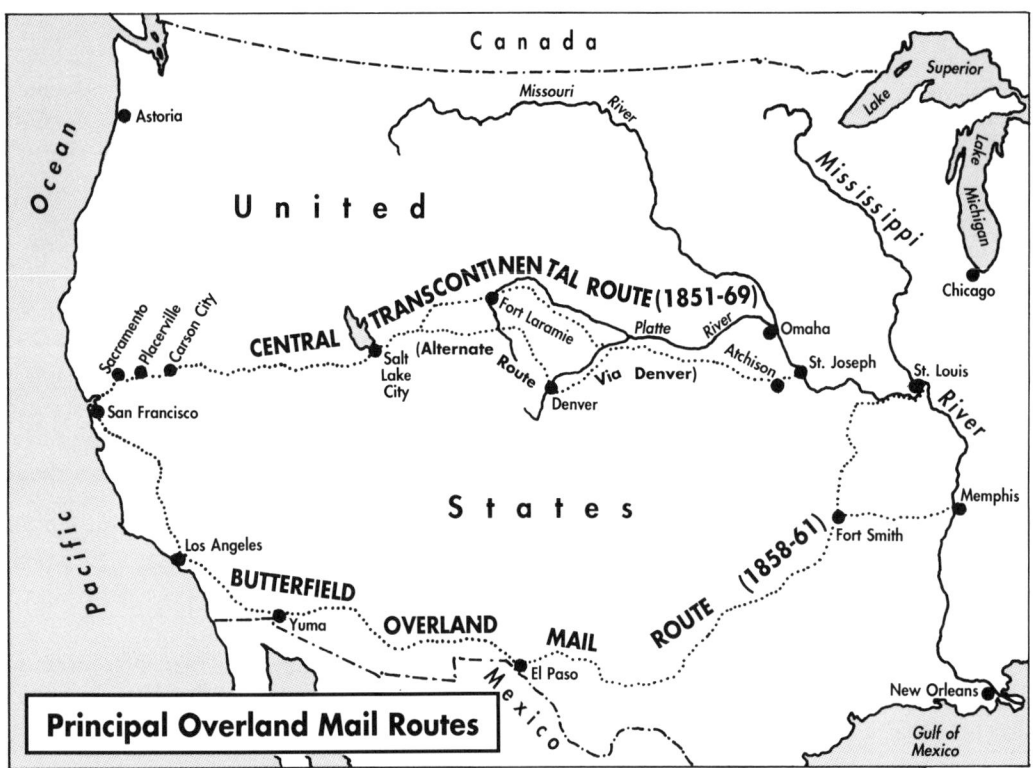

Figure 16-9. Principal overland mail routes.

Figure 16-10. Early woodcut of a Concord stagecoach carrying the mail over a mountain road in the West. (Courtesy of Richard J. Frajola Inc.)

Figure 16-10 shows a contemporary woodcut of a mail stagecoach with a team of six horses traversing the difficult terrain of the West.

By the end of 1858, the rate of expansion of postal routes to the Pacific had reached a peak. Postmaster General Brown received enthusiastic support from Western and Pacific coast populations for his rapid increase in postal service to their areas. Six lines were now in operation:

1. The central route, from Independence, Missouri, to Placerville, California, via Salt Lake City, weekly.

2. Kansas City, Missouri, to Stockton, California, via Santa Fe, monthly.

3. The Butterfield Route, from St. Louis to San Francisco, via El Paso, Texas, twice-weekly.

4. San Antonio, Texas, to San Diego, California, twice-monthly.

5. New Orleans to San Francisco, via Tehuantepec, twice-monthly.

6. New York to San Francisco, via Panama, twice-monthly.

Four of these six lines had been put in place during the first year and a half of Brown's administration, and his accomplishments were justly praised. The only adverse comments were generated because of his choice of a southern route, which could lead to that being the route of the anticipated railroad, and the fully justified suspicion that he favored the Southern states in his decisions.

Although discounted by some Californians, most of whom were in the San Francisco region, and the Northern congressmen, the Butterfield operation was quite successful. By 1859, it was carrying more letter mail than the Panama ship route, in spite of the fact that California postmasters directed all mail via Panama unless the letter was specifically endorsed to be sent overland. While successful from a mail-delivery standpoint, it was not a financial success. The large initial expenditures and cost of operation far exceeded the passenger and mail income, and Butterfield was forced to borrow money from Wells, Fargo. This problem was compounded by the failure of the Appropriations Act of 1859, which made it impossible for the Post Office Department to pay large sums of money it owed to Butterfield. This caused him to default on his loans from Wells, Fargo, and Wells, Fargo acquired control of the company.

During this period, limited mail services were still being conducted along the central route, and additional stage and mail routes were continually being added as new gold and silver strikes were being made in Nevada, Colorado and other Western territories. In February of 1860, William Russell and his associates, Majors and Waddell, formed the Central Overland and Pikes Peak Express Company (COC&PPE). The company had bought out the other contractors and now had a monopoly on the through mail via the central route. With the hope that the long-anticipated railroad would follow this route, which was almost 1,000 miles shorter than Butterfield's, it was set to reap a financial bonanza. Unfortunately, it was deeply in debt and needed some sort of spectacular success that would demonstrate the superiority of the central route and induce Congress to provide it with a substantial mail subsidy. Russell was a flamboyant operator, and with the support of Senator Gwin of California, proposed the idea of a Pony Express. This caught the imagination of the country and the support of the central-route adherents in Congress.

On April 3, 1860, riders simultaneously left San Francisco and St. Joseph, Missouri, for the 1,966-mile journey, each carrying 35 pounds of mail. The cost to the sender was not small. Letters were to be enclosed in government stamped envelopes, and a surcharge of $5 per ½ ounce was charged by the Pony Express. This was reduced on April 1, 1861, to $2, and again on July 1, 1861, to $1 per ½ ounce. Even at these substantial prices, the high costs of operation caused huge losses to the company. It was continued only in the hopes of receiving a large mail subsidy and future mail monopolies.

Although he was not a particularly astute businessman, there is little doubt that Russell's vision and ability to convince supporters of the merit of his ideas was instrumental in the establishment of most of the original stage lines in the Colorado and plains regions. A portrait of Russell is shown in **Figure 16-11**.

Several events occurred that sealed the demise of

Figure 16-11. William H. Russell, a pioneer organizer of the overland stage routes and the Pony Express. Flamboyant and well-liked, he was instrumental in the early development of Denver, Colorado.
(From Hafen's *The Overland Mails*, courtesy of Quarterman Publications Inc.)

the COC&PPE. In an attempt to stave off bankruptcy, Russell had borrowed $870,000 in negotiable bonds from the Indian Trust Fund maintained by the Department of the Interior. He covered this loan from a clerk in the department with unsecured notes on the COC&PPE and a promise to return the bonds by March 4, 1861, the date of the inauguration of the new president. After Lincoln's election, the clerk, a relative of John Floyd, Buchanan's secretary of war, became frightened and confessed to his part in the scheme. Russell and the clerk were arrested, and congressional hearings began. Later, Russell, Bailey, the clerk, and Secretary of War Floyd were indicted. Russell was excused from prosecution on a technicality, Floyd was excused for lack of evidence but immediately resigned his post under a cloud of suspicion. Bailey jumped bail and disappeared. Of course, after this, there was no possibility of Congress awarding any new contract to the COC&PPE with Russell at its head.

Soon after this, the Civil War became a reality. On February 1, 1861, Texas seceded from the Union, and immediately the horses and equipment of the Butterfield route were, wherever possible, confiscated by the Confederacy. The Overland Mail Co., which was now controlled by Wells, Fargo, was directed by the postmaster general to move north to the central route. It had little equipment, but was able to subcontract the portion of the route from Salt Lake City to St. Joseph, Missouri, to the COC&PPE. The western part of the route, between Salt Lake City and San Francisco, became part of the Wells, Fargo operation. The COC&PPE, in financial ruin, was acquired by Ben Holladay in March of 1862, who for the following four years controlled the eastern part of the transcontinental mail route as the owner of the Holladay Overland Mail and Express Company. Holladay was a smart and ruthless businessman. He expanded his stage and mail lines to as many locations in the West as possible, and eliminated most competition by reducing rates below cost until a competitor was forced out of business. Holladay then raised his prices as the only service available to more than compensate for his previous losses.

This brings the account of the transcontinental overland mail up to the eve of the appearance of the 1861 stamps.

The Pony Express was still operating, as a part of

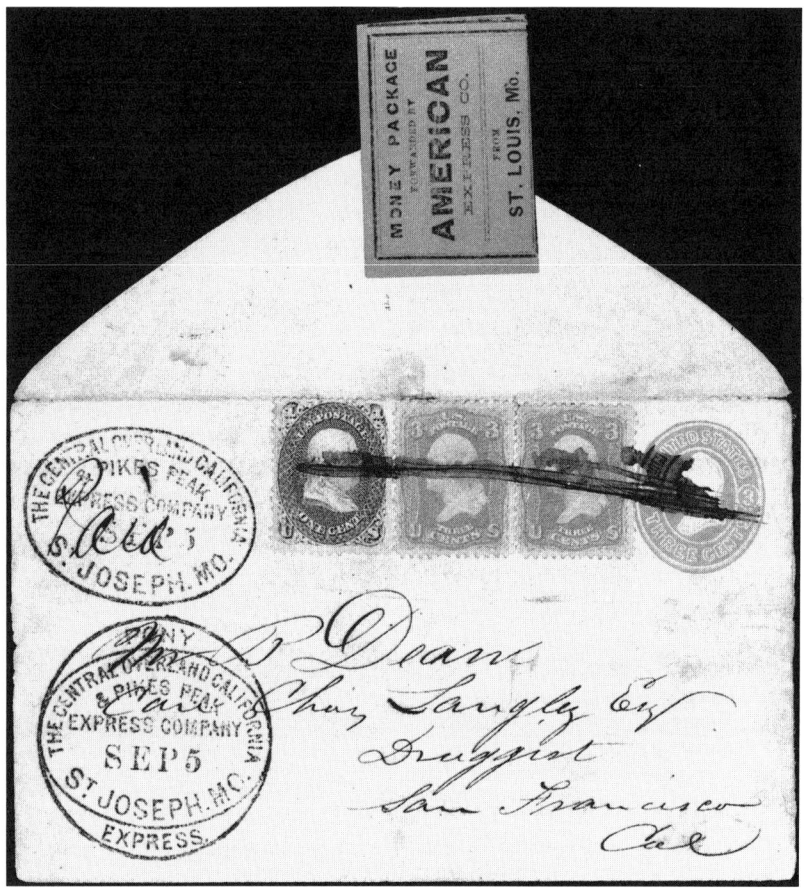

Figure 16-12. Rare use of the 1¢ Franklin on a Pony Express cover. This American Express money package with vermilion flap seal was sent from St. Louis to St. Joseph, Missouri, where it was transferred to the Pony Express operation of the COC&PPE for carriage to San Francisco. It is handstamped SEP 5. Use was during 1861. The 10¢ ("over the Rockies") postage was paid by a 3¢ stamped envelope (Scott U34), two 3¢ and one 1¢ stamps. The cover is opened to show the express label on the reverse.
(R.A. Siegel Auction Gallery photo)

the overland route. Postmaster General Blair noted in his 1861 annual report that the operators of the Overland Mail Co. (Butterfield route) were to discontinue their southern overland route, and instead "to provide for the conveyance, by the same parties, for a six-times-a-week mail by the 'central route,' that is, from some point on the Missouri River, connecting with the east, to Placerville, California."

The details of this new operation are of particular interest because they governed the transmission of the mails on the overland route for the duration of the Civil War. The entire letter mail was to be carried from St. Joseph, Missouri (or Atchison, Kansas) to Placerville, California, six times a week with a transit time of 20-23 days, depending on the time of year. The entire mail for Salt Lake City and Denver was to be carried three times per week.

All letter mail was to be carried to California no matter what its weight might be. If the letter mail amounted to less than 600 pounds, other types of mail were to be included to make up the 600 pounds. The balance of the mails was to be conveyed by the contractor in 35 days, with the privilege of sending them from New York to San Francisco in 25 days by sea. A pony express was to be run twice a week until the completion of the overland telegraph. The cost of the entire operation was to be $1 million per annum, to be paid from the general treasury. Service was to begin on July 1, 1861, and the contract was to continue for three years.

In his report of December 1, 1861, Blair went on to comment that the service had been initiated as scheduled, and that Salt Lake City was on the route selected so it would benefit from daily service. Complaints had been received concerning the handling of some of the mail. The contractor was supposed to make up any deficiency in a 600-pound load of letter mail by supplementing it with other types of mail. Evidently, since the the space occupied by newspapers and other printed matter could be used for passengers in a more financially rewarding manner for the stage operator, bags of printed-matter mail were being dumped by the side of the road so more paying passengers and express matter could be carried.

The Pony Express continued to operate until the completion of the telegraph line on October 26, 1861. Since the 1861 stamps were not available until August of 1861, the opportunity for a Pony Express cover to carry an 1861 1¢ Franklin existed for only a brief 13-week period. Such covers are very rare. **Figure 16-12** illustrates an exceptionally fine example of such use. The cover is opened to show the red American Express label on the reverse that sealed the envelope flap. The cover contained valuables, as denoted by the term "money package" on the label, and was carried from its origin in St. Louis to St. Joseph by the American Express Company.

At St. Joseph, it was turned over to the COC&PPE, and its handstamp, dated SEP 5, with "Paid" in manuscript, was applied in the upper-left corner. Immediately below this mark, the oval-in-circle Pony Express marking, also dated SEP 5, was applied. The required 10¢ postage was furnished by a 3¢ government stamped envelope with two 3¢ and one 1¢ 1861 stamps. The cover was then carried to its destination at San Francisco by Pony Express. The fee charged at this time was limited by law to $1 per ½ ounce.

A daily overland mail was now in operation, but the difficulties and interruptions to service continued. Indian depredations, which had been relatively light and sporadic in the past, began to become a serious danger to travelers and the transmission of the mails. The strength of many of the Western military forts had been reduced to provide men for the Civil War in the East, and some troops were diverted to deal with the Confederate attacks in New Mexico territory. The Indians finally decided that if they were going to limit the white man's encroachment onto their lands, drastic action had to be taken. From 1862 through 1865, tons of mail were destroyed, and hundreds of passengers and employees of the overland stages were killed.

The actions of the Indians, and also the winter weather in the high plains and Sierras, frequently required mail to be held at the terminals for extended periods, and at times it was necessary to send all mail by sea via Panama. Severe weather also caused the mail at times to pile up at stations on either side of the Rockies and High Sierras. Covers from correspondence during this period may have gone either by the normal overland route or by sea. Some correspondents, preferring the greater reliability of the ocean route, endorsed their letters for that route even though the transit time was longer.

The unprecedented floods in the West during the winter and spring of 1861-62, along with Indian depredations and some dereliction by the contractors, caused the postmaster general to report that the overland mail service had not been satisfactory. His annual report for 1862 went on to say that changes in the route and management of the overland mails had been made and that he expected the situation to improve. He further stated with regard to the overland mails:

> "Its importance, indeed, is becoming more and more manifest. Every day brings intelligence of the discovery of new mines of gold and silver in the region traversed by this mail route, which gives assurance that it will not be many years before it will be protected and supported throughout the greater part of the route by a civilized population. As an agency in developing these resources for the government the mail line is indispensable, and every needful protection and support should be given to the company, and some allowance made for failures in the beginning of the undertaking."

Figure 16-13 shows a transcontinental cover from Hazel Green, Wisconsin, to Jackson, California, in the heart of the Amador County gold country. The letter was paid with three 3¢ and one 1¢ stamps, canceled with four strikes of a Norton-type patent marker with a grid of eight parallel cutters. The blades, however, do not cut into the stamp. This cover reflects the new rate for transcontinental overland mail, effective July 1, 1861. The 10¢ rate, which had previously been required only for letters transmitted in excess of 3,000 miles, was revised to apply to all letters

Figure 16-13. This cover was sent from Hazel Green, Wisconsin, to Jackson, Amador County, California, on March 12. Three 3¢ and one 1¢ paid the 10¢ postage for the "over-the-Rockies" rate. The stamps are canceled by an eight-bar Norton-type patent marker.

Figure 16-14. Volcano, California, May 1, to Hannibal, Missouri. The 10¢ rate was paid by 10 1¢ Franklins. The cover is opened to show all stamps, four of which were applied to the reverse of the cover.

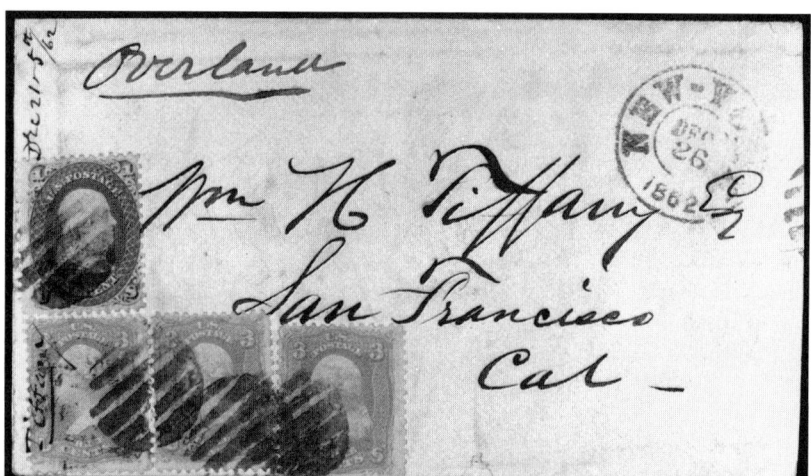

Figure 16-15. Endorsed "Overland," this cover was postmarked with a New York, December 26, 1862, CDS, and sent to San Francisco. This is an example of the 10¢ transcontinental rate.

from any point in the United States east of the Rocky Mountains to any state or territory on the Pacific, and vise versa, no matter what the mileage might be.

The main reason for this change was economic. Previously, much of the letter mail had been transmitted via Panama, with the distance well in excess of 3,000 miles, and requiring 10¢ for a single letter. With the shorter overland route, many letters now traveled a total distance of less than 3,000 miles and would normally qualify for a 3¢ rate. The cost of the overland-route mail contract was high, and the government wished to recoup some of that cost by ensuring that all through letters paid the higher rate.

Figure 16-14 shows a transcontinental cover that went in the opposite direction. This cover originated at Volcano, California, another gold rush town in Amador County during the 1860s. The destination was Hannibal, Missouri. The 10¢ rate was paid by 10 1¢ stamps applied to both the front and the back of the cover. The cover is opened up in the illustration to show all of the stamps.

The 1¢ Franklin is scarce on Western covers, and the use of 10 of them on a single cover is rarely seen. The year date is indistinct on the CDS but must be 1862 or 1863.

Figure 16-15 illustrates a transcontinental cover from New York City, dated December 26, 1862, to San Francisco. The envelope is endorsed "Overland" and probably traveled by that route. Postmaster General Blair noted in his annual report for fiscal 1863 that the floods of the previous year on the Pacific coast, and the "insurrection in the South Atlantic States, interrupted the overland mails for a few months on the west coast, and continues to interrupt them on the east." Blair had arranged to have the mails conveyed by sea during these periods, but the U.S auditor refused to pay the contractors for their services on the grounds that Congress had legislated that all letter mail was to go overland; therefore, sea transit was illegal. Blair petitioned Congress to provide him with the authority to pay for services that had already been performed, and to continue them where nec-

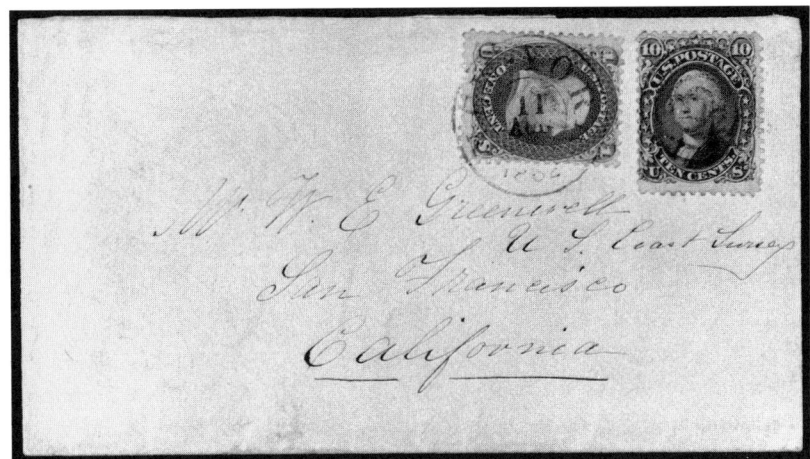

Figure 16-16. New York 11 AUG 1862 CDS to San Francisco. The 11¢ postage paid the transcontinental rate plus carrier collection at New York City.

Figure 16-17. Carrier collection letter from Boston, Massachusetts, bearing a red SEP 12 CDS, to San Francisco. The stamps paid the 1¢ carrier fee and 10¢ postage for distances in excess of 3,000 miles. The cover is part of the "Wetherbee" correspondence, as are the covers shown in Figures 16-5 and 16-6.
(James Lee collection)

essary. This situation was never satisfactorily concluded by Congress, and Blair continued to use whatever means he could to get the mails through.

Figure 16-16 shows a cover with 11¢ in postage. The 10¢ 1861 stamp paid for the transcontinental rate, and the 1¢ Franklin paid for the carrier fee to the mails at New York City. The double-circle New York postmark is dated August 11, 1862. The cover is addressed to a member of the U.S. Coast Survey at San Francisco. The "Greenwell" correspondence was well-preserved, and a relatively large number of covers have survived. Most are from New York City and bear the 11¢ franking.

Figure 16-17 illustrates a carrier-fee-to-the-mails use, mailed at Boston, Massachusetts, with a red Boston CDS dated SEP 12. The stamps are canceled with the usual boxed PAID handstamp of Boston. This cover is from the transcontinental correspondence between Mr. and Mrs. Henry Wetherbee. Other examples were shown in Figures 16-5 and 16-6.

On July 1, 1863, the domestic rate for letter postage became 3¢, regardless of distance. Transcontinental letters could now be sent at the lower rate. **Figure 16-18** shows a typical example of such use. This cover was mailed from Coloma, California, to New York. The Coloma CDS is dated FEB 1, with the "1" overwritten with a manuscript "10." Coloma was a gold-rush town in El Dorado County and the site of the first discovery of gold at Sutter's Mill. There is no year date on the cover, but obviously it was mailed subsequent to the reduction in the transcontinental rate. The cover is addressed to General J.W. Denver, at New York City. James William Denver had a varied and interesting career. He was a Midwestern lawyer and newspaper editor who served as a captain in the Mexican War. He then left the service and moved to California, where he was elected to the state legislature and later to the U.S. Congress. During this period, he killed a man in a duel for publicly criticizing him. His actions were excused as being justified, and no action was taken against him.

Figure 16-18. Transcontinental mail from Coloma, California, with a small 24mm double-circle CDS dated FEB 1 and with the "1" overwritten with a manuscript "10," to New York City. Three cents postage paid the domestic rate per ½ ounce, regardless of distance, effective July 1, 1863.

He later served as commissioner of Indian affairs and briefly as governor of the Territory of Kansas during the "Bloody Kansas" era. In 1861, he was appointed brigadier general, USV, and saw action at Shiloh and with the Army of the Tennessee. He resigned his commission in 1863, returned to the practice of law and later re-entered politics. Denver, Colorado, was named for him.

Indian attacks on the wagon trains and settlements continued to increase. The new postmaster general, William Dennison, in his annual report for 1864 noted that:

> "Owing to Indian depredations, the overland service was much interrupted during the months of August and September last, and for a period of four or five weeks the whole mail for the Pacific coast and the Territories was necessarily sent by sea from New York."

In October of 1864, the contract for the overland mails (including the sea transportation of paper and document mails) with Ben Holladay was renewed for an additional four years at a reduced cost of $910,000 per year.

With the conclusion of the Civil War in 1865, additional troops were available for assignment in the West, and the Indian problems with respect to the mails were generally suppressed. Armed troopers accompanied most of the mail stages, and the Indians concentrated their forays on targets where there was less protection. Construction of the railroad was accelerated, and Ben Holladay accurately forecast that the days of the overland stage were reaching their end. In 1866, he sold his control of the eastern portion of the overland route (The Holladay Overland Mail & Stage Express Company) to Wells, Fargo for the substantial sum of $1.8 million, and retired to the East to manage his other far-flung enterprises.

In 1862, Congress passed the Railroad Construction Act and the Homestead Act. The effect of both of these pieces of legislation was temporarily reduced by the problems of the Civil War, but as soon as the war was over, they were instrumental in acccelerating the settling of the West. Congress provided generous subsidies for the construction of the transcontinental railroad. Twenty square miles of land adjacent to the tracks was to be given to the railroad companies for each mile of track that was laid. In addition, government railway bonds were authorized, and low-interest loans of $16,000 to $48,000 per mile were made to finance construction. Congress commissioned the Union Pacific to begin building a line westward from Omaha, Nebraska, and the Central Pacific to start from Sacramento, California, eastward until the lines met. Of course with the huge subsidies for each mile, every effort was made to progress as rapidly as possible. Beginning in 1866, construction began in earnest, and in less than four years, 1,677 miles of track had been laid and the line was completed.

The Homestead Act recognized the need to populate the western part of the country, and the previous policy of selling public lands was reversed. Provisions were enacted so individuals could acquire 160 acres of public land at essentially no cost by the expedient of moving onto the land and improving it over a period of five years. This act and the construction of the transcontinental railroad combined to open the western areas to a flood of new emigrants and the establishment of permanent settlements, with the concurrent need for enlarged and improved postal services.

In 1867, serious Indian trouble again broke out. The postmaster general report for 1867 notes that the contractor for the overland mail, between April 1 and August 15, 1867, was robbed by the Indians of 350 head of stage stock, and 12 of his stage stations were burned, along with large amounts of grain and hay. Three coaches and express wagons were destroyed, severely wounding several of the passengers, and 13 of the contractor's most

Transcontinental and Western Mails

reliable employees were killed. Other Western mail routes were similarly besieged by Indians. The extensive loss of life and material prompted strong retaliation against the Indians by the U.S. Army. The military efforts and concurrent attempts to establish treaties provided periods of temporary relief, but the continuing expansion into Indian lands by the settlers and prospectors, and the resulting broken treaties, guaranteed the continuation of warfare. It was another decade before the high plains were relatively safe.

The rails of the Central Pacific Railroad from the west, and the Union Pacific Railroad from the east, met at Promontory Point, Utah Territory, on May 9, 1869. The nation was finally united by bands of steel that stretched from coast to coast. The transit time for mail was reduced to about seven days between New York and San Francisco, and posted schedules were met for the most part. The quality of service by the overland stages during the final year of their operation was a great disappointment to the Post Office Department, and to travelers. The overland stage companies, seeing the end of their major business approaching, were not particularly concerned with maintenance, schedules or the passengers' comfort. The stages were falling apart, along with the need for their existence. Some equipment was transferred to local routes to service areas that did not yet have railroads, but the great stage lines that had been built to handle the transcontinental overland mails and commerce disappeared from the scene.

Wells, Fargo prospered. In spite of a temporary lower income as a result of the unexpected rapidity with which the railroad had been completed, the company continued to expand, particularly in the express and financial areas. By the end of the century, it had more than 3,000 branch offices and operated more than 38,000 miles of express routes, becoming the major banking institution in the West.

Territorial Mails

The Pacific coast was not the only region to experience rapid growth during this period. Settlers were homesteading all over the West, and new discoveries of gold, silver and other minerals were attracting legions of new fortune-seekers. As the need for mail services expanded, the Post Office Department tried to establish new routes, but in the early years, most of the mails were handled by private expresses. As more and more post offices were established, territorial postmarks began to appear with greater frequency on letters, and some of those covers have survived the perils of the years. Covers from most territories are scarce, and some locations are rare. As with all mail of the 1861-70 period, the 1¢ Franklin can be found on only a small percentage of the surviving covers.

Figure 16-19 shows a local drop cover, mailed at Virginia City, Nevada Territory. The double-circle, "Virginia City/N.T." postmark is dated February 14. The discovery of the fabulous Comstock Lode in 1859 made Virginia City and nearby Carson City the preeminent settlements in the territory. The existence of Nevada as a territory was short-lived. It was carved out of Utah Territory on March 2, 1861, and on October 31, 1864, it became a state. Use of "N.T." in the CDS is known for an extended period following the date of statehood.

Figure 16-20 shows another Nevada Territory local drop cover from Carson City. The 1¢ stamp is canceled with one strike of a blue "Carson City/NEVT" postmarker, with another strike for the postmark. The postmark is dated May 27, 1863. The postmark designations for Nevada Territory differ on this and the previous example. In Figure 16-19, the initials "N.T." are used, while

Figure 16-19. Territorial cover from Virginia City, Nevada Territory (N.T.). The 1¢ Franklin paid the local drop rate. The cover is postmarked February 14. The date and the use of the "Present" address suggests that the cover may have contained a valentine. (James Lee collection)

Figure 16-20. Nevada territorial use. This local drop letter bears a Carson City/NEVT, MAY 27, 1862 CDS in blue. The 1¢ Franklin paid the drop rate and is canceled with another strike of the postmark.
(C.W. Christian collection)

Figure 16-21. Transcontinental territorial cover postmarked Salt Lake City UT, FEB 4 (1863). The cover is docketed on reverse with the year date. The 3¢ postage paid for the special rate accorded to Salt Lake City for letters, effective December 25, 1861. Letters between the East and Salt Lake City could be sent for 3¢ without regard to the over-the-Rockies provision.
(James Lee collection)

here "NEVT" is used. Carson City was first settled in 1851 by two men returning from the California gold fields. They built a trading post there and named it after Kit Carson.

The cover in **Figure 16-21** shows an interesting situation that occurred with mail originating or addressed to Salt Lake City, Utah Territory. Salt Lake City was a well-established city with a substantial volume of mail when the rate for mail that crossed the Rocky Mountains was increased to 10¢, effective May 1, 1861. Previous to this date, domestic letters that traveled less than 3,000 miles were rated at 3¢. Most of the correspondence of the Mormon settlement at Salt Lake City was probably to the eastern part of the country to destinations of less than 3,000 miles, and the sudden increase of postage to 10¢ caused understandable resentment among inhabitants.

Brigham Young was the governor of Utah Territory at that time, and he evidently requested his territorial delegate to Congress, John M. Bernhisel, to attempt to get some relief from this onerous situation. Excerpted from a letter from Bernhisel to Brigham Young is the following [5:592]:

> "Washington, Nov. 30th, 1861
> I have had an interview this morning with the Hon. Montgomery Blair, Postmaster General, also with the First Assistant Postmaster [General], in relation to the TEN CENT postage charged at Salt Lake City on letters not exceeding half an ounce in weight, and I have the satisfaction to inform you that it resulted in the issuing of an order for a letter to be written to Mr. Postmaster Bell, instructing him to charge only THREE cents on letters of the above mentioned weight."

This was followed by a public notice in the December 25, 1861, *Deseret News*, as follows,

> "G.S.L. CITY, Dec. 25, 1861
> On and after this date, the postage from Salt Lake City to the Eastern States, and vise versa, will be three cents.
> By order of the post office department.
> WM. BELL, P.M."

The Mormons had based their case on the fact that Salt Lake City was in the Rocky Mountains and not east or west of them, and this was evidently sufficient for they were granted special dispensation.

Surprisingly, this order only applied to Salt Lake City. Other Utah post offices continued to charge the 10¢ rate for letters to the East. No references to a policy concerning the situation for letters that were transmitted between Salt Lake City and the Pacific coast have been located by this writer. However, Richard C. Frajola, a respected authority on Western mails, has communicated that he has seen examples of letters between these two points with 3¢ and also with 10¢ postage. No postage due was marked on the 3¢ letters, so obviously the lower rate was accepted.

Naturally, since this special rate was in existence for only about 18 months, and only with a single post office, examples are scarce. Only letters mailed between December 25, 1861, and July 1, 1863, and originating at or addressed to Salt Lake City, with postage of 3¢, would qualify. Of course, subsequent to July 1, 1863, all domestic letters were rated at 3¢, so knowing the date of mailing is mandatory to identify this special rate.

The cover in **Figure 16-21** bears the corner card of the Salt Lake City office of the Overland Mail Co. and is docketed on the reverse with the year 1863. The balloon CDS for "Salt Lake City/U. T." is dated FEB 4, and the cover is addressed to Tiffin, Ohio. The date of mailing fell within the period of the 10¢ over-the-Rockies rate, and the cover is franked with three 1¢ Franklins. It therefore reflects the special rate accorded to Salt Lake City mail.

Colorado Territory produced some very interesting covers. With the discovery of gold at the present site of Denver in the summer of 1858, the gold rush was on, and the territorial population increased from just a handful of settlers to many thousands in a very short time. The town of Denver first consisted of two separate settlements, Auraria and St. Charles, on opposite sides of Cherry Creek where gold had been discovered. St. Charles was soon renamed Denver, after James W. Denver (see Figure 16-18), the territorial governor of Kansas Territory. Subsequently, Auraria was absorbed into Denver City. At that time, much of Colorado was still part of Kansas Territory. On February 28, 1861, Colorado Territory was formed out of parts of New Mexico, Utah, Nebraska and Kansas Territories, and on August 1, 1876, Colorado became a state.

Regular mail service to Denver was first provided by the Leavenworth City and Pike's Peak Express (LC&PPE) at cost of 25¢ for a 1-ounce letter, plus the cost of the government stamped envelope. This was a very low rate for private stages at that time, particularly in that part of the country. William H. Russell (of COC&PPE fame) was one of the organizers of the company and, as a shareholder of the town of Denver, did much to foster the town's rapid growth. A post office was opened in 1860 and received the first delivery of mail under government contract from the LC&PPE in August of 1860.

Figure 16-22 illustrates a territorial use of three 1¢ Franklins, mailed at Denver City, Colorado Territory, on November 19 to Binghampton, New York. While no year date is shown, the single-circle postmark is of the type first used with the Colorado Territory designation, and the latest reported use of this postmark is December 31, 1861. This would establish the year of use as 1861.

Figure 16-23 shows a similar cover, but in this case, the postmark is a double circle and the origin is shown as DENVER/COL, without the territorial designator. This type of marking is known to have been used between October 1863 and July 1865, a period when Colo-

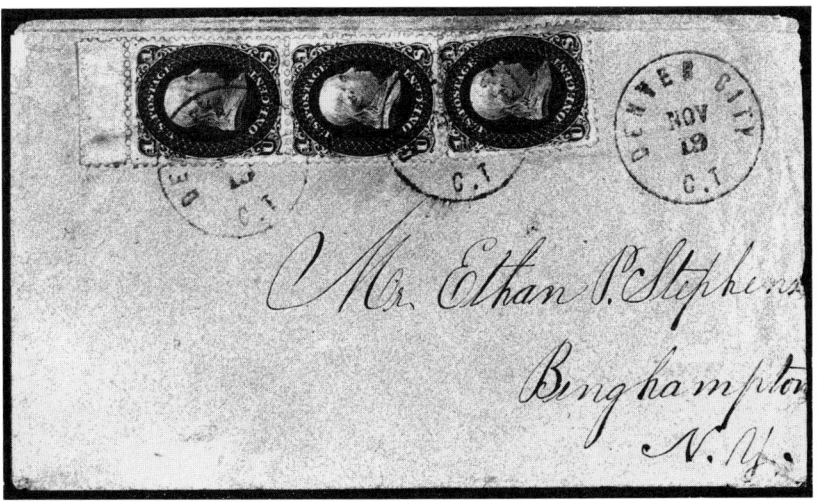

Figure 16-22. Early Colorado Territory use at Denver City, C.T. The single-circle CDS is dated NOV 19. The 3¢ postage was the correct rate for this letter since it did not cross the Rockies, and the total distance to its New York destination was less than 3,000 miles.
(James Lee collection)

Figure 16-23. This 3¢ rate cover bears a DENVER CITY COL SEP 22 double-circle duplex CDS. This type of postmark is recorded for the period October 1863 to July 1865. Colorado was a territory until August 1, 1876, but the territorial designator was not included in this postmark.
(James Lee collection)

Figure 16-24. Colorado Territory cover with the correct 10¢ rate to Canada. The cover bears a Mountain City, Colorado Territory, March 3, 1862, double-circle CDS to Montreal, Canada East, and a red "U.S. PAID 10" in oval exchange-office marking. It is backstamped with a Montreal, Canada East, receiving mark, dated March 18, 1862.

Figure 16-25. Stagecoach express receipt issued by Ben Holladay's *Overland Stage Line* at Denver City on November 22, 1864. The receipt is for a package of U.S. Treasury notes amounting to $3,000, to be carried to Central City, Colorado Territory, a mining town about 30 miles west of Denver. Note the advertisement for the "Great Through Mails."
(From Hafen's *The Overland Mails*, courtesy of Quarterman Publications Inc.)

rado was still a territory.

Figure 16-24 shows an exceptionally fine territorial use from Mountain City, Colorado Territory, to Montreal, Canada East. The 10¢ rate is paid by three 3¢ stamps and one 1¢. Mailed on March 3, 1862, this cover probably traveled to Denver by mail contract with a local stage operator. At that point, it is likely that a branch of the Overland Mail Co. carried it north to meet with the main overland route, and from there it went east to the overland terminus at St. Joseph, Missouri, where it continued by rail to a Canadian border exchange office at Detroit, Michigan. A red U.S. PAID 10 in oval marking was applied at the exchange office, and the letter continued to its destination at Montreal, Canada. The cover is backstamped Montreal, C.E., and dated March 18, 1862.

About four months later, the main overland route was moved south. Indian trouble had caused the route along the North Platte River to be untenable, and also the southern route was shorter. Beginning on July 21, 1862, the "Great Mails" of the overland route daily passed through Denver. This change helped accelerate the development of Denver into a major city in the West. Although the Indian attacks were publicized as the reason for the change, the subsidies and special privileges granted to Holladay's Overland Mail Co. by Governor John Evans and the Colorado territorial legislature may have played a major part in the decision.

Figure 16-25 shows a receipt from Ben Holladay's Overland Stage Line for a package worth $3,000 that was sent from Denver City to Central City, Colorado Territory, a distance of about 30 miles.

Figure 16-26 illustrates a territorial use at Omaha City, Nebraska. Nebraska became a territory on May 30, 1854, and achieved statehood on February 9, 1867. The letter was mailed on July 11, 1863, and addressed to Downington, Pennsylvania. Omaha City was at that time within the boundaries of the established railroad system, so it may be assumed that this particular letter reached its destination primarily by rail. During the early 1860s, Postmaster General Blair had to move the eastern terminus of the overland route to Omaha for a time because of fighting between the pro-slavery and anti-slavery factions in Kansas. Raids by lawless bands made the route from St. Joseph to Fort Kearny through the northern part of Kansas extremely dangerous, and it was moved northward.

Covers showing the use of the 1¢ Franklin probably exist from every territory west of the Mississippi; however, they are not easy to locate, and a representative showing from all of the territories would be a goal difficult to achieve.

The Western territories were all formed from earlier and larger areas and territories. In the process of finally achieving statehood, many of these went through a number of boundary and name changes. The evolution of the territories is historically important and of great philatelic interest. Unfortunately, the scope and space limitations of this book do not allow for a more comprehensive coverage of the subject.

Figure 16-27 is a list of the Western territories that had territorial status during the period of 1861 to 1870 and where examples of the use of the 1¢ Franklin might be expected to originate. The dates of their origination and conversion to statehood are also included [6].

Only a few highlights of the story of the U.S. mails in the Western states and their part in the settlement and development of the country have been presented in this chapter. Every cover from the West during the period before the completion of the transcontinental railroad has

Figure 16-26. Nebraska Territorial use with a double-circle Omaha City, Nebraska, CDS, dated JUL 11, 1863. Three 1¢ stamps paid the letter rate to Downingtown, Pennsylvania. Nebraska became a state on February 9, 1867.
(C.W. Christian collection)

NAME	TERRITORY	STATE	NOTES
Alaska	1867 (Oct. 11)	1959 (Jan. 3)	Purchased from Russia June 20, 1867
Arizona	1863 (Feb. 24)	1912 (Feb. 14)	Cut from New Mexico Territory
California	*	1850 (Sept. 9)	Ceded by Mexico Feb. 2, 1848
Colorado	1861 (Feb. 28)	1876 (Aug. 1)	Cut from Kansas, Nebraska, New Mexico and Utah
Dakota	1861 (March 2)	--------	From Minnesota and Nebraska (became North and South Dakota)
Idaho	1863 (March 3)	1890 (July 3)	Cut from Dakota, Nebraska and Washington
Kansas	1854 (May 30)	1861 (Jan. 29)	From unorganized area
Montana	1864 (May 26)	1889 (Nov. 8)	From Idaho
Nebraska	1854 (May 30)	1867 (Feb. 9)	From unorganized area
Nevada	1861 (March 2)	1864 (Oct. 31)	From Utah
N. Mexico	1850 (Dec. 13)	1912 (Jan. 6)	Ceded from Mexico Feb 2, 1848
N. Dakota	--------	1889 (Nov. 2)	Part of Dakota Territory
S. Dakota	--------	1889 (Nov. 2)	Part of Dakota Territory
Utah	1850 (Sept. 9)	1896 (Jan. 4)	From area ceded by Mexico
Washington	1853 (March 2)	1889 (Nov. 11)	From Oregon
Wyoming	1868 (July 29)	1890 (July 10)	From Dakota, Idaho and Utah

* Under U.S. military provisional government from Feb. 2, 1848, to statehood.

Figure 16-27. Western territories 1861-1870

its own particular tale to tell, and the philatelic research to unravel the secrets of when, how and why they came to be is one of the most interesting challenges to face the postal history collector.

References

1. Coburn, Jesse L. *Letters of Gold*. U. S. Philatelic Classics Society, Inc. 1984.

2. Hafen, LeRoy R. *The Overland Mail*. 1976 Quarterman reprint of *The Overland Mail 1849-1869*. Arthur H. Clarke Co. 1926.

3. Crowe, William T., Ed. *Western Roundup*. The Philatelic Foundation Seminar Series, Textbook No. 1. Philatelic Foundation. 1990.

4. *Report of the Postmaster General for 1863*. Reprinted by Theron Wierenga. 1977.

5. Perry, Elliott. *Pat Paragraphs*, Compiled and Arranged by George T. Turner and Thomas E. Stanton. Bureau Issues Association Inc. 1981.

6. Adapted from a list distributed widely by the U.S. Cancellation Club, Philip Bansner, and others. Credit for the data is attributed to Dr. Carroll Chase and R. McP. Cabeen.

CHAPTER 17

Foreign Mails

The crown jewels of a classic postal history collection are frequently found among the covers addressed to foreign countries. In these examples may be discovered the use of scarce high-denomination stamps and covers addressed to seldom-seen destinations. It is not only the rarity of foreign-mail covers and their stamps that appeals to philatelists, but also the challenge they present for analysis of the postal history of each example.

The determination of the rates charged by the various countries that might be traversed by a letter, and the routes and methods of transportation by which the cover reached its destination, can be an interesting and intellectually rewarding experience. Because of the lack of uniformity in pre-General Postal Union/Universal Postal Union agreements and conventions for the transmission of foreign mails, the search for the information needed to determine the rates, routing and meaning of the various markings can be at times somewhat intimidating. Fortunately several excellent reference books have been written on the subject. Among the most useful to the collector of classic-period U.S. covers are the *History of Letter Post Communication Between the United States and Europe, 1845-1875* by George Hargest [1], *U.S. Letter Rates to Foreign Destinations, 1847 to GPU-UPU* by Charles Starnes [2], and *North Atlantic Mail Sailings, 1840-75,* by Hubbard and Winter [3].

Most covers to foreign destinations are relatively simple to analyze, and the basic rates and routes describe their transmission in the mails. However, there are some letters for which analysis requires a substantial amount of research and specialized knowledge. Fortunately for the collector who has limited experience with the foreign mails, the vast majority of letters during the 1860s were addressed to Western European countries. The mail agreements governing these transmissions are well-documented, and most of the necessary information is available. At the beginning of the decade, the United States had postal conventions or treaties in force with four European nations and two city-states. These were England, France, Belgium, Prussia, and the city-states of Bremen and Hamburg. Mail to most other destinations in Europe, Africa, the Middle East and Asia was routed through these countries and handled by their postal systems.

A large amount of mail was exchanged between the British North American provinces and the United States. This was subject to special and generally mutually favorable postal arrangements. Postal treaties with some of the other nations in the Western Hemisphere and initial arrangements for transpacific mail routes came into being during the 1860s, but the volume of letters was very small compared to the correspondence with Europe and Canada.

The story of the mails to foreign countries during this period is fascinating. It reflects the rapid growth of communications and commercial shipping that occurred during this period. Much of this growth resulted from the reliability and rapid transit that was provided by the increased use of steamships. By the end of the Civil War, an unprecedented surge in the volume of foreign mail had occurred.

This period was also of extreme importance in changing the way the exchange of mail was handled throughout the world. The tenure of Postmaster General Montgomery Blair, from 1861 to 1864, resulted in many important and beneficial changes to the U.S. domestic postal service, some of which have been previously discussed throughout this volume. Blair and his able first assistant postmaster general, John A. Kasson, were keenly aware of the inefficiency of the foreign-mail arrangements. They initiated discussions with other countries aimed towards simplifying and standardizing existing treaties and conventions.

These discussions began at a meeting in Paris, France, on May 11, 1863. The conference was attended by the major postal countries of the world, and the United States was represented by Kasson. Although no new postal agreements immediately resulted, many innovative ideas were presented and general agreement was reached concerning the necessity for simplifying and standardizing the foreign-mail procedures. Subsequent to the conference, the United States continued to sponsor further and wide-reaching changes. These efforts finally resulted in improved conventions with most of the major European countries by 1868 and the eventual formation of the General Postal Union in 1875, which became the Universal Postal Union in 1878.

In his December 1, 1862, Annual Report to Congress and the President, Blair stated:

> "Our international mail system is extremely loose and defective. There is no common standard weight for the single rate. There is no common rate for the sea transit, or for overland transit . . .
> Rates upon closed mails are not uniform by distance, or by other common rule, and they vary greatly according to the route of carriage.
> The whole foreign system as now established is too complex to be readily understood by postmasters, and many mistakes and unfortunate delays arise from its complexity . . ."

Since much of the complexity to which Blair referred persisted throughout the decade of the 1860s, the resulting variation in rates and routings adds spice and challenge to the study of covers from the period. It may not have been an efficient system, but it is certainly an interesting one.

In this chapter, a representation of foreign-letter mail, which also shows the use of the 1¢ Franklin, during the period of 1860 to 1870, will be discussed and illustrated. This limits the number of examples that can be shown. While no attempt is made to cover the entire field of foreign communications, features of the applicable postal conventions, rates, routes and markings for representative destinations will be discussed. Incoming mail from foreign countries is part of the complete story of the foreign mails, but that interesting aspect will not be considered in this volume. The author wishes to emphasize that only a small portion of the vast subject of mail to foreign destinations will be included, and while this presentation will provide information sufficient to describe the more common uses, the analysis of complex routings and uncommon destinations will require additional references.

In earlier chapters, some mail to foreign countries has already been discussed. In Chapter 10, unpaid foreign letters that used carrier collection to the mails with the fee paid by the 1¢ Franklin were explained and illustrated. In Chapter 12, the use of the 1¢ stamp to pay the postage on printed circulars and newspapers to foreign addresses was covered. In this chapter, the remaining foreign letter uses will be discussed. In general, the covers will show the 1¢ Franklin in combination with other denominations. Prepaid letters to other countries with the postage paid entirely by 1¢ 1861 stamps are quite scarce. It would be possible to pay all of the postage with 1¢ stamps, but the large number of stamps that would be required makes this a very unusual occurrence. A letter part-paid with only 1¢ stamps was illustrated in Figure 14-20 of Chapter 14.

As a convenience to the reader, and particularly for the collector who is venturing into the analysis of foreign letter mail for the first time, some generally used terms are defined and described in the following paragraphs.

Foreign mail exchange offices: These are post offices that were specifically identified in a postal convention or treaty between the United States and another country. Their purpose was to rate and dispatch or receive mail between corresponding exchange offices in the two countries, and to record the debits or credits resulting from the transmission of each letter or item of mail. The postal personnel who manned these exchange offices were specially trained, and they removed much of the burden for understanding the complex features of foreign postal arrangements from the individual postmasters throughout the countries. Depending on the terms of the postal arrangement, an exchange office in one country might be limited to exchanging mail with a single office in the other country, or it might be possible to exchange with several listed offices. Exchange offices were normally, but not always, located at ports or borders. The principal exchange offices in the United States were New York City and Boston, although other cities also provided this service for specific routes. London, Paris and Hamburg are examples of exchange offices in foreign countries.

Open mail: mail transported from the dispatching exchange office to the first foreign exchange office on its route where the mail bags are opened, the mail sorted, accounted for and delivered domestically. If the final destination lies beyond the country, it enters again into the mail system and is forwarded towards destination as if it had originated at the foreign exchange office. This process may be repeated at the next exchange office if the mail was forwarded by open mail and the final destination is beyond the next country on the route. For example: Consider a letter sent from the United States to Switzerland by British open mail. The letter would depart a U.S. exchange office in a bag addressed to the corresponding British exchange office. Upon arrival, the letter would be processed and entered again into the British mail system and could be forwarded as open mail to France. In France the letter would again be processed and sent on to another exchange office in Switzerland, where it finally would be sent to its destination city. Obviously, this was not an efficient system, so mail was generally forwarded through intervening countries by closed mail (see next definition) when possible.

Closed mail: As the name implies, closed mail was transmitted between the originating and destination exchange offices in sealed bags. During transport through intervening countries, the bags remained sealed. Transit costs were accounted for on the basis of bulk weight. This is a more efficient way to handle mail, but requires that postal conventions be in force between the countries involved in the transport of the mail.

Sea postage: that portion of the total postage that was used to pay for the sea transport of a letter. It normally accrued to the country that paid for the sea transport of the mail. The amount that the ship received for the service did not necessarily equate to the amount of sea postage.

Inland postage: that portion of the total postage that accrues to originating and destination countries to pay for their own domestic postage under the postal-treaty provisions. The amount may or may not be equivalent to the amount paid by citizens for domestic-mail postage.

Transit postage: the amount of postage charged by a country to allow through transit of mail. The amount of postage was generally determined by the bulk weight of the closed bags.

Postal treaty: a postal agreement that is reached by two countries, and ratified by the legislatures and executive administrations of the parties to the treaty. Because of the involvement of Congress or equivalent bodies in the establishment of treaties, and conflicts between government agencies, they at times were difficult to conclude in an expeditious manner.

Postal convention: A postal convention could be agreed upon between the postal administrations of two countries, providing that the terms of the convention were not contrary to the postal laws that had been established by the contracting countries. Both treaties and conventions established postal routes and procedures, exchange offices, rates of postage, and methods for accounting and payment.

Forwarding agent: an individual or company who provided a multitude of postal services for patrons. Although forwarding agents were also used for domestic mail, their biggest use was to assist the senders and recipients of foreign mails. Because of the complexity, and occasional uncertainty, of foreign-mail systems, the expertise of the forwarders added reliability and speed to communications. They would accept responsibility for properly mailing and delivering letters, seeing that mail was forwarded to catch up with travelers, holding incoming mail pending arrival of the addressee, and other similar tasks.

The U.S. consuls in foreign countries were also authorized by Congress to act as postal agents, and in many of the smaller foreign port cities they performed this service for local U.S. citizens and travelers. However, the volume of mail in the larger and more commercial cities precluded this type of support, and commercial forwarders filled the need. Consuls would also handle mail for the crews of U.S. Naval ships stationed, or expected, at their locations.

The multiplicity of rates and procedures for letters to different countries makes it difficult to provide a general explanation of the foreign-mail systems. Instead, examples of letters to various destinations, and under differing mail arrangements, will be illustrated and discussed in detail. However, the handling of foreign letters prior to their leaving the United States followed standardized procedures in most cases.

If the sender desired to prepay the postage, letters were to be rated by the originating post office, which often was not an exchange office, in accordance to published postal rates. The rate was to be marked on the cover. Unpaid letters were to be forwarded to the appropriate U.S. exchange post office without rating. The rate could be a function of the routing of the letter and the foreign postal system that would handle it. For that reason, the Post Office Department suggested that letters be endorsed with the route and mail system desired. Dates of departure of ships and their destinations were published in the newspapers of many of the larger cities.

The need for endorsing the desired route to determine the rate resulted in some postmasters stamping or writing a rate on an unpaid letter, evidently assuming since different routes had specific rates, the amount would be an indication of the desired routing even if there was no endorsement. This practice was contrary to Post Office Department preferences, but no written notices to discourage it were published until 1867 [4:76]. Unpaid letters with handstamped or written rates on them are occasionally seen, and it should be noted that the exchange office did not always concur with the rate as indicated and charged a different amount.

At the exchange office, the rating on the letter would be determined, and it would be marked with a debiting or crediting postmark, depending on whether the letter was unpaid or prepaid. This debit or credit to the receiving nation would then be entered into the foreign-mail accounts to be later settled. If appropriate, the method of transport would also be indicated. Letter bills were prepared to accompany the letter, and it would be packaged for proper transmission. The method and route of travel would normally be in accordance with the instructions on the letter, but at times, it was necessary to use different ships or routes. If the letter had no endorsement or indication of preference, the postal clerk at the exchange office used his own discretion in making the selection.

The exchange-office markings were placed on letters when they arrived at the U.S. exchange office and not later when the mails were closed for dispatch. In effect, they were predated with the dates that they would be forwarded (either sent out on a locally departing steamer or sent to another location to catch a steamer). The date appearing in the exchange postmark is therefore of great importance in determining the method of transit of the cover since it can be correlated with the departure dates of mail steamers.

Transatlantic Mails

The majority of letters to foreign destinations during the 1860s was carried via the transatlantic mails, and most of these letters were addressed to England, France and the Germanic States. Two of the reference texts referred to earlier, the *History of Letter Post Communication Between the United States and Europe, 1845-1875* by George Hargest and *North Atlantic Mail Sailings, 1840-75* by Hubbard and Winter, are indispensable sources for information concerning rates and postal procedures. These books are each the result of many years of painstaking research by the authors, and they provide most of the collected data that is needed for the study of the transatlantic mails. In addition, they contain a wealth of interesting information concerning the development of the postal treaties and the shipping lines that carried the mail. These books, with the addition of *U.S. Letter Rates to Foreign Destinations, 1847 to GPU-UPU* by Charles Starnes, with its comprehensive listings of postal rates, are absolute musts for inclusion in the libraries of collectors with transatlantic foreign-mail covers. Much of the information presented in this chapter concerning postal conventions and the routes and dates of sailings was obtained from these references.

The most important postal agreements for mail carried during the 1860s were those with Great Britain, France, Prussia and the Hanseatic cities of Bremen and Hamburg. Mail addressed to most of the countries of Europe, Asia and Africa could be routed through these countries, and their mail systems assisted in transporting mail from the United States even to the Americas and Pacific Ocean countries.

Key elements of a postal agreement between two countries are the establishment of the routing of mail, rates to be charged for the internal postage for each country, the rate for sea transport, the provision and cost for the transit of closed mail bags through a country, and the accounting procedures for the division of the money collected for postage. In addition, specific post offices are named as the only points where mail can be exchanged between the countries.

British Treaty Mails

For most of the 1860s, the rates and procedures for mail to and via Great Britain were based on the U.S.-British postal treaty of December 15, 1848. This long-lasting arrangement was not substantially changed until January 1, 1868, when a new postal convention became effective. The new convention included a 50-percent reduction in rates, and two years later it was revised again, effective January 1, 1870, to further reduce the international rate. No further changes were made until the formation of the General Postal Union (GPU) in 1875.

The U.S.-British postal treaty of 1848, effective February 1849, established an international rate of 24¢ for a single-weight letter weighing ½ ounce or less. This rate was composed of inland postage of 5¢ for the United States and 3¢ inland postage for Great Britain. Sea postage was 16¢ and belonged to the country that furnished the sea transport. On letters addressed to or from the Pacific Coast, the U.S. inland postage was 10¢ instead of 5¢, in effect from July 1, 1851, to July 1, 1863, when the internal postage charged became 5¢ for all points in the United States.

Prepayment was optional, but part-payment was not recognized. Each country reserved the right to use the scale of progression (the increase of postage with additional weight) of its own country for charging inland postage. For the United States this was an additional single rate for each ½ ounce in weight over the basic ½ ounce. For Great Britain it was a single rate for the first ½ ounce, double rate for 1 ounce, and two additional single rates for each additional ounce or fraction thereof. This resulted in the curious situation where a letter weighing between 1 and 1½ ounces would require triple-rate inland postage for the United States and a quadruple-rate for the British inland postage.

This awkward system was in existence for only one month, February 15, 1849, to March 15, 1849, for the United States moved quickly to simplify the situation by adopting the British system of progression for U.S. inland postage on mail between the two countries. The result was that subsequent to 1849, and before 1866, there were no provisions for triple or other odd-numbered rates, beyond the initial single rate, for letters between the United States and Great Britain. This variance in the method of fixing the postage on multiple-rate letters for mail to Great Britain, with that for U.S. domestic mail, caused considerable confusion for postmasters. If care was not taken, it was easy to mistakenly charge triple-rate postage for a letter to Great Britain weighing between 1 and 1½ ounces. Since a quadruple rate was actually required, and partial payments were not recognized, the letter could be delivered in Great Britain as completely unpaid, and the prepayment of 72¢ entirely lost. Frequent announcements were printed in the USM&POA cautioning postmasters not to make this error. The British scheme progression with respect to weight, i.e., no odd multiples, was also included in the postal agreements that the United States made with Prussia and Belgium. France and the city-states of Bremen and Hamburg were major exceptions to this practice, and agreements with those nations required only a single additional rate to be charged for every single increase of the basic postal weight.

On April 1, 1866, the British Post Office declared that the new rate progression on letters to the United States from that time on was to be one rate for each ½ ounce or fraction thereof. This action was reciprocated by the United States for mail to England, and these changes finally eliminated the difficulties that had resulted from two different systems of progression.

Exchange offices were initially established at New York and Boston in the United States, and at London, Liverpool and Southampton in Great Britain, subject to revision in later years. The amounts to be credited or debited to the receiving country were to be stamped on the letters, credits in red and debits in black. Although not required, it was customary to also show the amount to be collected in black, and prepayments in red ink [1:27-29].

While letters between the United States and Great Britain had to be fully prepaid to destination or completely unpaid, letters posted for transit by open mail across Great Britain to another foreign country could be partially paid. For example, a letter addressed to Italy via the British mail system could be posted in the United States with a prepayment of 5¢ to pay the postage to the port of departure at New York or Boston, where the letter could be placed upon a British packet for transmission at British expense to Italy. Upon arrival at England, the letter would be deposited in the British mail system and treated as if it had originated in England as an unpaid

Figure 17-1. New York, December 21, 1861, to Liverpool, England. Double-weight, unpaid letter, with a 1¢ Franklin to pay for carrier service. The New York exchange marking in black debited Great Britain 42¢ for double-rate sea and U.S. postage. A red London exchange marking is on the reverse. The cover is marked 2 shillings (48¢) for collection. The destination arrival mark is dated "JA 4 62."
(Richard F. Winter collection)

New York exchange

letter to Italy. The additional required postage would be collected from the addressee. If the letter was to be conveyed to England by American packet, the U.S. prepaid postage must also include the packet postage. In this case the prepaid postage would necessarily be 21¢ (5¢ inland plus 16¢ sea). The arrangement for transit via open mail was fully reciprocal, and the key element was that the United States prepay all postage that would accrue to it prior to the letter's entry into the control of the British mail system, and vice versa.

Essentially, letters sent in the British open mails by British packet actually entered the British mail system when they went on board a British packet in a U.S. port. The British would recoup the transatlantic transit fees when they collected on these unpaid letters from the next country. The British mail system extended all the way to the U.S. port. Letters conveyed to Great Britain on American contract packets did not enter the British mail system until they reached a British port.

Exceptions to the above procedure were required for final destinations where there were no postal agreements with the transit country. In those cases, there was no way for the transit country to collect its postage due from the destination country, and prepayment of all postage costs was required.

The U.S.-Great Britain mail situation that existed in August of 1861, when the 1¢ Franklin was issued, was as outlined above except for new exchange offices. Philadelphia was added to the list, and Portland, Detroit and Chicago were established primarily to service mail handled under U.S. contract by the Allan Line (Montreal Ocean Steam Ship Line), which operated between Quebec, Portland and Liverpool [3:130].

The additional 5¢ postage required for letters to and from the Pacific coast was removed on July 1, 1863, when the U.S. 3¢ internal domestic rate became standard without regard to distance.

San Francisco became an exchange office in 1863, and Baltimore in 1865 [4:66]. The San Francisco office was authorized only to receive closed mail from Great Britain, not to send it. Mails from San Francisco to Great Britain had to be processed at one of the other authorized exchange offices, usually New York.

Examples of transatlantic mail carried under the provisions of U.S.-British postal treaty follow:

1861, double rate to England, unpaid: **Figure 17-1** shows an interesting example of a wholly unpaid foreign letter to England with a 1¢ Franklin used to pay the carrier fee for delivery to the post office at New York City. Carrier fees were established without regard to weight, and even though this was a double-weight letter, the fee remained at 1¢.

Postmarked at New York City on December 21, 1861, the cover received a black New York exchange "AmPkt" marking debiting Great Britain for 42¢, and departed the same day via the American mail contract steamship *Hansa* of the North German Lloyd Line. The *Hansa* arrived at Southampton, England, on January 3, 1862, and the cover was transported to the London exchange office where it was marked 2 shillings (48¢) for collection of the 2x24¢ rate and backstamped with a red London transit marking. The letter was then forwarded to Liverpool, where it received an arrival marking dated January 4, 1862. The manuscript date at the upper left of the cover was probably written by the addressee to note the date of reception. Upon collection, England retained 2x3¢ for inland postage, and the balance of the 42¢ was remitted to the United States to pay for 2x5¢ U.S. inland and 2x16¢ sea postage.

1862, single rate to England, forwarded to France: **Figure 17-2** illustrates a cover to England that finally ended up at Paris, France. The letter was mailed at Jamaica Plains, Mississippi, on August 19, 1862, and ad-

The United States 1¢ Franklin 1861-67

Figure 17-2. Jamaica Plains, Mississippi, August 19, 1862, to London, England, and then forwarded to Paris, France. 24¢ postage prepaid. Red, AUG 20, Boston/British packet marking, with 19¢ credited to Great Britain, 16¢ sea and 3¢ inland. Forwarded, with a red London paid exchange marking and a large red manuscript 4 (indicating 4 pence paid in cash). Black French receiving mark dated September 2, 1862, was applied on the Calais-to-Paris traveling office.
(C.W. Christian collection)

French entry marking   Boston exchange (red)

Figure 17-3. Portville, New York, cover dated December 9, 1862, to London, with arrival on December 25. The 24¢ was paid by two 10¢, a 3¢ and a 1¢. The cover re-entered British mails the same day for forwarding to Paris. The red London paid exchange marking and red PD in oval handstamp indicate prepayment of postage from London to Paris by two 2d British stamps (Scott 29). The French exchange marking is dated December 27, 1862, and the Paris receiving mark on reverse is dated the same day.
(Walter Cole collection)

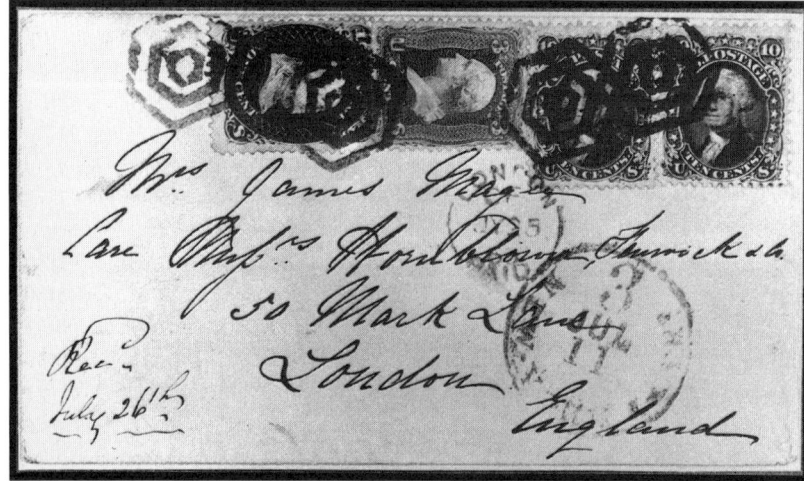

Figure 17-4. New York, July 11, 1863, to London. Prepaid with 24¢ for single-rate postage. The stamps are canceled by early use of a fancy New York Foreign Mail canceling device (Skinner 63-2). New York red American packet exchange postmark credited Great Britain with 3¢ inland postage. The red London exchange mark is dated "JY 25 63."
(Hubert C. Skinner collection)

New York exchange Paid - American packet (red)   NYFM (Skinner 63-2)

Figure 17-5. Braddocksfield, Pennsylvania, November 27 (1865), to Achbymagna, England, at the 24¢ rate. An exchange marking in red from New York credits Great Britain with 19¢ for sea and internal postage. The cover is backstamped at Lutterworth on "DE 12/ 65."
(C.W. Christian collection)

dressed to London, England. The 24¢ single rate was prepaid at the office of origin by a combination of 1861 stamps. At Boston, the exchange office marked the cover BOSTON BR PKT/AUG 20/19 PAID, crediting Great Britain with 19¢. The letter was dispatched on the Cunard ship *Arabia* the same day and arrived at Queenstown on August 29 and London on the following day, as shown by a red receiving mark. The letter was sent to the addressee in care of Baring Brothers & Co. in London. Upon receipt, it reposted the letter to Paris, paying the 4 pence per ¼-ounce postage rate to France.

The London exchange office applied the marking "SP 1./PAID," a PD in oval and a manuscript "4," all in red. The red "4" showed that 4 pence had been prepaid for the forwarding of the letter to Paris. Upon arrival in France, a black ambulant Calais entry marking for incoming British mail, dated "2 SEPT 62," was applied aboard the railway postal car between Calais and Paris

1862, single rate to England, forwarded to France: An unusual cover is pictured in **Figure 17-3**. This cover was mailed at Portville, New York, on December 9, 1862, as a fully prepaid letter to London, England, at the 24¢ rate. There is no evidence of a U.S. exchange marking, but there are three indistinct London receiving marks, dated "DEC 25/62." From this date it can be determined that the letter must have arrived aboard the HAPAG steamer *Saxonia*, which departed New York on December 13, 1862, and arrived at Southampton on December 25, 1862. The addressee at London had evidently moved to Paris, and the letter again entered the British mails with the addition of two blue 2-pence stamps to pay the forwarding postage. The cover was marked with a red paid circular marking of the London exchange office, dated December 25, 1862, and a red PD in oval to indicate that the cover was paid to destination. In France the cover received the Calais railway post office mark, dated "27/ DEC/62," and on the reverse a receiving mark at Paris for the same day. Covers with mixed foreign and U.S. postage are scarce, and are usually the result of a letter being forwarded.

1863, single rate to England: **Figure 17-4** illustrates a particularly interesting cover to England. This cover was postmarked in red at New York City on July 11, 1863, with a 3¢ credit to England to pay for the British inland postage. The four stamps that make up the 24¢ rate are canceled with four strikes of a concentric hexagon fancy cancel. This is a very early use of an elaborate "New York Foreign Mail" cancel. Fancy cancels on foreign mails at the New York Post Office were used extensively during the 1870s. The cover shows a red paid receiving mark applied at London on July 25, 1863. The *City of Baltimore* of the Inman Line, under contract to the U.S. Post Office, departed New York on July 11, 1863, and arrived at Liverpool on July 24, 1863 [3:205]. The fit of the dates of departure and arrival make it most likely that this was the means of sea conveyance for this cover.

1865, single rate to England: **Figure 17-5** illustrates the uncommon combination of four 1¢ Franklins with two 10¢ Washingtons to make up the postage. One stamp projects about an eighth-inch beyond the opened cover, and it is surprising that it has survived in undamaged condition through the years. This particular cover is addressed in a quaint and interesting manner to the addressee at "Achbymagna, Near lutterworth, LeicesterShire, old, England." Mailed at Braddocksfield, Pennsylvania, on November 27 (1865), the cover departed from New York via the Cunard steamer *Persia* on November 29, arriving off Queenstown on December 10, 1865. It was backstamped at Lutterworth on December 12, 1865. An exchange marking in red from New York credits Great Britain with 19¢ for sea and internal postage.

1861, British open mail to Spain, British packet: The

New York exchange unpaid - British packet

Forwarding agent mark (on reverse)

Figure 17-6. New York, October 1, 1861, to Barcelona, Spain. One 3¢ and two 1¢ stamps paid for postage by British packet via British open mail to London. The cover was backstamped at London on October 14 and Barcelona on October 17, 1861. It is marked 4 reales (20¢) for collection at destination. The cover is opened to show backstamp detail.
(James Lee collection)

folded letter, illustrated in **Figure 17-6**, was mailed at New York on October 1, 1861, to Barcelona, Spain, with 5¢ in stamps paying the British open-mail rate by British packet. No early sailing was available from New York, so the letter was forwarded to Boston, where it departed on the British packet *Europa* on October 2, 1861. It arrived off Queenstown on October 12. On the reverse is a London transit marking, dated "OC 14/61," a Junquera, Spain, transit mark dated "16/OCT/61," and a receiving mark from the destination at Barcelona, dated "17/Oct/61." The letter is marked in black, "4.R,ˢ" (4 reales, equivalent to 20¢), for postage due. The reverse also shows a marking of the New York forwarding agents, Rivera & Hall, with whom the letter was placed to expedite mailing. This is an early use of the 1861 series of stamps. The new issue was placed on sale at New York on September 16, 1861, just two weeks before this letter was mailed.

1867, British open mail to Spain, American packet: The cover shown in **Figure 17-7** was mailed at Rochester, New York, on April 25, 1867, to Malaga, Spain. It departed New York on "APR 27," per exchange marking. Postage of 21¢ prepaid the rate to the border of Great Britain by American packet, as endorsed. This paid for the U.S. internal 5¢ and the 16¢ sea postage, and was retained by the United States. The letter was carried by the Inman Line *City of Baltimore*, arriving at London on May 8, 1867, per receiving mark on the reverse of the cover. It was then treated essentially as an unpaid letter originating in England for delivery to Spain. The stamped notation PAID-ONLY/TO ENGLAND indicates that the cover is not paid to destination and should be forwarded as unpaid British open mail. This mark was applied at London, and from an examination of covers, probably was introduced in early 1866. The large red collection mark of "8.R."(8 reales, equivalent to 40¢) was applied in Spain. As mailed from the United States, this was a single-rate letter; however, the Spanish postage due is for a double-rate letter. The reason for this is that the letter probably weighed between ¼ and ½ ounce, and would have been considered a single-rate by U.S. and British progression. But the Spanish post office operated with a ¼-ounce progression like the French system, and charged it as a double-rate letter. The cover is backstamped with a Malaga receiving mark, dated May 12, 1867. Richard F. Winter advises that relatively few letters for Spain were sent by British open mail via American packet. The cover

Figure 17-7. Rochester, New York, April 25 (1867) to Malaga, Spain. The cover was paid to England by 21¢ in postage for U.S. inland and sea. It departed New York April 27, receiving a red American packet exchange marking. It is marked with a red 8.R (8 reales=40¢) for collection.
(C.W. Christian collection)

8.R
Spanish collection
8 reales
(red)

New York exchange
Paid - American packet (red)

Figure 17-8. New York, July 18, 1863, to Shanghai, China. The cover is prepaid to destination with one 1¢, two 10¢ and a 24¢ (Scott 78) making up 45¢ postage. The New York red paid exchange postmark shows conveyance by American packet. A London exchange marking in red credited Great Britain with 24¢. The cover proceeded to destination via Hong Kong. A Shanghai receiving mark is on the reverse, dated September 30, 1863.
(C.W. Christian collection)

New York exchange
Paid - American packet (red)

London exchange Paid (red)
(Letters C J refer to the postal brigade that processed mail.)

could be sent by British packet with only a 5¢ prepayment, as opposed to 21¢ by American packet, and the amount collected at destination was the same. Frugal and knowledgeable mailers, particularly businessmen with large correspondence, apparently took advantage of this situation to save 16¢ on each letter.

1863, British open mail to China, American packet: **Figure 17-8** shows a fine example of prepaid mail to China via the British mail system. This small cover was mailed at New York, where it received a red New York, American packet, paid exchange marking on July 18, 1863. The cover is prepaid 45¢ for the rate to Shanghai, China, via England. It was marked at New York with a red "24" for 24¢ credit to Great Britain. The cover was endorsed to be routed via Southampton. There were two steamship routes for letters from Great Britain to the Orient. One started at Southampton and went through the Mediterranean via Gibraltar and Malta to Alexandria. The other started at Marseilles, France. The routes actually converged at Suez, where the mails waited for the steamers to India and the Orient. Because the Marseilles route went via France, there was an extra charge. The "via Southampton" endorsement requests routing from Great Britain by Southampton steamer. The Inman Line *City of Washington* departed New York on July 18, and the letter was sent by that means. The cover arrived off Queenstown on July 28 and was marked at London for transit on July 30. The reverse of the cover shows a transit marking at Hong Kong on September 23 and an arrival mark at Shanghai dated September 30, 1863. The total time for transit was 75 days. Although addressed to China, this cover remained in the British mail system from En-

Figure 17-9. Emira, New York, October 28, 1865, to Kanagawa, Japan. The cover is a scarce use of the 1861 90¢ (Scott 72) denomination, plus a 10¢, 5¢ (76) and a 1¢, to a rare destination. The double-rate cover was prepaid (2x53¢) $1.06 for postage to destination via British open mail via Marseilles. It was marked in red crayon at London "2 96" to indicate 2 pence for the Shanghai colonial office and 96¢ credit to Great Britain from the United States. The cover is addressed in care of a forwarding agent at Shanghai for private transmission to Japan.
(Christie's New York auction photo)

gland to destination. The resident British Consul at Shanghai acted as the postal agent.

1865, British open mail to Japan, British packet: **Figure 17-9** illustrates a fabulous cover from the Ishikawa collection showing rare use of the 1861 90¢ denomination. This cover was mailed at Elmira, New York, on October 28, 1865, for delivery via Shanghai to Kanagawa, Japan. It was prepaid $1.06 in stamps for the 2x53¢ rate by British open mail via Marseilles. "Overland" in this endorsement refers to the fact the letter was to proceed overland across Egypt. The balance of the journey to the Orient would be accomplished over sea routes. The exchange office at New York City marked the cover PAID with an indistinct red exchange marking and "96" for credit to Great Britain. The remaining 10¢ would be retained for the 2x5¢ internal U.S. postage. The cover departed New York November 1, 1865, aboard the British packet *Scotia*.

Arriving off Queenstown on November 10, and at London on November 11, the cover received a red crayon accountancy marking of "2" indicating 2 pence credit to the British colonial office at Shanghai. The cover proceeded to Marseilles, and to the Orient via Suez and Singapore. The cover arrived at Shanghai as indicated by an indistinct receiving marking on the reverse, and was delivered to Messrs. Russell & Co., a forwarding agent, for private delivery to Kanagawa, Japan.

Letters to China and Japan could be sent at a lower 45¢ rate via Southampton, instead of Marseilles. While less expensive, it took longer for such letters to reach their destination.

The Postal Conventions of 1868

In 1868, several new postal conventions became effective. Extended negotiations had been under way for years with many of the European countries. Kasson was again the major negotiator for the United States. Since most of the resulting postal conventions have similar provisions, the general features will be collectively discussed at this point. Kasson was able to conclude new agreements between the United States and the North German Postal Union, Belgium, the Netherlands, Switzerland, Italy and Great Britain.

The principal provisions were:

a. Each country would adopt 15 grams as the standard weight for a single letter rate, with a single rate being added for each additional 15 grams or fraction thereof. Great Britain was the sole exception to this practice. It retained ½ ounce (14.18 grams) as its standard unit of weight, but now allowed odd multiples of a single rate.

b. The postal receipts for international mail were to be divided equally between the post offices of the two contracting countries. (Switzerland and the Netherlands were exceptions to this rule. In their cases, they received two-fifths and the United States received three-fifths.)

c. Because the collections were divided by percentages, there was no further need to mark individual letters with debits or credits, except in the case of transit open mail. Transit open mail was to be charged with the direct international rate, augmented by the postage due for transmission to a further destination.

d. Prepayment was optional, but a fine was to be levied on all unpaid letters. Partial payment was recognized, but the "unpaid penalty" was to be paid in addition to the deficient postage.

e. Sea postage was to be arranged and paid for by the dispatching country.

The standardization provided by the above features substantially decreased the complex handling of foreign mails and the requirements for involved rate and debiting determination. It was the first time that the United

States had used the metric system for postal weights, and a special law providing for the use of metric measurements had to be passed by Congress [1:148].

The British Conventions of 1868 and 1870

The postal agreement reached with Great Britain, effective January 1, 1868, provided for a standard international rate of 12¢ in the United States per 15 grams, or 6d in Great Britain for a single letter of ½ ounce. Sea postage was to be 8¢. Inland postage for both countries was set at 2¢ or the equivalent 1d. For open mail destined for countries beyond Great Britain, the postage was arrived at by charging 10¢ plus the British rate from England to the destination country. The combined rates for various destinations were listed in U.S. postal regulations and published in the USM&POA. The fine for unpaid or insufficiently paid letters was established at 5¢ in the United States. No fine for Great Britain was listed, but it has since been established to have been 6d. In January of 1869, when the treaty was amended, the British fine was established at 2d. Fines were retained by the collecting country.

On January 1, 1870, another new U.S.-British convention became effective. The international rate was further reduced to 6¢, with the amount being equally divided, 2¢ for sea postage and 2¢ for inland postage in each of the countries.

This drastic reduction in rates, while benefiting the public, caused substantial problems in the payment of mail contracts for sea transport. Legislation passed during the cost-cutting tenure of Postmaster General Holt in 1858 was still in force, restricting payment for sea transportation by foreign-owned vessels to the amount of sea postage on the mail carried. Payment to American-owned ships was limited to the total of the sea plus U.S. inland postage. The new lower postal reimbursements resulted in a legal requirement to reduce the amount paid to the shipping lines for mail contracts. This was unacceptable to the major foreign lines, and for a short period they threatened to stop carrying U.S. mail. Since almost all of the transatlantic mail was being transported aboard foreign-owned ships, this could have resulted in serious disruption in our foreign mails. The Canadian Allan Line continued to carry U.S. mail to England at the reduced payment, and the Guion Line received its first contract to carry mails by accepting the lower rates [3:308]. After a short impasse, the major lines reconsidered their position, and service was not compromised.

The French Mails

Difficulties were experienced in negotiating the first postal agreement with France. Although talks began shortly after the U.S.-British treaty became effective in 1849, it was another eight years before a postal treaty with France was concluded. One of the problems was the French insistence on retaining 7½ grams (¼ ounce) as the weight unit for rating, opposed to the ½ ounce rate-unit used by the United States, Great Britain and others. France refused to yield on this point, and the convention, as finally agreed upon, used 7½ grams for the French unit and ¼ ounce for the U.S. weight unit per single rate. Since ¼ ounce actually equals only 7.07 grams, the discrepancy between the weight units caused some problems with ratings and an unfair distribution of revenues.

The U.S.-French Postal Convention became effective on April 1, 1857, and remained in force, with minor changes, until abrogated at the end of 1869. The procedures for determining division and accounting for rates under the convention were complex and dependent upon routes and the method of sea transport, but fortunately for the postal history collector, those variations were hidden under a standard international rate of 15¢. A system of exchange-office marking and accounting was established, and the presence of elaborate French entry markings assists greatly in the analysis of covers to France and countries serviced by the French postal system. Drawings of many of these markings are shown in Hargest [1], and a complete listing is available in Raymond Salles' multivolume work on the French maritime mail [5]. These French entry marks are unusually descriptive and indicate the office, the complete date and the country that furnished the sea transport. Even the identity of the postal brigade that processed the letter was indicated in some of the markings (by a letter code).

Mail could be sent to France in closed bags via Great Britain, per the existing Anglo-French convention, or in closed bags direct via sea transport to a French port. Either of these methods were really closed mail, but in the philatelic literature, they are referred to simply as "French mail." This is in contrast to closed mail under the Prussian convention, which is always called "Prussian closed mail" as an indication that the mail bags passed closed through England and Belgium.

In 1861, the international rate between the United States and France (including Algeria) was 15¢ per ¼ ounce (or 7½ grams). Prepayment was optional, but if prepaid, full payment to destination was required. Partial payment was not recognized.

Exchange offices were operating in France at Havre and the traveling office from Calais to Paris. For the United

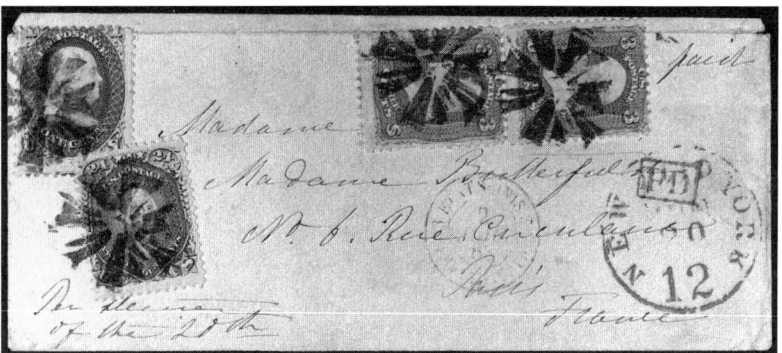

Figure 17-10. New York, June 20, 1863, to Paris France. This is an example of the double-weight rate of 2x15¢ made up by two 3¢ and a 24¢ (Scott 78), plus a 1¢ stamp for carrier delivery to the mails. It is postmarked in red at New York with 12¢ credit to France and endorsed "Per the Steamer of the 20th," and "paid." The French Calais entry marking in red denotes American sea service, and a boxed PD indicates prepayment to destination. It is backstamped Paris and Passy-les-Paris on July 2, 1863. (C.W. Christian collection)

States, the offices were New York, Philadelphia, Boston and San Francisco. The French offices were to mark the mail with the date of receipt and the method of transportation to them. Letters transported via England were to be marked in red and all others marked in blue (there are many exceptions to this requirement). U.S. exchange offices were to mark the date of dispatch; the method of transport, i.e. "American" or "British" packet; and the amount to be debited or credited. The U.S. offices did not always mark the method of sea transport, but it can usually be deduced from the debit and credit markings, and verified by the French exchange marks.

The division of the U.S. rate for letters was:

Via Great Britain		Direct	
U.S. inland	3¢	U.S. inland	3¢
Sea	6¢	Sea	9¢
British transit	2¢	French inland	3¢
French inland	4¢		15¢
	15¢		

Although the accounting and division of postage was different for the two methods of transport, the total cost for postage was the same. Direct routing rates also applied to ships that made only a single intermediate stop (without unloading French mail) at a British port before proceeding to a French port.

In June of 1864, the Compagnie Générale Transatlantique, also known as the French Line, established a direct service between New York and Havre. This service had been contemplated since the signing of the U.S.-French Convention of 1857, and the provisions of some of the articles were so worded that distinct advantages would accrue to France by the use of French-owned vessels in transatlantic service. Prior to this new service in 1864, only a small number of direct-mail sailings had been made, and none of these was by French-owned companies. The majority of French mail was routed via England, and even after the establishment of the French line, Great Britain continued to transit a substantial portion of the mail to France.

The United States was never completely satisfied with the 1857 postal agreement with France and in 1866 requested negotiations toward a more liberal and satisfactory postal convention. Kasson was again pressed into service to represent the United States, and after a long and frustrating series of conferences with no progress, the negotiations were broken off. The United States then gave notice to France that it intended to terminate the existing convention. This was effected on January 1, 1870, and the transmission of mail to France was continued after that date without benefit of a postal agreement. This meant that mail could only be transmitted directly as ship letters under the Act of 1864, which provided a rate of 10¢ per single rate of ½ ounce to pay for letters to the port of a foreign country with which the United States had no postal convention, and where the transportation was furnished by vessels regularly employed in the transportation of mails. Of course, mail could also continue to be sent as open mail through a country, such as Great Britain, with whom the United States had a postal convention and where a postal agreement also existed with France.

The arrangements during the following few years for mail to France, and to countries previously routed through France, are extremely interesting, but are outside the temporal scope of this book. While the abrogation of the familiar U.S.-French agreement caused considerable confusion, the letter mails continued to be delivered by alternate and sometimes complex procedures. Finally, effective on August 1, 1874, a new postal convention was enacted with France.

1863, double rate to France, with carrier fee: **Figure 17-10** shows a New York to Paris cover postmarked at New York on June 20, 1863. The red "Paid" exchange marking credits France with 12¢. The letter was prepaid

Foreign Mails

Figure 17-11. Newport, Rhode Island, December 4, 1866, to Paris, France. The cover was sent at the 3x15¢ rate with a 24¢ (Scott 78b), two 10¢ and a 1¢. It departed Boston December 5 per Cunard steamer as endorsed. The Boston exchange marking is in red, and the large "45" stamped in red-brown ink, applied at Newport, indicates total postage paid. The manuscript 36/3 in orange crayon shows 36¢ credit to France for a triple-rate letter. The cover bears a French Calais December 18, 1866, entry marking and was backstamped at Paris the same day. (C.W. Christian collection)

with one 24¢, two 3¢ and a single 1¢ stamp for a total of 31¢. This paid the 2x15¢ rate for a double-weight letter to France with an additional 1¢ to pay for carrier delivery to the mail. This was just 10 days before the carrier fee was abolished. The cover was endorsed by the sender, "Per Steamer of the 20th" and "paid." Two mail steamers left New York on June 20, 1863, the *Glasgow* of the Inman Line and the *America* of the North German Lloyd Line. The *Glasgow* carried only mail to Ireland, so it appears that this cover was carried on the *America*. The ship arrived off Southampton on July 1, where the mail bags were off-loaded for carriage to London and transport to France. In France, the cover was marked with a red boxed "PD" and a Calais exchange mark in red, indicating sea transport under American contract and transit via England. The cover was backstamped with receiving marks at Paris and Passy-les-Paris (a Paris suburb) on July 2, 1863. The postage was divided with 2x3¢ plus 2x6¢ to the United States for inland and sea, and 2x6¢ to France for its share, out of which it was to pay England for the closed-bag French mail transit charges. Actually, France paid for the transit charges by bulk weight and at a rate that was less than that received from the United States in credits for the service. This was one of the features of the U.S.- French postal convention to which the United States took exception.

1866, triple rate to France: **Figure 17-11** shows a triple-rate letter weighing between 1 and 1½ ounces, to Paris by French mail via England. The letter was mailed at Newport, Rhode Island, on December 4, 1866, and was endorsed, "per Cunard Steamer of Wed Dec 5th from 'Boston.' " The cover received a red "Boston Br. Pkt./PAID" exchange marking at Boston, without inclusion of the credit amount, and was stamped with a large brown-purple "45" to show the total amount paid. It was also marked with a manuscript "36/3" in red, indicating that France was to be credited with 36¢ for a triple-weight letter. The cover was dispatched on December 5, 1866, on the Cunard *Africa*, via England to France. The letter arrived in France on December 18, where it received a red marking at Paris, of the type illustrated in Figure 17-10, showing entry at Calais, and a red boxed "P.D." showing payment to destination.

Multiple-rate covers to France are relatively common. With a single rate being charged per ¼ ounce, many letters weighed enough to require an additional rate or more. Stationery stores in America evidently did not conveniently stock the extra-thin paper and envelopes that were common in France to reduce the weight of correspondence.

1867, double rate to France: **Figure 17-12** shows a government 3¢ stamped envelope with the addition of 27¢ in stamps to pay the 30¢ double-rate postage. The cover originated at Sing Sing (now Ossining), New York, on September 11, 1867, and was addressed to Dunkerque, France. At New York City, it received a red exchange marking dated "SEP 12," crediting France with 12¢ for payment of 2x2¢ British transit and 2x4¢ French inland postage. The United States retained 18¢ for inland and sea postage. The cover was transported as French mail aboard the American contract mail steamer *Hansa* of the North German Lloyd Line (NGL). It departed New York on September 12, 1867, and arrived off Southampton, England on September 23. From there, the cover was carried via British service through London to Calais, where a French receiving mark in black, dated September 24, 1867, was applied by the Calais to Paris traveling exchange office. It was backstamped on the Paris-to-Lille traveling office on the same day, and at Dunkerque upon arrival.

1863, part-paid to Switzerland: Illustrated in **Figure**

Figure 17-12. Sing Sing, New York, September 11, 1867, to Dunkerque, France. The double rate of 2x15¢ was paid by a nice combination of a 3¢ entire (Scott U58), a 24¢ (78) and three 1¢ Franklins. The cover departed New York September 12, 1867. The black entry marking and red boxed P.D. were applied at the ambulant Calais (A.C.) office September 24, 1867, with an A to identify the postal brigade on duty. It was backstamped on the Paris-to-Lille traveling post office, and at Dunkerque. (C.W. Christian collection)

Figure 17-13. Blackcreek, Ohio, May 11 (1863) to Orsières, Switzerland. The cover was sent at the single rate of 21¢, with attempted prepayment of 3¢. It departed New York on May 16, per black exchange marking debiting France with 9¢. It arrived in France on May 31, per red Calais entry marking. It proceeded via Paris and Neuchatel, Switzerland, to destination. It was marked 110 for collection of 110 Swiss centimes from addressee. There was no recognition of prepayment.

Figure 17-14. New York, November 16, 1864, to Neuchatel, Switzerland. The single-weight folded letter sheet was prepaid with 21¢ in stamps. France was credited with 18¢ per red New York exchange marking. British sea service was via Cunard *Persia*, as endorsed. The Calais red entry marking is dated "27 Nov 64." It was backstamped at Bern and Neuchatel, Switzerland, on November 28, 1864. (C.W. Christian collection)

Foreign Mails

Figure 17-15. Boston, October 31, 1865, to Vevey, Switzerland. The government 20¢ stamped envelope (U43) and a single 1¢ Franklin paid the 21¢ single rate to Switzerland. The Boston paid exchange marking in red credited 18¢ to France. The cover departed New York on November 1 aboard British packet *Scotia*. It arrived in France November 12, and received a black entry marking with a D (postal brigade) and A.C. (ambulatory Calais) entry marking dated "12 Oct 65" in error. It was forwarded to destination at Vevey, where it was backstamped on November 13, 1865. (Christie's New York auction photo)

17-13 is an example of a scarce part-payment of postage on a foreign cover. The letter originated at Blackcreek, Ohio, on May 11 (1863) with a manuscript cancellation and town/date marking. It is addressed to Orsières, Switzerland. Although not shown in the postmark, Ohio can be identified as the state of origin from the contents of the cover. Three cents postage was paid by three 1¢ Franklins, probably in a mistaken attempt to pay the U.S. postage to New York. The sender or originating post office evidently was unaware that partial payment was not recognized and that the letter would be forwarded from New York as completely unpaid, with no credit given for the postage affixed. The New York exchange office postmarked the cover on May 16 and debited France 9¢ for U.S. inland and sea postage. The cover departed on the Inman steamer, *City of Washington*, as American contract mail, and arrived at France, via England. On May 31, 1863, it received a red Calais exchange mark of the type shown in Figure 17-10 and was marked with a black manuscript "8" for collection of 8 decimes. This marking was probably applied in error, for the French office did not normally mark mail to Switzerland for collection. It may have been that the postal clerk mistakenly considered the letter as destined for a French city. In that case, the 8 decimes would have been correct. The cover continued as open mail and was marked in Switzerland with red crayon "110" (110 Swiss centimes, equivalent to 21¢ U.S.) for collection from the addressee for the total single-rate postage to Switzerland. Part of this amount was returned to France, which in turn, remitted 2¢ to Great Britain for transit, and 9¢ to the United States, leaving the balance to pay for the postage from France to Switzerland and Switzerland inland. The reverse of the cover shows transit marks at Paris, on May 31; Aarau-Neuchatel and Lausanne, Switzerland, on June 1; and Montreaux, Switzerland, on June 2, 1863.

1864, single rate to Switzerland: **Figure 17-14** shows a folded letter sheet from New York to Neuchatel, Switzerland. The New York exchange mark is in red and is dated "Nov 16," with 18¢ credit to France from the single letter rate of 21¢. The folded letter sheet is endorsed "per Persia" and was carried by the Cunard British packet *Persia*, arriving off Queenstown on November 25. At Paris, the cover received a Calais entry mark on November 27, and a red boxed "P.D." It was backstamped at Bern and Neuchatel, Switzerland, on November 28, 1864. The 18¢ credit that France received was divided thus: 6+2¢ to Great Britain for sea and transit postage, 4¢ for French inland postage, and the remaining 6¢ used to pay for the postage between France and Switzerland.

1865, single rate to Switzerland: A very unusual cover is pictured in **Figure 17-15**. It illustrates the scarce use of an 1861 20¢ entire envelope (Scott U43), together with a 1¢ Franklin, to make up the 21¢ rate to Switzerland. Prior to mailing, the sender reduced and refolded a large government stamped envelope to a smaller 130mm-by-79mm size. This may have been done to reduce weight. The cover is endorsed "Per French Mail" and has a red Boston exchange mark dated October 31 (1865). The next scheduled sailing for European mail was by the Cunard British packet *Scotia*, which departed from New York on November 1, so the letter was forwarded from Boston to New York for dispatch. It proceeded on the *Scotia* to England and arrived in France on November 12, 1865, where it received a black exchange mark and a black boxed "P.D." aboard the *Calais* to the Paris traveling post of-

Figure 17-16. This cover was prepaid at the 21¢ rate via French mail. It was mailed at Boston, where it received a red paid exchange marking with 9¢ credit to France on September 13. It departed New York on September 14, aboard the Havre Line *Arago*, an American mail packet. It received a French entry marking in black, dated September 27, 1861, and a small boxed P.D. in red was applied at Havre. The cover was forwarded to destination at Berlin, Prussia (C.W. Christian collection)

Figure 17-17. Rochester, New York, March 11, 1867, to Malaga, Spain. The cover was prepaid in stamps for the 21¢ rate. An exchange postmark was applied at New York on March 12, with 18¢ credit to France. The cover departed Boston March 12 on Cunard *Asia*. The French entry marking for Calais, March 26, 1867, indicated British service. The cover was marked "4R" in red at Malaga for collection. It was backstamped at Malaga on March 29, 1867. (C.W. Christian collection)

fice. This exchange marking is dated "12 Oct 65," and it should be "12 Nov 65." Evidently the postal clerk who changed the month date on the marker made a mistake. The cover is backstamped "Vevey/13 Nov 1865," showing arrival at destination.

1864, single rate to Prussia: **Figure 17-16** illustrates a cover originating at Boston on September 13 (1861), showing early use of the 1861 stamps that had been first issued the previous month. The cover received a red Boston paid exchange mark, with 9¢ credited to France. The 21¢ single rate to Prussia by French mail was paid by two 10¢ and a 1¢ stamp, which were canceled with a Boston PAID-in-grid design. The next sailing for mail to Europe was from New York by the New York & Havre Steam Navigation Company (Havre Line), one of the pioneer American steamship operators on the Atlantic crossing, and the only one still operating in the fall of 1861. The cover was forwarded to New York, where it departed on the Havre Line *Arago*, arriving at Havre on September 27, 1861, as shown by a black exchange marking. The Havre marking shows "SERV.AM.D," to indicate service by American packet on the direct route. The cover also received a customary red paid-to-destination "P.D." marking, and proceeded from there to destination by French open mail. The division of postage was 3¢ for U.S. internal, 9¢ for U.S. sea and the remaining 9¢ to pay for French internal and postage to Prussia.

This was the next to last voyage to Europe by the *Arago*. At the end of 1861, the two ships of the Havre Line, *Arago* and *Fulton*, were requisitioned by the U.S. War Department for use as contract transports in the Civil War.

1867, single rate to Spain: **Figure 17-17** shows a cover to the same addressee as that illustrated in Figure 17-7. This ladies' cover originated at Rochester, New York, on March 11, 1867. The 21¢ postage was prepaid in stamps for the single rate to Spain by French mail. At New York, the cover was postmarked with a red paid exchange marking dated March 12 and crediting France with 18¢. The next European mail sailing was from Boston via the Cunard *Asia*, which departed on March 13 and arrived off Queenstown on March 23. At Paris, the cover received a red French entry mark of the type shown in Figure 17-14, dated March 26, 1867, and indicating British service. The cover proceeded to destination at Malaga, Spain, via French open mail, and was marked 4R (4 reales, equiva-

Figure 17-18. New York, January 13, 1863, to Palermo, Sicily. Prepaid 22¢ in stamps. Single rate to Italy, by French mail, of 21¢ plus 1¢ for carrier fee. Stamps canceled by red New York/ Jan 13/ PAID foreign-mail marking. January 14 New York exchange marking in red with 18¢ credit to France. Departed New York on January 16, 1863, on the British Cunard packet *Asia*. Red Calais entry marking dated 30/JAN/63. Large red P.D. Backstamped with a boxed 5, and a transit marking at Genoa, Italy, on February 1, 1863, and a receiving mark at Palermo on February 3, 1863. (C.W. Christian collection)

Carrier mark

lent to 20¢) for collection of the double-weight (over ¼ ounce) for French transit.

1863, single rate plus carrier to Sicily: **Figure 17-18** shows a folded letter sheet from New York to Palermo, Sicily, at the prepaid 21¢ rate for French mail. Postage was paid by two 10¢ stamps and one 1¢. An additional 1¢ stamp was added to pay for carrier service to the mail at New York. The letter sheet was postmarked at New York on January 13, 1863, with two strikes of a large "New York/PAID" foreign-mail marking, which was also used to cancel the stamps. On January 14, an additional foreign exchange marking was added with a marked credit to France of 18¢. This indicates the letter was sent via British service. The Cunard *Asia* sailing scheduled for January 14 was delayed two days because of fog and finally departed on January 16, 1863, arriving off Queenstown on January 28. The letter received a Calais entry marking of the type shown in Figure 17-14, dated "30/ JANV./63." The letter sheet is backstamped with a transit marking at Genoa dated "1/FEB/63" and a receiving mark at Palermo dated "3/FEB/63." The cover is also backstamped with a large "5" in a square, showing the identification number of the carrier who delivered the letter.

It should be noted that during the decade of the 1860s, major portions of Italy were embroiled in wars of rebellion and attempts to form a unified state. Austria, France under Napoleon III, the Pope and Garibaldi all were involved. It was not until 1871 that all of Italy finally achieved its goal of becoming a single united country. The fact that mail seemed to be handled with little disruption underscores the fact that the frequent European wars of the 19th century seemed to have been waged primarily between armies and navies, with limited impact on the everyday lives of the general populace. Postal services to a large extent appear to have been exempted from political problems. In the latter part of the 1860s, articles were added to many foreign conventions, which guaranteed the freedom of mail access and transport in times of war.

1867, single rate to Italy: **Figure 17-19** shows a typical type of use to Genoa, Italy. This folded letter sheet was mailed at New York, probably by the forwarding agent "Jonas Phillips," whose handstamp, dated "APR 1867," was applied. The letter was prepaid by 21¢ in stamps for the single rate and received a red exchange mark at New York, dated May 1, with 18¢ credited to France. The sender endorsed the letter to be sent "per Steamer Scotia via Queenstown," and the letter departed New York as requested, on May 1. The folded letter sheet arrived off Queenstown on May 10 and was handstamped at the Calais office with a small red "P.D." and red exchange mark of the type shown in Figure 17-14, and dated May 13. It was backstamped with a receiving mark at Genoa, Italy, on May 15, 1867.

Mail under Conventions with the Germanic States

Germany in the early 1860s was not the monolithic country that now exists. It was composed of about 20 independent states with varying monetary systems, ranging from the large and very important Kingdom of Prussia to the small but also important city-states of Bremen and Hamburg. Since the 16th century, mail service to much of

Figure 17-19. New York, May 1, 1867, to Genoa, Italy. The cover was prepaid 21¢ in stamps for the single rate to Italy by French mail. The New York exchange marking in red, dated May 1, credited 18¢ to France. A circular forwarding-agent handstamp was applied in black. The cover departed New York on Cunard *Scotia*, as endorsed, on May 1, 1867. It received Calais entry marking dated May 13. It was backstamped with a receiving mark at Genoa on May 15, 1867. (C.W. Christian collection)

the region had been conducted under the auspices of the prince of Thurn and Taxis, who had an exclusive right by imperial decree to provide the service. The Thurn and Taxis postal system was efficient and remained in operation until 1867, when it was absorbed into the North German Postal District in return for a payment of 3 million marks for the franchise. This realignment was the result of the 1866 Treaty of Prague, which consolidated all of the northern German states into the North German Union (Confederation), with Prussia as the leading state.

In the early 1840s, the United States was beginning to feel a strong sense of national importance. A part of that feeling was a desire to establish a scheduled mail service with Europe and to provide that service by American-owned steamships. As of 1845, the United States had no formal postal treaties or conventions with any European nation, and mail to foreign addresses could not be sent fully prepaid, or fully collect, nor were there any accounting systems in effect. Also, the difficulty and complexity of forwarding the mail through one country to another required American businessmen to use the services of agents in foreign countries to expedite their correspondence. Pressure was placed on Congress to provide the means for better foreign postal service and lower rates.

In response, by the Postal Act of March 3, 1845, Congress authorized the postmaster general to contract for the transportation of U.S. mail between the United States and foreign countries. It stipulated that the contract was to be made with U.S. citizens, and the mail was to be transported by Americans in American ships [1:3]. The act also provided for a subsidy to an American steamship line to provide the service.

Postmaster General Cave Johnson invited bids for a steamship service between the United States and ports in Great Britain, or with countries along the Atlantic coast of Europe. There was a concerted response to his call for bids, and intense rivalry ensued concerning the location of the European terminus. Competing nations engaged in lobbying and offered various concessions to the American bidders. Bremen and Antwerp were strong contenders. Both were willing to grant special support to the operator of a mail line to their cities.

At the end of the competition, the bid of the Ocean Line (Ocean Steam Navigation Company) with Bremen as the European terminus was chosen and awarded a five-year contract. The Ocean Line was able to build only two of the four steamships required by the contract, and assigned part of its contract to the Havre Line (New York & Havre Steam Navigation Company) to build and operate the other two. The European terminus for this part of the operation was to be Havre, France. Each of these lines was to schedule a stop en route at Southampton, England, both going and coming, to off-load or acquire mail.

The Republic of Bremen was one of the Hanseatic free city-states. It was situated on the North Sea coast and had access to most of Europe. Bremen and Hamburg, a sister Hanseatic city-state 60 miles to the north, were the largest commercial ports in Europe. They provided excellent sites for the exchange of internatonal mail.

To further increase the American fraction of the transatlantic steamship operations, a similar contract was awarded in 1847 to the Collins Line (New York and Liverpool United States Steamship Company) for four ships to convey the mails between New York and Liverpool.

The combined operations of these three American lines were providing a service by 1855 that rivaled the weekly British packets. Unfortunately, the short-sighted efforts of the U.S. Congress and the Post Office Department in 1858 to decrease costs eliminated the mail subsidies and reduced the reimbursement to the value of the U.S. inland and sea postage on the mail that was carried. The Ocean Line and the Collins Line could not remain in business with the lower payments and discontinued operations in the latter part of the 1850s. The Havre Line managed to continue under the reduced contract and, except for a hiatus during the Civil War when its ships were used by the U.S. Navy, continued in operation. However, in 1867, it also succumbed to the problem of insufficient income and ceased operations.

Other small American transatlantic steamship mail operations were instituted during the 1850s and 1860s, but none was particularly successful. As a result, and primarily due to lack of government support and the exingencies of the Civil War, the potentially lucrative passenger and mail steamship routes were defaulted to foreign-flag operations. By the late 1850s, service was in operation every two weeks between Bremen and New York by the NGL Line, and another alternating service every two weeks between Hamburg and New York by the HAPAG (Hamburg-American Line). Both of these companies were German-owned. Their ships made a scheduled intermediate stop in Great Britain on each voyage.

Bremen Convention

Concurrent with the initial efforts to establish an American mail service to the Continent, negotiations were conducted with Bremen for a postal convention. This was the first postal convention or treaty to be considered by the United States. A successful arrangement for the exchange of mails between the United States and the Republic of Bremen was signed and became effective June 1, 1847. Bremen also acted as an intermediary for the United States in acquiring reduced and more standard rates within the German states [6:56-57]. In 1853, the original rate structure under the convention was revised and the postage for direct conveyance of a letter to Bremen became 10¢ per ½ ounce, prepayment optional. U.S. internal postage was 5¢. Recent information has been obtained from a cover that was carried on the July 17, 1858, inaugural eastbound trip of the NGL Line. This established that the rate charged by the United States for internal postage was reduced at the time of that voyage from 5¢ to 3¢ [7:63]. Official documentation to show this change has never been located, and until this recent analysis, only the fact that the change occurred sometime in the late 1850s was known. The total rate remained the same, so an additional 2¢ accrued to Bremen.

Hamburg Convention

On July 1, 1857, a postal convention with the Hanseatic City of Hamburg became effective. The HAPAG Line's scheduled sailings between Hamburg and New York were already operating, and this convention added another foreign-mail route. The provisions of the convention were essentially the same as for the Bremen convention, and the rates were the same. Taking advantage of the alternating weekly schedules of the NGL and HAPAG lines, it was now possible to send mail to Bremen via Hamburg, and to Hamburg via Bremen. For this alternate routing, 5¢ additional postage was charged. Mail that was addressed to countries in central, nothern and eastern Europe could now be sent via Bremen or Hamburg and, in general, at rates lower than those via France, Great Britain or Prussian closed mail.

The original conventions with Bremen and Hamburg had called for a progression modeled after the British system. But by 1860, modifications had been made to change to a system where the rate increased by ½-ounce units. This eliminated the practice of not allowing odd-numbered rates after the initial ½ ounce.

In contrast to Bremen mail, the internal U.S. rate for Hamburg mail remained at 5¢ until the fall of 1863, when the inland postage was reduced to 3¢ [8:160]. Other than this change, the original rates remained in force until January 1, 1868, when a new agreement was reached under the United States-North German Union Convention. The provisions of the new arrangement will be discussed in a following section.

1863, New York to Gratz, Austria, forwarded to Gurkfeld, Austria: A letter mailed under the Hamburg convention is illustrated in **Figure 17-20**. This cover was mailed at New York, where it received a red exchange marking dated May 16 (1863), showing prepaid postage via Hamburg packet and a 10¢ credit to Hamburg. The cover is endorsed "per Steamer/Via Hamburg." Sixteen cents postage was paid for the single rate to Austria of 15¢, plus 1¢ for carrier service at New York. The cover departed New York on the HAPAG steamship *Teutonia* on May 16 and arrived off Southhampton, England, on May 30. There it off-loaded mail transported under the American mail contract. It then continued on to Hamburg with the mail under the Hamburg convention and service, arriving on June 2, 1863. The cover was marked FRANCO at Hamburg to indicate that it was paid to destination. The postage was divided into 5+1¢, which was retained by the United States for inland and carrier, and 10¢ for Hamburg to pay for sea transport, transit and postage to Gratz. At Gratz, the cover was forwarded to Gurkfeld. The cover is backstamped at Hamburg on June 2, 1863, and Gratz and Gurkfeld on June 6.

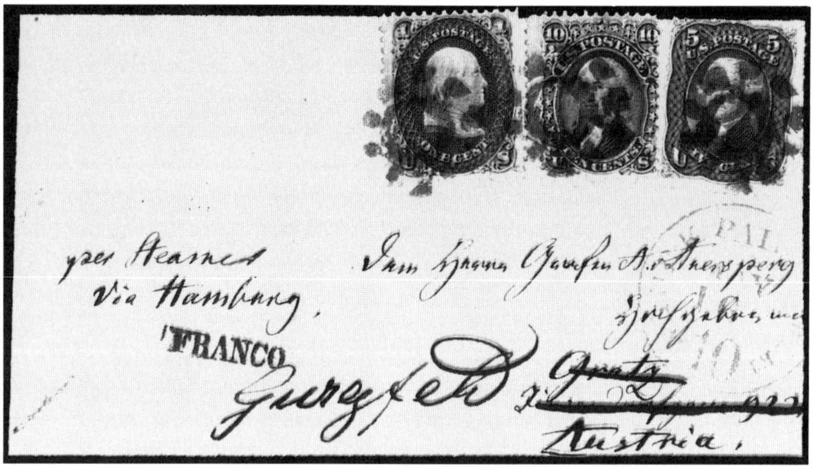

Figure 17-20. New York, May 16, 1863, to Gratz, Austria, forwarded to Gurkfeld, Austria, New York carrier service. The cover was mailed at the 15¢ single rate to Austria. Postage was paid by a 10¢ green plus 5¢ brown (Scott 76) of the 1861 issue. The carrier fee was paid by a 1¢ Franklin. The cover was carried by the HAPAG steamer *Teutonia* as Hamburg mail. It arrived at Hamburg on June 2, 1863, per receiving backstamp and was marked FRANCO. The cover is backstamped Gratz and Gurkfeld June 6. (James Lee collection)

Prussian Convention

In 1850, postal agreements between the German states laid the foundation for the German-Austrian Postal Union, which standardized procedures and reduced postage rates between the participants. This was followed by a desire to conclude a postal convention for the transmission of closed mail via England between Prussia and the United States. Effective October 16, 1852, this convention came into being with the following provisions. The international rate was set at 30¢ per ½ ounce, with the progression of rates following the British system. The mail from the United States was to be placed in closed bags at the exchange office at New York or Boston, conveyed by sea via American or British packet through Great Britain and Belgium to the exchange office at Aachen, Prussia, where the bags would be opened and the mail entered into the German postal system. Letters directed beyond the borders of the German states would be charged additional postage above the 30¢ rate. Letters sent under this convention are usually referred to as Prussian closed mail (PCM).

The United States exchange office accounting for outgoing Prussian closed mail was:

U.S. inland	5¢
Sea & British transit	18¢
Belgian transport	2¢
Prussian inland	5¢
	30¢

Paid letters credited Prussia with 7¢ to pay for Prussian inland and Belgian transit. If the destination was beyond Prussia, the credit would be 7¢ plus the postage to destination. The United States paid for sea transport and British transit, and retained 5¢ for U.S. inland postage.

Unpaid letters debited Prussia with 23¢. From this amount, the United States retained 5¢ for inland, and paid for sea transport and British transit.

A wide range of currency systems were in use in the German states, and rate markings on covers can be found in several different monetary units. A listing of the currency systems of foreign countries and the U.S. equivalents can be found in Starnes' *U.S. Letter Rates to Foreign Destinations, 1847 to GPU-UPU* [2:56-9]. This is useful for the analysis of covers to foreign destinations.

For German mail, the principal currency markings were in silbergroschen in the northern states and kreuzer in the southern states. The 30¢ international rate was equivalent to 13 silbergroschen or 45 kreuzer.

1861, to Athens, Greece: **Figure 17-21** illustrates a scarce use of the premiere gravure design of the 10¢ green 1861 issue, together with a 30¢ denomination and two 1¢ Franklins to make up the 42¢ rate on a mourning cover via Prussian closed mail to Greece. The stamps are canceled with a bright-red, eight-bar grid cancel, of a type used at New York. There is no city or exchange marking, but the cover shows a manuscript "19" in magenta, denoting 19¢ credit to Prussia. The cover is endorsed "Via Brussells." It received a Prussian exchange marking in red at Aachen dated "5 11," and was marked FRANCO as a prepaid letter. At Aachen the cover was also marked with a manuscript "fr 5" in stylized magenta script, an abbreviation for "weiterfranco 5," to show that the cover was paid 5 silbergroschen (equivalent to 12¢, U.S.) for postage beyond the German-Austrian Postal Union. The cover is docketed by the addressee, "Rec'd. Nov 14/1861." Working back from the dates on the cover, it can be determined that the letter probably departed from New York aboard the Cunard British packet *Asia* on October 23, 1861. It arrived off Queenstown on November 3, where the sealed Prussian closed mail bags were off-loaded and forwarded through England and Brussels, Belgium, to the exchange office at Aachen, Prussia, for futher transmission to Ath-

Figure 17-21. Probable New York, October 23, 1861, origin to Athens, Greece, via PCM. The 42¢ rate was paid by a 10¢ premiere gravure (Scott 62B), a pair of 1¢ Franklins and a 30¢ orange Franklin (71) of the 1861 issue, on a black-bordered mourning cover. A November 11 exchange marking was applied in red at Aachen. The cover was marked in magenta manuscript "19" for credit to Prussia and "fr 5" for postage paid to Greece. It was endorsed "Via Brussells" and docketed "Rec'd. Nov 11, 1861."
(R.G. Kaufmann auction photo)

Figure 17-22. New York, September 24, 1862, blue cover to Frankfurt-Am-Main, Germany. The 28¢ rate was prepaid by a 24¢ (Scott 78), 3¢ and 1¢. A red New York exchange marking credited Prussia with 7¢ by British packet. The cover departed New York aboard the Cunard *Australasian*. It bears a red Aachen exchange marking, dated October 7, and black circular marking with "D4/7 10."
(C.W. Christian collection)

ens, Greece.

1862, New York to Frankfurt-Am-Main, Germany: **Figure 17-22** shows a folded letter sheet with a red New York exchange marking, dated September 24 (1862), indicating British packet service, with 7¢ credited to Prussia. The cover departed New York on September 24 aboard the Cunard steamer *Australasian*, per endorsement, and arrived off Queenstown on October 4. A standard red Aachen exchange marking is dated October 7. The cover also has a circular handstamp receiving mark containing the inscription "D4/7 10." The single rate of 28¢ reflects the reduction of the previous 30¢ rate to 28¢, as a consequence of a lowering of the British transit rate. This change became effective for Frankfurt in May of 1862 and applied only to prepaid letters. The postage was divided with 7¢ to Prussia for its 5¢ internal postage plus 2¢ that Prussia paid to Belgium for transit. The United States retained 21¢ from which it paid Great Britain 16¢ for sea and transit postage. The remaining 5¢ accrued to the United States for internal postage.

1863, Gorham, Maine, to St. Petersburg, Russia: A scarce use to Russia is illustrated in **Figure 17-23**. This cover was mailed at Gorham, Maine, and received a distinctive, large circular postmark with bold lettering, dated July 18 (year unknown). It was prepaid with 35¢ in stamps to pay the single prepaid rate to Russia "by Prussian closed mail," as endorsed. This rate became effective in May of 1863. The cover was forwarded to New York, where a red exchange mark was applied showing prepayment and American packet service. This exchange marking is unusual in that it incorporates a seldom-seen year date in this type of marking. Unfortunately, the year date is too indistinct to identify. In addition, a large "14" handstamp in magenta was applied to show 14¢ credit to

351

Figure 17-23. Gorham, Maine, July 18, to St. Petersburg, Russia. The cover bears a red New York American "JUL 2(5)" packet paid exchange marking, with an unusual incorporated year date, and a magenta "14" credit to Prussia. The blue Aachen exchange marking has an unreadable date. Single-rate postage of 35¢ was prepaid by 24¢ (Scott 78), 10¢ and 1¢ of the 1861 issue.
(C.W. Christian collection)

Prussia, which included 7¢ to pay for the postage from Prussia to Russia. A blue boxed exchange marking was applied at Aachen (date unreadable). The earliest recorded date for the blue marking is March of 1865 [9:221]. There are no other markings on the cover to indicate routing or arrival at destination.

1863, Boston to Venezia, Austria (Venice, Italy): **Figure 17-24** illustrates a folded letter sheet from Boston to Venice. At the time of mailing, Venice was a part of Austria and did not become part of a united Italy until 1866. The folded letter sheet was mailed at Boston on August 25, 1863. The year of mailing is determined from the text of the letter sheet. The letter sheet received a red Boston exchange marking showing British packet service and 7¢ credit to Prussia. It was forwarded to New York to be transported on the next scheduled carrier for European mail. The Cunard packet *China* departed New York on August 26 and arrived off Queenstown on September 4. It received a red exchange marking at Aachen, dated September 6, and was backstamped with a receiving mark at Venezia on September 9 (1863). The 28¢ rate, paid in stamps, paid the letter to destination at the reduced rate, effective September 1861. Prussia was credited 7¢ to pay Belgian transit, internal postage and the postage to Venezia.

1865, Honolulu, to Neuchatel, Switzerland, forwarded to Havre, France: **Figure 17-25** is an example of an exceptionally interesting use from Honolulu to Switzerland, then forwarded to Havre, France. The cover was mailed at Honolulu on April 3, 1865, where it received a large brownish-red "Honolulu/U.S. POSTAGE PAID/APR 3" CDS. The internal Hawaiian rate was 5¢ and was paid in cash. Postage was prepaid by 38¢ in stamps. Effective December 3, 1864, and until September 26, 1867, the rate from Hawaii to the United States was 5¢. This essentially covered a 2¢ ship fee plus the 3¢ U.S. internal rate [2:53].

Figure 17-24. Boston, August 25, 1863, to Venezia, Austria (Venice, Italy) folded letter sheet. The red Boston exchange marking indicates British packet service and 7¢ Prussian credit. The cover departed New York aboard the Cunard packet *China*. At Aachen it received a red exchange marking dated September 6. The 28¢ PCM rate to Venice was paid with a 24¢ (Scott 78), 3¢ and 1¢. The letter sheet was backstamped "VENEZIA 9/9" as a receiving mark.
(C.W. Christian collection)

Foreign Mails

Figure 17-25. Honolulu, Hawaii, April 3, 1865, to Neuchatel, Switzerland, forwarded to Havre, France. The 38¢ in stamps paid United States-to-Switzerland PCM postage of 33¢ plus 5¢ for Hawaii to the United States. Hawaiian 5¢ internal postage was paid in cash. The cover was routed via San Francisco; New York; Boston; Cunard packet *Asia* to Queenstown; Aachen, Prussia; Neuchatel, Switzerland; and to final destination at Havre, France. (C.W. Christian collection)

Scheduled contract mail service between Honolulu and San Francisco did not start until 1867. Arriving at San Francisco, the uncanceled cover received San Francisco duplexed bull's-eye cancels and postmarks, dated April 21, 1865. The cover was then forwarded to New York, where it received a red New York exchange marking, indicating British packet service and dated May 23.

At this point, the balance of postage available was 33¢, which was the Prussian closed-mail rate to Switzerland. A large "12" handstamp in red was applied to show that 12¢ had been credited to Prussia. The cover was forwarded to Boston to catch the next British mail packet. It departed Boston aboard the Cunard *Asia* on May 24, 1865. The *Asia* arrived off Queenstown on June 3, 1865, and the Prussian closed mail was forwarded to Aachen, where it received a blue exchange office mark on June 6. At Aachen the cover also received a blue manuscript marking, "Wfr 2." This is the abbreviation for "Weiterfranco 2," which literally translates as "paid beyond 2." The meaning here, is that postage is paid in the amount of 2 silbergroschen (about 5¢) beyond the border of the German-Austrian Postal Union. Arriving at Neuchatel, Switzerland, on June 7, per backstamp, the cover was immediately forwarded to the addressee's new location at Havre. It received another June 7 backstamp at Neuchatel as it was processed for forwarding. The cover was also marked with an orange manuscript "6," probably at Neuchatel, to show that the internal Swiss postage of 6 kreuzers (about 4¢) had been paid. Of the 33¢ unaccounted-for postage remaining at New York on May 23, the United States retained 5¢ for internal postage and 16¢ to pay for sea and British transit. The balance of 12¢ was credited to Prussia to pay for Belgian transit (2¢), Prussian internal postage of 5¢ and 5¢ for postage to Switzerland. Forwarding postage to France was not indicated on the cover and may not have been

charged. A curious fact relating to this cover is that U.S. internal postage was collected twice: once for the Hawaii-to-New York segment (3¢), and once for New York to Switzerland (5¢).

This peripatetic cover, with its wealth of postal markings, is an excellent example of the interesting information that can be deduced with postal research, and consultation with reference materials, and (when needed) with experts in the philatelic community.

1867, Cincinnati, Ohio, to Brieg, Prussia: **Figure 17-26** shows a cover to Brieg, Ober-Schlesien (Upper Silesia), now part of Poland. Originating at Cincinnati on January 3, 1867, this cover was paid by 28¢ in stamps for the single closed-mail rate to Prussia and postmarked with the distinctive blue Cincinnati duplexed killer. At New York, it received a red exchange marking dated January 9, noting British packet and 7¢ credit to Prussia. The letter departed New York on the Cunard packet *Australasian*, arriving off Queenstown on January 22. The cover received a blue Aachen exchange marking on January 24, 1867.

In 1867, the formation of the new North German Union required negotiations to replace the treaties with the member states that were then in force. The general features of the new convention were discussed in an earlier section, titled The Postal Conventions of 1868. The special features specific to the United States-North German Union Convention were:

The establishment of U.S. exchange offices at New York, Boston, Philadelphia and Chicago. North German

Figure 17-26. Cincinnati, Ohio, January 3 (1867) to Brieg, Ober-Schlesien (Prussia). This cover received a blue duplex postmark at Cincinnati. It is endorsed "Prussia." The 28¢ rate was prepaid with a 24¢ (Scott 78), 3¢ and 1¢. The New York exchange marking in red, dated January 9, indicates British packet service and 7¢ credit to Prussia. The blue exchange marking was applied at Aachen, dated January 24. (C.W. Christian collection)

Union offices were established at Bremen, Hamburg, and the Traveling Post Office 10 between Cologne and Verviers. Bremen and Hamburg were to correspond with all U.S. offices, but the Traveling Cologne/Verviers office was to correspond only with New York for mail via England and Belgium.

The international rates for single letters of 15 grams were: direct between the United States and Hamburg or Bremen, 10¢; closed mail via England, 15¢.

Prepayment was optional, but unpaid or part-paid letters were subjected to a fine of 2 silbergroschen (4.8¢).

Open-mail letters were to be charged with the direct international rate, augmented by the postage due to foreign countries, plus any other monies due for exterior service [1:150].

1868, New York, to Naples, Italy: **Figure 17-27** illustrates an example of use under the new North German Union (NGU) convention. This folded letter sheet originated at New York, where it received a red PAID ALL circular exchange marking dated January 22, 1868, and a bold red "4" handstamp to show the credit to the NGU for transit beyond its borders. Postage of 21¢ was paid by two 10¢ Washingtons and a 1¢ Franklin of the 1861 issue. The rate for a single letter to Italy, not exceeding 15 grams, was 19¢ under the new convention. The reason for the 2¢ overpayment is not known; however, the new rates had become effective just three weeks previously, and there may have been some confusion regarding the correct rate. It is also possible that the sender anticipated the letter being transmitted by French mail, where the rate was 21¢ per single-rate of 7.5 grams. In any case, the New York exchange office elected to send it via closed NGU mail. The cover departed New York on January 22, 1868, by the Cunard steamer *Persia*, as endorsed on the letter.

This was an early voyage of the Cunard Line operating as an American mail packet under contract to the U.S. Post Office. The first voyage under this new contract had occurred two weeks earlier, and from that date

Figure 17-27. This folded letter sheet was sent from New York January 22, 1868, to Naples, Italy, by NGU closed mail. Postage was paid by 21¢ in stamps with 2¢ overpayment of the single rate. A red "Paid All" exchange marking and bold "4" handstamp were applied at New York. The letter sheet departed New York by the Cunard American packet *Persia*, as requested by endorsement. It received a red Verviers-to-Cologne exchange marking. The February 10, 1868, receiving mark was applied at Naples.

VERVIERS. B.
3 2 III
COELN
FRANCO

on, the Cunard eastbound mails were carried as American packet mail [3:56]. This ended almost three decades of continuous and exclusive mail service to the British Post Office and began an era where post office departments would enter into short-term competitive contracts with many steamship lines for sea transportation of mails.

The *Persia* arrived off Queenstown on February 1, and the letter was transported in sealed bags via England and Belgium to the new exchange office on the railway post office operating between Verviers, Belgium, and Cologne, Germany. The letter received a red VERVIERS.B./ COELN III/FRANCO marking dated February 3. A large red "P.D." was applied in Italy, indicating payment to destination. Backstamped transit markings were applied at Verona and Padova (Padua), Italy, on February 6, and a February 10 receiving mark was applied at Napoli (Naples), reflecting a somewhat leisurely trip down the Italian boot.

Belgian Conventions of 1859 and 1868

Although the writer has no 1¢ Franklin covers available to illustrate use under the Belgian, Netherlands, Switzerland and Italian conventions, short discussions of these conventions are included for completeness.

In anticipation of Belgium's establishing a scheduled direct steamship service between Antwerp and New York, early negotiations were initiated for a postal agreement. These negotiations were satisfactorily concluded, and a convention was signed on December 21, 1859. The agreement provided for the direct exchange of mail, if and when a satisfactory steamship route was inaugurated, and also for closed mail to be routed through Great Britain. In January of 1868, a new convention was agreed upon with the standard provisions of the other 1868 European conventions. The single-letter rate was established at 15¢, and the fine for underpaid or unpaid letters was to be 30 centimes (5.7¢). Exchange offices were to be Boston and New York for the United States, and Ostend and Antwerp for Belgium. The anticipated steamship service was not established until 1873. Mail to Belgium was relatively sparce during the 1860s, and examples are not easy to obtain.

The Netherlands (Holland) Convention of 1868

This convention followed the general provisions of the 1868 European conventions and became effective January 1, 1868. The rate for letter postage was 15¢ per 15 grams, and the mails were carried by Netherlands closed mail. Moerdyk, Netherlands, and New York were the exchange offices. The fine for unpaid or underpaid letters was established not to exceed 15¢ (Dutch) which is equivalent to 6¢ U.S. From covers showing the fine, it has been determined that the actual amount levied was only 10¢ Dutch.

Switzerland Convention of 1868

Effective April 1, 1868, this agreement also followed the general provisions of the 1868 European conventions. The postage rate per 15 grams was established as 15¢ for Swiss closed mail via England. The French service of 21¢ per 7.5 grams continued. Basel, Switzerland, and New York were designated as exchange offices. The fine for unpaid or underpaid letters (except for French service) was not to exceed 25 centimes (4.75¢). In actual practice, it was 20 centimes.

Italian Convention of 1868

Effective April 1, 1868, Italy entered into a similar convention with the United States. Postage rates per 15 grams were 14¢ if carried direct via the NGU and 19¢ if carried by NGU closed mail via England. (Although the name was officially changed by this date, the service was still frequently requested by letter-endorsement as Prussian closed mail.) A rate of 15¢ for direct closed mail to Italy via England was established. Under these new conventions, the previous meaning of "direct" mail was changed. Direct closed mail now included mail that was transported in sealed bags through another country. The existing rates for service under the French convention of 21¢ per 15 grams still remained in force. All of these rates had optional prepayment, but a fine of 30 centesimi (5.7¢) was assessed for underpayment (except for French service). The exchange office for the United States was to be New York, and the offices for Italy were originally established to be Susa, Camerlata and Arona. Each of these Italian exchange offices were traveling offices.

This concludes the limited discussion of the transatlantic mails. While examples of many of the more frequently used conventions and routes have been illustrated, the reader is cautioned that the coverage is by no means complete.

The mail transported across the Pacific is also an interesting subject. No contract-mail steamships were operating before 1867, and examples of transpacific service during the 1860s are quite scarce. Ship letters by private vessels between the South Pacific or the Orient and the United States also exist, but they too are consistently difficult to find.

A reasonable amount of correspondence occurred between the United States and Hawaii, particularly between Honolulu and San Francisco. Figure 17-25 showed a cover sent prior to the beginning of the scheduled steamship mail service, which began in 1867. This contract-mail route between the United States and the Hawaiian Islands was initiated by the California, Oregon & Mexico Steamship Line. This was one of the many enterprises of Ben Holladay, of "overland stage" fame, and made him the leading figure for U.S. mail transportation from the Missouri River to Honolulu. Two years later the transcontinental railroad was completed, and the stagecoach segment became a casualty of advancing technology.

Mail to Canada and the British North American Provinces

As a neighboring country and a country that shared many cultural and commercial interests with the United States, Canada exchanged a substantial amount of mail with the United States. The postal agencies of Canada and the United States worked closely together, and in the early 1800s even shared postmasters. According to Boggs, there were 13 exchange offices where, prior to 1843, the U.S. postmaster and the Canadian postmaster were the same individual. These included offices at Quebec, Toronto, Montreal, Niagara and Woodstock [10:58]. The reason for this was that in the pre-stamp period, Canadian postmasters could become agents of the United States and collect U.S. postage that was due on letters sent to Canada. They received a 20-percent commission for this service, and it was supported by Canadian postal officials who also benefitted from the commission.

During the period of interest to this text, present-day Canada was composed of several provinces and separately governed regions. Although all of these were part of the British Empire, they operated their own post offices and issued their own stamps. To better understand the impact of these divisions on the handling of mail to and from the United States, it seems advisable at this point to summarize a bit of Canadian history leading up to and including the period of 1860 to 1870.

In 1861, Canada consisted of only two provinces. These were the provinces of Upper and Lower Canada. Upper Canada consisted essentially of today's Ontario, and Lower Canada was present-day Quebec. These two most populous provinces had joined together under a common administration in 1841. Upper Canada, so-called because it was on the upper reach of the St. Lawrence River, was also referred to as "Canada West" or "C.W.," and this is the way most mail was addressed in the 1860s. Similarly, Lower Canada was also known as "Canada East" or "C.E." The boundary between the two parts of Canada was along the Ottawa River.

All other parts of present-day Canada were separate entities. They consisted in the east of the Maritime Provinces of New Brunswick, Nova Scotia (including Cape Breton), Prince Edward Island, and Newfoundland (including Labrador), and the crown colonies of British Columbia (ex-New Caledonia) and Vancouver's Island in the west. The vast tracts of land in between the west and east, and to the north, were sparsely populated. The western territory from Ontario to the Rockies, including present-day Manitoba, Saskatchewan and Alberta, was owned by the Hudson's Bay Company. This huge area was taken over by Canada in 1869 in return for a payment to the company of £300,000 and title to 5 percent of the fertile lands of the region, to be conveyed as they were surveyed.

In 1864, New Brunswick, Nova Scotia and Prince Edward Island were considering the possibility of joining together as a federal union. Canada met with them and convinced the participants that it would be more advantageous to become a part of Canada in a larger union. On July 1, 1867, the British Parliament passed the British North American Act and formed the first federal union in the British Empire. It was called the Dominion of Canada, and contained Upper and Lower Canada, New Brunswick and Nova Scotia. Prince Edward Island abstained from the union, but joined later in 1873. Newfoundland steadfastly refused to become a part and stayed separate until 1949.

In the west, Vancouver's Island merged with British Columbia on November 17, 1866, and in 1871 became a part of the Dominion of Canada. As a condition for joining the union, British Columbia exacted a commitment from Canada that construction on a transcontinental railroad to the Pacific would be initiated within two years and completed within 10 years of the date of union.

Obviously, the decade of the 1860s was a key period in the establishment of the government of Canada. While the many changes did not seriously impact the handling of mail, and in general, most procedures and rates were standardized across all of the provinces, there were some deviations. These deviations, as well as the standard rates and procedures, will be discussed and illustrated.

In 1861, the standard letter rate from the United States to Canada and all of British North America was 10¢ per ½ ounce for letters that traveled less than 3,000 miles from origin to the point of entry into Canada. For letters that originated from California or Oregon Territory, or where the distance was greater than 3,000 miles, the rate was 15¢. Prepayment was optional, but partial payment was not recognized (1859 PL&R, §150). Some minor variations in this general rate structure occurred between 1861 and 1868, and usually applied to the necessity for prepayment, or the difference in the dates that changes in postal arrangements were effective in the various provinces.

This 10¢/15¢ rate remained in force until April 1, 1868, when the standard rate, if prepaid, was lowered to 6¢. Unpaid letters continued at 10¢ for a single rate (rates to Prince Edward Island, Newfoundland, British Columbia and Vancouver's Island, since they were not yet part of the Dominion, remained at 10¢) [11:358,364].

A feature of the postal arrangements with Canada and the other British North American provinces that was an improvement over arrangements with most other countries was the provision that each would retain all of the postage it collected, either as a prepayment or from collection upon delivery. No accounts were to be kept with regards to postage by either country, nor any international charges levied. This simplified the transmission of mails and served as a model for this type of arrangement to be applied to other countries in the future.

Because of the many points of entry between Canada and the United States, there were approximately 40 exchange offices established on each side of the border. These included cities such as Detroit, Michigan; Buffalo, New York; Cleveland, Ohio; and Rutland, Vermont. The number and location of exchange offices changed as new postal arrangements were made over the years. Some major offices such as Boston and Albany acted as exchange offices with their distant counterparts at Hamilton, Ontario, or Montreal, Quebec, and other specified offices. In these cases the mail between the offices was forwarded by through bags. When changes in the specified offices were made, an updated list of current exchange offices was printed in the USM&POA to provide postmasters with the necessary information for routing their letters.

U.S. exchange offices were required by regulation to handstamp all letters to British North American provinces with "U. States." Prepaid letters were to be marked in red. Unpaid letters were to be marked in black ink and annotated with the amount due. Variations in the marking are common, such as "United States" or "Ud. States."

An excellent source for additional information concerning mail between the United States and the British North American provinces is the exhibit collection of the late Susan M. McDonald, titled *Cross Border Mails: United States and British North America to 1875* [12]. This 127-page exhibit is well-researched and described, and copies are available in photocopy form.

Canada

On July 1, 1859, the Canadian postal service converted from a currency expressed in pounds, shilling and pence to a decimal system of dollars and cents [10:21-B]. The equivalence was approximately 6d (pence) equal to 10¢. Most Canadian markings to be be found on 1860-70 covers are rated in cents, but occasionally a marking from the old monetary system was used.

According to regulations, letters could be sent to Canada with the postage prepaid in cash. This arrangement continued until July 1862. From that time, according to McDonald, prepaid letters to the British North American provinces were to be paid by postage stamps [12:110]. An official announcement in the July 1862 issue of the USM&POA states that payment in stamps will be required for Nova Scotia, effective June 1, 1862 [11:78]. It does not mention any of the other provinces in the notice, but they were possibly also affected. Of course, examples of this type of use would not have a 1¢ Franklin or any other U.S. stamp, unless they were unpaid covers with a 1¢ stamp showing carrier service to the mails. While examples of carrier payment are occasionally found on unpaid transatlantic mail covers, this writer has never seen one to Canada. It is understandable why the Post Office Department would want to discourage unpaid letters to Canada. Under the postal arrangements, Canada would retain all of the collect postage.

Figure 17-28 illustrates an example of an early use of the 1¢ Franklin on a cover to Cornwall, Canada West. This Boston cover was mailed on September 11, 1861. The year date is determined from a receiving stamp on the reverse dated "SP 12 1861." The cover is marked with a red UNITED STATES in a double-line oval marking of a type most frequently used at the Boston exchange office.

Figure 17-29 shows a Cincinnati, Ohio, to Oil Springs, Canada West, cover with a fancy corner card from a maker of sulphuric acid. There is no exchange marking as stipulated by the postal agreement with Canada, but this is not unusual, particularly for prepaid letters used in the mid-1860s and post-Civil War period. The three 3¢ and one 1¢ stamps is the most common combination used to pay the standard 10¢ rate.

The Pacific coast rate to Canada of 15¢ is illustrated in **Figure 17-30**. The cover is from Downieville, California, dated April 28, 1862, to Galt, Canada West. The day of the month was indistinct in the CDS, and the postmaster applied a "28" in manuscript to clarify the marking. The stamps are canceled with the well-known

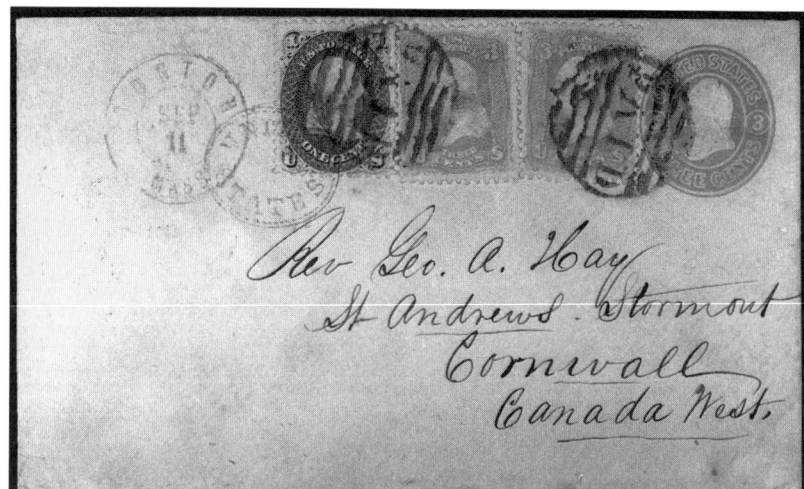

Figure 17-28. Combination franking on a 3¢ government stamped envelope (Scott U34), with 1¢ and two 3¢ stamps to make up the 10¢ rate from Boston, to Cornwall, Canada West. Markings include a red Boston CDS dated "SEP 11," a black PAID in circle with bars and a red UNITED STATES in oval exchange marking. The cover is backstamped "SP 12 1861."
(C.W. Christian collection)

Figure 17-29. A blue Cincinnati duplex cancel, dated "AUG 23," to Oil Springs, Canada West. Three 3¢ and one 1¢ combine to pay the 10¢ letter rate to Canada. The cover was backstamped at Oil Springs on August 30, 1862.
(C.W. Christian collection)

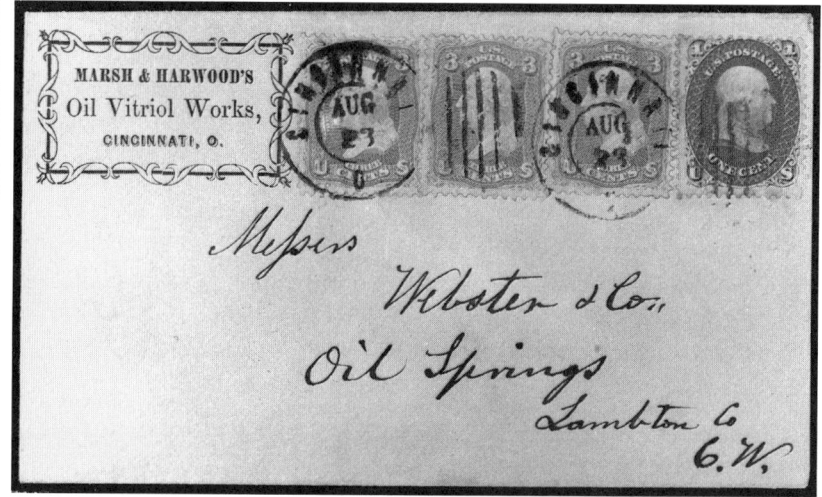

Figure 17-30. This cover is an example of the 15¢ rate for letters originating on the Pacific coast. It was sent from Downieville, California, April 28, 1862, to Galt, Canada West. The stamps were canceled with a "Downieville star" fancy cancel. The cover is marked "Paid 15" in black manuscript.
(C.W. Christian collection)

Figure 17-31. This mourning cover from New York to Hamilton, Canada West, was mailed June 7, 1863, and was received at Hamilton on June 8, 1863, per receiving mark on reverse. The 11¢ in postage makes up the standard rate to Canada plus a 1¢ carrier fee. (C.W. Christian collection)

and desirable "Downieville Star" fancy cancel. Covers with the 1¢ Franklin showing the 15¢ transcontinental rate, are relatively scarce. This reflects the limited period (from August 1861 when the stamp was issued until March 1864 when the rate was changed to 10¢ for any distance) and the scarcity of covers from the Pacific coast.

The elimination of the 15¢ rate for letters over 3,000 miles was diplomatically achieved by agreement between the post office departments of Canada and the United States. The postal treaty, which was effective on April 9, 1851, had called for the 15¢ rate to be charged on letters to and from Canada where the distance from point of origin to the line of crossing was in excess of 3,000 miles. The counterpart regulation of the Canadian Post Office did not mention the 3,000-mile restriction, but rather stated that the rate for letters addressed to or from California or Oregon was to be 9d (changed on July 1, 1859, to 15¢) [13:21B].

When the U.S. transcontinental domestic rate was lowered to 3¢ on July 1, 1863, without regard to distance, it was deemed desirable for the purpose of uniformity to eliminate the additional charge on letters to and from Canada where the distance exceeded 3,000 miles or where the destination or origin was on the Pacific coast. These rates were fixed under the treaty of 1851, and there was no desire at this time to enter into negotiations to amend the treaty. Instead, Postmaster General Blair entered into an agreement with the Canada Post Office to modify the postal arrangements so as to establish a uniform rate of letter postage between the United States and Canada of 10¢, regardless of distance or route of conveyance.

Blair used as the basis for this change the fact that since the overland distance from the Pacific coast to the line of crossing as presently traveled into Canada was less than 3,000 miles, it was no longer necessary to have the 15¢ rate. Blair's official order making this change was dated February 17, 1864. It was printed in the March 1864 issue of the USM&POA [11:266].

A small mourning cover is illustrated in **Figure 17-31**. This cover was posted at New York with carrier collection to the mails on June 7, 1863, and received at Hamilton, Canada West, on June 8, 1863, as attested by the receiving mark "HAMILTON/JU 8/1863/UC." The combination of a 10¢ and a 1¢ stamp to make up the rate plus carrier fee is relatively common.

Mailed just three weeks before the rate for letters to Canada was reduced to 6¢, the cover in **Figure 17-32** shows a Harrisburg, Pennsylvania, CDS dated March 13. The cover is addressed to Markham, Canada West, and is backstamped with the receiving mark of Whitby, Canada West, dated March 15, 1868.

Figure 17-33 shows an eye-catching cover to Canada East, paid with 10 1¢ Franklins. The cover originated at Burlington, Vermont, and was postmarked May 24. The year was 1867, as shown by the St. John's transit mark, dated the same day. St. John's is a Quebec city known more commonly as St. Jean, about 60 miles north of Burlington. From St. Jean, the letter was carried about 30 miles east to its destination at Knowlton, Canada East.

A cover from Albany, New York, to Caledonia, Canada West, about 40 miles west of Niagara Falls, is shown in **Figure 17-34**. The three 3¢ and one 1¢ stamps that make up the 10¢ rate are canceled with strikes of the Albany patent cancel. Examples of use of this Norton-type of duplex canceler are known at Albany from December 30, 1862, to November 20, 1863 [14:161]. No year date is shown on the Albany "APR 24" CDS, but the cover was backstamped in Canada on April 25, 1863. Albany was an exchange office and stamped the cover with

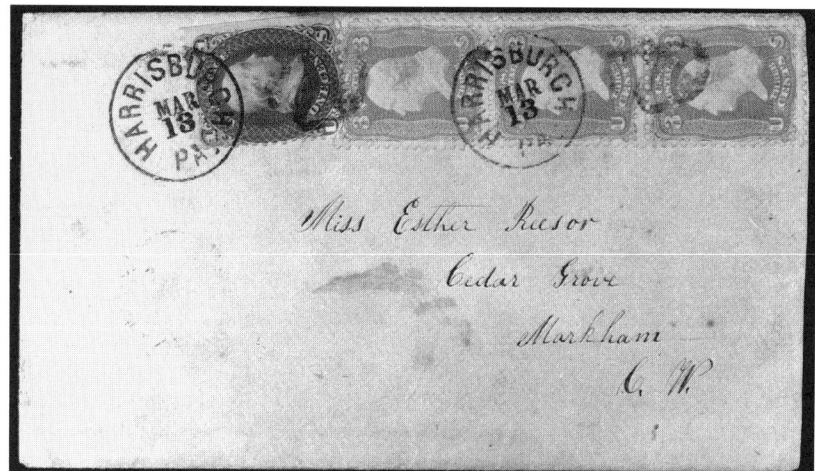

Figure 17-32. Harrisburg, Pennsylvania, CDS dated March 13 to Markham, Canada West. The cover was backstamped at Whitby, Canada West, on March 15, 1868. This is an example of use of the 10¢ rate just before the reduction to 6¢ on April 1, 1868.

Figure 17-33. This scarce cover is an example of the 10¢ rate prepaid by a pair and eight singles of the 1¢ Franklin. It was sent from Burlington, Vermont, to Knowlton, Canada East. The cover was postmarked at Burlington on May 24, (1867) and received at St. John's, Canada East, on the same day.
(C.W. Christian collection)

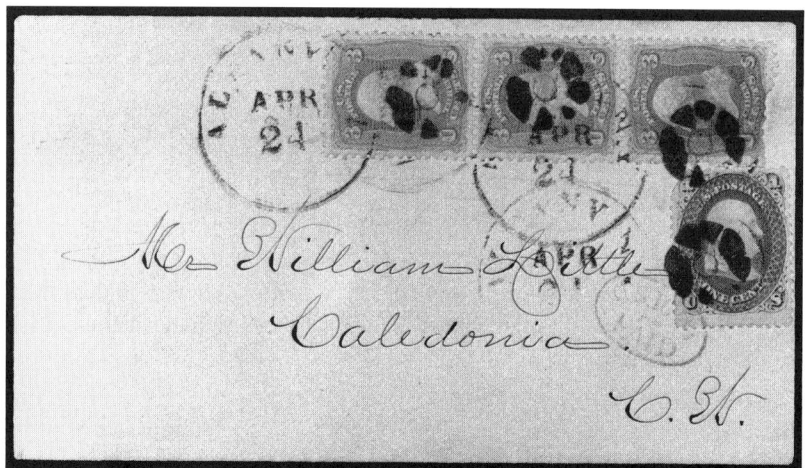

Figure 17-34. This cover was sent from Albany, New York, to Caledonia, Canada West, and is canceled "APR 24." The 10¢ letter rate was paid with stamps canceled by Norton-type patent duplex canceler. The cover was marked with a red "U.S. 10 cts/ PAID" exchange marking at Albany. It was backstamped on April 25, 1863.
(C.W. Christian collection)

Foreign Mails

Figure 17-35. This is an example of an early use of the 1861 stamps, paying the 10¢ rate to New Brunswick. The cover was sent from Lawrence, Massachusetts, September 2, 1861, to St. John, New Brunswick, via Portland and "Ship Chimborazo." It is stamped with red exchange markings of U. STATES in arc, PAID, and "10." It is backstamped SP 4/ 1861/ST. JOHN NEW BRUNSWICK.

a red "U.S. 10 cts/PAID" in oval marking.

A curious announcement appeared in the USM&POA in its first edition in October 1860 and continued in each issue until December 1865 when it was dropped without explanation. The announcement was in the Foreign Miscellany section, and read as follows:

> "Letters received from Canada, to which are affixed uncanceled United States postage stamps of sufficient value to prepay the full postage chargeable thereon, should be delivered without charge by the United States offices."

The notice is a direct quote from Section 150 of the 1859 Postal Regulations. This writer has never seen an example of such use, and certainly would be interested in obtaining further information concerning this unusual provision. Such a procedure was often used for mail originating at Vancouver's Island and British Columbia because of special circumstances that will be discussed later in this chapter, but the reason it was used for Canadian mail is unknown.

New Brunswick

New Brunswick followed in the footsteps of Canada with respect to postal arrangements and rates. The United States concluded its postal treaty with New Brunswick on July 6, 1851, just three months after its treaty with Canada, and with the same arrangements. The rates stayed the same as those for Canada except for a five-month period in 1864 when the elimination of the 15¢ Pacific coast rate was not applied to New Brunswick until August.

Figure 17-35 illustrates an interesting cover addressed to St. John, New Brunswick, from Lawrence, Massachusetts. The 10¢ rate includes the use of a "dot-in-U" variety of the 1¢ Franklin from the first plate, plate 9, and three rose-pink 3¢ stamps. The Lawrence CDS shows SEP 2 as the mailing date. The cover was backstamped at St. John on September 4, 1861, making this a very early use of the 1861 stamps.

The cover is endorsed to be sent via Portland on the "Ship Chimborazo," a coastal mail steamer. The cover has a red "U.STATES" in arc, together with a red handstamped PAID and "10." These markings were probably applied at Portland and met all of the regulatory requirements for a prepaid letter. A complete set of markings is more likely to be found on the early covers. As the decade of the 1860s progressed, the increase in the number of prepaid letters and the use of postage stamps negated the necessity for rate markings, and more and more covers were processed with no rate or country markings other than the origin CDS and possibly a receiving mark at the destination.

Figure 17-36 shows another cover to St. John, New Brunswick. This cover was mailed at Woburn, Massachusetts, on November 10, and received at St. John on November 13, 1862, per a receiving mark on the reverse. The cover carries an exchange office red "U.S. 10 cts/PAID" in a small oval marking.

A very rare and interesting cover is illustrated in **Figure 17-37**. The reason for the 2¢ rate on this cover caused much speculation for many years, and has at times erroneously been referred to as a "ferriage" use.

This is an example of a special rate established between specified exchange offices in the United States and their opposite exchange offices in Canada and New Brunswick. The rate was 2¢ for letters, without regard to weight, between certain exchange offices that were separated by only a short distance.

As explained by Susan M. McDonald in an informative article [15:56], the rate originated in 1851. With the

361

Figure 17-36. Woburn, Massachusetts, November 10 (1862), to St. John, New Brunswick. The cover bears a red "U.S. 10 cts/ PAID" in small oval exchange marking, probably applied at Boston. The stamps paid the 10¢ letter rate. The cover was backstamped with a receiving mark at St. John, New Brunswick, dated November 13, 1862.

Figure 17-37. Very rare, possibly unique, example of the 2¢ cross-border rate between exchange offices with the postage paid by 1¢ 1861 stamps. The cover was mailed at Houlton, Maine, to Woodstock, New Brunswick. It bears a black U. STATES in arc exchange marking and was backstamped at Woodstock, New Brunswick, on July 13, 1862. (James Lee collection)

increase in the cost of mail that resulted from the 1851 postal treaty between the United States and Canada, pairs of post offices on each side of the border that had been used to paying possibly only 1¢ or 2¢ for postage, now had to pay 10¢ or the equivalent 6d. This resulted in many complaints, and Canadian Postmaster General James Morris wrote to U.S. Postmaster General N.K. Hall on April 15, 1851, requesting a reduced rate between 10 pairs of exchange offices. A similar request was made by the postmaster general of New Brunswick. The United States agreed to a rate of 2¢ between selected line offices where the distance between them was less than five miles. These agreements were later expanded to other offices, and to short distances greater than five miles.

The earlier ferriage rates were used as a precedent to establish this new rate between exchange offices, and this is where the confusion in the terms probably originated. Ferriage was a Canadian surcharge to defray the cost of establishing and maintaining ferries for the transportation of mail across rivers. It was abolished in 1837, except for the case where a Canadian exchange office was the origin or destination of such mail. The fee was probably 1¢ or 2¢.

Only eight covers showing the 1851 exchange-office rate of 2¢ have been recorded. These are from the period of 1860 through 1870, and all of the covers originated at Houlton, Maine, and were addressed to Woodstock, New Brunswick. These two towns were listed as exchange offices.

Only one of the recorded covers has the postage paid by 1¢ 1861 Franklins, and that is the cover shown in Figure 17-37. This small cover was stamped with a black "U. STATES" in arc at Houlton, and on the reverse shows the receiving mark of Woodstock, New Brunswick, dated June 13, 1862. A large "2" in crayon is written on the front of the cover. All of the Houlton/Woodstock covers show some sort of marking with the figure "2" included. This may have been placed on the covers to emphasize that they were being mailed at the special exchange-office rate.

One of the most unusual aspects of the examples of this scarce rate is that they are all between the same exchange offices. Both Houlton and Woodstock were small towns with a limited amount of postal business. Large cities such as Detroit, Michigan, and Windsor, Canada, were also listed as being eligible for this special rate, but no known covers from them show use of the 2¢ rate. The absence of any known examples from these and other exchange cities of substantial size is very surprising, and the reason for this poses a philatelic conundrum that has yet to be solved.

A very interesting cover, originally from the Bruce Hazelton collection, is shown in **Figure 17-38**. This cover, dated December 15 (no year date), was mailed from Calais, Maine, to St. Stephens, New Brunswick. These two post offices were also exchange offices between the United States and New Brunswick, and are separated only by a bridge across the St. Croix River. The franking by a single 1¢ 1861 stamp suggests that this cover was mailed at a special rate, similar to that of the original ferriage rate.

When John Howe, postmaster general of New Brunswick, wrote to U.S. Postmaster General Hall, on November 19, 1851, asking for special rates between frontier exchange offices, he requested a local rate of 2¢ or 1d between St. Stephen and Calais, St. Andrew and Robbinstown, and Woodstock and Houlton. Hall replied with an agreement for a special rate of 2¢ only between St. Stephen and Calais, stating that the other towns were separated by a distance of more than five miles, and for the present, should not be allowed a reduced rate [15:57].

Although this cover is paid with only 1¢ in postage, it is likely that this was accepted as the special exchange-office rate. Other similar examples of 1¢ postage paid between exchange offices exist where the offices were separated only by a bridge, as in this case. It appears this is an example of a reduced special rate for these closely located offices; however, no documentation to support this has been found.

On July 1, 1867, New Brunswick, together with Nova Scotia and Canada, became part of the new Commonwealth of Canada, and from that time on, all postal arrangements for New Brunswick were the responsibility of the Commonwealth, and the rates and procedures were uniform.

Nova Scotia

During the decade of the 1860s, most of the mail to Nova Scotia was transported by ship. Nova Scotia is almost a separate island, with only an 18-mile-wide isthmus connecting it to New Brunswick on the mainland. There were no railroads between it and Canada. Overland mail from the United States was transported through Maine and New Brunswick. From the main commercial centers such as Philadelphia and New York, this route took about six days longer than the packet mail via Boston to Nova Scotia.

Although many rate tables list it separately, Cape Breton Island has been a part of Nova Scotia since 1820. They are separated only by a narrow waterway with the interesting name of the Gut of Canso. By the treaty of July 1851, Nova Scotia agreed to the same rates and procedures that were in effect for Canada at that time. Letter postage was 10¢ per ½ ounce up to 3,000 miles, and 15¢ for greater distances, prepayment optional. The over-3,000-mile rate for Nova Scotia was not eliminated until January 1, 1868. Some minor changes to procedures were reported in the USM&POA. The July 1862 issue stated that prepayment was required for letters to Nova Scotia, and this notice was continued until January 1863 when prepayment again became optional.

As a result of the British North American Act, Nova Scotia became part of Canada in 1867, and the new postal agreements, effective on January 1, 1868, resulting from the formation of the Commonwealth, also ap-

Figure 17-38. Rare use of a single 1¢ Franklin to pay a special international letter rate between the exchange offices at Calais, Maine, and St. Stephens, New Brunswick. Dated December 15 (no year date).

Figure 17-39. Boston, Massachusetts, December 2 (1861), to Annapolis, Nova Scotia. The 1¢ Franklin plus 10¢ premiere gravure (Scott 62B) paid the standard letter rate plus carrier fee. The cover is marked with Boston exchange office UNITED STATES in oval. Annapolis receiving mark dated December 3, 1861, appears on the reverse.
(James Lee collection)

Figure 17-40. Salem, Massachusetts, March 3 (1862) to Westport, Nova Scotia. The buff 3¢ pink entire (Scott U34) with two 3¢ and one 1¢ stamps paid the 10¢ rate. The cover has a Boston exchange mark, "U.S. 10 cts/ PAID" in oval and an oval backstamp "H/MR 13/1862/NS."

plied to Nova Scotia.

Figure 17-39 shows an early use to Nova Scotia mailed at Boston on December 2 (1861) to Annapolis, Nova Scotia. Annapolis, now known as Annapolis Royal, is the oldest city in Canada, first settled by the French in 1604. This carrier cover is postmarked by a red Boston CDS, with the 10¢+1¢ postage paying the standard letter rate plus carrier fee. The 10¢ stamp is the scarce premiere gravure or first design of the issue. The cover was backstamped at Annapolis on December 3, 1861.

Figure 17-40 shows an attractive use of the 1861 3¢ pink-on-buff government stamped envelope with two 3¢ and one 1¢ stamps added to make up the 10¢ rate. This cover was mailed at Salem, Massachusetts, on March 3 (1862) and addressed to Westport, Nova Scotia. Westport is located on a tiny island at the extreme southwestern tip of Nova Scotia. The cover has a red exchange marking, probably applied at Boston, and was backstamped with an oval receiving mark at Halifax, Nova Scotia.

Figure 17-41 illustrates an example of the special 5¢ packet rate that was in effect for mail via Boston to Nova Scotia and the other Maritime provinces. This rate has a curious history, and little is definitely known about the reason for it.

As of the July 6, 1851, postal agreement, packet mail from the United States to Nova Scotia was handled like other outgoing ship mail. Postage was 3¢, to be prepaid, to the port of departure. The British packet rate and any inland provincial rate was to be collected upon delivery. It could not be prepaid. The combined packet-plus-inland rate was 5d (8½¢) if the letter was addressed to Halifax and 8d if addressed to a destination beyond Halifax.

For some as yet unexplained reason, between June 20 and November 21, 1854, the U.S rate to the port for packet mail to Nova Scotia was raised to 5¢ [16:28]. This rate remained in force until January 1, 1868, when the packet rate was abolished. One explanation that has been advanced for the 1854 increase is that it was changed to bring it into line with the U.S. inland rate that was charged on British mail.

The folded letter sheet in Figure 17-41 was mailed at Baltimore where it received a March 31 (1862) blue CDS. It is endorsed, "Pr Mail Steamer America/Via Boston." The letter was most likely carried overland to Boston. Ship transport between Northern ports was at a premium during that time, as noted in the contents of the letter sheet, a portion of which is quoted:

> "Your order will have our attention as soon as Freight can be had either direct or via Boston such has been the demand by our Government for vessels to take troops and supplies south that our Steamers and Packets trading between this and Boston have been taken off and we now are depending on transient vessels which are scarce and Freights advanced to northern Ports . . ."

The letter sheet was carried by Cunard packet *America*, departing Boston on April 2, 1862, and arriving at Halifax on April 4, 1862, as attested by a backstamp dated the same day. The Halifax exchange office, or the postal agent aboard the Cunard packet, marked a large "5," for collection of 5 pence upon delivery. Although Nova Scotia converted to decimal currency in 1860, the old pence markings continued to be used for some time.

On May 1, 1862, the 8½¢ packet rate between Halifax and Boston was raised to 10¢. This did not affect the 5¢-to-the-port U.S. rate, but did result in letters sent by the packet route to be marked with a higher rate when addressed to Halifax. The additional 1½¢ accrued to the Halifax Post Office. Letters addressed beyond Halifax remained at the previous rate of 13½¢ (8d) for combined packet and inland postage, and the Halifax office received no additional fee.

This special packet rate between Boston and the Maritime provinces does not seem to be covered in any of the postal conventions, and the first official mention of it that has been located was in a Boston Post Office rate table dated November 1, 1856. Covers showing the rate do exist for earlier dates [16:29].

The USM&POA first cites the service in its August 1863 issue and describes it as follows:

> "Steamers of the Cunard line sail from Boston twice each month, touching at Halifax, and when letters are sent by that conveyance for Nova Scotia, Newfoundland, Cape Breton and Prince Edward Island, the U.S. postage is 5 cents the single rate, to be prepaid. The inland rate is collected upon delivery. On newspapers by this route, the postage is two cents each."

This announcement continued to appear each month until December 1867. The following issue listed only the 10¢ rate for all letters in accordance with the postal arrangement with the new Canadian Commonwealth.

A scarce combination of an 1861 12¢ and three 1¢ stamps to make up the 15¢ Pacific coast rate to Nova Scotia is shown in **Figure 17-42**. This cover originated at Stockton, California, on March 10, 1863, and was transported overland through Maine and New Brunswick to Nova Scotia, where it was backstamped at Amhurst on April 11, 1863, and again at Truro on April 13, 1863. From there it was delivered to its destination, a town with the picturesque name of Little Harlow Mountain. The cover is marked with a red "U.STATES" in an enclosed arc and was possibly applied at the Calais, Maine, exchange office.

Figure 17-43 shows a cover mailed after a reduction in rate. On April 1, 1868, the postal services of Canada, New Brunswick and Nova Scotia became integrated as a result of the previous July's confederation. The letter rate between the United States and Canada was now 6¢ if prepaid, for any distance, and 10¢ if not paid. Partial pay-

Figure 17-41. Special U.S. rate to British packet between Boston and Halifax, Nova Scotia. The 5¢ in stamps paid the U.S. inland postage. The cover bears a Baltimore, Maryland, blue "MAR 31" CDS to Halifax via Boston. It is marked "5" in black for collection upon delivery of 5d (8½¢) for packet postage. The cover was backstamped at Halifax on April 4, 1862.

Figure 17-42. The 15¢ rate for distances over 3,000 miles or Pacific coast origin was paid with a 12¢ (Scott 69) and three 1¢ stamps. The cover was sent from Stockton, California, March 10, 1863, to Little Harlow Mountain, Pictou, Nova Scotia. It bears an exchange office marking and was backstamped at Amherst, Nova Scotia on April 11, 1863, and at Truro, Nova Scotia, on April 13.

Figure 17-43. An example of the reduced 6¢ rate from Boston, Massachusetts, to Pictou, Nova Scotia. The rate, effective April 1868, was paid by an 1861 5¢ Jefferson plus a 1¢ Franklin. The cover was stamped with receiving marks on reverse. Halifax on July 26 and Pictou on July 27, 1869. (C.W. Christian collection)

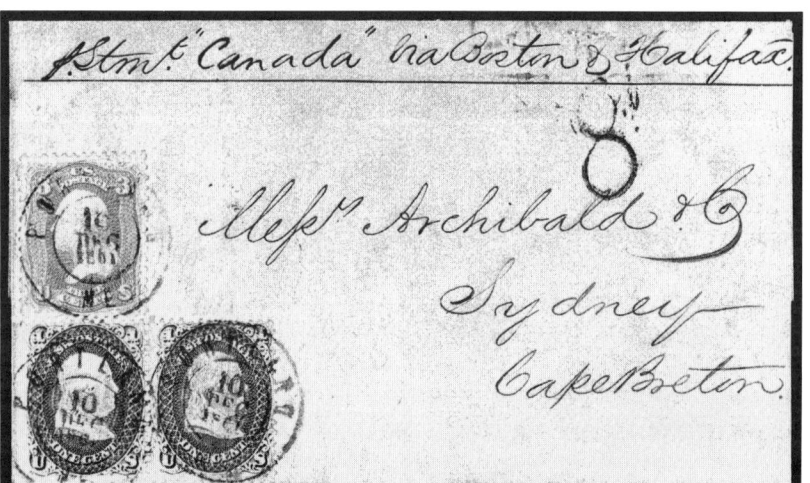

Figure 17-44. Cape Breton Island (Nova Scotia) from Portland, Maine, dated December 10, 1861. The stamps pay the 5¢ U.S. inland rate to packet for Halifax. The cover is endorsed to be sent by steamer *Canada* via Boston and Halifax. It was rated 8d for collection of Nova Scotia and packet postage.

ment was not recognized. This cover was mailed from Boston (date not legible) to Pictou, Nova Scotia. Three receiving marks are shown on the reverse: Halifax, dated July 26, 1869; Pictou, dated July 27; and one indistinct marking also dated July 27. The 6¢ rate is made up by single copies of the 1¢ Franklin and the 5¢ Jefferson of the 1861 issue.

Use to Cape Breton Island with the 1¢ Franklin included in the postage is difficult to find. **Figure 17-44** shows an example. The 3¢+1¢+1¢ franking pays for the U.S. internal rate from Portland, Maine, to Boston, where the cover was placed aboard a British packet to Halifax. The cover is endorsed "pStm^r 'Canada' Via Boston & Halifax." It is addressed to Sydney, Cape Breton. The stamps are canceled with strikes of the Portland CDS dated December 10, 1861. The cover was carried to Halifax by the Cunard steamer *Canada*, which departed Boston on December 11 and arrived at Halifax on December 13, 1861. Since the final destination was beyond Halifax, the cover was rated collect 8d.

Newfoundland and Prince Edward Island

Covers to both of these provinces are scarce, and when the requirement is added for use of the 1861 Franklin, examples become very scarce. Unfortunately, the author has not been able to find any examples to illustrate such use.

Vancouver's Island and British Columbia

The postal service of Vancouver's Island is possibly unique among the British colonies. During its entire existence as a crown colony from 1849 to 1866, it had no postal regulations, nor were the rates of postage ever fixed by legislative acts of the colonial government. The mail system to a large extent piggy-backed on the service of the U.S. Post Office and the express companies, such as Wells, Fargo and Co., that were indispensable to the western territories during the early years. The post offices regularly stocked U.S. stamps, and the majority of letters that departed from Vancouver's Island during the early 1860s had their postage paid with U.S. stamps and a handstamp marking from the colonial post office showing that internal postage had been paid.

Vancouver's Island and British Columbia were separated from the rest of British North America by 2,000 miles of almost impassable terrain, and there were no scheduled overland or sea routes in existence for the transport of mail. The only way mail could be exchanged on a regular basis was via the U.S. Post Office. This dependency resulted in a close relationship, and the establishment of procedures and agreements to effect the needed mail services. These arrangements were quasi-official and sufficed to provide a reasonably satisfactory international mail service for Vancouver's Island and British Columbia.

Although Vancouver's Island (later called Vancouver Island) and British Columbia were separate crown colonies until 1866, they operated very much in unison with respect to the handling of mail. For most cases there is no reason to consider them separately.

Until 1849, Vancouver's Island was an outpost of the Hudson's Bay Co. with a population of a few hundred people whose livelihood depended mostly on company activities. Mail service was provided free of charge by the company to all employees and residents. "Strangers" were also accommodated, but they had to pay a fee of $1 for a letter weighing ½ ounce and 25¢ for each additional ½ ounce. The mails were carried by the infrequent fur brigades, by canoes and by the once-a-year supply ship that arrived from England.

On January 13, 1849, Great Britain formally declared Vancouver's Island a crown colony and appointed a governor to represent the Crown and to conduct colonial business. At the same time, a grant for a period of 10 years was given to Hudson's Bay Co. to be the proprietors of the island. No postmaster was appointed, but the postal situation of the colony was given a boost by the inauguration of the U.S. mail steamship service from New York to San Francisco via the Isthmus of Panama, and the extension of this service to Astoria, Oregon, at the mouth of the Columbia River. There was now a way to get mail into a regular and reasonably reliable system by transporting mail by ship to Astoria, and from there to San Francisco, where it would enter the U.S. mails.

The coincident discovery of gold in California and the influx of thousands of gold-seekers and businessmen brought about the establishment of many private express services. When gold was also discovered in British Columbia in 1858, many of these express companies expanded their services into that area and provided mail service into the interior. The discovery of gold also elevated the importance of British Columbia. It was declared a crown colony in 1858, with the governor of Vancouver's Island, James Douglas, also acting as the governor of British Columbia.

The colonial legislature consistently refused to consider requests to establish a comprehensive post office department and postal service, citing the great expense that would be involved. They contended that the express companies and the U.S. services were adequately

Figure 17-45. Victoria, Vancouver's Island, to Princeton, Canada West. The ornate oval handstamp in black paid Vancouver's Island internal 5¢ postage. The cover was carried to San Francisco, where it entered the U.S. mails and received a NOV/25/1861 CDS. It traveled overland via Chicago to Canada, at the 15¢ rate. The cover received a CHICAGO/15 exchange marking and black PAID in oval handstamp. A PRINCETON/C.W./DE 21/1861 receiving mark is on the reverse.
(Walter Cole collection)

taking care of the problem. However, there did exist a postal service that just sort of grew in response to what was needed. Postmasters were designated, frequently as additional duties for government officials. For example, the postmaster at Victoria, was also the harbormaster and acted as the chief postmaster for the entire colony.

The story of the development of the postal services of Vancouver's Island and British Columbia, and its interaction with the U.S. postal system, is extremely interesting. Space here will allow only a few highlights of the complex and ever-changing mail situation to be recounted. Alfred S. Deaville's *The Colonial Postal Systems and Postage Stamps of Vancouver Island and British Columbia, 1849-1871* [17] is an excellent source for philatelic facts and historical background, and has provided much of the information for this section.

The beginning of the 1860s found the postal arrangements at Vancouver's Island in some disarray. The gold fields had petered out, and the economy of the colony was at a low ebb. The postmaster at Victoria, John D'Ewes, had absconded with most of the proceeds collected during his stewardship, leaving only $1.15 in the post office till. He kept no records of his transactions, and the colony treasurer, who was supposed to oversee the office, also engaged in improper activities and was subsequently indicted and convicted of fraud. These occurrences were a severe loss to a treasury that was on the brink of insolvency.

In 1860, the first postage stamp was issued for use by British Columbia (B.C.) and Vancouver's Island. It was a 2½ pence (5¢) adhesive and paid the single colonial domestic postage rate. It also paid the inland postage on outgoing letters that would use U.S. stamps to pay for the balance of the necessary postage. The stamps were somewhat unique in that they bore the names of both of the separate crown colonies of Vancouver's Island and British Columbia, and were available in each of them to pay the colonial postage. The money from the sale of these stamps went into the treasury of the colony of sale. In the history of the postage stamps of the world, this is a most unusual situation. It probably has never been duplicated elsewhere.

Covers showing the combined use of the stamps of the United States and B.C./V.I. stamps of 1860 and 1865 can be found, but they are scarce.

The postmaster of Victoria, Vancouver's Island, reported that for 1863, the outgoing and incoming letters for Vancouver's Island numbered about 60,000. About 45 percent were carried by the private express companies. This was in spite of the large additional expense of sending a letter by express. The reliability of the express companies was such that many individuals felt that the extra money was well-spent. A letter carried by Wells, Fargo required 5¢ for the colonial postage, which always was to be prepaid, 3¢ for U.S. postage (plus any domestic or foreign postage beyond the Pacific coast), plus the express charge, which would be 25¢ for a letter going to or from Victoria and could be $1 or more for towns in the interior of British Columbia.

Figure 17-45 illustrates the use of the U.S. mails to transport a letter from Victoria, Vancouver's Island, to Canada West. The prepayment of 5¢ internal postage for Vancouver's Island was shown by a black oval handstamp, and the U.S. postage of 15¢ for a letter originating on the Pacific coast was paid by a combination of 1¢, 3¢ and 10¢ stamps of the 1861 issue. The stamps were most likely affixed at Victoria, where the cover was prepaid to destination. The letter was then carried by closed bag aboard a steamer to San Francisco. For a period of time this service was provided to Vancouver's Island at no charge by the U.S. Post Office. At San Francisco, the cover received a CDS dated November 25, 1861, and the letter was dispatched overland to Chicago, where it received a red circular exchange office marking denoting 15¢ paid, and a black PAID in oval handstamp. From Chicago, it completed its journey to its destination at Princeton, Canada West, where it was backstamped December 21, 1861.

It is interesting to note here that the new 1861 stamps and stamped envelopes arrived at San Francisco, and were advertised on October 9, 1861, to be exchanged for the old style of stamps and envelopes up to October 15, 1861. After that date, the old designs would no longer be accepted for postage. Concurrently, Wells, Fargo advertised that it would exchange its franked envelopes for the new style, also until October 15. Evidently a supply of the new stamps was also sold to the Victoria post office for its use. Some of the stamps from that original shipment probably ended up on this cover.

The post office at Victoria sold handstamped envelopes for public use as colonial postage-paid envelopes. The cost was 6¢ each: 5¢ for postage and 1¢ for the envelope. The post office also serviced, at 5¢ each, the thousands of U.S. government stamped envelopes that carried the Wells, Fargo or other express company franks. This ensured that the Vancouver's Island postal service received its postage on the privately carried letters. Like the United States, it authorized, or at least condoned, the private carrying of mail as long as government postage was paid in addition to the express carrier's fee.

Figure 17-46 illustrates two of the handstamps used at Victoria post office to show prepayment of the 5¢ domestic colonial rate. The PAID in oval handstamp shown at the top in Figure 17-46 was used primarily as a prepayment marking until 1860. After that date, it was generally used as a canceling device on the Vancouver's

Figure 17-46. Handstamps of the Victoria Post Office at Vancouver's Island. The application of either of these markings served to indicate that the 5¢ domestic postage had been paid. After 1860, the device shown at top was generally used as a canceling device.

Island stamps, and only occasionally as a franking device. It was struck in both blue and black. Covers with U.S. stamps were forwarded without canceling the stamps.

The handstamp shown at the bottom in Figure 17-46 is the franking design more commonly seen on 1861-66 covers. This ornate oval handstamp was usually applied vertically at the upper left of an envelope, and the additional U.S. stamps that might be required were placed over the marking, partially obscuring it. It is usually struck in blue. Although it is known to have been used as a cancellation, that type of use is considered to be accidental [17:167].

Figure 17-47 shows an attractive cover to Manchester, England, posted at Victoria, where it was marked with the oval "Post Office/Victoria V.I." handstamp in blue, showing payment of internal postage. The cover is a U.S. 3¢ government stamped envelope with the printed paid frank of Wells, Fargo & Co. Twenty-one cents in additional postage was added to make up the 24¢ cent rate to England. The postage stamps were probably applied at the Wells, Fargo office and, as usual, overlap most of the Victoria handstamp. The cover was carried by

Figure 17-47. A Victoria Post Office frank in blue oval, partially obscured by a pair of U.S. 10¢ and a single 1¢ stamp on a 3¢ entire Wells, Fargo franked envelope (Scott U34). The cover was carried outside the mails to New York. It received a red NEW YORK BR. PKT./PAID 19 marking crediting Great Britain 19¢. The stamps cover the rate to Manchester, England. The auction description gives 1864 as the year date, possibly determined from a backstamp or contents.
(Christie's, New York, auction photo)

Figure 17-48. Rare and late use of the 5¢ rose (Scott 5) Vancouver's Island stamp to pay internal postage in combination with an additional 20¢ in U.S. postage to pay the rate to England. This pink on buff entire (Scott U59) with Wells, Fargo frank was carried outside the mails. It was entered into the mails at New York City, where it was marked with a 3¢ credit to Great Britain and forwarded by American packet. London arrival stamp in red is dated August 8, 1866. (Courtesy of Christie's, New York)

Wells, Fargo outside the mails to New York City, where the stamps were canceled with the distinctive New York "rosette within a rosette" foreign-mail marking. The cover also received a red exchange-office postmark showing a credit of 19¢ to Great Britain via British packet.

Figure 17-48 shows a rare combination of an 1865 Vancouver's Island 5¢ rose, paying the Vancouver's Island internal rate, with 24¢ in U.S. postage on a Wells, Fargo franked envelope to pay the 24¢ rate to England. This too was carried outside the mails to New York City, where it received a red "New York Amer Pkt/ 3" exchange marking crediting Great Britain for 3¢ for its internal postage. A London arrival is indicated by a red receiving mark dated August 8, 1866.

Just three months later, on November 17, 1866, Vancouver's Island and British Columbia joined together under the name British Columbia, primarily to eliminate the cost of duplicative government functions. In 1870, a postal convention was signed with the United States, and for the first time, British Columbia possessed a documented agreement for the exchange of mail. The terms of the convention paralleled those of the existing U.S.-Canadian agreement. The following year, on July 20, 1871, the crown colony joined the Canadian Confederation as one of the provinces of the Dominion of Canada, and the somewhat unorthodox and extremely interesting postal procedures of the colony faded into history.

St. Pierre & Miquelon

St. Pierre & Miquelon are two groups of small islands about 20 miles south of Newfoundland. The islands belong to France and are the sole remnants of the once extensive French colonial holdings in North America. Their proximity to the Grand Banks fishing areas, and the fact that possession of the islands retained for France valuable fishing rights, make them extremely important to French commerce.

The islands served as a base for the French fishing fleet and also for French naval vessels that guarded the fishing fleet. St. Pierre is the provincial capital. No direct mail service was available between St. Pierre and France. During the early years, some mail was transported on an irregular basis aboard fishing vessels and naval vessels arriving from or returning to France, or making port calls at Newfoundland or Nova Scotia. The post office at St. Pierre was established in 1854, and from that time, the postal markings of the office give some clues to the routes and charges for mail to and from the islands [18:2].

The primary route for mail during the 1860s was via the British Maritime Provinces. Mail was sent through Newfoundland or direct to Nova Scotia, and from there to destination. Scheduled mail service was maintained between St. John's, Newfoundland, and Nova Scotia. In the summer months the Nova Scotia port was Sydney, Cape Breton Island, and in the winter it was Halifax.

Most of the mail from the United States to St. Pierre was routed via the Boston-Halifax British Cunard packets (see the Nova Scotia section of this chapter for a discussion of this service). Infrequently, mail was routed overland through New Brunswick to Nova Scotia. Although the overland route was less expensive, it was considerably slower and consequently seldom used.

Because of the small population in the early years, St. Pierre & Miquelon is a difficult destination for postal-history collectors to acquire. The only cover showing the use of the 1¢ Franklin during the 1860s that the author has recorded is shown in **Figure 17-49**. This folded letter was mailed at New York City on August 6, 1862. It was endorsed "per Steamer Asia/fm Boston via Halifax." The

U.S. inland postage of 5¢ is paid by two 1¢ and a single 3¢ of the 1861 issue. It was forwarded to Boston, placed aboard the Cunard British packet *Asia* and carried to Halifax. The ship agent or the Halifax office marked the letter with a bold manuscript "8" to indicate 8 pence (13.5¢) due for the packet and inland postage to a Nova Scotia destination beyond Halifax. Although Nova Scotia had officially changed to the the decimal system, rate markings are found both in cents and pence during this period. Sometimes both systems were used on a single cover, as is the case here.

At Sydney, Cape Breton (summer route to St. Pierre & Miquelon), it is probable that the black "10" handstamp was applied to show the collect postage that was due to Nova Scotia from St. Pierre for transport to the island. At St. Pierre the cover was marked "1 25" in French-style script for 1.25-franc collection. This is equivalent to about 23½¢ U.S. The division of the postage due is not certain, but it would be reasonable for 13½¢ to be remitted to Nova Scotia for its service to Sydney, and the remaining 10¢ to pay the packet postage to the island. This 10¢ packet rate is listed by J.J. MacDonald [19:228] as the standard rate for Nova Scotia to St. Pierre-Miquelon. Any inland postage at the islands would be in addition to this. It is not known how the accounts for unpaid postage were handled between St. Pierre and the Maritime Provinces. The letter is backstamped with a Boston British packet marking and a transit marking at Sydney.

Mexico

The number of letters exchanged between the United States and Mexico during the decade of the 1860s was relatively small. There was only a limited commercial and consular correspondence, and there was no large exchange of populations such as had occurred with Europe. The internal postal rates of Mexico were prohibitively high, and the generally low income of the average person made the service too expensive for most communications. In addition, the literacy rate was very low. All of these factors contributed to few letters and consequently a scarcity of surviving covers from this period.

In 1860, there was no postal agreement between Mexico and the United States. Mail was exchanged primarily by ship, with the 10¢ ship rate being paid in advance and any internal Mexican postage being collected upon delivery. Most covers to Mexican destinations show the postage paid by a single 10¢ stamp, and covers showing the use of the 1¢ Franklin of 1861 are very rare.

Effective July 4, 1862, a postal convention with Mexico was announced [20:159]. The agreement did not make much difference in the way mail was exchanged, but did put the reciprocal postal relations between the countries on a solid documented basis. Its major provisions were: Letters to Mexico were to be prepaid per single ½-ounce rate with 3¢ internal U.S. postage and 7¢ sea postage to a Mexico port. Internal Mexican postage would be collected upon delivery. If the letter was sent overland across the Mexican border, only the 3¢ internal U.S. postage was to be prepaid for transport to the border. The internal Mexico postage would be collected at destination. There were to be no accounts kept between the countries, and each country retained the postage it collected. No exchange offices were specified.

No other changes in the mail procedures occurred during the 1860s except for the adoption of a decimal monetary system on April 8, 1864, which replaced the real

Figure 17-49. St. Pierre & Miquelon from New York City, August 6, 1862. The cover was sent by the British packet *Asia* from Boston to Halifax, Nova Scotia, to Sydney, Cape Breton Island, to destination. The 5¢ in stamps paid the U.S. postage to the packet. The cover was marked 8 (pence) for packet plus Nova Scotia inland postage, and 10(¢) for sea postage from Sydney to destination. The manuscript "1 25" (1.25 franc) due marking was for collection at St. Pierre. The cover was backstamped with a Boston British packet marking and Sydney transit marking. (Steve Ivy Auction photo)

Figure 17-50. Martinez, California, to Mazatlan, Mexico, dated April 17, 1863. The 10¢ rate paid the U.S. internal postage of 3¢ and the 7¢ sea postage. The cover was marked at Mazatlan 1 real for collection. This is a rare use to a destination on the Pacific coast of Mexico.

Figure 17-51. Twice-forwarded letter mailed at Williamsburgh, New York, on October 25 (year date not legible), to Vera Cruz, Mexico, and endorsed for routing via Havana. It was marked "24" in red for credit to Great Britain, handstamped 2 reales at Vera Cruz for collection and forwarded to a new address at Huatusco. It was forwarded again to San Andres Tuxtla via Tlactotalpan, where it was handstamped with a boxed "Tlactotalpan/ Franco" marking and another 2 (reales) for collection of additional forwarding postage. Original postage was paid by 30¢+3¢+1¢ of the 1861 issue. The 10¢ was retained by the United States for transport to Havana. (Robert A. Siegel Auction Galleries)

with the peso. One peso equaled 100 centavos, and 1 centavo was equal to 1¢ U.S.

The primary mode of mail transportation continued to be by ship. Scheduled U.S. mail steamships made regular stops at several of the Mexican ports. On the eastern seaboard, Vera Cruz was the main port of call, and on the Pacific, mail steamers called at Acapulco, Manzanillo and Mazatlan. Occasionally, mail addressed to a Mexican port city never entered the Mexican mail system. The letters could be picked up from the packet by the addressee or his agent, and at times, mail was received by an American consul for later delivery.

Figure 17-50 illustrates a cover from Martinez, California, dated April 17, 1863, with the 10¢ rate paid to Mazatlan, Mexico. The letter was probably carried by a coastal mail steamer on the route between San Francisco and Panama. At Mazatlan, the cover entered the Mexican mail system and was marked 1 real (12½¢) for collection. This rare example is the only cover to a Mexican destination on the Pacific coast showing the use of the 1¢ Franklin that this writer has ever seen.

Another rare usage is pictured in **Figure 17-51**. This cover originated at Williamsburgh, New York, on October 25 (year date is undecipherable). It was addressed to Vera Cruz, with endorsement to be sent via Havana. The cover was marked at New York City "24" in red to indicate that Great Britain was being credited 24¢ for its share of the prepaid 34¢ postage. The 34¢ rate establishes that the year of mailing must have been 1861 or 1862 since that rate stopped in May 1863. Ten cents was retained by the United States for carriage to Havana, there connecting with a British Royal Mail steamship bound for Veracruz. At this point the analysis of the cover becomes less straightforward. Although the year date on the cover is illegible, it was sent during the Civil War, and during that period, mail to Mexico by American packets was not as reliable as the long-established service of the British Post Office. The sender, to better ensure that his

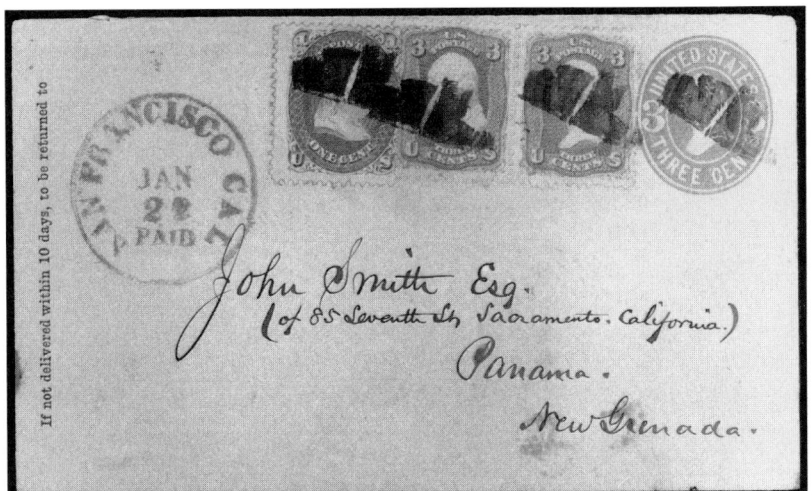

Figure 17-52. San Francisco to Panama, January 22 (year unknown); 1868 or later use. The 3¢ pink (Scott U59) Nesbitt envelope with two 3¢ F grills (94) and a 1¢ Franklin paid the ship rate of 10¢. The cover was hand-delivered at Panama, and never entered the postal system of New Granada (United States of Colombia).

letter would arrive promptly at its destination, was willing to pay an additional 24¢ to have the British mails take it on the last leg of the ocean route.

The internal postal rate for Mexico at this time was 1 real (12.5¢) for a letter weighing less than ½ ounce up to a distance of 16 leagues (approximately 50 miles). Beyond that distance, the rate was 2 reales. The rate progression was in quarter-ounces.

It can be assumed that the cover was marked at the Vera Cruz receiving office with a black "2" for collection of 2 reales (25¢) for Mexican inland postage. Since it was addressed for local delivery, the charge would normally be 1 real. It is probable that the Veracruz post office was advised by the person picking up the mail for Señores Stein and Sartorius that the addressee, Don Felipe Botleger, was no longer at Veracruz and had moved to Huatusco (about 75 miles inland). The post office then forwarded the letter, and this would account for the larger collection amount being charged. At Huatusco, it was found that the addressee had traveled on to San Andres Tuxtla, a town about 75 miles southeast of Veracruz. It was then forwarded via Tlactotalpan, where it received a boxed "Tlactotalpan/Franco" handstamp. Somewhere during its journey, the cover received an additional 2 reales collection mark, possibly for additional forwarding postage. Hopefully, the cover finally caught up with Señor Botleger at San Andres Tuxtla.

The above two covers are the only covers to Mexico with use of the 1¢ 1861 Franklin recorded by the author. Dale Pulver, a respected student and author on the philately of Mexico, assisted in the analyses of these covers, and has advised that he has seen two additional covers using the 1857 1¢ stamp as part of the postage. Those covers were addressed to Vera Cruz, but never entered the Mexican mail system.

Without question, examples of mail from the United States to Mexico during the 1860s are scarce without regard to what stamps were used to make up the postage, and when the additional requirement is made for the use of the 1861 1¢ Franklin, such covers are definitely rare.

Central and South America
New Granada (Colombia)

Figure 17-52 illustrates an example of a letter mailed under the provisions of Section 8 of the Postal Act of 1864, which provided for mail to countries where no postal arrangements were in force. The act provided for a 10¢ ship rate for a single letter addressed to, or received from, countries with whom the United States had no postal conventions and when conveyed by vessels regularly engaged in the transportation of the mails [1:165]. This particular cover was mailed at San Francisco and received a large 33mm magenta PAID CDS dated "JAN 22." Use of this distinctive marking has been recorded by John Mahoney, the author of a comprehensive listing of San Francisco postmarks [21], for several dates in the early 1870s. The cover is a buff 3¢ government stamped envelope (Scott U59) with additional postage paid by a pair of 3¢ F grills and a 1¢ Franklin, for a total of 10¢. Although there is no year date, the grilled stamps establish that the year of mailing was 1868 or later. The distinctive cancellation is known to have been used during 1868-69 [21:32].

The letter was addressed to a John Smith, Esq., which evidently was a common name at that time, as now, for under the name is written "(of 85 Seventh St, Sacramento. California)." With that additional information, there should have been no difficulty in determining which "John Smith" was the addressee. The cover most likely was

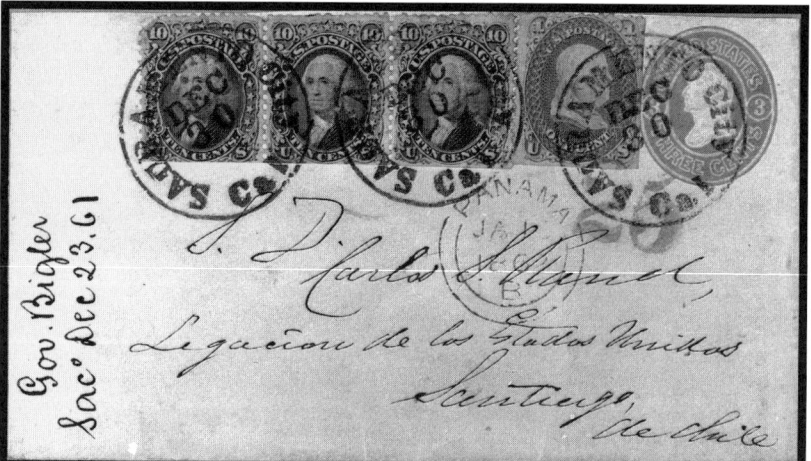

Figure 17-53. Sacramento, California, December 30, 1861, to Santiago, Chile. The 3¢ entire (Scott U34) with additional three 10¢ and one 1¢ stamps prepaid the 34¢ rate to Chile. The cover was carried from San Francisco to Panama by American packet, and from Panama to Santiago by British packet. It bears a British transit marking dated January 13, 1862, at Panama. The cover was handstamped with large "25" in red. (C.W. Christian collection)

sent via one of the scheduled mail ships of the Pacific Mail Steamship Line vessels operating between San Francisco and Panama. When it arrived at the Port of Panama, it apparently was delivered directly to the addressee or his agent. There is no evidence that the cover ever entered any foreign-mail system.

At the time of mailing of this cover, New Granada was actually the United States of Colombia, and the present country of Panama was one of its states. The name New Granada, by which the area had been known since the 16th century, continued in popular use for some years following the formation of the United States of Colombia in 1861.

Chile

Figure 17-53 shows a cover originating at Sacramento City, California, on December 30 (1861), and addressed to the American Légation in Santiago, Chile. The cover is docketed "Gov. Bigler/Sac° Dec 23.61," which probably identifies the writer and date of the contents. The cover was carried from San Francisco by an American coastal mail steamer to the British Consul at Panama, who acted as the mail agent for Great Britain. It was then transferred to a British packet for the remainder of the trip. The 3¢ government stamped envelope has additional postage of three 10¢ and one 1¢ stamps to make up the standard 34¢ single rate to Chile.

Government stamped envelopes were frequently used for correspondence by individuals residing in the Pacific states. The dependence on private express companies for the transmission of a large part of the mail, and the requirement that letters transported by private carriers be enclosed in government envelopes, made these envelopes a useful part of a writer's inventory. From the prepaid 34¢ postage, the United States retained 10¢ for the ship rate to Panama and credited Great Britain with the 24¢ balance. The cover is handstamped with a large red "25" (25 centavos equivalent to 25¢ U.S.) of the type used at Santiago to denote postage due. A British transit marking dated January 13, 1862, was applied at Panama.

In Conclusion

The decade of the 1860s saw great changes in the way U.S. mail to foreign destinations was handled. The time for transmission to destinations was markedly reduced, the reliability and the safety of mail steamships increased substantially, and the procedures for processing and accounting for the mails between countries were vastly simplified. From 1861 to 1870, the volume of foreign mail, as stated in the annual reports of the postmasters general, increased from approximately 3,684,000 letters to 18,359,000 letters, an increase of about 500 percent. During the same period, the average cost for the transmission of a foreign letter was reduced by about 75 percent, and the average time for the Atlantic crossing decreased substantially.

It was a pivotal period for this most interesting philatelic specialty, and certainly a period that saw political changes and military conflicts on a worldwide basis that had profound effects on the distribution of mail. This chapter has attempted to show some of those changes, and the philatelic importance and interest of a "foreign cover."

References

1. Hargest, George. *History of Letter Post Communi-*

cation Between the United States and Europe, 1845-1875. Second Edition, 1975. Quarterman Publications reprint.

2. Starnes, Charles J. *U.S. Letter Rates to Foreign Destinations, 1847 to GPU-UPU*. Published by Leonard J. Hartmann. 1989.

3. Hubbard, Walter and Richard F. Winter. *North Atlantic Mail Sailings, 1840-75*. U.S. Philatelic Classics Society Inc. 1988.

4. Winter, Richard F. "Exchange Marks on Trans-Atlantic Mails," *Postmarks and Cancellations*. The Philatelic Foundation Seminar Series, No. 3. New York. 1992.

5. Salles, Raymond. *La Poste Maritime Française Historique et Catalogue*. Volume 4, *Les Paquebots de l'Atlantique Nord*. Paris, France. 1971.

6. Winter, Richard F. and Wolfgang Diesner. "The Beginning Period of Bremen Line Mail Service, New Insights into the Bremen Postal Arrangement." *Chronicle*, No. 149. February 1991.

7. Conzelmann, Heinrich. "Accounting on Earliest North German Lloyd Cover from the United States to Württemburg Via Bremen." *Chronicle*, No. 165. February 1995.

8. Winter, Richard F. *Trans-Atlantic Mails (Steamship)*. Exhibit, 1988. Available from the Exhibition Photocopy Committee of the U.S. Philatelic Classics Society.

9. Hargest, George E., Editor. "Changes in Color of the Boxed Aachen Marking." *Chronicle*, No. 76. November 1972.

10. Boggs, Winthrop S. *The Postage Stamps and Postal History of Canada*. Quarterman Publications reprint. 1974.

11. *United States Mail and Post Office Assistant*. Collectors Club of Chicago reprint. 1975.

12. McDonald, Susan M. *Cross Border Mails: United States and British North America to 1875*. Exhibit, 1988. Available from the Exhibition Photocopy Committee of the U.S. Philatelic Classics Society.

13. Boggs, Winthrop S. *The Postage Stamps and Postal History of Canada*. Volume II. 1946.

14. Norona, Delf, Editor. *Cyclopedia of United States Postmarks and Postal History*. Quarterman Publications reprint. 1975.

15. McDonald, Susan M. "The Cover Corner." *Chronicle*, No. 69. February 1971.

16. McDonald, Susan M. "Cunard Packet Mail Between Nova Scotia and the United States." *Postal History Journal*. January 1972.

17. Deaville, Alfred S. *The Colonial Postal Systems and Postage Stamps of Vancouver Island and British Columbia, 1849-1871*. Quarterman Publications 1979 reprint of the original 1928 edition published by the Provincial Library, British Columbia.

18. Stone, Robert G. "St. Pierre." *Postal History Journal*. Vol. 14, No. 3. September 1970.

19. MacDonald J.J. *The Nova Scotia Post, Its Offices, Masters, and Marks 1700-1867*. The Unitrade Press, Toronto, Ontario, Canada. 1985.

20. *Report of the Postmaster General for 1862*. Reprinted by Theron Wierenga. 1977.

21. Mahoney, John M. *San Francisco Postal Markings, 1847-1900*. Vol. 8, La Posta Monograph Series. La Posta Publications. 1992.

The United States 1¢ Franklin 1861-67

CHAPTER 18

Monetary and Revenue Use

Monetary Use

Throughout the years, postage stamps have been used in lieu of money. Even today, advertisements frequently include a phrase, "Postage stamps of equal value accepted in payment." However, the 1861 stamps have the unique distinction of being the only postage stamps ever to be authorized by the U.S. government for use as legal tender.

In the mid-1800s, coins of all denominations were relatively scarce by today's standards. Even foreign coins were legally used until shortly before the Civil War. Prices for gold and silver that made it profitable to change coins into bullion almost guaranteed that coins would continue in short supply. Paper money was backed only by the banks that printed it and was viewed with some distrust, but coins of gold, silver and even copper had intrinsic value and were preferred over paper.

The Civil War turned what was a chronic shortage of coins into a complete absence of metal coinage of any type. First, the gold coins disappeared, followed shortly by silver, and finally even the copper and nickel small change vanished into jars, pots and safes. By the end of 1861, banks and the federal government suspended payments in specie, and by the spring of 1862, there was not a coin to be had to purchase even the smallest of items.

The impact on retail business, particularly in the large cities, was considerable. Merchants quickly responded to the crisis and began issuing small tokens embossed with their name and value, or paper coupons with similar information printed on them. These coin substitutes could be redeemed at the place of issue or wherever else a proprietor would accept them. The lack of a guaranteed value everywhere made their use somewhat restricted. Tokens were declared illegal in 1862 by the government, but they continued to be used for many years even though they were a poor substitute for real coins.

Concurrently, individuals began to use postage stamps for small purchases and merchants began to return change in the form of postage stamps. Here was a coin substitute that had an intrinsic value backed by the United States and that was difficult to counterfeit. Recognizing the need for some method of providing legal tender in small values, Salmon P. Chase, Lincoln's secretary of the treasury, proposed the idea of legalizing the use of postage stamps as money. On July 17, 1862, Congress passed an act authorizing the Treasury Department to sell and redeem postage stamps for use as legal tender. This act also prohibited the use of tokens and commercially produced scrip as money. There were two basic problems with this law. No one had bothered to consult with Postmaster General Montgomery Blair regarding the provision of postage stamps for this use, and little previous consideration seems to have been given to the fragile and sticky aspects of using pieces of gummed paper as coin of the realm.

Secretary Chase belatedly advised Blair by writing the following letter on Sunday, July 20, 1862, three days after the new law was passed.

> Sir:
> An Act of the last Congress provides for the use in payments of postage and other stamps of the U. States, and requires that the Secretary of the Treasury furnish them in such amounts as may be required to the Assistant Treasurer and selected designated depositories for the use and to be furnished to persons desiring them in exchange for U. States Notes.
> It has occurred to me that it will be advisable to take from your Department such quantities as may be needed immediately. Say 100,000 to 500,000 and pay for them direct in Treasury Notes, and that it may be expedient to have these stamps prepared without gum and perhaps on thicker paper than present stamps.
> I shall be obliged if you will favor me with your views on these, and any other points which seem to you to be proper to consider.
> As the Act will operate from the 1st. August it is desirable to have some arrangements promptly made.
> S.P. Chase
> Secretary of the Treasury [1:49]

Shortly after the the new law was publicized in the papers, there was a scramble to purchase stamps at the post offices. It is reported that sales in some of the larger urban areas experienced an increase of 700 percent. Stocks of stamps were soon exhausted. New York was selling $15,000 worth of stamps daily to be used as small change.

A byproduct of this act was a law passed on July 16, 1862, which for the first time prohibited the cleaning of cancellations from used stamps with the intent to reuse them. Such actions were considered to be a felony and carried a possible punishment of three years imprisonment and a $1,000 fine (with half of the fine to be paid to an informant). Previous laws had only prohibited the reuse of stamps but not the removal of their cancellations. This new law reflected the increased importance of cancellations now that stamps could be used as money [2:90].

Blair was evidently extremely displeased with the entire situation. In his annual report for 1862, he commented on the law:

> "... the Act ... has greatly embarrassed the depart-

377

ment in the performance of its duties connected with the distribution of postage stamps . . . Nearly the entire excess of stamps sold during the period under notice has been or is now in use as currency. Being ill adapted for circulation, large quantities of them have become so defaced as to be inapplicable to legitimate use for the payment of postage, and evil-disposed persons have availed themselves of the opportunity thus afforded to put into circulation stamps once used for postage, from which the canceling marks have been wholly or partially erased [3:131]."

The postmaster general reacted to the raid on his supply of stamps by writing letters and making announcements concerning the Post Office Department's disapproval of using postage stamps as currency. This culminated with the publication of a directive to his postmasters to cease selling stamps to be used as money, This directive was to be effective on September 20, 1862, and was also published in the October 1862 issue of the *U.S. Mail and Post Office Assistant*. The public was also to be advised that "postage currency" could only be procured from Treasury Department agencies, and not from postmasters [2:94].

Blair's order added to the problems of the users of "stamp money." The fact that they were made from thin paper and soon wore out was one of the major drawbacks to the use of stamps as coins. Another problem was that the gum frequently stuck to fingers and, if damp, to almost anything. A partial answer to these problems was to place the stamps in small envelopes. This decreased the wear and the handling problems somewhat, but added the problem of having to open each envelope and check the contents for agreement with the value printed on the outside. Even with the use of envelopes, stamps wore out and became soiled from constant handing. A better solution was still needed. **Figure 18-1** shows some examples of small envelopes that were privately manufactured to contain stamps and to be used as money for small transactions. The total value of the stamps contained was shown on the front of the envelope, and those envelopes that were furnished by merchants usually had advertising printed on them. Only stamps from the 1861 series were used since all stamps from the previous issues had been demonetized. The smallest denomination

Figure 18-1. Examples of envelopes that were used as small change, particularly during the years of 1862 and 1863. These small envelopes contained unused stamps whose total value was printed on the exterior of the envelopes. The examples without advertising could be purchased at retail stationers, and stamps were then enclosed by the buyer so that the envelope could be used in place of a coin. Those with advertising were provided as change when a purchase was made from the advertised establishment. They then could be reused as legal tender as necessary. Note that the "Mercantile Dining Room" envelope has no amount printed on it. Evidently, stamps to a desired amount would be placed in the envelope, the value would be written on the exterior, and the envelope proferred as change. These small envelopes are illustrated here approximately in their actual sizes. Examples are rare since the stamps were usually removed at some later date, and there was little reason to retain a generally worn small envelope. (Courtesy of David G. Phillips Co. Inc.)

Figure 18-2. Rare examples of "postage money" issued by William Newton & Co., Newport, Rhode Island. The stamps are unused and were trimmed before mounting. The money bills are dated July 4, 1862. (John A. Fox and R.A. Siegel auction photos)

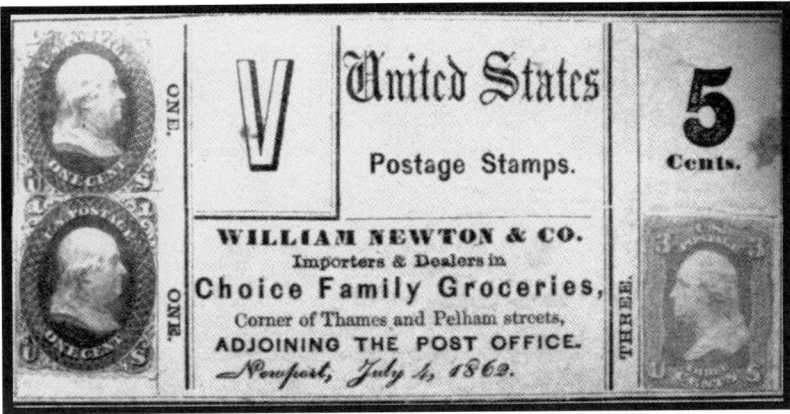

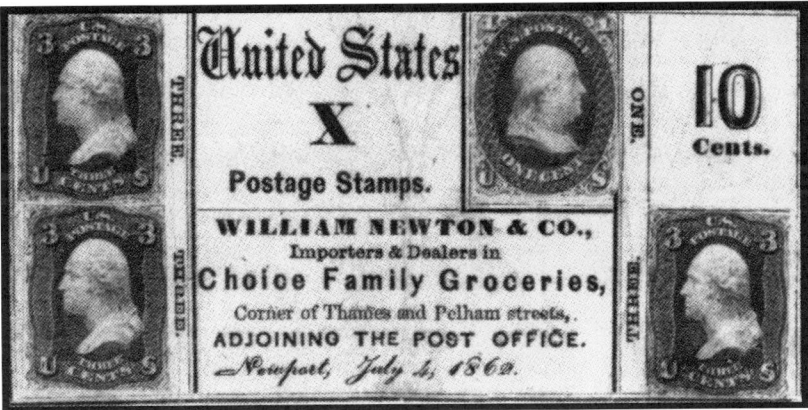

envelope that the author has seen recorded is for a 5¢ value [4:11]. This envelope was printed by O.H. Harpel of Cincinnati; however, almost all of the surviving examples of "envelope coins" were manufactured and used in New York City.

In the meantime, the decision of Blair not to allow the sale, exchange or redemption of stamps was causing friction between the Post Office and Treasury departments. A compromise was finally reached, and in December of 1862 provisions were made for a limited-time redemption of soiled or worn postage stamps that had been used for currency.

In his annual report to the president, dated December 1, 1862, Blair also wrote:

> "The issue of 'postage currency' by the Treasury Department will doubtless soon displace postage stamps from circulation; and although the redemption of stamps sold by postmasters is not required by existing law, in order to protect holders of the same against loss, so far as can be done without detriment to the interests of the department, I have determined to direct postmasters to exchange, for United States notes, under proper regulations, all evidently uncanceled stamps offered them for that purpose."

In New York, the redemption period was to be for one month, December 15, 1862, to January 15, 1863. The January 1863 issue of USM&POA relates that long lines of persons, eager to exchange their "gumbacks," formed each day at the New York Post Office, and that there were more applicants for the exchange than could be handled by the 10 clerks assigned to the task. Requests by the public for Blair to extend the redemption period were denied. He pointed out that the Post Office Department had never supported the idea of using stamps for money, and after the deadline for redemption, the only way to recoup the value of the stamps was to use them as postage.

Even prior to the legalization of postage stamps as currency, some enterprising merchants were pasting stamps on advertising cards and using them as money. Examples of this type of use are rare. **Figure 18-2** shows two stamp money bills that were issued by William Newton & Co. of Newport, Rhode Island. The perforations on the stamps were trimmed before being placed on the bills. The examples illustrate the 5¢ and 10¢ notes. The author has recorded three of these notes, the two shown and another 5¢ note that was illustrated in a Herman Herst article [5:20]. The Herst specimen is slightly different in that it has a larger bottom margin with the printed note, "Unless kept clean these Stamps will be useless for circulation and Post Office purposes."

Overtaking some of the events that have been related in the previous paragraphs were the actions of F.E. Spinner, the U.S. treasurer. Early in this period, Spinner, who is considered to be the father of "postage currency," suggested that postage stamps should be pasted on pieces of treasury paper to make them more resistant to wear. While this idea was never carried into production, it was only a short step to the idea of printing small bills with replicas of the current postal issue on their face to establish their denomination and worth. This resulted in the Treasury Department contracting with the National and American Bank Note companies to print what is now known as "postage currency." Postage currency, while never specifically authorized by Congress, was issued from August 21, 1862, to May 27, 1863, when it was replaced by small Treasury notes called "fractional currency," which were specifically authorized. The new fractional notes did not carry replicas of stamp designs, and their acquisition and study is a goal for numismatists rather than philatelists.

Postage currency, on the other hand, is collected by both stamp collectors and numismatists, and complete listings of the issues are contained in the Scott U.S. specialized. They were issued in denominations of 5¢, 10¢, 25¢ and 50¢, with replicas of the 5¢ and 10¢ 1861 designs on their fronts. Unfortunately, for the purposes of this volume, 1¢ denominations were not issued, nor was the 1¢ Franklin design depicted on any of the notes.

It should be noted that the use of actual postage stamps and treasury postage currency as a substitute for money occurred concurrently, with postage currency generally replacing the use of postage stamps as time progressed. In newspaper notices of the period, it is not always clear which of these two methods of using stamps or stamp designs for monetary purposes was being discussed, and it probably caused considerable confusion for the public regarding the regulations and procedures for their use.

Along with all of these government activities, private enterprise still flourished. Less than a month after the Act of July 17, 1862, John Gault was awarded a patent for encased postage. Gault's patent solved to some extent the problems of durability and ease of use, and the modern stamp-collecting fraternity has him to thank for producing these fascinating and desirable philatelic treasures. Encased postage stamps were made by placing a mint postage stamp between a circular brass frame fronted with a thin sheet of mica and a brass back that was embossed with the name of a merchant and a few words of advertising. The stamp could be readily viewed through the transparent mica face and its value determined. The brass case and mica protected the stamp, and its small 1-inch diameter made it easy to carry and use. A photo of the front and reverse of a 1¢ 1861 encased stamp with an advertisement from Joseph L. Bates, a Boston merchant, is shown in **Figure 18-3**. Bates was a well-known retailer of fine musical instruments, personal accessories and imported gift items. His shop was located adjacent to Tichnor's book shop, the home of the *Atlantic Monthly* and the epicenter of Boston's cultural elite.

Encased postage exists with all of the denominations of the 1861 issue, from 1¢ to 90¢, and there are more than 150 known varieties of cases. Thirty-five different varieties of cases enclosing the 1¢ Franklin have been recorded. **Figure 18-4** shows a scarce 1¢ encased postage stamp showing an advertisement of the Aerated Bread Company of New York on the reverse. Only the 1¢ value is known for this advertiser. Aerated bread was bread made by injecting the dough with carbon dioxide by a patented process before baking, thus negating the need for yeast. It was supposed to result in a better tasting bread and was favorably endorsed by Horace Greeley. Unfortunately, not enough New Yorkers shared Greeley's opinion, and the firm did not survive.

Records of the business affairs of Gault have proved to be very elusive, and little definitive information has been discovered. However, several writers have reported that the brass cases for the stamps were made by the Scoville Manufacturing Company in Middlebury, Connecticut. According to Arlie A. Slabaugh, a philatelic stu-

Figure 18-3. Front and reverse views of an encased postage stamp enclosing a 1¢ Franklin stamp issued by Joseph L. Bates, a leading Boston retailer. Examples are scarce, with 20-30 recorded. The reverse illustrates the usual "PAT AUG 12, 1862 J. GAULT." embossing.
(Bowers and Merena auction photo)

Figure 18-4. 1¢ Aerated Bread encased postage stamp. The reverse reads "AERATED BREAD/COMPANY/COR/ LA FAYETTE PLACE/AND/FOURTH ST/NEW-YORK," along with the Gault patent notice.
(Bowers and Merena auction photo)

dent and writer of note, encased postage was sold for $20 per thousand cases plus the cost of the enclosed stamp 6:7]. The Gault patent gained wide acceptance, and many merchants signed on as customers and had their personalized messages embossed on his brass coins. The Ayer's patent medicine firm of Lowell, Massachusetts, was the largest purchaser of the Gault tokens for distribution. This is not surprising since the Ayer's company was, by far, the biggest advertiser in the country at that time. While thousands of encased stamps were distributed, it is likely that many more would have been manufactured if Gault had not been limited in his supply of stamps by the postmaster general's edict against the sale of stamps to be used as money. By the time the prohibition was relaxed, the government was strongly in the business of printing postage currency notes, and the need for encased postage diminished. An article in the August 1939 *Numismatist* quotes Gault as saying "he could have made a million dollars in a year if the Post Office had not shut down on him [6:6]."

While most of the cases have a brass finish, some examples are found with a silvered finish, most of which has usually worn off. The silvering is probably tin plate. The presence of this silver finish raises the question of whether all of the cases were originally silvered, or if the silvered specimens were manufactured by a different supplier. Because of small differences in the construction and quality of the brass cases, students of encased postage consider that different manufacturers were possibly involved in their production [7:47]. The encased postage bearing the advertisement of G.G. Evans of Philadelphia is a case in point. The quality of manufacture is somewhat inferior, and the name of Gault and the accompanying patent notice is missing from the embossing.

A copy of an old piece of correspondence that suggests the possibility of other manufacturers was provided to the author by William Weiss of Weiss Philatelics. This letter, on the printed letterhead of the N.&G.Taylor Co., a large Philadelphia manufacturer of tin plate, is dated September 26, 1905. It is to Henry G. Pickels of Trenton who had evidently written to the company requesting information on encased postage, an example of which accompanied the letter.

The interesting response to Pickels follows:

"Dear Sir:-

The writer has the pleasure of acknowledging receipt of your favor of the 23rd, and in returning you herewith the little souvenir, which you possibly would like to keep. When the War of the Rebellion broke out in 1861 all coin quickly disappeared and with it all small change. Postage stamps were then offered where they could be used, and my firm conceived the idea of enclosing them like this little souvenir, intended as an advertisement in a general way on our part, but more especially intended to serve a useful purpose, and we issued a great many of them at that time, and, as you may infer, enclosing stamps of different denominations in the little case. I think that we enclosed stamps up to the value of twenty-five cents, certainly one cent, two cents, three cents, five cents, ten cents. Such methods of payment were extremely convenient. I came to the office in 1864, but have a very vivid impression for several years back of that in the use of these little coins. This is about all that I can recollect upon the subject, but probably the information will be at least interesting.

Believe me,
Dear Sir,
Very truly yours, N&G Taylor Co.
by Nathan A. Taylor"

The Scott catalog lists five denominations for the N.&G. Taylor & Co. encased postage, 1¢, 3¢, 5¢, 10¢ and 12¢. All are scarce and catalog well in excess of $1,000 each. The cases have the patent date and Gault's name embossed on the reverse, so evidently the recollection of Taylor with respect to his firm having "conceived the idea" was not correct. However, it is certainly possible that the firm may have manufactured some of the cases under Gault's license, or at least inserted the stamps and resealed the cases. It was a very large company, with plants and warehouses in several major cities.

Encased postage stamps are extremely attractive and interesting items. A specimen in good condition is a desirable addition to any collection containing mid-19th century material, but with the combined numismatic/philatelic interest, and their scarcity, they are not easy to obtain.

Revenue Use

The unexpected large expenditures during the first year of the Civil War had resulted in a severe drain on the U.S. Treasury. Additional means to raise money were urgently needed, and various taxes and bond-selling programs were put into effect.

For the first time in its history, the United States began to print money, the notorious "greenbacks." On February 25, 1862, the Legal Tender Act authorized the U.S. government to issue $150 million in noninterest-bearing notes that would be legal tender for most debts. This provided additional capital for the war effort, but the increasing rate of expenditures rapidly exhausted this source. In addition, public distrust of paper money contributed to the deficit by quickly depreciating the value of the new currency by almost half [8:184]. Government bonds, similar to the war bonds of World War II were also issued, and new taxes were instituted. More greenbacks were printed, and a special stamp tax was legislated.

This was the Revenue Stamp Tax Act of July 1, 1862, effective October 1, 1862. The legislation required that almost all legal and commercial paper, as well as some other items, be taxed, and that revenue stamps were to be affixed to show that the tax had been paid. Contracts, promissory notes, bills of lading and so on were not considered legal documents without the stamps, so there was a strong incentive to ensure that important documents carried an official revenue stamp.

A contract with the Butler and Carpenter bank note company of Philadelphia was concluded, and the first series of revenue stamps was printed and issued. The law stated that specially designated stamps must be used for each type of tax. For instance, there were stamps for bank checks, bills of lading, playing cards, proprietary items such as medicines and perfumes, certificates and telegrams. There were 27 different types of use in the original issue and many denominations, ranging from 1¢ to $200, for a total of 102 different stamps. Although the stamps were produced in sufficient quantities and on schedule, the many different types and denominations made the distribution and stocking of a specific stamp for every type of business transaction a logistical nightmare for both the Treasury Department and individual citizens and businesses.

Fortunately, the requirement that the stamp type must agree with its use was rescinded on Christmas Day, 1862; thereafter, any type of revenue stamp could be used to pay the stamp tax, with the exception of those for proprietary uses. The tax on proprietary items, such as medicine and drugs, had to be paid with the specific stamps designated for that purpose. The law, however, allowed manufacturers of proprietary goods to have special designs printed at their own expense for their exclusive use. The advertising potential of these labels induced many manufacturers to take advantage of this provision, and the attractive match and medicine stamps that are now collected are a result of these private printings.

The relaxing of the requirement for matching the stamp to the type of use made revenue stamps generally available for most needs. But occasions still arose where a document or item required a tax stamp, and there was

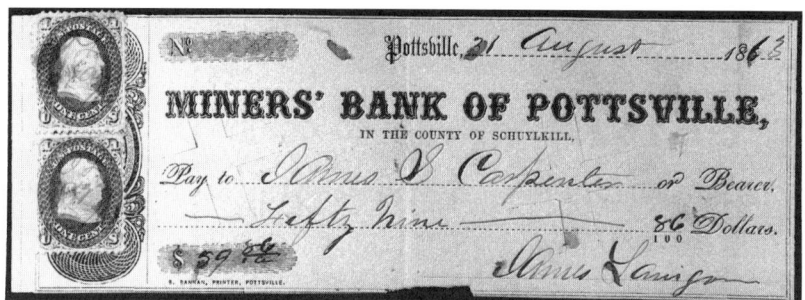

Figure 18-5. Check drawn on the Miners' Bank of Pottsville, (Pennsylvania), dated August 31, 1863, in the amount of $59.86. The correct revenue tax is illegally paid by two 1¢ Franklins, which are dated and canceled by the initials of the maker of the check, as required for revenue stamps.

Figure 18-6. Preprinted check of the William Bryce Co., dated August 31, 1863. This is the same date as the previous example, but in this case, the 2¢ tax was underpaid as well as being illegal because of the use of a single 1¢ Franklin postage stamp.

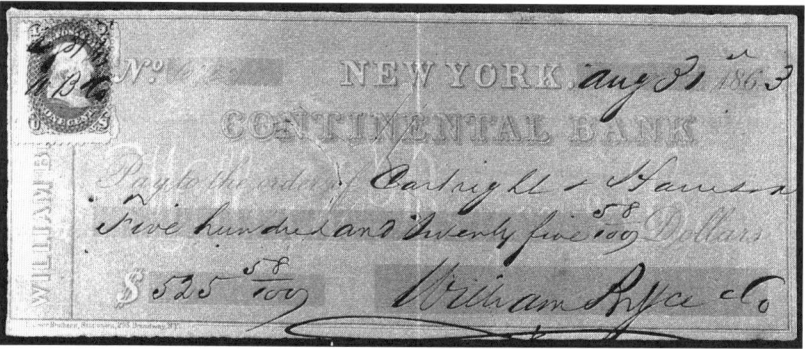

Figure 18-7. Counter check of the Herkimer County Bank, converted to use at the Central Bank. It is dated March 16, 1863, and drawn for $119.17. The tax was underpaid. An exceptional wide-margined 1¢ Franklin, in the scarce bright-ultramarine shade (Scott 63a), is illegally affixed to pay the stamp tax.

none at hand. These situations provided the stimulus that generated a class of philatelic items now referred to as "revenue use of postage stamps." In place of the required tax stamp, the user affixed a postage stamp. Although most users probably understood that this was not the proper or legal procedure, the fact that both revenue and postage stamp costs were paid to the government was considered by the public to imply that there was no attempt being made to evade the tax and that it was an acceptable practice to follow when no revenue stamp was available. **Figure 18-5** shows an example of a bank check where the tax was illegally paid by two 1¢ postage stamps of the 1861 issue. The tax for a bank check was established at a uniform 2¢ for any check written for $20 or more. In this example, the postage stamps were properly pen-canceled with date and initials by the signer of the check.

The illegal use of postage stamps, usually the 1861 issue, in place of revenue stamps for items like checks and receipts is believed to have been fairly common during the Civil War period. However, in the ensuing years most of the surviving pieces likely had their stamps removed by collectors. It has been estimated that this fate befell more than 99 percent of the original stamped documents [9:6].

The schedules of tax rates for the different transactions and documents were lengthy and somewhat complex, and were frequently revised with respect to the amount of tax required and the items that were to be taxed. A listing of rates and items can be found in reference [9]. The most important rates for philatelists are those for checks, notes, invoices and photographs. These are the types of documents where the revenue use of postage stamps is most likely to be found and the documents retained through the years. As previously mentioned, the tax on bank checks for any amount more than $20 was 2¢. Promissory note tax varied with the value of the note and the length of time to maturity, generally from a 1¢ to a 10¢ tax, and photographs were taxed from 2¢ to 5¢, depending on the cost of the photograph.

Figure 18-6 shows another bank check, written on the same day, August 31, 1863, as the check in Figure 18-5. This example is a preprinted orange check with the corner card of the William Bryce Co. A 1¢ Franklin is affixed to illegally pay the revenue tax. In this case the tax is also underpaid, since the correct tax for a bank check on this date was 2¢. The stamp is properly canceled with the date and initials of the maker.

The rates were evidently not too well-known or enforced on many of the low tax items. From the limited number of examples this author has seen with postage stamps used in place of revenue stamps, the majority either overpaid or underpaid the correct rate, with a preponderance of underpayments.

Figure 18-7 illustrates another example of underpayment on a bank check. This check, dated March 16, 1863, is written on what appears to be a Herkimer County Bank counter check with the words "Herkimer County" crossed out and replaced with "Central," where the maker evidently had his account. Payment was made by an exceptionally fine, wide-margined, straddle-pane copy of the 1¢ stamp printed in the scarce bright-ultramarine shade.

Figure 18-8 shows an unusual hand-written bank draft that reads as follows:

"1863
    Derry October 28
To the Treasurer of Haverhil
Savings Bank please pay the
Bearer Sixty Dollars of my
Deposit No 1792
Attest   Nancy Merrill"

The check is endorsed by a Harriet Hastings and has a blue handstamped "Paid/Oct 29 1863." The correct 2¢ amount was paid by two pen-canceled 1¢ Franklins. Subsequent to affixing the postage stamps, the signer of the draft evidently obtained a 2¢ bank check revenue stamp and pasted it over the postage stamps to legalize the transaction. The revenue stamp is canceled the same day as the postage stamps. One of the postage stamps is torn, suggesting that the maker of the check probably attempted to remove the postage stamps without success before applying the revenue stamp.

A payment order for $1,000, dated October 8, 1864, at Oil City (Pennsylvania) is illustrated in **Figure 18-9**. This instrument was written after the change in fees effective August 1, 1864, and falls under the category of "payment orders drawn on private individuals" for which the revenue fee was 2¢ for any amount over $10. This is another example of the fee being underpaid in addition to the illegal use of a postage stamp to pay the tax. There were very few documents where the fee was only 1¢. By the act effective October 1, 1862, express receipts up to the amount of 25¢ were charged 1¢. All express receipt fee taxes were eliminated March 3, 1863. Telegraph dispatches of fewer than 10 words, and costing less than 20¢, were taxed 1¢. This was rescinded on August 1, 1864. All other documents had tax rates greater than 1¢, and consequently most examples showing a tax paid by a single 1¢ stamp are underpaid, as well as being illegal.

Because of the scarcity of these philatelic gems, it is difficult to establish any pattern of use. The 1861 issue denominations of 1¢, 2¢, 5¢ and 10¢ on commercial documents or photographs have been seen by this author, and it should be assumed that other values possibly ex-

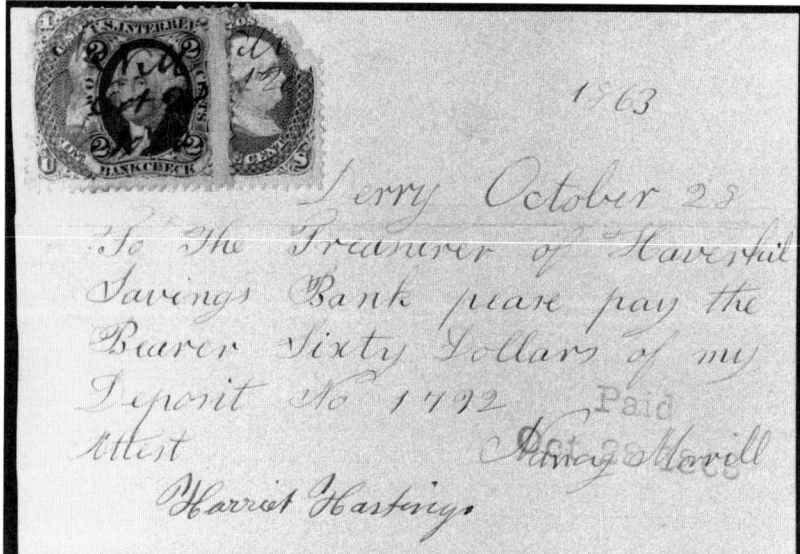

Figure 18-8. Illegal use of two 1¢ postage stamps to pay the revenue tax, corrected by the superposition of a 2¢ bank check revenue stamp (Scott R5). This handwritten payment order was made on the Haverhill Savings Bank of Haverhill, New Hampshire, and was paid on October 28, 1863, per "Paid" handstamp in blue.

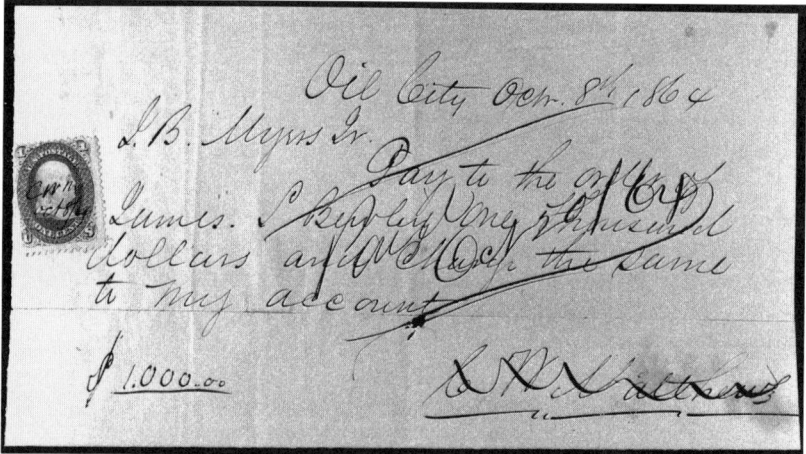

Figure 18-9. Payment order to an individual, possibly a broker, dated October 8, 1864, at Oil City (Pennyslvania) for the amount of $1,000. The order is marked "Paid/Oct 20/64" in manuscript. The use of a 1¢ Franklin to pay the tax on this order is not only illegal, but underpaid the fee. On this date, for payment orders on individuals the tax was 2¢ for any amount over $10.

Figure 18-10. Tax paid by the illegal use of a single 3¢ and two 1¢ postage stamps on a piece from a "true extract" of a bill of lading for items of cargo carried by the North German Lloyd steamship *Bremen*. The bill is dated April 15, 1863, with stamps canceled by a blue handstamp of Loeschick, Wesendonck & Co. of New York. Manuscript initials of customs inspectors and part of a red New York Customs House handstamp are visible on the piece.

ist. Surprisingly, the 3¢ denomination, in spite of its easy availability, has not been seen in any of these examples. The main reason is probably that there were few documents or items where the tax rate was 3¢. Higher tax rates could have been made up with the 3¢ in combination with other denominations, but if any examples exist, they are very elusive.

Examples of postage stamps used for revenue tax purposes that have been removed from the original documents are not always easy to identify. The character of the cancellation is the deciding factor in such identification. If the cancellation is in manuscript form and shows the complete date and a set of initials or a name, the stamp is probably from a revenue use. Examples of these cancellations were shown in Figures 18-5 through 18-9.

Cancellations by commercially manufactured stamping devices with the name of a company, such as the type used to mark the receipt of a document, also are likely to be found on postal issues used as tax stamps. **Figure 18-10** shows an example of this type of cancellation. The oval marking of Loeschick, Wesendonck & Co. of New York cancels two 1¢ stamps and a single 3¢ of the 1861 issue on a piece from what appears to be a true extract copy of a bill of lading. The bill contains the wording "... ent^d p'Bremen' April 15, 1863 ..." The *Bremen* was a well-known steamship of the North German Lloyd Line, and probably carried the cargo referred to in the bill of lading. The extract is written on ruled ledger paper and shows part of a red New York Customs Office handstamp in the lower-right corner of the piece. This handstamp is faint and does not show well in the illustration. There is enough information here to definitely establish that this is a revenue use.

While the tax fee was 25¢ to $1 for a bill of lading relating to the entry of goods to a custom house, depending on the value of the merchandise, it may be that since this was a copy of the bill of lading it was classified as a "certificate." The fee for a certificate was 5¢ and would make this a correctly paid item.

Figure 18-11 shows a cancellation on a pair of 1¢ Franklins that evidently were originally affixed to a receipt. The cancel is a large oval containing the words, "Received Payment/SEP/2/1862/Lane, Son & Co." Receipts were taxed at 2¢ for amounts in excess of $20, so this pair of stamps would represent a correct amount for payment.

Postage stamps where the cancel is from a commercially prepared marking device, and where the inscription contains a printed name or initials and a date, are probably from documents where they were used as revenue tax stamps. **Figure 18-12** shows two examples of such

Figure 18-11. A pair of off-document 1¢ Franklins marked with a "Received Payment" handstamp of the Lane, Son & Co., dated September 2, 1862. The stamps are probably from a receipt. Two cents was the correct revenue tax on a receipt. (C.W. Christian collection)

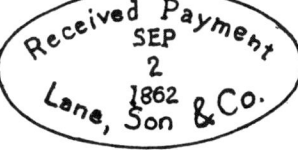

use. On the left is a CDS of E.T.H. Gibson, dated May 26, 1863. On the right example is a vertical straightline cancel with the initials and date "F.C.S./May. 4, 1863." The marking appears, from the sharpness of the impression, to have been made by a metallic canceler. Probably the only reason for having a commercial canceling device would have been a frequency of use that made it cost effective.

Another clue to revenue use is the presence of knife cuts on a stamp. Monetary instruments, such as checks and revenue stamps, were frequently canceled in this manner, and at times the cuts can be seen on the postage stamps.

Revenue Stamps Used for Postage

Covers showing the reverse situation of use of revenue stamps for postage stamps to pay the postal rates are quite scarce. Seldom did the revenue stamps get by

Figure 18-12. A single and a pair of off-document examples of 1¢ postage stamps showing evidence of use as revenue stamps. Handstamps with dates and names, used for cancellations, are characteristic of such use.

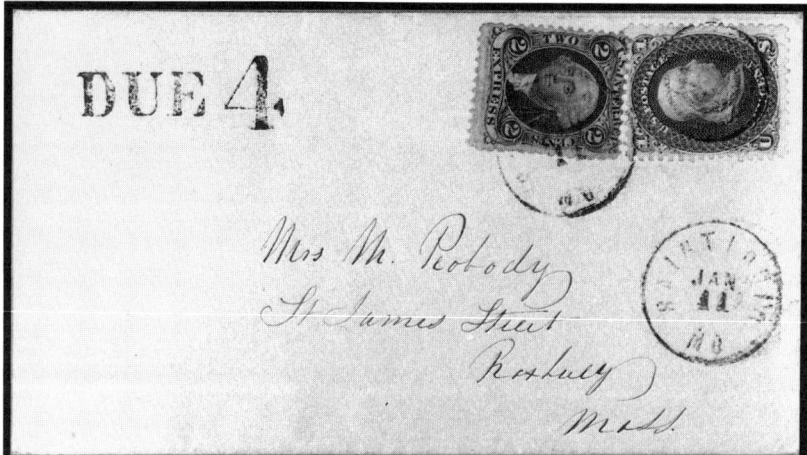

Figure 18-13. Illegal use of a 2¢ blue express revenue stamp (Scott R9), along with a 1¢ Franklin, to attempt payment of the 3¢ letter postage. The January 11 letter was posted at St. Louis, Missouri, and addressed to Roxbury, Massachusetts. It was marked "Due 4" as a penalty for partial payment, equal to twice the underpayment.
(C.W. Christian collection)

Figure 18-14. Attempted use of two 1¢ red Telegraph stamps (Scott R4), together with a single 1¢ Franklin, to pay the 3¢ postage rate. Payment was not recognized and the letter was treated as wholly unpaid. The postage "Due 6" notation in manuscript shows that a penalty equal to twice the postage required was being assessed for intentional underpayment. The cover is dated October 9, 1863, and was mailed from Eastport to Machias Port, Maine.
(C.W. Christian collection)

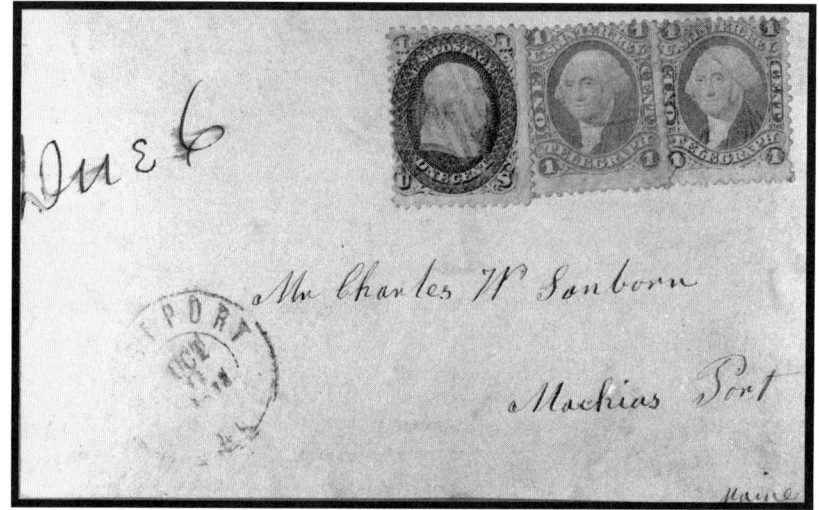

the watchful eyes of the postal clerks without a penalty.

The applicable postal laws and regulations that pertained to this situation were those related to the nonpayment or partial prepayment of postage. As far as the Post Office was concerned, revenue stamps were worthless labels.

During the 1860s, significant changes were made to the procedures for handling mail where the proper postage had not been paid. As previously discussed in earlier chapters, considerable leeway was exercised by the postmasters and postal clerks in assessing amounts of postage due. Their assessments did not always precisely reflect the laws and regulations that were in effect at the time. A brief restatement of some of the pertinent laws and regulations is provided here to assist in the interpretation of the postage-due markings on covers where the postage was partially or wholly paid by the illegal use of revenue stamps.

The Postal Regulations of 1859, in Section 106, state that part-paid letters were to be dispatched and charged with the additional postage due at the prepaid rate. If the underpayment was known to be intentional, the letter was to be treated as wholly unpaid. This meant that the addressee was to be notified of the underpayment and the additional postage requested. If this was not taken care of, the letter was sent to the Dead Letter Office.

These would be the provisions under which letters sent during the first year of the Stamp Tax Act, from October 1, 1862, to July 1, 1863, should have been rated.

The Act of March 3, 1863, effective July 1, 1863, revised this procedure. Section 26 of the law stated:

"If any matter on which by law the postage is required to be prepaid at the mailing office should reach its destination without such prepayment, double the prepaid rates shall be charged and collected on delivery."

In the instructions to this section it also stated:

"If postage is partly prepaid, the unpaid postage will be charged at double rates."

Figure 18-15. This cover is another example of attempted use of a 2¢ express revenue stamp (Scott R9) and a 1¢ postage stamp to pay the 3¢ letter rate, where the underpayment was assumed to be intentional and the the letter was considered to be unpaid. It is hand-stamped with a black "Due 6" in boxed oval for collection of postage at destination equal to twice the prepaid rate. The cover was mailed at Nelsonville, Ohio, on February 16, 1863 (date marked in pencil), and addressed to Lebanon, Ohio.

The following Postal Instruction, Number 27, further elaborated on the point as follows:

". . . This section intends, and postmasters are instructed, to use a liberal discretion in forwarding unpaid letters deposited for mailing where there is any reason to believe that such failure to prepay was the result of accident, ignorance, or any other cause than design, charging them with double rates of postage, to be collected on delivery. The former practice of notice to the party addressed is abolished.

In all cases where the failure to prepay postage on the letters of civilians, when the same are deposited for mailing, is evidently intentional, such letters should be forwarded with other 'unmailable' letters to the Dead Letter Office."

There is some ambiguity here with respect to a letter that is partially paid because part of the payment is considered illegal. In the examples shown in this section, it appears that postal clerks at times considered the postage paid to be acceptable and only charged double for the revenue stamp portion. In other similar cases, the postage as well as the revenue stamp were considered worthless, and the letter was deemed to have been intentionally underpaid. These examples are charged a double rate for collection at destination. Since none of the examples that will be discussed was processed through the DLO, it appears that the postal clerks liberally interpreted the specific wording of the regulations and assessed penalties using a combination of the provisions.

Figure 18-13 shows an example of the attempted use of a 2¢ express revenue stamp together with a 1¢ Franklin to make up the 3¢ domestic letter rate. Mailed at St. Louis, Missouri, on January 11 to Roxbury, Massachusetts, the cover is marked "DUE 4" for collection upon delivery. The 4¢ due rate was arrived at by allowing credit for the 1¢ stamp and charging a double-rate penalty for the underpayment of 2¢.

Figure 18-14 shows another attempted use of revenue stamps, but here the penalty is 6¢. This cover, from Eastport to Machias Port, Maine, dated October 9, 1863, was paid with two red 1¢ Telegraph revenue stamps and a single 1¢ Franklin to make up the required 3¢ rate. The revenue stamps were not recognized, and the cover was marked in manuscript, "Due 6." No credit was given for the 1¢ partial payment, and the letter was treated as a wholly unpaid letter because of intentional underpayment. Consequently double postage was due.

The cover illustrated in **Figure 18-15** was franked with a blue 2¢ express revenue stamp and a 1¢ Franklin. Mailed at Nelsonville, Ohio, on February 16, 1864, to Lebanon, Ohio, the cover was marked with a black "Due 6" in a boxed oval handstamp. This cover is another example of not crediting the partial payment and requiring the recipient to pay double postage.

The scarcest of all examples of revenue stamps being used for postage are those where the revenue stamps were accepted and no postage due was indicated. **Figure 18-16** shows such a cover. This small embossed lady's cover was posted at Notre Dame, Indiana, on March 21 (year unknown). The postage was paid with an orange 2¢ bank check revenue stamp and a 1¢ Franklin. Since both stamps are canceled with the same killer, it is evident that the originating post office accepted the illegal payment. It is surprising that the color of the bank check revenue did not alert the clerk to the fact that the cover was not correctly paid. This cover also passed the scrutiny of the delivering post office. Such oversights, whether accidental or otherwise, are very seldom seen, and the author has only recorded three examples with the use of the 1¢ Franklin.

The singular use of the 1861 stamps as money, and also their illegal use as revenue stamps, as well as the converse use of revenue stamps for postage, present some of the most unusual philatelic items available to the classic collector. The momentous events of the period

Figure 18-16. Rare example of the accepted use of a revenue stamp and a postage stamp to make up the correct 3¢ rate. A 2¢ orange bank check revenue stamp (Scott R6), together with a 1¢ Franklin, were canceled at the originating Notre Dame post office and delivered to the addressee at Shelburn, Indiana. No postage due was marked. This small embossed lady's cover is dated March 21, with no year date.

that led to these uses provide a backdrop of historical significance that enhances the inclusion of these bits of paper in any collection.

References

1. Mueller, Barbara R., editor. "Postage and Fractional Currency Production Problems." *The Essay-Proof Journal* No. 129. Winter 1976.

2. *United States Mail and Post Office Assistant.* Reprinted by the Collectors Club of Chicago. 1975.

3. *Report of the Postmaster General for 1862.* Reprints of the original documents. Theron Wierenga. Holland, Michigan. 1977.

4. Rothert, Matt. *A Guide Book to United States Fractional Currency.* Whitman Publishing Co. Racine, Wisconsin. 1963.

5. Herst, Herman Jr. "Stamps Used as Money." *Linn's Stamp News.* January 21, 1991.

6. Slabaugh, Arlie R. *U.S. and Foreign Encased Postage Stamps.* Hewitt Bros. Chicago, Illinois. 1967.

7. "Encased Postage Stamps, The Collection of James F. Ruddy." *Auction Catalog of Bowers and Merena Inc.* Wolfboro, New Hampshire. June 19, 1984.

8. Hargest, George. *History of Letter Post Communication Between the United States and Europe, 1845-1875.* Second Edition, 1975. Quarterman reprint.

9. Mahler, Michael, "Documents Bearing U.S. Revenue Stamps of the Civil War Era." A two-part article in the January and March 1982 issues of *American Revenuer.*

CHAPTER 19

Miscellaneous, Odd and Unusual

In any compendium such as this volume, there are always a number of interesting items that do not fit easily under the various chapter titles. This final chapter collects these bits and pieces of philatelic lore, and gives them a literary home.

Odd-Shaped Envelopes

In the 1860s, there seems to have been little restriction, if any, on the size, shape or material for postal envelopes. Ladies' envelopes of small size were manufactured and sold in large quantities, and examples of these miniature covers make an interesting collection. Covers were sometimes made from cloth and even leather. These were usually homemade envelopes. Odd shapes were also used. Rhomboid covers were commercially produced, together with specially cut and embossed paper, which when folded would fit nicely into the envelopes. Berlin & Jones of New York City held the patent on these, and while its output of rhomboid covers was probably never one of its most popular items, it did sell a lot of covers of various types. Records show that during the Civil War era, Berlin & Jones manufactured and sold approximately 600,000 envelopes per day [1:4-7].

Figure 19-1 illustrates an example of one of these rhomboid covers, which is slanted to the right. This example was mailed in March of 1863 at New York and received carrier collection to the mails. Envelopes angled to the left were also manufactured, and it might be that these were specifically designed for individuals who wrote with a reverse slant or possibly left-handed writers.

Figure 19-2 shows a pentagonal cover. This particular cover was homemade and is the only five-sided cover that the writer has ever recorded. The reverse of the cover has a black wax seal with the inscription "2.Tim.IV.9." The previous rhomboid cover in Figure 19-1 and this cover are both from the same "Bidwell" correspondence. Evidently the writer of the letters had a particular fondness for envelopes that were different from the norm.

The firm of Proctor & Clark of Boston manufactured envelopes in a triangular shape. Although a small number of examples with postage paid by the 1861 3¢ have been recorded, this writer has not seen any triangular covers showing use with the 1¢ Franklin. While it cannot be classed as an envelope, **Figure 19-3** shows an example of a rare small triangular folded letter. This three-sided letter with a 1¢ Franklin was mailed as an unsealed drop letter, addressed to "City," and canceled with a segmented cork killer. The letter is actually a printed invitation with manuscript notations from the Newburgh, New York, Young Men's Christian Association, dated February 15, 1869.

The postal clerks were probably quite happy that these odd shapes were not too common, for they certainly would have been difficult to stack, sort and handle.

Leeds & Franklin Patent Envelopes

The Leeds & Franklin envelopes are covers with one or more openings cut into their fronts through which postmarks, or stamps that would later be postmarked, could be affixed directly on the contents of the cover. These seldom-seen relics of a novel and ambitious scheme to provide correspondents with a record and proof of dates of mailing have been the object of much speculation through the years, and the story behind their development and use is extremely interesting.

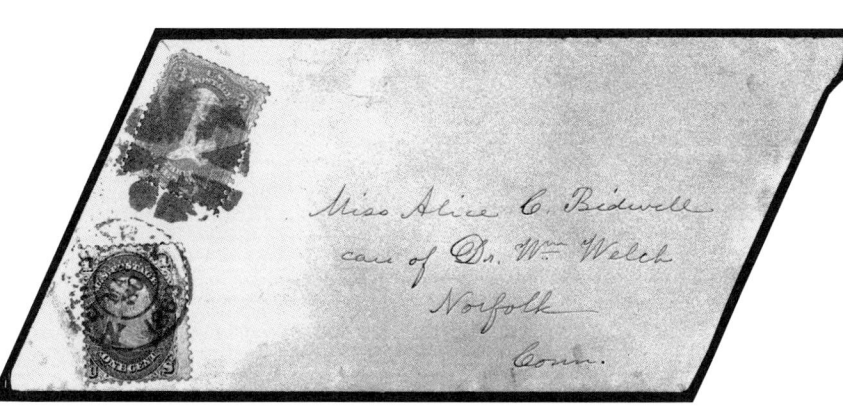

Figure 19-1. Berlin & Jones patent rhomboid envelope postmarked "MAR 30 1863" at New York City, to Norfolk, Connecticut. The stamps pay the 1¢ carrier-collection fee and 3¢ postage. A heavily embossed border design appears on the reverse.

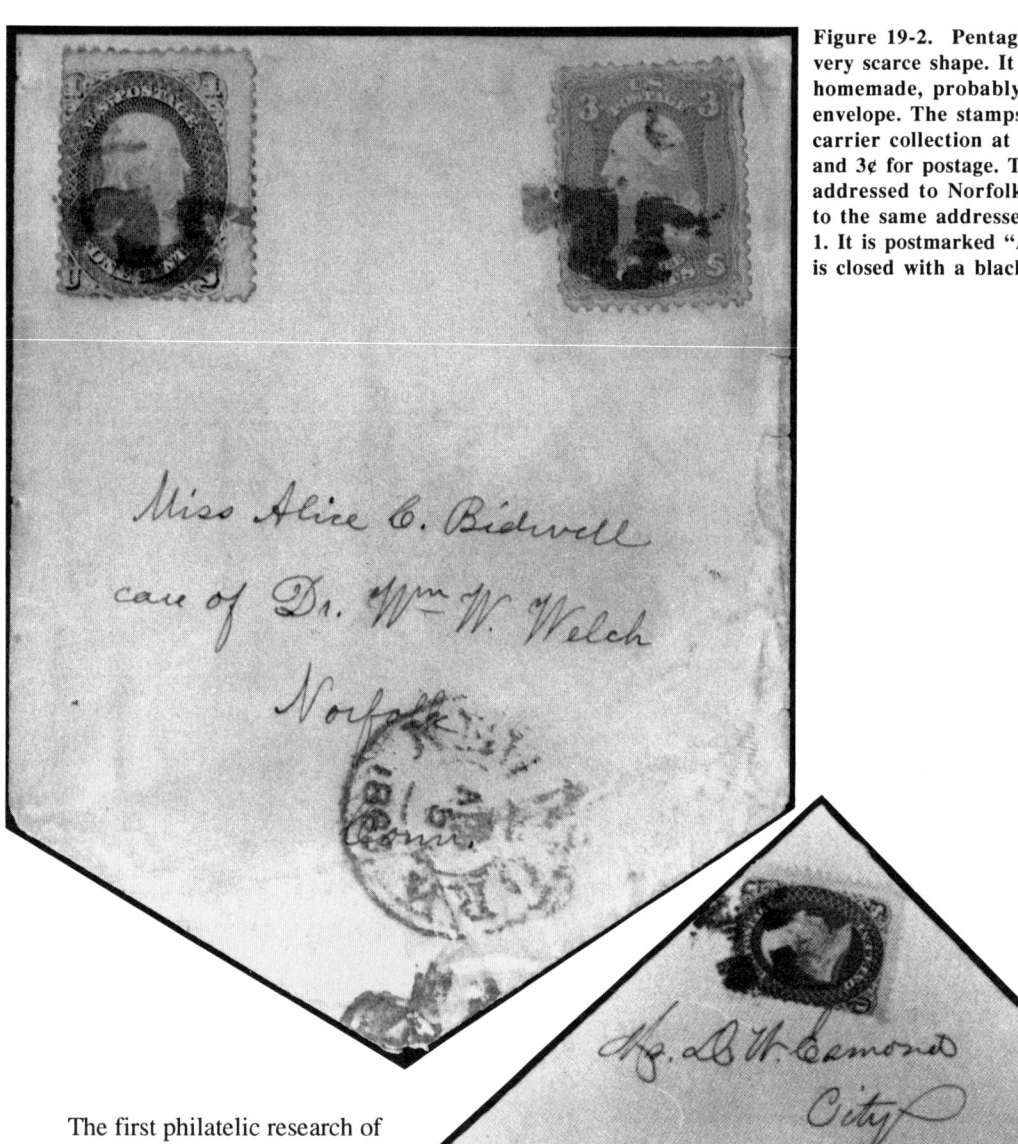

Figure 19-2. Pentagonal envelope, a very scarce shape. It appears to be homemade, probably from another envelope. The stamps paid the 1¢ carrier collection at New York City and 3¢ for postage. The cover is addressed to Norfolk, Connecticut, to the same addressee as Figure 19-1. It is postmarked "APR 5 1863." It is closed with a black wax seal.

Figure 19-3. Extremely scarce triangular shape. This unsealed folded letter at the 1¢ drop rate is addressed to "City." The letter is a folded YMCA invitation, dated February 15, 1869, at Newburgh, New York.
(Courtesy of Dr. James W. Milgram)

The first philatelic research of any consequence into the origins and purpose of these oddities was done by E. Tudor Gross, the pioneer collector of 1861 1¢ Franklin stamps and postal history. His investigations into philatelic matters were always exhaustive, with great attention to detail and a desire to find everything that he could about a subject. His search for the original source for the portrait of Franklin on the 1¢ stamp, as chronicled in Chapter 2 of this book, is another example of his thorough and continuing quest for information.

His efforts to discover the meaning of these "covers with holes" resulted in a series of articles in the *Collectors Club Philatelist* during 1942 and 1943 [2],[3],[4],[5] and are the main source for the material in this discussion. Little additional information has been discovered since that time, but new examples of use and two contemporary references to the envelopes from a Civil War-period publication have surfaced.

The story of the Gross investigations begins in 1926 when he discovered that a 1¢ 1861 on an unusual envelope had been sold in a Percy Doane auction in New York. The stamp was pasted on the contents of the envelope and had been canceled with a CDS dated January 24, 1864, through a die-cut oval opening in the cover. Gross contacted the purchaser, David C. Turnbull, with a re-

Figure 19-4. Patent envelope with local 1¢ drop-mail use at Flushing, New York. The 1¢ Franklin is pasted to the contents through an oval die-cut opening. The stamp is canceled with the Flushing postmark, dated "JAN 24 1862." This is a probable trial use to demonstrate correct use in the mails. (Illustration courtesy of the Collectors Club of New York)

quest to buy the cover. Turnbull did not want to part with it, and Gross repeated his offer once or twice a year for the next five years, until Turnbull finally acquiesced and sold him the cover in 1931. **Figure 19-4** shows a photograph of this historic item. Addressed to Leeds & Vaux at Flushing, New York, the envelope has an oval opening at the upper right. A 1¢ Franklin is affixed through the opening to the enclosure. The stamp, paying the local drop rate, was canceled at the Flushing post office on January 24, 1862, with a double-circle postmark showing the town and date. The enclosure was a folded sheet of blank paper, and the significance of this will be later explained.

After he acquired the cover, Gross mentioned that he had never seen or heard of anything like it. Actually, four philatelic references to similar types of covers had been previously published. John N. Luff had noted in the March 1902 issue of the *American Journal of Philately* in an article titled "An Interesting Study" that such items existed and explained their purpose. In the October 1929 issue of the *Collectors Club Philatelist*, Walter S. Scott described a cover with a hole in the upper right of the envelope through which a Philadelphia CDS dated February 1, 1862, had been applied to the contents. The cover also had a small embossed notation to the left of the opening with the message "POST MARK (pointing finger to the right)/PATENT/JUNE 19 1860." A 3¢ 1861 stamp was affixed on the lower-left corner of the cover and canceled with a bull's-eye killer.

Two months later a follow-up article by P.H. Thorp appeared in the December 1929 issue of *Scott's Monthly Journal*, which commented on the Scott article and noted that the writer also had one of these interesting envelopes. Scott's article had aroused his curiosity, and he queried Luff about them, as the expert in all matters relating to 19th-century U.S. philately. Luff promptly produced his article published 28 years previously, and the circle was complete as far as determining all that was known about the patent envelopes by 1930.

Gross obtained copies of these publications and began his long search to fill in the missing pieces of the puzzle. The labyrinthine unfolding of facts and clues regarding what actually occurred during the development and short life of these patent envelopes as Gross discovered them is a tale of philatelic detective work, but the length and complexity of his account makes it unfeasible to again relate all of the details. The reader, who desires to know more, will find the 1943-44 *Collectors Club Philatelist* articles to be most illuminating.

In summary, what occurred was that in the summer of 1861 Lewis W. Leeds, a heating and ventilation engineer in New York, had developed an idea for which he submitted a patent application to the Scientific American Patent Agency. The application was for an envelope that could be used to record the date of mailing on the contents of the envelope for reference and to legally verify the date of its entrance into the mails. There was a definite demand for such a capability, particularly for commercial and legal correspondence.

The patent agency informed Leeds that his idea had already been patented on June 19, 1860, by Benjamin Morison of Philadelphia, as "Improved Envelopes," patent 28767. An article containing this information and describing the Leeds invention later appeared in the *Scientific American* of July 12, 1862.

Essentially, Leeds had developed the idea of having a die-cut opening, somewhat larger than a normal postmark, in the upper-right corner of an envelope. The opening would be cut so that a latticework of narrow strips of paper would remain. An unused example of one of these envelopes is shown in **Figure 19-5**. A stamp

Figure 19-5. This unused Leeds and Franklin patent envelope features a die-cut opening with attached latticework. Attachments of the lattice to the main body of the envelope are extremely narrow so that when properly used the lattice will separate when the envelope is opened and leave the stamp glued to the lattice and to the contents beneath. This is a light canary-yellow envelope, frequently used for this patent. (C.W. Christian collection)

would be applied over the opening so that the gum adhered to both the latticework and the envelope's enclosure. When the letter was postmarked, the CDS, with the location and date of mailing, was to be applied as a cancellation directly on the stamp. When the envelope was later opened by the addressee and the contents removed, the fragile latticework would tear loose from the cover. The stamp with its dated cancel would remain glued to the contents and provide the necessary proof of mailing. The fact that the stamp adhered to the enclosure while in the mails, separated only by the easily broken lattice, was also supposed to alert the recipient to any surreptitious opening prior to receipt. Any attempt to open the letter would tear the lattice loose, and this would be evident to the addressee.

Although Morison had already patented the idea of having a hole (without the lattice) in an envelope through which a CDS could be applied, Leeds did not abandon his own version. He contacted Morison in Philadelphia and visited him in October of 1861 with an offer to purchase the patent. Morison had experienced little success in obtaining support for the idea from the Post Office Department. This support was important, because if the Post Office did not instruct its postmasters and postal clerks to carefully apply the CDS through the hole, and to always use postmarks that showed the complete date, the scheme would not be effective.

Later in 1861, Leeds again visited Morison in Philadelphia and concluded an agreement to purchase the patent on an extended payment plan. The patent was to be sold to Leeds and his partner, Calvet Vaux, for the sum of $1,000 to be paid in four equal monthly installments with the first payment to be made on January 1, 1862. Vaux was also a partner with Leeds in their heating-system business at 110 Broadway in New York City. In addition, Vaux was listed in the New York City Directory as an architect and doing business at that address.

The few sample envelopes that Morison produced had round holes in the upper right and were made of coarse brown paper. The Leeds envelopes were manufactured with approximately square or oval openings, and both with and without the lattice. The most common opening to be found on surviving covers is the type previously shown in Figure 19-5. Although this opening is not really square, its somewhat complex shape is not easy to describe and, for purposes of simplicity, will be referred to in this discussion as a square.

Gross recorded 18 covers showing use of the Morison or Leeds patent envelope with a postage stamp and actual use in the mails. Although additional examples have been found since he wrote his article, the total known probably does not exceed 30. Some of these are experimental covers that Leeds and Vaux mailed to themselves to show how the idea worked, and the majority of the recorded covers are franked by the 1861 3¢ stamp. Only a few covers have the 1¢ Franklin paying the postage.

Probably the finest existing example of a Leeds envelope with proper postal use is the cover shown in **Figure 19-6**. This magnificent cover is the only recorded example with three 1¢ Franklins. The stamp on the right was placed in the correct position, and although the circular postmark is larger than the opening, enough of it appears on the enclosure to show the month and day, and part of the town name. The postmark is also applied as a cancel to the other two stamps that are affixed to the cover. The letter was mailed at Stafford, Vermont, and addressed to South Hardwick, Vermont, with a date of June 29. The enclosure is still with the cover, and the stamp is affixed to the contents with the latticework still under it. The stamp has been lifted for viewing and replaced. The illustration also shows a portion of the enclosure with the right stamp attached.

Figure 19-6. Only known example of the use of three 1¢ stamps on a Leeds and Franklin patent envelope. Mailed at Stafford, Vermont, at the 3¢ letter rate to South Hardwick, Vermont, the envelope is canceled with a postmark dated "JUN 29." A portion of the enclosure with the right-hand stamp still attached is also illustrated.
(C.W. Christian collection)

Vaux soon dropped out of the enterprise, and his place was taken by Joseph F. Franklin, who was a broker and whose office at 110 Broadway, New York City, was located next door to that of Leeds and Vaux. Evidently, Franklin provided capital to the venture, and the money due to Morison for the patent was finally paid. The patent was officially assigned to Leeds & Franklin on May 7, 1862. Although Franklin's association with the firm was also brief, most of the circulars advertising the envelopes continued to carry the title "Leeds & Franklin's Patent Stamp-Sealing and Post-Mark-Preserving Envelopes." The name Leeds and Franklin patent envelopes has become the philatelic nomenclature for this type of window envelope.

On November 8, 1862, Franklin sold his share of the company to Barclay Leeds, the brother of Lewis Leeds. Barclay had earlier purchased a third of the partnership, and now the enterprise was wholly owned by the Leeds family, with Barclay owning two-thirds and Lewis, the remaining third.

During the early part of this period, Lewis and Vaux had produced samples and experimental envelopes. Lewis resided in Flushing, New York, and evidently requested the local postmaster to specially cancel the stamps on some of his patent envelopes with the Flushing postmark. The postmark was to be applied in such a manner that the postmark would clearly show on the stamp attached to the contents. One of the results from these trial mailings is the cover illustrated in Figure 19-5. The letter was a drop letter addressed to themselves, evidently to demonstrate the practicability of their invention. The blank paper enclosure was necessary to provide a recording of the Flushing postmark.

Leeds also asked the postmaster at Brooklyn, New York, to write the Post Office Department with a request that the Post Office authorize the special canceling that was needed for the Leeds patent. George B. Lincoln, the Brooklyn postmaster, complied and queried the Post Office on September 12, 1862. He received a reply four days later from St. John B.L. Skinner, who was acting for John Kasson, the first assistant postmaster general.

"Sir:
Your letter of the 12th inst. is received. Nothing appears on the records of the Department to show that Mr. Kasson ever took action in relation to the subject of your communication.

"If persons deposit letters in your office, with a request that the Post Mark may be placed upon a particular part of them, I see no reason why they should not be accommodated, unless the doing so would materially interfere with the business of your office.
Respectfully
Your obdt. Servt.
St John B.S. Skinner
Acting First Asst. P. M. Gen'l."

This letter, like many bureaucratic responses, did not address the key point of the request, which was the question of whether a postmark could be used to cancel a stamp. Skinner was evidently unaware of the order by Kasson's predecessor that stamps were not to be canceled with a postmarking device.

Leeds also wrote directly to the postmaster general and requested that he issue instructions to post offices to cancel stamps with postmarks. The letter was referred to Skinner's office for reply, and on September 19, 1862, Leeds and Franklin received the following reply:

"Your letter to the Postmaster General has been referred to this office.

> In answer I have to say, a new regulation which is about to be adopted and published forbids the use of the marking stamp in canceling stamps.
>
> Mr. Kasson is now absent and may not return until the last of October. In the mean time the Department will make no order in relation to your envelopes."

In the three days since his previous letter, Skinner must have been appraised that a prohibition against using a postmark as a cancel was going to be published (possibly a draft of the new proposed postal laws to be considered for passage in 1863). He obviously was still unaware that the prohibition order was already in effect.

The original of this particular prohibition order has been extremely elusive and has never been located. References have been found that establish that it was issued on July 23, 1860, by Horatio King, the previous first assistant postmaster general, and that it may have been originally transmitted only to some of the larger post offices. Gross spent several years trying to specifically find a copy of the original order without success.

Official references to the order give the text of the order, which later became a regulation, in some varying versions, but the essential points are contained in the 1866 compendium of Postal Regulations (§178), as follows:

> "The use of the office rating or post-marking stamp as a canceling instrument is positively prohibited, inasmuch as the post-mark, when impressed on the postage stamp is usually indistinct, and the cancellation effected thereby is imperfect. The postage stamp must, therefore, be effectually canceled with a separate instrument."

This, of course, made the Leeds patent without merit since the postmark would no longer be applied to the stamp. Philatelic writers throughout the years have made much of this fact and attribute the failure of the patent to achieve success to the existence of the prohibition against using a postmark to cancel a stamp.

This writer strongly disagrees with this contention. After all, if that were the only problem, the envelope could have been reconfigured. The desired position for application of the stamp at the upper right of the envelope could be indicated by a printed outline. This, together with a die-cut hole in the envelope at the position where a duplex canceler would postmark the cover when the stamp was canceled, would achieve the desired result of having the postmark stamped on the contents of the envelope. At the same time, the stamp would be canceled with a "separate instrument" as required by the regulations. This scheme would also work where duplex markers were not used. Of course, in that situation two entirely separate marking devices would necessarily be used.

The Post Office would still have had to issue instructions to ensure that legible postmarks were applied and that they were handstamped in the correct location.

Here is where the major shortcoming of the Leeds patent was evident. Handstamping of letters, particularly in the larger cities, was a huge task. Dozens of clerks postmarked and canceled tens of thousands of covers every day, usually as fast as they could move. To place the markings in a particular location on the envelope, and to ensure that the strike was legible, would decrease the speed with which the operation was conducted. Increases in personnel would be required with the attendant additional expense. Higher costs were always avoided by the Post Office whenever possible, and it is not surprising that it would not endorse the idea.

Poorly struck markings on the covers of mid-19th century were endemic. Legible and clear postmarks from that period are in the minority, and collectors prize them both for their attractiveness and their scarcity. It is not likely that any order from the postmaster general would have resulted in a meaningful improvement.

The Leeds organization did receive a substantial amount of publicity. The New York newspapers published accounts of the patent and its benefits. *The U.S. Mail and Post Office Assistant*, the quasiofficial publication of the Post Office Department, edited by J. Holbrook, a special agent of the Post Office, published a full-column discussion of the merits of the Leeds patent envelope in the July 1862 issue. The tone of the article was mostly in favor of the idea but with a qualified endorsement of some of the claims made by the inventor in his circulars. A lengthy reply to the column from Leeds & Franklin was printed three months later in the October 1862 USM&POA [6:85,87].

Leeds & Franklin circularized many commercial establishments across the country, and used its patent envelopes to mail the circulars. **Figure 19-7** shows one of these circulars with the 1¢ stamp still attached. Part of the "New York/October 23/1862" CDS remained on the original envelope, but sufficient information shows on the stamp to provide the desired date and point of origin. In an insert to the illustration is an enlarged photograph of the stamp and a small portion of the circular. It has been photographed with a light-box background so that the remnants of the latticework, which was separated from the original envelope, can be seen beneath the stamp. The envelope no longer accompanies the contents, but this is not surprising. There would not have been much desire to save an envelope with a hole torn in its front, even if the contents were interesting enough to save.

Figure 19-8 shows a cover that was saved along with its circular contents. This cover was mailed to the Platte Val(l)ey Bank in Nebraska City, Nebraska, from New York City on October 27. There is no year date, but it was probably mailed in 1862. The enclosed circular is most

Figure 19-7. Illustration of a 1¢ stamp still adhering to an enclosed circular that had been mailed in a Leeds and Franklin patent envelope. The envelope was postmarked at New York "OCT 23 1862." The insert shows the stamp when photographed against a light-box background, which outlines the remnants of the attached lattice-work beneath the stamp.
(Perry Sapperstein collection. Photos, Richard B. Graham)

interesting and lists 10 distinct advantages accruing to the users of Leeds & Franklin envelopes. It concludes with endorsements from 28 important personages of the period, including George Opdyke, mayor of New York; Horace Greeley, editor of the *New York Tribune* and author of the famous admonition, "Go West, young man"; the postmaster of New York City, Abram Wakeman; and J.G. Palfrey, the postmaster of Boston. The circular was printed by William P. Lyon, a local stationer and envelope manufacturer. Lyon was the exclusive producer of the patent envelopes and paid the patent-holders a small royalty on each envelope sold.

Leeds continued to add improvements, and developed an envelope with vertical perforations along one side. These were to facilitate the opening of the envelope and to negate having to tear open the flap. **Figure 19-9** shows an experimental version of this idea. The 1¢ Franklin is canceled by a special private "postmark," which Leeds & Franklin frequently used in its advertising or experimental samples. The same marking is also used as a postmark on the envelope. Another envelope, without the perforations is shown in **Figure 19-10**. A reproduction of the Leeds postmark is also illustrated. The 112 " B'W " is for 112 Broadway, the address of Franklin's brokerage office and the firm of Leeds & Franklin.

In spite of glowing recommendations, and favorable press, the enterprise did not prosper. The next important phase of the operation, at least from a philatelic point of view, was the involvement of Lewis Leeds with the U.S. Sanitary Commission.

Vaux, Leeds' partner in the heating and ventilating business, and his first partner in the patent-envelope operation, had also been involved with Frederick Law

Figure 19-8. 1¢ circular rate. Leeds and Franklin patent envelope with a square opening and latticework. The envelope was mailed at New York on October 27 (no year date) to the Platte Valley National Bank, Nebraska City, Nebraska. The circular contents are still enclosed, with the stamp and latticework affixed.
(Illustration courtesy of the Collectors Club of New York)

Figure 19-9. Experimental version of a Leeds and Franklin patent envelope with a series of vertical perforations to be used in "side opening" the envelope. The 1¢ stamp was applied over a square opening and canceled with the Leeds & Franklin private handstamp. This cover never entered the mails. (Illustration courtesy of the Collectors Club of New York)

Figure 19-10. An unaddressed sample Leeds & Franklin envelope with the private handstamp canceling the 1¢ Franklin stamp. The square die-cut opening is slightly different in design in this example, showing a point at the middle of each side. An enlarged reproduction of the private handstamp is also illustrated. (Photo courtesy of James Lee)

Olmstead, the most famous landscape architect of the period. They had collaborated in winning the design and construction competition for the landscaping of New York's Central Park. After the beginning of the Civil War, Olmstead was granted leave from his Central Park position to become general secretary of the U.S. Sanitary Commission in Washington, D.C.

Probably upon the recommendation of Vaux, Olmstead employed Leeds to inspect the heating and ventilating systems of some of the commission's buildings in Washington. Olmstead was evidently pleased with Leeds' work and appointed him "consulting engineer of ventilation and warming." He also requested that Leeds prepare for a trip to the West to inspect the general hospitals at Cincinnati, Louisville and so on.

Probably, Leeds convinced Olmstead or someone at the commission headquarters of the advantages of his patent envelope, and an order for envelopes in various sizes, both unprinted and printed with the U.S. Sanitary Commission corner card, was placed. The invoice that William P. Lyon, the manufacturer of the patent enve-

lopes, presented to Lewis Leeds on November 19, 1862, was for 29,500 envelopes for a total cost of $185.75. The consignment was shipped via Adams Express to Leeds at Washington.

The U.S. Sanitary Commission now possessed a large number of Leeds & Franklin envelopes, but what became of most of them has remained a philatelic mystery. Only a very few, probably no more than five, of the used covers with the imprinted corner cards have survived through the years and have been recorded.

It has been surmised by some philatelic writers that since the postal regulations negated the use for which the envelopes were designed, the commission destroyed most of its supply. This writer doubts this to be true. The mailing date and security features of the patent would not have been of much importance to the commission correspondence, and funds were short. It is much more likely that it used all of the envelopes and that the scarcity is just the result of the normal attrition of nonpersonal correspondence due to the discarding of envelopes and the removing of stamps by collectors over the years. Ratios of two in 10,000 for cover survival is not that unusual, particularly where the covers enclosed material that was frequently printed matter.

In his agreement with Leeds & Franklin to manufacture its patent envelopes, Lyon was required to produce advertising for its product. **Figure 19-11** shows one of the patent envelopes upon which Lyon had printed an advertisement for his wares. Lyon had also agreed to circularize the major banks in the country with advertisements of the envelopes. Most of the circulars that have been discovered with the patent envelopes, such as the cover previously shown in Figure 19-8, are a result of his work. Since the addressee of that circular was a bank in Nebraska, which was at the gateway to Indian territory in those days, it appears that Lyon did a commendable job in spreading the word. It should be noted that although Franklin sold his share in the enterprise in October of 1862, the partnership continued under the name of Leeds & Franklin for the remainder of its lifetime.

The number of Leeds patent envelopes used with the 1¢ Franklin where the cover actually entered the mails is limited. Only five recorded examples can be listed. They are:

1. January 24, 1862. Local use at Flushing, New York (Figure 19-4).

2. February 16 (?). Local use at Philadelphia addressed to Anna Leeds. No photo. The 1¢ stamp was not applied over the square lattice opening. The cover bears three strikes of a Philadelphia "Penny Mail" carrier postmark: one serving as a postmark, one canceling the stamp and one applied over the lattice opening.

3. June 29 (?). Stafford to South Hardwick, Vermont (Figure 19-6).

4. (?) 17 (?). New York to Nebraska City, Nebraska (Figure 19-8).

5. Unknown date. Melville, New Jersey, to Flushing, New York. Circular use with a 1¢ Franklin and a square lattice opening. A circular is enclosed. No photo. (Lot 2472. Knapp sale, Part II, October 1941).

In addition, at least one example of an enclosure with an attached canceled 1¢ stamp has been recorded (Figure 19-7).

Probably about a dozen examples of experimental envelopes using the 1¢ Franklin and off-cover 1¢ stamps with the Leeds & Franklin private postmark also exist. Even with these additions, the total number of Leeds & Franklin products with the 1¢ stamp is extremely small.

As previously noted, most of the recorded examples have their postage paid with an 1861 3¢ stamp; however, two covers are known with the 1862 2¢ Black Jack. In all of the examples of Leeds patent letters, correct use where the stamp is placed over the opening is scarce. On at least one occasion, the stamp was carefully placed under the lattice and affixed to the enclosure. In many cases, it was placed elsewhere on the envelope. Obviously, most users did not understand the purpose of the opening and lattice.

The earliest-known use of the Leeds/Morison patent envelopes with any denomination of stamp is October 26, 1861. The latest recorded use is July 3, 1865, with the majority being used during 1862.

Although the patent envelopes were never widely used, and their production was certainly not a profitable enterprise, records indicate that Leeds (see **Figure 19-12**) continued with his inventive proclivities. He designed significant improvements to heating and ventilating systems, and developed plans for better harbors. He left the United States in the 1870s and settled in London, England. While there, he proposed ideas for changing the London Underground to an elevated railway, for a railway to connect Europe and India, and for major changes in

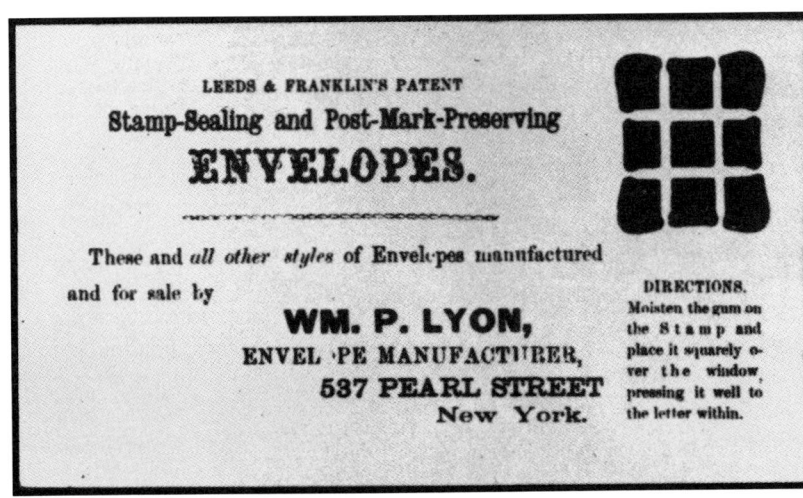

Figure 19-11. Advertising sample of the Leeds & Franklin envelope. (Illustration courtesy of the Collectors Club of New York)

Figure 19-12. Portrait of Lewis W. Leeds. (Courtesy of the Collectors Club of New York)

ship construction to improve ventilation in the interiors.

Possibly few, if any, of his ideas gained wide acceptance or great rewards, but philatelists will always be in his debt for those unusual and fascinating envelopes with the strange holes that are now so scarce and highly prized.

Turned Covers

A chronic shortage of paper in the Southern states, and some frugality in the North, resulted in the use of envelopes more than once. Since this multiple use was usually accomplished by turning the cover inside out and readdressing it, such covers are referred to as "turned covers."

Figure 19-13 shows a scarce example of a Northern reuse. This cover was originally used on April 24 to mail a letter from New York City to Albany, New York. Postage and carrier collection to the mails was paid by a 3¢ and a 1¢ stamp. The envelope was later turned inside-out, franked with a single 3¢ stamp and addressed back to New York City. The cover was postmarked "AUG 18 '64" at Albany for the return trip.

An exceptional turned cover that saw postal use with both the Confederate and the Union postal services is shown in **Figure 19-14**. A U.S. 3¢ stamped envelope of the 1853-55 issue was overprinted "Confederate States of America/Post Office Department/Official Business/Chief of the Contract Bureau." The embossed 3¢ stamp had no value in the Confederacy, and the envelope was used because of the scarcity of stationery. An authorizing franking signature was applied, and the cover was handstamped FREE and postmarked "OCT 14 1863" by the Confederate post office at Richmond, Virginia. It was addressed to Five Mile, South Carolina. Some time later, probably shortly after the war, the cover was turned and reused. This time, of course, the cover was handled by the U.S. Post Office. A 2¢ and 1¢ stamp of the 1861 issue paid the postage, and the cover was postmarked "AUG 19" at Five Mile. The stamps were canceled with what appears to be a manuscript "Five Mile SC."

1¢ Franklin Bisect Use

Since there were no ½¢ rates during the period of use of the 1861 1¢ stamp, there was never a need to bisect the stamp to achieve a particular rate. This was done at times with other values, particularly the 2¢ and 10¢ denominations.

A rare use of a bisected 1¢ Franklin is shown in **Figure 19-15**. This particular cover is a homemade wrapper mailed at New Orleans and postmarked on April 27, 1863. The 3¢ letter rate was paid by a 3¢ stamp, and a 1¢ stamp was torn in two to be used, along with the 3¢, as seals for the flap. The 3¢ and both halves of the 1¢ are canceled with a bull's-eye killer. The wrapper is addressed to East Franklin, Vermont. The normal rate for printed matter enclosed in a wrapper would be 1¢ at the time this item was mailed. However, there is a note written on the interior of the wrapper that conveys the following intelligence:

"The Rebs admit a loss on thier (sic) side of 50 men Killed 200 wounded and 500 Prissoners (sic) and 4 Gun boats."

This manuscript addition, of course, means that letter-rate postage must be paid.

While this is not a true bisect usage in the normal philatelic sense, it is as close as one can get with the 1¢ Franklin. The author has seen other examples where the 1¢ stamp was used singly or in multiples to seal an envelope, and also to pay postage, but this is the only example of a bisected stamp that he has listed.

There are many odd and interesting uses residing in collections and dealers' boxes that are yet to be recorded. There is always the desire to do something differently, and the American public has never been immune to the temptation to make their mail something special. Stamps are occasionally used on all four corners of an envelope. Some examples are known with artistic drawings and the 1¢ stamp incorporated into the design. The list is long, and these unusual items always bring a bit of spice to the search for something new to add to a prized accumulation of philatelic treasures.

Miscellaenous, Odd and Unusual

Figure 19-13. Scarce cover showing repeated use. It is partially opened to show both the interior and exterior of the envelope. The envelope was posted at New York City on April 24. The 1¢ Franklin paid for carrier collection to the mails, and a 3¢ 1861 paid for the letter postage to Albany. The cover was turned inside-out and reused with the addition of another 3¢ stamp to send another letter back to New York City. It is postmarked at Albany, "AUG 18 '64."

Figure 19-14. Turned Confederate States official-use cover. The cover was originally used at Richmond, Virginia, and postmarked "OCT 14 1863." It was handstamped FREE and addressed to "Five Mile, Pickens Dist., S.C." It was reused "AUG 19" (year unknown) at Five Mile and addressed to "Pickens C.H., S.C." Postage was paid with a 1¢ Franklin and a 2¢ Black Jack (Scott 73).
(Rorke collection, Christie's, New York, auction photo)

399

Figure 19-15. Rare, possibly unique, postally marked use of a bisected 1¢ Franklin. The cover was mailed at New Orleans, Louisiana, with an "APR 27 1863" CDS. The 3¢ 1861 Washington paid the letter postage. A single 1¢ Franklin was torn in half and used to help seal the flap of this homemade wrapper. (Lionel S. Newman auction photo)

References

1. Grant, Robert W. *The Handbook of Civil War Patriotic Envelopes and Postal History.* Vol. I. 1977.

2. Gross, E. Tudor. "The First 'Window' Envelope." *Collectors Club Philatelist.* April 1942.

3. Gross, E. Tudor. "The First 'Window' Envelope, Supplementary Notes." *Collectors Club Philatelist.* January 1943.

4. Gross, E. Tudor. "The First 'Window' Envelope, Supplementary Notes-Round Two." *Collectors Club Philatelist.* October 1943.

5. Gross, E. Tudor. "The First Window Envelope, Final Chapter." *Collectors Club Philatelist.* April 1944.

Index

-A-

Ackerman, Ernest 23, 28, 79, 81
Adams Express Company. *See* Covers: Western express
Advertised mail 90
Alexander, Thomas J. 101
Allan Line 335
Allen, Thomas F. 193
Altman, Sol 59
American and Commercial Advertiser 152
American Bank Note Company 2, 3, 10, 17, 18,
   21, 23, 56, 65, 76, 77, 79, 80, 380-381
American Journal of Philately 44
American Philatelic Congress 48
American Philatelic Congress Book 7, 41, 48, 59, 85
American Philatelic Society 10, 18, 81
American Philatelist 17, 54, 238, 391
Amos Press 8
Angell, Henry C. 274
Armed Forces mails 253, 255–266
Army Post Office 253
Ashbrook, Stanley B. 7, 138, 150, 186,
   197, 198, 238, 239, 246, 248, 277
Aspinwall, W.H. 310
Atlanta color proofs. *See* Special printings: 1881
   Atlanta color proofs
Atlanta Cotton Fair 22, 26
Atlantic Monthly 380
August issues 1, 6

-B-

Babcock, W.L. 249, 250, 251
Bacon, Edward Denny 79
Baker, Hugh 61
Baker, J. David 61, 101, 161
Bakers' U.S. Classics 62, 146
Bald, Cousland & Company 3
Baltimore carrier system 189–191
Banks, Nathaniel 269, 270
Barber, E.W. 73
Bartels, J.M. 70
Bates, Edward 281
Bates, Joseph L. 380
Battle of Bull Run 253
Baxter, DeWitt Clinton 281
Becker, John 206
Bell, William 326
Bellows, Henry W. 288
Bemrose and Sons 19
Bernhisel, John M. 326
Biddle, John R. 295

Bidwell correspondence 389
Bierman, Stanley M. 7, 80
Birney, David Bell 281
Bishop, Henry S. 193
Bishop's City Post 193
Blair, Francis P. 1
Blair, Montgomery 1, 2, 3, 4, 89, 93, 107, 118, 146, 149,
   158, 165, 166, 193, 203, 223, 232, 253, 254, 255, 259,
   278, 281, 313, 320, 322, 323, 331, 359, 377, 378, 379
Blake, Maurice C. 101
Blood's Penny Post 163-164, 176–178
Boell, W. 289
Boggs, Winthrop 19, 356
Bohn, C. 262
Bond, J.W. 277
Book mail 213–214
Bootlegging 189, 210
Boston carrier system 186–189
Boston Chronicle 186
Boston Philatelic Society 24
Bowen, Sayles J. 253
Bowers and Merena 380
Bowlsby essay 52-53, 59, 69
Bowlsby, George 59
Box letter. *See* Drop letters
Box mail. *See* Postal laws: Box mail
Boyd, Daniel M. 4, 6, 20, 152
Boyd's Dispatch 316
Branch post offices 91, 193–197
   Chicago, Illinois 195, 196
   Cleveland, Ohio 195
Brazer, Clarence 3, 7, 8, 9, 10, 11, 12, 13, 15,
   23, 26, 27, 28, 41, 43, 53, 54, 60, 63, 70, 77, 78, 79, 80, 84
Breckenridge, John C. 277
Brigham collection 49
British Guiana 1¢ magenta 46
British Mail Convention 218
British North American Act 363
British treaty mails 334–340
Brooklyn Institute of Science and Art 85
Brookman, Lester 19, 21, 29, 33, 41,
   44, 45, 46, 47, 48, 50, 73
Brown, Aaron V. 311
Brown, Shipley & Co. 175
Bruns, Franklin 82
Bruns, James H. 85, 86
Bryce, William, Co. 382, 383
Buchanan, James 263, 278, 319
Buffalo Boys of 21st Regiment 261
Bureau of Engraving and Printing 23, 24, 41
   Special printings 69–88
Bureau Specialist 85

401

Burns, Ronald A. 84, 85, 86
Butler & Carpenter 56, 382
Butler, Benjamin F. 266, 267, 278
Butterfield, John 317–318
Butterfield mail route. *See* Express mail: Butterfield

-C-

Cabeen, Richard McP. 80, 161, 195
California, Oregon & Mexico Steamship Line 356
Cameron, Simon 281, 288
Campbell, James 248
Cancellations .... 101, 127. *See also* Markings, postal
    Auxiliary markings 136
    Circle of wedges 172
    Colored 128, 147–148
    Fancy 128, 128–133, 147
        Chicago double K 132
        Dedham, Massachusetts 205
        Downieville star 359
        East Greenwich, Rhode Island, anchor 132, 133
        Greenfield, Massachusetts 132
        K D 132
        Masonic 132
        New Haven, Connecticut, star 133
        Rockford, Illinois, bluebird 132, 133
        Rockville, Connecticut 132
        Waterbury 128, 128–131
        West Eau Clair, Wisconsin, telephone dial 133
    Lazy date 140
    MAILS SUSPENDED 2
    Manuscript 128, 133–135, 136
    Paid 127, 135, 161, 186, 188, 193, 205
    Patent 128, 139–147
        Buffalo, New York 145
        Charleston, South Carolina 146
        Cookie cutter 144
        Eight-blade 141–143
        New York City 141, 145
        Norton, Marcus P. 139, 140, 141,
                142, 143, 144, 145, 146, 321, 360
        Robertson, T.J.W. 139
    Postal laws 91
    Postmarks used as cancels 135–137
    Prison bar 147
    Richmond, Virginia, negative shamrock 147
Cannon, Joseph G. 85
Carrier system
    U.S. Post Office Department 164–166
Carriers 91–92, 203, 267
    Baltimore 189–191
    Boston, Massachusetts 186–189, 198,
                      199, 260, 281, 284, 285

Carriers (continued)
    Brooklyn, New York 175
    Chicago, Illinois 193, 194
    Cincinnati, Ohio 166, 191, 192
    Cleveland, Ohio 192, 193
    Foreign destinations 172, 173, 175
    Local. *See* Collection and delivery: City carrier
    New Bedford, Massachusetts 193
    New York City ... 166–167, 172, 198, 199, 260, 280, 282,
                      283, 286, 298, 300, 302, 314
        Compound 3¢+1¢ envelope 172
    Philadelphia, Pennsylvania 175–186, 261, 272, 284,
                      285, 286, 296, 303
    Private 91–92, 316
    Smaller offices 191–193
    St. Louis, Missouri 166, 192, 193
    Washington, D.C. 290, 307
Caspary, Alfred 75
Census of U.S. Classic Plate Blocks 49
Centennial Exposition 72–76
Central Association of Relief 288
Central Overland Route 317
Central Pacific Railroad 325
Champagne, Richard A. 66
Chapin, John C. 29, 49, 76
Chase, Carroll 19, 70, 73, 150
Chase, Salmon P. 281, 377
Chicago North Branch Post Office 194
Chicago Post Office 97
Chicago Press and Tribune 250
Chicago Tribune 161
Christian, C.W. 13, 28, 29, 31, 36, 38, 45,
    54, 55, 59, 60, 65, 66, 67, 69, 70, 71, 75, 78, 86, 108, 114,
    115, 120, 121, 129, 133, 136, 154, 181, 183, 204, 205,
    221, 225, 226, 264, 265, 275, 276, 280, 281, 285, 286,
    296, 298, 303, 304, 326, 329, 336, 337, 339, 342, 343,
    344, 346, 348, 351, 353, 354, 358, 359, 360, 366, 374,
                      385, 386, 392, 393
Christie's, New York 14, 15, 30, 31, 35, 46, 51, 63,
    76, 131, 132, 138, 147, 153, 160, 340, 345, 369, 399
Chronicle 8, 29, 38, 42, 46, 51,
                56, 82, 141, 158, 197, 200, 239
Circular mail 213
    Advertisement 216
    Business cards 214, 217
    Domestic 214–218
    Foreign destinations 218–223
        Bremen 219, 220, 221
        Canada 218, 222, 223
        Italy 218, 219
        Netherlands 221
        Norway 221, 222

Circular mail (continued)
- Nova Scotia 363–367
- Scotland 219
- Spain 219, 220
- Switzerland 220, 221
- Junk mail 214
- Newspapers 213, 223–227, 276
  - Foreign destinations 227–229
  - Stagecoaches 223
- Pamphlets 213
- Prices current 213
- Third-class mail 215
- Unsealed 290, 302

Circulars ..... 136. *See also* Postal laws: Circulars
City carrier collection and delivery. *See* Collection and delivery: City carrier
City Despatch Post 127
Civil War .. 1, 2, 22, 103, 110, 122, 127, 149–162, 162, 182, 190, 215, 217, 236, 295, 297, 303, 304, 312, 313, 319, 320, 321, 324, 349, 372, 377, 396
Civil War military mails 253–293
Clark, Hugh 34
Cleveland Morning Leader 195
Coburn, Jesse L. 309
Cole, James 128
Cole, Walter 315, 336, 368
Collection and delivery
- City carrier 163
  - Blood's Penny Post 163
  - Brooklyn, New York 175
  - Foreign destination 172, 173
  - New York 166–167
  - Philadelphia, Pennsylvania 175–186
- Collection for delivery to the mails 171–175
- Post Office carrier system 164–166

Collectors Club of New York .. 81, 391, 395, 396, 397, 398
Collectors Club Philatelist 141, 390, 391
Collins Line 349
Colonial Postal Systems and Postage Stamps of Vancouver Island and British Columbia, 1849-1871 368
Colors
- 1861-67 1¢ Franklin 30, 32–34
  - Dark blue 33
  - Greenish blue 33
  - Indigo 33
  - Ultramarine 33
Compagnie Générale Transatlantique 342
Confederate Post Office Department 2, 254, 264
Confederate stamps 69
Continental Bank Note Company 23, 41, 74
Cook, I. 250

Cooper, David M. 18
Cotting, Roger B. 234
Cotton State and International Exposition 78
Counterfeit grills 54–55
Coupon essays. *See* Essays: Coupon
Covers
- 1861 1¢ Franklin
  - Earliest-known use 182
  - Advertising ..... 182, 183, 208. *See also* Covers: Illustrated: Advertising
  - Angell correspondence 274
  - Armed Forces 253, 255–266
  - Berlin & Jones patent envelope 389
  - Bidwell correspondence 389
  - Blockade 257, 259, 260
  - Boston carrier 186–189
  - Carried outside the mails 185
- Carrier
  - Brooklyn, New York 175
  - Foreign destination 175
  - Foreign-U.S. stamps 174
  - Markings 178
  - New York 260
- Carrier collection
  - Prepaid 173–175, 182
- Carrier fee prepaid 197–199, 277, 279, 296, 342
- Carrier to the mails ... 182, 183, 184, 186, 188, 190, 191, 192, 275, 292, 315, 323
- Chicago North Branch Post Office 194, 195, 196
- Chicago West Branch Post Office 196
- Collection fee paid by stamp 165, 199
- Compound envelopes 197–198
- Double-weight letter 175, 259, 284, 312, 314, 315, 335, 340, 342, 343
- Drop letter 203
  - Alexandria, Virginia 209
  - Blackstone, Massachusetts 211
  - Buffalo, New York 208
  - Concord, New Hampshire 209
  - Florence, Massachusetts 208
  - Free carriage 211
  - Gloversville, New York 306
  - Hartford, Connecticut 207
  - Holmes' Hole, Massachusetts 207
  - Marion, Massachusetts 306
  - Nevada Territory 326
  - New Orleans, Louisiana 208, 209
  - Penn Yan, New York 210
- Flag of Truce 263–264
- Foreign mails 331
  - British Columbia 367
  - British treaty mails 334–340

Covers (continued)
- Canada 357–361
- Central America 373
- Chile 374
- China 339–340
- Colombia 373
- France 341–347
- Hamburg 349
- Italy 334
- Japan 340
- Mexico 371–373
- Mixed frankings 337
- New Brunswick 361–363
- New Granada 373
- Newfoundland and Prince Edward Island 367
- Panama 374
- Prussia 350–355
- South America 373
- Spain 337, 338–340
- St. Pierre & Miquelon 370–371
- Switzerland 345
- Vancouver's Island 367
- Fort Monroe 257, 262, 263, 264, 278, 279
- Fort Warren 265
- Free 122-125, 184, 191
- Illustrated 215, 273–288, 295
  - Advertising 295, 295–301, 378–379
  - Bigler, J., & Co. 298, 299
  - Brandon, Vermont 301–303
  - Connecticut Life Insurance Co. 297, 298
  - Corner cards 295
  - Exhibiting 295
  - Fay, J.A., & Co. 301, 302
  - Hotel 297
  - India Ale 300–301
  - Johnson's Union Washing Machine 297, 298
  - Knickerbocker Ice Company 297
  - Late Jack's Hotel 297
  - Local government 295, 301–304
  - Logos 295
  - Love letters 295, 304–308
  - Magee of Philadelphia 303
  - Maine 303–304
  - Manhattan Life Insurance Company 296, 297
  - Montreal Telegraph Co. 297
  - New York City 301, 302
  - Pennsylvania 303
  - Phonography 299, 300
  - Putnam, John 297, 299
  - Romeo and Juliet 308
  - Sarony, Major & Knapp 301
  - Smith & Brother Brewers 300–301

Covers (continued)
- Soldier's Farewell 308
- State government 295, 301–304
- Temperance 295
- U.S. Patent and Bound Land Office 304
- Valentines 295, 304–308
- Water Cure and Hygeio-Therapeutic College ... 300
- Young America Nursery 301, 302
- Knickerbocker Ice Company 183, 297
- Lady's 198, 204, 306
- Leeds & Franklin patent envelopes 389–397
- Legal exchange-period use 158
- Lincoln campaign 206, 207, 277
- Masonic 205
- Massachusetts Volunteers 187, 266
- Mourning 123, 237, 351, 359
- Naval letter 257, 257–266, 275, 283
  - Key West 257, 260
  - Multiple rate 258
  - USS Bainbridge 257
  - USS De Soto 272
  - USS Florida 261
  - USS Henrick Hudson 260, 261
  - USS Mercedita 258
  - USS Patroon 260
  - USS San Jacinto 259, 260
  - USS Santiago de Cuba 257–259
  - USS Wabash 268, 269
- Occupation 266–273
  - Banks, Nathaniel 270
  - Fort Pickens 269
  - Fort Totten 269
  - New Orleans 266–267
  - Port Royal, South Carolinia 267, 268, 269
  - Shed's Corners, New York 271
- Odd-shaped 389
- Official business 190–191, 271–272, 273
  - Free 272
- Old Capitol Prison 265
- Old Stamps Not Recognized 159–161
- Outside the mails 314, 315, 316
- Overland 313–325
- Patriotic 162, 175, 182, 187, 198, 206,
                              253, 261, 262, 263, 273–288, 295, 303
  - Banks, Nathaniel 281
  - Campaign 275, 277
  - Cartoon 284
  - Davis, Jefferson 282, 285
  - Ellsworth, Elmer 278, 280
  - Farwell correspondence 278, 281, 286
  - Flag 286–287
  - Floyd, of the C.S.A. 278, 279

Covers (continued)
- Foreign destination 267
- Groupings 275
- Hale, Reuben C. 281, 282
- Hawley, J.R. 282
- Homemade 287–288
- Irish harp flag 287
- Kimmel and Magnus 277, 287
- King and Baird 281
- Lincoln's Cabinet 280
- Loyal to the Union 286
- Magee, James L. 282
- Magnus, Charles 283
- McClellan, George 281
- Mexican War 274, 276, 277
- Naval 275, 276, 283
- Printed on both sides 285
- Reagles and Co. 286
- Revolutionary War 280
- Valentine 307
- Wells, John G. 286
- Wyman, John 283–285
- Zouaves 281
- Prisoners of war 263–264, 265
- Proctor & Clark 389
- Registered 233–252
  - Foreign destination 234
- Revenue stamps used as postage 381–385
- Sanitary Fair 185, 253, 255, 288–292, 304
- Ship, steamboat and steamship 210, 236, 236–239, 242–244
  - Biddeford, Maine, to San Francisco 312, 313
  - Postage due 240–241
  - San Francisco to Cherryfield, Maine 313, 314
  - San Francisco to New York City 313
- Soldiers' letters 255–256, 257, 291
- South-to-North 264–265
- Stamps used as coins 378
- Supplementary mail 247–251
  - Chicago 249–251
  - New York 247–249
- Territorial 325–330
  - Canada destination 328, 329
  - Colorado 327–329
  - Nebraska 329
  - Nevada 325–326
  - Utah 326, 326–327
- Transatlantic mails 333–334
- Transcontinental 309, 321, 324
  - Denver, James William 323–324
  - Wetherbee correspondence 323
- Transcontinental letter rate 256, 316

Covers (continued)
- Turned 397–398, 399
- Unclaimed 270
- Volunteer Hospital 182, 289
- Way 242, 244–247
  - Canada 245–246
- Western 253–254, 309
- Western express 313–325
  - Adams & Co. 254, 314
  - Brents and Nelson's Express 316, 317
  - Canada destination 316, 317
  - Pony Express 320–321
  - San Francisco to Westfield, Massachusetts 315
  - Wells, Fargo 314, 316, 369
- Wisconsin Volunteers 256
- Craig, Benjamin 56
- Crane, Alanson 263
- Crawford, Earl of 23, 28, 79, 80, 81, 82
- Creswell, John A.J. 56
- *Cross Border Mails: United States and British North America to 1875* 357
- Curtis, Samuel L. 159
- Cutting, George W. 138
- *Cyclopedia* 141

-D-

- Danish Post Office 222
- Davis, Jefferson 282, 285
- Davis, Wilbur W. 101
- Dead Letter Office 2, 93, 111, 112–114, 115, 117–118, 119, 159, 254, 256, 270, 386
- Deaville, Alfred S. 368
- Demonetized stamps
  - 1847 stamps 149
  - 1851-57 stamps 1–2, 2, 73, 112, 149, 254
    - Completion dates 150, 151, 152, 155
    - Exchange period 155, 156
    - Held for Postage 157, 160
    - Legal exchange-period use 158
    - Mixed-issue use 158
    - Old Stamps Accepted 162
    - Old Stamps Not Recognized 159–161
    - Stamps not accepted 157
- Dennison, William 89, 90, 91, 112, 114, 146, 147
- Denver, James William 323, 324
- Denver Post Office 158
- Depew, Chauncey 85
- Die, premiere and issue design 13
- Dillaway, Guy 137, 138
- Distributing post offices 107
- Dix, John A. 103, 140, 141, 166, 167, 263, 264

405

Doane, Percy 390
Domestic registry fees and services 235
Douglas, Steven A. 277
Dred Scott case 1
Drews, Richard E. 29
Drop letters 111, 136, 145, 155, 163, 175, 179, 190,
  203. *See also* Covers: Drop lettters; Postal laws:
  Drop letters
DuBois, Warren 152
Durand, Cyrus 14, 18

-E-

Eastern Gulf Blockading Squadron 260
Ellsworth, Elmer 278, 280, 281
Elton, J.P. 129
Ely, Fred 205
Emerson, R.S. 274
Encased postage stamps 380–381
Encyclopedia of the Colors of
  United States Postage Stamps 32, 33
Engraving, stamp 3
Eno, Amos 101, 128, 146, 167
Envelope essays 82, 83
Errors
  1861-67 1¢ Franklin
    Cracked plate 34
    Perforation errors 36
    Preprinting fold 36, 37
  Production
    1861-67 1¢ Franklin 34–38
Essay-Proof Journal 7, 11, 13, 15, 23, 24, 59, 84
Essay-Proof Society 23
Essays
  1861 stamps 4, 7, 8, 10
  1¢ Franklin 10–11, 22, 26
  Bicolor 53–54
  Bowlsby 52–53, 59, 69
  Coupon 59–62
  Frame-only 53
  Grilled 52–54
  Monogram 53
Essays For U.S. Adhesive Postage Stamps 3, 9, 10, 11
Evans, G.G. 381
Experimental printings 59-67
  Bowlsby 52-53, 59, 69
  Gibson 66, 67
  Lowenberg 62-64, 67
  Macdonough 65-66, 67
  Wyckoff 64-65, 67
Express mail .... 309, 313–325. *See also* Covers: Western
  express
  Adams Express Company 254, 314

Express mail (continued)
  American Express 320, 321
  Brents and Nelson's Express 316, 317
  Butterfield 311, 313, 317–318, 318, 319, 320
  California mail routes 309
  Central Overland and Pikes Peak
    Express Company 319
  Central Overland Route 317
  Central route 311
  Holladay Overland and Express Company ... 319, 324,
                                                            329
  Holladay Overland Stage Line 328
  Leavenworth City and Pikes Peak Express 327
  Overland Mail Company 317–318, 319, 320, 329
  Pony Express 319, 319–320
  Texas mail routes 309
  Wells, Fargo 97, 217, 314, 314–315,
                                316, 318, 319, 324, 325, 369, 370

-F-

Fakes
  1861-67 1¢ Franklin 28, 29
Fancy Cancellations on Nineteenth Century United
  States Postage Stamps 101
Farragut, David G. 266
Finkelburg, Falk 11, 14, 64, 67
Fisher, L.S. 153
Floyd, John B. 278, 319
Floyd's Penny Post 193, 194
Foote, A.H. 272
Foreign Mail office 219, 221
Foreign mails .... 147. *See also* Covers: Foreign mails
  Belgium 355
  British Columbia 367
  British North America 356–357
  Canada 356–357, 357–361
  Central America 373
  Chile 374
  Closed mail 332, 334, 341
    North German Union 355
    Prussia 341, 350, 351, 353, 355
  Colombia 373–374
  Exchange offices 332
  Forwarding agents 333, 340
  French Line 342
  French mails 341–347
  German States mails
    Bremen 348–349, 349
    Hamburg 349
    Prussia 350–355
  Hawaii 356
  Inland postage 332

Foreign mails (continued)
- Italy mails 355–356
- Mexico 372–373
- Netherlands mails 355
- New Brunswick 361–363, 365
- New Brunswick and Prince Edward Island 367
- New Granada 373–374
- Nova Scotia 363–367
- Open mail 332
    - British 335, 337–339, 340
    - French 345
    - Prussia 354
    - Transit 340
- Panama 374
- Postal conventions 331, 332–333
    - 1868 340-341
    - Belgium 334, 340, 355
    - Bremen 349
    - France 341
    - German States 347–349
    - Great Britain 340, 341
    - Hamburg 349
    - Italy 340, 355–356
    - Netherlands 340, 355
    - North German Postal Union 340
    - Prussia 334, 350–355
    - Switzerland 340, 355
- Postal treaties 332
- Sea postage 332
- South America 373
- St. Pierre & Miquelon 370–371
- Switzerland 355
- Terms, glossary of 332–333
- Transatlantic 333–334
- Transit postage 332
- Vancouver's Island 367

Fort Monroe 257, 262, 263, 264, 278, 279
See also Old Point Comfort
Fortgang, Morris 156
Fourth-class post offices 102
Fowler, Isaac V. 248
Fox, John A. 379
Frajola, Richard 192, 318, 327
Franklin, Benjamin 3, 17
Franklin Engraving and Printing Company 41
Franklin, Joseph F. 393
Free 122-125, 135, 184, 191
Free Soil Party 1
Free-franking privilege ..... 104, 118, 122–125, 182, 190–191. *See also* Postal laws: Free franked
Frèmont, John C. 311, 317
French/Thurn and Taxis Convention 221

Friedman, Howard 77, 78, 79, 80, 85
Colonel Friedman's Cameron Regiment Dragoons 154
Fugitive Slave Acts 278
Fugitive-ink patent printings 64, 65, 66, 69
Fundamentals of Philately 18

-G-

Gault, John 380
General Postal Union 331
George V 79
German Postal Union 228
German-Austrian Postal Union 233, 350, 353
Gibson, Abraham 59, 66, 67
Gibson patent 66-67
Gold Rush 310–311, 313, 323
Goldbeater's skin 64
Graham, Andrew J. 300
Graham, Richard B. 2, 7, 8, 56, 102, 104, 105, 122, 123, 125, 129, 140, 141, 146, 149, 150, 158, 161, 195, 199, 206, 209, 214, 225, 234, 235, 240, 246, 257, 258, 259, 260, 266, 268, 270, 271, 297, 307, 308, 395
Grant, Robert W. 273, 277
Gray, David 138
Greeley, Horace 395
Green, Edward H.R. 29
Greenhow, Rose 265
Grills, 1867-69 issues 21, 41, 59, 70, 146
- 1867 3¢ 42
- A grill 45, 46
- B grill 45–46, 46, 56
- C grill 45, 46, 54, 60
- D grill 45, 46, 47
- E grill 43, 45, 46, 47, 48–50, 50, 52, 54, 210, 234
- F grill 43, 45, 47, 50–52, 54, 208, 209
- Z grill 45, 46–48, 54
- Bicolor essay 53–54
- Bowlsby essay 52–53, 54
- Counterfeit 54–55
- Discontinued 55
- Embossing device 44
- Essays 43, 52–54
- Fancy cancellations 129
- Female 44
- Frame-only essays 53
- History 41–43
- Male 44
- Monogram essay 53
- Points down 44
- Points up 44
- Production 43–45
- Steel patent 42, 43
- Varieties 49, 50, 51

Gross, E. Tudor 17, 21, 35, 153, 198, 390, 391, 392
Gum 18, 19, 20, 22, 28, 29, 33, 37, 42, 43, 44, 45, 53, 60, 61, 64, 66, 70, 73, 74, 81, 121, 139, 249, 377, 378, 392
Guthrie, John B. 56
Gutter spacing 9, 14, 15, 75
Gwin, William M. 311, 317, 319

-H-

Hackett, Robert P. 14
Hafen, LeRoy R. 309, 319, 328
Hahn, Calvet M. 46
Hall, N.K. 362, 363
Hallett, John H. 166
Hamburg-American Line 173, 222, 349
Hargest, George E. 90, 331, 333, 341
Harmer, H.R. 14, 29, 34, 49, 75
Harmer, Rooke and Company 81
Harpel, O.H. 379
Harper's New Monthly Magazine 3, 5, 19, 27, 32, 295
Havre Line 348
Hawkins, Rush 263
Hayton, L.G. 260
Hazelton, Bruce 363
Hazen, A.D. 69, 73
Herkimer County Bank 382, 383
Herst, Herman Jr. 101, 379
Herzog, William K. 21, 33, 41, 50, 52, 56
Higgins and Gage 34
Higgins, Judson 287
Hill, John W. 128, 129
Hind collection 49
History of Letter Post Communication Between the United States and Europe, 1845-1875 .... 90, 331, 333
Holbrook, J. 89
Holladay, Ben 319, 324, 328, 356
Holt, Joseph 103, 111, 139, 181, 198, 311, 341
Home Insurance Company 205
Home Journal 224
Homestead Act 324
Hoole, Edmund 141, 146
Hooper, R.M. 138
Houdon, Antoine 17
Howe, John 363
Hubbard, Norman 331, 333
Hudson's Bay Co. 367

-I-

Indian Trust Fund 319
International Cotton Exposition 77, 80
Ireland, William 24

Ishikawa, Ryohei 35, 46, 51, 131
Ivy, Steve 10, 35, 48, 131, 371

-J-

Jackson, Andrew 1
Jefferson, Thomas 3
Jennings, Clyde 36, 148
Johnson, Cave 127, 348
Jones, George T. 54, 56
Joyce, Morton Dean 11

-K-

Kantor, Alvin and Marjorie 289, 290
Kasson, John A. 159, 331, 340, 342, 393, 394
Kaufmann, John W. 50, 153, 182, 280, 290
Kaufmann, Robert G. 30, 351
Kelleher, Daniel 25, 28, 35, 75, 130, 233
Kimmel, Frederick 277, 287
King, Horatio 103, 394
Klein, Walter C. 30, 31
Klemann, John 24, 41, 79, 81
Knapp, Edward S. 295
Kochersberger, Charles 177
Kohlhepp, John 157, 200, 239
Kuhlman, Henry 47, 48
Kukstis Auction 308

-L-

La Tuchie, Herb 300
Lane, Maryette 167
Laurence, Robert 273
Lawrence, Ken 48
Laws and Regulations of the Post Office Department 89
Layton, C. Rodney 271
Leavy, J.B. 41, 86
Lee, James 37, 45, 48, 60, 67, 104, 113, 114, 115, 116, 117, 119, 124, 137, 139, 154, 161, 162, 171, 174, 188, 189, 196, 210, 211, 216, 222, 224, 226, 227, 228, 237, 241, 243, 251, 261, 265, 268, 271, 282, 284, 299, 316, 323, 325, 326, 327, 328, 338, 350, 362, 364, 396
Leeds, Anna 397
Leeds, Barclay 393
Leeds, Lewis W. 391, 393, 395, 396, 398
Legal Tender Act 381
Leominster, Massachusetts, Library 122
Leominster, Massachusetts, labels 121–122
Letters of Gold 309
Library Company of Philadelphia 176
Library of Congress 81

Lilly, Josiah 28, 79, 80, 81
Lincoln, Abraham 1, 206, 207, 254, 259, 277,
                                       278, 280, 281, 288, 319, 377
Lincoln, George B. 393
Lindquist, H.L. 249
Lindsay, James Ludovic. *See* Crawford, Earl of
Linn, George 135
Linn's Stamp News 8, 135
List of Post Offices in the United States 89
Local carrier services 163
   Bishop's City Post 193
   Blood's Penny Post 176–178
   Boyd's Dispatch 316–317
   Floyd's Penny Post 193, 194
   U.S. Penny Mail 178
   U.S.P.O. Dispatch 178
Local letter 203
Lodge, Henry Cabot 85
London Philatelist 79
Louisville Democrat 155
Lowenberg, Henry 59, 62, 63, 64, 67
Lowenberg patent 62-64, 67
Luff, John N. 6, 7, 8, 17, 19, 20, 21, 23, 28, 29,
                               41, 45, 49, 69, 70, 73, 75, 81, 150, 391
Lyon, William P. 395, 396

-M-

Macdonough, J. 5, 17, 19, 20, 23, 25, 43, 59, 63, 65, 66
Macdonough patent 65-66, 67
Madden, Edwin C. 84
Magee, James L. 277, 282, 303
Magnus, Charles 277, 282, 283
Mahoney, John 373
Mail classifications 92
Mandel, Henry G. 23, 25, 81, 82
Manifest Destiny 309
Markings, postal .... 101. *See also* Cancellations
   Advertised 101, 113, 283
   America Uber Bremen 274
   Auxiliary 101, 110, 118, 136
   Balloon marking 104
   Belonging to the Army 255
   Boston exchange 336, 337, 343, 346, 352, 357, 364
   Carrier
      Baltimore 189–191
      New York 167
      Washington, D.C. 189–191
   Chicago City 197
   Chicago double circle 195, 196
   Circular datestamps .. 102, 104, 105, 135, 158, 161, 163,
                               169, 175, 194, 204, 206, 211, 215

Markings, postal (continued)
   Dead Letter Office 111, 115, 117–118, 119
   Delayed delivery 110
   Devices, marking 101
   Drop letter 204
   Due 101, 110, 116, 118, 118–121, 121
   Duplex 102, 103, 104
   East Groveland, New York 106
   Fancy 105
   Follow the Regiment 94, 255, 271
   Foreign exchange 249, 333
   Foreign mails 101, 347
   Forwarded 113, 114–115, 116, 117
   Forwarding agent 338
   Free 118, 122–125, 135
   Free Service, H.M.B., P.M. 123
   French entry 336, 341, 342, 344, 346, 348
   French exchange 342, 343
   Hamburg exchange 174
   Hold for Mail 112
   Hold for Postage 111, 157, 160, 181
   Illegal Stamp 161
   Ink colors 105
   Leominster, Massachusetts, labels 121–122
   Loeschick, Wesendonck & Co. 384, 385
   London exchange 335, 336, 337, 339
   Mails Suspended 2, 253
   Missent 115–117
   MOB 135, 136, 137
   New York exchange 173, 335, 337, 338, 339,
                                         340, 344, 345, 346, 351, 352, 353
   New York Foreign Mail 336, 337
   Norton 103
   Not called for 113, 117, 118
   Not found 113, 114, 115
   Old Stamps Accepted 162
   Old Stamps Not Recognized 159–161, 253
   Outgoing mail 111
   Overland 322
   P/C, printed circular 219
   Paris exchange 173
   Penny Mail 272, 285, 298
   Philadelphia Post Office town marking 185
   Post Office Business 94
   Present 206
   Prussia exchange 350
   Railway 106–110
      AGT, AG'T 108
      Baltimore & Ohio Railroad 109
      Chicago & Northwestern Railroad 107
      Monrovia, Maryland, station marking 110
      Morris & Essex Railroad 108

Markings, postal (continued)
- New York & New Haven Railroad 108
- New York-to-Chicago route 109
- Railroad Business corner card 109, 110
- RPO 108
- Station markings 108–109
- Rate markings 135, 136
- Received 106, 181
- Redirected mail 114–115
- Registered 101, 110, 136, 231, 232, 233
- Returned to Writer 114, 115
- Route agent 236
- Rubber stamping devices 105
- San Francisco exchange 335
- Shed's Corner, New York, straightline 105
- Ship 136, 236, 236–239, 258–266
- Soldiers' letters 255, 257, 291
- SOUTHN LETTER/UNPAID 254
- Spanish collection 339
- Steamboat 135, 136, 236
  - STEAMBOAT PERRY 244
- Steamship 96, 239–242
  - N.Y. STEAMSHIP 240
- Stock circular town and date 102
- Straightline town 105
- Supplementary Mail 101, 247–251
- Too Late 137
- Town and date 102–106, 127, 135, 136, 204, 214
  - Boston 186
  - Transit, railroad 107
- U. States 357, 362, 365
- U.S. Penny Mail 122, 178, 179, 180, 181
- U.S.P.O. Dispatch 178, 179
- Uncalled for 113
- Unclaimed 110
- Undelivered mail 112–114
- Used as cancels 135–137
- VERVIERS.B./COELN III/FRANCO 355
- Washington, D.C., balloon marking 104
- Way 236, 242

Mason, E.H. 23, 61
Mason, James M. 259
Masonic covers 205
Massachusetts Historical Society 85, 215
Massachusetts Volunteer Militia 186, 266, 297–298
Matthies, Katherine 274
McCall, Francis J. 85
McClellan, George 281
McDonald, Susan M. 357, 361
Mead, John W. Jr. 258
Mekeel, C.H. 81
Mekeel's Weekly Stamp News 69

Mercury Stamp Company 70
Merrill, Nancy 383
Methuen Handbook of Color 32, 33
Metropolitan Museum of Art 17
Mexican War of 1845 186
Meyer, Henry 107, 244, 245
Meyersburg, Robert B. 82, 83, 169, 180, 185, 186, 187, 192, 198, 200, 247, 314
Milgram, James W. 204, 390
Military mail
- Western 253

Miller, Benjamin K. 47
Miner's Journal 218
Mitchell, J.S. 259
Mobile post office 107
Money orders 232
- *See also* Postal laws: Money orders

Montreal Ocean Steam Ship Line 335
Moody collection 49
Morganthau, J.C. 23
Morganthau, J.C., & Company 35
Morison, Benjamin 391, 392, 397
Morrill, Anson P. 291
Morris, James 362
Mozian, Vahan 76
Mueller, Barbara 232
Multiples
- 1861-67 1¢ Franklin 29–30, 31, 38
  - Plate inscription 30

Mustering Act 255

-N-

Nassau Stamp Company 24, 81
National Bank Note Company 3, 4, 5, 6, 8, 17, 18, 21, 35, 41, 42, 43, 55
- 1861 1¢ Franklin
  - Delivery 152, 255
  - Production 18–22
- 1861 contract 149, 151
- Encased postage stamps 380–381
- Essays 4, 62, 65
  - 1861 1¢ Franklin 10–11
  - Coupon 60–62
  - Envelope 82
- Premieres gravures 6, 12, 13
  - Hybrid proof 15
- Proofs 22–24, 25–26, 26, 27, 28
- Special printings 69–88

National Intelligencer 263
National Philatelic Society 6
National Postal Museum 85, 86
National Stamp Collection 24, 85, 86

Navy postal system 253, 257, 257–266
Neinken, Mortimer 29
New Harper's Magazine 20
New Orleans carrier system
    Markings 175
New York & Havre Steam Navigation Company 348
New York City carrier system 166–167, 186, 260
    Bootleg letter sheet 171
    Carrier covers 166, 172
    Foreign destination 173
    Foreign-origin cover 170, 171
    Free delivery, proposed 167
    Local service 167–171, 177
    Markings 167, 175
New York Post Office 103, 131, 157
New York postmaster's provisionals 127
New York Public Library 47
New York State Volunteers 261
New York Times 157
New York Tribune 157, 395
Newspaper wrappers 224–227
Newton & Co., William 379
Newton, Isaac 33
Norona, Delf 141, 250
North Atlantic Mail Sailings, 1840-75 .... 331, 333
North German Line 274, 349
North German Lloyd Line 335, 349, 384
North German Union 353
Norton, Marcus P. 103, 139, 140,
                             141, 142, 143, 144, 145, 146
Nowak, Henry 52, 70, 234, 247
Numismatist 381

-O-

Ocean Line 348, 349
Ocean Steam Navigation Company 348
Old Capitol Prison 265
Old Point Comfort post office 257, 261,
                                     262, 263, 264, 266
Olmstead, Frederick Law 395–396
Opdyke, George 395
Oregon Trail 317
Outside the mails 236
Overland mail .... 313, 313–325, 318. *See also* Covers:
    Overland; Express mail
    Routes 318
The Overland Mail 309, 319, 328
Overland Mail Company 317–318

-P-

Pacific Mail Steamship Company 310, 311, 374

Palfrey, J.G. 395
Panama-Pacific die proofs 85–87
Panama-Pacific Exposition 85
Paris International Exhibition 82–83
Parker, John 266–267
Passos, Cyril dos 7
Pat Paragraphs 20, 150, 151, 152, 200
Patent printings 59–67
Patents. *See* Cancellations: Patent
Pease, Joseph Ives 14, 17
Pennypost men 92
Perforations 9, 10, 15, 18-20, 22, 28, 34, 35, 36, 43, 44,
    45, 46, 50, 53, 60, 61, 62, 63, 65, 66, 67, 76, 161, 379, 395
Perkins, Jacob 18
Perry, Elliott 7, 15, 20, 21, 41, 47, 75, 149, 150, 151, 152,
                161, 165, 166, 178, 179, 180, 198, 200
Petrie, James A. 78, 79, 81
Peyton, J.E. 261
Philadelphia carrier system 175–186, 186
    Blood's Penny Post 175, 176–178
    Markings 175
    Outside-the-mails use 185
Philatelic Foundation 33, 35, 46, 47, 48, 70
Philatelic Journal of America 81
Philatelic Society of New York 139
Phillips, David G. 109, 110, 241, 247, 295, 378
Pickard, F.W. 70
Pickels, Henry G. 381
Piller, Stanley 34, 52
Piszkiewicz, Leonard 197
Plate, gutter spacing 9, 14, 15, 75
Plate margin markings 27
Polk, James 124
Pony Express. *See* Express mail: Pony Express
Postage due 118–121, 159–161, 169,
                           192, 226, 233, 240, 264
Postage Stamps of the United States 7, 17, 20, 23, 69
Postal Appropriation Act of 1859 .... 311, 312
Postal laws 89
    Act of March 3, 1863 .... 89, 90
    Advertised mail 90, 93
    Books 90–91
    Box mail 90
    Branch post offices 91, 193–197
    Canceling 91, 127
    Carrier collection and delivery 163–201
    Carrier fees 163–201
    Carriers 91–92
    Circulars 90, 92, 93, 213
    Collect/underpaid 92–93
    Dead Letter Office 93, 94, 159
    Domestic mail 90–100, 95

Postal laws (continued)
    Drop letters 90, 93–94
    Forwarding 94
    Free forwarding 89
    Free franked 94, 118, 122–125
    Free mail 94
    Insufficient postage 233
    Local letters 93–94
    Money orders 95
    Newspapers 95, 97
    Old Stamps Not Recognized 159–161
    Pamphlets 95
    Postal Law, 1860 113
    Postal stationery 96
    Private posts 176–177
    Refused mail 90
    Registered mail 95–96, 231–235
    Request letter 113
    Ship, steamboat, steamship 96, 97, 236, 242–244
    Soldiers and sailors letters 93, 96
    Stamped envelopes 96
    Supplementary mail 97
    Transient mail 95, 97, 213, 224
    Undelivered mail 112–114
    Underpaid letters 119–121
    Way letters 97, 244–247
Postal Laws and Regulations 89, 90, 101, 105
Postal rates. *See* Rates, postal
    Advertised mail 90
    Domestic mail 90–100
Postal stationery
    Wrappers 225–227
Postmasters, classified 102
Potts, Albert 176
Precancels 137–139
    Cumberland, Maine 138
    Harrisburg, Pennsylvania 138
    Weston W 137–138
Premieres gravures 1, 6–10, 75, 151
    Colors 8
    National Bank Note Company 12
        Hybrid proof 15
    Toppan, Carpenter & Company 11–12
Printed matter. *See* Circular and Transient mail
Printing
    1861 1¢ Franklin 18–22
        Plates 29–30
Proofs
    1861 1¢ Franklin 22–24
        Ackerman India proof sheets 24
        Autographed proof 25
        Engravers' die proofs 24

Proofs (continued)
    Hybrid 25
    India plate proofs 28, 33, 76
    Large die proofs 24–26, 33, 60, 61
    Plate proofs 26–29, 75
    Progressive die proofs 24, 26
    Small die proofs 26
    Trial color proofs 26
    Trial color proofs, experimental 62–67
1861 issue 5, 8, 10, 13
1879-93 cardboard 69
1881 Atlanta color proofs 69, 77–78
1895 Atlanta proofs 78–82
1903 Roosevelt die proofs 69, 83-85
1915 Panama-Pacific die proofs 85-87
Prussian closed mail 234, 267, 341, 350, 351, 353, 355
Puget Sound Herald 159
Pulver, Dale 373
Purnell, William 152

-Q-

Quarterman Publications Inc. 3, 10, 73, 319, 328

-R-

Railroad Construction Act 324
Railway markings. *See* Markings, postal: Railway
Railway post offices 107, 250
    Calais-to-Paris 219
Ralph, Joseph E. 23
Randall, Alex W. 42, 56
Rates, postal 89
    3¢ letter rate 105
    Advertised mail 90
    Advertising fee 98
    Armed Forces mail 255–266
    Books 90–91, 99
    Branch post offices 193–197
    British Columbia 367
    Canada and British North America 356–357
    Carrier fee 98, 163–201, 172, 190, 267
        Prepayment 197–199
    Carriers 91–92
    Central America 373–374
    Chile 374
    Circular mail 213
    Circulars 92, 99
    Closed mails 331
    Collect/underpaid 92–93
    Colombia 373–374
    Dead Letter Office 93
    Domestic rates and fees, 1860-70 98–99

Rates, postal (continued)
    Domestic registry fees and services 235
    Drop letter 21, 93–94, 104, 203
    Foreign 331
        British treaty mails 334–340
        France 341–347
    Forwarding fee 98
    Hawaii 352
    Letter 98
    Local letters 93–94
    Mexico 372–373
    Money orders 95
    New Brunswick 361–363
    New Granada 373–374
    Newspapers 95, 99, 223–224
    Nova Scotia 363–367
    Over the Rockies 321, 326
    Overweight letters 172
    Printed matter 92, 215, 223
    Registered mail 95–96, 231–235
        Foreign destinations 232
    Registry fee 98
    Ships, steamboats, steamships 96, 103, 236,
                            239–242, 242–244, 256
    Soldiers' and sailors' letters 96
    South America 373–374
    St. Pierre & Miquelon 370–371
    Supplementary mail 97, 247–251
    Third-class (miscellaneous) 99
    Transatlantic mail rates. *See* Transatlantic mails
    Transcontinental letter 256, 312–313,
                                316, 322, 323, 359
    Transient mail 97, 213, 266
    Unpaid/part-paid 99
    Vancouver's Island 367
    Way letters 97, 198, 244–247
Rawdon, Wright, Hatch & Edson 149
Reagan, John H. 1, 254
Refused mail. *See* Postal laws: Refused mail
Registered mail. *See* Postal laws: Registered mail. *See also* Special services
Remele, Charles 107
Report of the Postmaster General 193
Revenue Stamp Tax Act 381
Rieger, Barry 53
Robertson, T.J.W. 139
Rocky Mountain News 159
Rogers, C.R.P. 269
Rogers, William F. 261
Rohloff, Paul C. 129
Roosevelt, Franklin D. 24
Roosevelt presentation albums 23

Roosevelt small die proofs 83
Roosevelt, Theodore 84
Root, Elihu 85
Ropes, H., and Co. 175
Rorke collection 399
Route agents 107, 108
Royal Philatelic Collection 79
Rubricht 17
Russell, A.L. 261
Russell, Majors and Waddell 319
Russell, Messrs., & Co. 340
Russell, William 319

-S-

Salles, Raymond 341
Sanborne, Ray 129
Sanitary Commission 288–292, 304, 396
    Sanitary Fair envelopes 61, 185, 253, 255
    Sanitary Fair stamps
        Brooklyn, New York 289
        Women's Branch 291
Sapperstein, Perry 395
Sarony, Major & Knapp 301
Schaeffer, George C. 56
Schernikow reprints 11, 12
Schilling, Wilbur 47, 48
Schmalzriedt, Fred 141, 143, 146
Scientific American 391
Scott, J.W. 23, 139
Scott Publishing Company 11
Scott *Specialized Catalogue of United States Stamps* 7, 8, 9, 10, 11, 12, 14, 26, 33, 34, 35, 45, 46, 54, 60, 63, 66, 67, 69, 75, 76, 80, 249
Scott Stamp and Coin Company 7, 23
Scott *Standard Postage Stamp Catalogue* 7, 23
Scott, Walter S. 391
Scott, Winfield 274, 275, 280, 281
Scott's Monthly Journal 391
Scoville Manufacturing Company 380
Seward, William Henry 281
Shaver & Corse 146
Ship letters. *See* Covers: Ship, steamboat, steamship; Postal laws: Ship, steamboat, steamship
Ship, steamship, steamboat mail. *See* Special services
Shreves Philatelic Galleries 153
Siegel, Robert A. 10, 15, 29, 46, 48, 51, 61, 63, 79, 80, 81, 109, 160, 251, 274, 283, 299, 316, 320, 372, 379
Simmy's Stamp Company 153
Simons, Henry 182
Simpson's U.S. Postal Markings, 1851-61 101
Sisson, Vinton E. 70
Skinner, H.C. 101, 128, 131, 132, 146, 147, 167, 336

413

Skinner, St. John B.S. 393, 394
Slabaugh, Arlie A. 380
Slawson, George 158
Slidell, John 259
Smith, Caleb B. 281
Smith, William A. 23
Smithsonian Institution 85, 86, 194
Souren, Y. 29
South Atlantic Blockading Squadron 257, 260, 269
Special printings 69
    1875 reprints 69, 72–76
    1879-93 cardboard proofs 69, 76
    1881 Atlanta color proofs 69, 77–78
    1895 Atlanta printings 69, 76, 78–82
    Control-number overprints 69, 72
    Envelope essay 82, 83
    Manuscript overprint 71
    1900 Paris International Exhibition 82–83
    1903 Roosevelt small die proofs 69, 83
    1915 Panama-Pacific small die proofs 69, 85–87
    Specimen overprints 69
        15mm 70–71
        Large block-letter 71–72
        Small 69
    Specimens 69
Special services 231
    Registered mail 231, 231–235
        Domestic registry fees and services 235
        Foreign destinations 234
        Money orders 232
        Numbers 233
    Ship, steamship, steamboat mail 231, 236, 236–239,
                                                  239–242, 242–244
    Supplementary mail 231, 247–251
        Chicago 249–251
        New York 247–251
    Way letters 231, 244–247
Spelman, Henry M. 235
Stagecoach companies 309
Stamp Magazine 79
Stamp Specialist 249
Stamp Tax Act 386
Stamps 161
Starnes, Charles 90, 331
Steamboat and steamship letters. *See* Covers: Ship, steamboat, steamship; Postal laws: Ship, steamboat, steamship
Steamship routes ... 309–310, 311. *See also* Transcontinental mails: Steamship
Steel, Charles F. 5, 19, 41, 42, 59
Steele, Frederick 265
Stets, Robert B. 176, 178, 179, 200

Stevenson, William 41, 45, 47, 48
Stewart, Alexander T. 168
Supplementary mail. *See* Postal laws: Supplementary mail; Special services
Supplementary Mail Markings including Notes on Chicago, San Francisco, San Juan, Puerto Rico, and Honolulu 249

-T-

Taylor, N.&G. 381
Taylor, Richard 80, 81
Taylor, William B. 156, 157, 158
Territorial mails .... 325–330. *See also* Covers: Territorial
    Western territories chart 330
Third-class mail 215
Thorp, Prescott Holden 391
Thurn and Taxis 221, 268, 348
Tiffany, John 41, 81, 150
Toppan, Carpenter and Company
    1851-57 stamp contract 3, 41, 149
    1861 stamp contract 1
    Essays
        1861 1¢ Franklin 10–11, 11–12
    Perforations 19
Towle, Charles 107
Transatlantic mails 333–334. *See also* Covers: Transatlantic mails
    Belgium 355
    France
        Double rate 342–343
        Multiple rate 343
        Part-paid to Switzerland 343–345
        Single rate to Italy 347, 348
        Single rate to Prussia 346
        Single rate to Sicily 347
        Single rate to Spain 346–347
        Single rate to Switzerland 345–346
        Triple rate 343
    Great Britain
        Double rate 335
        Single rate 335
    Hamburg
        New York to Gratz, Austria 349, 350
    Italy 355–356
    Netherlands 355
    Prussia
        Athens, Greece 350–351
        Boston to Venezia, Austria 352
        Cincinnati, Ohio, to Brieg, Prussia 353, 354
        Gorham, Maine, to St. Petersburg, Russia . 351–352
        Honolulu to Neuchatel, Switzerland 352–353
        New York to Frankfurt-am-Main 351

Transatlantic mails (continued)
    New York to Naples, Italy 354–355
    Switzerland 355
Transcontinental mails 309
    Steamship 312–313
Transcontinental railroad 317, 324, 325, 329–330
Transient mail 213. *See also* Postal laws: Transient mail
    Advertisements 213
    Business cards 213
    Circulars 213
    Junk mail 214
    Newspapers 213, 223
        Foreign destinations 227–229
        Wrappers 225, 266
    Pamphlets 213
    Prices current 213
Travers, Arthur M. 84, 85
Treasure Island Golden Gate 1939 International
    Exhibition 152
Trent Affair 259
Trepel, Scott 42, 46, 47, 56
Trifit, F. 24
Turnbull, David C. 390

-U-

*U.S. Letter Rates to Foreign Destinations, 1847 to
    GPU-UPU* 90, 331, 333
U.S. Mail and Post Office Assistant 89, 96, 150,
        152, 186, 199, 227, 234, 242, 263, 378, 394
U.S. Penny Mail 178
U.S.P.O. Dispatch 178
Unicover Corporation Museum 153
Union Pacific 324, 325
United States Cancellations, 1845-1869 .... 101, 128
United States Mail Steamship Company 310
United States Philatelic Classics Society 8, 128
United States Post Office Department
    1851-57 stamps
        Demonetization 149–162
    1861 1¢ Franklin 22, 23, 24, 25, 27
        Atlanta card proofs 22, 26
        August 17, 1861, use 152–153
        Earliest-known use 152–153, 277
        First uses 152–155
        Special printings 69–88
    1861 stamp contract 1–16, 3, 4, 5, 6, 8, 20, 21, 255
        Chronology 8
        Premieres gravures 6, 75
    1867 stamp contract 41
    1868 stamp contract 54
    Postal Appropriations Act of 1859 .... 311, 312, 318

*United States Postage Stamps of the
    19th Century* 21, 33
United States Postal History Sampler 235
United States revenue stamps
    Ayer's patent medicine 381
    Used as postage stamps 381–385, 385–388
        Revenue stamps accepted 387, 388
United States stamped envelopes
    1860 1¢ star die 152, 196
    1860 3¢ star die 152
    Compound envelope 152
United States stamps
    1847 issue 149
    1847 reproductions 83
    1851 eagle carrier stamp 190, 191
    1851-57 stamps 1, 2, 21, 149–162, 193
        1¢ 70, 160, 161, 162
        3¢ 153, 154, 158, 160
        10¢ 156
    1857-60 reprints 83
    1861 1¢ 17
        Bisects 398
        Design 13, 17–18
        Dot-in-U variety 34, 152–153, 187, 190, 215, 262,
                              263, 275, 300, 361
        Earliest-known use 152–155
        Largest number on cover 234
        Mixed-issue use 158
        Multiples 29–30, 31
        Perforation 18–20
        Plate margin markings 27
        Plates 29
        Premieres gravures 8, 10, 13, 151, 350, 351
        Production 18–22
        Quantities 6, 20–21
    1861 2¢ 2, 167, 180, 197, 397, 399
    1861 3¢ 5, 6, 9, 21–22
        Envelope essays 82
        Grills 45
    1861 5¢
        Grills 45, 239
    1861 10¢ 315
    1861 10¢ premiere gravure 9
    1861 12¢ 6, 9
    1861 24¢ 6, 8, 9
    1861 30¢ 6, 8, 9
        Grills 45
    1861 issue 149
        Distribution 6, 151, 159, 253, 255
        Earliest-known use 6, 152–155, 181, 182, 277
        Essays 7, 8, 10
        First day of use 151, 152–153

United States stamps (continued)
- Issue date 5, 6
- Quantities 6, 85
- 1861 premieres gravures 1, 6, 6–10, 85
  - Colors 8
- 1861 stamp contract 1
- 1861-66 reprints 83
- 1863 2¢ Jackson 21, 134, 308
- 1866 15¢ black 235
- 1867-69 issue
  - Grilled issues .... 41. *See also* Grills: 1867-69 issues
- 1869 12¢ 235
- 1869 Pictorials 55–56
- 1875 reissue 72–76
- 1893 Columbians 77, 83
- Legal tender 377–381

U.S. stamps by Scott numbers (excepting No. 63)
- 62B 9, 350, 351, 364
- 63a 33
- 63b 33
- 63d 35
- 63e 34
- 63-E1 12
- 63-E2 12
- 63-E3 12
- 63-E9 12
- 63-E10 14
- 63-E11 14
- 63-E11e 10
- 63-E13 .... 61, 62
- 63-E13e 52
- 63P2 85
- 63P3 .... 28, 75
- 63P4 79
- 63S 70
- 63S B 70
- 63S J 72
- 63TC 26
- 63TC5 .... 63, 66, 67
- 63TC6 .... 63, 66, 67
- 64a 300
- 68 316
- 68P4 79
- 69 .... 274, 366
- 69P4 79
- 70 174
- 71 351
- 71P4 79
- 72 340
- 72P4 79
- 73 .... 196, 241, 274, 399
- 74P4 79

U.S. stamps by Scott numbers (continued)
- 76 340
- 76P4 79
- 77P4 79
- 78 .... 342, 352, 354
- 78a 234
- 78b 343
- 78P4 79
- 79 45
- 79-E 54
- 79-E29 53
- 79-E33 53
- 79-E79 53
- 80 45
- 81 45
- 82 45
- 82A 46
- 85A 46–48
- 86 .... 29, 48, 49, 54
- 89 234
- 92 .... 50, 51, 52, 54, 209
- 94 373
- 102 .... 74, 75
- 102TC 77, 78
- R5 384
- R6 388
- R9 .... 121, 386, 387
- U19 .... 196, 217
- U28-29 .... 152, 194
- U34 .... 154, 316, 320, 369, 374
- U36 188
- U40 314
- U43 345
- U58 344
- U59 .... 370, 373
- W20 .... 226, 266

United States Stamps of the 19th Century 41
Universal Postal Union 69, 331
Upham, Samuel C. 187, 280, 286

-V-

Valentines. *See* Covers: Illustrated: Valentines
Van Buren, Martin 123–125
Vanderbilt, Cornelius 312, 313
Varieties
- 1861-67 1¢ Franklin 34–38
  - Dot in U 34, 152–153, 187, 190, 215, 262, 263, 275, 300, 361
  - Double perforations 35
  - Double transfer 34
  - Imperforate 34, 35
  - Imperforate between 35

Varieties (continued)
    Paper 37–38
Vaux, Calvet 392, 393, 395, 396
Ventura Stamp Company 132

-W-

Wakeman, Abram 141, 395
Walborn 155, 177
Walcott, C.D. 86
Walcott, George 273
Wallis, S. Teackly 265
Wanamaker, John 168
War-related mails 253
Ward, Philip H. 7, 69
Ware, Joseph A. 89
Washington, D.C., carrier system 189–191
Washington, George 3
Waterbury Cancellations 128
Waterbury, Connecticut, Post Office 128–131
Way letters. *See* Postal laws: Way letters; Special services
Weill brothers 28, 80, 81
Weiss Philatelics 14, 77, 79, 80, 84, 273, 303
Weiss, William 273, 381
Welles, Gideon 281
Wells, Fargo
    Stamped envelopes 97, 217
Wells, John 286
West Indian Blockading Squadron 257
Western mails 309
Western Virginia 2
White, R.H. 32, 33
Wilder, Charles B. 258
Wiley, H.L. 41
Williams, L.N. 18
Williams, M. 18
Winter, Richard 218, 262, 268, 331, 333, 335, 338
Wisconsin Volunteers 256
Wolffers, Richard, Auctions 2, 51, 74, 122
Woodhull, D.E. 21
Worthington collection 45, 46, 48
Wrappers, newspaper 224–227
    Multiple rate 225
Wunderlich, Rudolph 35, 63
Wyckoff patent 64–67
Wyckoff, William 59, 63, 64
Wyman, John 283–285

-Y-

York, Norton 5, 7, 19
Young, Brigham 326

Young Lockwood & Co. 261

-Z-

Zahm, S.H. 274
Zevely, A.N. 5, 24, 42, 55, 56, 69, 118, 141, 151, 256
Zevely, Edmond S. 104

The United States 1¢ Franklin 1861-67

ABOUT THE AUTHOR

Don L. Evans

In 1932, at the age of nine, Don Evans purchased his first small album and a packet of assorted stamps. It was love at first sight, and within months, with his best friend, he started a stamp club and opened a vest-pocket stamp business. The club never gained any more members, and the business failed to sell a single stamp, but the fascination with stamps never paled.

At Hollywood High School and UCLA, collecting took a back seat to more immediate interests, and then World War II came along with a combat tour in B-24s. Then Korea and some more missions in B-26s, and the continuation of a 33-year Air Force career as a flyer and research and development officer for Air Force space systems.

During this hiatus from serious collecting, the old albums were occasionally taken from the bookcase and a few additions made to the collection. It wasn't until 1972, with two boys finally in college, and a wife who also had become enamored with the joys of philately, that really serious collecting and philatelic research began.

After a few years of specializing in 19th-century U.S. proofs, Evans, who retired from the military in 1975, settled on a small avocado ranch in Southern California. With more time to spend on his favorite avocation, a new focus of philatelic interest was discovered. The 1¢ blue Franklin of 1861 had everything that a collector might desire for a specialty. It is a beautifully designed stamp with a multitude of special and experimental printings. It was used in one of the most historic periods of our country's history, and its uses documented the interesting happenings and commerce of the day.

After several years of collecting, research and exhibiting the 1¢ Franklin, Evans realized that there just wasn't a single comprehensive reference for the stamp or for the postal history of the 1860-70 period. He decided to do something about filling that void, and this book is the result of that decision.

Evans has been active in exhibiting and has garnered several grand awards, and repeated entries into the APS Champion of Champion's competition. For some years he was chairman of the Southern California chapter of the U.S. Philatelic Classics Society and has been a frequent contributor to philatelic literature. For several years, he was an associate editor of the *U.S. Stamps & Postal History* magazine, where he wrote on 19th-century philately.

At the present, Evans, with his wife, Alyce, still manage and care for their avocado grove. She pursues her philatelic specialty of West Virginia postal history, and he maintains an active consulting role in the aerospace industry, but devotes the majority of his discretionary time to collecting, researching and, most of all, writing about 19th-century stamps and their postal history.

The late Calvin W. "Bert" Christian started collecting in the early part of this century while living in a small Midwestern farming community. In his early years, as a self-taught drummer, he toured with a Dixieland jazz band. After moving west to California, Christian became active in the restaurant business, and then owner and proprietor of drugstores in two Southern California communities.

About 1950, Christian began to assemble what were to become comprehensive national and international award winning collections of the 1¢, 3¢ and 10¢ denominations of the 1861 series of stamps.

He was a prolific writer of articles for society publications and the philatelic press, and in 1989 was inducted into the Writer's Unit #30 Hall of Fame.

C.W. "Bert" Christian

In addition to his collecting and writing, Christian also contributed his time and talents to many organizations. He was a member and accredited judge for the American Philatelic Society since 1965, a regional vice president and president of the U.S. Philatelic Classics Society and an officer of many philatelic groups located in Southern California.

Among his many awards are the 1993 APS Luff Award, and designation as a Fellow of the Royal Philatelic Society, London. The U.S. Philatelic Classics Society honored him with the Chase Cup, Lester Downing Award, Brookman Cup and Distinguished Philatelist Award.

Retiring from business in 1973 at the age of 78, Christian devoted himself entirely to philately, and to passing on the knowledge and information that he had accumulated during three quarters of a century of collecting and study to those who follow in his footsteps.